Watch America's courts in action with this FREE CD-ROM!

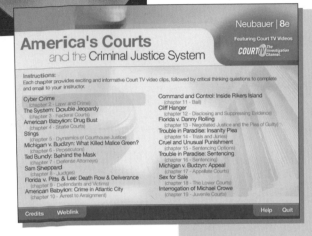

Neubauer | 8e

Featuring Court TV Videos

COURT TV *The Investigation Channel.*

America's Courts
and the Criminal Justice System

Instructions:
Each chapter provides exciting and informative Court TV video clips, followed by critical thinking questions to complete and email to your instructor.

Cyber Crime
(chapter 2 - Law and Crime)
The System: Double Jeopardy
(chapter 3 - Federal Courts)
American Babylon: Drug Bust
(chapter 4 - State Courts)
Stings
(chapter 5 - Dynamics of Courthouse Justice)
Michigan v. Budzyn: What Killed Malice Green?
(chapter 6 - Prosecutors)
Ted Bundy: Behind the Mask
(chapter 7 - Defense Attorneys)
Sam Sheppard
(chapter 8 - Judges)
Florida v. Pitts & Lee: Death Row & Deliverance
(chapter 9 - Defendants and Victims)
American Babylon: Crime in Atlantic City
(chapter 10 - Arrest to Arraignment)

Command and Control: Inside Rikers Island
(chapter 11 - Bail)
Cliff Hanger
(chapter 12 - Disclosing and Suppressing Evidence)
Florida v. Danny Rolling
(chapter 13 - Negotiated Justice and the Plea of Guilty)
Trouble in Paradise: Insanity Plea
(chapter 14 - Trials and Juries)
Cruel and Unusual Punishment
(chapter 15 - Sentencing Options)
Trouble in Paradise: Sentencing
(chapter 16 - Sentencing)
Michigan v. Budzyn: Appeal
(chapter 17 - Appellate Courts)
Sex for Sale
(chapter 18 - The Lower Courts)
Interrogation of Michael Crowe
(chapter 19 - Juvenile Courts)

Credits   Weblink   Help   Quit

Watch as prosecutors methodically prove the guilt of a serial killer. Think along with defense attorneys as they use cross-examination to question the evidence in police brutality cases. Ride with the police as they break up a knife fight and arrest commercial sex workers. Empathize with a mother as she pleads for the jury to spare her son's life.

These are some of the video clips presented on the FREE CD-ROM that accompanies every new copy of this book! The **Student CD-ROM** will take you on a fascinating, true-to-life tour of America's courts. Cases profiled run the gamut from selling drugs to murder. Taken from Court TV® episodes, the video clips offer a dynamic view of crimes like drugs, prostitution, rape and murder, and are based on actual criminal investigations and trials. All of the clips were carefully selected to cover important criminal justice issues like crime on the Internet, drugs, DNA evidence, and defendants falsely convicted.

To link the video clips to topics discussed in the book, each presentation is following by critical-thinking questions.

▶ The compelling Court TV® stories found on the CD-ROM are linked to Neubauer's text through *Court TV®* boxes. These sections include background information on key cases that relate to the various points covered throughout the text. The combination of text and CD-ROM helps bring important court cases and events into sharp focus.

COURT TV
Cyber Crime:
The Lawless Frontier

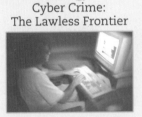

The Internet has revolutionized how we live and how we learn. But it has also provided new avenues for illicit activity. Identity theft has become a major problem with sophisticated criminals stealing credit card numbers and other important personal information, resulting in countless dollars lost. E-commerce also allows prostitutes to solicit clients on line, seemingly protected by jurisdictional voids.

Pedophiles also utilize the Internet to distribute child pornography. Specialized federal law enforcement agencies now monitor chat rooms and the like looking to arrest those who try to profit by selling images of children engaging in sexually explicit acts. At times, law enforcement personnel create fake Internet identities in order to identify and arrest pedophiles. But does law enforcement go too far at times? Do they entrap innocent citizens?

View a video clip of this case on your copy of the CourtTV CD-ROM. As you watch the video, keep the following questions in mind:

1. How has the Internet changed society?
2. What legal changes have been made in response to these societal changes?
3. What additional legal changes need to be made?
4. Does the media and law enforcement stress the negative side of the Internet and therefore impede legitimate uses of this new technology?
5. In reversing the conviction in this case, the appellate court suggests that law enforcement was wasting time on this type of enforcement practice. Do you agree or disagree? How would advocates of the crime control model of criminal justice differ in their answers from supporters of the due process model?

Explore this dynamic CD-ROM today!

www.wadsworth.com

www.wadsworth.com is the World Wide Web site f Wadsworth and is your direct source to dozens of online resoui s.

At www.wadsworth.com you can find out about suplements, demonstration software, and student resources. You can also send email to many of our authors and previewnew publications and exciting new technologies.

wadsworth.com
Changing the way the world learns®

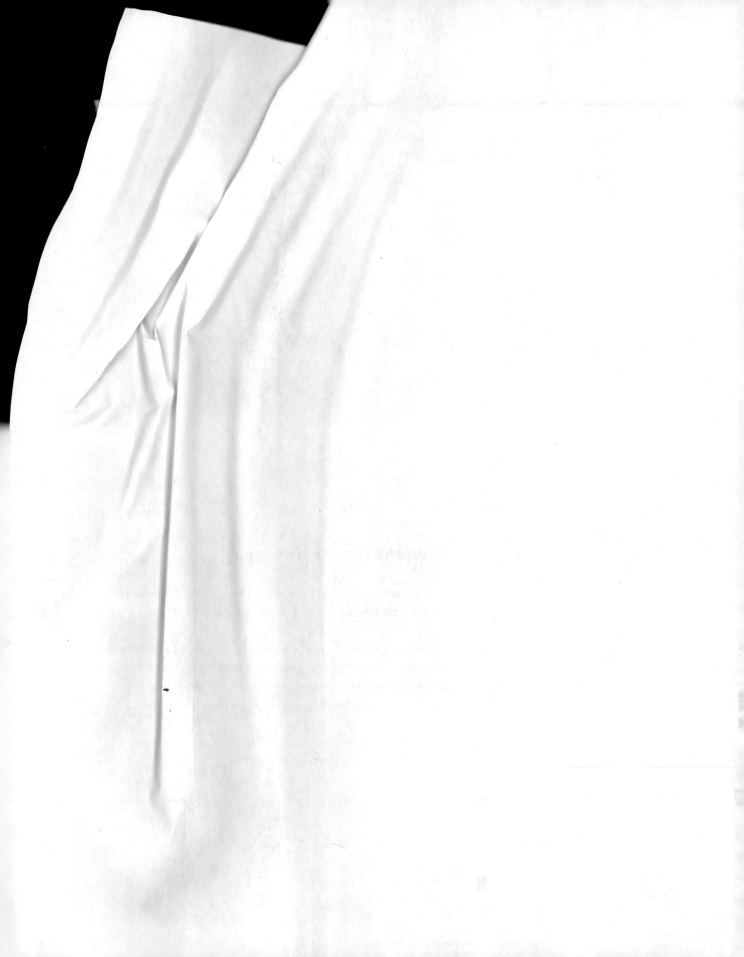

America's Courts
and the Criminal
Justice System

EIGHTH EDITION

America's Courts and the Criminal Justice System

EIGHTH EDITION

David W. Neubauer
University of New Orleans

THOMSON
™
WADSWORTH

Australia • Canada • Mexico • Singapore • Spain • United Kingdom • United States

THOMSON

WADSWORTH

Executive Editor, Criminal Justice: Sabra Horne
Developmental Editor: Shelley Murphy
Assistant Editor: Jana Davis
Editorial Assistant: Elise Smith
Technology Project Manager: Susan DeVanna
Marketing Manager: Terra Schultz
Marketing Assistant: Annabelle Yang
Advertising Project Manager: Stacey Purviance
Project Manager, Editorial Production:
    Matthew Ballantyne
Art Director: Vernon Boes
Art Editors: Carolyn Deacy; Yvo

Print/Media Buyer: Barbara Britton
Permissions Editor: Sarah Harkrader
Production Service: The Cooper Company
Text Designer: Delgado and Company
Copy Editor: Margaret C. Tropp
Illustrator: Lineworks, Inc.
Cover Designer: Yvo
Cover Image: Sky background © Jane Nelson/Getty
    Images; Stone steps © Thinkstock/Getty Images
Compositor: Thompson Type
Text Printer: Quebecor World–Taunton
Cover Printer: Coral Graphic Services

For more information about our products, contact us at:
Thomson Learning Academic Resource Center
1-800-423-0563
For permission to use material from this text or
product, submit a request online at:
http://www.thomsonrights.com
Any additional questions about permissions can be
submitted by email to thomsonrights@thomson.com

Library of Congress Control Number: 2003112736

Student Edition: ISBN 0-534-62892-3
Instructor's Edition: ISBN 0-534-62893-1

Thomson Wadsworth
10 Davis Drive
Belmont, CA 94002-3098
USA

Asia
Thomson Learning
5 Shenton Way #01-01
UIC Building
Singapore 068808

Australia/New Zealand
Thomson Learning
102 Dodds Street
Southbank, Victoria 3006
Australia

Canada
Nelson
1120 Birchmount Road
Toronto, Ontario M1K 5G4
Canada

Europe/Middle East/Africa
Thomson Learning
High Holborn House
50/51 Bedford Row
London WC1R 4LR
United Kingdom

Latin America
Thomson Learning
Seneca, 53
Colonia Polanco
11560 Mexico D.F.
Mexico

Spain/Portugal
Paraninfo
Calle/Magallanes, 25
28015 Madrid, Spain

To Jeff, Kristen, and Amy

Brief Contents

Contents

Preface

America's Courts and the Criminal Justice System, Eighth Edition, examines the history, traditions, and philosophy underlying our system of justice as it is played out in the criminal court. In a complex, sometimes contradictory, and often fragmented process, defendants are declared innocent or found guilty, and the guilty are sentenced to prison or placed on probation. This book is about the defendants caught up in the process: the three-time losers, the scared young first offenders, and the business executives who are before the court to answer an indictment. But most of all, this book focuses on the prosecutors, judges, defense attorneys, and jurors who are involved in the daily decisions about guilt or innocence, probation or prison.

The impact of these decisions on crime and criminals is the subject of widespread controversy. Concern over how the courts handle criminal cases has been a staple of American political rhetoric since the 1960s. The nature of this public debate, as well as solutions proposed to correct the problems, are integral parts of this book. To be sure, the last decades have witnessed significant deep-seated changes and readjustments in the criminal justice system—given all the public posturing, one would hardly expect less.

This book is written for undergraduate courses that deal with America's criminal courts. Such courses (or parts of courses) are taught in various departments: criminal justice, administration of justice, political science, sociology, psychology, and social welfare. This book highlights not only the pivotal role of the criminal courts within the criminal justice system but also the courts' importance and impact on society as a whole. America's Courts and the Criminal Justice System, Eighth Edition, focuses on the dynamics of the courthouse. Thus it differs from casebooks, which use appellate court decisions to highlight the history, structure, and philosophy of courts. Although these are important matters, casebooks often project a rather sterile image of courthouse justice and omit what courts do in practice, how they do it, and most important, why they do it.

This book's emphasis on the dynamics of courthouse justice grows out of my own field research. Since the 1960s, I have spent considerable time in state and federal courts in all parts of the nation. I have interviewed numerous judges, jurors, prosecutors, defense attorneys, probation officers, jailers, police officers, and defendants. I have observed these officials in action and discussed with them their problems and their views of possible solutions. By the luck of the draw, I have also served on juries in state and federal court. Throughout this book, I have tried to convey to the reader the sense of being in the courthouse.

Writing the Eighth Edition was gratifying and stimulating. It was gratifying to learn that numerous professors, and I hope their students as well, have found the book useful. It was stimulating because it involved closely examining recent changes in both scholarship and public dialogue. The Eighth Edition offers a current perspective on a continually evolving subject—the criminal court process. In this edition, the chapter structure remains the same as in the previous edition, but new topics are included and new special features have been added.

NEW TOPICS IN THIS EDITION

The courts remain at the center of public attention. I have tried to incorporate as many of these new issues as possible, as well as to highlight recent developments in old areas. Topics new to this edition or receiving expanded coverage include:

- Decreasing crime rates
- Expansion of drug courts
- Extension of right to jury

- Growth in drug prosecutions
- Increasing executions
- Innocents on death row
- Military tribunals
- Moratorium on the death penalty
- More limits on scientific evidence
- Nosier campaigns for judgeships
- Prosecuting white-collar criminals
- Recent threats to judicial independence
- Reduced spending on indigent defense
- Sexual assault prosecutions
- Swelling prison populations
- Three-strikes laws upheld

NEW FEATURES IN THIS EDITION

Simplified Presentation

Content within the chapters has been reorganized and streamlined for greater accessibility and student comprehension. The flow of cases through the court system is graphically illustrated throughout the text with a new "timeline" feature that appears on chapter-opening pages, enabling the student to connect the chapter material to the ongoing court process.

A Virtual Tour of American Courthouses

Each chapter contains a "virtual tour" that provides a set of links to courthouse Web sites across the nation. Some provide a dynamic look at what is happening inside the building, and others provide perspective on these activities.

New "America's Courts" Student CD-ROM

The Eighth Edition of *America's Courts and the Criminal Justice System* is accompanied by a new student CD-ROM packaged free with the book. The text is integrated with current high-interest court stories through Court TV vignettes in each chapter, where appropriate, in conjunction with a Court TV boxed feature. The CD-ROM contains video clips, with related essay questions for students to email to instructors, from those stories that illustrate key information from the chapter. Court TV videos, which feature clips tied to chapter content, are also available free to instructors.

FOUR CONTINUING FEATURES

The Eighth Edition incorporates the four features used in the previous edition.

The Murder Trial of Shareef Cousin

Cousin was for a time the youngest person on America's death row—he was only 16 when he was accused of murder. On appeal, however, the murder conviction was overturned, and the district attorney chose not to prosecute. Each chapter in the book focuses on an aspect of this case. The goal is to tie the chapter material to this one ongoing and controversial case.

A Day in Court

I have combed newspapers across the nation to find articles that give readers a sense of being in court, sitting with the decision maker. The purpose is to view the process through the eyes of that person, attempting to understand the pressures and frustrations that he or she faces on a daily basis.

Case Close-up

Each chapter highlights an important court decision that has affected our nation's criminal justice system. Some, like *Miranda* and *Gideon*, are familiar names. Others are less well known. But each highlights the dynamic nature of courts in the United States.

Controversy

These boxed features provide multiple perspectives on the topics discussed in the chapter. To better focus on the wide-ranging debate surrounding the criminal courts in the United States, these controversies have been given an expanded subhead. Thus, throughout the book, these features will discuss controversies centering on judicial administration, crime reduction, gender equity, racial discrimination, and economic inequality.

▌ THREE THEMES

In rewriting the Eighth Edition, I decided to continue with the three themes introduced in the previous editions. Although they have been with the book since the beginning, the new edition's emphasis on the themes of law on the books, law in action, and law in controversy provides a better focus.

Law on the Books

The starting point of this text is to provide readers with a working knowledge of the major structures and basic legal concepts that underlie the criminal courts. In deciding guilt or innocence and determining the appropriate punishment, the courts apply the criminal law through a complicated process termed criminal procedure. The structure of the courts, the nature of the criminal law they apply, and the procedures followed all have important consequences for how the courts dispense justice.

But to understand the legal system, one needs to know more than the formal rules. Also necessary is an understanding of the assumptions underlying these rules, the history of how they evolved, and the goals they seek to achieve. A discussion of the assumptions, history, and goals makes clear that America's criminal justice process is not monolithic but consists of a number of separate and sometimes competing units. It also points out conflicts over the goals the criminal courts are expected to achieve.

Law in Action

Many books leave the false impression that an understanding of the formal law and major structures of the court is all that one needs to know about the criminal courts. This kind of analysis provides only a limited view of how the courts administer justice. The law is not self-executing. It is a dynamic process of applying abstract rules to concrete situations.

In making decisions about charges to be filed, the amount of bail to be required, and the sentence the convicted person will receive, judges, prosecutors, and defense attorneys must make choices for which the formal law provides few precise guidelines. Thus, the second theme of this book is law in action, which emphasizes the dynamics of the criminal court process.

An examination of law in action reveals a gap between how the law is supposed to operate and how it is actually applied. For example, the law in theory suggests that the guilt of defendants should be decided by a jury trial. In practice, however, trials are rare. Most defendants plead guilty without a trial. Asking why there is a gap between the law on the books and the law in action is a big step toward understanding the dynamics of courthouse justice.

Courts in Controversy

No treatment of the criminal courts would be complete without a discussion of the problems they are confronting. Are the courts too slow? Are judges too soft in sentencing? Does the criminal court process discriminate against the poor? These are just a few of the questions about the operations of the criminal courts that this book will consider. In turn, many organizations, groups, and individuals have probed the problems facing the criminal courts and proposed reforms. The third theme of this book is to discuss and analyze the controversies surrounding courthouse justice and analyze the reforms that have been suggested for what ails the courts. Not everyone agrees on the types of changes needed. Some argue that certain reforms will produce greater difficulties without solving the original problems. This book examines competing perspectives on the changes and reforms that are being proposed.

PEDAGOGICAL INNOVATIONS

This edition contains an array of pedagogical aids to facilitate student learning. These include:

- Chapter outlines
- Chapter conclusions
- End-of-chapter critical thinking questions
- End-of-chapter glossary of key terms
- World Wide Web resources and exercises
- InfoTrac College Edition resources and exercises
- Suggestions for further reading
- Numerous exhibits and figures
- New visual timeline element showing court process

SUPPLEMENTS

An extensive package of supplemental aids has been developed to enhance the course and to assist instructors and students.

Instructor's Manual

The Instructor's Manual has been revised by Ray Kessler. It includes a detailed outline, key terms and concepts, discussion topics and student activities, recommended readings, critical thinking questions, and testing suggestions that will help time-pressed teachers communicate more effectively with their students and also strengthen coverage of course material. Each chapter has multiple-choice, true/false, and fill-in-the-blank test items, as well as sample essay questions.

Student Study Guide

The extensive Student Study Guide has been revised by Ray Kessler. Because students learn in different ways, a variety of pedagogical aids are included in the guide to help them. Each chap-

ter is outlined, major terms are defined, a summary is included, and sample tests are provided.

Student CD-ROM

The Student CD-ROM that accompanies this book provides compelling video clips of real police investigations and actual trials that have shaped our criminal justice system, including the Ted Bundy case. All of the clips are from Court TV, and were carefully selected to cover controversial issues like cyber crime, prostitution, false confessions, the war on drugs, and the insanity defense. Included are several trials of murderers, some of whom were later released.

Web Site

Designed exclusively for this edition of the text, this Web site—located at http://cj.wadsworth.com/neubauer_courts8e—provides a variety of informative resources and interactive exercises. It takes an in-depth look at chapter-specific cases with a summary of facts, court decision, majority opinion, why the verdict became a law, and related Web links.

Controversies is a topic-specific threaded discussion forum with related Web links. Flash Cards provide a glossary of terms. InfoTrac College Edtion allows the student and instructor access to a wealth of criminal justice articles. The polling feature gives students an opportunity to cast their vote on a particular issue. Links to reliable periodicals offer another way to search for information on specific topics. Statistics shows the cold facts. Other valuable resources include A Day in Court– Comparative Legal Systems, a link to CourtTV, just for fun links, and Critical Thinking Questions that require students to compare, contrast, analyze, and apply what they have learned.

ExamView®

This computerized testing software helps instructors create and customize exams in minutes. Instructors can easily edit and import their own questions and graphics, change test layout, and reorganize questions.

This software also allows instructors to test and grade online. It is available for both Windows and Macintosh.

CNN® Today Video Series

Exclusively from Wadsworth/Thomson Learning, the CNN Today Video Series offers compelling videos that feature current news footage from the Cable News Network's comprehensive archives.

Introduction to Criminal Justice, Volumes I through IV, provide a collection of three- to five-minute clips on hot topics in criminal justice, such as cybercrime, juveniles behind bars, gender and ethnicity, and more. Available to qualified adopters, these videotapes are great lecture-launchers as well as classroom discussion pieces.

The Wadsworth Criminal Justice Video Library

The Wadsworth Criminal Justice Video Library offers an exciting collection of videos to enrich lectures, including Court TV videos, many of which are directly correlated to the chapters. Qualified adopters may select from a variety of professionally prepared videos covering various aspects of policing, corrections, and other areas of the criminal justice system. The selections include videos from *Films for the Humanities & Sciences, A&E American Justice Series* videos, *National Institute of Justice: Crime File* videos, ABC News videos, and MPI Home Videos.

Careers in Criminal Justice Interactive CD-ROM

This engaging CD-ROM allows students to take an interactive look at the wide range of careers in criminal justice. The self-assessment feature helps steer students to suitable careers based on their personal profiles. They can gather information including job descriptions, salaries, employment requirements, sample tests, and video profiles of criminal justice professionals.

Crime Scenes CD-ROM

The first CD-ROM developed specifically for the introductory criminal justice course, this highly visual, interactive program casts students as the decision makers as they explore all aspects of the criminal justice system. Exciting videos and supporting documents put students in the middle of a juvenile murder trial, a prostitution case that turns to manslaughter, and several other scenarios. This product received the gold medal in higher education and the silver medal for video interface from *NewMedia* magazine's Invision Awards.

■ ACKNOWLEDGMENTS

Writing the Eighth Edition was made easier by the assistance and encouragement of people who deserve special recognition. First and foremost, I would like to thank the Wadsworth criminal justice team, who provided a fresh perspective on the new edition: Sabra Horne (executive editor), Shelley Murphy (developmental editor), Dory Schaeffer (marketing manager), Susan DeVanna (technology project manager), and Eno Sarris (assistant editor). I am also grateful to the gifted production team of Matthew Ballantyne, Barbara Britton, Sarah Harkrader, Cecile Joyner, Lisa Delgado, and Peggy Tropp, who turned raw manuscript into a polished book and dispensed good cheer along the way. As always, colleagues from a number of schools and institutions offered valuable critiques. They include George Cole (University of Connecticut), Paul Wice (Drew University), Stephan Meinhold (North Carolina—Wilmington), and Chris DeLay (University of Louisiana—Lafayette). At UNO, Patrick Hall and Mark Kaplinsky provided valuable research assistance.

Special thanks are due to the reviewers of this edition:

Barbara Belbot, University of Houston—Downtown

Frank Butler, Temple University

James A. Gazell, San Diego State University

Kimberly Keller, University of Texas at San Antonio

Jefferey M. Sellers, University of Southern California

I also wish to gratefully acknowledge the help provided by the reviewers of previous editions: Ruben Auger-Marchand, Indiana University/Purdue University; E. Stan Barnhill, University of Nevada at Reno; Anita Blowers, University of North Carolina—Charlotte; Paula M. Broussard, University of Louisiana—Lafayette; Kathleen Cameron-Hahn, Arizona State University; Bill Clements, Norwich University; Beverly Blair Cook, University of Wisconsin—Milwaukee; Mark Dantzker, Loyola University of Chicago; Max Dery, California State University—Fullerton; Frederick Van Dusen, Palm Beach Community College; Mary Ann Farkas, Marquette University; Roy Flemming, Texas A&M University; David Friedrichs, University of Scranton; Marc Gertz, Florida State University; Gary S. Green, Minot State University; Pamela L. Griset, University of Central Florida; Joseph Hanrahan, Westfield State University; Peter Haynes, Arizona State University; Michael Hazlett, Western Illinois State University; Ed Heck, San Diego State University; Ellen Hochstedler, University of Wisconsin—Milwaukee; Lou Holscher, Arizona State University at Tempe; N. Gary Holten,

University of Central Florida; Rodney Kingsnorth, California State University—Sacramento; Karl Kunkel, Southwest Missouri State University; Jim Love, Lamar University; Patricia Loveless, University of Delaware; David Lukoff, University of Delaware at Newcastle; James Maddex, Georgia State University; Larry Myers, Sam Houston State University; Elizabeth Pelz, University of Houston—Downtown; John Paul Ryan, American Bar Association; Joseph Sanborn, University of Central Florida; Jose Texidor, Penn State University; Douglas Thomson, University of Illinois—Chicago; David Thysens, Saint Martin's College; Donald Walker, Kent State University; Russell Wheeler, Federal Judicial Center; Nancy Wolfe, University of South Carolina; Sheryl Williams, Jersey City State College.

As always, my wife and children deserve a special note of thanks for their love and support. I dedicate the book to my children in response to their bemusement at the idea that Daddy was busy writing a book.

David W. Neubauer
Slidell, Louisiana

To the Student

Over the years, the nicest comment I have heard about this book is that students like it. In writing the latest edition, I have tried to build on the foundation of the earlier versions by making the book even more student-friendly. This book uses a spiral approach, beginning from a core of information and working outward to cover a wider range of relevant perspectives. I begin with basic building blocks of knowledge and then proceed to use them for a deeper analysis. In each chapter, the initial emphasis is on the basics—the later material deals with more complicated issues.

The Eighth Edition contains a number of special features that will help make this introduction to the criminal court process more informative and enjoyable.

Key Terms and Glossary

Any text should introduce readers to the basic terminology of a particular field. This is particularly important for a book on the criminal process because the law has a vocabulary all its own. Numerous students have suggested that this book needs a glossary. Indeed, one of my own students commented that the book has lots of "foreign" words—foreign not because they originated in another country but because they are so new.

To aid you, key terms are highlighted throughout the text in boldface type, and a list of key terms is provided at the end of each chapter. At the back of the book is a full glossary, which is a compilation of the key terms boldfaced in each chapter. Many of the most commonly used legal terms can be found there.

Key Developments

To provide a better sense of how the discussions in the chapters relate to material covered in other courses—such as Constitutional Law and Criminal Procedure—most chapters contain exhibits labeled "Key Developments," which summarize the major legal developments concerning the topic at hand. I suggest that you use these as cross-references for other courses and also update the material when the Supreme Court hands down new decisions or Congress passes new laws.

Important Material

In each chapter, I have also tried to highlight important material in exhibits. The idea is to provide information regarding law on the books (for example, definitions) as well as snippets of law in action (such as basic statistics). In particular, an exhibit summarizing the steps of the criminal court process is repeated (in an expanded version) in subsequent chapters. The intent is to direct your attention to the interrelated nature of the steps of the process. In addition, these figures provide an overview of the roles that each of the major actors—prosecutor, defense attorney, judge, and victim—play in the process. Because readers are often interested in particular states, a special effort has been made to provide important legal information for all 50 states.

Case Close-up

To complement the theme of law on the books, each chapter contains a Case Close-up. Many of these cases are landmark decisions of the U.S. Supreme Court. Others are less well known but chosen to illustrate the point. Throughout, I have tried to get beyond the often dry legal prose to look at the people involved and what happened after their temporary stay in the legal limelight. Thus, each chapter begins with a vignette, which is discussed in greater depth somewhere in the chapter.

A Day in Court

To complement the theme of law in action, each chapter contains the feature A Day in Court; it is designed to capture real-life experiences by looking at the people who make the decisions in the courthouse, emphasizing the frustrations they face. Juvenile judges, prosecutors, defense attorneys for those on death row, bounty hunters, and other key players are featured.

Controversy

To complement the theme of courts and controversy, each chapter contains a Controversy box, intended to involve readers in the ongoing debate. Thus, I start each Controversy with a question and then ask for your opinion at the end. Most important, I challenge you to get beyond the immediate, often emotional aspect and probe more deeply not only into the controversy but also into your own values.

I have tried to capture varying viewpoints in the Controversy sections. I have made no attempt to provide pro and con positions for every issue, but throughout the text as a whole I have tried to balance liberal and conservative views. I do not agree with all of the opinions expressed—and neither should you. However, understanding why people disagree about such matters as plea bargaining and the death penalty is an important part of understanding how courts operate in mediating between conflicting points of view.

The Murder Trial of Shareef Cousin

This feature puts a single face on the material examined in the text. Each chapter features one of the participants involved in this 1995 murder. These vignettes look at the prosecutor, judge, and defense attorney in the case. They also view the process from the perspective of the grieving father and the angry relatives of Shareef Cousin. I avoid trying to provide an answer to the dominant question: Was Shareef Cousin a brutal murderer who was let off on a legal technicality or an innocent defendant

wrongly convicted because of prosecutorial misconduct? I let you make your own decision.

A Virtual Tour of American Courthouses

Unlike some nations of the world, courts in the United States are open to the public. Anyone can go to the courthouse to observe a trial generating considerable public attention, or just sit in and watch the routine cases being processed each day. Likewise, courts are increasingly making Web sites available so you do not have to leave the comfort of your computer screen to gain a sense of what is happening inside these important government buildings. Each chapter, therefore, contains a new feature—A Virtual Tour of American Courthouses—that provides links to Web sites across the nation. Some provide a dynamic look at what is going on inside the building; others provide perspective on these activities. Some take a look into the future; others offer a glimpse of the past.

Court TV

Each chapter includes a Court TV feature box, which introduces a video clip found on the Student CD-ROM. The text provides an overview of the segment, ties it into the substance of the chapter and poses several critical thinking questions challenging students to apply concepts to the visual material.

Critical Thinking Questions

Each chapter ends with a set of critical thinking questions. The goal is to have you integrate material from several sections of the chapter. Stated another way, they encourage active learning. It is important that you not be content to let the words just pass in front of your eyes. Instead, you need to think about what you are reading and relate it to your own experiences and your own community. Along the way, I hope you come to appreciate how others with different experiences in other types of communities might react differently.

World Wide Web Resources and Exercises

In just a few short years, the Internet has moved into the mainstream of American life. Most immediately, the Web makes learning easier. The Net is chock-full of facts and figures, providing ready access to all matter of knowledge. But at the same time, it requires users to be more aggressive. Many Web pages are nothing more than thinly veiled propaganda pieces, presenting the world from the vantage point of one interest group. Often, factual claims are made without anything to back them up, and closer probing leaves one wondering if they were simply made up. Thus, using the Web as a learning tool requires that you analyze the arguments in terms of the perspective of the writer.

To encourage this kind of active, rather than passive, learning, each chapter contains three Web exercises. The first provides a useful URL, the second suggests a Yahoo search, and the third suggests a Web search. In addition, search terms, useful URLs, and uncommon URLs are highlighted.

InfoTrac College Edition Resources and Exercises

InfoTrac College Edition is a comprehensive and powerful reference resource for student research that is available 24 hours a day, seven days a week. For the subject of this book—courts and crime—InfoTrac College Edition is the perfect vehicle for finding supplementary information about a topic or locating recent developments. Search terms, recommended articles, and learning exercises are provided at the end of each chapter. In addition, relevant InfoTrac College Edition articles are noted throughout the text in special boxes.

Other Student Aids

Each chapter ends with a conclusion, and suggestions for further reading. References can be found in one place at the end of the book. A detailed index, including authors and subjects, is at the back of the book. Finally, a separate case index of all Supreme Court decisions discussed in the text can also be found at the back of the book.

About the Author

avid William Neubauer was born in Chicago. He grew up in Aurora, Illinois, graduating from West Aurora High School in 1962. After receiving an A.B. in political science from Augustana College in Rock Island in 1966, he began graduate work at the University of Illinois, receiving a Ph.D. in 1971.

Neubauer has previously taught at the University of Florida and Washington University in St. Louis. He is now a professor at the University of New Orleans, where he chaired the political science department from 1982 to 1986.

In the mid-1970s, Neubauer served as a consultant to the Federal Judicial Center on two court management projects. From 1978 to 1980, he worked with the American Judicature Society as principal investigator on a project (funded by the National Institute of Justice) concerning court delay reduction. Over the years he has served on review panels for the National Institute of Justice, the Bureau of Justice Statistics, the National Science Foundation, the National Institute of Mental Health, and the National Center for State Courts. He also served as a consultant to the Metropolitan Crime Commission of New Orleans.

Neubauer is the co-author of *Judicial Process: Law, Courts, and Politics in the United States,* Third Edition (2004), published by Thomson, and editor of *Debating Crime: Rhetoric and Reality* (2001), published by Wadsworth.

Courts, Crime, and Controversy

The murder was shocking, even in a city recently proclaimed murder capital of the United States. For their first date, Michael Gerardi gave Connie Babin a single red rose and took her out to dinner at the Port of Call restaurant on the edge of New Orleans' historic French Quarter. As they were returning to his truck, parked a block away, they were confronted by three black youths. Before Gerardi had a chance to hand over his wallet, he was shot in the face. The part-time bartender, who was also a medical student, provided emergency first aid but to no avail. Michael Gerardi was killed during what became known as New Orleans' bloodiest week.

Amid intense local media coverage, the majority African American jury convicted Shareef Cousin of first-degree murder and sentenced him to death. National attention soon focused on the case as well. Shareef Cousin became a poster child for the anti–death penalty movement; he was only 16 at the time of the murder and thus garnered the dubious distinction of being one of the youngest people on America's death row. ◄

The murder in front of the Port of Call restaurant provides but one poignant example that crime has been a pressing national concern for four decades. Newspapers headline major drug busts. Local television news broadcasts graphic footage of the latest murder scene. Not to be outdone, the national media offer tantalizing details on the latest sensational crime or prominent criminal. Meanwhile, official government statistics document that levels of crime are high (but declining), and unofficial pollsters report that Americans believe crime rates are too high. These concerns prompt governmental response. Candidates for public office promise that, if elected, they will get tough on criminals. Governmental officials, in turn, announce bold new programs to eradicate street crime, reduce violence, and end the scourge of drugs. Yet, despite all the attention and promises, street crime remains a volatile, persistent, and intractable issue in the United States (Scheingold 1991).

A good deal of the political rhetoric about crime focuses on the criminal courts. Judges and defense attorneys—much more so than police chiefs and prison wardens—are blamed for high crime rates. Prosecutors are viewed as being too ready to engage in plea bargaining. Judges are accused of imposing unduly lenient sentences. Appellate courts are blamed for allowing obviously guilty defendants to go free on technicalities. Meanwhile, the police complain that Supreme Court decisions handcuff the fight against crime. Victims of crime become frustrated by lengthy trial delays. Witnesses protest wasted trips to the courthouse.

The purpose of this chapter is to build on public perceptions of the criminal courts by focusing on a few basic topics. We begin by discussing where the courts fit in the criminal justice system. Next, attention shifts to the three activities that set the stage for the rest of the book:

- Finding the courthouse
- Identifying the actors in the courthouse
- Following the steps of the process

As we will see shortly, the judicial process is complicated, so throughout this book we will examine the courts from three perspectives:

- Law on the books
- Law in action
- Courts and controversy

THE COURTS AND THE CRIMINAL JUSTICE SYSTEM

Fighting crime is a major societal activity. Every year local, state, and federal governments spend $146 billion on the criminal and civil justice system in the United States (Bureau of Justice Statistics 2004). These tax dol-

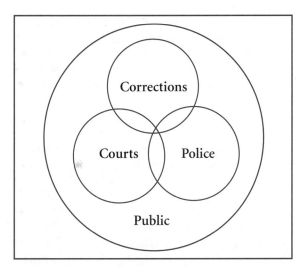

Figure 1-1
The Overlapping Circles of the Criminal Justice System

lars support an enormous assortment of criminal justice agencies, which in turn employ a large (and growing) number of employees; roughly 2 million people earn their living working in the criminal justice system. These government officials are quite busy: Every year the police make more than 14.5 million arrests, and every day correctional personnel supervise 6.3 million people. Yet as large as these figures are, they still underestimate societal activity directed against crime. A substantial number of persons are employed in the private sector in positions either directly (defense attorneys and bail agents) or indirectly (locksmiths and private security) related to dealing with crime (Hakim, Rengert, and Shachmurove 1996).

The numerous public agencies involved in implementing public policy concerning crime are referred to as the **criminal justice system.** Figure 1-1 depicts the criminal justice system as consisting of three overlapping circles: Police are responsible for apprehending criminals; the courts are responsible for deciding whether those arrested are legally guilty and, if so, determining the sentence; corrections is responsible for carrying out the penalty imposed on the guilty.

The major components of the criminal justice system do not make up a smoothly functioning and internally consistent organization. Rather, the criminal justice system is both interdependent and fragmented.

An Interdependent Criminal Justice System

Viewing the various components of criminal justice as a system highlights the fact that these different agencies are interdependent and interrelated (Walker 1992). Police, courts, and corrections are separate government institutions with different goals, histories, and operating procedures. Though separate, they are also tied together because they must interact with one another. The courts play a pivotal role within the criminal justice system because many formal actions pertaining to suspects, defendants, and convicts involve the courts. Only the judiciary can hold a suspect in jail prior to trial, find a defendant guilty, and sentence the guilty to prison. Alternatively, of course, the courts may release the suspect awaiting trial, find the suspect not guilty, or decide to grant probation.

The decisions that courts make have important consequences for other components of the criminal justice system. Judges' bail policies, for example, immediately affect what happens to a person arrested by the police; likewise, corrections personnel are affected because the bail policies of the judges control the size of the local jail population. If the decisions made by the courts have important consequences for police and prisons, the reverse is equally true: The operations of law enforcement and corrections have a major impact on the judiciary. The more felons the police arrest, the greater the workload of the prosecutors; and the more overcrowded the prisons, the more difficult it is for judges to sentence the guilty.

A Fragmented Criminal Justice Nonsystem

The system approach to criminal justice dominates contemporary thinking about criminal justice. But not everyone is convinced of the utility of this conceptualization. Some people point to a nonsystem of criminal justice. Although the work of the police, courts, and corrections must, by necessity, overlap, this does not mean that their activities are coordinated, or coherent. From the perspective of the nonsystem, what is most salient is the fragmentation of criminal justice. Fragmentation characterizes each component of the criminal justice system. The police component consists of more than 17,000 law enforcement agencies, with varying traditions of cooperation or antagonism. Likewise, the corrections component includes approximately 1,300 state and federal correctional facilities, to say nothing of thousands of local jails. But corrections also encompasses probation, parole, drug treatment, halfway houses, and the like.

The same fragmentation holds true for the courts. In many ways, talking about courts is misleading, because the activities associated with the "court" encompass a wide variety of actors. Many people who work in the courthouse—judges, prosecutors, public defenders, clerks, court reporters, bailiffs—are employed by separate government agencies. Others who work in the courthouse are private citizens, but their actions directly affect what happens in this governmental institution; defense attorneys and bail agents are prime examples. Still others are ordinary citizens who find themselves in the courthouse either because they are compelled to be there—defendants and jurors—or because their activities are essential to case disposition—victims and witnesses.

The fragmentation within the three components of the nonsystem of criminal justice is compounded by the decentralization of government. American government is based on the principle of federalism, which distributes government power between national (usually referred to as federal) and state governments. In turn, state governments create local units of government, such as counties and cities. Each of these levels of government is associated with its own array of police, courts, and corrections. This decentralization adds tremendously to the complexity of American criminal justice. For example, depending on the nature of the law allegedly violated, several different prosecutors may bring charges against a defendant, including the following: city attorney (local), district attorney (county), attorney general (state), U.S. attorney (U.S. district court), and U.S. attorney general (national).

Tensions and Conflicts

Criminal justice is best viewed as both a system and a nonsystem. Both interdependence and fragmentation characterize the interrelationships among the agencies involved in apprehending, convicting, and punishing wrongdoers. In turn, these structural arrangements produce tensions and conflicts within each component. For example, the prosecutor loudly condemns the actions of a judge, or a defense attorney condemns the jury for an unjust verdict.

Tensions and conflicts occur also between the components of criminal justice. The interrelationships among police, courts, and corrections are often marked by tension and conflict because the work of each component is evaluated by others: The police make arrests, yet the decision to charge is made by the prosecutor; the judge and jury rate the prosecutor's efforts.

Tensions and conflicts also result from multiple and conflicting goals concerning criminal justice. Government officials bring to their work different perspectives on the common task of processing persons accused of breaking the law. Tensions and conflicts among police, courts, and corrections, therefore, are not necessarily undesirable; because they arise from competing goals, they provide important checks on other organizations, guaranteeing that multiple perspectives will be heard (Wright 1981).

FINDING THE COURTHOUSE

The criminal justice system, as argued here, is both a system and a nonsystem, tied together by core tasks but also marked by tensions and conflicts. The same holds true for the courts. Judges, prosecutors, and defense attorneys, for example, share the common task of processing cases but at the same time exhibit different perspectives on the proper outcome of the case. In understanding this complexity, *America's Courts and the Criminal Justice System* examines the nation's judiciary from three complementary perspectives. Part I is about finding the courthouse, or the basic organization of our court system; Part II concerns identifying the actors in the courthouse; and Part III focuses on following the steps of the process from arrest to appeal.

By rough count there are 17,000 courthouses in the United States. Some are impos-

www A Virtual Tour of American Courthouses: Starters

Courts in the United States are readily accessible—almost every town of any size has a courthouse. Even better, American law mandates that court proceedings must be open to the public, so anyone can observe the dramatic as well as the mundane events that occur in courthouses every day. Hopefully, while reading this book, you will visit your local courthouse for the first time. Or if you have been to a court before, you will return and observe what is going on from a different perspective.

Web sites about courts are becoming increasingly common. Each chapter of this book includes a section called A Virtual Tour of American Courthouses. It is meant to call attention to some of these sites and provide a dynamic look at what goes on inside and outside of these important buildings. For starters, here are a few such Web sites.

Any tour of American courts must begin with our nation's most famous and important court—the United States Supreme Court. Northwestern University Professor Jerry Goldman offers an award-winning site at **http://oyez.itcs. northwestern.edu/oyez/tour/**. Alas, federal courts prohibit cameras, so it is harder to find Web sites offering good visual images. However, a few do exist. Historic photos are available from the Federal Judicial Center at **http://www. fjc.gov/newweb/jnetweb.nsf/fjc_courts**.

A growing number of state supreme courts offer virtual tours. You are just a click away from viewing the courtrooms where some of the nation's most important legal matters are argued, including

> North Dakota: **http://www.court.state.nd.us/Court/ VirtualTour/**
>
> Alabama: **http://www.judicial.state.al.us/tour.cfm**

Trial courts of general jurisdiction are developing Web sites, some of which are truly state of the art, including

> The Sixth Judicial Circuit of Florida: **http://www. jud6.org/**
>
> Washtenaw County, Michigan: **http://www.co. washtenaw.mi.us/depts/courts/index.htm**
>
> Maricopa County, Arizona: **http://www. superiorcourt.maricopa.gov/**
>
> San Diego, California: **http://www.sandiego.courts.ca.gov/superior/ tour/ct2khall.html**

If you travel abroad, take the time to check out other countries' courthouses. Here is a sampler of overseas virtual tours:

> Australia: **http://www.hcourt.gov.au/virtual/**
>
> Canada: **http://www.scc-csc.gc.ca/visitcourt/ inside/index_e.asp**
>
> England's Leeds Town Hall courtroom: **http://www. vrleeds.co.uk/town_hall_tour/source/courtroom. html**

For a true Internet experience, go to iCourthouse at **www. i-courthouse.com,** which offers a streamlined version of the judicial process that moves at Internet speed.

Finally, for sci-fi fans, a few Web sites offer a glimpse of what the courtrooms of the future might look like:

> Courtroom 21: **http://www.courtroom21.net/**
>
> Courtroom 23: **http://www.ninja9.org/courtadmin/ mis/courtroom_23.htm**

---

ing turn-of-the-century buildings noted for their elaborate architecture. Others are faceless modern structures marked by lack of architectural inspiration. A few courts, you might be surprised to learn, are in the front of a funeral parlor or the back of a garage, where justices of the peace preside in rural areas. To view the diversity of courthouses in the United States, see A Virtual Tour of American Courthouses: Starters. Buildings aside, courts are governmental organizations created to hear specific types of cases. Figure 1-2 offers a preliminary overview of different types of courts in the United States.

One distinction is between federal and state courts. The term *dual court system* refers to separate state and federal courts (rarely do cases move from one system to another).

Another important difference between courts relates to function. Most courts are trial courts. As the name implies, this is where trials are held, jurors sworn, and witnesses questioned.

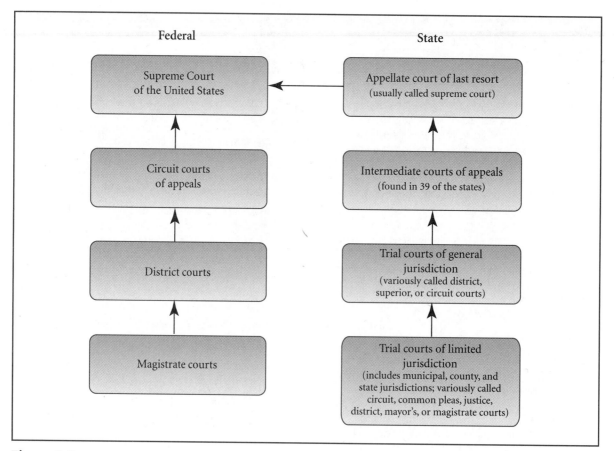

Figure 1-2
Overview of Court Structure in the United States

Trial courts are noisy places resembling school corridors between classes. Amidst the noisy crowd you will find lawyers, judges, police officers, defendants, victims, and witnesses walking through the building during working hours.

Trial courts, in turn, are divided between major and lower. Lower courts initially process felony cases (set bail, for example) but cannot find the defendant innocent or guilty and therefore cannot sentence. Their primary activity involves processing the millions of minor offenses such as public drunkenness, petty theft, and disorderly conduct. Major trial courts, on the other hand, are responsible for the final phases of felony prosecutions. It is in these courts that defendants charged with crimes such as murder, robbery, burglary, and drug dealing enter a plea of guilty (or occasionally go to trial), and the guilty are sentenced.

Other courts (fewer in number) are appeals courts that review decisions made by trial courts (usually only the major trial courts). Appeals courts review decisions made elsewhere, but no trials are held, no jurors employed, no witnesses heard. Rather, appellate courts are places where lawyers argue whether the previous decision correctly or incorrectly followed the law. In many ways appellate courts are like a monastery where scholars pore over old books and occasionally engage in polite debates. Given the growing volume of cases, the federal government and most states have created two levels of appellate courts—intermediate courts, which must hear all cases, and supreme courts, which pick and choose the cases they hear.

Although the U.S. Supreme Court stands atop the organizational ladder, it hears only a handful of the cases filed each year (fewer than

Exhibit **1-1**	Actors in the Courthouse

Police	Court administrator
Federal	Victim/witness assistance program
State	Rape crisis center
Sheriff	**Corrections**
Local	Probation officer
Special districts	Jail
Private security	Prison
Courts	Drug rehabilitation program
Lawyers	**Public**
Prosecutor	*Regular participants*
Public defender	Bail bondsman
Private defense attorneys	Newspaper reporter
Judge	*Irregular participants*
Law clerk	Defendant
Court support staff	Victim
Clerk of court	Witness
Court reporter	Juror
Pretrial services	Victim advocates
Bailiff	

80 per year). Thus its importance is measured not in terms of the number of cases decided but in the wide-ranging impact that these few decisions have on all stages of the process.

IDENTIFYING THE ACTORS IN THE COURTHOUSE

Part II focuses on the actors in the courthouse. Enter a trial courtroom and you will observe numerous people either busily engaged in doing something or seemingly doing nothing. Some of the actors in the courthouse are easily identifiable by the clothes they wear. The person sitting high above everyone else wearing the black robes is the judge. The person in handcuffs arrayed in a bright orange jumpsuit is the defendant. And the men and women dressed in uniforms are law enforcement officers. But the roles being performed by the others in attendance are not readily apparent. It is clear that those sitting in front of the railing are more important than those on the other side. Until court proceedings begin, the observer is never sure whether they are victims, defendants, family, witnesses, reporters, potential jurors, or retired citizens whose hobby is court watching. After the proceedings begin, the roles of those on the other side of the railing become more apparent.

Some participants are present on a regular basis, others only occasionally. Many are public employees, but some are private citizens. Using the categories applied to the criminal justice system, Exhibit 1-1 provides a chart of many of the actors one would expect to see in a courthouse on any given day. Some of the titles vary from place to place. Similarly, the participants vary depending on the type of case. In a murder case, for example, a scientist from the crime lab may be presenting evidence, but in a child sexual abuse case the actors will more likely include a social worker or psychiatrist. A brief overview of the main actors will help set the stage.

Prosecutors

The organization of prosecutors in the United States is as fragmented as the courts in which they appear. To limit ourselves only to state courts and state prosecutions, in most states you find one prosecutorial office for the lower courts (typically the city attorney), another for the major trial court (typically called the district attorney or the state's attorney), and yet another at the state level (almost uniformly called the attorney general).

Regardless of the level, prosecutors are the most influential of the courthouse actors. Their offices decide which cases to prosecute, which cases to plea-bargain, and which cases to try. They may also be influential in matters such as setting bail and choosing the sentence.

Defense Attorneys

The U.S. Constitution guarantees defendants the right to counsel. But for most defendants this abstract "right" collides with economic reality. Many defendants cannot afford to hire a lawyer, so the government must provide one at government expense, either a court-appointed lawyer or a public defender. Only a handful of defendants hire a private lawyer.

Our notions of defense attorneys have been shaped by fictional characters who are always able to show that their clients are innocent. Reality is strikingly different. Often defense attorneys urge their clients to plead guilty based on the assessment that a jury will find the defendant guilty beyond a reasonable doubt. Even when cases are tried, defense attorneys only occasionally are able to secure a not guilty verdict for their client.

Judges

Judges in state courts are by and large elected by the voters. Federal judges, on the other hand, are nominated by the president of the United States and confirmed by the U.S. Senate.

Judges are the ultimate authority figure in the courthouse because only judges can set bail, only judges can instruct jurors about the meaning of the law, and only judges can impose sentences. Exercising this authority, though, is limited by the reality of high caseloads. The quickest way to dispose of cases is by a plea of guilty. Thus judges must be responsive to prosecutors and defense attorneys if they are to achieve their principal goal of disposing of cases.

Defendants and Their Victims

Defendants are, by and large, young, poor, uneducated minority males. A large percentage stand accused of property crimes (theft and burglary) or low-level drug offenses. They are hardly the clever and sophisticated criminals portrayed in fiction. The fact that the defendants are disproportionately minorities means they are now center stage on the great fault line of U.S. politics—race. Whether the criminal justice system discriminates, either intentionally or unintentionally, against African Americans, Hispanics, or Native Americans is a hot topic and one for which there is no unequivocal answer.

The victims of crime are playing an increasingly important role in the criminal courts. Once banished to a bit part of testifying, they are increasingly demanding major roles in setting bail, agreeing to pleas of guilty, imposing sentences, and granting release from prison. Groups such as Mothers Against Drunk Driving (MADD) have become a potent political force. Rhetoric aside, it is important to remember that victims often share the same characteristics as their tormentors—they are, by and large, young, poor, undereducated minorities. But unlike defendants, victims are more likely to be female.

FOLLOWING THE STEPS OF THE PROCESS

From arrest to appeal, a case passes through numerous stages. Exhibit 1-2 presents the steps of criminal procedure in the order in which they typically occur. These steps are

Exhibit **1-2**	Steps of Criminal Procedure	
	Law on the Books	**Law in Action**
Crime	Any violation of the criminal law.	About 14 million serious crimes reported to the police yearly. Property crimes outnumber violent offenses eight to one.
Arrest	The physical taking into custody of a suspected law violator.	About 3 million felony arrests each year.
Initial appearance	The accused is told of the charges, bail is set, and a date for the preliminary hearing is set.	Occurs soon after arrest, which means the judge and lawyers know little about the case.
Bail	Guarantee that a released defendant will appear at trial.	Every day the nation's jails hold more than 650,000 pretrial detainees.
Preliminary hearing	Pretrial hearing to determine if probable cause exists to hold the accused.	Cases are rarely dismissed, but provides defense attorney a look at the evidence.
Charging	Formal criminal charges against defendant stating what criminal law was violated.	From arrest to the major trial court, half of cases are dropped.
Grand jury	A group of citizens who decide if persons accused of crimes should be charged (indicted).	Grand juries indict the defendants the prosecutor wants indicted.
Arraignment	The defendant is informed of the pending charges and is required to enter a plea.	Felony defendant's first appearance before a major trial court judge.
Evidence	Formal and informal exchange of information before trial.	Prosecutors turn over evidence of guilt in hopes of obtaining a plea of guilty.
	Defense may seek to have evidence suppressed because it was collected in a way that violates the Constitution.	Suppression motions are rarely granted but are at the heart of a major debate.
Plea negotiations	The defendant pleads guilty with the expectation of receiving some benefit.	About 90 to 95 percent of felony defendants admit their guilt.
Trial	A fact-finding process using the adversarial method before a judge or a jury.	Most likely only in serious cases; defendant is likely to be convicted.
Sentencing	Punishment imposed on a defendant found guilty of violating the criminal law.	There are 6.7 million persons in prison, on probation, or on parole.
Appeal	Review of the lower court decision by a higher court.	Only 6 percent of convicted defendants win a significant victory.

meant to provide only a basic overview. The specifics of criminal procedure vary from state to state, and federal requirements differ from state mandates. Moreover, prosecutions of serious crimes (felonies) are more complicated than prosecutions of less serious offenses (misdemeanors). Rest assured that the remainder of the text will complicate this oversimplification. But for now we will focus on a defendant charged with a noncapital state felony.

Crime

There is no way to quantify precisely the amount of crime in the United States, but compared to other industrialized nations it is high. Every year about 12 million serious crimes are reported to the police (many others are never reported and therefore never make the official statistics). Although the media focus on crimes of violence, the overwhelming majority of crimes involve burglary, drugs, and theft.

Legally, crimes fall into three categories: felonies (in most states punishable by one year or more in prison); misdemeanors (typically punishable by a sentence in the local jail); and ordinance violations (subject to fine or a short jail term). Felonies are filed in major trial courts, whereas misdemeanor and ordinance violations are typically heard in the lower courts.

Arrest

Every year the police make more than 14.5 million arrests for nontraffic offenses. Most are for minor crimes, but 3 million involve serious crimes such as murder, rape, assault, robbery, burglary, and theft. The police are able to make an arrest in only one out of five crimes known to the police. As a result, only a fraction of the nation's major crimes ever reach the courts.

Initial Appearance

An arrested person must be brought before a judge without unnecessary delay. For felony defendants the initial appearance is largely a formality because no plea may be entered. Instead, defendants are told what crime they are alleged to have committed and perfunctorily advised of their rights, and a date for the preliminary hearing is set. For misdemeanor defendants, the initial appearance is typically the defendant's only courtroom encounter; three out of four plead guilty and are sentenced immediately.

Bail

The most important event that occurs during the initial appearance is the setting of bail. Because a defendant is considered innocent until proven guilty, the vast majority of defendants have the right to post bail. But this legal right is tied to the defendant's economic status. Many defendants are too poor to scrounge up the ready cash to pay the bail agent's fee; thus they must remain in jail awaiting trial. The overriding reality, however, is that U.S. jails are overflowing. As a result, pretrial detention is limited largely to defendants who have committed serious crimes; judges set a very high bail because they don't want these defendants wandering the streets before trial. For defendants charged with less serious crimes, judges and prosecutors may want to keep them in jail while awaiting trial, but the citizens are not willing to invest the tens of millions of dollars needed to build more jails.

Preliminary Hearing

During the preliminary hearing the prosecutor must prove there is probable cause to believe the defendant committed the crime. Probable cause involves two elements: proof that a crime was committed and a linkage between the defendant and that crime. This isn't much of a standard of proof, so most of the time the judge finds that probable cause is present and orders the defendant held for further proceedings. In most courthouses, few cases are dismissed at the preliminary hearing for lack of probable cause.

Charging Decision

Sometime after arrest a prosecutor reviews the case, paying particular attention to the strength of the evidence but also keeping in mind office policies on case priorities. Half the time this review results in dismissal. One out of two defendants is lucky indeed; they are released without the filing of criminal charges. But the other half are in deep trouble; their chances of being found not guilty are now slim indeed.

Grand Jury

Like the preliminary hearing, the grand jury is designed as a check on unwarranted prosecutions. Grand juries are required in all federal felony prosecutions, but only about half the states use them. If the grand jury thinks there is enough evidence to hold the defendant for trial, they return an indictment (also called a true bill) charging the defendant with a crime. On rare occasions grand juries refuse to indict (such refusal is called a no bill or a no true bill). Legal theory aside, grand juries are dominated by the prosecutor, and they obligingly indict whomever the prosecutor wants indicted.

Arraignment

Although the two terms are often used interchangeably, arraignment differs from the initial appearance. During arraignment the defendant is given a copy of the formal charges, advised of his or her rights (usually more extensively than at the initial appearance), and for the first time is called upon to enter a plea. Not surprisingly, most defendants plead not guilty, but a handful admit their guilt then and there and enter a plea of guilty. Overall, little of importance happens during arraignment; this legal step is somewhat equivalent to the taking of class attendance.

Evidence

The term *discovery* refers to the exchange of information prior to trial. In some states (but not all) the prosecutor is required to turn over a copy of the police reports to the defense prior to trial. Generally, however, the defense is required to provide the prosecutor with little if any information. The formal law aside, many prosecutors voluntarily give defense attorneys they trust extensive information prior to trial, anticipating that the defense attorney will persuade the defendant to enter a plea of guilty.

Motions are simply requests that a judge make a decision. Many motions are made during trial, but a few may be made beforehand. The most significant pretrial motions relate to how the police gathered evidence. Defense attorneys file motions to suppress evidence— that is, to prevent its being used during trial. Motions to suppress physical evidence contend that the police conducted an illegal search and seizure (*Mapp*). Motions to suppress a confession contend that the police violated the suspect's constitutional rights during questioning (*Miranda*).

Plea Negotiations

Most findings of guilt result not from a verdict at trial but from a voluntary plea by the defendant. Ninety percent of all felony convictions are the product of negotiations between the prosecutor and the defense attorney (and sometimes the judge as well). Although the public thinks of plea bargaining as negotiating a lenient sentence, the reality is that each courthouse has an informal understanding of what a case is worth. Thus plea bargaining is governed by informal understandings of what sentence is appropriate for a given type of defendant.

Trial

Trial by jury is one of the most fundamental rights granted those accused of violating the criminal law. A defendant can be tried either by a judge sitting alone (called a bench trial) or by a jury. A jury trial typically begins with the selection of twelve jurors. Each side makes opening statements, indicating what they think the evidence in the case will show. Because the prosecutor has the burden of proving the defendant guilty beyond a reasonable doubt, he or she is the first to call witnesses. After the prosecution has completed its case, the defense has the opportunity to call its own witnesses. When all the evidence has been introduced, each side makes a closing argument to the jury, and the judge then instructs the jury about the law. The jurors retire to deliberate in secret. Though the details of trial procedure vary from state to state, one factor is constant: The defendant's chances for an acquittal are not good.

Sentencing

Most of the steps of the criminal process are concerned with determining innocence or guilt. As important as this question is, the members of the courtroom work group spend most of their time deciding what sentence to impose on the guilty. Indeed, defendants themselves are often more concerned about how many years they will have to spend in prison than about the question of guilt.

The principal decision the judge must make is whether to impose a prison sentence or place the defendant on probation. Fines are rarely

COURTᵀⱽ Overview

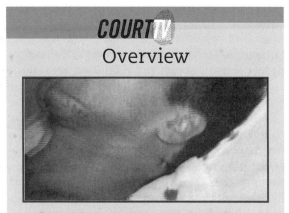

Ride with the police as they break up a knife fight and arrest commercial sex workers. Sit with federal law enforcement agents as they set an Internet trap for a child pornography distributor. Watch as prosecutors methodically prove the guilt of a serial killer. Think along with defense attorneys as they use cross-examination to question the evidence in police brutality cases. Observe judges as they make key rulings about the admissibility of evidence. Hear defendants recount how they came to be falsely convicted. Listen to jurors explain how they decided to convict or acquit. Empathize with a mother as she pleads for the jury to spare her son's life.

Video clips are presented on the CD-ROM that accompanies this book. Cases profiled run the gamut from selling drugs to murder. Taken from Court TV episodes, the video clips offer a dynamic view of crimes like drugs, prostitution, rape and murder, and are based on actual criminal investigations and trials. All of the clips were carefully selected to cover important criminal justice issues like crime on the Internet, drugs, DNA evidence, and defendants falsely convicted. To link the video clips to topics discussed in the book, each presentation is following by critical thinking questions.

used in felony cases. The death penalty is hotly debated but in actuality is limited to only some first-degree murder cases. Prison overcrowding is the dominant reality of contemporary sentencing; more than 1.5 million inmates are incarcerated in state and federal prisons, and the numbers increase by 8 to 12 percent each year. Only recently has attention begun to focus on the fact that the political rhetoric of "lock them up and throw away the key" has resulted in severe prison overcrowding.

Appeal

Virtually all defendants found guilty during trial contest their fate, filing an appeal with a higher court in hopes that they will receive a new trial. Contrary to public perceptions, defendants are rarely successful on appeal; only 1 of 16 appellants achieves a significant victory in the appellate courts. Moreover, appeals are filed in only a small proportion of all guilty verdicts; defendants who plead guilty rarely appeal. Appellate court opinions, however, affect future cases because the courts decide policy matters.

▌LAW ON THE BOOKS

An important first step in understanding how American courts dispense justice is to learn the basic law underlying the process. The structure of the courts, the legal duties of the main actors, and the steps in the criminal process are all basic to an understanding of how the courts dispense criminal justice. These elements constitute law on the books—the legal and structural components of the judiciary. In essence, the starting point in understanding the legal system is knowing the formal rules.

Law on the books is found in constitutions, laws enacted by legislative bodies, regulations issued by administrative agencies, and cases decided by courts. There is little doubt that decisions by the U.S. Supreme Court have far-reaching ramifications. To highlight the importance of court decisions, each chapter's Case Close-up provides an in-depth look at some of the court decisions that have shaped our nation's criminal justice system (see Case Close-up: Overview).

CASE CLOSE-UP

Overview

Each chapter of this book features a case that has had a major impact on the criminal justice system. Many of these cases are significant U.S. Supreme Court decisions. Indeed, some of these cases have been absorbed into the English language. Miranda and Mapp, for example, have almost become household names, and to actors in the system, they are a useful shorthand. Others are less well known but have affected the process in important ways. Throughout I have tried to stress not only the legal principles involved in the decisions but also the nature of the litigants themselves.

▌LAW IN ACTION

The ongoing public debate over the courts indicates that the criminal courts do not stand in splendid isolation, removed from the rest of society. Rather, their activities are intimately intertwined with other social institutions, community values, public opinion, and the actions of other members of the criminal justice system. This perspective has important consequences for how we study the criminal courts. We need to know not only what the law says (law on the books) but also how the rules are applied (law in action).

In many ways law on the books represents an idealized view of law, one that stresses an abstract set of rules that is so theoretical that it fails to incorporate real people. Law on the books provides only an imperfect road map of the day-to-day realities of the courthouse. The concept of law in action, on the other hand, focuses on the factors governing the actual application of the law. It stresses that in the criminal courthouses of the United States, few cases ever go to trial. Most defendants plead guilty rather than have their cases tried. Moreover, judges, prosecutors, and defense attorneys devote considerable time to determining the appropriate sentence to impose on the defendant after he or she is found guilty.

In short, there is a wide gap between legal theory (law on the books) and how that law is applied (law in action). Although some persons find this gap shocking, actually it is not; after all, no human institution ever lives up to the

A DAY IN COURT

Overview

Throughout this book A Day in Court sections focus on law in action, examining the reality of courthouse justice. Sometimes A Day in Court will examine a specific person; other times, an idea or a program. Here is what to expect:

high ideals set out for it. If you spend five minutes observing a stop sign on a well-traveled street, you will find that not all cars come to a complete stop, and some do not seem to slow down much at all. Yet at the same time, the stop sign (the law on the books in this example) clearly does affect the behavior of drivers (law in action).

In Exhibit 1-2, the law-on the-books column seems to suggest a streamlined criminal process, with defendants entering at arrest and steadily and methodically moving through the various stages until conviction and sentencing. This is not the reality. The criminal process is filled with numerous detours. At each stage officials decide to advance the defendant's case to the next step, reroute it, or terminate it. The result is that many cases that enter the criminal court process are eliminated during the early stages. Through-

out this book, A Day in Court boxes highlight key dimensions of law in action (see A Day in Court: Overview).

A law-in-action perspective helps us understand the dynamics of courthouse justice. High caseloads are the reality in courthouses across the nation. As a result, judges are under pressure to move cases lest a backlog develop. Similarly, in most cases the formal rules found in law on the books fail to provide answers to all the questions that arise in a case. As a result, prosecutors must make discretionary choices about matters such as what sentencing recommendation to make to the judge. Finally, cooperation, rather than conflict during trial, often characterizes the behavior of courthouse actors. As a result, defense attorneys often find that negotiating a plea of guilty, rather than going to trial, is in the best interest of their client.

Overview

Many of the issues facing other parts of the criminal justice system also confront the courts. Indeed the courts are often the focus of debates about what the justice system does wrong. Controversy surrounding the courts is widespread and involves a number of issues.

■ Controversy over judicial administration centers on issues such as reducing delay and establishing drug courts.

■ Controversy over crime reduction involves debates over forcing defendants to take a drug test and abolishing the insanity defense.

■ Controversy over gender equity involves debates over gender bias in the courtroom and whether the courts fail to treat domestic violence as a serious offense.

■ Controversy over racial discrimination centers on issues such as underrepresentation of minority judges and allegations of discriminatory sentencing.

■ Controversy over economic inequality centers on debate over underprosecution of white-collar crimes.

Each chapter of this book examines one or more controversies. To look ahead, here are some of the general controversies facing the courts and some of the specific issues that will be discussed.

▌COURTS AND CONTROVERSY

At the heart of the public's concern about crime has been a debate over the actions and inactions of the criminal courts. What the courts do (and don't do) and how they do it occupies center stage in the nation's continuing focus on crime. Numerous reforms have been suggested, but there is no agreement as to what types of change are in order. Throughout this book, Courts and Controversy boxes highlight many issues facing the courts that are debated today (see Courts and Controversy: Overview).

Exhibit **1-3**	Competing Values in the Criminal Justice System	
	Crime Control Model	Due Process Model
Key value	Repress crime.	Protect rights of citizens.
Causes of crime	Breakdown of individual responsibility.	Root causes are poverty and racial discrimination.
Police fact-finding	Most likely to determine guilt or innocence.	Only formal fact-finding can protect the innocent.
Goal of courts	Process guilty defendants quickly.	Careful consideration of each case.
Rights of defendants	Technicalities let crooks go free.	Price we pay for living in a democracy.
Sentencing	Punishment will deter crime.	Rehabilitation will prevent crime.
Advocacy groups	The National Center for Policy Analysis is an advocacy group often associated with the crime control model of criminal justice. For their views on a variety of criminal justice issues, go to **http://www.ncpa.org/pi/crime.htm.**	The American Civil Liberties Union (ACLU) is often identified with the due process model of criminal justice. For their views on a variety of criminal justice issues, go to **http://www.aclu.org.**

In the public dialogue on the issues facing the criminal courts, conservatives square off against liberals, hard-liners against those said to be soft on crime. This sort of terminology is not very helpful. Such phrases as "soft on crime" attract our attention to questions about the goals of the criminal courts, but they are not useful for systematic inquiry because they are ambiguous and emotional (Neubauer 2001).

More constructive in understanding the controversy over the criminal courts are the crime control and due process models developed by Herbert Packer (1968) and discussed by Samuel Walker (2001). In an unemotional way, these two models highlight competing values concerning the proper role of the criminal courts. The conservative crime control model proposes to reduce crime by increasing the penalties on criminals. The liberal due process model advocates social programs aimed primarily at reducing crime by reducing poverty. Exhibit 1-3 summarizes the two views.

Crime Control Model

The most important value in the **crime control model** is the repression of criminal conduct. Unless crime is controlled, the rights of law-abiding citizens will not be protected, and the security of society will be diminished. Conservatives see crime as the product of a breakdown of individual responsibility and self-control. To reinforce social values of discipline and self-control, and to achieve the goal of repressing crime, the courts must process defendants efficiently. They should rapidly remove defendants against whom there is inadequate evidence and quickly determine guilt according to evidence. The crime control model holds that informal fact-finding—initially by the police and later by the prosecutor—not only is the best way to determine whether the defendant is in fact guilty but also is sufficiently foolproof to prevent the innocent from being falsely convicted. The crime control model, therefore, stresses the necessity of speed and finality in the courts in order to achieve the priority of crime suppression.

According to the crime control model, the courts have hindered effective law enforcement and therefore have produced inadequate protection of society. Advocates of this model are concerned that criminals "beat the system" and "get off easy." In their view the cure is to eliminate legal loopholes by curtailing the exclusionary rule, abolishing the insanity defense, allowing for preventive detention of dangerous offenders, and increasing the certainty of punishment.

Due Process Model

In contrast, the **due process model** emphasizes protecting the rights of the individual. Its advocates are concerned about lawbreaking; they see the need to protect the public from predatory criminals. At the same time, however, they believe that granting too much leeway to law enforcement officials will only result in the loss of freedom and civil liberties for all Americans. This alternative diagnosis stresses different causes of crime. Liberals see crime not as a product of individual moral failure but as the result of social influences (Currie 1985). In particular, unemployment, racial discrimination, and government policies that work to the disadvantage of the poor are the root causes of crime; only by changing the social environment will crime be reduced (Currie 1989).

Although adherents of the due process model do not downgrade the need for controlling crime, they believe that single-minded pursuit of such a goal threatens individual rights and poses the threat of a tyrannical government. Thus the key function of the courts is not the speed and finality projected in the crime control model, but an insistence on careful consideration of each case. The dominant image is one of the courts as an obstacle course. The due process model stresses the possibility of error in the informal fact-finding process and therefore insists on formal fact-finding to protect against mistakes made by the police and prosecutors.

Proponents of the due process model believe that the courts' priority should be to protect the rights of the individual. Any resulting decrease in the efficiency of the courts is the price we must pay in a democracy based on individual liberties. The due process model emphasizes the need to reform people through rehabilitation. Community-based sentencing alternatives are considered preferable to the extensive use of prison sentences. Advocates of this approach are concerned that the court system is fundamentally unfair to poor and minority defendants; they therefore support the decisions of the Warren Court expanding protections for criminal defendants.

CONCLUSION

To some, the refusal of District Attorney Harry Connick to try Shareef Cousin a second time represented a miscarriage of justice—a brutal murderer was released on a legal technicality. In the words of Connie Babin, the victim's date for that evening: "You try and do the right thing, and you get kicked in the end" (Coyle 1999). To others, the reversal of the murder conviction meant that justice eventually prevailed—an innocent man had been freed from death row. Throughout the proceedings, the defendant's family alleged racism, prosecutorial misconduct, and underhanded police work. These contrasting reactions illustrate conflicting perspectives on the meaning of justice. They also mirror conflicting views of the purposes of the criminal justice process as summarized in the crime control versus due process models of justice.

Ours is a law-drenched age. Voters and elected officials alike see the solution to pressing social problems in terms of passing a law. Somehow we are not serious about an issue unless we have a law regulating it, and we are not really serious unless we have criminal laws. But laws are not self-enforcing. Some people delude themselves by thinking that passing a law solves the problem. This is not necessarily so. Indeed, if the problem persists, frustration sets in. Thus legislatures mandate that drivers purchase automobile insurance, but accident victims become frustrated when they discover the other party has no insurance. Similarly, judges require defendants to pay

THE MURDER TRIAL OF SHAREEF COUSIN

Acting on an anonymous tip, New Orleans police department detectives arrested Shareef Cousin at his home just a few blocks from where Michael Gerardi had been slain. Nine months later the case went to trial. The state's star witness was Connie Babin, the victim's date, who identified Cousin as the attacker. The defense countered with an alibi contending that Cousin was playing basketball about the time of the shooting. After three hours of deliberations, the jury in Judge Raymond Bigelow's courtroom unanimously found Cousin guilty of first-degree murder. Following the penalty phase of the trial, Shareef Cousin was sentenced to die by lethal injection.

Amid allegations that the prosecutor had improperly withheld evidence during the trial, the state's case unraveled on appeal, however. The Louisiana Supreme Court reversed on the basis of improper use of hearsay testimony. But there would be no retrial. In January 1999 District Attorney Harry Connick reluctantly dismissed the case. Yet Cousin would not walk away from death row a free man. Earlier he had pled guilty to four armed robberies and is now serving 20 years in Angola, the state's major penitentiary.

Throughout this book we will follow the murder trial of Shareef Cousin. Each chapter will examine one aspect of the prosecution, trial, and appeal of this case. The goal is to illustrate important aspects of the American justice system. Here is what to expect:

Chapter	The Murder Trial of Shareef Cousin
2	The Question of Civil Liability
3	A Federal Civil Rights Lawsuit Is Filed
4	Doing Time at Tulane and Broad (Part I)
5	Doing Time at Tulane and Broad (Part II)
6	DA Harry Connick Defends His Aggressive Tactics
7	Limitations Facing the Defense
8	Judge Raymond Bigelow, Ex-Prosecutor
9	The Anguish of the Victims
10	New Orleans' Bloodiest Week in Memory
11	Awaiting Trial in Foti's Fortress
12	The DA Fails to Disclose a Witness Statement
13	Pleading Guilty to Four Armed Robberies
14	Two Trial-Day Surprises
15	Doing Time on the Farm
16	The Jury Chooses Death
17	A Reversal on Narrow Grounds
19	Few Options or Safeguards in a City's Juvenile Courts

To learn more about the murder trial of Shareef Cousin, go to http://cj.wadsworth.com/neubauer_courts8e. This companion Web site provides additional resources, including timelines of key events, list of participants, photos, key documents in the case, newspaper stories of the case, court opinions, motions filed, and much more.

restitution, but crime victims discover that impoverished defendants (particularly those in prison) have no ability to pay. In the same vein, conservatives call for preventive detention, but jailers find that there are no jail cells available.

Although most people know something about the law, they also know much that is contrary to fact. Some of these public understandings and misunderstandings about law are the product of education. High school American government and history textbooks, for example, offer a simplified, formal picture of law and the courts, lawyers, and trials. Americans also learn about the legal system by going to the movies, watching television, and reading fiction. At times, persons who rely on these sources are badly misled. Entertainment programs misrepresent the nature and amount of crime in the United States. Because murder makes a much better show than embezzlement or burglary, entertainment rarely shows street crime other than drug offenses.

Television also offers a number of false or doubtful propositions. It tells us, for example, that criminals are white males between the ages of 20 and 50, that bad guys are usually businesspeople or professional criminals, and that crime is almost always unsuccessful in the end. Television and film also often misrepresent the roles of actors in the legal system.

With few exceptions, police are in constant action, chasing crooks in cars, running after them on foot, and capturing them only after exchanging gunfire. Perry Mason set the pattern for atypical portrayals of lawyers by always securing his client's acquittal. In addition, entertainment distorts important issues of civil liberties. As soon as we know who did it and that the guilty crook has been apprehended, the case is solved with no need for the prosecutor to prove the defendant guilty.

These understandings and misunderstandings form the backdrop for this book. The Epilogue will examine in greater depth how and why courts figure so prominently in the public rhetoric over crime.

CRITICAL THINKING QUESTIONS

1. On a sheet of paper, apply the general overview of court structure in the United States (Figure 1-2) to your local community.

2. On a sheet of paper, apply the list of Actors in the Courthouse (Exhibit 1-1) to your local community. If you live in a rural area, how does your list differ from that of someone who lives in a larger community? If you live in a large metropolitan area, how does your list differ from that of someone living a more rural area?

3. What private, nongovernmental organizations are important to the criminal justice system of your community?

4. Use newspapers, radio, and criminal justice discussion lists/chat groups to monitor discussions concerning the criminal justice system. Do citizens make distinctions about police, courts, or corrections, or do they lump everything under the general rubric of the criminal justice system?

KEY TERMS

crime control model (16)
criminal justice system (3)
due process model (17)

WORLD WIDE WEB RESOURCES AND EXERCISES

Web Guides

http://dir.yahoo.com/Society_and_Culture/Crime/
http://dir.yahoo.com/Government/Law/Criminal_Justice/
http://dir.yahoo.com/Government/U_S_Government/Judicial_Branch/
http://dir.yahoo.com/Society_and_Culture/Crime/Outlaws/

Web Search Terms

criminal justice
administration of justice

Useful URLs

The Bureau of Justice Statistics Web site provides the latest statistics on the criminal justice system at **http://www.ojp.usdoj.gov/bjs/**.

Sourcebook of Criminal Justice Statistics. This yearly publication runs over 600 pages. As new material becomes available, it is included in the online version: **http://www.albany.edu/sourcebook/**.

The National Consortium for Justice Information and Statistics provides a multifaceted resource for operational criminal justice agencies: **http://www.search.org/**.

The Justice Information Center maintained by the National Criminal Justice Reference Service provides the full text of hundreds of government publications: **http://www.ncjrs.org/**.

Uncommon URLs

Famous American Trials offers a fascinating glimpse into trials, old and new, that have shaped U.S. society: **http://www.law.umkc.edu/faculty/projects/ftrials/ftrials.htm**.

Crime Library is a gallery of famous and infamous criminals: **http://www.crimelibrary.com/**.

Journal of Criminal Justice and Popular Culture features articles on various topics as well as book reviews and movies: **http://www.albany.edu/scj/jcjpc/index.html**.

Famous Cases offers a walk through the history of the FBI: **http://www.fbi.gov/yourfbi/history/famcases/famcases.htm**.

Web Exercises

1. The Internet has been called the world's largest library, and as in any library, the easiest way to retrieve information is to go directly to the place where it is located. Each site on the Web has a unique location called a URL (Uniform Resource Locator). One site that contains a wealth of statistical data on the criminal justice system is maintained by the Bureau of Justice Statistics: **http://www.ojp.usdoj.gov/bjs**. Click on Expenditure & Employment, and update the employment statistics discussed in this chapter. You can also use this site to add to Exhibit 1-1 with basic data about numbers of criminal justice agencies and employees.

2. The Internet is not only the world's largest library but also the world's largest library without a card catalog. Unless you know specifically where to find information (the URL), you can waste a lot of time and become very frustrated in the process. Thankfully, several Web guides organize information around topics. In turn, this in-

formation is organized as a menu, which allows you to go from the most general topics (Society and Culture, for example) to specific ones. One of the most popular Web guides is Yahoo. You can access Yahoo either by clicking on Net Search on your browser and then clicking Yahoo or by going directly to Yahoo. The URL for Yahoo is **http://www.yahoo.com**. Once in Yahoo, here are the links to find information about the criminal justice system: Society and Culture/Crime/Organizations. Look for organizations that span different segments of the criminal justice system and see what they say about coordination.

3. Select the search engine of your choice and use the search term "administration of justice" to locate three or more groups active in the crime debate. Which Web sites articulate values associated with the crime control model? Which Web sites articulate values associated with the due process model?

INFOTRAC COLLEGE EDITION RESOURCES AND EXERCISES

Basic Search Terms

criminal justice *administration of crime*

Recommended Articles

John Diulio, "Federal Crime Policy: Time for a Moratorium"

Stephen Pomper, "Reasonable Doubts"

Rebecca Porter, "Public Attitudes about Justice System Explored in Survey, Conference"

InfoTrac College Edition Exercises

1. Using the search term "crime, causes of," locate one article that reflects the crime control model of criminal justice and another that is based on the due process model of criminal justice. How did you decide that the articles belong to one category

and not the other? Do these two articles make arguments similar to or different from those discussed in this book?

2. Using the search term "criminal justice, administration of," locate two or more articles that discuss the criminal justice system. To what extent do the articles emphasize the interdependent nature of the criminal justice system? To what extent do they stress the fragmentation of the criminal justice system?

FOR FURTHER READING

Conley, John. *The 1967 President's Crime Commission Report: Its Impact 25 Years Later.* Cincinnati: Anderson, 1994.

Friedman, Lawrence. *Crime and Punishment in American History.* New York: Basic Books, 1994.

Garland, David. *The Culture of Control: Crime and Social Order in Contemporary Society.* Chicago: University of Chicago Press, 2002.

Kappeler, Victor, Mark Blumberg, and Gary Potter. *The Mythology of Crime and Justice.* 2d ed. Prospect Heights, IL: Waveland Press, 1996.

Lock, Samuel. *Crime, Public Opinion, and Civil Liberties: The Tolerant Public.* Westport, CT: Praeger Publishers, 1999.

Marion, Nancy. *Criminal Justice in America: The Politics behind the System.* Durham, NC: Carolina Academic Press, 2002.

Neubauer, David. *Debating Crime: Rhetoric and Reality.* Belmont, CA: Wadsworth, 2001.

Neubauer, David, and Stephen Meinhold. *Judicial Process: Law, Courts, and Politics in the United States.* 3d ed. Belmont, CA: Wadsworth, 2004.

Robinson, Paul. *Would You Convict? Seventeen Cases That Challenged the Law.* New York: New York University Press, 1999.

Uviller, H. Richard. *Virtual Justice: The Flawed Prosecution of Crime in America.* New Haven, CT: Yale University Press, 1996.

Wilson, James Q. *Thinking about Crime.* Rev. ed. New York: Basic Books, 1983.

Part I The Legal System

art I examines the legal foundations of the American judicial system, with a particular emphasis on criminal law and the criminal courts.

Chapter 2 provides an overview of law, America's common law heritage, adversarial justice, and the rights of the accused. Particular attention is devoted to how the criminal law defines certain acts as illegal. Topics to be highlighted include the growing use of civil law for what traditionally had been criminal matters and how criminal law is both constant and changing.

Chapter 3 examines the federal court system with its four tiers of courts: magistrate courts, U.S. District Courts, U.S. Courts of Appeal, and U.S. Supreme Court. The federal courts also have an important array of administrative mechanisms. Some topics of interest include the rising volume of federal caseloads and efforts to federalize state crimes.

Chapter 4 focuses on the organization of state courts, which in most states consists of four levels: minor trial courts, major trial courts, intermediate courts of appeals, and state supreme court. Of special interest are efforts to reform court structures and the consequences of the diversity of judicial bodies. Drug courts are an example of current efforts to modernize the judiciary.

Chapter 2 | Law and Crime

o Bernhard Goetz the four black teenagers on the New York subway were not just a nuisance but a threatening pack. Before they could mug him, he pulled a .38-caliber pistol from his pocket and fired all five rounds, leaving 19-year-old Darrell Cabey paralyzed and suffering from brain injuries. Goetz quickly became known as the subway vigilante. To some he was a folk hero bold enough to take a stand against the all-too-frequent incidents of urban violence. But to others he was nothing more than a racist who illegally took justice into his own hands. These conflicting images would be played out in the courts over the next several years. The results were two jury decisions with somewhat contrasting verdicts. ◄

The multiple legal proceedings surrounding the events on the New York subway illustrate the complexities of U.S. law. And it is this law that constitutes the basic source of authority for the courts. Thus, before we can assess the type of justice produced by the courts, we need to know something about the law that is applied in reaching those results. Bear in mind that the United States has no uniform set of criminal or civil laws. Instead, each jurisdiction enacts its own set of criminal prohibitions, leading to some important variations from state to state.

This chapter begins by providing a working definition of law and then examines our common law heritage, including the adversary system and the rights of the accused. Next the discussion shifts from procedure to substance. After looking at differences between civil law and criminal law, we will concentrate on the elements of a crime and legal defenses. The chapter concludes with a discussion of the consequences of criminal law for the criminal court process.

THE BASIS OF LAW

The basis of law can be summarized in two words: human conflict. A controversy over how much money is owed, a quarrel between husband and wife, a collision at an intersection, and the theft of a television set are a few examples of the great number of disputes that arise and threaten to disrupt the normal activities of society. Business and everyday activities depend on mechanisms for mediating inevitable human conflicts. Without such mechanisms, individual parties might seek private, violent means of settlement. The legendary feud between the Hatfields and the McCoys illustrates the disruptiveness of blood feuds motivated by revenge—not only in the lives of the individual parties directly involved but also in the larger society.

Law is an everyday word, but as Law Professor Lawrence Friedman (1984, 2) suggests, "It is a word of many meanings, as slippery as glass, as elusive as a soap bubble." Although there are various approaches to defining the term, most scholars define **law** as a body of rules enacted by public officials in a legitimate manner and backed by the force of the state (Neubauer and Meinhold 2004). This definition can be broken into four phrases, and each has important implications for how we think about law.

The first element—law is a body of rules—is self-evident. What is not immediately obvious, however, is the fact that these rules and regulations are found in a variety of sources: statutes, constitutions, court decisions, and administrative regulations.

The second element—law is enacted by public officials—is of critical importance. All organizations of any size or complexity have rules and regulations that govern their members. But these private rules are not law under our definition unless they are recognized by public officials—judges, legislators, and executives in particular.

The third element—law is enacted in a legitimate manner—means that it must be agreed upon ahead of time how the rules will be changed. Thus, legislatures have methods for passing new laws, bureaucrats have procedures for applying those rules, and judges follow a well-known process in interpreting those rules.

The final element—law is backed by the force of the state—says that these rules and regulations would be largely meaningless without sanctions. Thus, what differentiates law from other societal rules is that law has teeth to it. As Daniel Oran's *Law Dictionary for Nonlawyers* (1985) puts it, law is "that which must be obeyed." In most instances, however, it is not necessary to apply legal sanctions, because the threat is enough to keep most people in line most of the time.

It is also important to stress what this working definition of law omits—namely, any mention of justice. In a representative democracy, public perceptions of law embody fundamental notions of justice, fairness, and decency (Walker 2001). It is the potential linking of law and justice (in the form of unjust laws) that also makes law so difficult to define. But law and morality do not necessarily equate. Our working definition of law deliberately excludes any reference to justice because there is no precise legal or scientific meaning to the term. Furthermore, people use justice to support particular political and social goals. In the public arena, *justice* is a catchall used in several different ways. As discussed in Chapter 1, backers of the crime control model see justice differently than do supporters of the due process model.

THE COMMON LAW HERITAGE

The American legal system traces its origins to England and is therefore referred to as Anglo-Saxon or **Anglo-American law.** Common law is utilized in English-speaking nations, including England, Australia, New Zealand, Canada, and the United States. (The only exception is the state of Louisiana, which derives its civil law from the Napoleonic Code and the Continental legal heritage; the state's criminal law, however, derives from the common law.)

The common law first appeared in medieval England after the Norman conquest in 1066. The new rulers gradually introduced central government administration, including the establishment of courts of law. Initially, the bulk of the law was local and was administered in local courts. A distinct body of national law began to develop during the reign of Henry II (1154–1189), who was successful in expanding the jurisdiction of the royal courts. The king's courts applied the common customs of the entire realm rather than the parochial traditions of a particular village. Thus, the term **common law** meant general law as opposed to special law; it was the law common to the entire land. During the development of the common law legal system, a distinctive way of interpreting the law gradually emerged. Three key characteristics of this common law heritage stand out: The law was judge-made, based on precedent, and found in multiple sources.

Judge-Made Law

One key characteristic of the common law is that it was predominantly **judge-made law** (rather than legislatively enacted). Until the late nineteenth century, there was no important body of statutory law in either England or the United States. Rather, judges performed the task of organizing social relationships through law. In the field of civil law, for example, the common law courts developed the rights and obligations of citizens in such important areas as property, contracts, and torts. Even today American law in these areas is predominantly judge-made.

Similarly, in the field of criminal law, by the 1600s the English common law courts had defined such felonies as murder, arson, robbery, larceny, and rape. Moreover, the legal defenses of insanity and self-defense had also entered the common law. These English criminal law concepts were transplanted to America by the colonists. After the Revolution, those common law crimes considered applicable to local conditions were retained. Although legislative bodies, not the courts, now define crimes, contemporary statutory definitions often reflect their common law heritage.

Precedent

A second key characteristic of the common law is the use of **precedent,** often referred to as

Exhibit 2-1   How to Read Legal Citations

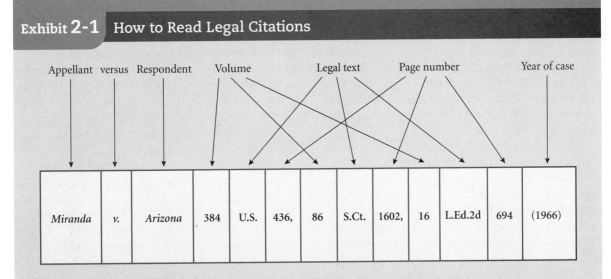

When first confronted with legal citations, students are often bewildered by the array of numbers. But with a few basics in mind, these citations need not be confusing; they are efficient aids in finding court decisions.

The full citation for Miranda is as follows: *Miranda v. Arizona*, 384 U.S. 436, 86 S.Ct. 1602, 16 L.Ed.2d 694 (1966). The lead name in the case usually refers to the party who lost in the lower court and is seeking to overturn that decision. That party is called the appellant. The second name refers to the other party (or parties) who won at the lower level (in this instance, the state of Arizona). The second party is called the appellee, or more simply, the respondent. Miranda is the appellant who is seeking to overturn his conviction. The state of Arizona is named as the respondent because criminal prosecutions are brought in the name of the state.

After the names of the parties come three sets of references. All decisions of the U.S. Supreme Court are reported in the *Supreme Court Reports*, which is published by the U.S. Government Printing Office. It is the official reporting system and is abbreviated U.S. In addition, decisions of the Supreme Court are reported in two private reporting systems: the *Supreme Court Reporter*, which is abbreviated S.Ct., and in *Lawyers Supreme Court Reports, Lawyers Edition*, which is abbreviated L.Ed.2d. The numbers preceding the abbreviation for the volume refer to the volume number. Thus, Miranda can be found in volume number 384 of the *Supreme Court Reports*. The numbers after the abbreviation refer to the page number. Thus the Miranda decision in volume 384 begins on page 436; in volume 86 of the *Supreme Court Reporter*, it is on page 1602. A library usually carries only one of the reporting systems, so the multiple references make it easy to locate the given case, no matter which of the three reporting systems is available. The final number in parentheses is the year of the case.

Decisions of other appellate courts at both the federal and state levels are reported in a similar manner in other volumes.

stare decisis ("let the decision stand"). The doctrine of precedent requires a judge to decide a case by applying the rule of law found in previous cases, provided the facts in the current case are similar to the facts in the previous cases. By following previous court decisions, the legal system promotes the twin goals of fairness and consistency. Exhibit 2-1 gives an example of the precedent-based citation system used in American law.

The common law's reliance on precedent reflects a cautious approach to problem solving. Rather than writing a decision attempting to solve the entire range of a given legal problem, common law courts decide only as much of the case as is necessary to resolve the individual dispute. Broad rules and policy directives emerge only through the accumulation of court decisions over time. Unfortunately, many Americans make the mistake of translating the common law heritage, particularly the doctrine of precedent, into a static view of the courts and the law. The entire history of Anglo-American law emphasizes the importance of common law courts' shaping old law to new demands. In the words of Justice Oliver Wendell Holmes (1920, 187): "It is revolting to have no better reason for a rule of law than that it was so laid down in the times of Henry IV. It is still more revolting if the grounds upon which it was laid down have vanished long since, and the rule simply persists from blind imitation of the past."

One way courts achieve flexibility is in adapting old rights to new problems. Another is the ability of courts to distinguish between precedents. Recall that the doctrine of precedent involves previous cases with a similar set of facts. Courts sometimes state that the present facts differ from those on which previous decisions were based and reach a different ruling. Finally, judges will occasionally (but very reluctantly) overturn a previous decision by stating that the previous court opinion was wrong. However, the common law is committed to gradual change in order to maintain stability; it is often said that the law and the courts are conservative institutions.

Multiple Sources of Law

The third key characteristic of the common law is that it is found in multiple sources (a concept sometimes expressed as *uncodified*). In deciding the legal meaning of a given crime (murder, for example), it is not sufficient to look only at the legislative act. One must also know how the courts have interpreted the statute. Depending on the issue, the applicable rules of law may be found in constitutions, statutes, administrative regulations, and court decisions.

Constitutions

Within the hierarchy of law, constitutions occupy the top rung. A **constitution** is the first document that establishes the underlying principles and general laws of a nation or state. The U.S. Constitution is the fundamental law of the land. All other laws—federal, state, or local—are secondary. Similarly, each state has a constitution that is the "supreme law of the state." State courts may use the state constitution to invalidate the actions of legislators, governors, or administrators.

Constitutions define the powers that each branch of government may exercise. For instance, Article III of the U.S. Constitution creates the federal judiciary (see Chapter 3).

Constitutions also limit government power. Some limitations take the form of prohibitions. Thus, Article I, Section 9, states, "The privilege of the Writ of Habeas Corpus shall not be suspended." Other limitations take the form of specific rights granted to citizens. The clearest example is the first ten amendments to the U.S. Constitution, known collectively as the Bill of Rights. For example, the First Amendment begins "Congress shall make no law respecting an establishment of religion, or prohibiting the free exercise thereof." State constitutions also contain bills of rights, many of which are modeled after their national counterpart.

Constitutions also specify how government officials will be selected. The U.S. Constitution provides that federal judges shall be nominated by the president, confirmed by the Senate, and serve during "good behavior." Similarly, state constitutions specify that state judges will be selected by election, appointment, or merit (see Chapter 8).

Statutes

The second rung of law consists of **statutes.** Laws enacted by federal and state legislatures are usually referred to as statutory law. A statutory law enacted by a local unit of government is commonly called a **municipal ordinance.**

Until the latter part of the nineteenth century, American legislatures played a secondary role in the formulation of law. It was not until the twentieth century that state legislatures became the principal source of law (Friedman 1984). A fundamental reason for the growing importance of legislatively enacted statutes was that new types of problems faced a rapidly industrializing society. Questions of how to protect the interests of workers and consumers were much broader in scope than those typically handled by the courts. The common law took decades to develop and refine legal rights and obligations, but the growing needs of an increasingly complex society could not afford the luxury of such a lengthy time frame. Legislators could enact rules of law that were not only much broader in scope than those adopted by judges but also more precise and detailed. Thus, a great deal of law today is statutory.

Administrative Regulations

The third rung of American law consists of **administrative regulations.** Legislative bodies delegate rule-making authority to a host of governmental bureaucracies variously called agencies, boards, bureaus, commissions, or departments. All levels of government—federal, state, and local—authorize administrative agencies to issue specific rules and regulations consistent with the general principles specified in a statute or municipal ordinance. The Internal Revenue Service, by rule, decides what constitutes a legitimate deduction. State boards, by rule, set standards for nursing homes. Local zoning boards, by rule, decide where restaurants may be built.

Administrative regulations are the newest, fastest-growing, and least understood source of law. The rules and regulations promulgated by government agencies are extensive. The federal bureaucracy alone issues thousands of pages of new rules and policy statements each year. Often administrative rules and regulations are interpreted by courts.

Judicial Decisions

Appellate court decisions also remain an important source of law. According to the common law tradition, courts do not make law, they merely find it. But this myth, convenient as it was for earlier generations, cannot mask the fact that courts do make law. This tradition, though, suggests a basic difference between legislative and judicial bodies. Legislative bodies are free to pass laws boldly and openly. Moreover, their prescription of the rules is general and all-encompassing. Courts make law more timidly, on a piece-by-piece basis, and operate much more narrowly.

Although American law today is primarily statutory and administrative, vestiges of judge-made law persist. The law governing personal injury (tort) remains principally judge-made law, as do procedural matters such as rules of evidence. The major influence of case law (another term for court decisions), however, is seen in interpreting the law of other sources. The Constitution is a remarkably short document of some 4,300 words, and it is full of generalizations such as "due process of law," "equal protection of the laws," and "unreason-

able searches and seizures." The founding fathers left later generations to flesh out the operating details of government. Supreme Court decisions have been primarily responsible for adapting constitutional provisions to changing circumstances. Through an extensive body of case law, the Court has supplied specific meaning to these vague phrases. For this reason, the Court has often been termed an ongoing constitutional convention (Chapter 17).

Case law is vital in determining the meaning of other sources of law as well. Statutes, for example, address the future in general and flexible language. The interpretations that courts provide can either expand or contract the statute's meaning. No lawyer is comfortable with his or her interpretation of an alleged violation of the criminal law without first checking to see how the courts have interpreted it.

THE ADVERSARY SYSTEM

Law is both substantive and procedural. **Substantive law** creates legal obligations. Tort, contract, and domestic relations are examples of substantive civil law. Murder, robbery, and burglary are examples of substantive criminal law. **Procedural law,** on the other hand, establishes the methods of enforcing these legal obligations. Trials are the best-known aspect of American procedural law, but trials do not exist alone. Before trial there must be orderly ways to start lawsuits, conduct them, and end them. An important aspect of procedural law centers on the roles lawyers and judges play in the legal process.

In many nations of the world, criminal investigations are conducted by a single government official whose function is to establish a unified version of what happened, seeking out facts that show the defendant's guilt as well those that indicate that he or she is innocent. France is an example of such an approach (see A Day in Court: The French Legal System). The Anglo-American legal system rejects such an approach. Its guiding premise is that a battle between two opposing parties will uncover more of the truth than would a single official, no matter how industrious and well-meaning. Under the **adversary system,** the burden is on

A DAY IN COURT

The French Legal System

 As the French government builds a legal case against seven photographers who pursued Princess Diana in the final hours of her life, prepare to set aside much of what you know about the American legal system. The French legal system is rooted in the Middle Ages, owing more to Napoleon than James Madison.

America boasts an adversarial process that weighs competing rights and turns lawyers into combatants. In France, from start to finish, the process is an inquiry in which the judge is the all-powerful truthseeker and lawyers are the supporting cast. "Après Dieu, c'est lui," says Pierre-Philippe Barkats, a lawyer licensed in France and Washington, referring to French judges. "After God, it's the judge." . . .

The first sign of major differences in the two legal systems came as the photographers were taken into custody after Saturday's tragedy. They were held two days without charges being filed. And they had no legal right to see their lawyers during the initial questioning—sure grounds for throwing out a case in the USA.

"The justice system in France would be unconstitutional here," says Tulane University law professor Thomas Carbonneau, who has practiced in France. "They have a very different sense of justice, that it's a job for professionals, not the people. They're less interested in public access to the process." . . .

The probe has no parallel in the U.S. system. The photographers have not been indicted, but a determination has been made that an investigation is warranted. "It's less than indictment, but it's still something significant," says Jonathan Wohl, an American lawyer in Paris. An investigating judge, who has no counterpart in the USA, will conduct the probe in close cooperation with the prosecutor. The judge's investigation could take months. If he decides no charges should be brought, the French prosecutor, unlike American district attorneys, could appeal. But if the judge decides some or all of the photographers should stand trial, the trial will get under way in a formal setting in which the lawyers must be civil and flamboyance is unwelcome. "Lawyers are rarely celebrities in France," says Axelle Hovine, aide to a judge in Paris. "The judicial process is much more closed."

A panel of judges would preside in the trial phase and question witnesses. Answers could include almost anything, even hearsay evidence that would be barred here. The lawyers can also ask questions, but have no right to cross-examine. The judges are civil servants, not elected or appointed as in the USA. But the fact that they are bureaucrats does not necessarily give them any greater independence, says Carbonneau. "In a celebrity case like this, the judge is going to follow what he believes is the position of the executive branch," says Carbonneau. The French government, he suggests, probably wants the paparazzi punished.

If the photographers are found guilty of anything, it will not be based on the U.S. standard of guilt "beyond a reasonable doubt" but rather the "conviction intime du juge"—the judge's [personal] belief of what really happened. . . .

In a "piggyback" process unfamiliar in the USA, the outcome of the criminal trial—guilt or innocence—will also determine the outcome of the civil suit filed this week by Dodi Fayed's father. There will be no separate civil trial. By contrast, O. J. Simpson was found not guilty of the crime of murdering his former wife and her friend, but a separate jury found him liable for their death.

SOURCE: Tony Mauro, "The French Legal System," *USA Today.* Copyright September 4, 1997. Reprinted with permission.

To explore how the legal systems of other countries differ from the U.S. system, go to any of these Web sites:

International Web sites from the National Center for State Courts http://www.ncsc.dni.us/COURT/SITES/courts.htm#international

The International Center http://www.ojp.usdog.gov/nij/international/

The United Nations Crime and Justice Information Network http://www.uncjin.org/

the prosecutor to prove the defendant guilty beyond a reasonable doubt, and the defense attorney is responsible for arguing for the client's innocence and asserting legal protections. The judge serves as a neutral arbitrator who stands above the fight as a disinterested party, ensuring that each side battles within the established rules. Finally, the decision is entrusted to the jury (although in some instances a judge alone may decide). The adversary system reflects two important premises: the need for safeguards and the presumption of innocence.

Safeguards

The guiding assumption of the adversary system is that two parties, approaching the facts from entirely different perspectives, will uncover more of the truth than would a single investigator, no matter how industrious and objective. Through cross-examination, each side has the opportunity to probe for possible biases in witnesses and to test what witnesses actually know, not what they think they know. The right to cross-examination is protected by the Sixth Amendment: "In all criminal prosecutions, the accused shall enjoy the right . . . to be confronted with witnesses against him."

By putting power in several different hands, the adversary system creates another type of safeguard. Each actor is granted limited powers, and each has limited powers to counteract the others. If the judge is biased or unfair, the jury has the ability to disregard the judge and reach a fair verdict; if the judge believes the jury has acted improperly, he or she may set aside the jury's verdict and order a new trial. This diffusion of powers in the adversary system incorporates a series of checks and balances aimed at curbing political misuse of the criminal courts.

In diffusing power, the adversary system provides a third safeguard: It charges a specific actor—the defense attorney—with asserting the rights of the accused. Defense attorneys search out potential violations of the rights of the accused. They function as perpetual challengers in the criminal court process and are ready at every juncture to challenge the government by insisting that the proper procedures be followed.

Presumption of Innocence

One of the most fundamental protections recognized in the American criminal justice process is the **presumption of innocence.** The state has the burden of proving defendants guilty of alleged crimes; defendants are not required to prove themselves innocent. In meeting the obligation to prove the defendant guilty, the prosecution is required to prove the defendant guilty **beyond a reasonable doubt.** This legal yardstick measures the sufficiency of the evidence; it means that the jury must be fully satisfied that the person is guilty. It does not mean the jury must be 100 percent convinced, but it comes close (Oran 1985). This criterion is more stringent than the burden of proof in a civil case, in which the yardstick is the **preponderance of the evidence,** meaning a slight majority of the evidence for one side or the other. Case Close-up: Two Verdicts in the O. J. Trial illustrates how differing burdens of proof can lead to different verdicts.

THE RIGHTS OF THE ACCUSED

Procedural law in the United States places a heavy emphasis on protecting the individual rights of each citizen. A key feature of a democracy is the insistence that the prevention and control of crime be accomplished within the framework of law. The criminal process embodies some of society's severest sanctions: detention before trial, confinement in prison after conviction, and, in certain limited situations, execution of the offender. Because the powers of the criminal courts are so great, there is concern that those powers not be abused or misapplied. The Judeo-Christian tradition places a high value on the worth and liberty of each individual citizen.

Restrictions on the use and application of government power take the form of rights granted to the accused. One of the most fundamental protections is the right to remain silent. Another is the right to a trial by jury. These protections exist not to free the guilty but to protect the innocent (see Exhibit 2-2). Basing the criminal justice process on the necessity of protecting individual liberties (of the innocent and guilty alike) obviously reduces

Two Verdicts in the O. J. Trials

 The trial of O. J. Simpson has been called the "trial of the century." While some argue that this phrase has become overused, there is little doubt that the trial of O. J. Simpson was the most watched event of its type in history. The reason for this intense viewer interest is that from the beginning the case seemingly had it all. The shocking news of the murder of Nicole Brown Simpson seemed like an event from a paperback novel: a beautiful blonde and her male companion brutally murdered near her home. The defendant was well known and well liked—a former star football player who after his playing days enjoyed a wide following as a TV sports personality. And to add even more interest, the suspect disappeared in the middle of the night, only to be seen days later by millions of television viewers as the police slowly pursued his white SUV in a surreal chase scene.

Nor was the trial itself an anticlimax. Prominent lawyers basked in the media attention while obscure prosecutors quickly became media celebrities, and a good-natured judge appeared, at times, unable to control the "media circus." For 37 weeks witnesses testified and experts offered their opinions, with lawyer pundits quick to label some "flaky" and others just plain wrong. Throughout, the defense kept the focus on the conduct of the Los Angeles Police Department during the case, alleging, at best, shoddy police work and, at worst, racial bias. But perhaps most important of all, the case was widely followed because there was an underlying dramatic tension to the proceedings: Was Simpson innocent or guilty? Finally, the case went to the jury. After only four hours of deliberation the jury returned a verdict of not guilty.

A year after O. J. Simpson was acquitted of criminal charges, the civil trial began. The underlying allegation—O. J. Simpson murdered his ex-wife and Ronald Goldman—remained the same, but the rules in the proceedings were fundamentally different. For one, the nature of the accusations differed. In the criminal trial Simpson was charged with homicide, but in the civil case the allegations involved wrongful death (a type of tort). Instead of having to prove guilty intent, the plaintiff had only to establish that O. J. Simpson was negligent, an allegation that is easier to prove because it is a broader concept. Moreover, because this was a civil action, the plaintiff only had to prove its case with a preponderance of evidence.

Constitutional protections likewise differ in criminal and civil proceedings. In a criminal case the defendant has a right to remain silent, and during the criminal trial the defense did not call Simpson to the stand. But in a civil case the defendant can be forced to testify, and testify Simpson did. Prior to the trial the plaintiff's attorneys took Simpson's deposition. And during trial they called him to the stand as a plaintiff witness.

Finally, the Simpson cases illustrate important differences in remedies. If Simpson had been found guilty of murder, he most certainly would have gone to prison. In the civil case the jury awarded compensatory damages of $8.5 million and $25 million in punitive damages. But the plaintiffs are unlikely to recover anything near the $33.5 million jury award because Simpson said he was broke and could not pay.

The verdicts divided American citizens largely along racial lines. Whites strongly believed that Simpson literally got away with murder, whereas African Americans were more supportive. These sentiments were reversed after the civil trial, with many arguing that justice had finally been done.

To read more about the O. J. Simpson criminal trial and to view some of the evidence, just click on **http://www.cnn.com/US/OJ/index.html**.

the effectiveness of that process in fighting crime. To ensure that innocent persons are not found guilty, Anglo-American criminal law pays the price of freeing some of the guilty.

The primary justification for providing constitutional safeguards for those caught in the net of the criminal process is to ensure that innocent persons are not harassed or wrongly convicted. The American legal system is premised on a distrust of human fact-finding. The possibility of wrongly convicting an innocent person arises when honest mistakes are made by honorable

Provisions of the U.S. Constitution Dealing with Criminal Procedure

	Constitutional Language
Crime	Article I Section 9.3: No bill of attainder may be passed by the legislature.
	Article I Section 10.1: No state may pass any bill of attainder.
	Article I Section 9.3: The legislature may not pass an ex post facto law.
	Article I Section 10.1: No state may pass an ex post facto law.
Arrest	None
Initial appearance	Amendment VI: Right to know charges.
Bail	Amendment VIII: Right against excessive bail.
Preliminary hearing	Amendment VI: Right to assistance of counsel.
Charging	None
Grand jury	Amendment V: Right to a grand jury for a capital or otherwise infamous crime.
Arraignment	Amendment VI: Right to know charges.
Evidence	Amendment IV: Right against unreasonable search and seizures.
	Amendment V: Right against self-incrimination.
Plea bargaining	None
Trial	Amendment V: Right not to be tried twice for the same crime.
	Amendment VI: Right to a speedy trial; right to an impartial jury; right to a public trial; right to be confronted by witnesses against oneself; right to a jury from state or district where crime shall have been committed; right to obtain witnesses in one's favor; right to conduct cross-examination; right to speak at trial.
Sentencing	Amendment VIII: Right against excessive fines; right against cruel and unusual punishment.
	Amendment XIII: Right against involuntary servitude.
Appeal	Article I Section 9.2: Privilege of the writ of habeas corpus shall not be suspended.

people. But it also arises when dishonorable officials use the criminal justice process for less-than-honorable ends. In countries without built-in checks, the criminal justice process provides a quick and easy way for government officials to dispose of their enemies. For example, a common ploy in a totalitarian government is to charge persons with the ill-defined crime of being an "enemy of the state." The possibility of political misuse of the criminal justice process by a tyrannical government or tyrannical officials is a major concern in the Anglo-American heritage.

Another reason that democracies respect the rights of those accused or suspected of violating the criminal law is the need to maintain the respect and support of the community. Democratic governments derive their powers from the consent of the governed. Such support is undermined if power is applied arbitrar-

ily. Law enforcement practices that are brutal or overzealous are likely to produce fear and cynicism among the people—lawbreakers and law abiders alike. Such practices undermine the legitimacy that law enforcement officials must have to enforce the law in a democracy.

Due Process

The principal legal doctrine for limiting the arbitrariness of officials is due process. Due process of law is mentioned twice in the Constitution:

■ "No person shall . . . be deprived of life, liberty or property without due process of law." (Fifth Amendment)

■ "No state shall deprive any person of life, liberty or property without due process of law." (Fourteenth Amendment)

The concept of **due process of law** has a broad and somewhat elastic meaning, with definitions varying in detail from situation to situation. The core of the idea of due process is that a person should always be given notice of any charges brought against him or her, that a person should be provided a real chance to present his or her side in a legal dispute, and that no law or government procedure should be arbitrary. The specific requirements of due process vary somewhat, depending on the Supreme Court's latest interpretations of the Bill of Rights.

Bill of Rights

The major obstacle to the ratification of the Constitution was the absence of specific protections for individual rights. Several of the most prominent leaders of the American Revolution opposed the adoption of the Constitution, fearing that the proposed national government posed as great a threat to the rights of the average American as had the king of England. Therefore, shortly after the adoption of the Constitution, ten amendments, collectively known as the **Bill of Rights,** were adopted. Many of these protections—particularly the Fourth, Fifth, Sixth, and Eighth Amendments—deal specifically with criminal procedure.

Originally, the protections of the Bill of Rights restricted only the national government. Through a legal doctrine known as **incorporation,** however, the Supreme Court ruled that the due process clause of the Fourteenth Amendment made some provisions of the Bill of Rights applicable to the states as well. Although not all the protections of the Bill of Rights have been incorporated into the Fourteenth Amendment, all of the major protections now apply to the states as well as the national government (Exhibit 2-3). The major provisions of the Bill of Rights incorporated through the due process clause of the Fourteenth Amendment are protections against unreasonable searches and seizures (Fourth Amendment); protection against self-incrimination (Fifth); the right to counsel and trial by jury (Sixth); and the prohibition against cruel and unusual punishment (Eighth).

CIVIL LAW

Most disputes that come to court involve private parties. Conflicts over failure to pay money owed or injuries suffered in an automobile accident are settled on the basis of the body of rules collectively known as **civil law.** These suits are brought because the courts possess powers that private parties do not; courts can, for example, order a person to pay a business money owed under a contract or award monetary damages suffered for an injury received in an automobile accident.

A civil suit is brought by a private party. But "private parties" are not limited to individual citizens. They may include groups of citizens (advocacy groups and homeowners' associations, for example) as well as businesses and the government. Given these "legal fictions," it is best to view civil law as every lawsuit other than a criminal proceeding.

Basis for Filing a Civil Suit

Civil law is considerably more voluminous than criminal law. Exhibit 2-4 summarizes the major branches of civil law, which form the basis for filing suit in court. **Tort** law involves the legal wrong done to another person. Injuries suffered during automobile accidents are a prime example of tort law. When lawyers speak of an *injury,* however, they do not necessarily mean a physical injury. The term has a broader meaning, including any wrong, hurt, or damage done to a person's rights, body, reputation, or property.

Another type of private law involves **contracts,** or agreements between two or more persons involving a promise (termed a *consideration*). Money owed on a credit card and bank loans for buying a new car are considered contracts.

Property, which centers on the ownership of things, is another division of private law. But property does not have to be tangible. It may also include ideas. An area of property law that is increasingly important in the computer age is the law of *intellectual property* (formerly called *patent and copyright*).

Domestic relations constitutes a major and growing area of law. These family law matters mainly involve divorce and related issues

Exhibit 2-3   Cases Incorporating Provisions of the Bill of Rights into the Due Process Clause of the Fourteenth Amendment

First Amendment

Establishment of religion	*Everson v. Board of Education*	1947
Free exercise of religion	*Cantwell v. Connecticut*	1940
Freedom of speech	*Gitlow v. New York*	1925
Freedom of the press	*Near v. Minnesota*	1931
Freedom to peaceably assemble	*DeJong v. Oregon*	1937
Freedom to petition government	*Hague v. CIO*	1939

Second Amendment

Right of the militia to bear arms	[*Presser v. Illinois*, 1886]	NI

Fourth Amendment

Unreasonable search and seizure	*Wolf v. Colorado*	1949
Exclusionary rule	*Mapp v. Ohio*	1961

Fifth Amendment

Grand jury	[*Hurtado v. California*, 1884]	NI
No double jeopardy	*Benton v. Maryland*	1969
No self-incrimination	*Malloy v. Hogan*	1964
Compensation for taking private property	*Chicago, Burlington and Quincy Railroad v. Chicago*	1897

Sixth Amendment

Speedy trial	*Klopfer v. North Carolina*	1967
Public trial	*In re Oliver*	1948
Impartial jury	*Parker v. Gladden*	1966
Jury trial	*Duncan v. Louisiana*	1968
Venue	[Implied in Due Process]	NI
Notice	*Cole v. Arkansas*	1948
Confrontation of witnesses	*Pointer v. Texas*	1965
Compulsory process	*Washington v. Texas*	1967
Assistance of counsel	*Gideon v. Wainwright* (felony)	1963
	Argersinger v. Hamlin (some misdemeanors)	1972

Seventh Amendment

Jury trial in civil cases	[*Walker v. Sauvinet*, 1875]	NI

Eighth Amendment

No excessive bail	[*United States v. Salerno*, 1987]	NI
No excessive fines		NI
No cruel and unusual punishment	*Robinson v. California*	1962

Ninth Amendment

Privacy*	*Griswold v. Connecticut*	1965

*The word "privacy" does not appear in the Ninth Amendment (nor anywhere else in the Constitution), but in *Griswold* several justices viewed the Ninth Amendment as guaranteeing that right.

NI—Not incorporated

Adapted from Marvin Zalman and Larry Siegel, *Criminal Procedure: Constitution and Society*, 2d ed. (Belmont, CA: West/Wadsworth, 1997).

Exhibit 2-4 Major Areas of Civil Law

	Law on the Books	Law in Action
Tort	A legal injury (other than contract) resulting from violating a duty.	Examples: negligence, assault, false arrest, trespass.
Contract	An agreement between two or more parties creating a legally enforceable contract.	Money owed is the major source of cases in small claims courts.
Property	Ownership of a thing.	Lawsuits disputing ownership of property are rarer today than 100 years ago.
	Real property: Land and things on it.	
	Personal property: Everything else.	
Domestic relations	Law relating to the home.	Domestic relations constitutes the single largest category of cases filed in the major trial courts.
	Divorce: The ending of a marriage by court order.	At times civil and criminal issues overlap, most obviously in domestic abuse cases (Chapter 9).
	Custody: Court determination of care and keeping of children after divorce.	
	Support: Financial obligation to provide for children after divorce.	Formally or informally, some big cities have created family courts, which handle both civil and criminal matters involving juveniles (Chapter 19).
	Alimony: Court-ordered payments by a divorced husband (or wife) to the ex-wife (or husband) for ongoing personal support.	Nonpayment of child support (often called deadbeat dads) is a growing problem.
	Adoption: Legally taking a child of another (or, in some states, an adult) as one's own, with all the rights and duties there would have been if the child had been one's own originally.	
Inheritance	Receipt of property from a dead person.	Courts routinely process probate cases because the will is clear and the amount of money in question is small. On occasion, though, the heirs of the rich and famous have been known to publicly contest distribution of the large sums of money left behind.
	Will: A document in which a person tells how his or her property should be handed out after death.	
	Intestate: Dying without making a will.	
	Probate: The process of proving that a will is genuine and giving out the property in it.	

such as child custody, child support, and alimony. Some areas of domestic relations overlap with juvenile law (Chapter 19). Domestic disputes are also a common reason that police may be summoned, and at times criminal conduct may be involved (see Chapter 9 for a discussion of domestic violence).

Property received from a person who has died is governed by laws on **inheritance.** The best-known example is a *will*, a written document telling how a person's property should be distributed after his or her death.

Remedies

Individuals, groups, or governments sue because they want something from the other party. What they want is termed a **remedy.** A court's official

Exhibit 2-5   Major Civil Remedies

	Law on the Books	Law in Action
Declaratory judgment	A court decision declaring the legal rights of the parties.	Principal outcome of divorce cases.
Monetary damages	*Compensatory damages:* Payment for actual losses suffered by a plaintiff.	Principal outcome of tort cases.
	Punitive damages: Money awarded by a court to a person who has been harmed in a malicious or willful way by another person. The purpose is to warn others.	Rarely awarded. Major source of debate over product liability.
Equity	*Temporary restraining order (TRO):* A judge's order to a person to keep from taking certain action before a full hearing can be held on the question.	Can be granted without the other party present. Expires after a few days.
	Preliminary injunction: A judge's order to a person to keep from taking action after a hearing but before the issue is fully tried.	During the hearing, both sides present their case. Plaintiff must be able to show that irreparable damages will occur if the injunction is not issued.
	Permanent injunction: A judge's order to a person to keep from taking certain action after the issue has been fully tried.	As with all injunctions, violations are punishable by contempt of court, which can include fines but also jail time.

decision about the rights and claims of each side in a lawsuit is known as a **judgment.** Thus, if the plaintiff wins, the judgment also contains a remedy, which is the relief granted by the court. Exhibit 2-5 summarizes the major civil remedies.

Most civil cases involve a request for monetary damages. The **plaintiff** (the person who starts a lawsuit) demands that the **defendant** (the person against whom a lawsuit is brought) pay money to the plaintiff. For example, in a case involving an automobile accident, the injured party may request a sum of money to pay for hospital expenses, doctors' fees, lost wages, and general "pain and suffering." **Monetary damages** are sums of money that a court orders paid to a person who has suffered a legal injury.

Another type of remedy occasionally requested is a **declaratory judgment,** which is a judicial determination of the legal rights of the parties. For example, in prisoner litigation, lawyers seek declaration that prison conditions violate constitutional standards (see Chapter 15).

A third type of remedy is called an **injunction** (and comes from the type of law found in England termed *equity* or sometimes *chancellory* law). An injunction is a court order that requires a person to take an action or to refrain from taking an action. For example, a court may issue an injunction prohibiting a company from dumping industrial wastes into a river. To qualify for an injunction, the plaintiff must demonstrate to the court that it will suffer irreparable damages. An injunction is a powerful measure that can be enforced by the contempt power of the court. Thus, a person who violates an injunction can be fined or sent to jail.

Using Civil Remedies to Fight Crime

Civil law is having an increasing impact on the criminal justice system (Ross 2002). Victims of crime are increasingly resorting to civil litigation, in addition to victim compensation and restitution, as a means of recovering from the ill effects of crime (National Center for Victims of Crime 2002). Moreover, victims' rights advocates are advocating civil remedies as one way for victims to reassert control (see Chapter 9). In criminal prosecutions the prosecutor essentially makes all decisions, but in civil litigation it is the plaintiff and plaintiff's lawyer who make the decisions. Although parallel civil and criminal proceedings have been brought for years, they are being used today more frequently than ever before (McCampbell 1995). Two areas—drugs and rape—illustrate the blending of criminal and civil law.

The overlap between civil and criminal law is highlighted by a number of recent efforts to fight drugs. Legislators at both the state and national levels are passing laws that allow for the eviction of residents from public housing if they are convicted of drug possession and permit drug testing of employees. Likewise, nuisance abatement suits have targeted so-called crack houses. These essentially civil laws increase the arsenal of legal weapons law enforcement officials may use against the sale and use of illegal drugs. But some people now wonder whether the use of civil remedies, particularly asset forfeiture, may have gone too far (see Courts, Controversy, and Reducing Crime: Should Asset Forfeiture Be Limited?).

Rape victims are pursuing justice in the civil courts at a growing rate, seeking damages from almost anyone they can find who may have shared liability for the rape. These lawsuits often proceed on the basis of the legal theory of *premises liability*. In premises liability cases, the victim alleges that the owner and/or manager of the property failed to provide adequate security and thereby contributed to the occurrence of the crime. The claims raise issues concerning inadequate security caused by poorly trained security guards, too few security guards, or environmental design flaws. In short, premises liability lawsuits argue that the crime that occurred was foreseeable and the defendant had a legal duty to provide adequate security (Gordon and Brill 1996).

In recent years civil justice has become almost as controversial as criminal justice. Perhaps nowhere is this more apparent than in efforts to curb drunk driving. Seemingly every session, legislatures vote even tougher penalties for driving while intoxicated (see Chapter 18). But at the same time, civil lawsuits filed by persons injured in automobile accidents caused by drunk drivers are viewed with skepticism. Tort reformers often implicitly suggest that such lawsuits unnecessarily drive up the already high cost of automobile insurance.

The principal downside of civil remedies is the obvious: Few criminal defendants have the economic resources to make litigation financially worthwhile. Indeed, in the most prominent civil lawsuits, the plaintiffs' motives have been primarily vindication, with little likelihood of collecting a dime from Bernhard Goetz or anything close to the $8.5 million O. J. Simpson was ordered to pay (see Exhibit 2-6).

Civil Liability of Criminal Justice Officials

In the modern era, it is not just criminal defendants who find themselves hauled into civil court but police officers and prison guards as well. Increasingly, criminal justice officials find that they must defend themselves against a variety of civil lawsuits. Perhaps the best known are cases filed by prison inmates alleging that conditions of confinement constitute cruel and unusual punishment in violation of the Eighth Amendment. These lawsuits have reshaped American prisons in recent years (see Chapter 15).

Other civil lawsuits seek monetary damages for misconduct on the part of law enforcement personnel. Most commonly these lawsuits allege that the police used excessive force or were negligent in using deadly force. Conversely, some lawsuits center on the inactions of law enforcement or correctional personnel. Local governments have been found liable for the death of a person in detention when police officers failed to prevent suicide (Kappeler, Vaughn, and Del Carmen 1991). Similarly, prison officials have been held liable for failure to prevent inmate-against-inmate assaults (Vaughn 1996).

Criminal justice officials also find themselves in civil court as defendants in growing numbers of cases filed by their own employees.

Should Asset Forfeiture Be Limited?

NBC's *Dateline* television series focused on two small Louisiana sheriff's departments accused of targeting innocent motorists on heavily traveled I-10 and seizing their cars for a hefty departmental profit. The law lets police seize property from drivers who they think may be violating drug laws, even if they don't find any drugs. To recover their property, motorists must first post a bond and then wage a long court battle. The local officials blasted the NBC report as "trash journalism designed to boost ratings," but did acknowledge that their rural jurisdictions totaled $19 million a year—37 percent of all asset forfeitures in the state (Wardlaw 1997). This TV report focused national attention on complaints that some law enforcement officials have abused their powers under asset forfeiture.

Asset forfeiture involves government seizure of the personal assets obtained from, or used in, a crime. Assets refer to property, businesses, cars, cash, and the like. For example, a car used in the distribution of illegal drugs may be forfeited to the government. Asset forfeiture was part of British common law as early as 1660. More recently, it is identified with the Racketeer Influenced and Corrupt Organizations Act (RICO for short) enacted by Congress in 1970. Congress was concerned about the infiltration of organized crime into the regular business marketplace and sought to discourage such activities by taking away the profits.

One form of asset forfeiture is criminal: A defendant convicted under the RICO law is subject not only to criminal penalties (fines and imprisonment) but also forfeiture of property obtained from the profits of the illegal enterprise. Thus, drug dealers who pour their profits into a restaurant can have the restaurant seized by government agents.

But asset forfeiture is not limited to criminal actions. The more potent form of asset forfeiture is civil in nature. The government is proceeding not against a person but against the property in what is termed an **in rem** procedure (a lawsuit brought against a thing rather than against a person). Once the property is seized, the burden of proof is on the property owner to show that the property was not used illegally (Cassella 1996). Through the years Congress has greatly expanded the scope of asset forfeiture, and all states except one have enacted asset forfeiture laws (Jensen and Gerber 1996).

The major concern over asset forfeiture laws is that they make it too easy for law enforcement officials to seize the assets of innocent persons (Levy 1996). The Supreme Court has begun to rein in the government's forfeiture power. In the case of a South Dakota man who had his mobile home and auto body shop seized after being convicted of selling two grams of cocaine, the Court unanimously ruled that the amount seized (almost $43,000) was disproportionate to the crime (*Austin v. U.S.* 1993; Giffuni 1995). The next term, the Court held that the same provisions of the Bill of Rights also apply in asset forfeiture (*U.S. v. James Daniel Good Real Property* 1993). But innocent owners can have their assets seized (*Bennis v. Michigan* 1996; *U.S. v. Ursery* 1996).

After years of debate, Congress passed the Civil Asset Forfeiture Act of 2000, which shifts the burden of proof to the government. The new law also awards lawyers' fees to those who successfully challenge confiscation of property. These changes, though, were strongly opposed by the U.S. Department of Justice. Moreover, proponents labeled the law only a first step.

What do you think? Should more limits be placed on law enforcement officials' ability to seize assets of suspected wrongdoers? Do large financial incentives like these provide too great a temptation?

To continue the debate, you can visit the following Web sites:

Forfeiture Endangers Americans' Rights (FEAR)
http://www.fear.org/

U.S. Department of Justice, Asset Forfeiture Program
http://www.usdoj.gov/jmd/afp/

Some lawsuits allege discrimination in hiring or promotion. Others argue that the plaintiff was sexually harassed. Chapter 3, on federal courts, will explore how a wide range of federal laws shape the internal operations of law enforcement and corrections.

▌ CRIMINAL LAW

Some disputes are viewed as so disruptive to society that they require special treatment because civil law remedies are not enough. There

Exhibit 2-6 Prominent Examples of Civil Actions Following Criminal Prosecutions

Person	Criminal	Civil
Bernhard Goetz	Criminal jury convicted the subway vigilante of illegally having a gun but acquitted him of more serious charges after the 1984 shooting of a youth Goetz claimed was trying to rob him. The shooting had clear racial overtones (Goetz is white, his victim black).	A 1996 civil jury ordered Goetz to pay $43 million to the man he left paralyzed. It is unlikely that Darrell Cabey, who was paralyzed and suffered brain damage, will be able to collect from the unemployed electrician.
O. J. Simpson	In the televised "trial of the century," the jury acquitted O. J. Simpson of murdering his former wife Nicole Brown Simpson and her friend Ronald Goldman. The verdict divided the nation along racial lines.	A civil jury found Simpson liable for the killings of his ex-wife and her friend. The jury awarded $8.5 million in compensatory damages to Goldman's parents and $25 million in punitive damages. Plaintiff's ability to collect on the judgment is limited because Simpson placed most of his money in retirement accounts that cannot be seized.
Rodney King	Two Los Angeles police officers were acquitted in state court of beating Rodney King, but they were later convicted in federal court (Chapter 3).	The City of Los Angeles settled the civil lawsuit for $3.8 million.
Randall Weaver	After a months-long standoff, federal agents arrested Randall Weaver at his mountain home in Ruby Ridge, Idaho. During the arrest a firefight broke out, and Weaver's wife was killed. A criminal jury acquitted Weaver of a variety of gun charges.	The U.S. Justice Department paid $3.1 million to settle wrongful death claims against federal agents for the 1992 death of Randall Weaver's wife and son.
Amadou Diallo	Four NYPD officers were acquitted of murder. The Justice Department will not file federal charges.	The city of New York settled the case for $3 million.

are several important differences between civil law and **criminal law** (see Exhibit 2-7). One difference centers on who has been harmed. Whereas a breach of the civil law is considered a private matter involving only the individual parties, violations of the criminal law are considered public wrongs. As such, criminal law relates to actions that are considered so dangerous, or potentially so, that they threaten the welfare of society as a whole.

A second difference involves prosecution. Unlike the civil law, in which private parties file suit in court alleging an infringement of private rights, violations of public wrongs are prosecuted by the state.

The type of penalties imposed on law violators is a third difference. In civil law the injured party receives compensation. Violators of the criminal law, however, are punished. In setting penalties, American law often makes a distinction between a misdemeanor and a felony. In general, a **misdemeanor** is a criminal offense less serious than a **felony,** punishable by a fine or up to a year in jail. But there is no uniform usage or definition of these terms in the United States. One common method is to define felonies by the place of imprisonment: The convicted are sentenced to death or to imprisonment in the state prison. The alternative approach is to define felonies

Exhibit 2-7	Differences between Civil and Criminal Law	
	Civil	Criminal
Moving party	Plaintiff	State
Defending party	Defendant	Defendant
Burden of proof	Preponderance of the evidence	Guilty beyond a reasonable doubt
Jury verdict rules	Less than unanimous (many states)	Unanimous (most states)
Remedy	Monetary damages	Prison or probation
Defendant's testimony	May be forced to testify	Constitutional right to silence
Right to counsel	No constitutional right to counsel	Constitutional right to counsel
Prosecution	Must hire own lawyer	The government through the district attorney
Examples	Tort, contract, property, probate	Assault, theft, burglary

on the basis of the duration of imprisonment: The convicted are sentenced to death, life imprisonment, or imprisonment for more than one year (Bureau of Justice Statistics 1987).

The stress on punishment derives from the goal of criminal law to prevent and control crime. It is important to recognize that the criminal law is intended to supplement, not supplant, the civil law. Thus, as discussed earlier, a person may be prosecuted criminally and the victim may also seek to recover civil damages for the same act (see Case Close-up: Two Verdicts in the O. J. Trials). In automobile accidents involving drinking, for example, the drunk driver may be charged criminally with drunk driving, and the injured party may also file a civil suit seeking monetary damages.

ELEMENTS OF A CRIME

Corpus delicti, a Latin phrase meaning "body of the crime," refers to the essential **elements of a crime.** In defining the elements of a particular offense, criminal laws are based on five general principles. No behavior can be called criminal unless

- a guilty act is committed, with a
- guilty intent, and
- the guilty act and the guilty intent are related.

In addition, a number of crimes are defined on the basis of

- attendant circumstances and/or
- specific results.

An understanding of the basic concepts embodied in the statutory definitions of crime is essential for correctly interpreting definitions of crime. In turn, these basic concepts produce numerous categories of criminal activities (murder, voluntary manslaughter, and involuntary manslaughter, for example).

Guilty Act

Before there can be a crime, there must be a **guilty act (actus reus).** Thus, criminal liability occurs only after a voluntary act that results in criminal harm. The requirement of a guilty act reflects a fundamental principle of American law: No one should be punished solely for bad thoughts. Depending on the crime, there are different types of guilty acts. In the offense of possession of an illegal drug, for instance, the guilty act is the possession. Differences in the nature of the guilty act account for many gradations of criminal offenses. To choose one obvious example, stealing property is considered separately from damaging property.

An important subdivision of the guilty act is a class of offenses labeled as **attempts** (for example, attempted burglary or attempted murder). The law does not want a person to avoid legal liability merely because someone or something prevented the commission of a crime. Typically, though, the penalties for attempt are less severe than if the act had succeeded. One result is that in some states, defendants often plead guilty to attempt to reduce the possible severity of the prison sentence.

Guilty Intent

Every common law crime consists of two elements, the guilty act itself and the accompanying mental state. The rationale is that criminal sanctions are not necessary for those who innocently cause harm. As Justice Holmes once pithily put it, "Even a dog distinguishes between being stumbled over and being kicked." The mental state required for a crime to have been committed is referred to as **guilty intent** or **mens rea** ("guilty mind").

Despite its importance in criminal law, guilty intent is difficult to define because it refers to a subjective condition, a state of mind. Some statutes require only general intent (intent to do something that the law prohibits), but others specify the existence of specific intent (intent to do the exact thing charged). Moreover, legislatively defined crimes have added new concepts of mental state to the traditional ones. Thus crimes differ with respect to the mental state the prosecution must prove existed in order to secure a criminal conviction. Larceny (termed theft in some states), for example, typically requires proof of a very great degree of intent; the prosecutor must prove that the defendant intentionally took property to which he knew he was not entitled, intending to deprive the rightful owner of possession permanently. Negligent homicide, on the other hand, is an example of a crime involving a lesser degree of intent; the prosecution need only show that the defendant negligently caused the death of another. Most crimes require that the defendant knew he or she was doing something wrong. Also, the law assumes that people know the consequences of their acts. Thus, a person cannot avoid legal liability by later saying, "I didn't mean to do it."

Fusion of Guilty Act and Guilty Intent

The criminal law requires that the guilty act and the guilty intent occur together. Here is an example that illustrates this concept of **fusion of the guilty act and guilty intent:** Suppose a husband planned to kill his wife; he purchased some poison but never got around to putting the poison in her drink. The husband returns home late one night, an argument ensues, and he stabs her. In this situation the intent to kill necessary for a murder conviction did not occur along with the death. Therefore, the correct charge would be voluntary manslaughter.

Attendant Circumstances

Some crimes require the presence, or absence, of **attendant (accompanying) circumstances.** Most states differentiate between classes of theft on the basis of the amount stolen. In Illinois, for example, the law provides that theft of less than $300 is treated as a misdemeanor and more than $300 as a felony. The amount stolen is the attendant circumstance.

Results

In a limited number of criminal offenses, the **result** of the illegal act plays a critical part in defining the crime. The difference between homicide and battery, for example, depends on whether the victim lived. Similarly, most states distinguish between degrees of battery, depending on how seriously the victim was injured. Note that the concept of results differs from that of intent. In all of the preceding examples, the defendant may have had the same intent. The only difference was how hearty the victim was or perhaps how skillful the defendant was in carrying out his or her intentions.

Based on the five general principles—guilty act, guilty intent, fusion, attendant circumstances, and results—the corpus delicti of each crime (murder, robbery, rape, and burglary, for example) differs (Exhibit 2-8). The elements of a particular crime provide the technical (that is, legal) definitions of a crime. For this reason, criminal statutes must be read

Exhibit 2-8   Characteristics of the Most Common Serious Crimes

	Law on the Books	Law in Action
Homicide	The willful (nonnegligent) killing of one human being by another.	Homicide is the least frequent violent crime. Most often murderers are relatives or acquaintances of the victim.
Rape	The carnal knowledge of a female forcibly and against her will.	Most rapes involve a lone offender and a lone victim, at night.
Robbery	The taking or attempting to take anything of value from the care, custody, or control of a person or persons by force or threat of force or violence and/or by putting the victim in fear.	Half of all robberies involve one offender. Half of all robberies involve the use of a weapon.
Assault	*Aggravated assault* is an unlawful attack by one person upon another for the purpose of inflicting severe or aggravated bodily injury. This type of assault is usually accompanied by the use of a weapon or other means likely to produce death or great bodily harm. *Simple assault* is an unlawful attack by one person upon another for the purpose of inflicting less than severe bodily injury. This type of assault does not involve the use of a weapon or other means likely to produce death or great bodily harm.	Simple assault occurs more frequently than aggravated assault. Simple assault is the most common type of violent crime.
Burglary (breaking or entering)	The unlawful entry of a structure to commit a felony or a theft.	Residential property is targeted in two out of three burglaries.
Larceny (theft)	The unlawful taking, carrying, lending, or riding away of property from the possession or constructive possession of another.	Pocket picking and purse snatching occur most frequently inside businesses or on street locations.
Motor vehicle theft	The theft or attempted theft of a motor vehicle. A motor vehicle is self-propelled and runs on the surface, not on rails.	Motor vehicle theft is relatively well reported to the police.
Arson	Any willful or malicious burning or attempt to burn, with or without intent to defraud, a dwelling house, public building, motor vehicle, aircraft, or personal property of another.	Single-family residences are the most frequent targets of arson.

SOURCE: Federal Bureau of Investigation, *Uniform Crime Reports* (Washington, DC: U.S. Department of Justice, 2003); Bureau of Justice Statistics, *Report to the Nation on Crime and Justice,* 2d ed. (Washington, DC: Government Printing Office, 1988).

closely, because each clause constitutes a critical part of the offense. Before a defendant can be convicted, all the elements of a crime must be proven.

LEGAL DEFENSES

Under the law, individuals may have performed illegal acts but still not be found guilty of a criminal violation because of a legally recognized justification for the actions or because legally they were not responsible for their actions. These **legal defenses** derive from the way crime is defined.

The requirement of a guilty act gives rise to several legal defenses. Above all, criminal acts must be voluntary. Thus, a person who strikes another while suffering an epileptic seizure would not be guilty of battery, because the act (hitting) was not voluntary. Similarly, the law recognizes the defense of duress—unlawful pressure on a person to do what he or she would not otherwise have done. Duress includes force, threat of violence, and physical restraint. In a defense of duress, the defendant is contending, in essence, that he or she should be treated as a victim rather than as a criminal.

The requirement of guilty intent gives rise to several other legal defenses. Some types of persons are considered legally incapable of forming criminal intent and therefore cannot be held criminally responsible for their actions. Children are prime examples. Until children reach a certain age (7 in most states), they are presumed not to be responsible for their actions and therefore cannot be criminally prosecuted. After reaching this minimum age, but before becoming an adult, a child's criminal violations are treated as acts of juvenile delinquency (Chapter 19). The premise of **juvenile delinquency** acts is that people under a certain age have less responsibility for their actions than adults do. The exact age at which a person is no longer considered a juvenile, and can thus be prosecuted as an adult, differs from state to state. As more and more youths are committing violent crimes, states are lowering the age for prosecuting a minor as an adult (see Chapter 19).

Similarly, the law assumes that persons with certain types of mental illness are incapable of forming criminal intent. Indeed, the best-known, and also most controversial, legal defense is insanity. In Chapter 14 we will examine how insanity and other legal defenses are occasionally used at trial.

EFFECTS OF THE CRIMINAL LAW ON THE COURTS

Because the criminal code constitutes the basic source of authority for law enforcement agencies, the way crimes are defined has an important bearing on the entire administration of criminal justice. Chapter 5 will consider in greater detail the relationship between law and discretion. For now we will examine the criminal law and inconsistencies, plea bargaining, and sentencing.

Criminal Law and Inconsistencies

Inconsistencies exist within each criminal code (sometimes referred to as the penal code). All too often criminal statues resemble a crazy quilt of inconsistent sets of criminal definitions and penalties. Because legislatures change criminal codes piecemeal, the end product is a set of criminal laws with obsolete prohibitions and inconsistent penalties. Typically such contradictions indicate a lack of agreement in American society about what behavior should be criminalized and what penalties are appropriate (Sigler 1981).

In practice, judges and prosecutors attempt to rectify these inconsistencies by informally developing a consistent set of penalties. It should be obvious that the courts must apply the law as they find it. The corollary is that the courts often must rectify inconsistencies in that law. Disparities in possible sentences as provided in state statutes require judges, prosecutors, and defense attorneys to arrive at a workable penalty structure. Society would be outraged if serious crimes elicited the same punishment as minor ones, even if the law

THE MURDER TRIAL OF SHAREEF COUSIN

The Question of Civil Liability

 After the criminal charges were dropped against Shareef Cousin, legal attention shifted to the civil law. At first glance the issue seems straightforward. After all, Shareef Cousin's rights were apparently violated—he spent almost two years on Louisiana's death row and almost as long in jail awaiting a new trial that never occurred. But the legal issues are much more complicated and evolving. Legislatures and courts across the nation are debating the question: If an inmate turns out to be wrongfully convicted, does the state owe compensation for the years lost in prison? Or is the restoration of freedom compensation enough? (Coyle 2000a). These have become pressing questions in the wake of a wave of persons who have been freed from death row or long prison terms. Only a handful of states, however, have enacted laws that create a rational system for paying compensation. In the other jurisdictions, these issues are being decided by courts.

In Louisiana the question of compensating the wrongfully incarcerated arose in a lawsuit that was winding its way through the courts at about the same time that Shareef Cousin was being convicted and sentenced to death. Roland Gibson was convicted for the 1967 murder of a New Orleans cab driver and sentenced to life imprisonment. After he had spent 17 years in prison, Gibson's boyhood friend and codefendant, Lloyd West, recanted his claim that Gibson had been the triggerman. A new trial was ordered, but the DA decided not to conduct a retrial. Nonetheless, Gibson spent another 8 years in prison after the problem of perjured testimony surfaced.

Following a bench trial, civil court judge Carolyn Gill-Jefferson ruled that the New Orleans police had lacked probable cause to arrest Gibson and ordered the city to pay the plaintiff and his family $10.7 million in damages (Finch 1998). But the Louisiana Supreme Court unanimously held that civil trials should not "second-guess" a criminal court finding of probable cause to arrest, even when that evidence later turns out to be false. The court also chastised the trial judge for putting too much weight on the testimony of West, a convicted felon (*Gibson v. New Orleans* 2000).

Given these legal standards, it would be hard for Shareef Cousin to successfully sue the New Orleans Police Department. And even if he were to win, it would be difficult to collect because the city of New Orleans is cash-starved. In a lawsuit against a private party, the plaintiff is entitled to seize the defendant's assets to pay the judgment, but the federal courts have exempted cities from such possibilities. Thus in the past when plaintiffs have successfully sued the city of New Orleans over matters such as police brutality, the city has delayed paying for years. Indeed, some may never collect.

Because state law allows little likelihood that Shareef Cousin could successfully win a civil lawsuit for wrongful conviction, his lawyers turned to federal court, filing a federal civil rights lawsuit (see Chapter 3).

technically allowed both categories of offenses to be treated the same way.

Criminal Law and Plea Bargaining

Variations in the definitions of crimes make the criminal courts fertile ground for plea bargaining. In particular, differences in degrees of seriousness provide the means for charge bargaining (the defendant pleads guilty to a less serious offense than the one charged). For example, in some states, assault and battery involves five degrees (categories). Although the law must attempt to differentiate between, say, a punch thrown in anger and a deliberate gunshot wound that leaves its victim permanently paralyzed, the existence of many different degrees of seriousness facilitates pleas to less serious offenses. Thus, prosecutors may deliberately overcharge in hopes of inducing the defendant to later plead guilty to a lesser charge (see Chapter 13).

Criminal Law and Sentencing

The most obvious way criminal law affects the operations of the criminal courts is in sentencing. As we will discuss in greater detail in Chap-

COURT TV
Cyber Crime: The Lawless Frontier

The Internet has revolutionized how we live and how we learn. But it has also provided new avenues for illicit activity. Identity theft has become a major problem with sophisticated criminals stealing credit card numbers and other important personal information, resulting in countless dollars lost. E-commerce also allows prostitutes to solicit clients on line, seemingly protected by jurisdictional voids.

Pedophiles also utilize the Internet to distribute child pornography. Specialized federal law enforcement agencies now monitor chat rooms and the like looking to arrest those who try to profit by selling images of children engaging in sexually explicit acts. At times, law enforcement personnel create fake Internet identities in order to identify and arrest pedophiles. But does law enforcement go too far at times? Do they entrap innocent citizens?

View a video clip of this case on your copy of the CourtTV CD-ROM. As you watch the video, keep the following questions in mind:

1. How has the Internet changed society?

2. What legal changes have been made in response to these societal changes?

3. What additional legal changes need to be made?

4. Does the media and law enforcement stress the negative side of the Internet and therefore impede legitimate uses of this new technology?

5. In reversing the conviction in this case, the appellate court suggests that law enforcement was wasting time on this type of enforcement practice. Do you agree or disagree? How would advocates of the crime control model of criminal justice differ in their answers from supporters of the due process model?

pressures are strong to increase penalties. As a result, legislatures increase the harshness of sentencing, and the courthouse mitigates that harshness. According to Rosett and Cressey (1976, 95), such legislative action and courthouse reactions follow a predictable pattern:

> Step I. Laws calling for severe punishments are passed by legislatures on the assumption that fear of great pain will terrorize the citizenry into conformity.
>
> Step II. Criminal justice personnel soften these severe penalties for most offenders (a) in the interests of justice, (b) in the interests of bureaucracy, and (c) in the interests of gaining acquiescence.
>
> Step III. The few defendants who then insist on a trial and are found guilty, or who in other ways refuse to cooperate, are punished more severely than those who acquiesce.
>
> Step IV. Legislatures, noting that most criminals by acquiescing avoid "the punishment prescribed by law," (a) increase the prescribed punishments and (b) try to limit the range of discretionary decision making used to soften the harsh penalties.
>
> Step V. The more severe punishments introduced in the preceding step are again softened for most offenders, as in Step II, with the result that the defendants not acquiescing are punished even more severely than they were at Step III.

This book will return often to the question of whether the legislatures or the courts have adopted the more appropriate stance.

CONCLUSION

The verdicts in the subway vigilante case left citizens divided over where justice lay. Was the criminal jury right (or wrong) in finding Goetz guilty only of a minor misdemeanor? Was the civil jury equally right (or wrong) in awarding civil damages? As for Goetz, he remained unrepentant, eagerly stating that he would do it all over again if he were confronted by four black teenagers. In the end, both sides became symbols of the contrasting views associated with the crime control and due process models of

ters 15 and 16, the legislature establishes sentencing options from which judges must choose. Because of the public's concern about crime,

A Virtual Tour of American Courthouses: American Law

A useful place to begin a virtual tour of American law is with the basic documents of our nation. Historical legal documents such as the Constitution and the Magna Carta are available at **http://www.constitutioncenter.org/** under Historical Documents. You can view the original copy of the Bill of Rights on the Internet thanks to the National Records and Archive Administration at **http://www.nara.gov/exhall/charters/billrights/billmain.html**. For an interpretive look at the Constitution, visit the newly opened National Constitution Center, the first museum dedicated to honoring and explaining the U.S. Constitution, found at **http://www.constitutioncenter.org/**.

After you've developed a general feel for our nation's constitutional heritage, you are ready to branch out to examine more general legal concepts. A good first stop for mastering the language of the law is Oran's dictionary, which provides nontechnical definitions (**http://www.wld.com/conbus/orans/**). To explore legal concepts, go to the Virtual Law Library provided by the Indiana University School of Law–Bloomington: **http://www.law.indiana.edu/v-lib/**. More specific legal resources are available online for your state; just click on **http://dir.yahoo.com/Government/Law/U_S__States/** and then select your state.

To check out today's legal news, click on **http://www.cnn/law** for a summary of important court decisions and major crimes across the nation. To dig deeper into the criminal law from the perspective of criminal defense lawyers, visit **http://www.crimelynx.com/**.

---

criminal justice. In the end, both sides also suffered, and neither will ever be the same again. Goetz is penniless and unemployable, which means that Cabey will collect little or nothing of the civil damage award.

The Goetz trials also illustrate the importance of understanding both law on the books and law in action. The law on the books—first-degree murder, in this case—is abstract. The law in action—what victims, defendants, lawyers, judges, and jury do—is concrete. Ultimately the meaning of the law is not what the judge instructs to the jury (law on the books) but the decision reached by the jury (law in action). By voting not guilty, the first jury decided that this conduct was not criminal. By deciding that Goetz was liable, another jury decided that his conduct violated community standards.

What activities should be labeled criminal is a source of constant political discussion. Actions viewed as bad in the past may no longer be considered bad. As society changes, so do public perceptions of public wrongs, and pressures develop to add more activities to the list of officially proscribed ones. Through all of this change, we must not lose sight of the essential fact that law is an integral part of society. Law is not imposed on society; rather it reflects the sociology, economy, history, and politics of society. Law was created to help society, not the other way around.

CRITICAL THINKING QUESTIONS

1. Constitutional rights of the accused is, of course, a controversial topic. The crime control model, in particular, decries letting the obviously guilty go free on "technicalities," whereas the due process model emphasizes basic rights. Examining Exhibit 2-2, what common ground do these two approaches share? Where do they disagree most?

2. All non-English-speaking industrial democracies use the inquisitorial system rather than the adversary system. In this system the judge, not the prosecutor and not the

defense attorney, calls witnesses and questions them. Would you prefer being tried under the adversary system or the inquisitorial system? Would you have confidence in the willingness of the judge to search out equally evidence for conviction and evidence for acquittal?

3. If O. J. Simpson had been tried in France, what procedural differences in the case would have occurred? Would the substantive findings also have been different?

4. One of the biggest societal changes in recent years has been the rapid expansion of computer technology. How have legislatures responded to crimes involving the use of computers? How has the Internet changed the debate over pornography?

KEY TERMS

administrative regulations (29)
adversary system (29)
Anglo-American law (26)
attempt (41)
attendant (accompanying) circumstances (42)
beyond a reasonable doubt (31)
Bill of Rights (34)
civil law (34)
common law (26)
constitution (28)
contract (34)
corpus delicti (41)
criminal law (40)
declaratory judgment (37)
defendant (37)
domestic relations (34)
due process of law (34)
elements of a crime (41)
felony (40)
fusion of the guilty act and guilty intent (42)
guilty act (actus reus) (41)
guilty intent (mens rea) (42)
incorporation (34)
inheritance (36)
injunction (37)
in rem (39)
judge-made law (26)
judgment (37)
juvenile delinquency (44)
law (25)

legal defense (44)
misdemeanor (40)
monetary damage (37)
municipal ordinance (28)
plaintiff (37)
precedent (26)
preponderance of the evidence (31)
presumption of innocence (31)
procedural law (29)
property (34)
remedy (36)
result (42)
stare decisis (27)
statute (28)
substantive law (29)
tort (34)

WORLD WIDE WEB RESOURCES AND EXERCISES

Web Guides

http://dir.yahoo.com/Government/Law/
http://dir.yahoo.com/Government/Law/Cases/
   OJ_Simpson_Case/

Web Search Terms

law
common law
criminal law
asset forfeiture
O. J. Simpson
subway vigilante

Useful URLs

The Legal Information Institute offers a menu of federal and state sources: **http://www.law.cornell.edu/topics/criminal.html**.

The federal Web locator from the Center for Information Law and Policy is at **http://www.infoctr.edu/fwl/**.

The state Web locator from the Center for Information Law and Policy is at **http://www.law.vill.edu/**.

For state resources, go to **http://www.findlaw. com** and select your state.

Legal research on the Web is at **http://www. accd.edu/sac/leassist/la1103/webres.htm**.

Internet Legal Resource Guide is a categorized index of more than 4,000 Web sites in 238 nations: **http://www.ilrg.com**.

Uncommon URLs

Anatomy of a Murder offers a trip through our nation's legal system: **http://library.thinkquest. org/2760/homep.htm**.

Legal History and Philosophy is a site with links to many of the common law classics: **http://www.commonlaw.com/**.

About.Com/Law shows today's legal headlines: **http://law.about.com/newsissues/law/**.

Nolo Press is the leading publisher of legal self-help materials: **http://www.nolo.com/**.

United Kingdom Web sites explain another common law jurisdiction with some important differences: **http://www.leeds.ac.uk/law/ ccjs/ukweb.htm**.

The Subway Vigilante Board Game is a beer-and-pretzel game: **http://waggle.gg.caltech.edu/ ~jeff/games/subwayv.html**.

The Five-Hour Law School is a primer that was designed for nonlawyer employees of Thomson Publishing: **http://members.aol.com/ ronin48th/hope.htm**.

Web Exercises

1. One of the major links for doing legal research is FindLaw. Its URL is **http://www.findlaw.com/**. You can find the U.S. Constitution by following this path: Laws: Cases and Codes/Constitution. Click on Article III—Judicial Department to read the full article.

   Also click on one of the amendments in the Bill of Rights to find annotated information about the meaning of that provision. In particular, examine the Second Amendment and the bearing of arms.

2. Each year more laws are added to the Web. Check to see what is available in your state. Again we will use FindLaw: **http://www. findlaw.com/**. On the menu click State Law Resources. Click on your state to get a general sense of what is available. Is the criminal law for your state online? If so, compare the burglary section of your state code to the one in a neighboring state. In what ways are the laws similar? In what ways are they different?

3. Update the debate over asset forfeiture by doing a Yahoo search. Access Yahoo at **http://www.yahoo.com**; then click Society and Culture/Crime/Asset Confiscation.

   You may also want to go directly to Forfeiture Endangers American Rights (FEAR) at **http://www.fear.org**. This group says it is dedicated to helping forfeiture victims, working to reform draconian forfeiture laws, assisting legal counsel in difficult forfeiture cases, and acting as a watchdog over governmental forfeiture practices. Where do they fit in the crime control versus due process debate?

INFOTRAC COLLEGE EDITION RESOURCES AND EXERCISES

Basic Search Terms

criminal law   *United States Constitution*
asset forfeiture   *First to Tenth Amendments*
common law

Recommended Articles

Hossein Esmaeili, Jeremy Gans, "Cultures Colliding in Court"

Mark Goldie, "The Bill of Rights, 1689 and 1998"

Kent Greenawalt, "Justifications, Excuses, and a Model Penal Code for Democratic Societies"

Harper's, "This Is Your Bill of Rights"

InfoTrac College Edition Exercises

1. One of the most hotly debated proposed criminal laws involves hate crimes. Using the search term "hate crime, analysis," locate one article on either side of the debate. To what extent does the debate over passage of hate crime laws parallel the divisions discussed by Herbert Packer using the concepts of the due process and crime control models of criminal justice? Here is one article that debates the topic: Elizabeth Birch, Paul Weyrich, "Symposium: Debate for Specific Hate Crime Legislation Protecting Homosexuals."

2. Another hotly debated criminal law is the Internet Decency Act, which Congress has passed twice only to have it struck down as unconstitutional by the U.S. Supreme Court. After entering the search term "Telecommunications Act of 1996," limit the search with the term "pornography." Locate at least one article on each side of this issue. To what extent do the arguments parallel the debate between adherents of the crime control model and proponents of the due process model of criminal justice? To what extent does the debate cross traditional ideological lines? Here are two articles of relevance: William F. Buckley Jr., "Internet: The Lost Fight"; Christopher Harper, "How Free Is the Net?"

FOR FURTHER READING

Bodenhamer, David. *Fair Trial: Rights of the Accused in American History.* New York: Oxford, 1991.

Brunet, James. "Discouragement of Crime through Civil Remedies: An Application of Reformulated Routine Activities Theory." *Western Criminology Review* 4 (2002): 68–79.

Friedman, Lawrence. *American Law in the 20th Century.* New Haven, CT: Yale University Press, 2002.

Gardner, Thomas, and Terry Anderson. *Criminal Law.* 8th ed. Belmont, CA: Wadsworth, 2003.

Payne, Dennis. *Police Liability: Lawsuits against the Police.* Durham, NC: Carolina Academic Press, 2003.

Pollock, Joycelyn. *Ethics in Crime and Justice: Dilemmas and Decisions.* 4th ed. Belmont, CA: Wadsworth, 2004.

Samaha, Joel. *Criminal Law.* 7th ed. Belmont, CA: Wadsworth, 2002.

Scheb, John, *Criminal Law.* 3d ed. Belmont, CA: Wadsworth, 2003.

lfonso Lopez, Jr., a twelfth-grader at Edison High School in San Antonio, Texas, thought he had found an easy way to make a quick buck. "Gilbert" would pay him $40 to take a .38-caliber pistol to school and deliver it to "Jason," who planned to use it in a "gang war." Based on an anonymous tip, school officials confronted Lopez, who admitted carrying the unloaded weapon (but he did have five bullets on his person). Lopez was charged in federal court with violating the Gun-Free School Zones Act of 1990. After a bench trial, Lopez was found guilty and sentenced to six months in prison. The Supreme Court reversed the conviction, however, concluding that the U.S. Congress had no authority to outlaw guns in schools. ◀

The Supreme Court's decision in *United States v. Lopez* first attracts our attention because it deals with gun control—one of the truly hot-button issues of American politics. But a closer probing raises other, even more important questions. What should be a federal crime? After all, weapons offenses are usually violations of state law, and indeed Lopez was initially charged in state court; but these charges were dropped after federal officials stepped in. How is it that five conservative judges, appointed by Republican presidents and pledged to getting tough on crime, reversed a conviction that was certainly popular with the American public? After all, Republicans have accused liberal federal judges (seemingly those appointed by Democratic presidents) of being soft on crime.

The issues, both direct and indirect, raised in the case of *U.S. v. Lopez* trace their origins to the early days of the Republic. The founding fathers were deeply divided over which cases federal courts should hear. Indeed, the drafters of the U.S. Constitution were deeply divided over whether there should be any federal courts besides the U.S. Supreme Court. A principal task of this chapter, therefore, is to discuss how the current federal judicial structure—magistrate, district, appellate courts, and the Supreme Court—is a product of more than 200 years of political controversy and compromise about the proper role of the federal judiciary. The remainder of the chapter focuses on the specialized courts and the administrative structure. Most important, we will discuss the contemporary debate over how many cases are too many for the federal courts

to handle, thus illustrating that the controversies continue. But first, to establish some common ground about the often confusing topic of court organization, we begin this chapter by examining some basic principles.

BASIC PRINCIPLES OF COURT ORGANIZATION

Even lawyers who regularly use the courts sometimes find the details of court organization confusing. Court nomenclature includes many shorthand phrases that mean something to those who work in the courts daily but can be quite confusing to the outsider. Learning the language of courts is like learning any foreign language—some of it can come only from experience. Before studying the specifics of federal and state courts (Chapter 4), it is helpful to understand the basic principles of court organization. Three concepts—jurisdiction, trial versus appellate courts, and the dual court system—underlie the structure of the American judiciary.

Jurisdiction

Court structure is largely determined by limitations on the types of cases a court may hear and decide. **Jurisdiction** is the power of a court to decide a dispute. A court's jurisdiction can be further classified according to three subcomponents: geographical jurisdiction, subject matter jurisdiction, and hierarchical jurisdiction.

Geographical Jurisdiction

Courts are authorized to hear and decide disputes arising within a specified **geographical jurisdiction.** Thus, a California court ordinarily has no jurisdiction to try a person accused of committing a crime in Oregon. Courts' geographical boundaries typically follow the lines of other governmental bodies such as cities, counties, or states.

One major complication arising from geographical jurisdiction occurs when a person is arrested in one state for committing a crime in another state. **Extradition** involves the surrender by one state of an individual accused of a crime outside of its own territory and within the territorial jurisdiction of the other state. If an American fugitive has fled to a foreign nation, the U.S. Secretary of State will request the return of the accused under the terms of the extradition treaty the United States has with that country (but a few nations of the world do not have such treaties).

Subject Matter Jurisdiction

Court structure is also determined by **subject matter jurisdiction.** Trial courts of *limited jurisdiction* are restricted to hearing a limited category of cases, typically misdemeanors and civil suits involving small sums of money. State courts typically have traffic courts or juvenile courts, both of which are examples of subject matter jurisdiction. Trial courts of *general jurisdiction* are empowered to hear all other types of cases within the jurisdictional area. In the state court systems (to be discussed in the next chapter), the county trial court fits here.

Hierarchical Jurisdiction

The third subcomponent of jurisdiction is **hierarchical jurisdiction,** which refers to differences in the courts' functions and responsibilities. **Original jurisdiction** means that a court has the authority to try a case and decide it. **Appellate jurisdiction** means that a court has the power to review cases that have already been decided by another court. Trial courts are primarily courts of original jurisdiction, but they occasionally have limited appellate jurisdiction—for example, when a trial court hears appeals from lower trial courts such as mayor's courts or a justice of the peace court. Appellate courts often have a very limited original jurisdiction. The U.S. Supreme Court has original jurisdiction involving disputes between states, and state supreme courts have original jurisdiction in matters involving disbarment of lawyers.

Trial and Appellate Courts

The second concept embodied in the American court system is the relationship between trial and appellate courts. Virtually all cases begin in the **trial court.** In a criminal case, the trial court arraigns the defendant, conducts a trial (or takes a guilty plea), and if the defendant is found guilty, imposes sentence. In a civil case, the trial court operates in much the same way, ensuring that each party is properly informed of the complaint and conducting a trial or accepting an out-of-court settlement. Because only trial courts hear disputes over facts, witnesses appear only in trial courts. Trial courts are considered finders of fact, and the decision of a judge (or jury) about a factual dispute normally cannot be appealed.

The losing party in the trial court generally has the right to request an appellate court to review the case. The primary function of the **appellate court** is to ensure that the trial court correctly interpreted the law. But appellate courts may also make new law.

Appellate and trial courts operate very differently because their roles are not the same. In appellate courts, no witnesses are heard, no trials are conducted, and juries are never used. Moreover, instead of a single judge deciding, as in trial courts, a group of judges makes appellate court decisions; there may be as few as 3 or as many as 28 judges. In addition, appellate judges often provide written reasons justifying their decisions; trial court judges rarely write opinions.

Dual Court System

The United States has a **dual court system:** one national court system plus separate court systems in each of the 50 states and the District of Columbia. The result is more than 51 separate court systems. Exhibit 3-1 shows the ordering of cases in the dual court system.

Exhibit 3-1	Overview of Court Structure in the United States

Federal	State
Hears cases everywhere in the United States. Decides 46,000 criminal cases a year.	Important variations from state to state. State felony filings outnumber federal by 87 to 1.
U.S. Supreme Court Most powerful court in the world. Virtually complete control over cases it hears. Decisions have completely changed the criminal justice system. Hears only a handful of state criminal cases.	**Supreme Court** Typically has almost total control over cases to be heard. Major policymaker for the state. Final decider of questions of state law. Decides a handful of criminal appeals.
U.S. Courts of Appeals Twelve circuits are organized regionally. Must hear all requests for review. Last stop for the vast majority of defendants convicted in federal court.	**Court of Appeals or Appeals Court** Thirty-nine states have intermediate courts of appeals. Must hear all requests for review. One in 16 appellants win a significant victory.
U.S. District Court Eighty-nine courts in the continental United States. Criminal cases: drugs, fraud, and embezzlement. Civil cases: civil rights, federal statutes, diversity of citizenship.	**District, Superior, or Circuit Court** Organized by county (or groups of counties). Criminal cases: burglary, theft, drugs, murder, robbery, rape. Civil cases: automobile accidents, divorce, contract, probate.
U.S. Magistrate Court Responsible for preliminary stages of felony cases. Hears a fair volume of minor crimes on federal property. Has responsibility (but not authority) over habeas corpus petitions.	**Municipal, City, or Justice of the Peace Court** In rural areas, judges may be nonlawyers. Handles preliminary stages of felony cases. Criminal cases: petty theft, public drunkenness, disturbing the peace, disorderly conduct. Civil cases: small claims.

The division of responsibilities is not as clear-cut as it looks, however. State and federal courts share some judicial powers. Some acts—for example, selling drugs or robbing banks—are crimes under federal law and under the laws of most states, which means the accused could be tried in both federal and state courts. Moreover, litigants in state court may appeal to the U.S. Supreme Court, a federal court.

One of the most immediate consequences of the dual court system is the complexity it adds to the criminal justice system. In essence, the framers of the U.S. Constitution created two parallel criminal justice systems consisting of their own law enforcement, court structure, and correctional systems. Of all the levels of complexity created by the dual court system, perhaps the most confusing is the application of the constitutional prohibition against double jeopardy (see Courts, Controversy, and the Administration of Justice: Should the Double Jeopardy Clause Prohibit Parallel State and Federal Prosecutions? and CourtTV: *Double Jeopardy*). It is to the complexities created by federalism that we now turn.

COURTS, CONTROVERSY, AND THE ADMINISTRATION OF JUSTICE

Should the Double Jeopardy Clause Prohibit Parallel State and Federal Prosecutions?

Lemrick Nelson, Jr., who is black, was acquitted of state charges of murdering Jewish scholar Yankel Rosenbaum during a 1991 race riot in Brooklyn (see CourtTV: Double Jeopardy). Yet he was convicted in 1997 in federal court of violating the victim's civil rights. To some, the federal conviction meant that justice was finally done. But to others, the federal prosecution was itself a miscarriage of justice.

Of all the complexities created by the dual court system, perhaps the most confusing to laypersons and lawyers alike is the application of the constitutional prohibition against double jeopardy. The Fifth Amendment provides, "Nor shall any person be subject for the same offense to be twice put in jeopardy of life or limb." How, then, can a defendant be tried in both state court and federal court for the same crime? The answer is that the double jeopardy clause prevents only trial by the *same* government for the *same* offense (*Bartkus v. Illinois* 1958). This justification has been termed the *dual sovereign* doctrine, because two different sovereign governments (state and federal) are prosecuting the defendant for actions that happen to violate their separate criminal laws. Consider a defendant arrested for robbing a bank. The federal government can try the defendant for robbing a federal bank, and the state government may try the same defendant for robbery. Although the event is the same, it violates both federal and state laws.

The Supreme Court justified its decision in terms of federalism; the Court felt that a jurisdiction's interest would be impaired if the jurisdiction (state or federal) were unable to try an individual who had been tried elsewhere facing lesser penalties. Not all agree with this interpretation, however. Critics argue that the dual sovereign exception has no legal or historical basis (Piccarreta and Keenan 1995). The ACLU would bar parallel prosecutions by different governments for the same event, a view shared by sundry defendants who have been acquitted in one court only to be convicted in another.

The application of the double jeopardy clause has in recent years engendered considerable controversy in several highly publicized cases:

■ Two Los Angeles police officers were acquitted of state charges in the 1991 beating of Rodney King but were later convicted in federal court of violating his civil rights.

■ Four white New York police officers were acquitted in state court of murdering Amadou Diallo in 2000. The U.S. Justice Department later decided against federal prosecution.

These few cases aside, separate state and federal prosecutions are rare. As a practical matter, policies of the U.S. Department of Justice establish a strong presumption against federal reprosecution of a defendant already prosecuted by a state for the same conduct (Litman and Greenberg 1996).

What is perhaps most striking about the controversy over parallel prosecutions by dual sovereigns is that it cuts across the ideological dimensions that structure so much of our nation's debate concerning crime policy. In the Rodney King case, for example, members of the police union readily accepted the ACLU position. Similarly, some groups that are otherwise noted for conservative positions oppose parallel prosecutions. In short, the crime control and due process models are not particularly helpful in understanding this controversy.

As for Lemrick Nelson, a federal appellate court reversed his conviction, citing irregularities with jury selection. But on retrial, the jury returned a mixed verdict, finding Nelson had violated Mr. Rosenbaum's civil rights but did not cause his death. After years of denials, Nelson admitted during the retrial in Federal District Court in Brooklyn that he had stabbed Mr. Rosenbaum (Glaberson 2003).

What do you think? Are federal prosecutions after failed state prosecutions a good way to remedy miscarriages of justice, or are the rights of defendants unnecessarily placed in jeopardy?

To continue the debate over parallel prosecutions and double jeopardy, visit the Opposing Viewpoints Research Center at http://www.galegroup.com/opposingviewpoints and use the search term "double jeopardy" to locate additional articles on the topic. Here are two: Kelly McMurry, "Fourth Circuit Opens Door to Double Jeopardy"; Donald Dripps, "The Continuing Decline of Finality in Criminal Law."

COURT TV

The System: Double Jeopardy

A jury in state court acquitted Melvin Ignatow of murdering his fiancée. A year later new evidence turned up that proved he did indeed kill her. Moreover, he confessed to the crime. The double jeopardy clause protects him from being tried again in state court for murder, but is he guilty of another crime—the federal offense of perjury?

View a video clip of this trial on your copy of the CourtTV CD-ROM. As you watch the video, keep the following questions in mind:

1. Why does the double jeopardy clause of the U.S. Constitution apply in this case?

2. Was it correctly applied?

3. On occasion, defendants acquitted in state court are later tried in federal court. Should that have happened in this case? Why or why not?

4. Does the prosecution for perjury violate the spirit (but perhaps not the letter) of the double jeopardy clause?

HISTORY OF THE FEDERAL COURTS

At first glance the history of the federal courts appears to be a debate over details of procedure. But a closer look reveals that the political controversies that have shaped the federal judiciary go to the heart of the federal system of government, often involving the allocation of power between the national and the state governments. Thus, any discussion of the federal courts in the early twenty-first century must begin with two eighteenth-century landmarks— Article III of the U.S. Constitution and the Judi-

ciary Act of 1789. Although there have been important changes since, the decisions made at the beginning of the Republic about the nature of the federal judiciary have had a marked impact on contemporary court structure.

The Constitutional Convention

One major weakness of the Articles of Confederation was the absence of a national supreme court to enforce federal law and resolve conflicts and disputes between courts of the different states. Thus, when the delegates gathered at the Constitutional Convention in Philadelphia in 1787, a resolution was unanimously adopted that "a national judiciary be established." There was considerable disagreement, however, on the specific form that the national judiciary should take. Article III was one of the most hotly debated sections of the Constitution.

The dominant question of whether there should be a federal court system separate from the state systems produced two schools of thought. Advocates of states' rights (later called Anti-Federalists) feared that a strong national government would weaken individual liberties. More specifically, they saw the creation of separate federal courts as a threat to the power of state courts. As a result, the Anti-Federalists believed that federal law should be adjudicated first by the state courts; the U.S. Supreme Court should be limited to hearing appeals only from state courts. On the other hand, the Nationalists (who later called themselves Federalists because they favored ratification of the Constitution) distrusted the provincial prejudices of the states and favored a strong national government that could provide economic and political unity for the struggling new nation. As part of this approach, the Nationalists viewed state courts as incapable of developing a uniform body of federal law that would allow businesses to flourish. For these reasons, they backed the creation of lower federal courts.

The conflict between Federalists and Anti-Federalists was resolved by one of the many compromises that characterized the Constitutional Convention. **Article III** is brief and sketchy, providing only an outline of a federal judiciary: "The judicial Power of the United

States, shall be vested in one Supreme Court, and in such inferior Courts as the Congress may from time to time ordain and establish." The brevity of this provision left Congress with the task of filling in much of the substance of the new judicial system.

The Judiciary Act of 1789

Once the Constitution was ratified, action on the federal judiciary came quickly. Indeed, the first bill introduced in the Senate dealt with the unresolved issue of inferior federal courts. The congressional debate included many of the same participants, who repeated all the arguments involved in the judiciary debates at the Constitutional Convention. After extensive debate, Congress passed the Judiciary Act of 1789, which laid the foundation for our current national judicial system. The Judiciary Act of 1789 represented a major victory for the Federalists; they were successful in creating separate federal district courts. At the same time, the act was a compromise that allayed some of the Anti-Federalists' fears. The organization of the federal judiciary supported state interests in three ways (Richardson and Vines 1970).

First, the boundaries of the district courts were drawn along state lines; no district encompassed more than one state. Thus, from the outset, the federal judiciary was "state-contained." Even though district courts enforced national law, they were organized along local lines, with each district court responsible for its own work under minimal supervision.

Second, by custom the selection process ensured that federal district judges would be residents of their districts. Although nominated by the president, district judges were to be (and are today) local residents, presiding in their home area, and therefore subject to the continuing influence of the local social and political environment (see Chapter 8).

Third, the act gave the lower federal courts only limited jurisdiction. The Federalists wanted the full range of federal jurisdiction granted by the Constitution to be given to district and circuit courts. However, to achieve a lower federal court system, they were forced to reduce this demand greatly.

But this issue would reappear repeatedly over the next 100 years.

1789–1891

The Judiciary Act of 1789 provided only a temporary compromise on the underlying disagreements between Federalists and Anti-Federalists. The Federalists immediately pushed for expanded powers for the federal judiciary. These efforts culminated in the passage of the Judiciary Act of 1801, which created many new judgeships and greatly extended the jurisdiction of the lower courts. The Federalist victory was short-lived, however. With the election of Thomas Jefferson as president, the Anti-Federalists in Congress quickly repealed the act and returned the federal judiciary to the basic outlines of the previous court system. The 1801 law is best remembered for the resulting lawsuit of *Marbury v. Madison* (1803) in which Chief Justice John Marshall created the power of judicial review (the Court can strike down as unconstitutional an act of Congress) (Neubauer and Meinhold 2004).

Between 1789 and 1891 there was general agreement on the inadequacy of the federal judicial system, but the underlying dispute persisted. Congress passed numerous minor bills modifying the system in a piecemeal fashion. Dissatisfaction centered on two principal areas: circuit riding and the appellate court workload.

One of the most pronounced weaknesses of the 1789 judicial structure was circuit riding. The Supreme Court justices, many of them old and ill, faced days of difficult and often impossible travel. In 1838, for example, the nine justices traveled an average of 2,975 miles. There were numerous complaints from the justices about the intolerable conditions that circuit-riding duties imposed on them.

Beyond the personal discomforts some justices encountered, the federal judiciary confronted a more systemic problem—mounting caseloads. Initially the federal judges of the newly created trial courts had relatively little to do because their jurisdiction was very limited. The Supreme Court likewise had few cases to decide. But the initially sparse workload began to expand as the growth of federal activity, the increase in corporate business, and the expansion of federal jurisdiction by court interpretation created litigation for a court system that was ill equipped to handle it. From the end of the Civil War until 1891, it was not uncommon for an appeal to wait two or three years before it was argued before the Supreme Court. The essential cause was that the high court had to decide every case appealed to it.

Court of Appeals Act of 1891

At first glance the creation of the court of appeals in 1891 appears to be an automatic response to increased federal litigation resulting from a rapidly expanding population and the growth of business following the Civil War. A closer look indicates that it was the culmination of "one of the most enduring struggles in American political history" (Richardson and Vines 1970, 26). There was no debate over the difficulties facing the federal court system. All parties to the controversy agreed that the federal judiciary needed relief; what was in dispute was the nature of the relief.

To solve the burden of mounting litigation in the federal courts, the supporters of states' rights wanted to return cases to the state level by reducing the jurisdiction of federal courts. The supporters of national power, on the other hand, argued for expanding the jurisdiction of federal courts by creating a system of federal appellate courts that would take a great deal of the burden off the high court and also allow the trial courts to function as true trial courts.

The landmark Court of Appeals Act of 1891 represented the climactic victory of the nationalist interests. The law created new courts known as circuit courts of appeals. Under this new arrangement, most appeals of trial decisions went to the circuit court of appeals. In short, the creation of the circuit courts of appeals released the high court from hearing many types of petty cases. The high court now had much greater control over its workload and could concentrate on deciding major cases and controversies.

Federal Courts Today

In 1925 Congress passed the Judges Bill, which among other things gave the Supreme Court much greater control over its docket. In 1988 Congress eliminated even more mandatory appeals to the high court. Exhibit 3-2 summarizes other key developments in the federal judiciary.

The current structure of federal courts is best understood in terms of four layers of courts: magistrate, district, appellate, and Supreme Court. In addition, the federal judiciary includes specialized courts and administrative structures.

■ U.S. MAGISTRATE JUDGES

U.S. magistrate judges are the federal equivalent of state trial court judges of limited jurisdiction. Although they are officially a subcomponent of the district courts, their duties and workload merit separate discussion. Congress created **U.S. magistrate judges** in 1968 to replace the former position of U.S. commissioners. The purpose was to provide a new type of judicial officers in the federal judicial system to alleviate the increased workload of the U.S. district courts (Puro 1976; Smith 1992).

Magistrate judges perform quasi-judicial tasks and work within the judicial branch of government. They are not, however, Article III judges. Magistrate judges are selected by the district court judges. Full-time magistrate judges are appointed for eight-year terms and part-time magistrate judges for four years. They may, however, be removed for "good cause." Except in special circumstances, all must be lawyers. According to the Administrative Office of the U.S. Courts, there are 422 full-time magistrate judges and 77 part-time magistrate judges (the part-time magistrate judges serve primarily national parks, where the work is seasonal).

Magistrate judges are authorized to perform a wide variety of duties. In felony cases, they are responsible for preliminary proceedings, including holding initial appearances, conducting preliminary hearings, appointing counsel for indigents, setting bail, and issuing search warrants. In misdemeanor and petty offense cases, the jurisdiction of magistrate judges is more extensive; they may preside over trials, accept pleas of guilty, and also im-

Exhibit 3-2	Key Developments in the Federal Judiciary	
U.S. Constitution	1787	Article III creates U.S. Supreme Court and authorizes lower federal courts.
Judiciary Act of 1789	1789	Congress establishes lower federal courts.
Marbury v. Madison	1803	The Court has the authority to declare an act of Congress unconstitutional.
Courts of Appeals Act	1891	Modern appellate structure is created.
Judges Bill	1925	Supreme Court is given control over its docket.
Court Packing Plan	1937	FDR's attempt to pack the Court is defeated.
Administrative Office Act	1939	Current administrative structure is created, including judicial conference and judicial councils.
Federal Judicial Center	1967	Research and training unit is created.
Federal Magistrate Act	1968	Commissioners are replaced by U.S. magistrates (later the name is changed to magistrate judges).
Sentencing Commission	1984	Commission is charged with developing sentencing guidelines.
Congressional Act of 1988	1988	Some mandatory appeals to the Supreme Court are eliminated.
Antiterrorism and Effective Death Penalty Act	1996	Right of state prisoners to file habeas corpus petitions in federal court is severely limited.
USA Patriot Act	2001	The government's ability to gather domestic antiterrorism intelligence is expanded, allowing for less court scrutiny and closing some court proceedings to the public.

pose sentences. On the civil side they supervise discovery, review Social Security disability benefit appeals, and even conduct full civil trials with the consent of the litigants. In short, under specified conditions and controls, magistrate judges may perform virtually all tasks carried out by district court judges, except trying and sentencing felony defendants (Smith 1992; Seron 1988; *Peretz v. U.S. 1991*).

Caseload of U.S. Magistrate Judges

Magistrate judges play an increasingly important role in helping district court judges dispose of their growing caseloads. In a typical year, for example, they handle approximately 880,000 matters for the federal courts, including being involved in some way in 494,000 felony matters. In addition, they dispose of more than 100,000 misdemeanor and petty offenses.

Given the rising workload of felony cases on the district court docket, magistrate judges are increasingly involved in civil matters—about 163,000 in the most recent year for which statistics are available. Indeed, in recent years magistrate judges have presided over 17 percent of civil trials.

Finally, they review but do not decide prisoner petitions, a topic we will address shortly. During 1999, for example, magistrate judges reviewed approximately 30,000 prisoner litigation matters.

U.S. DISTRICT COURTS

Congress has created 94 U.S. **district courts,** of which 89 are located within the 50 states. There is also a district court in the District of Columbia and four territorial district courts located in Guam, Puerto Rico, the Virgin Islands, and the Northern Mariana Islands.

There is at least one district court in each state; moreover, based on the compromise that produced the Judiciary Act of 1789, no district

| Exhibit 3-3 | Case Filings in the U.S. Courts |

	Total	Criminal	Civil	Prisoner Petitions	Minor Criminal
Supreme Court	7,924				
Courts of Appeals	57,555	11,569	17,227	18,272	
District Courts	385,886	67,000	263,591	55,295	
Magistrate Judges	880,129	494,000	298,109	30,000	72,109

Note: Some of these numbers have been rounded.

SOURCE: "Judicial Facts and Figures" Administrative Office of the U.S. Courts, http://www.uscourts.gov/judicialfactsfigures/contents.html, accessed August 13, 2003.

court crosses state lines. Some states have more than one district court: California, New York, and Texas, for instance, each have four. Because district courts often encompass large geographical areas, some hold court in various locations, or divisions. Some districts have only one division while others have several.

Congress has created 680 (667 permanent and 13 temporary) district court judgeships for the 94 districts. The president nominates district judges, who must then be confirmed by the Senate (see Chapter 8). Once they take the oath of office, they serve during "good behavior," which for practical purposes means for life. The number of judgeships in each district depends on the amount of judicial work as well as the political clout of the state's congressional delegation and ranges from 2 in sparsely populated Wyoming to 28 in densely inhabited Manhattan (officially called the U.S. District Court for the Southern District of New York).

Judges are assisted by an elaborate supporting cast of clerks, secretaries, law clerks, court reporters, probation officers, pretrial services officers, and U.S. marshals. The larger districts also have a federal public defender. Another important actor at the district court level is the U.S. attorney. There is one U.S. attorney (see Chapter 6) in each district, nominated by the president and confirmed by the Senate, but unlike the judges, he or she serves at the pleasure of the president.

The work of the district judges is significantly assisted by 326 **bankruptcy judges.** Although bankruptcy judges are adjuncts of the district courts, they are appointed for 14-year terms by the court of appeals in which the district is located. The bankruptcy workload of the district courts is enormous, with more than 1.5 million petitions filed annually. The vast majority of these bankruptcy filings are non-business-related, typically involving consumers who cannot pay their bills. The others are filed by businesses big and small.

Caseload of U.S. District Courts

In the federal system, the U.S. district courts are the federal trial courts of original jurisdiction. Exhibit 3-3 provides an overview of case volume in the federal courts. The volume of cases is large and growing. Each year, around 385,000 civil and criminal cases are filed in the U.S. district courts (not including bankruptcy, misdemeanors, and the like). These numbers represent a dramatic increase in workload over the last several decades.

The district courts are the trial courts for all major violations of federal criminal law (magistrate judges hear minor violations). Each year, U.S. attorneys file approximately 67,000 criminal cases, primarily for drug violations, embezzlement, and fraud. For many years federal prosecutions remained fairly constant (roughly 30,000 per year), only to shoot up beginning in 1980. A major part of this upsurge has been due to a dramatic increase in drug prosecutions. Today, drug prosecutions account for 29 percent of all federal criminal cases. Moreover, trials of criminal cases are now more frequent (and also longer) than in years past. Thus although civil, not criminal,

A DAY IN COURT

Bunton's Rocket Docket

 In Pecos, Texas, a procession of prisoners captured in the war on drugs is paraded before U.S. District Judge Lucius Bunton. There are no lunch breaks or continuances, and the cases are a blur. Lawyers call it "Bunton's Rocket Docket." The judge has no choice if he wants to keep up with the volume. "You are just running them through here like cattle," he says. . . .

Some in government say the war [on drugs] has made significant progress. But a growing number of judges, defense lawyers and prosecutors say it has had a host of unintended consequences that are jeopardizing the 200-year-old federal court system: Court dockets are choked; probation officers, marshals, and public defenders are overwhelmed; and the balance of power in the courtroom has shifted substantially to the prosecution, impairing the quality of justice that is meted out.

Federal courts . . . now resemble assembly lines, raising serious questions about the integrity of the system.

"It's tenuous," Bunton said, "and in some places, it's broken."

Perhaps most disturbing, although the nation's prisons are bloated, many on the front lines say there has been no serious dent in the drug trade or the violence that attends it.

Congress and the White House declared war on drug traffickers in 1986 by hiring thousands of new law-enforcement officers and passing sweeping laws that carry long, mandatory sentences.

The result has been a record number of arrests and prison terms. . . .

Because they feel overburdened, some judges have placed themselves in the uncharacteristic role of lobbyists with the senators who nominated them.

Bunton has this evidence to make his case: The seven federal judges in the Western District of Texas average 164 cases a year, more than triple the national average. Each judge also averaged 87 trials a year, compared to a national average of 35. Drug cases increased to 886 in 1989 from 272 in 1985.

Bunton's answer is more judges, politics be damned. "I don't care if it's a Republican or a Democrat. What I need is a body on the bench to try lawsuits." . . .

Asked what he thinks the war on drugs is accomplishing, Bunton responded: "It's accomplishing full prisons."

---

cases account for most of the work of the district courts, in some districts criminal filings are limiting the ability of these courts to decide civil cases. (See A Day in Court: Bunton's Rocket Docket.)

Civil lawsuits consume considerably more of the federal courts' time than criminal cases do. Although only a small number of all civil cases are filed in federal courts, these cases typically involve considerably larger sums of money than the cases filed in state court. Federal court jurisdiction is limited to a few types of cases, primarily involving questions of federal law, diversity of citizenship, and prisoner petitions.

Federal Questions

Article III provides that federal courts may be given jurisdiction over "Cases, in Law and Equity, arising under this Constitution, the Laws of the United States, and Treaties made, or which shall be made under their authority." Cases that fall under this type of jurisdiction are generally referred to as involving a **federal question.** Most federal question cases are filed alleging a violation of a congressional statute. Some of the principal federal laws that are the basis of litigation include Social Security, civil rights, the Americans with Disability Act, and truth in lending. These federal laws are having an increasing impact on state and local criminal justice (see Exhibit 3-4).

Diversity Jurisdiction

Diversity of citizenship cases involve suits between citizens of different states or between a

Exhibit 3-4   Federal Laws Affecting State and Local Criminal Justice

The impact of federal law on the criminal justice system of the states is most apparent in the decisions of federal courts expanding the rights of those accused of crimes. Under Chief Justice Earl Warren the U.S. Supreme Court sparked a due process revolution (Chapter 17) giving defendants the right to counsel (Chapter 7), broadening notions of a fair trial (Chapter 14), and expanding the right to appeal (Chapter 17). Perhaps most in the public eye have been decisions restricting police gathering of evidence (Chapter 12).

But indirectly, civil lawsuits also play an important role. Federal civil law affects the internal operations of criminal justice agencies as well as how these organizations deal with the general public. Here are four types of federal civil cases that have important consequences for state and local criminal justice officials.

■ *Civil Rights Violations*   Under Section 1983 (originally passed by Congress in 1871) city or state employees may be sued civilly for depriving an individual of his or her constitutional rights (*Monroe v. Pape*, 1967). Moreover, the government, and not just the individual, is liable for damages (*Monell v. Department of Social Services*, 1978). Section 1983 has become second only to prisoner petitions in the number of cases filed in the federal courts (Barrineau 1994). Police officers are sued for brutality, and prison guards are now regularly sued for alleged physical mistreatment.

■ *Equal Employment Opportunities*   Federal laws relating to equal employment opportunity prohibit discrimination on the basis of race, color, religion, sex, age, or national origin. Bona fide occupational qualifications, however, are exempt. Thus, valid job-related requirements necessary to normal business operations are allowed. Criminal justice agencies, though, should avoid height and weight requirements that are not related to job performance.

■ *Sex Discrimination*   Several federal laws prohibit sex discrimination. Except in rare instances, employers are required to ignore gender when hiring or promoting, provide equal pay to all employees, and treat pregnancy like any other temporary disability (Rubin 1995).

■ *Discrimination against the Disabled*   The 43 million Americans with disabilities are now protected against discrimination in employment and in their use of public facilities and services (Dooley and Wood 1992). Police departments, in particular, are covered (Smith and Alpert 1993). The Americans with Disabilities Act has had a noticeable impact on the docket of the federal courts, with a significant number of lawsuits being filed.

U.S. citizen and a foreign country or citizen. For example, a citizen from California claims to be injured in an automobile accident in Chicago with an Illinois driver and sues in federal court in Illinois because the parties to the suit are of "diverse citizenship." In deciding diversity of citizenship cases, federal courts apply state (not federal) law (Sloviter 1992).

Overall, diversity cases constitute almost one fourth of the civil docket of the district courts, thus making a significant contribution to the workload of the district courts. In an effort to restrict the types of minor disputes that may be filed in federal court, Congress in 1996 raised the amount-in-controversy to $75,000. Despite some speculation to the contrary, this change in jurisdictional amount has indeed significantly decreased the number of diversity cases filed in federal courts each year (Flango 1991; Kramer 1990). Overall, total diversity filings today remain well below levels of a decade earlier.

Prisoner Petitions

A controversial area of district court jurisdiction involves **prisoner petitions.** Prisoners incarcerated in either federal or state penitentiaries may file a civil suit alleging that their rights under federal law are being violated. (Similar suits may also be filed in state court, where they are called habeas corpus petitions.) Some prisoner petitions contend that the prisoners are being illegally held because they were improperly convicted; for example, they were denied the effective assistance of counsel at trial (discussed further in Chapter 7). Other prisoner petitions relate to the conditions of confinement; for example, the penitentiary is overcrowded or provides inadequate medical assistance (mentioned in Chapter 15). Peti-

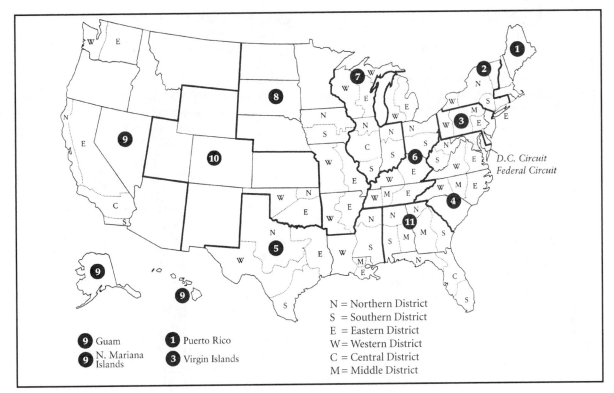

Figure 3-1
The Federal Judiciary

Source: Russell Wheeler and Cynthia Harrison, *Creating the Federal Judicial System,* 2d ed.
(Washington DC: Federal Judicial Center, 1994), 26.

tions from state and federal inmates have increased significantly, from about 3,500 filings in 1960 to more than 55,000 today. Thus, prisoner petitions constitute 25 percent of the total civil caseload as measured by filings. These numbers are being driven by the sharp increase in the prison population. U.S. magistrate judges hear most of these prisoner petitions but are limited to making a recommendation to the U.S. district judge (who typically follows the recommendation). Thus, these cases add volume but take little of the district judges' time.

U.S. COURTS OF APPEALS

As mentioned previously, Congress created the courts of appeals in 1891 to relieve the Supreme Court from hearing the growing number of appeals. The courts of appeals are the intermediate appellate courts of the federal system. Originally called circuit courts of appeal, they were renamed and are now officially known as the United States Court of Appeals for the ____ Circuit. Eleven of the circuits are identified by number, and another is called the D.C. Circuit (see Figure 3-1).

The courts of appeals are staffed by 179 judges nominated by the president and confirmed by the Senate. As with the district courts, the number of judges in each circuit varies, from 6 (the First Circuit) to 28 (the Ninth Circuit), depending on the volume and complexity of the caseload. Each circuit has a chief judge (chosen by seniority) who has supervisory responsibilities. Several staff positions aid the judges in conducting the work of the courts of appeals. A circuit executive assists the chief judge in administering the circuit. The clerk's office maintains the records. Each judge is also allowed to hire three law clerks. In addition, each circuit has a central legal staff that screens appeals and drafts memorandum opinions.

In deciding cases, the courts of appeals normally use rotating three-judge panels. Along with active judges in the circuit, these panels often include visiting judges (primarily district judges from the same circuit) and senior judges. By majority vote, all the judges in the circuit may sit together to decide a case or rehear a case already decided by a panel. Such **en banc** hearings are relatively rare, however; in a typical year fewer than 100 are held throughout the entire nation.

Caseload of U.S. Courts of Appeals

Over the last four decades, the caseload of the courts of appeals has skyrocketed. This dramatic increase in caseload has not been matched by an equivalent increase in judgeships, however. In 1960 there were 68 judgeships, compared to 179 today. As a result, the number of cases heard per panel has increased from 172 (1960) to 964 today.

Approximately 57,000 cases are filed annually. Appeals from criminal convictions in the U.S. district courts constitute about 20 percent of the workload of the courts of appeals. Appeals from decisions in civil cases make up the backbone of their caseload. Finally, the courts of appeals review a large number of prisoner petitions each year. As Chapter 17 will discuss in greater depth, prisoners petitioning the court are rarely successful except in death penalty cases.

A decision by the court of appeals exhausts the litigant's right to one appeal. The losing party may request that the Supreme Court hear the case, but such petitions are rarely granted. As a result, the courts of appeals are the "courts of last resort" for virtually all federal litigation. Their decisions end the case; only a tiny percentage will be heard by the nation's highest court.

■ U.S. SUPREME COURT

The highest court in the nation is composed of nine justices: eight associate justices and one chief justice, who is nominated specifically to that post by the president. Like other judges appointed under Article III of the Constitution, Supreme Court justices are nominated by the president, require confirmation by the Senate, and serve for life.

Cases proceed to the Supreme Court primarily through the **writ of certiorari,** an order to the lower court to send the case records so that the Supreme Court can determine whether the law has been correctly applied. The Court reviews decisions from the U.S. courts of appeals and state appellate courts of last resort. Although the Supreme Court is the only court in the nation to have authority over all 51 separate legal systems, its authority is actually limited.

Caseload of U.S. Supreme Court

With few exceptions, the Court selects which cases it will decide out of the many it is asked to review each year. In deciding to decide, the Court uses the *rule of four:* Four judges must vote to hear a case before it is placed on the docket. As a result, only a small percentage of the requests for appeals are ever granted. By law and custom, a set of requirements must be met before a writ of certiorari (or *cert,* as it is often called) is granted. In particular, the legal issue must involve a "substantial federal question." This means state court interpretations of state law can be appealed to the Supreme Court only if there is an alleged violation of either federal law or the U.S. Constitution. For example, a suit contending that a state supreme court has misinterpreted the state's divorce law would not be heard because it involves an interpretation of state law and does not raise a federal question. As a result, the vast majority of state cases are never reviewed by the Supreme Court.

Through its discretionary powers to hear appeals, the high court limits itself to deciding about 80 cases a year. The Court does not operate as the court of last resort, attempting to correct errors in every case in the nation, but rather marshals its time and energy to decide the most important policy questions of the day. The cases granted certiorari reflect conflicting legal doctrines; typically, lower courts have decided similar cases in very different ways.

Exhibit 3-5 Specialized Federal Courts

Courts with Permanent Judges

Court		Level	Jurisdiction
Tax Court	Article I	Trial	Tax disputes
Court of Federal Claims	Article I	Trial	Monetary claims against the federal government
Court of Veterans Appeal	Article I	Trial	Federal veterans' benefits
Court of International Trade	Article III	Trial	Imports of foreign goods
U.S. Court of Appeals of the Armed Forces	Article I	Appellate	Uniform Code of Military Justice
Court of Appeals for the Federal Circuit	Article III	Appellate	Trademarks, patents, foreign trade, claims against the federal government

Courts with Judges Borrowed from Other Federal Courts

Court	Level	Jurisdiction
Alien Terrorist Removal Court	Trial	Decides whether an alien should be removed from the United States on the grounds of being an alien terrorist
Foreign Intelligence Surveillance Court	Trial	Electronic surveillance of foreign intelligence agents
Foreign Intelligence Surveillance Court of Review	Appellate	Electronic surveillance of foreign intelligence agents

SOURCE: Adapted from Lawrence Baum, *American Courts: Process and Policy*, 2d ed. (Boston: Houghton Mifflin, 1990), 37; Lawrence Baum, "Specializing the Federal Courts: Neutral Reforms or Efforts to Shape Judicial Policy?" *Judicature* 74 (1991): 217–224.

Although the Supreme Court decides a fraction of all cases filed in the courts, these decisions set policy for the entire nation.

SPECIALIZED COURTS

The magistrate, district, appeals courts, and Supreme Court handle the bulk of federal litigation and therefore are a principal focus of this book. To round out our discussion of the federal judicial system, however, we also need to discuss briefly several additional courts that Congress has periodically created. These courts are called specialized federal courts because they are authorized to hear only a limited range of cases—taxes or patents, for example. They are created for the express purpose of helping administer a specific congressional statute.

Exhibit 3-5 gives an overview of the specialized federal courts and highlights two important distinctions. First, most specialized courts have permanent, full-time judges appointed specifically to that court. A few specialized courts, however, temporarily borrow judges from federal district courts or courts of appeals as specific cases arise (Baum 1991).

The second distinction relates to the specialized courts' constitutional status. Judicial bodies established by Congress under Article III are known as **constitutional courts.** The Supreme Court, courts of appeals, and district courts are, of course, constitutional courts. Judicial bodies established by Congress under **Article I** are known as **legislative courts.** Courts presided over by bankruptcy judges and U.S. magistrate judges are examples of legislative courts. The constitutional status of federal courts has important implications for judicial independence. Article III (constitutional court) judges serve for a period that amounts to a lifetime appointment, but Article I (legislative court) judges are appointed for a specific term of office. Moreover, Article III judges are protected against salary reductions while in office. Article I judges enjoy no such constitutional protection. In short, constitutional courts have a greater degree of independence from the other two branches of government than do the legislative courts. The specialized federal courts are overwhelmingly civil in their orientation, handling such matters as patents and tariffs on imported goods. But three specialized courts bear directly on criminal matters: tribal courts, military courts, and noncombatants.

Tribal Courts

In 1789 Congress designated the Native American tribes as foreign nations to enable the government to sign land and boundary treaties with them. During the nineteenth century U.S. policy was to force Native Americans onto reservations west of the Mississippi River. Today there are about 285 federal and state protected land bases, colloquially called *reservations* but technically termed *Indian Country* (18 U.S.C. sec. 151). The Bureau of Indian Affairs manages federal reservations. On the reservations today, Native Americans enjoy a degree of self-determination and sovereignty, but the degree of self-government varies from tribe to tribe. Moreover, state governments often seek to exert some authority over Indian reservations (Resnik 1995).

The *tribe* is the basic unit of federal Indian law. Federal legislation protects Native American groups and grants them rights against the federal government. Treaties, for example, give tribes rights to land and hunting, fishing, and water rights. The key elements of American law regarding Native Americans are (1) federal acknowledgment of sovereign governmental powers possessed by Native American groups and (2) a federal trust obligation toward and special federal powers over such groups and their members (Goldberg-Ambrose 1994).

Native American law is a jurisdictional maze of civil and criminal courts affecting Native Americans, as well as non-Native Americans living or operating a business within the jurisdiction of a Native American government (Nielsen and Silverman 1996). Tribal courts total 248, staffed by 271 trial and 39 appellate judges in 27 states. Most were created under the Indian Reorganization Act of 1934, which encouraged self-government through tribal constitutions, organized government, and tribally created courts.

Today 1.2 million Native Americans live on or near these reservations ("Courts Try . . ." 2001). According to the Bureau of Justice Statistics (1999a), Native Americans experience a high rate of violent crimes and are more likely to be victimized by someone of another race; also, 46 percent of all violent victimizations involve a drinking offender. As a result, the federal government is rethinking its policies and experimenting with ways to strength tribal courts (Baca 2001).

Military Justice

Congress adopted the Uniform Code of Military Justice in 1950, extending significant new due process rights in courts-martial. The law created the U.S. Court of Appeals for the Armed Forces, composed of three civilian judges appointed by the president for 15-year terms. The intent was clearly to extend civilian influence to military law. The Military Justice Act of 1968 contributed to the further civilianization of courts-martial. The code covers criminal acts but can also punish acts that are not criminal for civilians (for example, disrespect of an officer). Moreover, on a military base, military justice applies not only to members of the armed services but also to civilian employees, and it covers acts committed by military personnel on and off a military base (Sherman 1987).

As with other systems of criminal law, the objective of military justice is to provide a forum for determining guilt or innocence. But in addition, courts-martial serve the purpose of enforcing order and discipline in the military. In the words of the U.S. Army: "The purpose of military law is to promote efficiency and effectiveness in the military establishment, and thereby to strengthen the national security of the United States." Thus, although military justice is not exempt from the Constitution, it is certainly distinctive. Military justice differs from state and federal justice in the following ways:

- Proceedings are secret.
- Rules of evidence are less demanding.
- Six-person juries are used.
- The jurors are military personnel.
- A two-thirds majority is sufficient to convict.
- Convictions are automatically appealed to a higher military court.

The principal concern with military courts is that jurors may be unduly influenced by military commanders.

In recent years a few high-profile cases have thrust military justice into the news. Some of the more prominent cases include these:

- Drill Sergeant Delmar Simpson was sentenced to 25 years in military prison for raping and abusing more than a dozen trainees at the Aberdeen, Maryland, Army base.
- The Army charged its top enlisted man, Sergeant Major Gene McKinney, with 18 counts of adultery, maltreatment, and sexual misconduct toward subordinates.
- A U.S. soldier raped a young girl in Okinawa.
- Two Illinois air national guard pilots were charged with involuntary manslaughter for accidentally dropping bombs on Canadian troops in Afghanistan.

Military Noncombatants

In response to September 11, the United States invaded Afghanistan, capturing hundreds of persons suspected of being members of the Al Qaeda terrorist organization. The military decided that those captured did not qualify as prisoners of war (and therefore subject to the Geneva Convention) but instead would be considered military noncombatants. Hundreds were held at the Navy base in Guantanamo Bay, Cuba, because they were not subject to the jurisdiction of the U.S. federal courts.

By 2003 the Bush administration decided that these military noncombatants would be tried in military courts, where the proceedings would be secret and the potential punishments could include the death penalty. Pending trials have created an international furor, with critics arguing that the United States is not living up to its tradition of respecting the rule of law.

Closer to home, the American Bar Association condemned the decision that those tried would not be able to talk to their lawyers in private.

It is also possible that Zacarias Moussaoui, charged with being the twentieth hijacker on September 11, will be tried by a military tribunal to avoid making key prosecution evidence public, as would be required in a trial before a U.S. district court.

FEDERAL JUDICIAL ADMINISTRATION

The Administrative Office Act of 1939, which largely created the current administrative structure of the federal judiciary, illustrates the interplay between judicial administration and politics. During the mid-1930s, the conservative majority on the Supreme Court declared many pieces of New Deal legislation unconstitutional. After his reelection in 1936, President Franklin Delano Roosevelt put forth his Court-packing plan: The Court would be expanded from 9 to 15 justices, thus allowing FDR to pack the Court with justices more sympathetic to his policies. There was no legal barrier to such action because the Constitution fails to specify how many justices shall serve on the Court. But the political obstacles proved insurmountable; many of Roosevelt's backers felt that tampering with the Court was a bad idea. The Court-packing plan never passed, but it did call attention to the president's complaints that the administration of federal courts was inefficient. At the same time, some judges were dissatisfied with the old system of court management because it was located in the Department of Justice, an executive agency. Thus, a movement arose among federal judges and national court reformers to clean their own house. The result was a compromise plan—the Administrative Office Act of 1939. The act expanded the responsibilities of the Judicial Conference, created the Administrative Office of the U.S. Courts, and established the judicial councils. These agencies, along with the office of the chief justice, the Federal Judicial Center, and the more recently created U.S. Sentencing Commission, are the main units involved in administering the federal courts.

THE MURDER TRIAL OF SHAREEF COUSIN

A Federal Civil Rights Lawsuit Is Filed

Late on the afternoon of January 7, 2000, attorney Clive Stafford-Smith walked the five blocks from his office to the federal courthouse at 500 Camp Street. The date was important. Federal law mandates a one-year statute of limitations in cases like this one. Thus the lawsuit was filed exactly one year after District Attorney Harry Connick decided not to retry Shareef Cousin for the Port of Call murder.

Smith, the state's leading anti–death penalty lawyer, had represented Shareef Cousin in the state criminal trial and appeal. But now he was filing a federal civil rights lawsuit. Proceeding to the intake desk of the clerk's office, he paid the $150 filing fee, and the office time-stamped the lawsuit, titled "Shareef Cousin versus Anthony Small." The complaint was given the number 00-0069, indicating that it was the sixty-ninth civil lawsuit filed during the year 2000. The case was then randomly allotted to U.S. district court judge Sarah Vance, who had been appointed to the federal bench in 1994 by President Clinton. As a practicing lawyer, she had worked in the civil litigation section of one of the city's largest law firms. As a presiding judge, she was noted for running a tight ship, particularly in cases involving felony prosecutions of some of the state's top elected officials (Gyan 1997).

Some of the defendants were the prosecutors in the state criminal prosecution. The others were New Orleans police officers. The 83-page lawsuit began: "This civil action arises from the malicious prosecution, wrongful arrest, incarceration and prosecution of plaintiff Shareef Cousin." The lawsuit alleged that the plaintiff's rights were violated under the Civil Rights Act (Chapter 42 of the U.S. Code), particularly Section 1983.

The document offered a broad-based indictment of both police and prosecution. Detective Anthony Small, the lead homicide detective in the murder of Michael Gerardi, was accused of being corrupt and fabricating evidence. Assistant District Attorney Roger Jordan was accused of repeatedly not turning over favorable evidence to the defense. The complaint concluded with a broad-based indictment of racial bias in the police department and Connick's office. The complaint requested an unspecified amount of damages. In a later letter from one of Cousin's attorneys, however, the lawyer suggested that, based on past cases, $2.5 million would constitute a justifiable settlement.

The City Attorney for New Orleans defended the police officers. His reply simply denied the allegations, thus providing little guidance as to the defense the city might use in the case. More interesting was the reply from Harry Connick's lawyer, who asserted that the district attorney enjoys absolute immunity from lawsuits (see Chapter 6). The reply also termed the complaint redundant and immaterial. The judge would later call the document convoluted but refused to dismiss it on procedural grounds.

A month before filing the civil rights lawsuit, attorney Clive Stafford-Smith and other defense lawyers held a news conference to bestow their first Chef Menteur award (which in French means "big liar"). The recipient was an NOPD homicide detective who allegedly falsified evidence in a trial that resulted in the defendant's being acquitted. A longtime homicide detective, who requested that he not be identified by name, scoffed. He said the lawsuits had little to do with the case they claimed to address but instead were part of an effort to undermine the credibility of detectives who testified in future cases (Coyle 2000b).

The cases never went to trial. The judge dismissed the case on substantive grounds, ruling that both the police and prosecutor were immune from prosecution.

Chief Justice

The chief justice is the presiding officer of the Supreme Court and has supervisory authority over the entire federal judicial system. In fulfilling these duties, the chief justice is allotted an extra law clerk and an administrative assistant to help with the administrative tasks for both the Court and the judicial system as a whole. As head of the federal judiciary, the chief justice is an ex officio member of several important administrative organizations and also appoints persons to key administrative posts. Current Chief Justice William Rehnquist has often spoken about the need for Congress to increase the number of federal judges, increase the salaries of judges to be competitive with the private practice of law, and reduce the workload of the courts.

Judicial Conference of the United States

The Judicial Conference of the United States is the administrative policymaking organization of the federal judicial system. Its membership consists of the chief justice, the chief judges of each of the courts of appeals, one district judge from each circuit, and the chief judge of the Court of International Trade. The conference meets semiannually for two-day sessions. Because these short meetings are not sufficient to accomplish a great deal, most of the work is done by about 25 committees. The committees consist of judges and a few lawyers appointed by the chief judge. The recommendations of the committees set the agenda for the conference (Fish 1973).

The Judicial Conference directs the Administrative Office in administering the judiciary budget and makes recommendations to Congress concerning the creation of new judgeships, increases in judicial salaries, revising federal rules of procedure, and budgets for court operations. The Judicial Conference also plays a major role in the impeachment of federal judges (a topic discussed in greater depth in Chapter 8). In short, the Judicial Conference is a vehicle through which federal judges play a major role in developing policy for the federal judiciary.

Administrative Office of the U.S. Courts

Since 1939, the day-to-day administrative tasks of the federal courts have been handled by the Administrative Office of the U.S. Courts, a judicial agency. The director of the Administrative Office is appointed by the chief justice and reports to the Judicial Conference. Acting as the Judicial Conference's official representative in Congress, the Administrative Office's lobbying and liaison responsibilities include presenting the annual budget requests for the federal judiciary, arguing for the need for additional judgeships, and transmitting proposed changes in court rules. The Administrative Office (AO) is also the housekeeping agency of the judiciary responsible for allotting authorized funds and supervising expenditures. Throughout the year, local federal court staff send the AO a vast array of statistical data on the operations of the federal courts, ranging from the number of filings to the speed of the disposition of cases. The data are published in three separate volumes. The heftiest is the *Annual Report,* which runs hundreds of pages long and is now available on the Internet.

Federal Judicial Center

The Federal Judicial Center is the research and training arm of the federal judiciary. Its activities are managed by a director appointed by the board, which consists of the chief justice, the director of the Administrative Office, and judges from the U.S. district court, courts of appeals, and bankruptcy court. One of the principal activities of the Federal Judicial Center is education and training of federal judicial personnel, including judges, probation officers, clerks of court, and pretrial service officers. The center also conducts research on a wide range of topics, including the work of the magistrate judges, ways of measuring the workload of the courts, and causes of delay.

Judicial Councils

The judicial council (sometimes referred to as the circuit council) is the basic administrative unit of a circuit. The membership consists of both district and appellate judges of the circuit. A judicial council is given sweeping authority to "make all necessary and appropriate orders for the effective and expeditious administration of justice within its circuit." Working within this broad mandate, the councils monitor district court caseloads and judicial assignments. Although the law specifies that "all judicial officers and employees of the circuit shall promptly carry into effect all orders of the judicial council," the actual enforcement powers are limited. The major weapons at the councils' disposal are persuasion, peer group pressure, and publicity directed at the judge or judges who are reluctant to comply with circuit policy. At times, for example, circuit councils have ordered that a district judge receive no new cases until his or her docket has been brought up to date. Judicial councils are also authorized to investigate complaints of judicial disability or misconduct (a topic probed in greater detail in Chapter 8).

U.S. Sentencing Commission

The U.S. Sentencing Commission is an independent agency in the judicial branch of government. The commission was created by the Sentencing Reform Act of 1984. Its original purpose was to develop federal sentencing guidelines. Today the commission is charged with evaluating the effects of the sentencing guidelines on the criminal justice system, recommending to Congress appropriate modifications of substantive criminal law and sentencing procedures, and establishing a research and development program on sentencing issues (see Chapter 16).

RISING CASELOADS IN THE FEDERAL COURTS

Rising caseloads in federal court are nothing new. The onset of the Industrial Revolution increased the caseload of the federal courts, a trend that was later accelerated by Prohibition, then the New Deal, and even further by federal lawmaking often associated with President Lyndon Johnson's "Great Society" programs. Growing caseloads in turn prompted changes and additions to the federal judiciary; appellate courts have been added and specialized courts created.

What is new is the pace of that expansion. For most of our nation's history the growth in federal cases was gradual. No longer! Over the past 50 years, district court filings have increased more than sixfold, and court of appeals cases have increased more than tenfold. According to the Administrative Office of the U.S. Courts, federal judges today are faced with unprecedented levels of work. By and large federal judges across the country face a greater number of cases this year than last, and in some instances are encountering record levels of work.

The caseload problem is particularly acute in some metropolitan jurisdictions, where federal judges must postpone civil trials for months and even years to accommodate criminal trial schedules (particularly of major drug dealers) in accordance with the Speedy Trial Act (see Chapter 5). Developments like these have given rise to the term "federal judicial gridlock" (Williams 1993).

The solutions most often suggested for the problem of rising federal court caseloads are increasing the number of federal judges and reducing federal jurisdiction.

Increase the Number of Federal Judges?

Through the years, increases in the number of cases filed in federal court have been followed by an increase in the number of federal judgeships. More recently, however, the dramatic increases in federal court cases have not been accompanied by a corresponding increase in the number of federal judgeships. Particularly at the appellate level, the creation of new judgeships has lagged far behind the increase in filings.

It is unlikely that in the short term the number of federal judgeships will be increased. Only Congress can authorize additional judgeships, and Congress has been locked in a decades-long partisan battle over the federal judiciary. Chapter 8 will explore ongoing political battles between Republicans and Democrats over who should fill existing vacancies on the federal bench. Given this partisan divide, it is unlikely that additional judgeships will be created anytime soon because new judgeships would become political spoils for the party temporarily in control.

Reduce Federal Jurisdiction?

To cope with rising caseloads, federal judges have proposed not only creating more judgeships but also reducing the types of cases that can be filed in federal court. According to the *Report of the Federal Courts Study Committee* (1990), Congress created most of these problems by unwisely expanding federal court jurisdiction, and therefore Congress should act immediately to pass remedial legislation. Alas, having been labeled as the culprit, it is hardly surprising that Congress gave the report a chilly reception (Biskupic 1993). In short, the nation's top elected lawmakers have been at odds with the nation's top appointed law interpreters for most of the past century, and this disagreement is not likely to change.

Arguments based on numbers of cases stress issues of efficiency but typically need to be understood within a broader framework of political winners and losers. Thus, some disagree-

Exhibit 3-6	The Limited Scope of Federal Criminal Involvement		
Activity	State and Local	Federal	
Law enforcement personnel	796,518	88,496	11%
Supreme Court justices	357	9	2%
Courts of appeals judges	874	179	17%
Major trial court judges	10,000	680	6%
Lower trial court judges	18,317	422	2%
Prison inmates	1,304,260	136,395	10%
Prisoners under sentence of death	3,562	19	0.5%
Correctional officers	352,847	25,515	7%

Source: Bureau of Justice Statistics, http://www.ojp.usdoj.gov/bjs/, accessed on August 13, 2003.

ments reflect divisions along the lines of the due process versus crime control models of justice. But other disagreements reflect institutional differences: The views of federal judges (whether appointed by Republican presidents or Democratic ones) contrast with the views of federal lawmakers. Part of the political battle over federal court jurisdiction involves the scope of federal criminal law. Courts, Controversy, and Reducing Crime: Should State Crimes Also Become Federal Violations? explores why this topic cuts across typical ideological perspectives.

CONSEQUENCES OF FEDERAL INVOLVEMENT IN THE CRIMINAL JUSTICE SYSTEM

Crime has been a pressing national concern for decades. As a result, national elected officials, whether members of Congress or the president, have often made crime a key campaign issue. In turn, the crime policies of nonelected officials, whether bureaucrats or judges, have been closely scrutinized. Despite all this clamor at the national level, crime remains primarily the responsibility of state and local governments. This imbalance between federal officials' need to be seen as doing something about the crime problem and their limited jurisdiction to do anything explains a good deal

of the political dynamics surrounding the role of the federal government (and the federal judiciary) in the criminal justice system.

Limited Scope

Although crime receives extraordinary attention from the national government, the role of the federal government in the criminal justice system is limited. The majority of events labeled as crime are violations not of federal law but of state law; as a result, the capacity of the federal justice system is limited. Exhibit 3-6 makes the point. The federal system has 11 percent of the nation's law enforcement personnel, 10 percent of prison inmates, and 7 percent of major trial court judges.

Forum for Symbolic Politics

In spite of the limited scope of its involvement in crime, the federal government remains the focal point of the national debate. Crime is a powerful issue and therefore has attracted a variety of interest groups. Some focus on crime issues directly—for example, the National Association of Chiefs of Police, and Mothers Against Drunk Driving (MADD). Other interest groups find that crime and crime issues are related to other concerns—the American Civil Liberties Union (ACLU) and the National Organization of Women (NOW).

Interest groups have a major impact on public policy. Most directly, they lobby on behalf of

COURTS, CONTROVERSY, AND REDUCING CRIME

Should State Crimes Also Become Federal Violations?

 Walk into federal court for the first time and you probably won't expect to see defendants like Alfonso Lopez. We associate federal courts with big cases and important issues. Bank embezzlers and big-time drug dealers are what we expect to see. Street criminals like Lopez are more likely to be found in state courts. But increasingly, the dockets of federal courts are being crammed with such criminals. Deciding what should be a federal offense and what should be a state crime reflects both issues of law and political disagreements.

Under federalism, one of the powers reserved to the states is the power to regulate persons and property in order to promote the public welfare (commonly referred to as *police powers*). Based on these police powers, state governments and their local subdivisions pass laws to promote the public health, welfare, and safety. Thus, most crimes are defined by the states (see Chapter 2).

Congressional Expansion

Over the years Congress has extended federal criminal jurisdiction beyond the basics centering on federal property and interstate commerce. The underlying motivation has been public concerns (some would say public hysteria) about public morality (Meier 1994). Thus, the Mann Act of 1910 prohibited the interstate transportation of prostitutes, the Harrison Act of 1914 outlawed drugs associated with deviants, and the Volstead Act ushered in Prohibition in 1919.

Contemporary demands to expand federal criminal jurisdiction typically reflect contrasting partisan and ideological positions. Conservatives generally favor reducing federal court caseloads but have called for increasing federal criminal jurisdiction to include car-jacking and transferring numerous gun cases from state to federal courts. These efforts, if successful, would potentially result in numerous violent offenders who were armed with a weapon being prosecuted in federal, not state, court.

Democrats oppose such efforts but tend to support expansion of federal criminal law to cover citizens with limited political power. Thus, they favor expanding federal criminal legislation to cover hate crimes, stalking, and violence against women. And most of all they back gun control as the best strategy for controlling crime. Republicans oppose such efforts.

The *Lopez* and *Morrison* Decisions

Federal judges, whether appointed by Republican or Democratic presidents, almost uniformly oppose the federalization of state crimes (Schwarzer and Wheeler 1994). Chief Justice Rehnquist (1993) has decried what he calls the near transformation of some federal courts into national narcotics courts.

Thus, the *Lopez* case is ultimately significant not because it involves guns but because the Court set limits on what crimes Congress may federalize. Chief Justice William Rehnquist's majority opinion stressed that in passing the Gun-Free School Zones Act in 1990, Congress "did not issue any findings showing a relationship between gun possession on school property and commerce."

More recently, a bare conservative majority of the Court declared part of the Violence Against Women Act of 1994 unconstitutional (*United States v. Morrison*, 2000). In particular, victims of rape and other violent felonies "motivated by gender" can no longer sue their attackers in federal court (although state remedies are still available). These decisions have sparked intense debate. To some, overexpansion of federal jurisdiction is a genuine concern in matters like this. But to others, the concern over caseload appears to be a façade masquerading conservative antipathy toward gun control and protecting the rights of vulnerable members of society.

> Use the term "crime, federal" to locate additional articles on the topic. Here are two:
> John Mountjoy, "The Federalization of Criminal Laws"; James Gondles, "The Federalization of Criminal Justice."

United States v. Miller and the Right to Bear Arms

 It is no small irony that in the polemics over gun control the U.S. Constitution is very salient while the U.S. Supreme Court has been very silent. The Second Amendment reads: "A well regulated Militia, being necessary to the security of a free State, the right of the people to keep and bear Arms, shall not be infringed." The high court has addressed the meaning of these archaic words only five times in its history, most recently in 1939.

Why Jack Miller and Frank Layton drove from Claremore, Oklahoma, to Siloam Springs, Arkansas, is unknown. In the quaint words of *The New York Times* ("Supreme Court Bars Sawed-Off Shotgun" 1939), "The record in the case of Miller and Dayton [sic] does not show for what purpose they were taking the sawed-off shotgun across State lines." Both were arrested for transporting a sawed-off shotgun in interstate commerce. The U.S. district court dismissed the indictment on grounds that the National Firearms Act "violates the Second Amendment to the Constitution of the United States" (*United States v. Miller et al.,* 1939). Alas for Miller and Layton, the nation's high court reached a very different conclusion.

Writing for a unanimous court, Justice James McReynolds (a jurist noted for his conservative views) explored the history of the Second Amendment, emphasizing that the drafters inserted the phrase "well regulated Militia" very purposefully. "The sentiment of the time strongly disfavored standing armies; the common view was that adequate defense of country and laws could be secured through the Militia—civilians primarily, soldiers on occasion." In short "the right of the people to keep and bear Arms" applied only to militia and not to individual citizens.

Since *Miller,* the Supreme Court has declined to address the issue directly. Lower federal courts have upheld firearms regulations either on grounds

that the Second Amendment is a collective, not an individual, right or because it has not been incorporated—that is, it limits only the national government, but not state or local entities. Recently, however, the high court (in the tradition of *Lopez*) struck down the part of the Brady Act dealing with background checks, reasoning that the Tenth Amendment prohibits Congress from compelling state law enforcement officers to "administer or enforce a federal regulatory program" (*Printz v. United States,* 1997).

The decision in *United States v. Miller* is often mentioned by gun control advocates and just as often ignored by gun rights supporters. The ongoing debate over the meaning of the Second Amendment illustrates the interplay between law on the books and law in action. In terms of law on the books, the Supreme Court has the final say. But in terms of law in action, other branches of government and citizens themselves play a vital role. The Constitution is an important symbol of American society. Labeling a governmental program as constitutional (or unconstitutional) has tremendous consequences. No matter what the Court (and lawyers and judges for that matter) might say, a significant minority of the American public interprets the Second Amendment as creating a personal right to bear arms (not limited to the militia). Moreover, these views are reinforced by powerful interest groups—most notably, the National Rifle Association.

To continue the debate over gun control and the right to bear arms, visit the Opposing Viewpoints Resource Center at http://www. galegroup.com/opposingviewpoints and use the search term "gun control" to find articles that express opposing viewpoints on this topic. Here are two possibilities: George Detweiler, "Gun Control Denies Citizens' Rights"; Melissa Huelsman, "Gun Control Is Constitutional."

their members for favorable government policies. They can also mount campaigns encouraging their members to write federal officials in favor of (or in opposition to) specific proposals. Some organizations likewise make campaign contributions to selected officials.

The National Rifle Association (NRA), for instance, contributes to officials who are dubious about gun control, whereas Handgun Control, Inc., supports candidates who favor gun control (Marion 1995). The rhetoric over gun control typically focuses on the right to

A Virtual Tour of American Courthouses: Federal Court

Alas, federal courts prohibit cameras, so it is hard to find Web sites offering good visual images. However, a few do exist. Historic photos are available from the Federal Judicial Center at **http://www.fjc.gov/newweb/jnetweb.nsf/fjc_courts**. Also readily available is the Federal Circuit Courtroom found in the Old Post Office in Columbus, Ohio, at **http://www. bricker.com/firminformation/tour/**.

"The Supreme Court: A Journey through Time" is presented by CourtTV at **http://www.courttv.com/multimedia/ supremecourt/index.html**.

bear arms (see Case Close-up: *United States v. Miller* and the Right to Bear Arms).

Federal Dollars

A basic rule of American politics is that citizen demands for services exceed the willingness of voters to raise taxes to pay for those services. Those who one day vocally demand a tax reduction are quick to demand expanded government services the next day. Funding the criminal justice system illustrates this rule. Citizens demand that courts "get tough with criminals" but are unwilling to raise taxes to build new prison cells. Likewise, pleas for more cops on the beat are seldom followed by requests for increased taxes to pay for such increased people power. Faced with these limitations, local and state officials often turn to Washington as a source of "free" money (with free defined as no local taxes). In turn, federal officials find that appropriating federal money is one way of assuring voters that they take the crime problem seriously.

Congress has authorized spending for a variety of anticrime programs. Some are general in nature—for example, block grants for local projects that reduce crime and improve public safety. Similarly, 60 percent of the research budget of the National Institute of Justice—the principal federal agency involved in the war on crime—is spent on developing new technology for law enforcement and the criminal justice system. Other spending programs are targeted toward specific concerns—for example, domestic violence and victim assistance programs (see Chapter 9).

Overall, though, the amount of federal dollars is small compared to what local and state governments spend. Moreover, federal money is often limited to a short period of time (typically three years). After federal funding ends, state or local units of government are expected to take over funding, but often these agencies are strapped for cash, meaning that successful programs are canceled.

CONCLUSION

Street punks like Alfonso Lopez were no doubt on Justice Scalia's mind when he spoke in New Orleans a few years ago, condemning what he called the deterioration of the federal courts. In the 1960s the federal courts had few judges and small caseloads, but the cases they did hear were "by and large . . . cases of major importance." Today, he argued, the federal courts have more judges and larger caseloads, but many of these cases are "minor" and "routine," concerning "mundane" matters of less import or even "overwhelming triviality" (quoted in Galanter 1988). Thus, to one of the Court's leading conservatives, the federal courts should be returned to their rightful role of deciding major controversies; lesser ones would be banished to state courts.

Other federal judges, whether noted for their liberal, moderate, or conservative views, have also expressed concern about the federalization of state crimes, calling for drug cases to be sent back to state courts where they rightfully belong. But in an era when crime remains a major political issue, rolling back federal jurisdiction to the "good old days" (whenever that might have been) is unlikely to happen. What we learn ultimately is that the jurisdiction of federal courts is determined in no small measure by decisions of elected officials in Congress. In an earlier era, federal officials decided that federal law should cover matters such as prostitution, consumption of alcoholic beverages, gambling, and organized crime. Today they focus more on drug dealers, crooks who use guns, and wife beaters.

Federal prosecutions often grab the headlines because the crimes are large or audacious or because the accused are people of prominence. In turn, the public by and large identifies the judiciary with federal courts. But we should not be misled. The federal courts are a relatively small part of the nation's judicial system. A major city such as Chicago or Los Angeles prosecutes more felons in a year than the entire federal judiciary. The nature of the crimes brought to federal court differs strikingly from those appearing in state judiciaries, though. State courts handle primarily street crimes that require immediate action—burglary, armed robbery, and murder, for example. By contrast, federal crimes are often paper crimes requiring no immediate action—bank embezzlement and money laundering, for instance. It is to the more common state courts that we turn our attention in the next chapter.

CRITICAL THINKING QUESTIONS

1. To what extent are contemporary debates over the role of the federal government similar to, but also different from, the debates in the late eighteenth century?

2. How would the criminal justice system be different today if the founding fathers had decided not to create a separate system of federal courts and instead allowed federal laws to be enforced in state courts?

3. How would you reduce the federal court caseload? In considering where you would reduce federal court jurisdiction, also consider where you might increase it. What do your choices reflect about your political values?

4. To what extent does the debate over federalization of state crimes cut across traditional ideological values as represented in the due process model and the crime control model?

5. Federal law enforcement is limited in scope but subject to considerable public attention. Why?

6. Why do opponents of gun control so often ignore *U.S. v. Miller*?

KEY TERMS

appellate court (53)
appellate jurisdiction (53)

Article I (65)
Article III (56)
bankruptcy judge (60)
constitutional courts (65)
district courts (59)
diversity of citizenship (61)
dual court system (53)
en banc (64)
extradition (53)
federal question (61)
geographical jurisdiction (53)
hierarchical jurisdiction (53)
jurisdiction (52)
legislative courts (65)
original jurisdiction (53)
prisoner petition (62)
subject matter jurisdiction (53)
trial court (53)
U.S. magistrate judges (58)
writ of certiorari (64)

WORLD WIDE WEB RESOURCES AND EXERCISES

Web Guides

http://dir.yahoo.com/Government/U_S_Government/Judicial_Branch/

Web Search Terms

federal courts
federalization of crime
double jeopardy

Useful URLs

The Supreme Court of the United States maintains an official Web site, which is very good for recent opinions, arguments, and schedules: http://www.supremecourtus.gov/.

The Administrative Office of the U.S. Courts Web site, complete with up-to-date statistics, can be accessed at http://www.uscourts.gov/.

The Federal Judicial Center Web site is located at http://www.fjc.gov/.

The United States Sentencing Commission Web site is located at http://www.ussc.gov/.

The U.S. Marshals Service is America's oldest federal law enforcement agency: http://www.usdoj.gov/marshals/.

The Federal Court Clerks' Association offers insights into the work of clerks of court at http://www.id.uscourts.gov/fcca.htm.

The Federal Magistrate Judges Association maintains a Web site at http://www.fedjudge.org/.

Uncommon URLs

Emory Law School's Federal Court Finder provides a U.S. map with easy links: http://www.law.emory.edu/FEDCTS/.

The Library of Congress provides resources for the U.S. judicial branch: http://lcweb.loc.gov/global/judiciary.html.

National Tribal Justice Resource Center was established by the National American Indian Court Judges Association (NAICJA) to provide support and assistance to tribal justice systems nationwide: http://www.tribalresourcecenter.org/courts/.

The Third Branch, the magazine of the U.S. courts, often contains articles on federal court caseloads: http://www.uscourts.gov/ttb/.

See the Commission on Structural Alternatives for the Federal Courts of Appeal at http://app.comm.uscourts.gov/.

The American Bar Association provides a report, "The Federalization of Criminal Law": http://www.abanet.org/crimjust/fedreport.html.

Federal Justice Statistics on the Web are available at http://fjsrc.urgan.org.

Web Exercises

1. The home page for the federal courts contains links to all the federal courts and federal judicial agencies. The URL is http://www.uscourts.gov/. Click on the Web sites for the Administrative Office of the U.S. Courts and for *The Third Branch* (the newsletter published by the Federal Judicial Center). Examine recent discussions of federal court caseloads.

2. Yahoo also has numerous links to federal courts. To access them, first go to Yahoo at http://www.yahoo.com; then click on Government/Judicial Branch/Federal Courts. Don't be dismayed to find many of the same sites as on the U.S. courts home page. The Web is interrelated, which means there is more than one way to access a specific site. Which route you take is entirely your preference. Click on the site for the circuit that governs your state, and see what information is available. In particular, does the site provide information about the number of criminal cases decided each year? Do the data give any indication of the nature of the crimes involved (drugs, bank robbery, for example)? Who do you think the audience is for the Web site—practicing lawyers, potential jurors, the general public?

3. U.S. Supreme Court opinions are available on the Web, which saves the drudgery of walking to the law section of the library and getting your hands dirty on all the dust

of older volumes. One of the major links, FindLaw, is at **http://www.findlaw.com/**. Choose Laws: Cases and Codes/Supreme Court Opinions and search for the court's opinion in *U.S. v. Lopez* using either the citation search (U.S.) or the party (Lopez). (The option of full-text search is not recommended for the novice.)

INFOTRAC COLLEGE EDITION RESOURCES AND EXERCISES

Basic Search Terms

federal courts
crime, federal
tribal courts
courts-martial
military courts
constitutional
  convention
gun control
Rodney King
double jeopardy

Recommended Articles

Donald C. Dilworth, "Blue Ribbon Judicial Panel Will Recommend Fate of Federal Ninth Circuit"

Carrie E. Johnson, "Rocket Dockets: Reducing Delay in Federal Civil Litigation"

Clarissa Campbell Orr, "Court History"

InfoTrac College Edition Exercises

1. Using the search term "crime, federal," find articles that discuss what types of behavior should be made a federal violation. Based on these articles, discuss what arguments are made suggesting why a crime should be a federal offense. What arguments are made against such proposals? Overall, do disagreements reflect philosophical differences of the crime control versus due process model of justice? Here are two suggested articles: Brian Levin, Bruce Fein, "Q. Does America Need a Federal Hate-Crime Law?"; David Savage, "The Chief Lays Down the Law."

FOR FURTHER READING

Banks, Christopher. *Judicial Politics in the D.C. Circuit Court.* Baltimore: Johns Hopkins University Press, 1999.

Brody, David. "The Misuse of Magistrate Judges in Federal Criminal Proceedings: A Look at the Non-Ministerial Nature of Sentencings." *Justice System Journal* 23 (2002): 259–262.

Carp, Robert, and Ronald Stidham. *The Federal Courts.* 4th ed. Washington, DC: CQ Press, 2001.

Frederick, David. *Rugged Justice: The Ninth Circuit Court of Appeals and the American West, 1891–1941.* Berkeley: University of California Press, 1994.

Fritz, Christian. *Federal Justice in California: The Court of Ogden Hoffman, 1851–1891.* Lincoln: University of Nebraska Press, 1991.

Hall, Kermit, and Eric Rise. *From Local Courts to National Tribunals: The Federal Courts of Florida, 1821–1990.* Brooklyn, NY: Carlson, 1991.

"Indian Tribal Courts and Justice: A Symposium." *Judicature* 79 (1995): 110–156.

Levenson, Laurie. "The Future of State and Federal Civil Rights Prosecutions: The Lessons of the Rodney King Trial." *UCLA Law Review* 509 (1994): 509–583.

Lurie, Jonathan. *Military Justice in America: The U.S. Courts of Appeals for the Armed Forces, 1775–1980.* Lawrence: University of Kansas Press, 2001.

"Native Americans in the Criminal Justice System: Issues of Self-Determination." *Journal of Contemporary Criminal Justice* 14:1 (1998).

Sayer, John William. *Ghost Dancing the Law: The Wounded Knee Trials.* Cambridge, MA: Harvard University Press, 1997.

Smith, Christopher. *Judicial Self-Interest: Federal Judges and Court Administration.* Westport, CT: Praeger, 1995.

Spitzer, Robert. *The Politics of Gun Control.* Chatham, NJ: Chatham Publishers, 1994.

Wilkins, David. *American Indian Sovereignty and the U.S. Supreme Court: The Masking of Justice.* Austin: University of Texas Press, 1997.

Zelden, Charles. *Justice Lies in the District: The U.S. District Court, Southern District of Texas, 1902–1960*. College Station: Texas A&M University Press, 1993.

Zimring, Franklin, and Gordon Hawkins. "Toward a Principled Basis for Federal Criminal Legislation." *Annals of American Academy of Political and Social Science* 543 (1996): 14–26.

Chapter 4 State Courts

A fter attending several judicial conferences around the nation, two judges had little trouble identifying the major problems facing the Los Angeles County municipal courts: Soaring drug prosecutions were further crowding jails that were already full. Implementing a solution, however, proved a more troublesome and time-consuming process. In order to establish a drug court, the judges needed the active cooperation of other judges, the district attorney, the public defender, treatment providers, and the sheriff. To ensure that these agencies had a voice in the process, a coordinating council was formally established. Finally, after months of meeting and planning, two drug courts were created (Torres and Deschenes 1997). ◀

Discussions of state courts usually contain references to major cases such as armed robberies and automobile accidents. But this is only part of their workload. State judges must also adjudicate cases involving wives who want divorces from unfaithful husbands and husbands who physically abuse their wives; juveniles who rob liquor stores and juveniles who simply drink liquor. The contemporary realities reflect an increase in the number of cases placed on the dockets of state courts and rising societal expectations about the administration of justice—while staffing levels remain constant. Thus, although an earlier generation viewed court reform in terms of a neater organizational chart, contemporary discussions are more likely to focus on such topics as finding a better way to handle drug cases.

This chapter examines the structure and functions of state courts. We begin with a discussion of the development of American courts and then divide the somewhat confusing array of state courts into four levels: trial courts of limited jurisdiction, trial courts of general jurisdiction, intermediate appellate courts, and courts of last resort. (Chapter 18 examines the lower courts in depth, and we will discuss juvenile courts in Chapter 19.) We will examine the efforts of court reformers to reorganize state court structure as well as the consequences of court organization for the administration of justice.

HISTORY OF STATE COURTS

Just as American law borrowed heavily from English common law, the organization of American courts reflects their English heritage. But the colonists and later the citizens of the fledgling new nation that called itself the United States of America adapted this English heritage to the realities of the emerging new nation. Issues such as the clash of opposing economic interests, the debate over state versus national power, and outright partisanship have shaped the development of America's 50 diverse state court systems.

Colonial Courts

Early colonial courts were rather simple institutions whose structure replicated English courts in form but not in substance. The numerous, complex, and highly specialized English courts were ill suited to the needs of a small group of colonists trying to survive on the edge of the wilderness, so the colonists greatly simplified the English procedures. As towns and villages became larger, however, new courts were created so that people would not have to travel long distances to have their cases heard. Moreover, a notion of separation of governmental powers began to emerge. In the early days the same governmental body often held executive, legislative, and judicial powers. The county courts, for example, stood at the heart of American colonial government. Besides adjudicating cases, they also performed important administrative functions (Friedman 1985). Gradually, different institutions began to perform these tasks.

Diversity was the hallmark of the colonies, with each colony modifying its court system according to variations in local customs, different religious practices, and patterns of commercial trade. Some of these early variations in legal rulings and court structures have persisted and contribute to the great variety of U.S. court systems today (Glick and Vines 1973).

In the northern colonies, biblical codes were often adopted. In the South, laws governing slavery were enacted. Overall, public punishments like the pillory and the stock were commonly used, but the death penalty was used less often than in England.

Early American Courts

After the American Revolution, the functions of state courts changed markedly. Their governing powers were drastically reduced and taken over by the legislative bodies. The former colonists distrusted lawyers and harbored misgivings about English common law. They were not anxious to see the development of a large, independent judiciary. Thus, state legislatures often responded to unpopular court decisions by removing some judges or abolishing specific courts all together.

A major source of political conflict between legislatures and courts centered on the issue of free money. Legislators were more responsive to policies that favored debtors, usually small farmers. Courts, on the other hand, reflected the views of creditors, often merchants. Out of this conflict over legislative and judicial power, the courts gradually emerged as an independent political institution.

In the northern states, European immigration generated cultural and religious tensions between new arrivals and native residents. In the South, the justice system focused on tracking down escaped slaves. Meanwhile, the nation was steadily moving west, and a unique form of frontier justice emerged.

Courts in a Modernizing Society

Rapid industrialization following the Civil War produced fundamental changes in the structure of the American judiciary. Increases in population led to a higher volume of litigation. Just as important, the growing concentration of people in the cities (many of whom were immigrants) meant the courts were faced with a new set of problems. Thus by the end of the 19th century, the nation had to respond to a new type of social problem—crimes committed by juveniles (see Chapter 19).

The American courts, still reflecting the rural agrarian society of the early nineteenth century, were inadequate in the face of rising demands for services (Jacob 1984). States and localities responded to societal changes in a number of ways. City courts were created to deal with new types of cases in the urban areas, including public drunkenness, gambling, and prostitution. Specialized courts were formed to handle specific classes of cases (for example, small claims courts and family relations courts). Additional courts were created, often by specifying the court's jurisdiction in terms of a geographic boundary within the city.

The development of courts in Chicago illustrates the confusion, complexity, and administrative problems that resulted from this sporadic and unplanned growth. In 1931 Chicago had 556 independent courts; the majority were justice of the peace courts that handled only minor offenses (Glick and Vines 1973). The jurisdiction of these courts was not exclusive; that is, a case could be brought before a variety of courts depending on the legal and political advantages that each one offered. Moreover, each court was a separate entity; each had a judge and a staff. Such an organizational structure meant there was no way to shift cases from an overloaded court to one with little to do. Each court also produced patronage jobs for the city's political machines.

The sporadic and unplanned expansion of the American court system has resulted in an often confusing structure. Each state system is different (see A Virtual Tour of American Courthouses: State Courts). Although some states have adopted a unified court structure, others still have numerous local courts with overlapping jurisdictions. To reduce confusion, we will examine state courts at four levels: trial courts of limited jurisdiction, trial courts of general jurisdiction, intermediate appellate courts, and courts of last resort. Exhibit 4-1 summarizes the tremendous volume of cases decided each year by state courts.

TRIAL COURTS OF LIMITED JURISDICTION: LOWER COURTS

At the first level of state courts are **trial courts of limited jurisdiction,** sometimes referred to as *inferior courts,* or more simply, *lower*

Exhibit 4-1	Case Filings in State Courts					
	Civil	Criminal	Domestic	Juvenile	Traffic	Total
Court of last resort						85,400
Intermediate courts of appeals						187,000
Trial courts of general jurisdiction	7,400,000	4,800,000	3,800,000	1,300,000	14,100,000	31,400,000
Trial courts of limited jurisdiction	8,400,000	9,200,000	1,500,000	700,000	41,600,000	61,400,000
Total	15,800,000	14,100,000	5,300,000	2,000,000	55,700,000	92,800,000

Note: These are estimates based on percentages; therefore, the numbers may not total.

SOURCE: Brian Ostrom, Neal Kauder, and Robert LaFountain, eds., *Examining the Work of State Courts, 2002* (Williamsburg, VA: National Center for State Courts, 2003).

courts. There are more than 13,500 trial courts of limited jurisdiction in the United States, staffed by about 18,000 judicial officers. The lower courts constitute 85 percent of all judicial bodies in the United States. The number of trial courts of limited jurisdiction varies from none in Idaho, Illinois, Iowa, Massachusetts, Minnesota, South Dakota, and the District of Columbia (where their functions have been absorbed by the major trial courts) to more than 2,900 in New York and 2,500 in Texas.

Variously called district, justice, justice of the peace, city, magistrates, or municipal courts, the lower courts decide a restricted range of cases. Most of these courts are created by city or county governments and therefore are not part of the state judiciary. Thus, lower courts are typically controlled only by the local governmental bodies that create them and fund them.

The caseload of the lower courts is staggering—more than 61 million matters a year, the overwhelming number of which are traffic cases (more than 41 million in any given year) (see Exhibit 4-1). The caseload indicates that these are the courts that the average citizen is most likely to come into contact with. For this reason, Chapter 18 will examine the lower courts in more depth, highlighting their role in conducting the preliminary stages of felony cases and deciding misdemeanor, traffic, and small claims cases.

TRIAL COURTS OF GENERAL JURISDICTION: MAJOR TRIAL COURTS

At the second level of state courts are the **trial courts of general jurisdiction,** usually referred to as *major trial courts.* There are an estimated 2,000 major trial courts in the 50 states and the District of Columbia, staffed by more than 11,000 judges (Rottman et al. 2000). The phrase *general jurisdiction* means that these courts have the legal authority to decide all matters not specifically delegated to lower courts. The specific division of jurisdiction between the lower courts and the major trial courts is specified by law—statutory, constitutional, or both. The most common names for these courts are *district, circuit,* or *superior.* The specific names used in all states are listed in Exhibit 4-2.

The geographical jurisdictions of the major trial courts are defined along existing political boundaries, primarily counties. Each court has its own support staff consisting of a clerk of court, a sheriff, and others. In most states the trial courts of general jurisdiction are also grouped into judicial districts or cir-

A Virtual Tour of American Courthouses: State Courts

Some state court administrators' offices now provide interesting overviews of their states' judicial systems, including

Minnesota: **http://www.courts.state.mn.us/home/**

Oklahoma: **http://www.oscn.net/applications/oscn/start.asp**

North Carolina: **http://www.aoc.state.nc.us/**

Trial courts of general jurisdiction are developing Web sites, some of which are truly state-of-the-art, including

The Sixth Judicial Circuit of Florida: **http://www.jud6.org/**

Washtenaw County, Michigan: **http://www.co.washtenaw.mi.us/depts/courts/index.htm**

Maricopa County, Arizona: **http://www.superiorcourt.maricopa.gov/**

San Diego, California: **http://www.sandiego.courts.ca.gov/superior/tour/ct2khall.html**

The quickest way to determine if your local courts have Web sites is to go to **http://www.ncsc.dni.us/court/sites/Courts.htm**. You may wish to compare the Web site of your local court to one listed above to gauge what is good (and perhaps not so good) about your local Web site.

Information about drug courts is increasingly available on the Web. Read "What Is a Drug Court?" on the Web site of the National Association of Drug Court Professionals: **http://www.nadcp.org/**. For a more critical discussion, read "Drug Courts and Coerced Treatment" on the Web site of Friends of the Addicted for Comprehensive Treatment: **http://www.factadvocates.org/factsheets/**.

Some drug courts have Web sites that let you see some of the process and also some of the problems that these courts face. Several possibilities are

California's Drug Court Project: **http://www.courtinfo.ca.gov/programs/drugcourts/**

King County, Washington: **http://www.metrokc.gov/kcscc/drugcourt/**

St. Mary's Parish, Louisiana: **http://drugcourt.com/dc/index.html**

Utah's Drug Courts: **http://www.hsdsa.state.ut.us/Drug_Court.htm**

One way to gauge the history of courts is through courthouse architecture. The courthouse was often built in the center of the major town in the county and was also the biggest building in the county. Here's a sample of state courthouses that you can see on the Internet:

Texas: **http://www.telalink.net/~scaevola/chtexas.htm**

California: **http://www.courtinfo.ca.gov/courts/trial/historic/**

Georgia: **http://www.cviog.uga.edu/Projects/gainfo/courthouses/**

Indiana: **http://members.iquest.net/~browns/county/**

---

cuits. In rural areas these districts or circuits encompass several adjoining counties. Here the trial court judges are true generalists who hear a wide variety of cases as they literally ride circuit, holding court in different counties on a fixed schedule. More populated counties have only one circuit or district for the area. Here judges are often specialists assigned to hear only certain types of cases, such as criminal, family, juvenile, or civil. Refer back to Exhibit 4-1 for some basic workload data on the major trial courts.

As discussed in Chapter 3, the lion's share of the nation's judicial business takes place at the state, not the federal, level. About 31 million cases are filed each year in the nation's state trial courts, more than 80 times the number of similar filings in the federal district courts. Moreover, the types of cases filed in the state courts differ greatly from those going to the federal courts. Litigants in federal courts are most often big businesses and governmental bodies. In sharp contrast, litigants in state courts are typically individuals and small businesses.

Exhibit **4-2**	Major Trial Courts in Different States

Circuit Court

Alabama, Arkansas,[a] Florida, Hawaii, Illinois, Indiana,[b] Kentucky, Maryland, Michigan, Mississippi,[a] Missouri, Oregon, South Carolina, South Dakota, Tennessee,[a] Virginia, West Virginia, Wisconsin

Court of Common Pleas

Ohio, Pennsylvania

District Court

Colorado, Idaho, Iowa, Kansas, Louisiana, Minnesota, Montana, Nebraska, Nevada, New Mexico, North Dakota, Oklahoma, Texas, Utah, Wyoming

Superior Court

Alaska, Arizona, California, Connecticut, Delaware,[a] District of Columbia, Georgia, Maine, Massachusetts, New Hampshire, New Jersey, North Carolina, Rhode Island, Vermont,[c] Washington

Supreme Court

New York[d]

[a]Arkansas, Delaware, Mississippi, and Tennessee have separate chancery courts with equity jurisdiction.

[b]Indiana uses superior and circuit courts.

[c]Vermont also uses district courts.

[d]New York also uses county courts.

SOURCE: David Rottman, Carol Flango, Melissa Cantrell, Randall Hansen, and Neil LaFountain, *State Court Organization 1998* (Washington, DC: Bureau of Justice Statistics, 2000).

Criminal Cases

Whereas federal courts hear a high percentage of white-collar crimes and major drug distribution cases, state courts decide primarily street crimes. The more serious criminal violations are heard in the trial courts of general jurisdiction. The public associates felonies with crimes of violence such as murder, robbery, and rape, but as we will see in Chapter 10, 90 percent of criminal violations involve nonviolent crimes such as burglary and theft. State courts must also process a rising volume of drug-related offenses, ranging from simple possession of small amounts of illicit drugs to sale of large quantities of cocaine and heroin. Over the last decade and a half, criminal cases filed in general jurisdiction courts (primarily felonies) increased 25 percent. Most criminal cases do not go to trial. Thus, the dominant issue in the trial courts of general jurisdiction is not guilt or innocence but what penalty to apply to the guilty.

Civil Cases

The focus on criminal cases in the media might lead one to believe that criminal cases account for the majority of court business. In reality, civil cases dominate the dockets of major trial courts. Press attention also suggests that personal injury lawsuits dominate civil filings. In reality, tort cases make up a relatively small percentage of the docket.

Domestic relations constitutes the single largest category of cases filed in the major trial courts. These family law matters mainly involve divorce and related issues such as determining child custody, setting levels of child support, allocating economic resources (homes, cars, and savings accounts), and in some states providing for spousal support (alimony and the like). Domestic relations cases account for a full one third of case filings. Moreover, domestic relations cases constitute the fastest growing part of the civil caseload.

Estate cases (often referred to as *probate*) are the second most common type of case filed in the states' major trial courts. For those who made a will prior to their death, the courts supervise the distribution of assets according to the terms of the will. For those who failed to make a will before dying, the courts determine which heirs will inherit the estate. Most estate matters present the judge with little if any controversy.

Personal injury cases constitute the third most common type of case filings in state trial courts of general jurisdiction. Tort law covers a wide range of legal injuries. Most involve a physical injury, which can vary from a sprained ankle to wrongful death. Although tort cases may involve a wide range of activities, most stem from accidents involving motor vehicles. Tort cases constitute only about 8 percent of all filings in trial courts of general jurisdiction, but they are the most likely to go to trial. Only the handful that involve large sums of money are likely to be covered in the press. Contrary to popular belief, there has been no "litigation explosion" (Neubauer and Meinhold 2004); tort case filings have been steadily decreasing since 1996 (Ostrom, Kauder, and LaFountain 2003).

A variety of other types of civil cases are also filed in state trial courts of general jurisdiction. Contract cases arise when one party claims that the other party has failed to live up to the terms of a contract and asks for monetary damages as compensation. Other cases allege violations of property rights, which typically involve mortgage foreclosures. Thus, most of the other cases are commercial matters, involving businesses in one form or another. Most commercial cases involve debt collection in one form or another.

INTERMEDIATE COURTS OF APPEALS

A century ago state court systems included only a single appellate body—the state court of last resort. Like their federal counterparts, however, state courts have experienced a significant growth in appellate cases that threatens to overwhelm the state supreme court. State officials in 39 states have responded by creating **intermediate courts of appeals,** or **ICAs** (Exhibit 4-3). The only states that have not followed suit are sparsely populated ones

with a low volume of appeals. The ICAs must hear all properly filed appeals. Subsequent appeals are at the discretion of the higher court. Thus a decision by the state's intermediate appellate court is the final one for most cases.

The structure of the intermediate courts of appeals varies in several ways. Twenty-four states organize their ICAs on a statewide basis and the rest on a regional basis. In most states these bodies hear both civil and criminal appeals. Alabama and Tennessee, however, have separate courts of appeals for civil and criminal cases. The number of judges in the intermediate courts of appeals ranges from 3 to the 105 in the California Court of Appeal. Like their federal counterparts, these courts typically employ rotating three-judge panels for deciding cases.

The ICAs handle the bulk of the caseload in the appellate system, and their workload has increased dramatically in the last decade. States have created these courts and given them additional judgeships in hopes of relieving the state supreme courts from crushing caseloads, only to find that the ICAs experience the same problems (see Chapter 17).

In the future, criminal defendants are increasingly likely to appeal their convictions but will find appellate courts markedly unsympathetic to their legal arguments; only 1 of 16 achieves a major (even if temporary) victory. As we will shortly see, the intermediate appellate courts represent the final stage of the process for most litigants. Very few cases make it to the appellate court in the first place, and of those cases only a handful will be heard by the state's highest appellate court.

COURTS OF LAST RESORT: STATE SUPREME COURTS

The court of last resort is generally referred to as the **state supreme court.** The specific names vary from state to state, and to further complicate the picture, Texas and Oklahoma have two courts of last resort—one for civil appeals and another for criminal appeals. The number of supreme court judges varies from a low of five to as many as nine (see Exhibit 4-4). Unlike the intermediate appellate courts, these courts do not use panels in making decisions; rather, the

THE MURDER TRIAL OF SHAREEF COUSIN

Doing Time at Tulane and Broad (Part I)

Emergency vehicles with lights and sirens a-go-go are so frequent here that no one seems to notice. Also missed in the daily bustle is the grand building on the corner. . . . The Orleans Parish Criminal Courthouse is so familiar and dirty and, at night, so poorly lit that it fades into background despite the jolting tales of the city inside. . . .

Morning light filters in the north windows in the grand foyer, gray light turning yellow, illuminating dust particles above the expansive marble floor. . . . "It's like a church," one bystander affirms. "It makes you feel guilty before you even get to the courtroom." . . .

There are 12 criminal court sections . . . and each day's docket reflects anywhere from 20 to 40 cases in progress. Hundreds of people flock through the courthouse doors for bond hearings, status hearings, arraignments, motions, and pretrial arguments on cases from crack possession to murder, on and numbingly on, all of this dispensed with before actual trials begin later in the day.

Many of the accused in these cases shuffle along wearing international safety orange prison fatigues stamped with "OPP"—Orleans Parish Prison—on the back, their wrists and ankles shackled, deputies flanking them. Down the center of the hall they walk, past the innumerable "bench people" who gather on the seats outside each courtroom. The bench people are witnesses to crimes, victims of crimes, and, mostly, friends and relatives of the accused. . . .

The improbably named Lark Fall administers to the hurt and the fallen here. Fall, 33, is the answer desk clerk just inside the front door. Her job is to provide courthouse visitors with directions to various courtrooms and agencies, but sometimes she takes on extra duty. Dressed in a sequined "Amazing Grace" T-shirt and poring over sheet music while making notes in the margins, Fall sings. . . .

Numa Bertel loves this story. . . . "Bertel is a veritable lifer here, the chief of the public defender's office and the man to see if you want to know what it's like to love this place. "The colloquial expression would be: I like to be where the action is," Bertel explains. "The actual expression is: I like life. This is much closer to real life than sitting in a high-rise law office watching corporations function. . . . I've been coming into this building every day since '63 and there's hardly a day goes by that there isn't some high drama going here if you know where to look for it—and usually you don't have to look for it. In and out come all the misfortunes and tragedies of the city."

In a first floor corner is Magistrate Court, the first stop in the criminal justice system after arrest and booking. . . . Magistrate Court is a microcosm of the criminal justice system, a quick picture. The defendants have generally all been arrested within the past 12 to 24 hours. Dressed in various combinations of OPP fatigues and street clothes, they are, on this day, 20 men in serious need of a good night's sleep, bleary-eyed and unshaven. Statistics tell us at least three-quarters of them are coming down off a buzz from drugs or alcohol.

Bail bondsmen sit in the audience hungrily eyeing these prospective clients like carrion-eaters over road kill. Magistrate Judge Gerard Hansen whips through the docket. The first guy is fittingly named Lawless. He threw a boat propeller at a guy. Hansen puts bond at $2,000 and moves on. . . . In about 24 minutes, Hansen has dispensed with the entire docket. In a few hours there will be another Magistrate Court session . . . 20 more morose citizens will enter the revolving door that is the Orleans parish criminal justice system.

SOURCE: Christopher Rose, "Doing Time at Tulane and Broad," *The Times Picayune*, 27 September 1998.

entire court participates in deciding each case. All state supreme courts have a limited amount of *original jurisdiction* in dealing with matters such as disciplining lawyers and judges. In most states the high court has a purely *discretionary docket*. As with the U.S. Supreme Court, that is, the state supreme court selects only a few cases to hear, but these cases tend to have broad legal and political significance. In states without an intermediate court of appeals, however, the supreme court has no power to choose which cases will be placed on its docket.

| Exhibit **4-3** | Intermediate Courts of Appeals (Number of Judges in Different States) |

Appeals Court

Massachusetts (25)

Appellate Court

Connecticut (9), Illinois (40)

Appellate Division of Superior Court

New Jersey (32)

Appellate Divisions of Supreme Court

New York (55)

Appellate Terms of Supreme Court

New York (15)

Commonwealth Court

Pennsylvania (9)

Court of Appeals

Alaska (3), Arizona (22), Arkansas (12), Colorado (16), Georgia (12), Idaho (3), Indiana (15), Iowa (9), Kansas (10), Kentucky (14), Michigan (28), Minnesota (16), Mississippi (10), Missouri (32), Nebraska (6), New Mexico (10), North Carolina (12), North Dakota (3),[a] Ohio (68), Oregon (10), South Carolina (9), Tennessee (12),[b] Utah (7), Virginia (11), Washington (22), Wisconsin (16)

Courts of Appeal

California (105), Louisiana (55), Texas (80)

Court of Civil Appeals

Alabama (5), Oklahoma (12)

Court of Criminal Appeals

Alabama (5), Tennessee (12)

Court of Special Appeals

Maryland (13)

District Court of Appeals

Florida (62)

Intermediate Court of Appeals

Hawaii (4)

Superior Court

Pennsylvania (15)

None

Delaware, District of Columbia, Maine, Montana, Nevada, New Hampshire, North Dakota, Rhode Island, South Dakota, Vermont, West Virginia, Wyoming

[a]Temporary

[b]Civil only

SOURCE: National Center for State Courts, *State Court Caseload Statistics, 2002* (Williamsburg, VA). Available at http://www.ncsconline.org/D_Research/csp/2002_Files/2002_SCCS.html.

Exhibit **4-4**	Courts of Last Resort in Different States (Number of Judges)

Supreme Court

Alabama (9), Alaska (5), Arizona (5), Arkansas (7), California (7), Colorado (7), Connecticut (7), Delaware (5), Florida (7), Georgia (7), Hawaii (5), Idaho (5), Illinois (7), Indiana (5), Iowa (8), Kansas (7), Kentucky (7), Louisiana (7), Michigan (7), Minnesota (7), Mississippi (9), Missouri (7), Montana (7), Nebraska (7), Nevada (7), New Hampshire (5), New Jersey (7), New Mexico (5), North Carolina (7), North Dakota (5), Ohio (7), Oklahoma (9),[a] Oregon (7), Pennsylvania (7), Rhode Island (5), South Carolina (5), South Dakota (5), Tennessee (5), Texas (9),[a] Utah (5), Vermont (5), Virginia (7), Washington (9), Wisconsin (7),Wyoming (5)

Court of Appeals

District of Columbia (9), Maryland (7), New York (7)

Supreme Judicial Court

Maine (7), Massachusetts (7)

Court of Criminal Appeals

Oklahoma (5),[a] Texas (9)[a]

Supreme Court of Appeals

West Virginia (5)

[a]Two courts of last resort in these states.

SOURCE: National Center for State Courts, *State Court Caseload Statistics, 2002* (Williamsburg, VA). Available at http://www.ncsconline.org/D_Research/csp/2002_Files/2002_SCCS.html.

The state supreme courts are the ultimate review board for matters involving interpretation of state law. The only other avenue of appeal for a disgruntled litigant is the U.S. Supreme Court, but successful applications are few and must involve important questions of federal law. Chapter 17 will probe why many state supreme courts have in recent years emerged as significant governmental bodies. In state after state, the supreme courts are deciding issues that have a major impact on the law and government of their jurisdiction.

COURT UNIFICATION

For more than 100 years, the organization of American courts has been a central concern to court reformers who believe that the multiplicity of courts is inefficient (because judges cannot be shifted to meet the caseload needs of other courts) and also inequitable (because the administration of justice is not uniform). His-torically, court reform has been associated with implementing a unified court system. Figure 4-1 provides a diagram of a state (Florida) with a unified court system; Figure 4-2 offers a contrasting diagram of a state (Texas) with limited unification.

The principal objective of a **unified court system** is to shift judicial administration from local control to centralized management. The loose network of independent judges and courts is replaced by a coherent hierarchy with authority concentrated in the state capital. Although court reformers differ about the exact details of a unified court system, their efforts reflect five general principles: a simplified court structure; centralized administration, rule making, and budgeting; and statewide financing (Berkson and Carbon 1978).

Simplified Court Structure

Court reformers stress the need for a simple, uniform court structure for the entire state. In

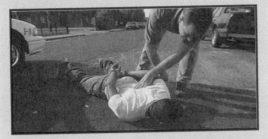

COURT**TV**
American Babylon: Drug Bust

Follow detective Jeff Fauntleroy, an undercover vice detective, as he prowls the streets of Atlantic City, New Jersey. At first we see him make an arrest. Next he sneaks down an alley to make a drug arrest. The detective comes upon an apparent drug sale and finds a lot of cash readily in sight. After placing the suspect under arrest, he searches and finds apparent drug paraphernalia. The woman protests, however, that it is her money and that she did not make it from selling drugs.

 View a video clip of this trial on your copy of the CourtTV CD-ROM. As you watch the video, keep the following questions in mind:

1. Does Detective Fauntleroy have probable cause for the arrest?
2. Is this a lawful search and seizure (see Chapter 12)?
3. Is this arrest likely to result in a conviction? Why or why not?
4. What does the neighborhood suggest about drugs and drug use?
5. Is this the type of apparent drug trafficking that should be the focus of the war on drugs?
6. What would advocates of the crime control model of criminal justice find most important about this drug arrest?
7. What would proponents of the due process model of criminal justice stress about this drug arrest?

particular, the multiplicity of minor and specialized courts, which often have overlapping jurisdiction, would be consolidated in one county-level court. This would mean that variations between counties would be eliminated and replaced by a similar court structure throughout the state. Overall, the court reformers envision a three-tier system: a state supreme court at the top, intermediate courts of appeal where the volume of cases makes it necessary, and a single trial court.

Centralized Administration

Reformers envision the state supreme court, working through court administrators, as providing leadership for the state court system. The state court system would embody a genuine hierarchy of authority, in which local court administrators would be required to follow the policy directives of the central office and would in turn be held accountable by the state supreme court. Thus, a centralized state office would supervise the work of judicial and nonjudicial personnel.

Centralized Rule Making

Reformers argue that the state supreme court should have the power to adopt uniform rules to be followed by all courts in the state. Examples of such rules include procedures for disciplining errant attorneys and time standards for disposing of cases. In addition, judges could be temporarily assigned to other courts to alleviate backlogs and reduce delay. Centralized rule making would shift control from the legislature to judges and lawyers.

Centralized Judicial Budgeting

Centralized budgeting would give the state judicial administrator (who reports to the state supreme court) the authority to prepare a single budget for the entire state judiciary and send it directly to the legislature. The governor's power to recommend a judicial budget would be eliminated. Likewise, lower courts would be dependent on the supreme court for their monetary needs and unable to lobby local representatives directly. Thus, decisions about allocating funds would be made at the state and not the local level.

Statewide Financing

Along with centralized judicial budgeting, reformers argue for the adoption of statewide

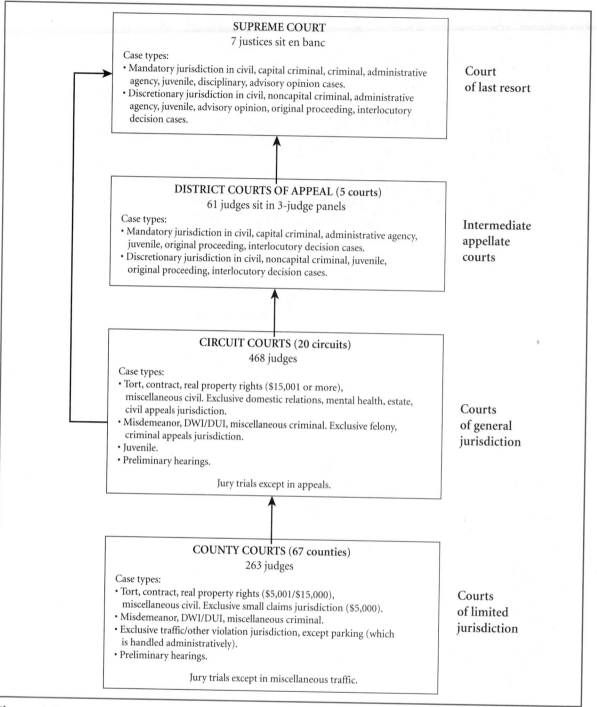

Figure 4-1

Example of a State with a Unified Court Structure: Florida Court Structure

financing of the judiciary. Although courts are mandated by state law, they are often financed in whole or in part by local governments. Given that courts are often not a high priority for local government, they end up with less than adequate local financing. State government, in contrast, has more money and could better support necessary court services.

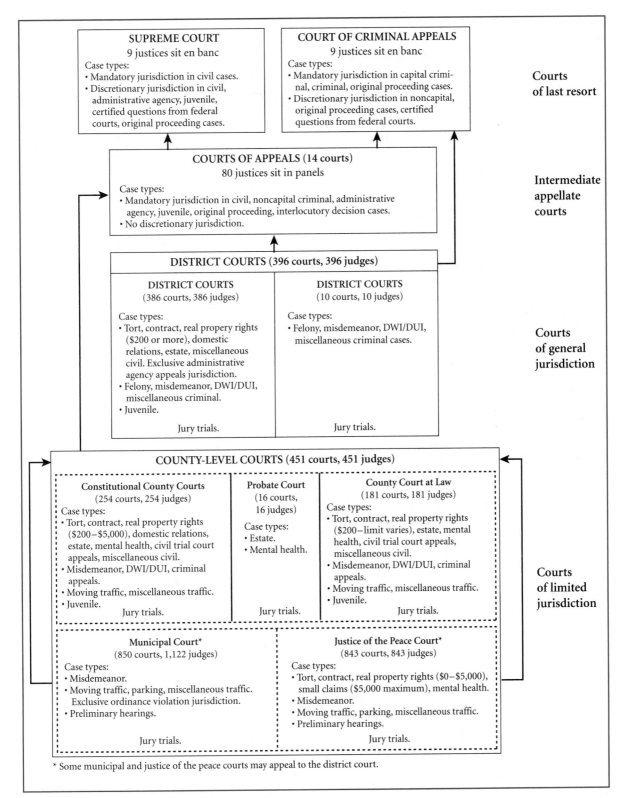

Figure 4-2
Example of a State with Limited Court Unification:
Texas Court Structure

COURT REFORM: THE EMERGING AGENDA

The assumptions and philosophy of traditional notions of court reform have been called into serious question. A new generation of scholars believes that the old principles of court reorganization hamper creative thinking about the direction court reform should take (Lamber and Luskin 1992; Flango 1994). One concern is that the concept of a unified court system does not allow for a desirable diversity. The standard blueprint of court organization fails to consider, for example, important differences in the working environment of courts in densely populated cities as opposed to those in sparsely inhabited rural areas.

Modern critics have also charged that traditional concepts of court reform stress abstract ideals of court organization (law on the books) to the neglect of the realities of the courthouse (law in action) (Baar 1980). As a result, court reformers suffer from elite bias. Their perceptions of the problems of the courthouse extend only to cases with policy significance involving major community actors and rarely extend to ordinary cases affecting average citizens. In the biting words of Laura Nader (1992), court reformers talk about ridding the courts of "garbage cases," which include domestic violence, substance abuse, and neglected children. The solutions proposed by lawyer elites seem unresponsive to the realities of ordinary cases heard in the nation's trial courts. A judiciary with a clearly delineated organizational structure staffed by judges selected on the basis of merit (see Chapter 8) will face the same problems of large caseloads and types of cases—juvenile delinquency, for example—that are difficult to decide. Moreover, courts, no matter how well organized, must cope with public sentiments demanding getting tough with crime (see Case Close-up: *Ewing v. California* and Three Strikes Laws).

Today court reform concentrates more on improving the quality of justice meted out by American courts and less on providing a neater organizational chart. The emerging agenda of court reform includes topics such as reducing trial court delay (Chapter 5), improving the efficiency of the appellate courts (Chapter 17), creating alternative dispute resolution (Chapter 18), and establishing community courts (Chapter 18). For now, we will examine the general concept of therapeutic jurisprudence and its most widely known application—drug courts.

Therapeutic Jurisprudence

Contemporary court reform involves the creation of specialized courts to deal with specific types of cases. Initially these were called *designer courts* or *boutique courts,* indicating their specialized nature. Common examples include drug court, domestic violence court, family court, juvenile drug court, gun court, drunk driving court, elder court, and reentry court (which deals with prisoners reentering the community).

More recently these specialized courts have been said to rely on **therapeutic jurisprudence** (Wexler and Winick 1996; Rosenthal 2002). Such courts have five essential elements:

1. Immediate intervention
2. Nonadversarial adjudication
3. Hands-on judicial involvement
4. Treatment programs with clear rules and structured goals
5. A team approach that brings together the judge, prosecutors, defense counsel, treatment provider, and correctional staff (Rottman and Casey 1999)

Drug treatment courts are the best-known examples of therapeutic jurisprudence.

Drug Courts

The emergence of **drug courts** illustrates how the judiciary is responding both to increases in caseload and changes in the types of cases being brought to court. In the mid-1980s, drug caseloads increased dramatically in courts throughout the country. As a centerpiece of the so-called war on drugs, elected officials across the nation backed efforts to arrest, prosecute, and imprison persons possessing or selling illegal drugs. As a result, arrests for drug abuse violations represent the largest single category of police activity—more than 1.5 million per year. Particularly in the nation's major urban areas, drug arrests have become the single most dominant police activity.

CASE CLOSE-UP

Ewing v. California and Three Strikes Laws

 Forty-year-old Gary Ewing was caught moments after he attempted to steal three golf clubs hidden in his pants leg. Under normal circumstances Ewing would have been prosecuted for a misdemeanor violation. But his background of several previous convictions marked the case as unusual. Thus the Los Angeles District Attorney decided to prosecute Ewing under California's "three strikes and you're out" law; as a result, he was sentenced to 25 years in prison without parole.

Three strike laws have become an increasingly popular reaction to citizen frustrations over crime. As discussed further in Chapter 16, these laws systematically increase potential prison sentences for defendants who have been convicted of violent offenses. In California, however, only one of the convictions must be for a violent crime, thus adding to the controversy in the nation's most populous state. Critics argue that such laws are fundamentally unfair because the sentence is disproportionate to the actual crime committed. However, in *Ewing v. California,* a majority of the U.S. Supreme Court rejected this argument, holding that the sentence was not disproportionate and hence not a violation of the Eighth Amendment prohibition against cruel and unusual punishment.

Justice O'Connor's opinion for the majority stressed that in enacting three strike laws the California legislature had made a deliberate policy choice that individuals who repeatedly engage in serious or violent criminal behavior have not been deterred by conventional punishments and therefore society can protect itself by isolating the defendant. Justice Stevens and three other justices dissented, arguing that a 25-year sentence for such a petty offense was "grossly disproportionate" and therefore constituted cruel and unusual punishment.

Legislatively mandated get-tough-on-criminal policies like "three strikes and you're out" laws most immediately impact corrections. Across the nation, the prison population has risen steadily (see Chapter 15). But these policies also impact the judiciary in several ways.

These laws increase the volume of criminal prosecutions. Note that Ewing would normally have been tried in a misdemeanor court, where costs are low and trials are few. Instead he was prosecuted in a more costly felony court, where trials are more likely and also more time-consuming. In Los Angeles, for example, only 4 percent of felonies go to trial, compared to 25 percent of three strike cases (Schultz 2000).

Get-tough policies affect the judiciary because of uneven application of the laws. Some prosecutors choose to apply the laws, but others do not. Thus critics contend that three strike laws distort the justice process. In the words of law professor Charles Weisselberg, an innocent person facing a third-strike offense runs the risk of going to trial. Because of the previous convictions, the prosecutor has an enormous advantage in forcing a plea bargain (Ryan 2002).

In deferring to the state legislature, the Court's decision in *Ewing* is strikingly different from the *Lopez* decision discussed in Chapter 3. Recall that in *Lopez* the Supreme Court struck down a federal law that threatened to add to the growing caseloads of federal courts, but in *Ewing* the Court seemed unconcerned that state legislatures were greatly adding to the docket of state courts.

Some court officials feared that the first major casualty of the war on drugs would be the nation's urban trial courts (Lipscher 1989). Fears of a system breakdown, however, were somewhat overdrawn (Mahoney 1994). One reason is that many prosecutions are straightforward—pleas of guilty are entered shortly after arraignment. Another reason is that some courts began to experiment with new ways of processing cases by creating drug courts.

Drug courts emphasize treatment. The assumption is that treatment will reduce the likelihood that convicted drug offenders will be rearrested. Dade County (Miami) Circuit Court is an example of a treatment approach to drug offenders. It has received extensive national publicity because it was the first in the nation.

A DAY IN COURT

County Wants Drug Court

Joseph Traficanti Jr. calls himself the "original skeptic." Through the mid-1990s, the former Ulster County judge believed in the state's Rockefeller Drug Laws and the notion that all drug offenders should receive harsh punishment. Courts, he said, had no business getting involved with social work or community partnerships that promote treatment over incarceration. But Traficanti, now a state deputy chief administrative judge, had a change of heart after he attended a drug court commencement in Rochester and saw a tearful graduate thank the judge for saving his life. Similar programs for nonviolent drug offenders were being formed across the country, and the former skeptic himself was later responsible for the formation of treatment courts in 62 New York counties.

"What really impressed me was there's no politics to it," Traficanti told an audience of police officers, judges, health-care workers and human service workers at the Madison County Domestic Violence Coalition's semiannual meeting Wednesday at New Beginnings Free Methodist Church in Wampsville. "All sides of the political spectrum seemed to be supportive of this." Today, Traficanti said, every county in New York state either has one drug court or is forming one. Madison County would be the last Central New York county to start a drug-treatment court. . . .

The program allows defendants to have criminal charges dismissed after successfully completing the treatment program under judicial supervision. In order to graduate, candidates must get a job or earn a General Education Development diploma if they don't already have a high school diploma, and remain sober for one year. In some counties or cities, participants see the judge every day.

"Most thought it was the easy way out. It's not," Traficanti said. "They tell you they're afraid to disappoint you. The black robe helps. Street thugs say, 'I'm afraid to mess up because I'm afraid to face the judge.'

"I thought at first, giving them a (graduation) certificate was kind of Mickey Mouse," Traficanti said. "But for some of these folks, it's the first time in their entire life they had something with their name on it that they could hang on their wall. They absolutely cherish it. And how many of these folks have ever had anybody applaud for them?"

A successful drug-treatment court program requires tremendous collaboration between the courts, social services departments and other agencies that can help the drug offender with transportation, child care and financial issues. In the beginning, Traficanti said, judges, prosecutors and defense lawyers may have difficulty grasping its non-adversarial approach. "Just changing the culture, the thinking, is very difficult for us lawyers," he said. "It's a hard sell in some places." Yet the intensive team effort saves the state and counties money, Traficanti said. It costs about $30,000 a year to house a drug offender in jail. By contrast, he said, inpatient treatment for nonviolent drug offenders is $18,400 per year and outpatient treatment is $5,100.

A 1999 Erie County Department of Social Services study found that the Lackawanna Drug Court saved the county $2.1 million in Medicaid, child foster care, food stamps and cash assistance programs. Its graduating class of 152 people avoided public entitlements because they were able to work, maintain custody of their children, remain healthy and give birth to healthy babies, the study said. . . .

SOURCE: Aaron Gifford, "County Wants Drug Court; Treatment Program Already Established in Other Counties," *The Post-Standard* (Syracuse, NY), 12 June 2003. The Herald Company © 2003 The Post Standard. All rights reserved. Reprinted with permission.

To be eligible, defendants must have no prior felony convictions, must be charged with possession only (not sale), and must admit their drug problem and request treatment. These offenders are diverted into treatment. The sentencing judge, rather than a probation officer, monitors offenders' progress. Participants must periodically report to the drug court judge, who assesses their progress and moves them through the phases of the program.

Within a decade, drug courts have moved from experimental innovation to well-established programs. More than 1,200 drug courts have been started or planned in all 50 states (Nolan 2002). (See A Day in Court: County Wants Drug Court.) Initial evaluations gave favorable rates of success. For example, compared to defendants not in the program, offenders in the Miami drug court treatment program had lower incarceration rates, less frequent rearrests, and longer times to rearrest (Goldkamp and Weiland 1993). More sophisticated evaluations, however, have highlighted the complex impact of drug courts. In Washington, D.C., participation in a drug court treatment program has been poor— only 41 percent of those eligible chose to participate. Moreover, completion of the program took much longer than anticipated; cases were open an average of 11 months as opposed to the 6 months estimated (Harrell, Cavanagh, and Roman 2000). Overall, there is sufficient evidence to conclude that drug courts have a positive impact, but their impact varies by time, manner, and place (Goldkamp 2002).

CONSEQUENCES OF COURT ORGANIZATION

What activities legislatures define as illegal has a major impact on the courts (see Courts, Controversy, and Crime Reduction: Is It Time to End the War on Drugs?). In turn, how the courts are organized and administered has a profound effect on the way cases are processed and on the type of justice that results.

Decentralization and Choice of Courts

Although people often talk about the American legal system, no such entity exists. Instead, America has 51 legal systems—the federal courts and separate courts in each of the 50 states. As Chapter 2 stressed, there are significant differences in the law among these separate systems. As a result, lawyers sometimes try to maneuver cases so that they are heard in courts that are perceived to be favorable to their clients. For example, some criminal offenses violate both state and federal laws. As a general rule, federal officials prosecute major violations, leaving more minor prosecutions to state officials.

The prosecution of the DC-area snipers illustrates the importance of the choice of courts. The U.S. Attorney General decided to transfer the defendants to Virginia because that state's law makes the death penalty more likely than in the other jurisdictions where murders occurred—Maryland and the District of Columbia.

Local Control and Local Corruption

The 50 state court systems are in actuality often structured on a local basis. The officials who staff these courts—judges and lawyers, prosecutors and defense attorneys—are recruited from the local community they serve and thus reflect the sentiments of that community. As a result, the U.S. system of justice has close ties to local communities and the application of "state" law often has a local flavor. Jurors in rural areas, for example, often have markedly different attitudes toward guns than jurors in suburban areas.

Local control of justice has the obvious advantage of closely linking courts to the people they serve. But local control has also been an incubator of corruption and injustice. Every state invariably has a town or two where gambling and prostitution flourish because the city fathers agree to look the other way. Not surprisingly, they often receive monetary benefits for being so nearsighted. Increasingly, though, such activities attract the attention of state police, state attorneys general, and federal prosecutors.

The locally administered criminal justice system has also been marked by pockets of injustice. At times the police and the courts have been the handmaidens of the local economic elite. In the South, historically, the police and the courts hindered efforts to exercise civil rights by arresting or harassing those who sought to register to vote, eat at whites-only lunch counters, or simply speak up to protest segregation. The dual court system has provided a safety valve for checking the most flagrant abuses of local justice. Often, it is federal—not state or local—officials who prosecute corrupt local officials.

CONCLUSION

The implementation of drug courts in Los Angeles County (and numerous other areas across the nation) illustrates a major shift in thinking

COURTS, CONTROVERSY, AND REDUCING CRIME

Is It Time to End the War on Drugs?

The association of drugs with social problems begins to explain why the war on drugs enjoys considerable public support. There is no doubt that drug addiction produces untold human suffering in the United States. And there is little doubt that drugs are also associated with crime; indeed, two out of three people arrested by the police show evidence of recent use of illegal drugs (crack, methamphetamines, marijuana, for example) and/or legal drugs (primarily alcohol).

Public support for the war on drugs is also fueled by its link to controlling marginal groups. Historians suggest that medical or scientific knowledge about the harm of drugs has never played a significant role in formulating U.S. drug policy. Rather U.S. policy has been driven by the desire to control groups considered threats to the existing social order. Thus the Harrison Narcotics Act of 1914 targeted opium (used by Chinese in California), marijuana (smoked by Mexican Americans in the Southwest), and cocaine (allegedly being used by blacks in the South).

Beneath the broad consensus supporting the war on drugs, however, is a growing disquiet. Off the record, some criminal justice officials guardedly express reservations about the war on drugs. In public, some scholars are now voicing the urgent need to rethink the war on drugs. In *Drug War Politics: The Price of Denial*, Eva Bertram and her colleagues (1996) argue that despite spending billions of dollars on reducing the supply of drugs and punitive approaches to those who use illegal drugs, the war on drugs is a failure. Failure, however, only convinces the advocates of the war on drugs that greater efforts need to be made. In short, in the war on drugs, nothing succeeds like failure.

It is not just the failure to reduce drug supply (or demand) that concerns critics, but also the social impact of these efforts. In *Reckoning: Drugs, the Cities, and the American Future*, sociologist Elliott Currie (1993) condemns current drug policy for destroying inner-city communities by swelling prison populations with the unemployable minority poor.

The public support and the private disquiet over the war on drugs reflects the differences between the crime control and due process models of criminal justice. Three points—focusing on causes, equality, and punishment—are at issue.

■ The crime control model begins with the judgment that drug abuse is caused by a breakdown of individual responsibility. The due process model views substance abuse as a disease that needs to be treated.

■ According to the crime control model, the solution is punishment. Arrest and conviction will serve as a lesson to the violator and will also deter others. The due process model replies that filling the prisons is costly and ineffective. It is therefore more effective and also less costly to emphasize rehabilitation programs.

■ The due process model is very concerned that current drug policies fall unequally on racial minorities. The crime control model counters with seeming banal indifference: "You do the crime, you serve the time."

What do you think? Does the nation need to change its drug policies to place more emphasis on treatment and prevention, and less on arrest, conviction, and imprisonment?

To continue the debate over the war on drugs, visit the Opposing Viewpoints Resource Center at www.galegroup.com/opposingviewpoints and use the search term "narcotics, control of" to find articles that express opposing viewpoints on this topic.

---

about court reform in the United States. Whereas traditional court reform emphasized consolidating various judicial bodies, the emerging agenda encourages the creation of specialized courts. Modern court reform also actively encourages working with members of the community, whereas the older tradition stressed notions of professionalism that disdained popular input. Likewise, court reform in the contemporary context stresses the importance of working with other agencies rather than viewing the judge as a lone authority figure. The next chapter focuses on these other agencies, elaborating on the concept of the courtroom work group.

What is perhaps most striking is that the ideas that have dominated discussion of court reform for most of this century are now being quietly buried. Instead of stressing organizational charts and other abstract notions, most efforts to reform the judiciary now focus on more specific matters—reduce court delay and target drug cases for special treatment, for example. Thus, today's court reform is marked by tremendous experimentation at the local level. Judges and other court actors identify a problem and seek solutions, adapting local resources and local understandings in the process. This adaptation to change has always been the hallmark of the American judiciary. Perhaps the only differences today are the rapid pace of change and the public attention paid to these ongoing efforts at judicial reform.

CRITICAL THINKING QUESTIONS

1. Although we typically talk of state courts (as opposed to federal courts), would it be better to talk about local courts? To what extent are there major variations within your state?

2. Compare your state to Figures 4-1 and 4-2. How unified is your state court structure?

3. Have there been discussions in your state of court reorganization? What major interest groups are urging court reform, and what advantages do they suggest? What interest groups are opposing court reform, and what disadvantages do they cite?

4. Why do crime control advocates often oppose drug courts, and why do due process proponents support drug courts?

5. Make a list of state and local politicians who have been tried in federal court. Were there parallel state investigations or prosecutions? To what extent would corrupt local officials be better off if federal court jurisdiction were limited?

KEY TERMS

domestic relations (84)
drug courts (92)
estate (84)
intermediate courts of appeals (ICAs) (85)
personal injury (85)
state supreme court (85)
therapeutic jurisprudence (92)
trial court of general jurisdiction (82)
trial court of limited jurisdiction (81)
unified court system (88)

WORLD WIDE WEB RESOURCES AND EXERCISES

Web Guides

http://dir.yahoo.com/Government/U_S_Government/
    Judicial_Branch/State_Courts/
http://dir.yahoo.com/Government/Law/U_S_States/

Web Search Terms

courts   *court reform*
state courts   *courthouses*
drug courts

Useful URLs

The National Center for State Courts provides a variety of reports on caseloads and latest trends at **http://www.ncsc.dni.us/**.

The Bureau of Justice Statistics offers a summary of court organization statistics: **http://www.ojp.usdoj.gov/bjs/courts.htm**.

The Conference of State Court Administrators (COSCA) provides a national forum for improving justice systems: **http://cosca.ncsc.dni.us/**.

The American Judicature Society champions court reform at **www.ajs.org**.

The State Justice Institute was established by federal law to award grants for the improvement of state courts: **http://www.statejustice.org/**.

The National Drug Court Institute disseminates drug court information and provides training: **http://www.drugcourt.org/ndci.htm**.

The American University's Drug Court Clearinghouse and Technical Assistance Project can be accessed at **http://www.american.edu/justice/**.

Uncommon URLs

The Legal Justice Reform Network is a self-help site for those who believe they have been "judicial victims": **http://www.atps.com/uclr/**.

See courthouses recorded by the Historic American Buildings Survey (HABS) and the Historic American Engineering Record (HAER): **http://www.loc.gov/rr/print/list/171_cour.html**.

Learn about records kept at courthouses; see the Librarian's Guide to Helping Patrons with Genealogical Research, "Visiting Courthouses," at **http://home.tampabay.rr.com/centans/courthou.html**.

Read about "Pennsylvania Court Reform Issues" on the Web site of the Pennsylvanians for Modern Courts: **http://www.libertynet.org/pmcpms/Issues.htm**.

See "Strategies for Effective Court Reform" on the Web site of Justice for All: **http://www.wordwiz72.com/courts.html**.

Web Exercises

1. FindLaw has information not only on state law but also on state courts. To locate specific information about your state, go to **http://www.findlaw.com/**. On the menu, click State Law Resources and then your state. Examine state-level courts. Based on this information, where would you rank your state on a continuum from consolidated to fragmented?

2. Information on state courts is also available in Yahoo at **http://www.yahoo.com**. Choose Government/Judicial Branch/State Courts, or Government/U.S. States/Your State. Using either path (or, preferably, both), find information on trial courts in your state. How easy or difficult is it to locate information? In some states information is easier to locate on the executive and legislative branches than on the judiciary. Is this true in your state? If so, why?

3. Using a search engine of your choice, look for information on drug courts. Look for a drug court near you, and examine the site to see if it is similar to or different from the therapeutic justice model discussed in the text.

4. Using the search engine of your choice, use the phrase "court reform" to locate two or more Web sites that deal with this topic. What range of specific topics is included under the general rubric of court reform? To what extent are they consistent or inconsistent with your notions of court reform?

INFOTRAC COLLEGE EDITION RESOURCES AND EXERCISES

Basic Search Terms

courts   *drug courts*
state courts   *National Center for State Courts*

Recommended Articles

Jet, "Blacks Have Little Confidence in State, Local Courts"

"In Los Angeles County, Two Courts Are Better Than One"

Alcoholism & Drug Abuse Weekly, "New York Drug Reforms Call for Drug Treatment, Not Incarceration"

Spectrum: The Journal of State Government, "Drug Crime: The Impact on State Courts"

InfoTrac College Edition Exercises

1. Using the search term "court administration," select two articles that discuss state efforts. Does the approach discussed reflect traditional court reform ideas or the emerging agenda of court reform? Here are two possibilities:

   Major B. Harding, "Preparing Florida Courts for the New Millennium"

   Donald C. Dilworth, "BJA Reports Measurement System for Trial Court Performance"

2. Using the search term "drug court," select two or more articles that discuss this growing phenomenon. What advantages do the writers see for drug courts? What pitfalls do they discuss? Here are two possibilities:

   Robert Curley, "Drug Court Boom May Bust Treatment Availability"

   Alcoholism & Drug Abuse Weekly, "Justice-Treatment Relationship Crucial to Drug Court Success"

FOR FURTHER READING

Abadinsky, Howard. *Drugs: An Introduction.* 4th ed. Belmont, CA: Wadsworth, 2001.

Belknap, Michael. *To Improve the Administration of Justice: A History of the American Judicature Society.* Chicago: American Judicature Society, 1993.

Boersema, Craig. "Simplifying the Maze of Nevada's Courts." *Judicature* 78 (1995): 299–303.

Edelman, Mark, and Terry Raun. "Does Rural Court Consolidation Save Costs?" *Judicature* 79 (1995): 86–90.

Harrell, Adele, John Roman, and Emily Sack. *Drug Court Services for Female Offenders, 1996–1999: Evaluation of the Brooklyn Treatment Court.* Washington, DC: Urban Institute Justice Policy Center, 2001.

Jacob, Herbert. "The Governance of Trial Judges." *Law and Society Review* 31 (1997): 3–27.

Lurigio, Arthur, Amy Watson, Daniel Luchins, and Patricia Hanrahan. "Therapeutic Jurisprudence in Action: Specialized Courts for the Mentally Ill." *Judicature* 84 (2001): 184–189.

Meier, Kenneth. *The Politics of Sin: Drugs, Alcohol, and Public Policy.* New York: M. E. Sharpe, 1994.

Nolan, James. *Reinventing Justice: The American Drug Court Movement.* Princeton, NJ: Princeton and Oxford University Press, 2001.

Stojkovic, Stan, John Klofas, and David Kalinich. *The Administration and Management of Criminal Justice Organizations: A Book of Readings.* 3d ed. Prospect Heights, IL: Waveland Press, 1998.

Wice, Paul. *Court Reform and Judicial Leadership.* Westport, CT: Praeger, 1995.

Part II Legal Actors

The law is not self-executing. Prosecutors, defense attorneys, and judges must exercise discretion. The types of people recruited to these positions, the nature of the work they perform, and the pressures they must deal with are the concerns of the five chapters of Part II.

Chapter 5 analyzes the dynamics of courthouse justice, with particular emphasis on how these separate actors work together as a group.

Chapter 6 discusses why the prosecutor is the most important member of the courtroom work group. The discretionary powers of the office structure virtually all the decisions of the criminal courthouse.

Chapter 7 examines the defense attorney. The nature of the attorney's clientele, the lack of great monetary rewards, and the effects of other members of the courtroom work group help explain why most defense attorneys act nothing like Perry Mason, the famous television figure.

Chapter 8 considers the role of the judge. Of prime concern is how the judge's actions shape and in turn are affected by the courtroom work group.

Chapter 9 discusses the importance of witnesses, victims, and defendants in the decisions made by members of the courtroom work group.

PART II
Legal Actors

Chapter 5
The Dynamics of Courthouse Justice

Chapter 6
Prosecutors

Chapter 7
Defense Attorneys

Chapter 8
Judges

Chapter 9
Defendants and Victims

Chapter 5 · The Dynamics of Courthouse Justice

PART II
Legal Actors

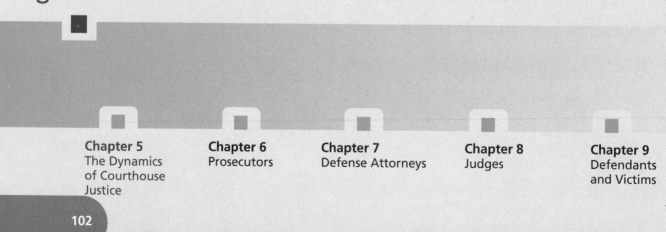

ixteen times Willie Barker's murder case was set for trial, and sixteen times it was continued. At first the defense readily agreed, gambling that Barker's codefendant would be found not guilty. Thus, some of the continuances were caused by the six separate trials before the codefendant was finally convicted. Other continuances were granted because of the illness of the police investigator. It was not until five years after arrest that Barker was convicted of murder. To Barker's lawyer, this lengthy delay clearly violated the Sixth Amendment's right to a speedy trial. The Kentucky prosecutor replied that the delay did not jeopardize Barker's right to a fair trial. ◄

Barker v. Wingo underscores three key points about criminal case processing in contemporary courts. First, courts deal with lots of cases. From the perspective of victims and defendants, criminal cases are discrete life events, but from the vantage point of judges, prosecutors, and defense attorneys, the docket consists of numerous cases, each demanding the court's time. The pressure to move cases, often referred to as assembly-line justice, is the first concept discussed in this chapter.

Second, the problems in prosecuting and convicting Barker indicate that discretion is often needed in interpreting the law. After all, the meaning of "speedy trial" is not self-evident. As we shall see, the concept of discretion begins to grapple with the day-to-day realities of courthouse dynamics.

Third, the *Barker* case shows that case dispositions involve far more than the isolated actions of individual judges. From arrest through trial and sentencing, case dispositions require mutual activity on the part of prosecutors and defense attorneys, to say nothing of police officers and probation officers, bail agents and bailiffs. This chapter uses the concept of the courtroom work group to analyze the complexities of interaction among courthouse regulars.

This chapter examines the dynamics of courthouse justice by analyzing three major explanations for the great difference between textbook images of criminal procedure and the realities of the courtroom. We will then apply these concepts to one of the most often mentioned problems of American justice—delay. As in the *Barker* case, though, we will see that deciding how long is too long is a knotty ques-

tion. But first let us begin with a tour of a typical U.S. courthouse.

THE COURTHOUSE AND THE PEOPLE WHO WORK THERE

Concepts of court jurisdiction and court structure are admittedly intangible notions. Courthouses, on the other hand, are concrete. To be sure, from the outside courthouses appear to be imposing, even forbidding, government buildings. But on the inside they are beehives of activity. Most immediately, courthouses are places where you find lawyers arguing before juries, talking to their clients, and conversing with one another. But courthouses also employ numerous nonlawyers who perform vital roles; without clerks and probation officers, bail agents and bailiffs, courthouses could not function. Not to be overlooked, ordinary citizens (whether victims or defendants, witnesses or jurors) also perform important roles in the courthouse.

In trying to understand how lawyers and nonlawyers, regular participants and occasional ones, dispense courthouse justice on a daily basis, it is helpful to start with a walking tour of a courthouse. What goes on inside a courthouse, of course, varies in important ways. In the courthouses of small towns, for example, one finds only a few courthouse regulars who handle many different types of matters. By contrast, in the courthouses of major cities you will find numerous courthouse regulars

A Virtual Tour of American Courthouses: Other Courthouse Actors

To take a virtual tour of a courtroom in Orange County (California), go to Courtroom 23 at **http://www.ninja9.org/courtadmin/mis/courtroom_23.htm**.

Have you ever wondered if you have what it takes to become a court reporter? Visit **http://www.depo.com/becr.htm**.

For photos of Judge Ito's courtroom in Los Angeles, see **http://ww.ncsc.dni.us/ncsc/ito_ctrm/ito_ctrm.htm**.

FAQs about the Cook County (Illinois) courts are just a click away at **http://www.cookcountycourt.org/jury/faq-courthouse.html**.

For a close-up of the victim advocates program of the Adams County (Colorado) Sheriff's Office, just click on **http://www.co.adams.co.us/SheriffWeb/victim~20advocate.htm**.

The National Crime Prevention Council has a Web site for court watchers: **http://www.ncpc.org/3bias2dc.htm#top**.

FAQs from the American Translator Association can be found at **http://www.atanet.org/frequently.htm**.

To read about how one MADD chapter provides victim advocacy, go to **http://www.columbiasc.com/maddsc/MADD4.htm**.

who specialize in specific duties. Moreover, in some courthouses civil and criminal cases are heard in the same courtroom at the same time; in other jurisdictions civil and criminal cases are separated in time and place. These variations aside, the following provides an overview of a typical day in a medium-sized courthouse in the United States.

The Courthouse

One indication of the low status of the criminal courts is their location. In some cities the criminal courts are found in isolated and inconvenient locations. Security is the main reason. Since the pretrial detention facilities have often been built next to the courthouse, the entire criminal justice complex is located away from the downtown business center. As a result, victims and witnesses face a difficult task in getting to the courthouse. Those using public transportation require several transfers; for those who drive, parking is at a premium because the large parking lots are invariably reserved for the courthouse regulars (Wice 1985).

Having located the courthouse complex, visitors are struck by the architecture of their surroundings. Clustered nearby are older buildings, occupied by bail agents and defense attorneys.

Garish neon signs proclaiming "Bail Bonds, 24 Hour Service" compete with unpainted wooden structures to provide a general sense of urban decay. The courthouse building likewise often has a haggard and unkempt look about it. Beneath the veneer of decades of uncleaned grime, though, one sees a once grand building built during an era when citizens took great pride in their public buildings. Although criminal court buildings are constructed in a variety of architectural styles, they nevertheless all seem to present an image of stolidity and unyielding strength.

Entrance is usually gained by climbing an excessive number of steps. For security reasons there is often only one door open, funneling all visitors through a crowded, narrow entranceway. Once inside, visitors find themselves in a massive lobby with an impressively high arched ceiling. In the center of the lobby is the omnipresent information booth, which is invariably unattended. A nearby bulletin board offers the only clue as to what cases are to be found in which courtrooms, but the notices are usually outdated. (See A Virtual Tour of American Courthouses: Other Courthouse Actors.)

The lobby and hallways resound with animated conversations between lawyers, bail agents, bailiffs, defendants, family members, witnesses, and a variety of other interested parties. Indeed, for many bail agents and private criminal lawyers these hallways are their daytime offices. Although courthouses often provide witness reception areas and lawyers' lounges, nearly everyone prefers to be near the action so as not to miss out on a business opportunity or a choice bit of gossip.

The Courtroom

After some difficulty, most first-time visitors manage to locate the specific courtroom of interest, entering through a double set of heavy doors, which suggests that this is not an ordinary public building. This initial impression of orderliness under law quickly gives way to a sense of social anarchy. One is immediately confronted with a visual and audio reality far different from that portrayed on television or in the movies. What is happening inside the courtroom is best viewed in terms of sets of actors who congregate in different locations.

In the front is an imposing bench, which dominates the courtroom, literally elevating the black-robed judge on a pedestal. Court begins by the customary call of the crier: "All rise, the court for _____ County is now in session, the Honorable _____ _____ presiding." On cue, the judge strides mindfully from behind a hidden door, law book or case folder tucked under one arm. Just below the bench sits the clerk of court (sometimes called the calendar clerk), who controls the scheduling of cases and keeps the judge apprised of the relevant details of the case. To one side of the bench sits the court stenographer, whose machine mysteriously makes a shorthand record of the proceedings. Also in attendance is a bailiff, who tries to maintain order in the courtroom. The judge's staff also may include a law clerk and a secretary (who jealously guards access to the judge when he or she is not presiding in the courtroom). Typically, the personal staff has worked with the judge for extended periods of time.

Ten to 20 feet from the front of the bench are two tables reserved for the defense and prosecution, respectively. The district attorney's table is piled high with case folders needed for the day's activities. Somehow, no matter how high the pile of case folders, a file or part of a file is invariably

missing, resulting in last-minute scurrying by frantic assistant district attorneys trying to rectify the periodic lapses of the prosecutorial bureaucracy. The mountain of files on the public defender's table nearly matches that of the prosecutor's. The public defender (PD) likewise finds that files are missing or incomplete, resulting in scurrying around looking for missing pieces of paper. When a case involving a private criminal lawyer is called, the PD temporarily gives up the seat at the defense table, but the files remain, an indication that it is really the PD who dominates. Between the bench and the lawyers' table stands a battered wooden podium, which is typically used only for ceremonial occasions—most notably, when the defendant enters a plea of guilty or the lawyers argue before a jury. Otherwise, lawyers typically argue while sitting behind the table.

To the side of the bench is the jury box. On trial day, jurors occupy these seats; when no jury trial is being conducted, a variety of folks can be found in and around the jury box, waiting, socializing, and occasionally conducting business. Often the easiest to identify are police officers in court to provide testimony. Also in attendance are probation officers, substance-abuse counselors, and pretrial services representatives. Bail agents also often drop in to make sure that the persons they have posted bail for have indeed arrived as scheduled.

Often sitting in the jury box, too, are defendants who have been detained before trial. Defendants out on bail sit in the public sector, but those in jail sit in brightly colored uniforms with the name of the county jail readily displayed. Often they are manacled together and are temporarily unchained when their cases are called. Surrounding the defendants, hovering like brooding hens, are the sheriff's deputies. The number of deputies in court provides a pretty good indication of the perceived threat of the defendants; the higher the ratio of guards to prisoners, the more serious the crime and the criminal.

A railing separates the courthouse regulars from the occasional participants. The first row or two are reserved for lawyers waiting for their cases to be called. Sitting in the remaining rows are the defendants (those who have been free on bond or released on their own

Exhibit 5-1 Courthouse Actors

	Main Activities
Law Enforcement	
Court security staff	Provide security throughout the courthouse
Sheriff 's deputy	Transports prisoners to and from jail
Bailiff	Maintains order in courtrooms
Courts	
Lawyers	
Prosecutor	Government official who conducts criminal proceedings
Public defender	Government attorney who represents indigents
Private defense attorney	Lawyer paid by defendant for representation
Judge	Officer who presides in a court of law
Law clerk	Performs legal research for the judge
Court Support Staff	
Clerk of court	Record keeper, often responsible for jury selection
Court reporter	Makes verbatim transcript of proceedings
Secretary	Handles routine work of judge's office
Translator	Renders another language into English
Court administrator	Supervises and performs administrative tasks for the court
Corrections	
Probation officer	Recommends defendants for probation and monitors their activities
Pretrial services	Handles release of qualified pretrial detainees
Drug rehabilitation program	Recommends defendants for drug rehabilitation and monitors progress
Public	
Bail agent	Secures pretrial release of defendants for a fee
Newspaper reporter	Provides media coverage of key events
Defendant	Person accused of violating the law
Victim	Person who has suffered a loss due to crime
Witness	Anyone who will testify in court
Jurors	Citizens who will decide guilt or innocence
Rape crisis center	Provides counseling to rape victims
Child advocate	Person who speaks up for child's best interest
Court watchers	Retirees whose hobby is coming to court
Victim/witness assistance	Public or private agency seeking to improve treatment program of victims and witnesses

recognizance), family members, and perhaps a variety of other observers—for example, senior citizens, who enjoy rooting for the prosecutor. Increasingly in contemporary courthouses, one will also find victim advocates affiliated with organizations such as victim/witness assistance programs, Mothers Against Drunk Driving, child advocates, and rape crisis centers. Like senior citizens, these people make known their desire for harsh punishments. Exhibit 5-1 summarizes the courthouse actors and their main activities.

A DAY IN COURT

Those People behind the Scenes

 To David Lawrence, the world of common pleas court depends on a vast, seldom-noticed army that rarely visits a courtroom—a workforce that he divides into "paper people" and "people people." "Every case has a judge, a defendant, a prosecutor, a defense attorney, two court officers, a stenographer, at least one witness, and two sheriff's deputies if the defendant is in jail," said Lawrence, the court's chief deputy administrator.

"That's what you see in the courtroom. What goes on behind the scenes involves many, many more." Lawrence oversees his two groups of non-courtroom employees as they guide each criminal case from arrest to final disposition. The "paper people"—largely clerks and secretaries—track and update the paperwork essential to the resolution of any criminal case.

The "people people" coordinate the work of clerks, stenographers, janitors, and other employees who make sure each case has its day in court. Together, these two groups account for more than half the 2,000 Common Pleas Court employees. The rest work in other sections—the civil section of the trial division and Family and Orphan courts.

The court employees whose duties relate primarily to criminal cases work for a dozen key agencies that try to move those cases efficiently through the system. From the time of arrest, Lawrence said, those agencies are busy. One as-

sesses a defendant's ability to afford counsel and eligibility for bail; another coordinates court appearances of the defendant with the schedules of police officers to reduce overtime; another makes sure clerks and defendants are scheduled for court when the case is called.

"There just aren't enough people" in the hidden bureaucracy, he said. For example, he said, judges outnumber stenographers. That makes it impossible for every judge to be on the bench every day, since some courtrooms wouldn't have anyone to make the official record. . . .

Most significantly, he added, the hidden bureaucracy operates amid other competing bureaucracies. The interests of each of those bureaucracies—primarily the Police Department, defense bar, district attorney's office, prisons, and sheriff's office—"have a tremendous impact" on case flow, Lawrence said.

"Every action that takes place in the process depends on each of those agencies," he said. "But when the system doesn't work, what do people say? The courts are screwed up."

"Should the courts be the focal point? I guess, because we're the ones charged with dispensing justice and the courts are charged with balancing the diverse interests of all those agencies."

SOURCE: P. Maryniak, "Those People behind the Scenes," *Philadelphia Daily News*, 13 March 1990, 16. Reprinted by permission.

What is disconcerting to the newcomer to the courtroom is that these actors seem in constant motion. Small groups form and re-form as cases are called and defendants summoned before the bench. In one corner an assistant district attorney (DA) can be seen conversing with an assistant PD, while in the back of the room a private defense attorney is engaged in whispered conversations with the defendant and his mother. Moreover, the cast of characters is ever changing. Many actors are in court for a specific case, and when that case has finished, they leave, often walking to another courtroom where they have other cases to attend. Most exasperating of all, the courtroom alternates

between bursts of energy and periods of lethargy. Cases are called, only to be put on hold because one of the needed participants is temporarily busy elsewhere in the courthouse.

Behind the Scenes

Outside the great hall of the courthouse and behind the individual courtrooms are areas where visitors seldom venture. What is immediately obvious is that the steady march of people and the accompanying din of noise are absent. Behind the scenes work the actors who provide essential support for courtroom activities (see A Day in Court: Those People behind the Scenes).

Courts are paperwork bureaucracies. Even the simplest case requires sheets and sheets of paper: the initial charge, later the indictment, bail release forms, pretrial motions, notice of appearance of counsel, and so on. Most of the behind-the-scenes people process this paperwork. Their actions are almost never visible, but their inaction can make headlines.

Other behind-the-scene actors are managers. A constant complaint is that the courts are mismanaged. Alas, trying to define management in a court setting proves to be elusive. Part of the difficulty is that in many jurisdictions there are three distinct sets of court managers—clerks of court, chief judges, and court administrators—and these three sets of managers are often in competition. Just as important, it is difficult to define what the managers should be doing. There is a fundamental conflict between management—standardized work processes and standard outputs—and the profession of law—individual attention to cases that are fundamentally different. Thus, at the heart of the problem of managing the courthouse is the tension between the rationality of bureaucracy and the antibureaucratic philosophies of judges (Saari 1982).

The **clerk of court,** variously referred to as *prothonotary, register of probate,* and *clerk,* is pivotal in the administration of local judiciaries. They are responsible for docketing cases, collecting fees, overseeing jury selection, and maintaining court records. These local officials have enormous power (Gertz 1977). Since they are elected officials in all but six states, they can operate semiautonomously from the judge. Thus, they have traditionally competed with judges for control over judicial administration (Mays and Taggart 1986).

Judges are responsible for court administration, but they have most often been ineffective managers. This is primarily due to the unique environment in which the courts operate. Judges may be held responsible, but they seldom have the necessary authority (Jacob 1997). Moreover, they are not trained in management. The end result is that the lawyers who become judges are not accustomed to analyzing patterns of case dispositions or managing large dockets—the essential skills a manager needs. These problems are reflected in the position of chief judge. Although the chief judge has

general administrative responsibilities, the position is really one of "first among equals." Particularly when the chief judge assumes the position by seniority, as many do, there is no guarantee that the person will be interested in management or will be effective at it.

One of the most innovative approaches to court problems has been the creation of a professional group of trained administrators to assist judges in their administrative duties. In short, management—like law—is a profession, and therefore well-trained managers can give the courts what they have often lacked: managerial skill and bureaucratic knowledge. The development of the professional position of court administrator has been sporadic (Lawson and Howard 1991; Flanders 1991). By the 1980s, every state had established a statewide court administrator. The primary duties of these officials are preparing annual reports, summarizing caseload data, preparing budgets, and troubleshooting. Usually, they report to the state supreme court or the chief justice of the state supreme court. Increasingly, trial courts are also employing court administrators. Few, if any, major metropolitan areas are without professional judicial employees (Reinkensmeyer 1991).

Tension between judges and the court administrator may arise. Some judges are reluctant to delegate responsibility over important aspects of the court's work, such as case scheduling (Mays and Taggart 1986). In practice, the distinction between administration and adjudication is not clear-cut. A court administrator's proposal to streamline court procedures may be viewed by the judges as an intrusion on their role in deciding cases. For example, it is not easy to determine whether transferring a judge from one assignment to another is a judicial or nonjudicial responsibility (Stott 1982; Hoffman 1991).

DYNAMICS OF COURTHOUSE JUSTICE

The brief tour of the courthouse indicates that justice is very unlike the dramatizations one sees on TV or in the movies. First-time observers find scant relationship between the dynamics of courthouse justice (law in action)

Exhibit 5-2	Three Concepts Explaining the Dynamics of Courthouse Justice	
Concept	Definition	Examples
Assembly-line justice	The operation of any segment of the criminal justice system with such speed and impersonality that defendants are treated as objects to be processed rather than as individuals	War on drugs has greatly increased case volume. Judges feel pressure to move cases.
Discretion	The authority to make decisions without reference to specific rules or facts	Prosecutors decide whether to file criminal charges. Judges choose between prison or probation.
Courtroom work group	The regular participants in the day-to-day activities of a particular courtroom; judge, prosecutor, and defense attorney interacting on the basis of shared norms	Cooperation more than conflict governs working relationship of courtroom actors. Case disposition requires joint actions of judge, prosecutor, and defense attorney. Rules of thumb guide bail release and sentencing.

and widely held cultural images (law on the books).

■ Expecting to see individual trials, they instead witness a parade of defendants and their cases. In particular, newcomers to the courthouse are often struck by the sheer volume of cases.

■ Expecting the law to provide guidance, they instead find that decisions are not necessarily clear-cut and that some leeway is available. How else can one explain disagreements over lengths of prison sentences and terms of probation?

■ Expecting to observe the conflict (and perhaps even hostility) projected by the adversarial model, courthouse watchers discover cooperation among judges, prosecutors, and defense attorneys. At times conversations become animated, but by and large the verbal exchanges reflect a good amount of badinage.

In exploring these differences, practitioners and scholars have employed three concepts—assembly-line justice, discretion, and courtroom work group (see Exhibit 5-2).

■ Assembly-line justice explains why few cases receive individual treatment.

■ Discretion emphasizes that decisions, although guided by law, are not totally determined by rules found in statutes or court decisions.

■ The courtroom work group concept stresses the importance of the patterned interactions of judges, prosecutors, and defense attorneys.

As we shall see, each of these explanations is useful in understanding the dynamics of courthouse justice.

ASSEMBLY-LINE JUSTICE

The most commonly advanced reason that criminal courts do not administer justice according to the textbook image is **assembly-line justice.** This explanation was put forth by the President's Commission on Law Enforcement and Administration of Justice (1967, 31): "The crux of the problem is that there is a great disparity between the number of cases and the number of judges." It is not only judges who are in short supply. There are not enough prosecutors, defense attorneys, and probation officers. The deluge of cases is reflected in every aspect of the courts' work, from overcrowded corridors and courtrooms to the long calendars that judges, prosecutors, and defense attorneys face each day.

Strengths of the Explanation

The assembly-line justice explanation highlights some important features of the contemporary courthouse. No one disputes that the volume of cases is large and growing (see Chapter 10). Every year approximately 14 million persons are arrested by the police—3 million for felonies and the rest for misdemeanors. Because of the large volume, overworked officials are often more interested in moving the steady stream of cases than in individually weighing each case on the scales of justice. Particularly in large cities, there are tremendous pressures to move cases and keep the docket current lest the backlog become worse and delays increase. In short, law on the books suggests a justice process with unlimited resources, whereas law in action stresses an administrative process geared to disposing of a large volume of cases.

In order to cope with large caseloads, prosecutors, defense attorneys, and judges often apply several mass-production techniques. Thus actors often specialize in specific tasks. In big-city public defender's offices, for example, one assistant will conduct the initial interview with the defendant, another will represent him or her at the initial appearance, and still another will negotiate the plea. Another mass-production technique is group processing. During the initial appearance, felony defendants are often advised of their rights in one large group rather than individually. Moreover, in the lower courts, sentences are often fixed on the basis of the defendant's membership in a given class rather than detailed consideration of the individual case (see Chapter 18).

Weaknesses of the Explanation

Although the assembly-line justice explanation draws our attention to some important aspects of the criminal courts, it also obscures many important considerations. First of all, this orthodox explanation stresses that excessive caseloads are a modern problem. Repeated references are made to the "rise" of plea bargaining, and the "decline" of the trial. However, these vivid metaphors distort history. American courts have been faced with caseload pressures for more than a century. Even more important, plea bargaining predates any of the "modern" problems of the courthouse. Indeed, plea bargaining "began to appear during the early or mid-nineteenth century and became institutionalized as a standard feature of American urban criminal courts in the last of the nineteenth century" (Haller 1979, 273). In short, the historical evidence must be ignored if one tries to explain how justice is administered in the courthouse simply in terms of too many cases resulting from the growth of big cities.

Emphasizing excessive caseloads also fails to consider the types of cases trial courts must decide. Most trial court cases, criminal or civil, present no disputed questions of law or fact. Rather, most case dispositions reflect **routine administration:** "A matter is routine when a court has no disputed question of law or fact to decide. Routine administration means the processing or approving of undisputed matters" (Friedman and Percival 1976, 267). Most cases, therefore, end with a plea of guilty (rather than a trial), not because the courthouse has too many cases but because the courts are confronted with a steady stream of routine cases in which the only major question is the sentence to be imposed.

Although heavy caseloads are part of the conventional wisdom surrounding the operations of criminal courts, several studies cast serious doubt on this proposition. A study in Connecticut compared two courts—one with a heavy caseload, another with a light one. It would be logical to expect major differences in how cases were processed and in the substance of justice handed out, but the results indicated that the courts were remarkably similar. Neither court had many trials. In neither did the defense attorneys engage in pitched battle with the prosecution. Both courts set bail in approximately the same amounts and imposed roughly similar sentences. Each court spent the same amount of time per case, moving through its business "rapidly and mechanically." The only difference was that the busier court was in session longer than the court with fewer cases (Feeley 1979).

THE MURDER TRIAL OF SHAREEF COUSIN

Doing Time at Tulane and Broad (Part II)

 On this day at the courthouse, the elevators are out of order, the bathrooms are filthy, their fixtures marginally functional. The majesty of this great building stands without human assistance; the mayor's Keep-It-Clean campaign has not made it to Tulane and Broad. The marble floors are unwaxed, the main hallway is un-air-conditioned, and the basement corridor smells like fish. . . .

The defendant in a burglary case in Section B is shackled at the limbs with steel braces. In the courtroom behind him, his wife or girlfriend is crying. He motions with his head for her to come closer but his lawyer raises a hand from across the room to tell her: No. She sits back down, looking across the courtroom at him, searching. He averts his eyes at first, then looks, sees her misery and arches his eyebrows, mugs a little, tries to cheer her up. Two friends on either side of her rub her shoulders. The voices of lawyers arguing motions and the buzzing white noise of the courtroom air-conditioner join together in a fluorescent-tinged droning, the kind of sound into which everything slips away sometimes. . . .

Down in the basement, prospective jurors, culled from state voter and driver's license rosters, are packed into windowless waiting rooms. Josie Windhorst, a state jury commissioner, is in charge here. She paints the best face on the bleak-looking place, talking about the great ideals of democracy, honor, civic duty, and such. The worst thing, really, are the occasional odors that creep in from the coroner's office in the basement annex.

She is like a schoolteacher on a rainy day, trying to keep everyone happy while they fidget and wait. She handles the legion of excuses from those who'd prefer to jettison their duty to the commonwealth. "People have a tendency to reveal to me their entire medical history when all I really want is a doctor's note," she says.

On this day, there will be five trials, about the average number. Windhorst dispatches dozens of prospective jurors to each court for voir dire, the preliminary examination by lawyers of the jurors' fitness to serve. . . .

On this day of five trials, two are for heroin distribution, one is for possession of marijuana and a pistol, and two are for possession of a crack pipe. "They're kind of legendary around here," says one court official with a roll of his eyes. "Crack pipe cases." They eat the building's resources. The afternoon in both Sections F and J is consumed by cases trying to prove some sorry looking guy was in possession of a piece of drug paraphernalia.

It is the state's duty to do this. But both cases deadlock at five to one in the jury rooms. A holdout for not guilty in each case prompts mistrial rulings. The juries are thanked and dismissed; the suspects are led back to jail, but not before one of them, in an ill-fitting gray suit, asks for a moment with his father. It turns out not to be a Kodak moment it promised to be; the two start arguing over the defendant's clothes. . . .

It is now late afternoon and trial results trickle in from around the building. In the drugs and weapons case in [Judge] Alarcon's court, the defendant is found guilty. An hour later, the day's third mistrial is declared in one of the heroin cases; this time because of an assistant DA's improper introduction of prejudicial evidence.

At 5:30 p.m., the building is clear except for Judge Julian Parker's courtroom, where the heroin distribution trial of Paul Washington is winding up. Washington was busted with 25 packets of heroin and a loaded .45. If convicted, he'll likely get a life sentence. . . . A 12-member jury finds Washington guilty, to which the defendant has no visible reaction. As the jurors file out of the courtroom, only one—like Washington, a young black man—looks him in the eye. One of the sisters bolts from the room sobbing while the other quietly buries her head in her hands. As he is led away, Washington looks back over his shoulder to wave good-bye but neither of them sees him.

At 6:45 p.m., two defense attorneys hardly older than the girls' brother comfort them at the top of the steps of the courtroom at Tulane and Broad, and for today at least, court is adjourned.

SOURCE: Christopher Rose, "Doing Time at Tulane and Broad," *The Times Picayune*, 27 September 1998.

This and other studies clearly suggest that the criminal court process cannot be understood solely on the basis of excessive caseloads, because such an explanation omits too many important considerations (Heumann 1975; Nardulli 1979).

DISCRETION

Law on the books projects an image of a legal system that seemingly runs by itself—a mechanical process of merely applying rules of law to given cases. Law in action, however, emphasizes a legal system in which the legal actors exercise discretion because choices must be made.

Discretion lies at the heart of the criminal justice process. From the time a crime is committed until after sentence is imposed, discretion is exercised every time key decisions are made. After arrest, the prosecutor may decide not to prosecute. Once charges have been filed, a lower court judge must set the amount of bail and decide whether there is sufficient probable cause to hold the defendant for the grand jury. In turn, grand juries have discretion over indictments, trial juries over conviction, and the judge over sentencing.

 Discretion is best defined as the lawful ability of an agent of government to exercise choice in making a decision. Viewed from this perspective, discretion has three major sub-components: legal judgments, policy priorities, and personal philosophies (Cole 1970).

Many discretionary decisions in the criminal court process are made on the basis of legal judgments. An example would be a prosecutor who refuses to file a criminal charge because in her legal judgment there is insufficient evidence to prove all the elements of the offense. Some legal judgments stem from a prediction about the likely outcome of a case at a later stage in the proceedings. The prosecutor, for example, may believe that the defendant did violate the law but that no jury would convict.

Other discretionary decisions reflect policy priorities. Because criminal laws are so broad and general, they must be selectively enforced. The number of crimes that could be charged is virtually unlimited, but the resources devoted to detecting wrongdoers and processing them through the courts (and later incarcerating

COURT TV
Stings

Stings are one of law enforcements most effective weapons. But by using deception and hidden cameras does law enforcement sometimes go too far? The defense argues that the government improperly pressures a defendant to commit a crime that he or she would otherwise not commit.

Washington, D.C., Mayor Marion Barry was the subject of an undercover sting operation. So was boat builder Phillip Johnson. Did the government go too far in investigating and prosecuting them?

View a video clip of these events on your copy of the CourtTV CD-ROM. As you watch the video, keep the following questions in mind:

1. Was the verdict in the Mayor Barry case an example of the jury finding entrapment or an example of jury nullification (Chapter 14)?

2. Was the verdict in the Phillip Johnson case an example of the jury finding entrapment or an example of jury nullification (Chapter 14)?

3. Is Phillip Johnson the type of person whom law enforcement should, or should not, target in the war on drugs (Chapter 4)?

4. In these two cases, what specifics would advocates of the crime control model emphasize when arguing that complaints about entrapment are overstated? What specifics would backers of the due process model of criminal justice point to in arguing that law enforcement does indeed engage in entrapment?

them) are limited. Thus, discretionary decisions are often made on the basis of policy priorities. Through policy priorities, court officials try to devote more resources to prosecuting serious crimes, such as murder, rape, and armed robbery, rather than minor offenses.

Other discretionary decisions reflect the decision makers' personal values and attitudes—their personal philosophies. Judges and prosecutors have varying views of what offenses are serious and deserving of a high priority. Differences among judges in the same courthouse are readily apparent. Some differences center on the purpose of the criminal law. Those who believe that the courts can deter crime (through heavy sentences, for example) behave differently from those who discount the role the courts can play in deterrence. Stated another way, the same differences of opinion about crime that characterize society as a whole likewise divide courthouse actors.

THE COURTROOM WORK GROUP

Every day, the same group of courthouse regulars assembles in the same courtroom, sits or stands in the same places, and performs the same tasks as the day before. The types of defendants and the nature of the crimes they are accused of also remain constant. Only the names of the victims and defendants are different. Whereas defendants come and go, the judges, prosecutors, defense attorneys, clerks, and probation officers remain. To even the most casual observer, the courthouse regulars occupy a special status. They freely issue instructions to the temporary visitors to the courthouse (don't smoke, don't talk, don't read the newspaper), although they smoke, talk, and read the newspaper themselves. The ordinary citizens sit on hard benches in the rear of the courtroom and may approach the bench only when specifically requested. The courthouse regulars, on the other hand, enjoy easy access to the front part of the courtroom.

The activities of the courthouse regulars represent a complex network of ongoing social relationships (Blumberg 1970; Neubauer 1974; Flemming, Nardulli, and Eisenstein 1992). These relationships are as important as they are complex. James Eisenstein and Herbert Jacob (1977) have proposed that the best way to analyze the network of ongoing relationships among the courthouse actors is through the concept of the **courtroom work group.**

Judges, prosecutors, and defense attorneys are representatives from separate, independent sponsoring institutions. They are drawn together by a common task: Each must do something about a given case. As a result, courthouse regulars work together on a daily basis in ways not envisioned by the formal adversary model (Jacob 1991). In Philadelphia, for example, 83 percent of the district attorneys and public defenders report that they cooperate always or often (Lichtenstein 1984). To understand the extent as well as the limits of this cooperation, we need to examine why courtroom work groups form in the first place and their impact on the administration of justice.

Mutual Interdependence

The criminal courthouse is not a single organization but rather a collection of separate institutions that gather in a common workplace. Whereas most large organizations consist of distinct divisions operating under a central leadership, the criminal courthouse consists of separate institutions without a hierarchical system of control. A judge cannot reward a prosecutor or a public defender who performs well. Rather, each of the courthouse regulars is a representative of a sponsoring institution, which hires and fires them, monitors their activities, and rewards their performance.

None of these actors can perform his or her tasks independently; they must work together. These interactions are critical because none of the courthouse regulars can make decisions independently; each must consider the reactions of others. This is most readily seen in the work of the defense attorney. In representing his or her client, the defense attorney must consider the type of plea agreement the prosecutor may offer, the sentencing tendencies of the judge, and the likelihood of a jury verdict of guilty. Prosecutors and judges are interdependent in similar ways.

Each member of the work group can achieve individual goals and accomplish separate tasks only through work group participation. The actors come to share common interests in disposing of cases. Hence, cooperation—mutual interdependence—within the work group is viewed as leading to mutual benefits. Assistant prosecutors, for example, are judged by their superiors not so much on how many cases they win but on how few they lose. Thus to secure their primary goal of gaining convictions, they must depend on defense attorneys to sell their clients on the advantages of the bargain offered and also on judges to impose the agreed upon settlement.

Shared Decision Making

Courtroom work groups reflect shared decision making. Judges retain the legal authority to make the major decisions, such as setting bail and imposing sentences, but they often rely on others. They routinely follow the bail recommendations of the prosecutor and accept guilty plea agreements reached by the defense and prosecution. This does not mean that the judge is without power; the other actors must be sensitive to what the judge might do. Prosecutors (and defense attorneys) know the amount of bail a particular judge has set in past situations, so that is what they recommend in the current case.

This shared decision making is highly functional because it diffuses responsibility. Judges, prosecutors, defense attorneys, and others are aware that the decisions they make can turn out to be wrong. Since such dire results cannot be predicted ahead of time, the members of the courtroom work group share a sense that when one of their members looks bad, they all look bad. Decisions, therefore, are made on a joint basis. If something later goes wrong, work group members have protected themselves: Everyone thought it was a good idea at the time (Clynch and Neubauer 1981).

The hallmark of work groups is regularity of behavior. This regularity is the product of shared norms about how each member should behave and what decisions are desirable. Courthouse workers can make their common worksite a fractious and unpredictable place for carrying out assigned tasks or, through cooperation, a predictable place to work. The greater the certainty, the less time and resources they need spend on each case. Newcomers learn these important informal norms of cooperation through a process referred to as *socialization.*

Socialization

A problem common to all organizations, courts included, is the need to break in new members,

a process known as socialization. Through socialization newcomers are taught not only the formal requirements of the job (how motions are filed and so on) but also informal rules of behavior. One veteran court aide put it this way:

> Most of the judges are pretty good—they rely on us. Sometimes you get a new judge who wants to do things his way. We have to break them in, train them. This court is very different. We have to break new judges in. It takes some of them some time to get adjusted to the way we do things. (Wiseman 1970, 99)

Thus, newcomers learn not only from their peers but also from other members of the social network. One of the most important things they learn is the importance of shared norms. It is the shared norms that provide structure to what otherwise would appear to be an unstructured, almost chaotic, process. These shared norms are referred to as *normal crimes.*

Normal Crimes

As discussed earlier, most of the matters before the courts are routine. Although each case is unique, most fall into a limited number of categories. Based on similarities among cases, members of the work group develop certain ideas about types of crime and criminals. One study has aptly labeled this phenomenon as the concept of the **normal crime** (Sudnow 1965). The legal actors categorize crimes on the basis of the typical manner in which they are committed, the typical social characteristics of the defendants, and the types of victims. Once a case has been placed into one of these categories, it is usually disposed of on the basis of a set pattern. In essence, normal crimes represent a group sense of justice.

Rewards and Sanctions

Actors who violate these rules of personal and professional conduct can expect sanctions from the other members of the work group. A variety of rewards (carrots) are available as benefits to those who follow the rules. For example, defense attorneys who do not unnecessarily disrupt routines are able to negotiate a sentence that is slightly less severe than normal. In turn, some sanctions (sticks) may be applied to those who do not cooperate. Judges can sanction uncooperative private defense attorneys, for instance, by making them wait for their case to be called. By far the more effective approach is the carrot, because it operates indirectly and is less disruptive. The imposition of sanctions can lead to countersanctions, with the result that the network is disrupted even further.

Variability in Courtroom Work Groups

Virtually all criminal courts studied to date exemplify the patterns just discussed of how courtroom work groups operate, but some important variations need to be considered (Flemming, Nardulli, and Eisenstein 1992).

The stability of the work groups varies (Church 1985). Work groups are much more stable in Chicago than in Baltimore, for example, where rotation of key officials' jobs occurs more often and produces numerous disruptions of the ongoing network of relationships (Eisenstein and Jacob 1977).

Mavericks can be found in most courthouses. Some defense attorneys engage in hostile relations with prosecutors and exhibit many "Perry Mason" attributes of adversarial behavior. They do so at a price, however: They are seldom able to negotiate effectively for good deals.

The content of the policy norms varies from community to community. Property crimes are viewed as more threatening in rural areas than in urban ones, so the appropriate penalty for a defendant convicted of burglary in a rural area is more severe than for a defendant convicted in a big city. In recent years, one set of major concerns about the policy norms relates to gender equity (see Courts, Controversy, and Gender Equity: Is Gender Bias a Significant Problem in the Courts?).

To the general public, perhaps the most visible variation between work groups concerns delay. Each courthouse has, over time, evolved a set of expectations about the proper pacing of case dispositions. Some courthouses process cases in a timely fashion, others less so.

THE PROBLEM OF DELAY

A commonly mentioned problem affecting many of the nation's courts is that too many cases take too long to reach disposition. The magnitude of the backlog and the length of the delay vary greatly, however, depending on the court involved (Mahoney et al. 1988). Clearly, there are degrees of delay. The 17 courts listed in Exhibit 5-3 fall into three relatively distinct clusters. Seattle and Cincinnati are examples of faster courts—median time of 100 days or less from arrest to disposition. Moderately fast courts—Tucson and Omaha, for example—have disposition times ranging from 100 to 150 days. Finally, in slower courts such as Austin and Baltimore, the median time is greater than 150 days (Ostrom and Hanson 2000). Stated another way, delay appears to be a problem in some jurisdictions, but a number of American trial courts handle their cases very expeditiously.

In a general sense, the term **delay** suggests abnormal or unacceptable time lapses in the processing of cases (Neubauer et al. 1981). The inherent subjectivity of the term becomes apparent when we try to define *unnecessary delay* (Neubauer 1983). There is no consensus about how long is too long. Past commissions have provided yardsticks ranging from six months to two years (American Bar Association 1968; President's Commission 1967; National Advisory Commission 1973). The most commonly used benchmark is the recommendation of the American Bar Association that all felony cases reach disposition within one year of filing.

Consequences of Delay

Concern that "justice delayed is justice denied" is as old as the common law itself. In the thirteenth century, the nobles forced King John to sign the Magna Carta and promise not to "deny or delay right or justice." In the nineteenth century, the novelist Charles Dickens condemned the tortuous process of litigation in the English courts. Today judicial reformers and critics argue that case delay undermines the values and guarantees associated with the legal system. The three most often cited negative consequences of delays in the courthouse center on defendant, society, and citizen.

COURTS, CONTROVERSY, AND GENDER EQUITY

Is Gender Bias a Significant Problem in the Courts?

The last several decades have witnessed a monumental change in the gender composition of the American workforce. Not only are a higher percentage of women working outside the home, but women are also increasingly working in what were once considered male professions. Law most certainly is a case in point. Today, women constitute anywhere from one third to one half of all law students, and make up more than 10 percent of the nation's judges.

One of the areas of most concern to the women's rights movement is gender bias. Thirty-six states have created task forces to investigate gender bias in the legal system. Some state task forces define gender bias as making decisions based on stereotypes about men and women; others stress insensitivity toward certain aspects of men's and women's lives; still others emphasize intentional bias and ill will. Regardless of the precise definition, a team of researchers from Boise State University found these reports to be remarkably consistent. The state task forces consistently found gender bias in four areas of the legal system: domestic violence, sexual assault, divorce, and behavior toward female workers (Hemmens, Strom, and Schlegel 1997).

Domestic violence is one area in which the state task force studies found gender bias to be most common. Some members of the courtroom work group believe that domestic violence is a private matter and should not be dealt with in the court system. Indeed, one male district judge was quoted as saying slapping around the wife was justified.

Sexual assault is another area in which women experience gender bias. Sexual assault is underreported because women believe they will not be believed and will themselves be blamed. Moreover, women perceive that reporting sexual assault will result in a revictimization, with past sexual history of the female (more so than the male) thrown open to scrutiny.

Divorce cases are another area in which the possibility of gender bias looms. The state task force reports unanimously found that women suffer from gender bias in terms of awarding alimony, division of property, and child support. The courts, on the other hand, appear to be biased against fathers in child custody awards.

Finally, all 36 state task force reports found gender bias against female lawyers and court employees. Of principal concern were offensive and intolerable actions toward female participants in the legal system. The most common form of gender bias mentioned was the practice of judges' and attorneys' addressing female lawyers in a demeaning manner.

Female lawyers, more so than their male counterparts, were addressed by their first names. Moreover, terms like "sweetie," "little lady lawyer," "pretty eyes," and "dear" were used. Another com-

Historically, court delay was considered a problem because it jeopardized the defendant's right to a speedy trial. The Sixth Amendment provides that "in all criminal prosecutions, the accused shall enjoy the right to a speedy and public trial. . . ." Defendants may languish in jail for a number of months before guilt or innocence is determined. A number of states have enacted speedy-trial laws premised on the need to protect the defendant's rights.

More recently, delay has been viewed as hampering society's need for a speedy conviction. This view stresses harm done to the prosecution's case. As the case becomes older and witnesses' memories diminish, the defendant's chances of acquittal increase. In short, the state is also viewed as possessing the right to a speedy trial. Thus in recent years some jurisdictions have enacted speedy-trial laws to try to increase conviction rates.

Regardless of the costs or benefits to either the defense or the prosecution, a third perspective emphasizes that delay erodes public confidence in the judicial process. Citizens lose confidence in the swiftness or certainty of punishment. Additionally, victims and witnesses may be forced to make repeated, needless trips to the courthouse. Such appearances can cost

mon form of gender bias suffered by female attorneys (and judges as well) is sexist remarks or jokes. Gender bias also affects hiring and promotion. Female lawyers perceive that it is harder to get hired, and once hired they are paid less and have fewer opportunities for promotion.

It is important to underscore that these findings are based on reports of specific events ("Have you ever had remarks made about your looks?") as well as perceptions of gender bias or problems. Women consistently reported problem areas at higher levels than men. Answers to questions like those asked in surveys, of course, can be understood in different ways. Perhaps women are oversensitive to these issues (or alternatively, males are oblivious). Another stumbling block is the difficulty in estimating the true extent of the gender bias problem. Perceptions of bias could be the product of an isolated few who have contact with many female lawyers and judges, or they could be the result of persistent practices by numerous male lawyers and judges.

Given the problems of using perceptions alone to document a social problem such as gender bias, it is important to look for independent validation. For this reason, this book examines domestic violence (Chapter 9).

Perceptions of gender bias are a serious matter because they affect litigants' perceptions of the fairness of justice. If litigants and/or their lawyers perceive that they are treated differently, they have less confidence in the process of justice, irrespective of the outcome of the case. It is also important to underscore that the gender bias issues investigated must be taken seriously because they directly affect the lives of many women and their children as well. Moreover, the issues are some of the most explosive facing the justice system and have become, in a relatively few years, important public issues.

Gender bias is not a problem created by the court system but a reflection of prevailing attitudes in society. Although "current laws and affirmative action plans have furthered women's equality, they cannot by themselves change the attitudes of individuals. It is the individual attitudes that require change if gender bias is to be eradicated" (Hemmens, Strom, and Schlegel 1997, 31).

What do you think? Is gender bias a serious problem in the nation's courthouses? Have you seen or experienced biased behavior by lawyers, judges, or other court personnel? If you are troubled by using individual reports to make the case for gender bias, what alternative methods would you use to study the problem?

To learn more about gender bias, visit The Clearinghouse on Racial/Ethnic and Gender Bias at the National Center for State Courts, http://www.ncsc.dni.us/is/clrhouse.htm, and the National Judicial Education Program Task Force on Gender Bias in the Courts, http://www.nowldef.org/html/njep/history.htm.

citizens time and money and ultimately discourage them from prosecution. Overall, delay in disposing of cases strains the resources of the criminal justice system.

Assessing the Costs of Delay

Assertions about the costs of delay require careful scrutiny. A general consensus has emerged that delay is a problem facing the courts, but there is no agreement about the particulars. The three perspectives just described stress varying reasons that delay is a problem. Some perceive that lengthy pretrial incarceration forces defendants to enter into detrimental plea bargains. Others, however, portray caseload pressures as forcing prosecutors into offering unduly lenient negotiated bargains.

The National Center for State Courts has noted that few of the assertions about the social costs of delay have been subjected to empirical examination (Church and McConnell 1978). They find some evidence to indicate that jail overcrowding and defendants' skipping court appearances (Chapter 11) are related to case delay. But they find no support

| | Exhibit 5-3 | Felony Case Disposition Time in Selected Cities (Days from Arrest to Disposition) |

City	Median Days from Arrest to Disposition
Faster courts	
Seattle, WA	59
Cincinnati, OH	79
Portland, OR	85
Santa Clara, CA	86
Des Moines, IA	100
Moderate courts	
Grand Rapids, MI	104
St. Petersburg, FL	105
Tucson, AZ	113
Omaha, NE	115
Baltimore County, MD	135
Oakland, CA	143
Slower courts	
Baltimore City, MD	162
Austin, TX	193
Fort Worth, TX	195
Sacramento, CA	224
Birmingham, AL	304
Hackensack, NJ	314
All courts combined	**126**

SOURCE: Brian Ostrom and Neal Kauder, *Examining the Work of State Courts, 1998* (Williamsburg, VA: National Center for State Courts, 1999).

for the assertions that case delay causes deterioration of cases or pressures prosecutors to offer lenient plea bargains.

LAW-ON-THE-BOOKS APPROACH TO COURT DELAY

The law-on-the-books approach to court delay focuses on resources and procedures (Church and McConnell 1978). It is an article of faith among many commentators that the problem of delay results from an imbalance between available resources and mounting caseloads.

A common response is to supplement resources—add judges, prosecutors, clerks, and so on. Beyond adding more resources, traditional court reformers emphasize streamlining procedures. They view procedural stages such as preliminary hearing, grand jury indictment, and pretrial motions as sources of delay.

This conventional wisdom about court delay has been called into serious question (Church 1982; Gallas 1976). In *Justice Delayed* (Church et al. 1978), the National Center for State Courts studied 21 courts across the nation and found that the level of court resources was not associated with court delay. The relative size of court caseloads, for example, bore little relationship to case processing time. Sim-

How does delay affect it

Barker v. Wingo and the Right to a Speedy Trial

The police arrested two suspects—Willie Barker and Silas Manning—for beating an elderly couple to death with a tire iron in Christian County, Kentucky. The district attorney had a stronger case against Manning and believed that Barker could not be convicted unless Manning testified against him. Thus, the DA first sought a conviction against Manning. The court-appointed lawyer initially had no objection to continuing the trial; after all, an acquittal could only help Barker.

The Commonwealth of Kentucky, however, encountered more than a few difficulties in its prosecution of Manning. Altogether, six trials were conducted. Two ended in hung juries, and two others in convictions that were reversed on appeal. Finally, Manning was convicted of murdering one victim, and a sixth trial resulted in a conviction for the other murder.

During these legal maneuverings, Barker was in jail for 10 months, which largely explains why it wasn't until the twelfth continuance was requested that the defense filed a motion to dismiss the charges. By the time the Commonwealth was ready to try Barker, another problem arose: The chief investigator on the case was ill; two continuances resulted. Eventually the judge announced

that the case would be dismissed if it wasn't tried during the next setting. The trial finally commenced with Manning as the chief prosecution witness; Barker was convicted and given a life sentence.

In assessing these lengthy delays, the opinion of the Court notes that "the right to speedy trial is a more vague concept than other procedure rights. It is, for example, impossible to determine with precision when the right has been denied. We can not definitely say how long is too long in a system where justice is supposed to be swift but deliberate" (p. 522). In essence, the right to a speedy trial is relative, not absolute. The test would be a balancing test in which the conduct of both the prosecution and the defendant are weighted. Calling the delay "extraordinary," the Court nonetheless ruled that Barker was not seriously prejudiced by the more than five-year delay.

Only in extraordinary circumstances has the Court ordered criminal charges dismissed for lack of timely trial. One such situation involved an eight-year gap between indictment and arrest. The government was negligent in making any effort to track down the defendant, and the defendant was entitled to go free without a trial (*Doggett v. U.S.* 1992).

ilarly, court procedures were poor predictors of delay. Courts that emphasized plea bargaining (as opposed to trying cases) were as fast (or as slow) as their opposite numbers.

These findings explain why the law on the books approach—issuing more and more rules and regulations—is often ineffective in speeding up case dispositions and reducing excessive caseloads. Speedy-trial laws are a case in point.

Speedy-Trial Laws

Besides the provisions of the U.S. Constitution, 35 state constitutions have speedy-trial guarantees, but these provisions apply only when the delay has been "extensive." What constitutes un-

necessary delay, however, is difficult to pinpoint (see Case Close-Up: *Barker v. Wingo* and the Right to a Speedy Trial). Given the vagueness of these constitutional standards, legislatures have shown considerable interest in putting some teeth into the guarantee of a speedy trial. The best-known such effort is the Speedy Trial Act of 1974 (amended in 1979), which specifies time standards for the two primary stages in the federal court process. Thirty days are allowed from arrest to indictment, and 70 days from indictment to trial. Certain time periods, such as those associated with hearings on pretrial motions and the mental competency of the defendant, are considered excludable time.

Speedy-trial statutes exist in all 50 states (Misner 1983), but they have a different orientation than their federal counterpart. Most state laws are defendant centered; that is, they are designed to protect defendants from suffering extensive delay, particularly if they are incarcerated prior to trial. By contrast, the federal law is designed to protect the interests of society; that is, a speedy trial is viewed as an important objective irrespective of whether the defendant's interests are in jeopardy.

Limits of Speedy-Trial Laws

Efforts to mandate speedy trials are striking in their lack of specifics. These laws are not based on an analysis of why delay occurs. Moreover, they do not provide for any additional resources (more judges or prosecutors) to aid the courts in complying. This can produce unforeseen consequences. In a number of federal courts, compliance has come at the price of delaying civil cases. Potential difficulties also arise because not all cases fit easily into the mandated time frames. A major murder case or a large drug-smuggling case takes longer to prepare than an ordinary burglary prosecution.

Researchers approach speedy-trial laws with considerable skepticism. Various studies find that such laws have had limited impact in speeding up the flow of cases through the state criminal court process (Nimmer 1978; Church et al. 1978; Mahoney et al. 1988). The primary reason is that most state laws fail to provide the court with adequate and effective enforcement mechanisms. As a result, the time limits specified by speedy-trial laws are seldom a guide to actual practice. One study found that North Carolina's speedy-trial law did indeed speed up the criminal docket, but Connecticut's law did not (Marvell and Luskin 1991). The federal speedy-trial law has proven effective. The average criminal case filed in the federal courts in the early 1970s took seven months to reach a disposition. By the early 1980s, the average case was disposed of in less than three months. Thus, the federal approach of court planning followed by fixed standards works to reduce delay (Garner 1987). Overall, researchers stress that law-in-action approaches to reducing court delay are ultimately more effective.

LAW-IN-ACTION APPROACH TO COURT DELAY

Law-on-the-books approaches to reducing court delay are ineffective because they ignore the dynamics of courthouse justice. All too often, the impression conveyed is that case flow management is somehow removed from other issues in the criminal court process. Delay is related not to how many cases a court must process but to the choices that the actors make in how they process these cases. Defense attorneys seek continuances to avoid harsh judges or to pressure the client to pay the agreed upon fee. Prosecutors use delay to increase the stakes of plea bargaining or to postpone weak cases they are likely to lose. Judges acquiesce in continuances so as not to disrupt the dispositional process (Flemming, Nardulli, and Eisenstein 1987).

For these reasons, lawyers and judges are generally content with the existing pace of litigation in their courts. Practitioners were asked to provide appropriate case-processing times for typical cases. Within the four courts studied—the Bronx, Detroit, Miami, and Pittsburgh—there was little systematic disagreement among judges, defense counsel, and prosecutors on the appropriate pace of case dispositions (Church et al. 1978). Findings like these show why law-in-action approaches to court delay seek to alter practitioners' attitudes regarding proper case disposition times. Improving case scheduling and trying to achieve better coordination among courtroom work group members are two such approaches.

Case Scheduling

Waiting is one activity that people in the courthouse inevitably engage in. A busy courtroom can grind to halt because an important witness fails to show up or a lawyer is temporarily detained in another courtroom. From an administrative perspective, the courts are extremely complex institutions. The disposition of a case often requires the presence of the following individuals: judge, clerk, court reporter, bailiff, defendant, prosecutor, defense attorney, police officer, victim, and witness. Depending on the procedural stage, jurors, a probation officer, a pretrial services representative, and an interpreter may also need to appear.

Many of these people have several different courts to appear in during a single day. For example, defense attorneys, prosecutors, and probation officers may have several cases set for the same time. There can be administrative problems, too. Because of an illegible address, the defendant never receives a notice. Or the jailer may inadvertently forget to include the needed defendant on the day's list. If just one person is late, the others must wait, and if one person never shows up at all, the hearing must be rescheduled.

Efforts at Coordination

As we have noted previously, the court is actually a collection of agents from separate and independent organizations: judge, police, prosecutor, sheriff, clerk, and probation officer. Most of these organizations are headed by elected officials or, like the police, report to elected officials. They have their own bases of power and their own separate legal mandates. Judges thus have limited administrative control (although they are often held responsible when something goes wrong). Not surprisingly, judges typically mention as a significant problem "inadequate" control over organizations that provide necessary support for court operations (Beerhalter and Gainey 1974).

In turn, each of these separate organizations has scheduling problems. Each tries to establish a schedule of court appearances that is best for itself. But such schedules often inconvenience other agencies. A major study of the federal courts concluded that most of the best-run district courts held regular meetings of top officials of the various organizations to iron out administrative problems. In the other, less well run courts, each agency head criticized operating procedures of the others as causing delay

and inconvenience, but the agency heads never met to work out a coordinated plan (Flanders 1977). A report on the success of four state trial courts in reducing delay pointed to improved communications between the principal agencies as a chief factor. Meeting periodically, the heads of the court agencies were able to share information and work out common problems (Ryan et al. 1981).

■ CONCLUSION

Discussions of court delay and its consequences all too often are conducted in abstract terms. *Barker v. Wingo,* however, forces one to deal with some of the realities. The Court's opinion is clearly mindful of the fact that to interpret the right to a speedy trial in a manner understood by the drafters of the Constitution would, in all likelihood, result in a brutal murderer's being set free.

Barker v. Wingo and our discussion of the problem of delay show that the actual operations of the criminal courts differ greatly from official expectations. Three concepts—excessive caseloads, discretion, and the courtroom work group—have been used to explain this gap between the law in action and the law on the books. Although courts are burdened with too many cases, excessive volume of cases is at best only a partial explanation for the behavior of the criminal courts. More important is the role discretion plays in the court system, shaping the dictates of formal law to the actual cases and defendants that come to the criminal courts. The courtroom work group concept emphasizes the interactions among the key actors in court. The next three chapters will examine in greater depth how prosecutors, defense attorneys, and judges work within the courtroom work group, and why.

CRITICAL THINKING QUESTIONS

1. Take a tour of your local courthouse. How does the description match the one at the beginning of this chapter? Compare notes

with other classmates; perhaps they focused on features that you did not.

2. Place yourself in the position of a felony court prosecutor. In what ways does the cooperation of other members of the courtroom work group work to your

benefit? How would your answer be different if you approached the question from the vantage point of the judge or the defense attorney?

3. Of the several consequences of delay, which one do you think is the most important? Which one is the least important?

4. In *Barker v. Wingo* the Court stressed the legitimate reasons for the 16 trial continuances. But is there a danger that prosecutors might illegitimately seek continuances?

KEY TERMS

assembly-line justice (109)
clerk of court (108)
courtroom work group (113)
delay (115)
discretion (112)
normal crime (114)
routine administration (110)

 # WORLD WIDE WEB RESOURCES AND EXERCISES

Web Search Terms

speedy trial
court congestion and delay
clerk of court
court reporter
court watchers
court services
court administrator

Useful URLs

The National Association for Court Management focuses on improving the administration of justice. Visit their Web site at http://www.nacmnet.org/.

The Bureau of Justice Assistance stresses agency collaboration and crime prevention: http://www.ojp.usdoj.gov/BJA/.

The National Court Reporters Association serves the court reporting and captioning profession. Their Web site is http://www.verbatimreporters.com/.

FindLaw's discussion of the right to a speedy and public trial can be found at http://caselaw.findlaw.com/data/constitution/amendment06/02.html#1.

Uncommon URLs

Achieving success as a court reporter requires doing two things at once: http://www.modbee.com/reports/jobs/20000325_06.html.

These court watchers in Skokie, Illinois, even have their own Web page: http://www.skokienet.org/cccwatc1/.

These court watchers are concerned about gender bias: http://www.leswhaley.org/watchers.html.

Cook County court watchers rank the local judges: http://www.kentlaw.edu/legal_resources/cccw/.

To read about the Court Security Survey, go to http://aja.ncsc.dni.us/Ctsecurity.html.

Concerns about courtroom safety are apparent in the following article: http://sequimgazette.com/News/CountyNews/Courtjudgesfearviole991222.html.

The Court Reform Committee of the Colorado Bar Association can be accessed at http://www.cobar.org/comms/crtreform/index.htm.

Courtroom 21 is a joint project of the William and Mary College of Law and the National Center for State Courts; this Web site emphasizes technology in the courtroom: http://www.courtroom21.net/.

Court services bureaus are a major part of sheriff's offices in major cities. See, for example:

San Diego
http://www.co.san-diego.ca.us/cnty/cntydepts/safety/sheriff/csb/index.html

Chicago
http://www.cookcountysheriff.org/court/

Indianapolis
http://www.open.org/~msheriff/court.htm

Web Exercises

1. Summaries of how the amendments that make up the Bill of Rights have been interpreted can be found at the following site: http://www.findlaw.com/laws/constitution. Click on the Sixth Amendment to find a full legal discussion of the right to a speedy and public trial. You might want to bookmark this section for future reference, for two reasons: (1) You won't forget where the information came from, and (2) you won't have to type all those letters next time.

2. Court reform is a topic of constant conversation in legal circles. Do a search on the topic by going to Yahoo: http://www.yahoo.com. Then, under Search, type the phrase "court reform." Select several of these discussions, and ask yourself to what extent the right to a speedy trial figures in the call for action. Moreover, ask yourself how court reform is viewed by various groups. Is court reform needed to protect the values of the crime control model or the values of the due process model?

3. A growing number of newspapers now have online editions. Some browsers make this service easily available under bookmarks that are built in. Click on Bookmarks and then Newsstand. Or you can go directly to the service at http://www.naa.org/. Click the box with the words "Select a State" inside, and then click on your state. Find the newspaper in your town (or the closest one). Also find a newspaper in a city that is similar to yours in terms of size. Compare the discussion of courts and crime in these two papers. What common elements do you find? How unique is your community?

INFOTRAC COLLEGE EDITION RESOURCES AND EXERCISES

Basic Search Terms

discretion
court administration
court congestion and delay

InfoTrac College Edition Exercises

1. Using the search terms "court congestion and delay" and/or "speedy trial," locate two or more articles that discuss court delay. To what extent do the articles stress law-on-the-books solutions or law-in-action reforms? Here are two possible articles: Dwight Aarons, "Getting Out of This Mess," and Major Harding, "Preparing Florida Courts for the New Millennium."

2. Using the search term "criminal justice, administration of," select two or more articles that discuss problems in the criminal justice system. To what extent do the articles stress assembly-line justice, discretion, or the courtroom work group? To what extent does the choice of problems reflect differences summarized by the due process versus crime control models of justice discussed in Chapter 1? Here are two suggestions: Stephen Pomper, "Reasonable Doubts," and Barbara Dority, "The U.S. Criminal Injustice System."

FOR FURTHER READING

Church, Thomas, and Milton Heumann. *Speedy Disposition: Monetary Incentives and Policy Reform in Criminal Courts.* Albany: State University of New York Press, 1992.

Harris, John, and Paul Jesilow. "It's Not the Old Ball Game: Three Strikes and the Courtroom Workgroup." *Justice Quarterly* 17 (2000): 185–204.

Hays, Steven, and Cole Graham, Jr., eds. *Handbook of Court Administration and Management.* New York: Marcel Dekker, 1992.

Lipetz, Marcia. "Routines and Deviations: The Strength of the Courtroom Workgroup in a Misdemeanor Court." *International Journal of the Sociology of Law* 8 (1980): 47–60.

Martin, John. *Strategic Planning in the Courts: Implementation Guide.* Denver: Center for Public Policy Studies, 1995.

Stojkovic, Stan, John Klofas, and David Kalinich, eds. *The Administration and Management of Criminal Justice Organizations,* 3d ed. Prospect Heights, IL: Waveland Press, 1999.

Walker, Samuel. *Taming the System: The Control of Discretion in Criminal Justice, 1950–1990.* New York: Oxford University Press, 1993.

Zaffarano, Mark. "Team Leadership: Using Self-Directed Work Teams in the Courts." *Justice System Journal* 17 (1995): 357–372.

Chapter 6 Prosecutors

PART II
Legal Actors

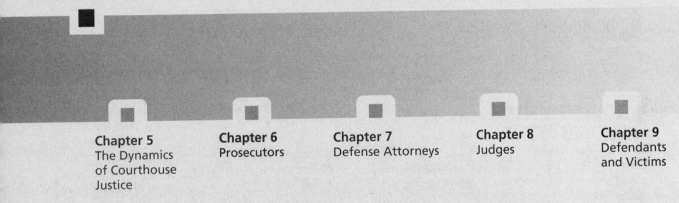

Chapter 5
The Dynamics of Courthouse Justice

Chapter 6
Prosecutors

Chapter 7
Defense Attorneys

Chapter 8
Judges

Chapter 9
Defendants and Victims

Even though it might result in some "incompetent, lousy prosecutors getting off," prosecutors should be immune from civil lawsuits, argued an assistant solicitor general in the first Bush administration. Granting total immunity to prosecutors will only result in "shredding the Constitution to tiny bits," countered the lawyer for Cathy Burns. At issue was the conduct of Chief Deputy Prosecutor Rick Reed of Muncie, Indiana, who had given poor legal advice to the police. As a result, Cathy Burns had been held on attempted murder charges (later dropped), partly because the prosecutor deliberately misled the trial court judge (Campbell 1990). ◀

MAKE SURE YOU KNOW PROSECUTOR

The difficulties the nation's highest court faced in trying to draw the line between permissible advocacy and prosecutorial misconduct underscores the influential role prosecutors play in the criminal justice system. More so than judges and defense attorneys, the prosecutor is the most powerful official in the criminal courts. From initial arrest to final disposition, how the prosecutor chooses to exercise discretion determines to a large extent which defendants are prosecuted, the type of bargains that are struck, and the severity of the sentence imposed.

This chapter discusses several factors involved in the work of the prosecutor. We begin by examining the prosecutor's role in the criminal justice system and then consider separately the structure of federal and state prosecutors' offices. Our focus then shifts to actual courtroom behavior, looking at prosecutors at work. But prosecutors do not work in isolation. Thus, the later parts of this chapter look at prosecutors within the context of the courtroom work group and their expanding domain in the criminal justice system.

ROLE OF THE PROSECUTOR

The prosecutor is of critical importance because of the office's central position in the criminal justice system. Whereas police, defense attorneys, judges, and probation officers specialize in specific phases of the criminal justice process, the duties of the prosecutor bridge all of these areas. This means that on a daily basis the prosecutor is the only official

who works with all actors of the criminal justice system. As Justice Robert Jackson once remarked, "The prosecutor has more control over life, liberty, and reputation than any other person in America."

Prosecutors stand squarely in the middle of the fragmented nonsystem of criminal justice discussed in Chapter 1. Naturally, the various actors have conflicting views about how prosecutorial discretion should be used—the police push for harsher penalties, defense attorneys for giving their clients a break, and judges to clear the docket. Thus, prosecutors occupy a uniquely powerful and highly visible position in a complex and conflict-filled environment. Amid the diffusion of responsibility that characterizes the criminal justice system, power has increasingly been concentrated in the hands of the prosecutor (Misner 1996).

Broad Discretion

A key characteristic of the American prosecutor is broad discretion. Although the prosecutor works in the courthouse, the office of prosecutor is part of the executive branch of government. This independence from the judiciary is vital for the proper functioning of the adversary system, since prosecutors at times challenge judicial decisions. The breadth of prosecutorial power stems from numerous court cases since 1833. Typical is *People v. Wabash, St. Louis and Pacific Railway*, an 1882 decision in which the Illinois Court of Appeals stated that the district attorney "is charged by law with large discretion in prosecuting offenders against the law. He may commence public

Exhibit 6-1 Role of the Prosecutor in Steps of Criminal Procedure

	Law on the Books	Law in Action
Crime	Must enforce all laws to the fullest.	The impossible legal mandate means that priorities must be established.
Arrest	Little involvement.	In major crimes, may advise the police whether there is sufficient evidence of probable cause to arrest.
Initial appearance	Represents the government.	Manages the chaos in the lower court, where there are many cases and little is known about the crime or the defendant.
Bail	Can make a bail recommendation to the judge.	Typically recommends a high bail amount to the judge.
Charging	Exclusive domain of the prosecutor.	Often decides which defendants will be charged with what crime.
Preliminary hearing	Dominates this step because of authority to call witnesses.	Highly successful in having defendants bound over for further proceedings.
Grand jury	Acts as legal adviser to the grand jury.	Largely decides which cases will be heard and indicted.
Arraignment	Formally presents the charges against the defendant in open court.	By taking the case this far, the prosecutor has indicated that the defendant very likely will be found guilty.
Evidence		
Discovery	Important variations in state law regarding how much information must be disclosed prior to trial.	Informally provides trusted defense attorneys with information to induce a plea of guilty.
Suppression motions	Argues that police acted legally in searching and/or interrogating the suspect.	Argues that police acted legally in searching for evidence to be admitted.
Plea bargaining	DAs have considerable discretion in plea bargaining.	Based on normal penalties, dictates the terms under which defendant pleads guilt.
Trial	Presents witnesses proving defendant guilty and urges jury to return a verdict of guilty.	Very successful in gaining convictions.
Sentencing	In many jurisdictions, the DA can make a sentencing recommendation to the judge.	Judge is more likely to follow the DA's sentencing recommendation that the defense attorney's.
Appeal	Argues before the appellate court why the lower court conviction should stand, and often wins.	Wins a significant victory in most appeals.

prosecutions . . . and may discontinue them when, in his judgment the ends of justice are satisfied." In decisions like this one, appellate courts have allowed the modern prosecuting attorney to exercise virtually unfettered discretion relating to initiating, conducting, and terminating prosecutions (Jacoby 1980; Albonetti 1987). Exhibit 6-1 provides an overview of the role of the prosecutor throughout the criminal justice process.

It is only during the trial itself that appellate courts have placed restrictions on the exercise of prosecutorial power. In the context of the adversary system, the prosecutor is expected to advocate the guilt of the defendant vigorously. But the prosecutor is also a lawyer and is therefore an **officer of the court;** that is, he or she has a duty to see that justice is done. Violations of the law must be prosecuted, but in a way that guarantees that the defendant's rights are respected and protected. In 1935 the Supreme Court spelled out the limitations imposed on prosecutors by their obligation as officers of the court: "He may prosecute with earnestness and vigor—indeed, he should do so. But while he may strike hard blows, he is not at liberty to strike foul ones. It is as much his duty to refrain from improper methods calculated to produce a wrongful conviction as it is to use every legitimate means to bring about a just one" (*Berger v. U.S.* 1935).

In recent years, the Supreme Court has expressed repeated concern about prosecutorial misconduct. Convictions have been reversed because prosecutors were too zealous in their advocacy. But at the same time, the nation's highest tribunal has also decided that prosecutors enjoy absolute immunity from civil lawsuits when acting as courtroom advocates. However, under other conditions, prosecutors may be sued civilly (see Case Close-up: *Burns v. Reed* and Prosecutorial Misconduct).

Decentralization

Another characteristic of the office of prosecutor is decentralized organization. Although the American prosecutor represents the state in the prosecution of criminal cases, the office is not centralized, as it is in England and most of Europe (Flemming 1990). Instead, prosecution is highly decentralized; there are more than 8,000 federal, state, county, municipal, and township prosecution agencies.

Commensurate with the nation's often confusing dual court system, separate prosecutors are found in federal and state courts. The structure, however, is not parallel with court structure; that is, each court does not have attached to it a specific prosecutor. District attorneys, for example, often conduct the trial in the trial court of general jurisdiction and then appeal through both layers of state courts and, on rare occasions, even to the U.S. Supreme Court (a federal judicial body).

Moreover, different prosecutors' offices may handle the same case; sometimes, the city attorney conducts the preliminary stages of a felony case in the lower courts and the district attorney prosecutes in the trial court of general jurisdiction.

Exhibit 6-2 provides a rough overview of typical state and federal prosecutorial structure. Be aware, however, that the apparent hierarchy of prosecutorial structure is an illusion. In the federal courts, the U.S. attorneys enjoy considerable autonomy from the U.S. Justice Department, and in the states, local district attorneys are totally separate from state attorneys general. We will begin with prosecution in federal courts and then turn to the more complex realities of state prosecutions.

PROSECUTION IN FEDERAL COURTS

Prosecutions in federal courts are conducted by the U.S. Department of Justice. Billed as the world's largest law firm, the Department of Justice represents the U.S. government in all legal matters not specifically delegated to other agencies. The department is headed by the **U.S. attorney general,** who is a member of the president's cabinet. Top-level officials are presidential appointees who reflect the views of the administration on important policy issues. Day-to-day activities are carried out by a large cadre of career lawyers who enjoy civil service protection and have, over the years, developed invaluable expertise in particular areas of law (Landsberg 1993, 276).

The Department of Justice has grown tremendously in recent years. As a direct result of the nation's continuing focus on crime as a major political issue, the Justice Department quadrupled in size from 1981 to 1993 (McGee and Duffy 1997). The nation's efforts to combat terrorism will likewise lead to further expansion.

The Department of Justice is a sprawling series of bureaucracies including investigatory and law enforcement offices such as the FBI, the Drug Enforcement Administration (DEA), the U.S. Marshals Service, and the Federal Bureau of Prisons. Also in the Department of

Burns v. Reed and Prosecutorial Misconduct

On the evening of September 2, 1982, Cathy Burns called the Muncie, Indiana, police and reported that an unknown assailant had entered her house, knocked her unconscious, and shot her two sons while they slept. The police came to view Burns as their primary suspect, even though they had no physical evidence to support their conclusion. Speculating that Burns had multiple personality disorder, the officers decided to interview her under hypnosis, but they were concerned that hypnosis might be an unacceptable investigative technique. They therefore sought the advice of Rick Reed, chief deputy prosecutor, Delaware County, Indiana, who told the officers they could proceed with the hypnosis. Under hypnosis, Burns allegedly confessed, but neither the police nor the district attorney informed the judge that the "confession" was obtained under hypnosis (and therefore not admissible).

Cathy Burns spent four months in the psychiatric ward of a state hospital. During this time, she was fired from her job as a dispatcher with the Muncie Police Department and the state obtained temporary custody of her sons. Medical experts concluded that she did not have multiple personalities, and she was released. The criminal charges against her were later dropped when the judge ruled that the evidence obtained under hypnosis was not admissible.

Cathy Burns filed a civil rights suit (section 1983, discussed in Chapter 2) in the U.S. District Court for the Southern District of Indiana. Before trial, the Muncie Police Department settled for $250,000 (Campbell 1991). But the court dismissed Burns's suit against the DA, holding that Reed enjoyed absolute immunity, a position upheld by the U.S. Court of Appeals for the Seventh Circuit (894 F.2d 949, 1990).

In situations like this, should the DA be immune from a civil lawsuit? Yes, said the Supreme Court, arguing that without this type of legal protection, prosecutors would hesitate to provide legal advice for fear of being harassed by civil lawsuits. Prosecutors enjoy immunity for their actions during trial and pretrial court proceedings. Therefore, Reed could not be sued for his actions in supporting the application for a search warrant and presenting evidence at the probable cause hearing. But there are limits, the Court decided: Advising police during the investigative phase of criminal cases was not intimately associated with the judicial phase of the criminal process. Therefore, Reed was potentially liable for the legal advice he provided the police.

The Court revisited the issue two years later and laid down a slightly more discernable line of permissible and impermissible conduct. The Court restated that prosecutors have absolute immunity from civil damage suits for actions in connection with the traditional role of courtroom advocacy. But DAs enjoy only "qualified immunity" for other actions. The Court unanimously held that statements made in a news conference were not protected by absolute immunity. But the justices split 5-4 on whether investigative actions by the DA were subject to suit. The bare majority held, "There is a difference between the advocate's role in evaluating evidence, and interviewing witnesses as he prepares for trial . . . and the detective's role in searching for the clues and corroboration that might give him probable cause to recommend that a suspect be arrested" (*Buckley v. Fitzsimmons* 1993).

Justice is the Office of Justice Programs, which oversees Bureau of Justice Assistance and other entities.

In terms of prosecution, three entities—solicitor general, criminal division, and U.S. attorneys—are particularly important. We will examine them from the top down, although, as we shall see, there is no hierarchy and considerable autonomy.

Solicitor General

The **solicitor general** is the third-ranking official in the Justice Department. The solicitor general's principal task is to represent the executive branch before the Supreme Court. But at the same time, the justices depend on the solicitor general to look beyond the government's narrow interest. Because of the solicitor general's dual

Exhibit 6-2	Overview of Prosecutors in the Dual Court System

Federal	State
Solicitor general	**Attorney general**
Represents the U.S. government before the U.S. Supreme Court in all appeals of federal criminal cases.	Chief legal officer of the state.
	Civil duties more extensive than criminal.
Often appears as amicus in appeals involving state criminal convictions.	Has limited authority in criminal prosecutions.
Criminal division	**Chief prosecutor**
Prosecutes a few nationally significant criminal cases.	Has great autonomy in prosecuting felony cases.
Exercises nominal supervision over U.S. attorneys.	Typically argues cases on appeal.
U.S. attorney	**Local prosecutor**
Prosecutes the vast majority of criminal cases in federal courts.	Handles preliminary stages of felony cases.
Enjoys great autonomy in actions.	Prosecutes the large volume of cases in the lower court.

To learn more about the vast bureaucracies included in the U.S. Department of Justice, click on http://www.usdoj.gov/.

responsibility to the judicial and executive branches, the officeholder is sometimes called the Tenth Justice, an informal title that underlines the special relationship with the Supreme Court (Caplan 1988; Meinhold and Shull 1993).

The office of the solicitor general is in essence a small, elite, very influential law firm whose client is the U.S. government. The staff consists of 23 of the most able attorneys found anywhere. As the representative of the United States in litigation before the Supreme Court, the solicitor general's office argues all government cases before the Court. For example, the assistant solicitor general argued the major issues in *Burns v. Reed*. But the influence of the office extends further.

Roughly half the work of the solicitor general's office involves coordinating appeals by the federal government. With few exceptions, all government agencies must first receive authorization from the solicitor general to appeal an adverse lower court ruling to the Supreme Court. The office requests Supreme Court review only in cases with a high degree of policy significance and in which the government has

a reasonable legal argument. In turn, the solicitor general has a high rate of success in petitioning the Supreme Court and in winning cases argued on their merits.

Criminal Division of the Justice Department

The criminal division formulates criminal law enforcement policies over all federal criminal cases, except those specifically assigned to other divisions. The criminal division, with the U.S. attorneys, has the responsibility for overseeing criminal matters under more than 900 statutes, as well as certain civil litigation. The criminal division is organized into a number of units that handle matters such as fraud, organized crime, and public integrity. Several of the units deal with international matters and have become more visible with U.S. efforts to fight terrorism.

Criminal division attorneys prosecute many nationally significant cases—for example, the Unabomber and the Oklahoma City bombing. In the wake of 9/11, the criminal division has directed prosecutions of several alleged terrorists and overseen the detainment of enemy noncombatants on federal military bases. Through the years, the criminal division has also received extensive press coverage for cases involving corrupt government officials, alleged members of organized crime, and major drug-dealing enterprises.

U.S. Attorneys

The **U.S. attorneys** serve as the nation's principal litigators under the direction of the attorney general. Ninety-three U.S. attorneys are stationed throughout the United States, Puerto Rico, the Virgin Islands, Guam, and the Northern Mariana Islands.

U.S. attorneys are appointed by, and serve at the discretion of, the president, with the advice and consent of the Senate. One U.S. attorney is assigned to each of the judicial districts, with the exception of Guam and the Northern Mariana Islands, where one serves in both districts. Each U.S. attorney is the chief federal law enforcement officer of the United States within his or her particular jurisdiction. The 93 U.S. attorneys are assisted by 4,700 assistant U.S. attorneys, who increasingly have become career employees (Lochner 2002).

U.S. attorneys represent the federal government in court in many matters. They have three statutory responsibilities:

- Prosecution of criminal cases brought by the federal government
- Initiation and defense of civil cases in which the United States is a party
- Collection of certain debts owed the federal government

The volume of litigation varies considerably among the districts. U.S. attorneys along the Mexican border, for example, initiate a large number of drug prosecutions. Nonetheless, each district handles a mixture of simple and complex litigation. U.S. attorneys exercise wide discretion in the use of their resources to further the priorities of local jurisdictions and the needs of their communities. According to the U.S. Department of Justice Web site, "United States Attorneys have been delegated, and will continue to be delegated, full authority and control in the areas of personnel management, financial management, and procurement." Although the criminal division supervises all federal prosecutions, in practice U.S. attorneys enjoy considerable autonomy. This is partly because of remoteness from Washington, D.C.— the 93 U.S. attorneys are widely dispersed geographically. The selection process also plays a role. Many U.S. attorneys owe their appointments primarily to persons other than the attorney general or, in some cases, even the president (Bell 1993). Thus, in the vast majority of cases, the decisions are made by U.S. attorneys scattered across the nation rather than by the central office based in Washington, D.C.

PROSECUTION IN STATE COURTS

Decentralization and local autonomy characterize prosecution in state courts. The result is divided responsibility, with state prosecution authority typically found in three separate offices: state, county (or district), and local. At times, the relationship among these separate agencies is marked by competition; various prosecutors jockey to be the first to prosecute a notorious defendant. We will examine the three major state prosecutors from the top down, but bear in mind that each office is separate and not necessarily subject to the dictates of the office above it.

State Attorney General

The position of attorney general, the state's chief legal officer, is typically spelled out in the state's constitution. Among the most important duties are providing legal advice to other state agencies and representing the state in court when state actions are challenged. In recent years, attorneys general have focused on their civil responsibilities by emphasizing their role in protecting consumers from various forms of fraud. Thus, the typical home page of the attorney general of a state proclaims how many individual consumer complaints (many of which involve motor vehicles and home repair fraud)

| Exhibit **6-3** | Chief Prosecutors Who Handle Felony Cases in State Courts |

Title	States
District attorney	Alabama, California, Colorado, Georgia, Kansas,* Louisiana, Maine, Massachusetts, Mississippi, Nevada, New Mexico, New York, North Carolina, Oklahoma, Oregon, Pennsylvania, Texas,* Wisconsin, Wyoming*
County attorney	Arizona, Iowa, Kansas,* Minnesota, Montana, Nebraska, New Hampshire, Texas,* Utah
State's attorney	Connecticut, Florida, Illinois, Maryland, North Dakota, South Dakota, Vermont
Prosecuting attorney	Arkansas, Hawaii, Idaho, Indiana, Michigan, Missouri,* Ohio, Washington, West Virginia
Commonwealth attorney	Kentucky, Virginia
County prosecutor	New Jersey
District attorney general	Tennessee
County and prosecuting attorney	Wyoming*
Solicitor	South Carolina
Circuit attorney	Missouri* (City of St. Louis)
No local prosecutor	Alaska, Delaware, Rhode Island

*Kansas, Missouri, Texas, and Wyoming use varying names depending on the jurisdiction.

SOURCE: DeFrances, Carol, "Prosecutors in State Courts, 2001," *Bulletin* (Washington, DC: Bureau of Justice Statistics, National Institute of Justice, 2002).

are handled annually. Many state attorneys general have also been visible in filing consumer lawsuits against major U.S. businesses. The biggest of all involves the suits by more than 30 states against the tobacco industry.

State attorneys general have chosen to emphasize their civil responsibilities because they typically have limited authority over criminal matters. Local autonomy is a key characteristic of the office of prosecutor. Generally, state officials do not monitor the activities of local prosecutors. Although the **state attorney general** is the state's chief law enforcement official, his or her authority over local criminal procedures is quite limited. Indeed, in a handful of states, the attorney general has no legal authority to initiate or intervene in local prosecutions. In other states, this authority is limited to extreme situations.

Thus, the state attorney general exercises virtually no control or supervision over chief prosecutors at the county level. This lack of supervisory power, coupled with the decentralization of the office, means that local prosecutors enjoy almost total autonomy. Only the local voters have the power to evaluate the prosecutor's performance, by means of their votes.

Chief Prosecutor

The American prosecutor has few direct parallels elsewhere in the world (Flemming 1990). Compared to their counterparts in England and Europe, American prosecutors enjoy unmatched independence and discretionary powers (Albonetti 1987).

Variously called the district attorney, county attorney, or prosecuting attorney (see Exhibit 6-3), the **prosecutor** is the chief law enforcement official of the community. Altogether there are 2,341 chief prosecutors across the nation, employing a staff of almost 80,000. Structure and workload differ according to the

| Exhibit 6-4 | Profile of Chief Prosecutors' Offices |

| | | Population Served | | | |
	All offices	1,000,000+	250,000 to 999,999	Under 250,000	Part-time offices
Number of offices	2,341	34	194	1,581	532
Population served*	36,052	1,478,630	449,737	41,319	9,589
Staff size*	9	456	112	10	3
Salary of chief prosecutor*	$85,000	$136,700	$115,000	$90,000	$39,750
Total budget*	$318,000	$32,115,000	$6,100,000	$379,000	$95,000

*Medians

SOURCE: Carol DeFrances, "Prosecutors in State Courts, 2001." *Bulletin* (Washington, DC: Bureau of Justice Statistics, National Institute of Justice, 2002).

size of the population. The typical office serves a population of 36,000 people, with 250 adult felony cases in the district, a staff of 9, and a budget of $318,000. But deviations are readily apparent (DeFrances 2002). The great majority of the nation's prosecutors' offices are small ones (see Exhibit 6-4). Frequently, rural prosecutors are part-time officials who also engage in private law practice.

Elections are a key characteristic of the office of prosecutor, as 95 percent of chief prosecutors are locally elected officials who typically serve four-year terms. The exceptions are Alaska, Connecticut, Delaware, the District of Columbia, New Jersey, and Rhode Island, where chief prosecutors are either appointed or are members of the state attorney general's office.

Because of elections, the work of the American prosecutor is deeply set within the larger political process (Worden 1990). For a lawyer interested in a political career, the prosecutor's office offers a launching pad. Indeed, prosecutors "virtually own the politically potent symbols of 'law and order' politics" (Flemming, Nardulli, and Eisenstein 1992).

Numerous government officials—governors, judges, and legislators—have begun their careers as crusading prosecutors (Schlesinger 1966). Most prosecutors, however, do not plan to enter politics. Studies in Wisconsin and Kentucky, for example, indicated that more than half of the prosecutors had no further political ambitions. They viewed the office as useful for gaining visibility before establishing a private law practice (Jacob 1966; Engstrom 1971). Thus, after serving one or two terms in office, former district attorneys typically practice private law or assume other positions in the public sector—primarily judge (Jones 1994).

The tremendous power of the prosecutor means that political parties are very interested in controlling the office. The chief prosecutor has numerous opportunities for patronage. In some communities, partisan considerations play a large role in the hiring of assistant district attorneys (Eisenstein, Flemming, and Nardulli 1988). Political parties may also want one of their own serving as district attorney to guarantee that their affairs will not be closely scrutinized and to act as a vehicle for harassing the opposition.

Local Prosecutor

Little is known about the activities of local prosecutors—variously called city attorneys, solicitors, or the like—although recent estimates place their numbers at about 5,700. In some jurisdictions, **local prosecutors** are responsible for the preliminary stages of felony cases as they are processed in the lower courts. In these jurisdictions, it is the local prosecutor (not the chief prosecutor) who represents the government at the initial appearance, argues bond amounts, and conducts the preliminary hearing. These decisions may have important consequences for later stages of the felony prosecution, but the chief prosecutor's office has no direct control over these matters.

Local prosecutors, however, are primarily responsible for processing the large volume of minor criminal offenses disposed of in the lower courts. Public drunkenness, petty theft, disorderly conduct, and minor assaults are the staple of these judicial bodies (see Chapter 18).

THE PROSECUTOR'S OFFICE AT WORK

In the courtroom one's attention normally gravitates toward the individual lawyers as they call witnesses, ask questions, and cross-examine the opponent's witnesses. These individual activities, however, must be understood within the larger context in which they occur. The day-to-day work of the prosecutor's office is executed by more than 79,000 attorneys, investigators, and support staff. How these persons are hired, trained, and supervised has a major bearing on the exercise of prosecutorial discretion.

Assistant District Attorneys

Most assistant district attorneys (sometimes called deputy district attorneys) are hired immediately after graduation from law school or after a short time in private practice. Usually, they have attended local law schools rather than the nation's most prestigious law schools (whose graduates prefer higher-status, better-paying jobs in civil practice).

In the past, many prosecutors hired assistants on the basis of party affiliation and the recommendations of elected officials. Increasingly, however, greater stress is being placed on merit selection, a trend exemplified by the Los Angeles prosecutor's office—the nation's largest, with more than 1,000 lawyers—where hiring is done on a civil service basis.

The turnover rate among assistant district attorneys is high. Most serve an average of two to four years before entering private practice.

Low salaries are one reason for the high turnover. Although starting salaries are generally competitive with those in private law offices, the salary levels after a few years are markedly lower.

Turnover is also a product of assistants' growing tired of the job. With its never-ending stream of society's losers, the criminal courthouse can become a depressing place to work (see A Day in Court: The Good Fight Takes Its Toll). Moreover, regular trial work creates numerous physical and psychological pressures. In the words of a former New Orleans prosecutor, "The average trial assistant leaves work every day with a huge stack of papers under his arm. The grind can really wear you down. There's just too much work" (Perlstein 1990).

Although many assistants view their job as a brief waystation toward a more lucrative and more varied private practice, some see it as a permanent career position. In Wisconsin the average tenure is about six years, and perhaps just as important, some assistants advance to become the elected DA in their county, run for the position in a neighboring county, or make other lateral moves (Jones 1994). Across the nation, there is now a marked trend toward a prosecutorial "civil service," with assistants moving from office to office (Jones 2001).

Learning the Job

Law schools provide an overview of law on the books—criminal law, criminal procedure, evidence, and constitutional law, to name just a few. But they give their students very little exposure to law in action. Thus, the typical assistant DA comes to the job having little familiarity with the day-to-day realities of the profession. Here is how one lawyer described his first days on the job:

> For the first week or two, I went to court with guys who had been here. Just sat there and watched. What struck me was the amount of things he [the prosecutor] has to do in the courtroom. The prosecutor runs the courtroom. Although the judge is theoretically in charge, we're standing there plea bargaining and calling the cases at the same time and chewing gum and telling the people to quiet down and setting bonds, and that's what amazed

A DAY IN COURT

The Good Fight Takes Its Toll

 I chose to become an assistant district attorney for that most noble and banal of reasons: I wanted to help people. Growing up in New York City, I had always been appalled by the crime and thought I could do something about it. At law school graduation I was a fireball, full of energy and the conviction that I could make a difference. But I wasn't prepared for the kind of uphill battle I would face.

My colleagues and I jumped right into combat together, and for a while it was exhilarating. Our first year was a blur of thousands of misdemeanors and countless hours in court. Cases such as shoplifting, marijuana possession, and disorderly conduct landed on our desks in heaps and were disposed of in short order. We took our mission seriously and gave our all (at first) to insisting on a few more days of community service or a few more dollars in restitution. We were proud to be the good guys, and we had some great times together. Several nights a week we would make a beeline to the local bar to blow off steam, shoot some pool, and trade horror stories.

There were crazies of all kinds, like the defendant who mooned the judge or the guy who was convinced he was being stalked by Roberta Flack. We laughed through our exhausted haze and formed friendships that would last a lifetime. As we gained experience our cases got more serious, but the problems remained the same. A victim called police demanding that someone be arrested. A few days later, when the legal machine had been set in motion and that someone was in jail, the victim would refuse to cooperate. Others were too terrified to testify, and who could blame them? They knew all too well how the system worked and that there was no guarantee the defendants would stay in jail.

Star Witnesses

Then there were those who were a little too enthusiastic about testifying. An alarming number of people, I discovered, thought nothing of lying under oath for revenge in hopes of getting money in future civil lawsuits—or simply because they liked being the center of attention. I was suckered by a flaky yet sympathetic girl who wept in my office and showed me horrifying photos of bruises inflicted by her boyfriend. She was a nobody, and the boyfriend was wealthy and powerful. He was convicted based mainly on those photos and the testimony of the girl's friend. It was only months later, after the defense attorney hired an expert to examine the photos, that we realized they were fakes and our victim was a liar.

Witnesses were not our only frustration. Defense attorneys called us racists and zealots, and they reserved even worse epithets for the police. The judges indulged these attacks, which was even more infuriating. They sneered at us and scorned our determinedly polite requests for higher bail, longer sentences. In most courtrooms, there was no limit to what the defense could insinuate or even claim outright without a shred of evidence to back it up. Assistants who objected were silenced and overruled. Ridiculous requests for obscure, irrelevant paperwork were granted, delaying trials for days. Endless, frivolous motions were entertained, necessitating reams of wasted paper. We were expected to live up to an unrealistic standard, and as frustrating as that was, it was somehow a source of pride. Nobody in the outside world could ever comprehend what our lives were like. We stood up to unbelievable pressure, and we fought the good fight; in spite of the stress, we loved what we did.

Burnout Begins

I left all that behind when I experienced the predictable burnout. The bad times had begun to outweigh the good, and worse than that I had stopped caring. I dreaded what fresh horrors each day would bring instead of looking forward to the challenges. I was disillusioned and discouraged and really just wanted to wash my hands of the whole thing: the crumbling building, the endless parade of ruined lives and misery, the wasted time, the constant arguing.

So I turned in my badge and became a civilian. There wasn't that much about the office that I expected to miss. But I was wrong. I miss it every day—from the lousy coffee to the camaraderie of the court officers to the 2 A.M. giddiness of the complaint room. The work I have done since then feels like a pale shadow of the life I used to lead. And while the stress is gone, so too is the thrill. Nothing else will ever match the terror, the joy, the pride, and the sorrow I felt as an assistant district attorney in Manhattan.

SOURCE: Page Bondor, "The Good Fight Takes Its Toll," *ABA Journal* 86 (2000), 104. Used by permission.

Vertical + Horizontal

me. I never thought I would learn all the terms.

What bothered me also was the paperwork. Not the Supreme Court decisions, not the *mens rea* or any of this other stuff, but the amount of junk that's in those files that you have to know. We never heard about this crap in law school. (Heumann 1978, 94)

For decades, training in prosecutor's offices was almost exclusively on the job; it was not unusual for recent law school graduates with no experience to be sent into court on their first day on the job. One assistant summed up the office tradition as follows: "They have a very unique way of breaking people in. They say, 'Here's a file. There's the jury. Go try it.'" (Flemming, Nardulli, and Eisenstein 1992). More recently, large prosecutors' offices have begun to train new employees more systematically. After a week of general orientation to the different divisions of the office, new assistants are allowed to watch various proceedings and observe veteran trial attorneys at work.

New assistants quickly learn to ask questions of more experienced prosecutors, court clerks, and veteran police officers. Through this socialization process, assistants learn important unwritten rules about legal practice relating to what types of violations should be punished and the appropriate penalties to be applied to such violations. Assistants also learn that their performance (and chances for promotion) are measured by how promptly and efficiently they dispose of cases. They become sensitive to hints—for example, if a judge complains that a backlog is developing because prosecutors are bringing too many minor cases, the new assistant usually gets the message that his or her plea-bargaining demands are too high.

Promotions are also related to the candidate's reputation as a trial attorney. Assistants are invariably judged by the number of convictions they obtain. In the courthouse environment, however, not losing a case has a higher value than winning. Thus, assistants learn that if the guilt of the defendant is doubtful or the offender is not dangerous, it is better to negotiate a plea than to disrupt the courtroom routine by attempting to gain a jury conviction.

Promotions and Office Structure

As assistants gain experience and settle into the courthouse routine, they are promoted to more demanding and also more interesting tasks. Promotions are related to office structure (Flemming, Nardulli, and Eisenstein 1992). Small prosecutors' offices usually use vertical prosecution, in which one prosecutor is assigned responsibility for a case from intake to appeal (Nugent and McEwen 1988). In these offices, assistants are promoted by being assigned more serious cases. However, such an assignment system is administratively burdensome in large courthouses; assistants would spend much of their time moving from one courtroom to another and waiting for their one or two cases to be called. Therefore, most big-city prosecutors' offices use horizontal prosecution, in which prosecutors are assigned to specific functions, such as initial appearance, charging, preliminary hearing, grand jury, trial, or appeal. On a regular basis, one or two attorneys are systematically assigned to one courtroom with a given judge. Through time, prosecutors come to know the judge's views on sentencing and the like. Under horizontal prosecution, assistants are promoted by being assigned to courtrooms with more serious felonies.

Over the past decades, specialization has become increasingly common in chief prosecutors' offices, particularly in densely populated jurisdictions. Often it is the most experienced trial attorneys who staff these positions. Specialized units dealing with murder, sexual assault, armed robbery, and major drug crimes are the most prestigious, mainly because trial work is both plentiful and challenging.

Supervision

Assistant district attorneys are supervised by a section head, who is supposed to ensure that they follow policies of the office. However, for several reasons, assistant DAs enjoy fairly broad freedom.

Office policies are often general and somewhat vague. In small offices, they are seldom even put in writing. Official and unofficial policies are simply part of what the assistant learns informally; for this reason, it is hard for the bureau chief to enforce them. In large offices, decentralized work assignments mean that supervisors can exert only limited control over specific cases or individual assistants. Assistant district attorneys spend most of their time not in the central office but in the courtroom. Indeed, in crowded courthouses, trial assistants often have offices adjoining the judge's chambers and only rarely appear in the prosecutor's office at all. It is therefore difficult for supervisors to observe and monitor the assistant district attorney's activities. Each assistant has dozens of cases that require individual decisions on the basis of specific facts, unique witness problems, and so on. A supervisor has no way to monitor such situations except on the basis of what the assistant orally reports or writes in the file. Here, as elsewhere, information is power. Assistants can control their supervisors by selectively telling them what they think they should know (Neubauer 1974).

Attempts at Greater Supervision

The traditional form of prosecutorial management is centered on autonomy; each individual assistant district attorney is granted a great deal of freedom to make his or her own decisions. The Erie, Pennsylvania, DA's office is typical; it "promulgated few formal written policies, gave most of its assistants fairly wide latitude to dispose of cases in ways consistent with the general aim of the office, and relied on informal supervision" (Eisenstein, Flemming, and Nardulli 1988, 215).

Concerned that autonomy allows too much unchecked discretion, some prosecutors have attempted to exert greater supervision by adopting a rigid system of office policies. Some forbid any charge reductions whatsoever for some types of defendants (habitual offenders) and for serious charges such as violent offenses and major drug dealers (Eisenstein, Flemming, and Nardulli 1988). To ensure compliance with these detailed office policies, formal, detailed, bureaucratic enforcement mechanisms are imposed. Typical is DuPage County, Illinois, where the DA's office "was highly centralized, rigidly enforcing the 'bottom-line' pleas established by the indictment committee. The DA's office relied on a formally structured hierarchy to administer its policies" (215). Chief prosecutors believe that these management systems monitor prosecutorial discretion, minimize differences among individual assistants, and concentrate scarce crime-fighting resources (Jacoby 1980).

Attempts by supervisors to control the work of the assistants tend to erode the morale of the office. Office review of all case files (to ensure that policies have been followed) makes some assistants feel uncomfortable because they feel that they are not completely trusted. Reductions in individual discretion increase the general level of tension in the office. One trial assistant related how a colleague was summarily fired on the same day he violated office policy on plea bargaining. All the assistants resented and feared the administrator who fired him (Eisenstein, Flemming, and Nardulli 1988, 215).

PROSECUTORS AND COURTROOM WORK GROUPS

Prosecutors spend most of their time working directly with other members of the courtroom work group. Even when interviewing witnesses or conducting legal research, the prosecutor is anticipating the reactions of judges and defense attorneys. Thus, the activities of prosecutors can be understood only within the setting of the courtroom work group (Worden 1990).

The prosecutor is the most important member of the work group. Prosecutors set the agenda for judges and defense attorneys by exercising discretion over the types of cases filed, the nature of acceptable plea agreements, and the sentences to be handed out. Prosecutors also control the flow of information about cases by providing access to police arrest reports, laboratory tests, and defendants' past criminal histories. By stressing certain information or withholding other facts, prosecutors can influence the decisions of judges and defense attorneys.

As the dominant force in the courtroom work group, prosecutors clearly set the tone for plea bargaining. This is how one veteran explained his perspective:

I get so damned pissed off and tired of these guys who come in and cry, "My guy's got a job" or "My guy's about to join the army," when he's got a rap sheet as long as your arm. His guy's a loser, and he's wailing on my desk about what a fine man he is. What really wins me is the guy who comes in and says, "O.K., what are we going to do with my criminal today? I know he has no redeeming social value. He's been a bad son of a bitch all his life, so just let me know your position. But frankly, you know, my feeling is that this is just not the case to nail him on. We all know if he does something serious, he's going." And before long the guy who approaches it this way has you wrapped around his little finger. (Carter 1974, 87)

Prosecutors' actions, in turn, are influenced by other members of the courtroom work group. Through the socialization process, assistant district attorneys internalize the accepted ways of doing things in the courthouse, learning to plead cases out on the basis of normal crimes (discussed in Chapter 5). Prosecutors who stray too far from the shared norms of the courtroom work group can expect sanctions. The judge may informally indicate that the state is pushing too hard for a harsh sentence or may publicly chastise a district attorney in open court, thus threatening the attorney's status among peers. The defense attorney may not agree to a prosecutor's request for a continuance or may use delaying tactics to impair the state's efforts to schedule cases, thus further disrupting the prosecutor's efforts to move cases. (The prosecutor, of course, is not without countersanctions. These will be discussed in the next two chapters.)

Operating within the constraints of the courtroom work group, effective assistant DAs are those who make tactical decisions that maximize their objectives. Experienced prosecutors, for example, know which defense attorneys can be trusted, granting these people greater access to information about the case and listening to them more when the case involves unusual circumstances. Prosecutors also quickly learn the tendencies of the judge. No experienced prosecutor can afford to ignore how the judge wishes the courtroom to be run.

Although the prosecutor is generally the most important member of the courtroom work group, work groups show considerable variability. There are differences between one community and the next, and in big-city courthouses, there are often differences from court-room to courtroom. Conflicting goals and varying political styles are two factors that account for contrasting work groups.

Conflicting Goals and Contrasting Work Groups

On the surface, the goals of prosecutors seem the model of simplicity: Their job is to convict the guilty. But a closer examination shows that the goals are not as clear-cut as they first appear. Prosecutors define their main job in different ways. Some stress working closely with law enforcement agencies. Thus, they serve as police advocates in court and stress punishing the guilty. Others emphasize their role as court-based officials. Thus, they define their job as impartially administering justice and emphasize securing convictions (Eisenstein 1978; LaFave 1965).

The uncertainties about which goals should come first produce marked diversity among prosecutors (McDonald, 1979). A study of prosecutors' offices in San Diego and Oakland discovered contrasting operating styles (Utz, 1979). The prosecutor's office in San Diego reflects an adversarial model. Assistant district attorneys presume that cases are serious, they routinely overcharge, and they set plea-bargaining terms so high that many cases are forced to trial. Because there is a pronounced distrust of defense attorneys, plea bargaining involves a gamelike atmosphere. In general, the San Diego office is dedicated to the "full enforcement" of the law.

The operating style in Oakland, on the other hand, reflects an administration of justice model. Office policies determine which types of cases represent serious violations of the law and set strict standards in terms of charging. The office philosophy is that if the case is not "prison material," there should be no trial. Plea bargaining proceeds on the basis that defense attorneys are fellow professionals. Overall, there appears to be more of a search for the truth in Oakland than in San Diego.

Political Styles and Contrasting Work Groups

The prosecutor's role within the courtroom work group also needs to be understood within

THE MURDER TRIAL OF SHAREEF COUSIN

DA Harry Connick Defends His Aggressive Tactics

District Attorney Harry Connick, Sr., was a fixture in New Orleans political life for three decades. (His son, Harry Connick, Jr., is a popular musician and actor.) In 1973 he challenged embattled District Attorney Jim Garrison and won. New Orleans District Attorney Jim Garrison had arrested businessman Clay Shaw in 1965 on the charge of conspiracy to assassinate President John F. Kennedy. At first, Garrison spoke of a "homosexual thrill killing" but later expanded the investigation to include conspiracy theories. Two years later the jury deliberated less than an hour in acquitting Shaw. Nationally, the city became associated with conspiracy theories and government plots to kill the president. Locally, community leaders thought that Garrison had embarrassed the city and sought a candidate who would restore civic pride. Connick proved to be their man.

Throughout his long tenure as DA, Connick was often at the epicenter of controversy, mostly of his own making. Internally, some assistants chafed under his tight management control. One hardworking assistant who thought she was unfairly fired appealed all the way to the U.S. Supreme Court (only to lose). Externally, Connick was quick to condemn publicly those who didn't share his law-and-order philosophy. Numerous judges (some of whom had previously worked in his office) were singled out for harsh criticism.

By the mid-1990s the Orleans Parish district attorney was again attracting national attention, this time over the issue of prosecutorial misconduct and innocents on death row (see Chapter 17). In *Kyles v. Whitely* the U.S. Supreme Court used strong language to condemn the office for not disclosing exculpatory evidence in a death penalty case (see Chapter 12). After five trials, Connick eventually dismissed the charges in that case.

The same issue became pivotal in the murder trial of Shareef Cousin. On the night of the murder, Connie Babin told police that things were so confusing that she doubted she could identify the killer. Yet this key witness statement was not given to the defense. Connick and his assistants contended that they were under no legal obligation to disclose such information, but the vast majority of lawyers and judges strongly disagree.

The Shareef case is not the only case to cause Connick public embarrassment in recent years. A dying former prosecutor told his best friend that he had concealed evidence that could have cleared John Thompson, who had been convicted of murder and sentenced to death (Bell 2001). For the first time in his 25 years as district attorney, Connick asked a judge to put off the execution of a man his office had put on death row.

Harry Connick, Sr., easily won reelection in 1978, 1984, and 1990. But the 1996 campaign resembled a bare-knuckled political brawl, with the candidates attacking the fitness of their opponent to hold public office. The underlying issue was race. Connick, who is white, ran for reelection in a city with a 64 percent black voting population. His major challenger was former judge Morris Reed, an African American, who charged that Connick's office was racially biased and it was time to elect a black DA. Connick won, though, by putting together a biracial coalition, benefiting greatly from the backing of Mayor Marc Morial, the city's top black elected official.

In 2002, Connick retired. His successor is former U.S. Attorney Eddie Jordan, who is black. Jordan swiftly moved to hire more African Americans in the office and quietly reversed some of the office's most controversial anti–defense attorney positions.

A good Web site on New Orleans and the Garrison investigation can be accessed at http://mcadams.posc.mu.edu/garrison.htm. The home page of the New Orleans District Attorney is located at http://www.noda.new-orleans.la.us/. For more about the Shareef Cousin trial, go to http://cj.wadsworth.com/neubauer_courts8e.

the broader political context in which the office functions. This was the conclusion of Roy Flemming's (1990) study of nine prosecutors' offices in three states. Because they exercise broad discretion (in the context of decentralization and local autonomy), elected prosecutors choose political styles. This choice is both personal and strategic. It depends first on the prosecutor's satisfaction or dissatisfaction with the office's status within the courthouse community. It also depends on the prosecutor's perception of the value of conflict as a means of changing the office's status.

Prosecutors satisfied with the status of the office adopt an "office conservator" style. Office conservators accept the status quo. Continuity is often a key consideration; former assistants are elected with the blessings of the previous officeholder and the support of the local political establishment. Once in office, conservators do not deliberately step on toes; if they push for change, it generally comes as a response to the requests of others. Montgomery County, Pennsylvania, provides an example. The newly elected DA retained the preexisting staff intact. He did fashion some guidelines regarding guilty pleas, but they were flexible, symbolic gestures—signals that a changing of the guard had taken place, not a revolution. Most important, however, the DA tolerated the judges' traditional dominance of the courthouse community.

Prosecutors who are less content with the status of their offices face a more complicated set of choices. They must decide whether conflict is an effective tool for them to use.

Courthouse insurgents are very dissatisfied with the status quo and are prepared to do battle to change it. They do not shy away from open conflict, nor do they hesitate to challenge the courthouse community in pursuit of their goals. DuPage County, Illinois, is an example. The state's attorney was an outsider to the county who won the office by narrowly defeating the Republican party's favored candidate in a bitterly fought, mud-slinging primary. Perceiving that the office failed to stand up to defense attorneys, the new state's attorney turned the office inside out. Immediately after election, he eliminated the part-time staff, hired aggressive assistants, and instituted policies severely restricting plea bargaining. Moreover, the insurgent DA minced no words in publicly criticizing judges and defense attorneys.

Policy reformers are also dissatisfied with the status quo, but unlike courthouse insurgents, they are cautious, often conciliatory, in their approach. Upon taking office, they gradually move to tighten their offices' guilty plea policies, encourage more assertive attitudes among their assistants, and try to develop innovative approaches to prosecutorial work. They do not shrink from trying to alter their relationships with judges. Erie, Pennsylvania, provides a case in point. Embittered by the decline of the office when he left as an assistant to enter private practice, the new Erie prosecutor bucked the political establishment and decisively trounced the incumbent in the Democratic party primary to win the office. However, his plans to restore the respect of the office clashed with the docket policies of the court. Rather than fighting openly, the Erie DA mounted an indirect campaign to wrest control of the docket from the judges.

Flemming's study highlights two aspects of prosecutorial behavior that are not immediately obvious. First, differences in political styles cross party lines; these are not Republican or Democratic styles. Second, differences in political styles are not necessarily constant through time. In several communities, a district attorney was initially elected as an insurgent or a policy reformer but through the years came to adopt a conservator style.

THE EXPANDING DOMAIN OF THE PROSECUTOR

The domain of the prosecutor has been expanding throughout the past century, and pressures to place greater authority in the hands of the prosecutor are likely to continue (see Exhibit 6-5). Within the fragmented, sometimes nonsystem of criminal justice, the prosecutor is in the best position to provide coordination. Moreover, with crime as a dominant issue in elections, the prosecutor is uniquely able to capitalize on his or her role as the community's chief law enforcement official and to promise the voters to expand crime-fighting efforts. To sample the expanding domain of the prosecutor, take A Virtual Tour of American Courthouses: Prosecutors.

We will examine two types of programs that exemplify the contemporary expansion of the domain of the prosecutor: improving police–prosecutor relationships and community prosecution.

COURTS, CONTROVERSY, AND GENDER EQUITY

Are Sexual Assaults against Women Underprosecuted?

In *The Accused* (1988) Sarah Tobias (Jodie Foster) is raped by three men in a bar while several bystanders cheer on the assailants. Her sexual assault complaint is handled by Kathryn Murphy (Kelly McGillis), an assistant district attorney who sees showing compassion to crime victims as an impediment to her principal task of winning at all costs in the arena of the courtroom. Winning this case will be extremely difficult. Sarah had been drinking the night of the assault, her live-in boyfriend is a drug dealer, and she had flirted with one of her assailants before the assault. Because her questionable moral character severely weakens the prospects of victory, the district attorney plea-bargains the case down to "aggravated assault."

To some, this fictional account of a sexual assault comes too close to reality. The movie portrays Sarah as victimized twice—assaulted by the rapist the first time and the legal system the second.

Sexual assault is one of the most visible gender-equity controversies in the criminal justice system. Along with domestic violence (see Chapter 9) and gender bias in the courtroom (Chapter 5), it is the topic that feminists have most identified as involving systematic bias throughout the criminal justice system.

A report of the U.S. Senate Judiciary Committee—*The Response to Rape: Detours on the Road to Equal Justice* (1993)—forcefully concludes that the justice system creates serious barriers to women who are sexually assaulted. For one, many of the 876,000 sexual assaults occurring every year are not prosecuted (Bureau of Justice Statistics, 1995). According to this line of thinking, prosecutors and police are prone to view allegations of rape skepti-

cally. There is a widespread belief that many allegations of rape are false, even though the FBI reports that false allegations occur in only 2 percent of all reported cases.

But not all are convinced that the evidence supports the allegation that sexual assaults are underprosecuted. Skeptics counter that rape rates have declined by more than 50 percent in recent years (Bureau of Justice Statistics 2003). Nor is there evidence that the "moral character" of the victim plays a significant role. A study in Detroit assessed the influence of blame and responsibility factors in decisions of police and prosecutor to go to court. The authors concluded that there is little evidence that victim characteristics affected case outcomes. Rather, the presence of evidence—the victim's ability to identify her assailant, for example—was the dominant reason that cases were prosecuted or not (Horney and Spohn 1996).

What do you think? Are sexual assaults underprosecuted or not? If so, is the reason because criminal justice officials fail to adequately consider the plight of the victim or because these cases are more likely to have evidence problems?

 The following articles available on InfoTrac College Edition provide important information on the topic:

Cathy Young, "Excluded Evidence: The Dark Side of Rape Shield Laws"

Ronet Bachman, "The Factors Related to Rape Reporting Behavior and Arrest"

Janice Du Mont and Terri L. Myhr, "So Few Convictions: The Role of Client-Related Characteristics in the Legal Processing of Sexual Assault"

Gloria Cowan, "Beliefs about the Causes of Four Types of Rape"

Improving Police–Prosecutor Relationships

Police and prosecutors are commonly viewed as members of the same crime-fighting team, but a closer look reveals a more complex reality. Police and prosecutors have differing perspectives on the law. To the police, the case is

closed when the suspect is arrested, but prosecutors stress that they often need additional information to win in court (Stanko 1981).

Inadequate police reports present a classic illustration of noncoordination within the criminal justice system. The thoroughness of police investigations and the quality of their arrests directly affect the likelihood of the

Exhibit **6-5**	Key Developments Concerning the Prosecutor	
Berger v. United States	1935	The prosecutor's primary interest is in doing justice, not simply winning cases.
Imbler v. Pachtman	1976	Prosecutors enjoy absolute immunity from civil liability when initiating and pursuing a criminal prosecution.
Morrison v. Olson	1988	Independent counsel law is constitutional.
Burns v. Reed	1991	Prosecutors enjoy only qualified immunity from lawsuits concerning advice given to the police.
Buckley v. Fitzsimmons	1993	Prosecutors enjoy only qualified immunity from civil lawsuits for actions during criminal investigations and statements made during news conferences.
Kalina v. Fletcher	1997	A prosecutor may be sued for making false statements of fact in an affidavit in support of an arrest warrant.

prosecutor's obtaining a conviction. In a survey of 225 (mostly big-city) prosecutors, 66 percent cited inadequate police preparation of crime reports as a major problem in their offices (Nugent and McEwen 1988). Among commonly mentioned problems were that names and addresses of victims and witnesses were lacking, full details of how the crime was committed were missing, and vital laboratory reports were not forwarded on time. Faced with incomplete or inaccurate police reports, the prosecutor may be forced to drop charges (see Chapter 10).

Police and prosecutors in several jurisdictions have adopted strategies to improve coordination and communication among themselves (Buchanan 1989). In Indianapolis, for example, the prosecutor has funded a computer message system that enables attorneys in the office to transmit notes, case dispositions, and subpoenas directly to police officers at their work location. In Alameda County, California, and Montgomery County, Maryland, "street jump" narcotics officers and prosecutors consult frequently, both in person and over the telephone, to build cases that meet the requirements of the search-and-seizure law.

A few agencies have gone further, institutionalizing teamwork and making communication between investigators and prosecutors a top priority. In Multnomah County, Oregon, the Organized Crime/Narcotics Task Force has brought together 12 investigators from several area agencies and 2 prosecutors from the district attorney's office. There is daily informal contact about the progress of pending cases. Moreover, prosecutors act as consultants to the police during the investigative phase. Thus, investigators can get answers to difficult legal questions in a few minutes, just by walking down the hall.

Programs like these indicate that, despite a long history of difficulties, some agencies apparently are bridging the gap. But a word of caution is in order. No research to date has systematically evaluated these programs to indicate their overall effectiveness. Until such research is conducted, there is no way of knowing which programs may or may not prove effective in other communities.

Community Prosecution

The historic image of the district attorney stresses case processing: The DA files charges and doggedly pursues a conviction. But this traditional image is becoming blurred as locally elected prosecutors respond to a wide variety of social problems such as domestic violence (Chapter 9), drug abuse (Chapter 10), disorder on city streets (Chapter 18), and growing numbers of juvenile offenders (Chapter 19). In responding to these types of social problems, which often reflect disintegrating neighbor-

A Virtual Tour of American Courthouses: Prosecutors

Lawyer shows have long been a staple of American television. For the latest offerings, point your browser to **http://dir.yahoo.com/Entertainment/Television_Shows/Dramas/Lawyer_Shows/**. In an earlier era, the defense attorney was often the hero, fighting to prove his client innocent. More recently, however, crusading DAs have become the focal point, seeking to punish the bad guys, often by defeating the sly and unscrupulous tactics of the defense. A long-running drama of this type is *Law and Order*, which has several Web sites, including **http://www.uni-television.com/laworder/**.

Prosecutors' offices increasingly maintain Web sites that offer insight into the more prosaic activities of real-life prosecutors. To locate the Web page of the U.S. attorney in your area, go to the following address: **http://www.usdoj.gov/usao/eousa/usa_websites.html**. To find the home page of your state attorney general, click on **http://www.naag.org/index2.html** and then go to "About Your Attorney General." Ask yourself, What is the balance in workload between civil and criminal matters?

The bulk of serious criminal cases are prosecuted by locally elected district attorneys. Here are four prosecutors' offices with informative Web sites:

Marion County (Indiana)
http://www.ci.indianapolis.in.us/pros/index.htm

San Angelo (Texas)
http://www.tgcl.co.tom-green.tx.us/datty/

Mercer County (New Jersey)
http://www.mercerpros-nj.com/

Morris County (New Jersey)
http://www.morrisnjpros.org/

The latest reform (or some would say fad) is community prosecution. To learn more about community prosecution across the nation, go to the following:

National Center for Community Prosecution
http://www.ndaa-apri.org/apri/programs/community_pros/cp_home.html

Indianapolis
http://www.ci.indianapolis.in.us/pros/street_level_advocacy.htm

Washington, D.C.
http://www.usdoj.gov/usao/dc/cp/cp.html

Maryland
http://www.lib.jjay.cuny.edu/len/97/10oct/html/feature.html

For an up-to-date list of Web links, go to **http://cj.wadsworth.com/neubauer_courts8e**.

---

hoods, prosecutors today are more likely to stress problem-oriented approaches. At times the specifics are hard to pin down because the approaches are truly shaped to local needs rather than national program guides (Coles and Earle 1996). But these new approaches have three elements in common (Jacoby 1995):

■ Crime prevention is recognized as a legitimate prosecutorial goal.

■ The most effective results are obtained within small, manageable geographic areas.

■ Change is more likely to occur through cooperative efforts or partnerships, rather than prosecutorial dictates.

The Neighborhood District Attorney approach in Multnomah County (Portland, Oregon) provides a case in point. Business leaders in Lloyd District (an inner-city neighborhood) called for more police protection as well as the assignment of a special prosecutor to the district (for which they provided one year's funding). Citizen demands were invariably expressed in traditional law enforcement terms—more police, more arrests, and more convictions, particularly of repeat offenders. The Lloyd District special prosecutor, however, quickly saw that people's concerns were more immediate than he had imagined. "They wanted something done about prostitution, public drinking, drug use,

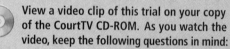

COURT TV
Michigan v. Budzyn: What Killed Malice Green?

Two white Detroit police officers were tried for bludgeoning to death an African-American outside a crack house. Police saw a violent criminal but the community saw police brutality. To the defendants, racial politics, not justice, was the dominant reality.

Michigan v. Budzyn provides a good illustration of many issues facing the nation's criminal justice system because the typical roles of police and accused criminal are reversed.

After the jury found both officers guilty, Budzyn's conviction was reversed by the Michigan Supreme Court and Nevers' conviction was reversed by the U.S. District Court.

View a video clip of this trial on your copy of the CourtTV CD-ROM. As you watch the video, keep the following questions in mind:

1. What aspects of this case would proponents of the crime control model of criminal justice emphasize?

2. What aspects of this case would advocates of the due process model of criminal justice stress?

3. How does this case illustrate the key steps of the criminal justice process?

4. How does this case illustrate the roles played by the major actors in the criminal justice process?

5. How do community attitudes affect the prosecution of the case?

vandalism, [minor] assaults, littering garbage, and 'car prowls' (thefts from cars)" (Boland 1996, 36). Although none of these problems (except thefts from cars) fits traditional notions of serious crime, they nonetheless raise serious concern among citizens. (This approach clearly emphasizes the activities of the local courts, discussed in Chapter 18.)

As the program developed, several distinctive features became apparent. For one, the assistant DA used the laws in new ways, including using civil remedies to fight crime (see Chapter 2). Perhaps most important, the program was problem-oriented: Rather than focusing on individual arrestees, the Neighborhood District Attorney addressed problems from a larger perspective, with long-term goals in mind. Ultimately what emerged was an approach, not a program. Rather than being guided by clear-cut procedures, Portland has adopted a highly flexible organization that can meet the different needs of different neighborhoods (Boland 1996).

Overall, community prosecution stresses a proactive approach: Rather than reacting to crime through prosecution, these programs stress crime prevention (Coles and Kelling 1999). And often the crimes stressed are minor ones that are nonetheless serious irritants to local residents (Goldkamp, Irons-Guynn, and Weiland 2002).

▌CONCLUSION

The impact of *Burns v. Reed* is still unfolding. Carol Burns was last reported working as a supervisor in a discount department store in Muncie, richer by her civil settlement with the police (minus lawyers' fees). Her suit against Reed, however, was still pending: The nation's highest court held only that she had a right to sue, not that she would win that suit. As for Rick Reed, the aftermath has been more promising: He is now the district attorney for Delaware County, Indiana, the voters evidently not convinced that his behavior was out of line.

From a broader perspective, *Burns v. Reed* and other lawsuits claiming prosecutorial misconduct are likely to have minimal impact. For years courts have granted prosecutors wide-ranging discretionary powers. The exercise of this discretion shapes the dynamics of the courthouse. In effect, all others involved in the criminal courts—judges, defense attorneys, probation officers, juries, witnesses, and so on—must react to the decisions made by the prosecutor. But the law imposes few formal restrictions on the use of these discretionary powers. Prosecutors' offices are decentralized, autonomous, and headed by locally elected officials.

This does not mean that prosecutorial discretion is uncontrolled; rather, it is influenced by other members of the courtroom work group. Through the socialization process and the occasional application of sanctions, new prosecutors are educated in the norms of the courtroom work group.

CRITICAL THINKING QUESTIONS

1. Robert Misner (1996) argues that given the fragmented nature of the criminal justice system (see Chapter 1), over the past 30 years responsibility has increasingly been centralized in the hands of the district attorney. What factors support this assessment?

2. Should state attorneys general be given authority to supervise locally elected district attorneys? How would such increased authority alter the criminal justice system?

3. How much authority should assistant district attorneys be given? As licensed attorneys, should they be given a large amount of discretion to dispose of cases according to their best judgment, or should they have more limited authority so that the office has a uniform policy?

4. Of the three political styles—office conservator, courthouse insurgent, and policy reformer—which best describes your local prosecutor?

5. Community prosecution stresses the need for the prosecutor to reach out to the community, but what does "community" mean? Is this reform based on a naive assumption that all members of the same geographic entity share similar views? How might different "communities" within the same city (or perhaps county) stress different law enforcement priorities?

KEY TERMS

local prosecutors (133)
officer of the court (128)
prosecutor (132)
solicitor general (129)
state attorney general (132)
U.S. attorney general (128)
U.S. attorneys (131)

WORLD WIDE WEB RESOURCES AND EXERCISES

Web Guides

http://dir.yahoo.com/Society_and_Culture/Crime/Law_Enforcement/District_Attorneys/

Web Search Terms

attorney general
solicitor general
U.S. attorney
United States
 Department of Justice
prosecutor
prosecutorial
 misconduct

Useful URLs

For an update on the organizational chart of the criminal division of the Justice Department, click on http://www.usdoj.gov/dojorg.htm.

For up-to-date statistics on prosecution from the Bureau of Justice Statistics, go to http://www.ojp.usdoj.gov/bjs/pros.htm.

Visit the National Association of Attorneys General at http://www.naag.org/.

Visit the Web site of the National District Attorneys Association, "The Voice of America's Prosecutors," at http://www.ndaa.org/.

The American Prosecutors Research Institute—the research, training, and technical affiliate of the National College of District

Attorneys—provides continuing legal education and training for prosecutors: **http://www.law.sc.edu/ncda/index.htm**.

The Eaton County (Michigan) prosecutor's office provides links to thousands of prosecution-oriented sites across the nation at **http://www.co.eaton.mi.us/ecpa/proslist.htm**.

Uncommon URLs

Read about "The Epidemic of Prosecutorial Misconduct" on the Web site of the Association of Americans for Constitutional Laws and Justice: **http://www.pixi.com/~itmc/ProsecutorialMisconduct.html**.

Visit the Mean Justice home page: **http://home.earthlink.net/~ehumes/**.

Truth in Justice works to free wholly innocent men and women convicted of crimes they did not commit, and to prevent wrongful convictions: **http://www.truthinjustice.org/**.

Web Exercises

1. The U.S. Department of Justice maintains a major Web site. Access it using the following URL: **http://www.usdoj.gov**. Under Justice Department Press Releases, sample the press releases of the attorney general and those of the U.S. attorneys. To what extent do they reflect a focus on similar types of crimes? To what extent do they reflect an emphasis on very different types of activities? Overall, what does this Web site suggest about the difference between federal prosecutors and state prosecutors?

2. A growing number of district attorneys' offices have created Web pages. To access these sites, conduct a search by going to Yahoo: **http://www.yahoo.com**. Then choose Society and Culture/Crime/Law Enforcement/District Attorneys. Select two home pages and compare them. Do the Web pages stress contrasting operating styles, as discussed in the text? Overall, do you think these home pages provide useful information, or does the information amount to little more than public relations?

3. A growing number of communities are instituting some form of community prosecution. Access these programs using the search engine of your choice. Type in the phrase "community prosecution," and select three different programs. Compare the information with the discussion in the text. Do these programs appear to differ in major ways from the way prosecutors have historically run their offices, or are these programs just old wine in new bottles?

INFOTRAC COLLEGE EDITION RESOURCES AND EXERCISES

Basic Search Terms

United States Department of Justice
prosecution
malicious prosecution
public prosecutors
state attorneys general
special prosecutor

community prosecution
prosecutorial misconduct
city attorney
attorneys
government attorneys

Recommended Articles

Welsh White, "Curbing Prosecutorial Misconduct in Capital Cases"

Anthony Annucci, "Effective Strategies for Managing Litigation and Working with Attorneys General Offices"

Eric Waltenburg and Bill Swinford, "Tactics of State Attorneys General"

InfoTrac College Edition Exercises

1. Use the search phrase "community prosecution," and answer the following questions: What advantages are portrayed for community prosecution? What negatives are mentioned? In general, do the articles support or refute the discussion in the text of the expanding domain of the prosecutor? Here are two articles: Catherine M. Coles and George L. Kelling, "Prevention through Community Prosecution," and Susan Weinstein, "Community Prosecution: Community Policing's Legal Partner."

2. Using the search term "prosecutorial misconduct" and/or "malicious prosecution," locate two or more articles on the topic. How significant do the authors consider the problem to be—is it major or minor? What remedies do they recommend? Here are two articles: Rick Bierschbach, "Fixing a Broken Frame" and "One Bite at the Apple."

FOR FURTHER READING

Baker, Mark. *D.A.: Prosecutors in Their Own Words.* New York: Simon & Schuster, 1999.

Baker, Nancy. *Conflicting Loyalties: Law and Politics in the Attorney General's Office, 1789–1990.* Lawrence: University Press of Kansas, 1992.

Clayton, Cornell. *The Politics of Justice: The Attorney General and the Making of Legal Policy.* Armonk, NY: M. E. Sharpe, 1992.

Forst, Brian. "Prosecutors Discover the Community." *Judicature* 84 (2000): 135–141.

Gomme, Ian, and Mary Hall. "Prosecutors at Work: Role Overload and Strain." *Journal of Criminal Justice* 23 (1995): 191–200.

Harriger, Kathy. *Independent Justice: The Federal Special Prosecutor in American Politics.* Lawrence: University Press of Kansas, 1992.

Heilbroner, David. *Rough Justice: Days and Nights of a Young D.A.* New York: Pantheon, 1990.

Jones, David. "Judicial Federalism and Prosecutorial Vindictiveness: State Responses to *Bordenkircher* and *Goodwin*." *Journal of Crime and Justice* 20 (1997): 73–96.

Salokar, Rebecca. *The Solicitor General: The Politics of Law.* Philadelphia: Temple University Press, 1992.

Sanders, Andrew, ed. *Prosecution in Common Law Jurisdictions.* Brookfield, VT: Dartmouth Publishing, 1996.

Chapter 7 Defense Attorneys

PART II
Legal Actors

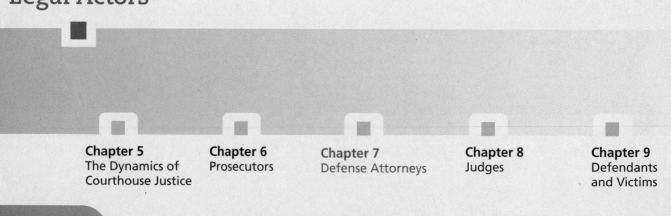

larence Earl Gideon had been in and out of prison since the age of 14. His brushes with the law had been minor—public drunkenness and petty theft primarily—but now he faced a much more serious charge: burglarizing a poolroom in Bay Harbor. As he stood before the judge, he appeared to be a shipwreck of a man; his wrinkled face and trembling hands suggested a person much older than 51. Yet "a flame still burned inside Clarence Earl Gideon . . . he had a fierce feeling that the State of Florida had treated him wrongly" (Lewis 1972, 6). He demanded that the court appoint a lawyer to defend him. The trial judge flatly refused; unrepresented by counsel, Gideon was found guilty. But on appeal he was luckier. The Supreme Court plucked this obscure case from the bowels of the criminal justice system to issue a landmark decision: All indigent defendants were entitled to court-appointed counsel in felony trials. *Gideon v. Wainwright* (1963) was not only a victory for Clarence Earl Gideon but, more important, sent shock waves through the criminal justice system. ◄

The Court's decision in *Gideon* underscores the importance of the lawyers in the criminal justice system. In the United States, the phrase *defense attorney* makes most people think of Perry Mason. As rerun on late-night television, the fictionalized character of Perry Mason embodies our image of the defense attorney fighting to free his falsely accused client—and always succeeding. The public often contrasts this favorable image with a less complimentary one of real attorneys. Concerned about rising crime rates, many Americans view the defense attorney as a conniver who uses legal technicalities to free the guilty. In the eyes of other members of the legal profession, the defense attorney is a virtual outcast who knows little about the law and who may engage in unethical behavior. To a client, the one whose future is literally in the lawyer's hands, the defense attorney is often perceived as just another member of the courthouse gang who does not fight hard enough.

This chapter assesses these conflicting images in terms of the daily realities of the small proportion of the legal profession who represent defendants accused of violating the criminal law. The picture is a complicated one. Some defense attorneys suffer from the shortcomings mentioned by their critics; others do not. But all face day-to-day problems and challenges not usually encountered by the bulk of American lawyers who represent higher-status clients. The key topics of this chapter are the factors influencing the type of legal assistance available to those who appear in criminal courts: the legal right to counsel, the tasks defense attorneys perform, their relationship with courtroom work groups, the nature of the criminal bar, the relationship between lawyer and client, and, finally, the various systems for providing legal assistance to the poor.

THE RIGHT TO COUNSEL

Like many other provisions of the Constitution, the Sixth Amendment has a different meaning today than it did when it was first ratified. In a landmark decision, the U.S. Supreme Court held that, based on the Sixth Amendment's provision of **right to counsel,** indigent defendants charged with a felony are entitled to the services of a lawyer paid for by the government (see Case Close-up: *Gideon v. Wainwright* and the Right to Counsel). Later, the Sixth Amendment right to counsel was extended to juvenile court proceedings as well (*In re Gault* 1967). But as so often happens, answering one question raised several new ones. In the wake of the *Gideon* decision, the Court wrestled with issues involving the right to counsel with regard to (1) nonfelony criminal prosecutions, (2) stages of the criminal process, (3) ineffective assistance of counsel, and (4) self-representation. Exhibit 7-1 summarizes key developments in the right to counsel.

Nonfelony Criminal Prosecutions

The *Gideon* ruling was limited to state felony prosecutions. In *Argersinger v. Hamlin* (1972), the

CASE CLOSE-UP

Gideon v. Wainwright and the Right to Counsel

 From his prison cell, Clarence Earl Gideon drafted a petition that, despite the garbled prose of a man with no real education, nonetheless raised a major legal principle:

When at the time of the petitioners trial he ask the lower court for the aid of counsel, the court refused this aid. Petitioner told the court that this [Supreme] Court made decision to the effect that all citizens tried for a felony crime should have aid of counsel. The lower court ignored this plea. (Lewis 1972)

Every year thousands of pauper petitions like this are sent to the Supreme Court; few are ever heard. But this petition struck a responsive cord. The Court signaled the importance of the issue when it appointed Abe Fortas, one of the best-known lawyers in Washington, D.C., to represent Gideon. (Fortas would later be appointed to the Court.)

In what became officially known as *Gideon v. Wainright,* the Court forcefully noted that "in our adversary system of criminal justice, any person, haled into court, who is too poor to hire a lawyer, cannot be assured a fair trial unless counsel is provided for him. This seems to us to be an obvious truth. . . ."

The Sixth Amendment states that "in all criminal prosecutions, the accused shall enjoy the right . . . to have the assistance of counsel for his defence." As written by the framers more than 200 years ago, this constitutionally protected right to counsel meant only that the judge could not prevent a defendant from bringing a lawyer to court. (In England defendants had been convicted despite requests to have their lawyers present.) Thus, the Sixth Amendment affected only those who could afford to hire their own lawyers.

Beginning in the 1930s, the Supreme Court took a more expansive view of the right to counsel. Criminal defendants in federal cases were entitled to a court-appointed lawyer if they were too poor to hire their own. But a different rule prevailed in the state courts. Only defendants accused of a capital offense were entitled to court-appointed

counsel; indigent defendants charged with ordinary felonies or misdemeanors were not (*Betts v. Brady*). Thus, a significant number of defendants in state courts had to face the legal maze of criminal proceedings by themselves.

Gideon v. Wainwright (1963) significantly expanded the legal meaning of the right to counsel. As occasionally happens, the Court reversed its earlier precedent in *Betts.*

That the government hires lawyers to prosecute and defendants who have the money hire lawyers to defend are the strongest indications of the widespread belief that lawyers in criminal courts are necessities, not luxuries. The right of one charged with crime to counsel may not be deemed fundamental and essential for fair trials in some countries, but it is in ours.

Now, all indigent defendants charged with a felony were entitled to the services of a lawyer paid by the government, irrespective of whether they were on trial in state or federal court.

Gideon proved to be a major transforming event in the American criminal justice system. It was the first major decision of the Warren Court's revolution in criminal justice. But unlike other decisions, it proved not to be controversial. The Court's rationale, focusing on basic fairness and the importance of lawyers, gave it widespread legitimacy. Moreover, *Gideon* focused on the need for a lawyer at the trial itself. Later decisions—*Miranda* in particular— restricted police gathering of evidence and proved to be highly contentious.

You can view Clarence Gideon's handwritten petition by clicking on **http://www. constitutioncenter.org/resources/supreme _court/4b2.asp** or **http://www.aclumontana.org/ rights/gideon.html**. The full opinion in *Gideon v. Wainwright* is available at **http://supct.law.cornell. edu/supct/**. In the Quick Search box, type "Gideon." To listen to the oral argument in *Gideon,* go to **http://oyez.at.nwu.edu/cases/cases.cgi**. Under Search by Title, insert "Gideon."

Court refused to extend the newly discovered constitutional right to court-appointed counsel to those accused of minor violations (misdemeanor or ordinance violations), holding that

"absent a knowing and intelligent waiver, no person may be imprisoned for any offense, whether classified as petty, misdemeanor, or felony, unless he was represented by counsel." Later the

Exhibit 7-1 Key Developments in the Right to Counsel

Sixth Amendment	1791	"In all criminal prosecutions the accused shall enjoy the right . . . to have the assistance of counsel for his defence."
Powell v. Alabama	1932	Indigent defendants in a capital case in state court have a right to court-appointed counsel.
Johnson v. Zerbst	1938	Indigent defendants in federal court are entitled to court-appointed counsel.
Betts v. Brady	1942	Indigent defendants in a noncapital case in state court have no right to appointed counsel.
Gideon v. Wainwright	1963	Indigents in state court have the right to appointed counsel (*Betts* overruled).
Douglas v. California	1963	Indigents have a right to court-appointed counsel during the first appeal.
In re Gault	1967	Juveniles are covered by the Sixth Amendment's right to counsel.
Argersinger v. Hamlin	1972	Limited the right of nonfelony defendants to have court-appointed counsel.
Faretta v. California	1975	Defendants have the right to self-representation.
Strickland v. Washington	1984	Defense attorney is ineffective only if proceedings were unfair and the outcome would have been different.
Martinez v. Court of Appeal of California	2000	Defendants have no Sixth Amendment right to represent themselves on appeal.
Roe v. Flores-Ortega	2000	A lawyer's failure to file an appeal does not necessarily constitute ineffective assistance of counsel.
Alabama v. Shelton	2002	Indigent entitled to a court-appointed attorney even if facing only a suspended jail term for a minor charge.
Wiggins v. Smith	2003	The failure of an inexperienced defense attorney to conduct a reasonable investigation of the defendant's troubled personal background constituted ineffective assistance of counsel.

justices narrowed the *Argersinger* decision, ruling that a defendant is guaranteed the right to legal counsel, paid by the state if necessary, only in cases that actually lead to imprisonment, not in all cases in which imprisonment is a potential penalty (*Scott v. Illinois* 1979). The net effect of the *Scott* case was to limit the right to counsel in nonfelony prosecutions, particularly if the guilty faced only paying a fine (see Chapter 18).

Stages of the Criminal Process

The *Gideon* ruling spawned another important question: When in the criminal process does the right to counsel begin (and end)? Note that the Sixth Amendment provides for the right to counsel in "all criminal prosecutions," so it is not limited to the trial itself. The Supreme Court adopted a "critical stages" test, under which a defendant is entitled to legal representation at every stage of prosecution "where substantial rights of the accused may be affected," requiring the "guiding hand of counsel" (*Mempa v. Rhay* 1967). As Exhibit 7-2 summarizes, indigent defendants have a right to court-appointed counsel from the time they first appear before a judge until sentence is pronounced and the first appeal concluded. (The only exception is the grand jury, whose peculiar practices will be examined in Chapter 10.) As a general rule, defendants have a Sixth Amendment right to the assistance of counsel once any adversary proceedings have begun (*Brewer v. Williams* 1977).

Exhibit 7-2 Right to Counsel during Steps of Felony Crime Procedure

	Extent of Right	Supreme Court Case
Crime	No lawyer required	
Arrest	No lawyer required	
Initial appearance	Lawyer required if critical stage	*Coleman v. Alabama* (1970)
Bail	Lawyer required if critical stage	*Coleman v. Alabama* (1970)
Charging	No lawyer required	
Preliminary hearing	Lawyer required	*Coleman v. Alabama* (1970)
Grand jury	No lawyer allowed	
Arraignment	Lawyer required	*Hamilton v. Alabama* (1961)
Evidence		
Interrogation (preindictment)	Lawyer on request	*Miranda v. Arizona* (1966)
Interrogation (postindictment)	Lawyer required	*Massiah v. U.S.* (1964)
Lineup (preindictment)	No lawyer required	*Kirby v. Illinois* (1972)
Lineup (postindictment)	Lawyer required	*U.S. v. Wade* (1967)
Plea bargaining	Lawyer required	*Brady v. U.S.* (1970)
		Tollett v. Henderson (1973)
Trial	Lawyer required	*Gideon v. Wainwright* (1963)
Sentencing	Lawyer required	*Mempa v. Rhay* (1967)
Probation revocation	Lawyer in court's discretion	*Gagnon v. Scarpelli* (1973)
Parole revocation	Lawyer in board's discretion	*Morrissey v. Brewer* (1972)
Appeal		
First appeal	Lawyer required	*Douglas v. California* (1963)
Discretionary appeal	No lawyer required	*Ross v. Moffitt* (1974)

The right to counsel in the pretrial stage is much more limited, however. Applying the critical stages test, subsequent decisions held that defendants have the right to court-appointed counsel during custodial interrogations (*Miranda v. Arizona*) and police lineups (*U.S. v. Wade* 1967; *Kirby v. Illinois* 1972). However, merely being detained by the police is not sufficient grounds to guarantee a right to counsel (*United States v. Gouveia* 1984). (The controversy surrounding the extension of the right to counsel in the police station will be examined in Chapter 12.)

The right to counsel also extends to certain posttrial proceedings, but as in pretrial proceedings, the right to counsel is more limited. Working on the assumption that a person's right to an appeal can be effective only if counsel is available, the Court held that indigents have the right to court-appointed counsel for the appeal (*Douglas v. California* 1963), as well as free trial transcripts (*Griffin v. Illinois* 1956). The Burger Court, however, rejected attempts to extend the *Douglas* ruling beyond the first appeal. Thus, in discretionary appeals and appeals to the Supreme Court, indigent defendants have no right to court-appointed counsel (*Ross v. Moffitt* 1974). One consequence of the *Ross* decision is that defendants sentenced to death must rely on voluntary counsel in pursuing post-conviction remedies.

Some state supreme courts, however, have gone considerably further in mandating counsel for situations in which the Supreme Court has not required counsel under the Sixth Amendment (Bureau of Justice Statistics 1988a).

Ineffective Assistance of Counsel

But is it enough to have a lawyer? Must the lawyer also be competent and effective? The Supreme Court has recognized the effective assistance of counsel as essential to the Sixth Amendment guarantee (*McMann v. Richardson* 1970). The Court's most significant holding came in 1984 in *Strickland v. Washington,* in which an "objective standard of reasonableness" was set forth as the proper criterion to be applied in making a determination of the ineffectiveness of counsel. Speaking for the Court, Justice Sandra Day O'Connor emphasized that the "benchmark for judging any claim of ineffectiveness must be whether counsel's conduct so undermined the proper functioning of the adversarial process that the trial cannot be relied on as having produced a just result." In short, appellate courts must reverse only if the proceedings were fundamentally unfair and the outcome would have been different if counsel had not been ineffective.

This standard places a heavy burden on the claimant; there are few appellate court reversals on these grounds. Indeed, the Court recently held that a lawyer's failure to file an appeal does not necessarily constitute ineffective assistance of counsel (*Roe v. Flores-Ortega* 2000). However, applying *Strickland,* the Court ordered a new sentencing hearing in a death penalty case because the inexperienced defense attorney failed to conduct a reasonable investigation of the defendant's troubled personal background (*Wiggins v. Smith* 2003).

Self-Representation

Can defendants represent themselves if they wish? An important qualification was added to *Gideon* when the Supreme Court ruled that defendants have a constitutional right to self-representation. This means that criminal defendants have the right to proceed *pro se* (Latin for "on his or her own behalf").

The Court, however, did establish limits. Defendants who wish to represent themselves must show the trial judge that they have the ability to conduct the trial. The defendant need not have the skills and experience of a lawyer, and the judge may not deny self-representation simply because the defendant does not have expert knowledge of criminal law and procedure (*Faretta v. California* 1975). This decision has been qualified by the Court's recognition that the trial judge may appoint standby counsel when defendants choose to represent themselves (*McKaskle v. Wiggins* 1984). Standby counsel is available during the trial to consult with the defendant, but it is the defendant, not the standby lawyer, who makes the decisions.

Although self-representation occurs rarely, these cases have the potential to become media spectacles. Perhaps the oddest case of self-representation was that of Colin Ferguson. Ferguson fired into a crowded Long Island Railroad commuter train, killing 6 passengers and wounding 19 others. Ferguson claimed that he acted out of a sense of "black rage"; his lawyer argued he was insane. Ferguson then dismissed his court-appointed lawyer, who objected that the trial would become a complete circus because "a crazy man cannot represent himself." The prediction proved accurate. During his opening statement Ferguson said there were "93 counts in the indictment, only because it matches the year 1993" (McQuiston 1995). Broadcast nationwide on CourtTV, the trial, with its inevitable guilty verdict, was perceived as not a trial but a spectacle and underscored the limits of self-representation. More recently, Dr. Jack Kevorkian represented himself in an assisted suicide case in Michigan and Zacarias Moussaoui represented himself against charges that he was the twentieth participant in the terrorist attack of September 11.

DEFENSE ATTORNEYS AND COURTROOM WORK GROUPS

Lawyers are expected to be advocates for their clients' cases, arguing for legal innocence. As one defense counsel phrased it, "If the attorney does not appear to be taking the side of the defendant, then no one will" (Neubauer 1974, 73). But the zealous advocacy of a client's case is not the same thing as winning at all costs. As a member of the legal profession, a lawyer's advocacy of a client's case is limited by professional

Exhibit 7-3 Role of Defense Attorney in Typical Felony Case

	Law on the Books	Law in Action
Crime		Counsels the client about the crime charged.
Arrest		Rarely present.
Initial appearance	Allowed to be present.	Typically advises client to say nothing during the court proceedings.
Bail	Argues for client's release on bail.	Judge more likely to listen to the DA's recommended bail.
Charging		May urge the prosecutor to charge the client with a less serious offense.
Preliminary hearing	Allowed to be present but typically cannot call witnesses.	Good opportunity to find out what really happened in the case.
Grand jury	Only in some states may defense attorney be present.	Grand jury transcripts may be useful for discovery.
Arraignment	Allowed to be present.	Chance to talk to the client; may suggest entering a plea of guilty.
Evidence	Requests discovery information from the prosecutor; files motions to suppress confession and/or search and seizure.	Cooperative defense attorneys receive greater discovery information from the DA. Rarely successful in winning suppression motions.
Plea bargaining	Often a direct participant in plea discussions.	Negotiates for most beneficial deal possible.
Trial	Advocate for defendant's rights.	Typically stresses that the prosecutor has not proved the defendant "guilty beyond a reasonable doubt."
Sentencing	Makes a sentencing recommendation to the judge.	Argues for sentence at the low end of the normal penalty scale.
Appeal	Files notice of appeal and writes appellate brief.	Rarely successful on appeal.

obligations. Like prosecutors, defense attorneys are officers of the court, who must fulfill their responsibilities within the framework established by legal ethics. They cannot deliberately mislead the court by providing false information. Nor can they knowingly allow the use of perjured testimony.

Assessing how well lawyers represent their client is difficult because there are different ways of assessing the work performed. How do we define winning? Our popular culture suggests that winning means an acquittal. But experienced lawyers reject such simplistic notions. A veteran Los Angeles public defender explains:

What is our job as a criminal lawyer in most instances? Number one is . . . no kid-

ding, we know the man's done it, or we feel he's done it, he may deny it, but the question is: Can they prove it? The next thing is: Can we mitigate it? Of course you can always find something good to say about the guy—to mitigate it. Those are the two things that are important, and that's what you do. (Mather 1974b, 278)

Thus, many defense attorneys define winning in terms of securing probation, or accepting a plea to a misdemeanor. One attorney put it this way: "Given the situation, what is the best that can be done for my client?" (Neubauer 1974, 74). At virtually all stages of the criminal justice process, defendants may have the guiding hand of counsel (see Exhibit 7-3).

How defense attorneys seek to reach the best solution possible to the plight of their client is directly related to their relationship with other members of the courtroom work group. Usually, assistant public defenders are permanently assigned to a single courtroom and work every day with the same judge, the same prosecutor(s), the same court reporter, and the same clerk of court. Similarly, private defense attorneys—although they practice before several judges—are a permanent fixture in the criminal courts, for a handful of lawyers dominate the representation of fee-paying criminal defendants in any city. This daily interaction of the criminal bar with the court community shapes the type and quality of legal representation received by those accused of violating the law. Whereas the adversary system stresses the combative role of the defense attorney, the day-to-day activities of the courtroom work group stress cooperation (see A Day in Court: Legal Friend of the Down-and-Out Is Retiring).

The legal system, civil and criminal, is based on controversy. Norms of cooperation work to channel such controversy into constructive avenues. All too often, advocacy is falsely equated with antagonism. Although defense attorneys exchange pleasantries with judges and prosecutors, their personal contacts with these officials outside the courtroom are limited (Mather 1974b).

Another qualification to bear in mind is that cooperative attorneys do not bargain every case; they also take cases to trial. If the defense attorney thinks the prosecutor is driving too hard a bargain or that the state cannot prove its case to the jury, a trial will be recommended. Furthermore, there is no evidence that cooperative attorneys do not argue the case to the best of their abilities during a trial.

Rewards and Sanctions

Defense attorneys who maintain a cooperative stance toward judges, prosecutors, and clerks can expect to reap some rewards. Defense attorneys have limited (in some instances, nonexistent) investigative resources. Prosecutors can provide cooperative defense attorneys with information about the cases by letting them examine the police reports, revealing the names of witnesses, and so on.

The court community can also apply sanctions to defense attorneys who violate the norms. Some sanctions work indirectly, by reducing a lawyer's income-generating ability. The clerk may refuse to provide beneficial case scheduling, or the judge may drag out a trial by continuously interrupting it for other business. Other sanctions are more direct. A judge can criticize a lawyer in front of his or her client (thus scaring away potential clients in the courtroom) or refuse to appoint certain attorneys to represent indigents—a significant source of income for some lawyers (Nardulli 1978). A final category of sanctions involves the prosecutor's adopting a tougher stance during bargaining by not reducing charges or by recommending a prison sentence that is longer than normal.

Sanctions against defense attorneys are seldom invoked, but when they are, they can have far-reaching effects. Every court community can point to an attorney who has suffered sanctions, with the result that the attorney either no longer practices criminal law in the area or has mended his or her ways.

Variations in Cooperation

Defense attorneys are the least powerful members of the courtroom work group. Because of the numerous sanctions that can be applied to defense attorneys, they are forced into a reactive posture.

Prosecutors assess a defense attorney in terms of "reasonableness"—that is, ability to "discern a generous offer of settlement and to be willing to encourage his client to accept such an offer" (Skolnick 1967, 58). Based on this criterion, Skolnick put attorneys into three categories. One category consisted of defense attorneys who handled few criminal cases. One might suppose that prosecutors would prefer dealing with such inexperienced attorneys, but they did not. Because these attorneys did not know the ropes, they were too unpredictable and often caused administrative problems. In another category were attorneys who had active criminal practices and maintained a hostile relationship with the prosecutor's office. Known as "gamblers," these attorneys exemplified the aggressive, fighting advocate, but

> ### A DAY IN COURT

Legal Friend of the Down-and-Out Is Retiring

 Public Defender Carl C. Holmes, the blunt-talking barrister who spent 30 years fighting for the indigent and indefensible in Orange County [California] criminal courts, announced Thursday that he will retire this month.

Holmes, who defended a rogues' gallery of clients during his tenure, said some of his most gratifying cases ended with convictions. The true reward came in sparing his clients the death penalty. "In this line of work, keeping a person from the death penalty is a success," said Holmes, 61. "Saving a person's life is about as good as it gets."

News of Holmes' retirement was met with sadness Thursday in Orange County's legal community, with friends and adversaries hailing his dedication in making sure that every defendant received a fair trial. "He's always given the best honest defense he could put forth," Dist. Atty. Tony Rackauckas said. "I don't find him doing any of the sneaky, dishonest shenanigans some defense attorneys get known for."

Fighting on behalf of killers and ne'er-do-wells didn't always win him friends. But Holmes said he relished the times that his efforts helped in tough cases. Holmes said his dedication to defending the penniless is rooted deeply in his experience while growing up poor in the Midwest and in his opposition to the death penalty. "I've got a real weak spot for the poor and a real chip on my shoulder," Holmes said. "Some people feel it in their guts. Others, we have to teach."

Paul Meyer, a criminal defense lawyer and former prosecutor who faced Holmes numerous times as a prosecutor, said the outgoing public defender holds an almost mythic reputation in the courthouse. "He's the Atticus Finch of Orange County," Meyer said, referring to the lawyer in the novel *To Kill a Mockingbird*. "He's got great integrity. He's the essence of a public defender. He's placed his stamp on the public defender's office and raised it to a noble profession."

Holmes said he was gratified by the release of DeWayne McKinney, who spent 20 years in prison for a murder he likely did not commit. Holmes led the effort to win McKinney's release but was named as a defendant in a federal lawsuit against the public defender's office and the Orange Police Department. Based in part on McKinney's release, Holmes also joined the district attorney's office in an unusual project to review potential wrongful convictions using DNA technology.

Rackauckas said Holmes' reputation as a forthright and ardent public defender made such a pioneering project possible. Rackauckas said Holmes was also instrumental in the implementation of Proposition 36, the law intended to divert nonviolent, first-time drug offenders into treatment programs instead of prison. "There was quite a fear that if the public defender took an obstructionist position and took a lot of these cases to trial, it could have bogged down the system," Rackauckas said. "That could have caused a crisis. Carl hasn't done that. He's been very practical."

Holmes, who will step down Jan. 24, supervised about 200 deputy public defenders for the last five years. Before that, he was chief deputy public defender for 15 years. . . . Holmes said he decided to become a public defender even before he entered law school. His classmates, he said, never quite understood his conviction. "They'd ask me, 'Don't you want to make money?'" Holmes recalled. "I told them, 'I don't care about money.'"

Noting that 30 years is a long career for a public defender, Holmes said he decided on retirement now because "it was time to smell the roses." He said he plans to pursue his hobbies of photography, fly fishing and computers. While he doesn't have immediate plans to continue practicing law, Holmes said he wasn't withdrawing entirely from the criminal defense world. He said he would continue to lobby for an amendment to the state's three-strikes law. "I'm going to continue to fight for that," Holmes said. "When the law was passed, there was a gross misrepresentation of what it was we were voting for."

www To learn more about the Orange County Public Defender, point your browser to http://www.pubdef.ocgov.com/index.htm.

SOURCE: Monte Moris, "Legal Friend of the Down-and-Out Is Retiring," *Los Angeles Times*, 3 January 2003. Reprinted by permission.

because they either won big or lost big, they also served to show the other attorneys the disadvantage of this posture. The final category of attorneys consisted of public defenders and private attorneys who represented large numbers of defendants. These attorneys worked within the system.

An Assessment

Are criminal defense attorneys, especially public defenders and regular private attorneys, the co-opted agents of a court bureaucracy or simply calculating realists? This question has been a preoccupation of research on defense attorneys for decades (Flemming 1986b).

Some studies argue that defense attorneys' ties to the court community mean that defendants' best interests are not represented. David Sudnow (1965) argued that public defenders became co-opted when public defenders and prosecutors shared common conceptions of what Sudnow called "normal crimes." Public defenders were more interested that a given case fit into a sociological cubbyhole than in determining whether the event met the proper penal code provisions. As a result, the public defenders seldom geared their work to securing acquittals for their clients. Thus, from the beginning, the presumption of guilt permeated the public defenders' assessment of cases.

Similarly, Abraham Blumberg (1967b) concluded that all defense attorney regulars were double agents. His study of a large New York court likened the practice of law to a confidence game in which both the defendant and the defense attorney must have larceny at heart; a con game can be successful only if the "mark" is trying to get something for nothing. Judges and prosecutors depended on the defense attorneys to pressure defendants to plead guilty. In short, both Sudnow and Blumberg portray defense attorneys as ideological and economic captives of the court rather than aggressive advocates.

However, other studies have concluded that defendants' best interests are not eroded when their attorneys adopt a cooperative posture within the courtroom community. Indeed, Jerome Skolnick (1967) suggested that the clients do better as a result of a cooperative posture. Working within the system benefits the client, because the prosecutor will be more amenable to disclosing information helpful to the defense, the bargains struck will be more favorable, and the defendant will not be penalized for the hostility of the defense attorney. Furthermore, attorneys identified as agitators may harm their clients' causes because prosecutors and judges will hand out longer sentences. Neubauer's (1974) study of Prairie City, Illinois, also found that attorneys who remained on good terms with other members of the courtroom work group functioned better as counselors, because they were better able to predict the reactions of the court community to individual cases. In short, the studies by Skolnick (1967), Neubauer (1974), and Mather (1974b) conclude that attorneys who work within the system are better able to develop a realistic approach to their work, based on experience and knowledge of how their clients will fare.

■ THE CRIMINAL BAR

Law offices of solo practitioners are a permanent feature of urban architecture. They can be found huddled around the stone edifice of the criminal courts and near the neon lights proclaiming "Harry's 24-Hour Bail Bonds." In Detroit they are called "the Clinton Street Bar" and in Washington, D.C., "the Fifth Streeters"—titles that are not meant to be complimentary. These lawyers spend little time in their offices; they are most often at the courthouse, socializing with other members of the courtroom work group. Their proximity to the criminal courts and the sparseness of the law books in their offices are good indicators that the law practiced from these offices bears little resemblance to images of defense attorneys presented on television. A number of factors account for the low economic and professional status of the criminal bar.

Diversity and Stratification of the Legal Profession

Law is a diverse profession based partially on the law school attended and the place of work

A Virtual Tour of American Courthouses: Lawyers at Work

Fictional Lawyers

How we think about lawyers is greatly influenced by fictional lawyers. To find out more about your favorite lawyers on TV, go to **http://dir.yahoo.com/Entertainment/Television_Shows/Lawyer_Shows/**. Movies that features lawyers can be found at **http://dir.yahoo.com/Entertainment/Movies_and_Film/** (use the term *lawyer* to search the category).

Real-Life Lawyers

Alas, the work of defense attorneys in the real world is often not as exciting as that of their fictional counterparts. To learn how defense attorneys defend drug cases, click on **http://dpa.state.ky.us/~rwheeler/drugs/leo.htm**. And to see how public defenders function in neighborhoods, read "A Harlem Law Office Stresses Teamwork, Early Investigation": **http://www.ncjrs.org/txtfiles/163061.txt**. In addition, several states provide close-ups of the functioning of their public defender offices, including Colorado at **http://www.state.co.us/gov_dir/pdef_dir/pd.htm**, Florida at **http://www.nettally.com/fpda/**, and Georgia at **http://www.gidc.com/**.

Need a Lawyer Quick?

For practical tips on what to do (and not say) until your lawyer arrives, look at **http://www.indygov.org/pubdef/case.htm**. And if you need to hire a defense lawyer quickly, here is a sample of some Web sites:

> **Extraordinary Criminal Defense Attorneys:** Crime attorneys exclusively practice criminal defense nationwide. Our attorneys have successfully represented thousands of clients facing serious criminal matters. **http://www.fightforme.com**.

National DUI/DWI Attorney Directory-USA: Facing a DUI/DWI charge? Click here to connect to a highly respected criminal defense attorney in your state. An arrest is not a conviction! Visit **http://www.drunkdrivingdefense.com**.

When the FBI Comes Calling: Call McNabb, fight federal charges. 100% federal criminal defense attorney. Never a prosecutor. When you need a trusted advocate, a preeminent lawyer, click on **http://www.Federalcrimes.com**.

For "Ten Tips on Hiring a California DUI Lawyer over the Telephone," see **http://topgundui.com/hiring.htm**.

Need a Lawyer, but Can't Afford One?

See FAQs from the Marion County, Indiana, public defender at **http://www.indygov.org/pubdef/FAQ.htm**. Here are three Web sites that provide an overview of the functions and structures of public defenders' offices:

> Maryland Office of Public Defender:
> **http://www.opd.state.md.us/**
>
> Oklahoma Indigent Defense System:
> **http://www.state.ok.us/~oids/**
>
> South Carolina Commission on Indigent Defense:
> **http://www.scoid.state.sc.us/**

Lawyer Jokes

Have you heard any good lawyer jokes recently? If not, point your browser to **http://www.fulljokes.com/categorylist.asp?category=Lawyer**. For another source of jokes about the profession that Americans seem to hold in low repute (until they themselves get into trouble), go to **http://www.nolo.com/humor/jokes/index.html**.

(see A Virtual Tour of American Courthouses: Lawyers at Work). An interdisciplinary team, law professor John Heinz and sociologist Edward Laumann, conducted a comprehensive study of the diverse tasks that characterize the social role of lawyers. Based on extensive interviews with practicing attorneys, *Chicago Lawyers: The Social Structure of the Bar* (1982) reported dramatic differences among several sorts of lawyers.

The most important differentiation within the legal profession involved which clients were served. Some lawyers represent large organizations (corporations, labor unions, or government). Others represent mainly individuals. By and large, lawyers operate in one of these two hemispheres of the profession; seldom, if ever, do they cross the equator separating these very different types of legal work. The corporate client sector involves large corporate, regulatory, general corporate, and political lawyers. The personal client sector is divided into personal business and personal plight lawyers (divorce, tort, and so on).

The bulk of the attorneys who appear in criminal court are drawn from the personal client sector. They are often referred to as solo practitioners because they practice alone or share an office with another attorney. For this group of courtroom regulars, criminal cases constitute a dominant part of their economic livelihood. Thus, studies of private attorneys in different cities report that the bulk of nonindigent defendants are represented by a handful of attorneys (Nardulli 1986; Neubauer 1974).

Environment of Practice

It is no accident that in many large cities there is a distinct criminal bar. Low status, difficulty in securing clients, and low fees are three factors that affect the availability of lawyers to represent those accused of violating the law.

Most lawyers view criminal cases as unsavory. Representing criminal defendants also produces few chances for victory; most defendants either plead guilty or are found guilty by a judge or jury. Moreover, many lawyers who represent middle-class clients do not want accused drug peddlers brushing shoulders in the waiting room with their regular clients. Also, despite the legal presumption of innocence, once defendants are arrested, the public assumes they are guilty. As a result, the general public perceives attorneys as freeing known robbers and rapists to return to the streets. "Realistically, a lawyer who defends notoriously unpopular clients becomes identified in the public's mind, and not infrequently in the mind of his own profession, with his client" (Kaplan 1973).

To earn a living, lawyers first need clients. Attorneys working in the personal client sector of the legal profession seldom have a regular clientele. Accordingly, a part of their time is spent securing clients. The criminal lawyer's most important commodity in securing clients is his or her reputation, which often develops on the basis of the lawyer's handling of a specific case. A lawyer's reputation is important in several ways. First, defendants want a specific attorney to represent them, not a firm of lawyers. Second, attorneys who do not practice criminal law often refer clients to a specific lawyer who does. Finally, a repeat offender may seek out the previous attorney, if he or she felt the lawyer provided good representation in the past. In securing clients, some defense attorneys rely on police officers, bail agents, and court clerks to give their names to defendants who need counsel (Wice 1978).

Obtaining clients is only half the problem facing private attorneys who represent criminal clients. The second half is getting paid. "Criminal lawyers are more concerned than other lawyers with collection of the fee—after all, their clients are mostly criminals" (Lushing 1992, 514). The lawyer's fee in a criminal case is generally a flat fee paid in advance. The three most important considerations in setting the fee are the seriousness of the offense, the amount of time it will take the lawyer to deal with the case, and the client's ability to pay. Well-known criminal lawyers, for example, often charge their prosperous clients considerable fees. There has been a myth that criminal lawyers receive fabulous salaries. Although a few have become quite wealthy, most earn a modest middle-class living (Wice 1978). Of course, many defendants are so impoverished that they cannot afford to hire a private attorney at all.

PROVIDING INDIGENTS WITH ATTORNEYS

Indigents are defendants who are too poor to pay a lawyer and therefore are entitled to a lawyer for free. Three quarters of state prison inmates had a court-appointed lawyer to represent them for the offense for which they were serving time. In urban courthouses, the indigency rate is a little higher: 80 percent of felony defendants are too poor to hire their own lawyer (Smith and DeFrances 1996). Obviously, the Supreme Court's decision in *Gideon,* requiring the state to provide attorneys for indigents, applies to a substantial number of criminal defendants.

Although the Supreme Court has essentially mandated the development of indigent defense systems, it has left the financing and type of delivery system up to states and counties, which have considerable discretion in adopting programs (Worden and Worden 1989). As with other aspects of the American dual court system, the characteristics of defense systems for the indigent vary considerably (Lee 1992). In

THE MURDER TRIAL OF SHAREEF COUSIN

Limitations Facing the Defense

"I could win most of my cases if it weren't for the clients. . . . They will waltz into the witness box and blurt out things which are far better left unblurted" (Mortimer 1984, 11). This sentiment from the fictional British defense attorney Rumpole is shared by many real-life American attorneys, who might add, "Clients blurt out things to the police that are better left unblurted."

Late on the afternoon of March 27, 1995, the police arrested the defendant at his house and took him to the homicide division (located in central police headquarters). With his mother present, the police interrogated Cousin. Although he confessed to participating in four armed robberies, he did not directly admit to murdering Michael Gerardi in front of the Port of Call restaurant. However, when he was handed a copy of a police report about the murder, he immediately noted that the murder occurred on March 3, not February 3, as the report erroneously recorded. If he had taken the stand in his own defense, then the jury would almost certainly have been able to learn this damning tidbit.

Shareef Cousin was also very unlikely to take the stand in his own defense because of his past conduct. During police questioning, he admitted to participating in four armed robberies, and he later pled guilty to those crimes (see Chapter 13). As discussed in Chapter 14, defendants enjoy the protection against self-incrimination; that is, they cannot be forced to testify against themselves. But if a defendant takes the stand, then the prosecution can impeach the defendant's credibility by introducing evidence of past felony convictions. Thus, if Cousin took the witness stand in his own defense, the jury would learn of these crimes, several of which appeared to parallel the murder in front of the Port of Call restaurant.

Another limitation the defense had to work around was the defendant himself. It appears from the court record that Cousin was unpredictable. Outside of the presence of the jury, the defense hinted at medical and psychiatric issues but never presented them to the jury. This much is known, however. In the fall of 1994 Cousin spent several months in a hospital, and the admitting physician was a child psychiatrist. Moreover, during the sentencing phase of trial, Cousin made an angry statement of innocence, one that most certainly worked to the advantage of the prosecution.

Finally, the defense was forced to defend Cousin without any help from his family. Jumping ahead to material covered in Chapter 16, by the time of the penalty phase of the first-degree murder trial, family members firmly believed that the justice system was racist and would therefore not participate, not even to the extent of the mother's pleading for the jurors to spare her son's life.

Given these limitations, the defense proceeded on two fronts. One was to stress that Shareef Cousin had an alibi. The other was to limit the evidence the state could present at trial. Toward this end the defense filed a series of motions, one of which was successful. The prosecution wanted to introduce the testimony of the victims of the four previous armed robberies. The trial judge ruled that the evidence of such signature crimes could be introduced at trial. But the appellate court overturned the trial judge, ruling, "The four prior armed robberies are not sufficiently distinctive or similar to the offense charged to justify their admission in evidence." But the other efforts by the defense to limit the evidence that the prosecution could introduce—motions to suppress physical evidence and motions to suppress identification—were not successful.

To read more about the Shareef Cousin trial, type in the search words "dead teen walking," and read the section "The Defense."

most jurisdictions, local governments (counties) are solely responsible for providing criminal defense for the poor. In 17 states, the state government is responsible. To confuse matters further, six states' defense systems for the indigent are organized on both state and county levels.

How best to provide legal representation for the poor has been a long-standing vital issue for the courts and the legal profession. In the United States, there are three primary methods: assigned counsel (attorneys appointed by the judge on a case-by-case basis), contract systems (attorneys hired to provide services for a specified dollar amount), and public defender (a salaried public official representing all indigent defendants). The ongoing debate over the advantages and disadvantages of these three systems highlights some important issues about the quality of legal representation provided the poor.

Assigned Counsel

The assigned counsel system reflects the way professions such as law and medicine traditionally respond to charity cases: Individual practitioners provide services on a case-by-case basis. **Assigned counsel systems** involve the appointment by the court of private attorneys from a list of available attorneys. The list may consist of all practicing attorneys in the jurisdiction or, more commonly, those attorneys who volunteer (Houlden and Balkin 1985). The assigned counsel system is used in half of all U.S. counties but serves less than one third of the nation's population. It predominates in small counties with less than 50,000 residents, where there is not a sufficient volume of cases to support the costs of a public defender system.

Critics contend that the assigned counsel system results in the least qualified lawyers' being appointed to defend indigents. In most counties, the only attorneys who volunteer are either young ones seeking courtroom experience or those who seek numerous appointments to make a living. Even where appointments are rotated among all members of the practicing bar (as in New Jersey and Houston, Texas), there is no guarantee that the lawyer selected is qualified to handle the increasing complexity of the criminal law; the appointee may be a skilled real estate attorney or a good probate attorney, but these skills are not readily transferable to the dynamics of a criminal trial.

The availability of lawyers willing to serve as assigned counsel is directly related to financial compensation. In the past, a number of jurisdictions expected attorneys to represent indigents as part of their professional responsibility, without being paid (*pro bono*). Today, however, the majority of assigned counsel are paid. Most commonly, lawyers are compensated for such defense work on the basis of separate hourly rates for out-of-court and in-court work. However, hourly fees for in-court felony work usually range far below the fees charged in private practice. Critics contend that inadequate compensation pressures attorneys to dispose of such cases quickly in order to devote time to fee-paying clients.

The widely held assumption that rates of compensation are directly related to the quality of criminal defense representation has been challenged by a recent study. The extent of effort of lawyers in Michigan who handled appellate representation did not vary significantly in relation to the rate of compensation. Overall, professional role expectations of lawyers may be of greater influence on their work than financial considerations (Priehs 1999).

Contract Systems

Contract systems are a relatively new way to provide defense services. A **contract system** involves bidding by private attorneys to represent all criminal defendants found indigent during the term of the contract, in return for a fixed payment (Worden 1991; 1993). Contract systems are most often found in counties with populations of less than 50,000, where the key feature is that they place an absolute budget limit on defense services for the indigent.

The primary advantage of contract systems is that they limit the costs government must pay for indigent defense. Critics counter with two types of concerns. The first is that contract programs will inevitably lead to a lower standard of representation through the bidding system, which emphasizes cost over quality. The second is that the private bar will no longer play an important role in indigent defense (Spangenberg Group 2000).

The contract system was held unconstitutional in Arizona when the Arizona Supreme Court held that the Mohave County contract system, which assigned defense representation of the indigent to the lowest bidder, violated the Fifth and Sixth Amendments because the system (1) did not take into account the time the attorney is expected to spend on a case, (2) did not provide for support staff costs, (3) failed to take into account the competence of the attorney, and (4) did not consider the complexity of the case (*Smith v. State* 1984). Likewise, courts in several other states have found legal defects in contract systems that result in inadequate funding levels (Spangenberg Group 2000).

Public Defender

The **public defender** is a twentieth-century response to the problem of providing legal representation for the indigent. Public defender programs are public or private nonprofit organizations with full- or part-time salaried staff who represent indigents in criminal cases in the jurisdiction.

Started in Los Angeles County in 1914, public defender offices spread slowly. By 1965 the National Legal Aid and Defender Association—the national organization that promotes better legal representation for indigents in civil as well as criminal cases—reported programs in only 117 counties. Since 1965 public defender programs have spread rapidly because of Supreme Court decisions (*Gideon* and later *Argersinger*), as well as increased concern for more adequate representation of indigents. Today the public defender system represents approximately 70 percent of all indigents nationwide. It predominates in most big cities and has also been adopted in numerous medium-sized jurisdictions. Seventeen states have established statewide, state-funded programs. The remaining public defender programs are funded by local units of government and operate autonomously, without any central administration (DeFrances and Litras, 2000).

Proponents of the public defender system cite several arguments in favor of its adoption. One is that a lawyer paid to represent indigents on a continuous basis will devote more attention to cases than a court-appointed attorney who receives only minimal compensation. Moreover, many members of the practicing bar like the idea that they no longer have to take time away from fee-paying cases to meet their professional obligations.

A second advantage often claimed for the public defender system is that it provides more experienced, competent counsel. Because public defenders concentrate on criminal cases, they can keep abreast of changes in the law, and the day-to-day courtroom work keeps their trial skills sharp. The public defender is also likely to be more knowledgeable about informal norms and is therefore in a better position to counsel defendants and negotiate the best possible deal.

Finally, a public defender system assures continuity and consistency in the defense of the poor (Silverstein 1965). Public defenders are usually able to provide early representation, entering the case at the initial appearance. Moreover, issues that transcend individual cases—criteria for pretrial release, police practices, and so forth—are more likely to be considered by a permanent, ongoing organization than under appointment systems.

Assessing the Merits of Public Defenders

Critics contend that public defenders—as paid employees of the state—will not provide a vigorous defense because they are tied too closely to the courtroom work group. Several studies have investigated this concern by comparing the adequacy of representation provided by assigned counsel to that of public defenders' offices. The dominant conclusion is that there is not much difference (Flemming 1989; Wice 1985; Eisenstein, Flemming, and Nardulli 1988). The National Center for State Courts drew the following conclusions from the nine jurisdictions it studied: (1) Attorneys for indigent defendants resolved their cases more expeditiously than did privately retained counsel. (2) Defense attorneys for the indigent gained as many favorable outcomes (acquittals, charge reductions, and short prison sentences) for their clients as privately retained attorneys did for their clients. (3) Indigent defense attorneys and prosecuting attorneys were equally experienced (Hanson, Hewitt, and Ostrom 1992). Likewise, the outcomes of criminal appeals do not vary between public defenders and privately retained counsel (Williams 1995).

The Public Defender: The Practice of Law in the Shadows of Repute offers a radically different view of public defense attorneys. In this book, Lisa McIntyre (1987) demonstrates that public defense lawyers are indeed free to defend their clients zealously. She found that in the courts of Cook County, Illinois, public defenders are adversarial and even combative opponents of the state's prosecutorial apparatus. McIntyre argues, in fact, that the office of the public defender survives because its effective advocacy for its clients bolsters the legitimacy of the court system.

Why, then, does the public defender's image not reflect this? The freedom to defend against the state cannot include the freedom to embarrass it. Hence, the complexity of the public defender's institutional role requires that the office not advertise its successes. McIntyre shows that the public defender's office deliberately retains its image of incompetency in order to guarantee its continued existence. Public defenders may practice good law, but they must do it in the darker shadows of repute.

The long-standing debate over the adequacy of court-appointed counsel is beginning to give way to a new reality—large governmental expenses. Images and myths play a central role in the debate over funding levels for court-appointed lawyers (see Courts, Controversy, and Economic Inequality: Are We Spending Too Little or Too Much on Indigent Defense?).

LAWYERS AND CLIENTS

One of the most important tasks of defense attorneys is counseling. As advocates, defense attorneys are expected to champion their clients' cases. But as counselors, they must advise their clients about the possible legal consequences involved. Lawyers must fully and dispassionately evaluate the strengths and weaknesses of the prosecutor's case, assess the probable success of various legal defenses, and—most important—weigh the likelihood of conviction or acquittal. In appraising risks and outlining options, lawyers interpret the law to their clients, who are often unversed in what the law considers important and what the law demands.

In order to be an effective advocate and counselor, the lawyer must know all the facts of a case. For this reason, the American legal system surrounds the attorney–client relationship with special protections. Statements made by a client to his or her attorney are considered **privileged communication,** which the law protects from forced disclosure without the client's consent. The attorney–client privilege extends not only to statements made by the client but also to any work product developed in representing the client.

Based on trust and a full exchange of information, the attorney assumes the difficult task of advocating a client's case. In civil litigation, the relationship between lawyer and client is often (but not always) characterized by trust and full disclosure (Cox 1993). In criminal cases, however, the relationship is more likely to be marked by distrust and hostility. Indeed, more than half of defendants are described by their attorneys as passive participants in the overall defense, and 10 percent are described by their attorneys as recalcitrant—that is, rarely or never accepting the attorney's advice (Bonnie et al. 1996).

Lawyers View Their Clients

Getting along with clients is one of the most difficult tasks of public defenders. Client disrespect irritates attorneys and sours their associations with clients. As one public defender complained, "It is frustrating to have to constantly sell yourself" to clients. "The standard joke around this county is, 'Do you want a public defender or a real attorney?'" (Flemming 1986a, 257–258). Many eventually leave the job because of the difficulty of dealing with their clients (Platt and Pollock 1974).

Refusal to cooperate, deception, and dishonesty are serious problems public attorneys face in dealing with their clients (Flemming 1986a). At times, defendants tell their attorneys implausible stories, invent alibis, or withhold key information. The defendant's lack of candor greatly complicates the job of the attorney in representing him or her. Evasions and deceptions can affect tactical and strategic decisions.

Lynn Mather (1974b) describes a case in which a public defender went to trial at the request of a client who claimed she had no prior record. To the attorney's surprise, the defendant's presentence report revealed that she had a five-year history of similar crimes. She was sentenced to prison. The public defender said that his client "fooled everyone."

The lack of trust in the lawyer–client relationship may stem from the necessity for the lawyer to prepare the client for less than total

COURTS, CONTROVERSY, AND ECONOMIC INEQUALITY

Are We Spending Too Little or Too Much on Indigent Defense?

 To mark the fortieth anniversary of *Gideon v. Wainwright,* Quitman County, an impoverished area of the Mississippi delta, filed an unusual lawsuit contending that the county was too poor to provide indigent defendants with anything more than assembly-line justice. At issue was who should pay for public defenders. To the county board, it is the state's responsibility to pay these expenses. But officials of the state countered that its budget was in dire straits, and therefore it was unable to afford such services (Liptak 2003).

Beyond the immediate question of which level of government should pay, the lawsuit also illustrates important ideological differences over court-appointed counsel. Although all camps agree that basic notions of equity and fairness require that indigents have counsel during trial, the scope of this right is disputed. Crime control advocates are concerned that government spends too much money on providing the poor with lawyers, whereas due process proponents are worried that government is spending too little.

Crime Control Perspective: We Spend Too Much

Over the years, the cost of providing defense services for the indigent has increased dramatically, tripling between 1982 and 1999 (DeFrances 2001). Hardest hit by the expansion of legal rights and consequent increase in costs have been local governments and, secondarily, state governments. Indeed, the burden is highest in communities with the greatest needs and fewest resources—those with high crime rates and large populations of the poor.

As expenditures for defense services for the indigent have risen dramatically, there has been a noticeable trend toward containing the costs. One technique is the adoption of stringent indigency standards. Traditionally, big-city judges rarely inquired into the financial capabilities of defendants to determine whether they satisfy the court's definition of indigency. However, a report funded by the National Institute of Justice stresses that courts should screen applications "to ensure that only the truly indigent are provided representation at public expense" (Spangenberg et al. 1986, 69).

Another way of containing government expenses is cost recovery. In screening applications for defense services for the indigent, many courts now distinguish between defendants so poor that they are exempt from paying any costs of their defense and a new category of "partially indigent" defendants who may be able to pay a portion of the costs (Lee 1992). Thus, some jurisdictions try to collect contributions from the partially indigent prior to disposition of the case. "From a practical standpoint, defendants appear to be more willing to voluntarily contribute to their costs of representation before disposition than being requested to pay after entering a plea or having been found guilty" (Spangenberg et al. 1986, 70).

Due Process Perspective: We Spend Too Little

Due process advocates, on the other hand, are concerned that government is spending too little on indigent defense. Typical is a *Chicago Tribune* editorial headlined "Paying for Justice" (2000), arguing that it "is not too much to say that many poor people are in prison who would be free if they had the legal representation that many affluent people do—and vice versa."

From the perspective of the due process model, oppressive caseloads are the single greatest obstacle to effective representation (Gershman 1993). Underfunding indigent defense produces high caseloads. The National Advisory Commission on Criminal Justice Standards and Goals recommends that a maximum effective felony caseload per attorney per year be 150 cases. Yet in many jurisdictions it is typically much higher, sometimes approaching 1,000 clients per year (Cauchon 1999). Such high caseloads undermine the ability of lawyers to even meet their clients in a timely fashion.

The lack of attorneys available to defend death row inmates is a major point of contention regarding the death penalty (see Chapters 15 and 17).

By 2003 the issue of funding indigent defense has become a pressing problem in many states. In the wake of the economic downturn of the early twenty-first century, state after state has often been forced to reduce funding for indigent defense.

What do you think? Should government be spending less money or more money on court-appointed counsel for the indigent?

victory. The defense attorney may at some point have to inform the defendant that imprisonment is a likely result, given the crime, prior record, facts of the case, and so forth. Since defendants involved in the criminal process often don't look beyond the present, postponing bad news from day to day, such statements are not to their liking. Preparing the client for the possibility of conviction clashes with traditional notions that the attorney should always win.

Ultimately, it is the defendant's choice whether to accept the attorney's advice to plead guilty or to go to trial. Lawyers differ in their ability to influence their clients. Private attorneys find their advice accepted more readily than court-appointed lawyers do. This difference in part reflects the type of commitment the defendant has made. The indigent defendant has no choice in receiving the services of a public defender or assigned counsel, whereas defendants with private attorneys have a choice and have shown their commitment by paying a fee.

Defendants View Their Lawyers

Public clients are skeptical about the skills of their lawyers and are worried about whose side the lawyers are on. Thus, many defendants view their lawyers, whether public or private, with suspicion, if not bitterness. This is particularly the case with court-appointed attorneys, whom many defendants consider the same as any other government-paid attorney. Some defendants think that public defenders will not work hard on their cases because they are paid whether they win or not. To others, the defense attorney has ambitions to become a judge or prosecutor and therefore does not want to antagonize the court system by fighting too hard. Overall, then, many defendants view the public defender as no different from the prosecutor. In prison, "PD" stands not for "public defender" but for "prison deliverer." In what has become a classic statement, a Connecticut prisoner responded to Jonathan Casper's (1972) question as to whether he had a lawyer when he went to court with the barbed comment, "No, I had a public defender."

A partial explanation for a breakdown of trust between the client and public defender involves the absence of one-to-one contact. Most public defenders' offices are organized on a zone

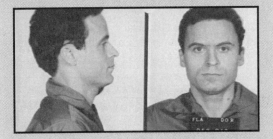

COURT TV

Ted Bundy: Behind the Mask

In the modern era, the name Ted Bundy is synonymous with serial killer. The police suspected that he killed over 30 women. But Bundy hardly fit the stereotype. Handsome, bright, and well educated, he initially maintained his innocence. Later, while on death row, he began to confess to numerous murders, evidently in an effort to postpone his execution.

Bundy was tried in Tallahassee, Florida, for the murder of several sorority coeds. At first he agreed to plead guilty and receive life imprisonment. But he abruptly withdrew the plea of guilty and fired his defense attorneys, choosing to represent himself at trial. Bundy clearly enjoyed the extensive media attention he received and appeared to play the role of a lawyer, but in the end he became solely an actor impersonating a lawyer.

View a video clip of this trial on your copy of the CourtTV CD-ROM. As you watch the video, keep the following questions in mind:

1. Would the outcome of the trial have been different if Ted Bundy had not represented himself at trial?

2. If Bundy had been represented by counsel, would counsel have attempted to persuade the jury to return a verdict of not guilty or would they have chosen a strategy to have the jury spare his life?

3. Did the judge err in allowing Ted Bundy to represent himself? For example, if the defense planned to raise an insanity defense, how could an insane person knowingly waive his right to counsel?

4. Why would the prosecution offer a guilty plea, and a sentence of life, in this case?

basis. Attorneys are assigned to various courtrooms and/or responsibilities—initial appearance, preliminary hearing, trial sections, and so on. Each defendant sees several public defenders, all of whom are supposed to be working for him or her. This segmented approach to representation for indigents decreases the likelihood

A Virtual Tour of American Courthouses: Thinking about Going to Law School?

Searching for Advice

Advice is plentiful on the Internet, and also free. The American Bar Association, for example, offers a set of guidelines for preparing for law school, available online at http://www.abanet.org/legaled/prelaw. In addition, prelaw handbooks are available, including The University of Richmond's Prelaw Handbook at http://oncampus.richmond.edu/academics/as/polisci/prelaw/. Louisiana State University's Prelaw Web site offer good prelaw advice at http://www.artsci.lsu.edu/poli/prelaw.html.

Taking the LSAT

Information about when and where the Law School Admissions Test (LSAT) is offered is available at the Web site of the Law School Admission Council: http://www.lsac.org. Even better, the LSAC offers a sample test for free. If you think you need help in preparing to sit for the exam, several commercial options are available, including Test-Master LSAT Preparation, http://www.testmasters180.com/; PowerScore Law School Preparation, http://www.powerscore.com/lsat/help/links_school.htm; and the Princeton Review, http://www.princetonreview.com/law/default.asp.

Choosing Which Law School to Attend

In deciding where to go to law school, a useful first stop is http://dir.yahoo.com/Government/Law/Law_Schools/, which provides links to hundreds of law schools. To find out which ones are accredited, make sure you look at The Official Guide to ABA Approved Law Schools, searchable by tuition, region, LSAT scores, and other variables at http://www.abanet.org/legaled/publications/officialguide.html. As for the debate over which law schools are the best, U.S. News and World Report publishes its annual rankings of law schools, readily available at http://www.usnews.com/usnews/edu/grad/rankings/law/lawindex_brief.php.

Applying to Law School

In applying to law school, it is a good idea to apply to several. The application forms are available from the Web site of the law school. In addition, the Law School Admission Council publishes a CD-ROM that includes the applications for many law schools (http://www.lsac.org). If you are interested in financial aid, make sure you visit The Access Group at http://www.accessgroup.org/. If you wonder what they teach in law school, check out this Web site of law school course outlines: http://www.ilrg.com/students/outlines/.

---

that a bond of trust will develop between attorney and client. It also increases the probability that some defendants will be overlooked and no attorney will work on their cases or talk to them. One can certainly understand the frustration of this 33-year-old accused murderer with no previous record:

> "I figured that with he being my defense attorney, that as soon as that grand jury was over—because he's not allowed in the hearing—that he would call me and then want to find out what went on. After that grand jury I never saw him for two months." "You stayed in jail?" "Yeah." (Casper 1972, 8)

Quite clearly, not all defendants' criticisms of their attorneys are valid. But valid or not, defendants' lack of trust and confidence in their lawyers is a major force in shaping the dynamics of courthouse justice. Defendants try to con their attorneys, and the lawyers respond by exhibiting disbelief when defendants state unrealistic expectations or invent implausible alibis. For an attorney, failure to gain "client control" can lead to a bad reputation in the courthouse and jeopardize his or her own position within the courtroom work group (Eisenstein, Flemming, and Nardulli 1988).

CONCLUSION

From the bleak perspective of his prison cell, Clarence Gideon had no way of knowing that his petition to the Supreme Court would have the impact it did. Overnight Gideon went from defending himself to having Abe Fortas—one of the nation's most prestigious lawyers—represent him. Following the Supreme Court reversal of his conviction, Clarence Earl Gideon was given a new trial. His court-appointed lawyer discovered evidence suggesting that the man who had accused Gideon of burglarizing the poolroom had himself committed the crime. Moreover, as a result of the *Gideon* decision, thousands of other prison inmates in Florida and elsewhere were freed.

Nor could Gideon have realized that his name would become associated with a landmark Supreme Court decision. He achieved no small degree of legal immortality. His case was chronicled by *New York Times* reporter Anthony Lewis (1972) in the book *Gideon's Trumpet. Gideon v. Wainwright* transformed the law, signaling a due process revolution in the rights of criminal defendants. Gideon himself was not transformed, however. He avoided any more major brushes with the law, but he died penniless on January 18, 1972, in Ft. Lauderdale, Florida.

The travails of Clarence Earl Gideon illustrate the importance of legal access to the justice system. Perhaps nowhere else is there a greater contrast between the images and the realities of the criminal court process than in the activities of the defense attorney. Unlike Perry Mason, who always defended innocent clients successfully, most defense attorneys deal with a steady stream of defendants who are in fact guilty, and their representation focuses on plea bargaining.

CRITICAL THINKING QUESTIONS

1. The public generally views defense attorneys as too zealous in their advocacy of obviously guilty clients, while many scholars portray an image of defense attorneys, particularly public defenders, as too willing to plead their clients guilty. What do you think? What evidence would you cite for either position?

2. In what ways have contemporary decisions by the U.S. Supreme Court modified the original meaning of the Sixth Amendment? Is the original intent of the Sixth Amendment relevant in today's world?

3. What factors hinder a defense attorney in his or her attempt to protect the rights of the defendant? Think of both system factors and individual ones.

4. What are the major contrasts in the workaday world of private defense attorneys and court-appointed lawyers?

5. Should all attorneys be required to provide pro bono defense for indigents? Would such activities improve the image of the bar? Would such activities be in the best interests of the defendants?

6. If you were arrested, which would you rather have, a private lawyer or a public defender?

KEY TERMS

assigned counsel system (161)
contract system (161)
indigents (159)
privileged communication (163)
public defender (162)
right to counsel (149)

WORLD WIDE WEB RESOURCES AND EXERCISES

Web Guides

http://dir.yahoo.com/Entertainment/Humor/Jokes/Lawyer_Jokes/
http://dir.yahoo.com/News_and_Media/Television/Shows/Lawyer_Shows/

Web Search Terms

adversary system   *right to counsel*
defense attorneys   *Gideon v. Wainwright*
public defender   *indigent defense*

Useful URLs

The American Bar Association Division for Legal Services is the nation's leading advocate for greater legal services for the poor: http://www.abanet.org/legalservices.

The National Legal Aid and Defender Association is a nationwide network of persons, programs, and organizations committed to equal access to justice for the poor: **http://www.nlada.org/**.

The American Civil Liberties Union (ACLU) is a longtime advocate of increased access to defense attorneys: **http://www.aclu.org**.

The National Association of Criminal Defense Lawyers (NACDL) discusses issues in criminal defense: **http://www.criminaljustice.org/**.

The Law Reform Network advocates reforming the adversary system: **http://www.lawreform. net/adversary.htm**.

The Association of Federal Defense Attorneys (AFDA) hosts a Web site for criminal defense attorneys, law school students, and the interested general public: **http://www.afda.org**.

The Office of Justice Programs has a Web page on indigent defense: **http://www.ojp.usdoj. gov/indigentdefense**.

Uncommon URLs

To view a photo of the nine young black men dragged off the train in Scottsboro, Alabama, click on **http://www.aclumontana.org/rights/powell. html**. The case became known as *Powell v. Alabama.*

To learn more about the Sixth Amendment and the right to counsel, go to **http://caselaw. findlaw.com/data/constitution/amendment06/ 10.html**.

The Colorado Public Defender's Office can be accessed at **http://www.state.co.us/gov_dir/ pdef_dir/pd.htm**.

The Florida Public Defender's Office is at **http://www.nettally.com/fpda/**.

The Georgia Indigent Defense Council can be found at **http://www.gidc.com/**.

The New York State Defenders Association offers defense news and hot topics: **http://www. nysda.org/**.

Web Exercises

1. The American Bar Association has always had an active interest in providing legal services for the poor. Here is their URL: **http://www.abanet.org/legalserv/**. What services does the ABA provide, and what changes would they like to see?

2. A limited amount of information on indigent defense is available from the Bureau of Justice Statistics at **http://www.ojp.usdoj. gov/bjs/**. Choose Courts and Sentencing Statistics/Indigent Defense, and update the material in this chapter on the major methods of providing indigents with defense attorneys.

3. The reality of being a defense attorney is strikingly different from the fictional images portrayed by Perry Mason and others. One way to explore what defense attorneys really do is to examine their role in defending those accused of violating drug laws. Go to the Web site **http://dpa.state.ky.us:80/ ~rwheeler/drugs/leo.htm**. How does this discussion differ from fictional notions of defense attorneys' defending clients who are factually innocent?

⛭ INFOTRAC COLLEGE EDITION RESOURCES AND EXERCISES

Basic Search Terms

defense attorney
defense, criminal
right to counsel
attorneys
solo practitioners
attorneys, bar association

Gideon v. Wainwright
attorneys, attorney and client
public defender

Recommended Articles

Lev Grossman, "The Accidental Advocate"

Donald A. Dripps, "Ineffective Assistance of Counsel"

Joseph Hall, "Guided to Injustice . . . Indigent Defendants and Public Defense"

Tamara Rice Lave, "Equal Before Law," in which a public defender wrestles with the question, How can you represent *those* people?

Joseph McSorley, "'Criminal Lawyers' or 'Lawyer Criminals'"

Michael Depp, "Defensive Starters"

InfoTrac College Edition Exercises

1. Using the search term "right to counsel," locate articles on the subject and answer the following question: In discussing the concept of right to counsel, do the articles proceed from a crime control or a due process perspective? Here are two possibilities: Martin Gardner, "The Sixth Amendment Right to Counsel," and Burke Kappler, "Small Favors."

2. Using the search term "defense, criminal" or "public defender," select two or more articles on the topic. Do they discuss the role of lawyers more in terms of law on the books or in terms of law in action? Here are two possibilities: Spencer M. Aronfeld, "Go Solo without Starving," and Cornelius Nestler, "Faulty System or Ineffective Defense Counsel?"

FOR FURTHER READING

Bright, Stephen. "Counsel for the Poor: The Death Sentence Not for the Worst Crime, But for the Worst Lawyer." *Yale Law Journal* 103 (1994): 1835–1884.

Clarke, Cait, and Christopher Stone. *Bolder Management for Public Defense: Leadership in Three Dimensions.* Boston: Harvard University, John F. Kennedy School of Government, Bulletin #1, 2001.

Gershman, Bennett. "Themes of Injustice: Wrongful Convictions, Racial Prejudice, and Lawyer Incompetence." *Criminal Law Bulletin* 29 (1994): 502–515.

Hanson, Roger, William Hewitt, Brian Ostrom, and Christopher Lomvardias. *Indigent Defenders: Get the Job Done and Done Well.* Williamsburg, VA: National Center for State Courts, 1992.

Schrager, Sam. *The Trial Lawyer's Art.* Philadelphia: Temple University Press, 1999.

Seron, Carroll. *The Business of Practicing Law: The Work Lives of Solo and Small-Firm Attorneys.* Philadelphia: Temple University Press, 1996.

The Spangenberg Group. *Keeping Defender Workloads Manageable.* Washington, DC: Bureau of Justice Statistics, 2001.

Uphoff, Rodney. "The Criminal Defense Lawyer: Zealous Advocate, Double Agent, or Beleaguered Dealer?" *Criminal Law Bulletin* 28 (1992): 419–456.

Williams, Marian. "A Comparison of Sentencing Outcomes for Defendants with Public Defenders Versus Retained Counsel in 'Florida Circuit Court.'" *Justice System Journal* 23 (2002): 249–258.

Chapter 8 Judges

PART II
Legal Actors

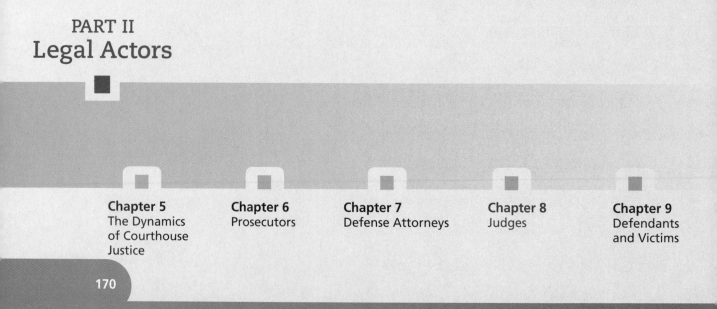

Chapter 5
The Dynamics
of Courthouse
Justice

Chapter 6
Prosecutors

Chapter 7
Defense Attorneys

Chapter 8
Judges

Chapter 9
Defendants
and Victims

o U.S. District Judge Paul Cassell, the recommended sentence (30 to 37 months in prison) for an ex-felon's selling a sawed-off shotgun to a pawnshop was too severe. After all, the defendant, Paul VanLeer, had never committed a violent crime. So Cassell imposed 18 months in prison. To U.S. Attorney General John Ashcroft, this type of lenient sentencing (termed *downward departures* under federal sentencing guidelines) was all too typical of federal judges. So he ordered federal prosecutors across the nation to report every case to the Justice Department. To some, Ashcroft's actions were justified, because federal judges have been imposing lenient sentences in 18 percent of federal cases (U.S. Sentencing Commission 2003). Thus, his new policy would ensure that federal judges would be held accountable for their actions. But to others, the attorney general's actions were just the latest example of judge bashing, because federal prosecutors had found only 19 downward deviations objectionable. Thus, this new policy would serve only to erode judicial independence. ◀

The debate over federal judges' imposing sentences below those recommended by Congress is at one level a continuation of the debate over sentencing, with advocates of the crime control model calling for tougher sentences and supporters of the due process model calling for sentences based on rehabilitation. Beyond this ideological debate, however, this issue illustrates that judges do not judge in a vacuum. Rather, they are directly and indirectly influenced by other courthouse actors and broader trends in society.

The purpose of this chapter is to untangle the conflicting notions about what judges do and how they do it. The chapter begins by examining the position of judge and how various pressures (the large number of cases, for example) have eroded the ideal image of a judge's power. Next, the judge will be considered as a member of the courtroom community. A judge's actions are shaped and influenced by the actions of prosecutors and defense attorneys, among others. At the same time, the type of justice handed out varies from one judge to another. A persistent concern is whether judges are as qualified as they should be. Therefore, two suggestions for improving the quality of the judiciary will be examined: merit selection and mechanisms for removing unfit judges.

■ THE POSITION OF JUDGE

For most Americans, the judge is the symbol of justice. Of all the actors in the criminal justice process, the public holds the judge most responsible for ensuring that the system operates fairly and impartially. And most certainly the trappings of office—the flowing black robes, the gavel, and the command "All rise!" when the judge enters the courtroom—reinforce this mystique. As important as these symbols are, they sometimes raise obstacles to understanding what judges actually do and how they influence the criminal justice process. The vast array of legal powers often causes us to overestimate the actual influence of the judge by ignoring the importance of the other actors in the courtroom work group. At the same time, the mystique of the office often results in an underestimation of the role of the judge. Judges are not merely impartial black-robed umpires who hand down decisions according to clear and unwavering rules. "This view of the judge as an invisible interpreter of the law, as a part of the courtroom with no more individual personality than a witness chair or a jury box, is a fiction that judges themselves have done much to perpetuate" (Jackson 1974, vii).

Powers of the Judge

The formal powers of judges extend throughout the criminal court process. From arrest to final disposition, the accused face judges whenever decisions affecting their futures are made (Exhibit 8-1). Judges set bail and revoke it; they determine whether there is sufficient probable cause to hold defendants; they rule on pretrial motions to exclude evidence; they accept pleas of guilty; if there is a trial, they preside; and after conviction, they set punishment.

Although we tend to think of judges primarily in terms of presiding at trials, their work is much more varied. In the course of their workday, they conduct hearings, accept guilty pleas, impose sentences, or work in their offices (called **chambers**). In carrying out the responsibilities of the office, judges mainly react to the work of prosecutors and defense attorneys.

Benefits of the Job

In discharging their duties, judges enjoy some distinct benefits of the office. Traditionally, they have been given a high level of prestige and respect (Wice 1991). Lawyers address the judge as "your honor," and everyone rises when the judge enters or leaves the courtroom. Judges also enjoy other trappings of the office. Federal judges enjoy life terms, as do judges in a handful of states. More commonly, terms of office for state judges range from six to ten years, considerably longer than those of other public officeholders—a reflection of the independence of the American judiciary.

For many lawyers, a judgeship is the capstone to a successful career. Judicial salaries are not the highest incomes in the legal profession, but they are higher than the average of other criminal justice personnel. Annual salaries of general jurisdiction trial judges range from $82,600 to $150,000 (National Center 2002). The average is about $100,000. For some lawyers, a judicial salary represents an increase over that received in private practice, and it is certainly more secure. For others, however, a judgeship represents a significant decrease in earning power. For example, it is not at all unusual to find lawyers in federal court who are paid more than the judges.

Many judgeships carry with them considerable patronage powers. Court positions—bailiffs, clerks, court reporters, probation officers, and secretaries—must be filled. Because these positions are usually not covered by civil service, judges can award jobs to friends, relatives, campaign workers, and party leaders. In some cities, judicial staff positions are significant sources of party patronage.

Frustrations of the Job

Because of the pressures of today's criminal justice system, the ideals surrounding the judge are not always borne out by the reality. One of the most frustrating aspects of being a judge is the heavy caseload and corresponding administrative problems (Rosen 1987). Thus, instead of having time to reflect on challenging legal questions or to consider the proper sentence for a convicted felon, trial judges must move cases, acting more like administrators in a bureaucracy than as judicial sages. As a New York judge put it:

> It is clear that the "grand tradition" judge, the aloof brooding charismatic figure in the Old Testament tradition, is hardly a real figure. The reality is the working judge who must be politician, administrator, bureaucrat, and lawyer in order to cope with a crushing calendar of cases. A Metropolitan Court Judge might well ask, "Did John Marshall or Oliver Wendell Holmes ever have to clear a calendar like mine?" (Blumberg 1967a, 120)

Moreover, the judge's actions are limited by the system—lawyers are late, court documents get lost, jails are crowded. Added to these general constraints is the overall low prestige of criminal court judges, who occupy the lowest rung within the judicial system. Like the other actors in the criminal justice system, the judge becomes tainted by close association with defendants who are perceived as society's outcasts.

Thus, the frustrations of the criminal trial court judge are many. Some judges prefer the

Exhibit **8-1**	Role of Judges in the Steps of Criminal Procedure (Typical Felony Case)		
	Lower Court	Major Trial Court	Appellate Court
Crime			Appellate court opinions are the final word on interpreting criminal laws passed by the legislature.
Arrest	Occasionally signs arrest warrants.		Wrestles with legality of police arrest in context of question of illegal search and seizure.
Initial appearance	Informs defendant of pending charges; appoints counsel for indigents.		
Bail	Sets initial bail amount.	May alter bail amount.	Rarely decides that bail is excessive.
Charging		No authority to intervene.	
Preliminary hearing	Presides over preliminary hearing.		
Grand jury		Chief judge has nominal supervision over the grand jury.	
Arraignment		Informs defendant of pending charges and enters defendant's plea.	
Evidence	Signs search warrants.	Rules on suppression motions involving illegal search and seizure and custodial interrogation.	Rulings establish boundaries for search and seizure and custodial interrogation.
Plea bargaining	Judges rely on pleas to dispose of large dockets.	Some judges actively participate, whereas others are passive.	Rarely rules that plea of guilty was not voluntary.
Trial	Rarely held.	Presides at trial. Rules on admissibility of evidence. Instructs jury as to law applicable to the case.	Decides if evidence was properly admitted. Decides if trial judge properly instructed jury as to the law.
Sentencing	Typically imposes "normal penalties."	Increasingly difficult and controversial task.	In some jurisdictions, must interpret sentencing guidelines.
Appeal	Rare except in some drunk driving convictions.	Notice of appeal filed in trial court.	Rarely reverses trial judge.

relative peace of civil court, where dockets are less crowded, courtrooms quieter, legal issues more intriguing, and witnesses more honest than in the criminal court atmosphere of too many cases, too much noise, too many routine (and often dull) cases, and too many fabricated stories. Other judges, however, like the camaraderie of the criminal court.

JUDGES WITHIN THE COURTROOM WORK GROUP

The public believes that judges are the principal decision makers in courts. Often they are not. Instead, they are constrained by the actions of other members of the courtroom work group—prosecutors, defense attorneys, jail wardens, and probation officers. Thus, judges often accept bail recommendations offered by prosecutors, plea agreements negotiated by defense attorneys, and sentences recommended by the probation officer. In short, although judges still retain the formal legal powers of their office, they often informally share these powers with other members of the courtroom work group.

Sanctions can be applied against judges who deviate from the consensus of the courtroom work group. Defense attorneys and prosecutors can foul up judges' scheduling of cases by requesting continuances or failing to have witnesses present when required. Particularly in big-city courts, judges who fall too far behind in disposing of the docket feel pressure from other judges, especially the chief judge. Judges who fail to move their docket may be transferred to less desirable duties (for instance, traffic court or juvenile court).

By no means are judges totally controlled by the courtroom work group. As the most prestigious members of the group, they can bring numerous pressures to bear on prosecutors, defense attorneys, and others. A verbal rebuke to a defense attorney in open court or an informal comment to the head prosecutor that the assistant is not performing satisfactorily are examples of judicial actions that can go a long way toward shaping how the courtroom

work group disposes of cases (see A Day in Court: "Frustrated" Judge Gets the Gridlocked System Moving).

The amount of influence judges actually exert on the other members of the courtroom work group varies. Some judges are active leaders of the courtroom work group; they run "tight ships," pressuring attorneys to be in court on time, for example. These judges participate fully in courthouse dynamics. On the other hand, some judges have a laissez-faire attitude, allowing the attorneys as many continuances as they request.

In large courts, "judge shopping" is a common practice. Through the strategic use of motions for continuances and motions for a change of judge, defense attorneys maneuver to have their clients' cases heard by the judge they perceive as most favorable. Such judge shopping is the most direct evidence of variations among judges. Although organizational pressures work to provide a certain degree of consistency among judges, any examination of a multijudge court immediately shows that judges differ in terms of the sentences they hand out, the way they run their courtroom, and the number of cases pending. A knowledge of these judicial differences is often as necessary for the practicing attorney as mastery of the law and rules of procedure.

VARYING ROADS TO A JUDGESHIP

Which lawyers are selected to be judges is determined by both formal selection methods and informal procedures. Exhibit 8-2 presents the major formal selection methods used in the states, including partisan elections, nonpartisan elections, merit selection (usually referred to as the *Missouri Bar Plan*), and appointment. Note, though, that some states use different selection procedures for different levels of the judiciary.

However, formal selection methods (law on the books) are far less important than informal methods (law in action) in determining which lawyers reach the bench. How selection is conducted establishes the actual routes to who becomes a judge (Graham 1990a). When a judicial vacancy occurs, interim selection

A DAY IN COURT

"Frustrated" Judge Gets the Gridlocked System Moving

 It's the criminal justice version of a run-down rowhouse—a small, utilitarian courtroom with little charm and no amenities. Four of the 14 overhead fluorescent lights are out; the strip of blue carpeting under the defense and commonwealth tables looks as if it's never been vacuumed; aged parchment shades cover the windows.

It's not pretty. And neither is the situation that Common Pleas Judge Norman Ackerman has to deal with on this Monday morning in Courtroom 615. As Assistant District Attorney Tariq Karim El-Shabazz put it, "This is a real Murphy's Law day." Defense attorneys who are scheduled to appear are at trials in other counties, states and City Hall courtrooms; defendants and complaining witnesses show up only to leave frustrated over more delays; there are snafus and postponements and long, long waits.

"This case is 546 days old, you'd better have a good reason," Ackerman admonishes Shabazz and public defender Pat Mandracchia, who seek a continuance in a drug case for reasons they refuse to disclose—probably because the defendant is cooperating with the state's investigation. Throughout the morning, as he reviews the status of cases before him, Ackerman expresses frustration with the delays. The cases before him have been pending for an average of 462 days— more than a year and three months.

Ackerman is a waiver judge who presides over non-jury trials and proceedings. There are 15 cases before him. Six will be continued. One was listed in error. Eight will proceed, but only because of his diligence. He stays on the bench all day—from 9:30 A.M. until 5:15 P.M. with one 10-minute recess and a 50-minute lunch break, through interminable waits for private counsel and other delays—virtually forcing cases through the system.

Case in point: Attorney J. Michael Farrell, scheduled to be in court on a drug case, sent a message that he was in court in New Jersey on a last-minute matter. Ackerman was angry. "If you practice law in Philadelphia, I expect Philadelphia cases to take precedence. This case is 497 days old, which is bothersome to the court." And instead of continuing the case again, Ackerman waited it out. "We'll be here all afternoon. Tell him to call when he gets back," Ackerman instructed the court crier to tell Farrell's office.

When Farrell finally called, he was told to report immediately. He roared down I-95 from Trenton—calling from his car with reports of heavy traffic—and finally burst into the courtroom in a breathless rush, well after 4 P.M., to have his case heard.

"We need 30 more like him," court crier Pat West says of Ackerman, a gray-haired man with a calm temperament who is uniformly described as dedicated and hard-working.

In an interview later, Ackerman acknowledges his frustration with the system. "Sure I'm frustrated. What do you do? I was practicing law for close to 30 years before I came on the bench and you reach a situation when you're elevated to the bench and you want to make a significant contribution to the court system. . . ." He said he and the other judges who are new to the bench . . . are trying to make defense attorneys realize that repeated continuances will not be tolerated.

That attitude and some innovative programs are making things better, he said. Waiver judges are now disposing of more cases on a daily basis than are coming into the system, and "that's a great sign." . . .

At 5:30 P.M., as dusk begins to fall and Judge Ackerman takes off his robe, he ends a day that was as productive as possible; a day in which he was tough and human and determined to get some work done.

They should all be like him.

SOURCE: J. Porter, "'Frustrated' Judge Gets the Gridlocked System Moving," *Philadelphia Daily News*, 13 March 1990, 5. Reprinted by permission.

---

methods are needed. Appointment by governors and merit selection predominate in filling temporary vacancies. Indeed, nationwide, half of all trial judges initially received their position through some form of interim selection (Ryan et al. 1980).

We will examine the three major methods of judicial selection—executive appointment,

Exhibit 8-2 Initial Selection of State Judges (Trial Courts of General Jurisdiction)

Partisan Election	Nonpartisan Election	Merit	Appointment
Alabama	California	Alaska	Maine (G)
Arkansas	Florida	Arizona	New Hampshire (G)
Illinois	Georgia	Colorado	New Jersey (G)
Indiana	Idaho	Connecticut	Rhode Island (G)
Louisiana	Kentucky	Delaware	South Carolina (L)
Mississippi	Michigan	District of Columbia	Virginia (L)
Missouri*	Minnesota	Hawaii	
New York	Montana	Iowa	
North Carolina	Nevada	Kansas	
Pennsylvania	North Dakota	Maryland	
Tennessee	Ohio	Massachusetts	
Texas	Oklahoma	Nebraska	
West Virginia	Oregon	New Mexico	
	South Dakota	Utah	
	Washington	Vermont	
	Wisconsin	Wyoming	

L = Legislative appointment; G = Gubernatorial appointment
*Partisan election in nonmetropolitan circuits

SOURCE: American Judicature Society, *Judicial Selection in the United States: A Compendium of Provisions*, 2d ed. (Chicago: American Judicature Society, 1993).

popular election, and merit selection—and explore the influence of both formal and informal selection practices.

Executive Appointments

In the early years of the Republic, judges were selected by executive appointment or elected by the legislature. Today, these methods of judicial selection are used in only a handful of jurisdictions. Three states use election by the legislature, and a few others still use appointment by the governor. All Article III federal judges are selected by executive appointment. A number of studies have examined the political dynamics involved in the selection of federal judges (Goldman 1997; Holmes and Savchak 2003).

The U.S. Constitution specifies that the president has the power to nominate judges with the advice and consent of the Senate. Based on this constitutional authorization, both the president and the Senate have a voice in the selection process. When a judgeship becomes vacant, the deputy attorney general of the U.S. Department of Justice (the executive official authorized by the president to handle judicial nominees) searches for qualified lawyers by consulting party leaders of the state in which the vacancy has occurred, campaign supporters, U.S. senators, and prominent members of the bar. This initial private screening has been known to take a year or longer when there are conflicts within the president's party over who should be selected.

After the president has submitted his nomination for the vacant judicial post, the process shifts to the Senate. Most nominations are routine. After a hearing by the Senate Judiciary Committee, the full Senate usually confirms, most often without a negative vote being cast. If the nomination is controversial, the committee hearings and Senate vote become the focus of great political activity. Over the past decade, major partisan wrangling has surrounded nominations to the federal bench. During 2003, for example, most of President Bush's nominees to the federal bench were confirmed, but Democrats filibustered three nominations to the Courts of Appeals.

Senators also influence federal judicial selections through the informal power of senatorial courtesy. Senators expect to be consulted before the president nominates a person for a judicial vacancy from their state if the president belongs to the same party. A senator who is not consulted may declare the nominee personally unacceptable, and senators from other states—finding strength in numbers—will follow their colleague's preferences and not approve the presidential nomination. Through this process, senators can recommend persons they think are qualified (former campaign managers come to mind) or exercise a direct veto over persons they find unacceptable (political enemies, for example). This process produces federal judges with two defining attributes: They belong to the president's party, and they have often been active in politics.

Although the **American Bar Association (ABA),** the national lawyers' association, enjoys no formal role in the screening of nominees for the federal bench, it plays an increasingly influential role through its Standing Committee on Federal Judiciary (Slotnick 1983). The committee investigates potential nominees by consulting with members of the legal profession and law professors. It then ranks the candidates as "exceptionally well qualified," "well qualified," "qualified," or "unqualified." Although the president has the sole power to nominate, most presidents do not wish to name someone who will later be declared unqualified. Therefore, the deputy attorney general usually seeks the ABA's recommendations prior to nomination, and some potential nominees are eliminated in this way.

State appointive systems resemble the presidential system for selecting federal judges, except that with **gubernatorial appointments** there is no equivalent of senatorial courtesy at the state level. As with federal appointees, governors tend to nominate those who have been active in their campaigns. At times, governors have been known to make appointments to strengthen their position within a geographical area or with a specific group of voters. In recent years, some governors have allowed bar associations to examine the qualifications of potential nominees. State bar associations are gaining influence, much like the ABA influence on federal judicial appointees. However, governors have greater independence to ignore bar association advice.

Election of Judges

More than half the states select judges through popular **judicial elections.** The concept of an elected judiciary is a uniquely American invention at democratizing the political process. It is based on the notion that an elitist judiciary does not square with the ideology of a government controlled by the people (Dubois 1980). According to this philosophy, there should be no special qualifications for public office; the voters (not the elites) should decide who is most qualified.

In some states, judges are selected using partisan elections (the nominee's political party is listed on the ballot). Historically, this approach enabled party bosses to use judicial posts as patronage to reward the party faithful. In other states, judges are selected using nonpartisan elections (no party affiliations are listed on the ballot). Nevertheless, even where nonpartisan elections are used, partisan influences are often present (law in action); judicial candidates are endorsed or nominated by parties, receive party support during campaigns, and are readily identified with party labels.

Traditionally, campaigns for American judgeships have been low-key, low-visibility affairs marked by the absence of controversy and low voter turnout (Hojnacki and Baum 1992; Champagne and Thielemann 1991). Judicial candidates often stressed general themes like doing justice and being tough on criminals in their campaigns, thus providing voters few guides to possible differences between the candidates. The general lack of information and the low levels of voter interest give incumbent judges important advantages in running for reelection. The prestigious title "Judge" is often listed on the ballot in front of the judge's name. For this reason, few local lawyers wish to challenge a sitting judge. Once a judge is selected, either through an election or an appointment to fill a midterm vacancy, the chances of being voted out of office are small. Few sitting judges are even opposed for reelection; of those challenged, few are ever voted out of office (Dubois 1984).

Times are changing, however. In recent years, some judicial elections have become nastier, noisier, and costlier (Schotland 1998). Mudslinging and attack advertising has become common in some states. Interest groups backed by business or plaintiff lawyers are spending millions to back their candidates (Goldberg, Homan, and Sanchez 2002). Thus today races, particularly at the state supreme court level, are hard-fought affairs. Moreover, the U.S. Supreme Court recently ruled that candidates for judicial office are free to announce their views on key issues (*Republican Party v. White* 2002). One consequence is that incumbent judges are now being defeated for reelection at a higher rate than before (although at the trial level incumbents still often win).

Merit Selection

"Remove the courts from politics" has been the long-standing cry of judicial reformers, who oppose popular election of judges because voters have no way to know which lawyers would make good judges. Moreover, election suggests the appearance of impropriety because it provides an incentive for judges to decide cases in a popular manner (National Advisory Commission 1973). To cure these ills, legal reformers advocate merit selection, also known as the **Missouri Bar Plan** because that state was the first to adopt it in 1940.

Merit plans are actually hybrid systems incorporating elements from other judicial selection methods: gubernatorial appointment, popular election, citizen involvement, and—most important—a formalized role for the legal profession. Merit selection involves the establishment of a judicial nominating commission composed of lawyers and laypersons, who suggest a list of qualified nominees (usually three) to the governor (Henschen, Moog, and Davis 1990). The state's chief executive makes the final selection but is limited to choosing from those nominated by the commission.

After a short period of service on the bench (usually one year), the new judge stands uncon-

tested before the voters. The sole question is, "Should Judge X be retained in office?" If the incumbent judge wins a majority of affirmative votes, he or she earns a full term of office. Each subsequent term is secured through another uncontested "retention ballot" (Hall and Aspin 1992). Most judges are returned to the bench by a healthy margin, often receiving 70 percent of the vote. Only a handful of judges have been removed from office. Over a 30-year period, for example, 50 court judges from trial and appellate courts were defeated in 3,912 retention elections in 10 states; 28 of these defeats occurred in Illinois, which requires a judge to receive a minimum of 60 percent of the popular vote to remain on the bench (Aspin et al. 2000).

Although backers of the Missouri Bar Plan contend that it will significantly improve the judges selected and remove the courts from politics, studies of the merit selection system in operation have reached different conclusions. The politics of judicial selection has been altered but not removed; in fact, removing politics does not seem possible. What the reformers presumably mean is the removal of "partisan" politics. In operation, the Missouri Bar Plan has reduced the influence of political parties while at the same time greatly increased the power of the legal profession (Watson and Downing 1969).

Merit selection has won increasing acceptance. A majority of states use the merit system, at least at some level of their state court system (see again Exhibit 8-2). In addition, a number of other states have actively considered adopting merit selection. As evidence of the growing importance of merit selection, all states that have altered judicial selection techniques in recent years have adopted some form of the Missouri Bar Plan. Even in states that have not formally adopted merit selection, governors often use "voluntary merit plans" to fill temporary vacancies (Dubois 1980).

CONSEQUENCES OF JUDICIAL SELECTION

The debate over the best method for selecting state judges has raged for decades. Partisan and nonpartisan elections, used in a majority

THE MURDER TRIAL OF SHAREEF COUSIN

Judge Raymond Bigelow, Ex-Prosecutor

Raymond Bigelow first ran for a judgeship in 1992, but lost. The following year another vacancy opened up. In a crowded field of five, Bigelow won a plurality in the first election and won outright with 54 percent of the vote in the runoff, defeating Harry Tervalon, a former policeman, prosecutor, and public defender. During his campaign Bigelow stressed the rights of victims. "It seems to me that the victims are kind of lost, kind of shuffled aside," he said, promising to devise "creative ways to provide victims with comfort" (Cooper, 1993).

Before becoming a judge, Bigelow was first assistant district attorney in Orleans Parish, a powerful position that runs the day-to-day operations of the office. Thus he enjoyed the political backing of his boss, DA Harry Connick (see Chapter 6). Indeed, Bigelow is one of several judges who had previously worked for Connick. But once on the bench, Bigelow's former boss and political mentor became his sharpest critic. In more than a dozen trials of defendants charged with possessing crack cocaine, Judge Bigelow found them innocent, ruling that simply possessing a crack pipe with residue invisible to the naked eye does not prove a defendant intended to possess cocaine. To Connick, the law was clear: They were smoking crack and should be punished. The appellate court, though, upheld Judge Bigelow's rulings. (The DA could have charged the defendants with the less serious offense of possession of drug paraphernalia, but chose not to.)

The long-running legal battle over the status of crack pipes was the second time Connick and Bigelow had faced off. In another case, the judge ordered prosecutors to give defense attorneys a list with potential jurors' arrests and convictions, saying both sides should have access to the same information. Connick refused and appealed, but the state supreme court let Bigelow's order stand.

In terms of case processing time (see Chapter 5), Orleans Parish Criminal District Court is one of the fastest in the nation. Some judges, though, are faster than others, and Judge Bigelow is certainly one of these. In his section of court, the median time from arraignment to disposition is approximately 31 days. But even in speedy sections of court, complicated cases like murder take longer to reach disposition than simpler cases like possession of illegal drugs. Nonetheless, in the murder trial of Shareef Cousin, Judge Bigelow moved with dispatch; the case was tried 7 months after indictment and less than 11 months after the crime.

Predictably, both sides strenuously disagreed with some of Judge Bigelow's decisions during the trial. The defense objected to the improper use of rebuttal witnesses (an issue they would win on appeal). On the other hand, the prosecution objected to the decision to allow the defense several extra days to prepare for the penalty phase of the trial. Most important, the judge refused to grant a motion for a new trial. Cousin's supporters were quick to claim that the black defendant was being "railroaded." They speculated that Bigelow did not want to appear to be soft on crime by granting a new trial for an accused killer because he was up for reelection in a few months. In the words of Reverend Raymond Brown, a local minister and supporter of the Cousin family, "The judge is afraid of the backlash" (Charles, 1996).

Bigelow was reelected to a full six-year term, easily defeating veteran defense attorney Donald Ray Pryor. Bigelow, then 49, garnered all the major endorsements in the race. He promised to keep his court's docket as low as possible and to refuse unjustified requests for continuances. According to Pryor, Bigelow's attitude often works to the disadvantage of low-income defendants.

of states, are supported by those who believe elections are the most appropriate method for guaranteeing the popular accountability of state judicial policymakers. Critics, on the other hand, assert that elections are fundamentally inconsistent with the principle of ju-

dicial independence, which is vital for neutral and impartial judicial decision making. Less philosophically, these competing perspectives find expression in tension between the legal profession and political parties over influencing judicial selections. The different methods

COURT TV

Sam Sheppard

The murder of Marilyn Sheppard remains one of the most intriguing mysteries of the twentieth century. Was she brutally beaten to death by her husband, as police and prosecutor allege, or was she slain by an unknown assailant, as Dr. Sheppard and his son maintain?

Public fascination with this case was fanned by extensive media coverage, especially in the newly emerging communication vehicle—television. For the first time, average citizens could from their living rooms watch on television the investigation, arrest and trial involving a sensational crime. This media coverage resulted in a major Supreme Court decision—*Sheppard v. Maxwell*—which for the first time established guidelines for media coverage of trials, guidelines that still prevail (see Chapter 14).

By modern standards the quality of the television images is limited. Nonetheless watching the video clips as this case unfolds offers important glimpses into a case that 50 years later remains in the public's mind and helped shaped contemporary law.

View a video clip of this trial on your copy of the CourtTV CD-ROM. As you watch the video, keep the following questions in mind:

1. Would the media cover this case differently today? What contemporary trials have attracted this level of media attention and why?

2. How has television changed the criminal justice process? Has the Internet had a similar impact?

3. The Sheppard trial has been called a mockery of justice, a Roman holiday, and a media circus. Do you agree with these sentiments? Why or why not? Who do you think was principally responsible—the media, the police, the prosecutor, the coroner, or the judge? Was the judge influenced too heavily by popular sentiments?

4. Judges are elected in Ohio. What would have been the judge's re-election prospects if he had been perceived as siding with Sam Sheppard?

of judicial selection heighten or diminish the influence of the bar or the influence of political parties.

This debate indicates that methods of judicial selection are perceived to have important consequences. Three topics stand out. One centers on which system is "best." The second relates to similarities in judges' backgrounds. The third involves efforts to produce a more diverse judiciary.

Which System Is Best?

In evaluating which selection system is best, a key criterion is whether one system produces better judges than another. Judicial folklore has long held that particular systems may produce superior judges. Several studies have systematically analyzed this folklore. Because it is impossible to evaluate a normative concept such as "best," it is necessary to rephrase the question empirically. That is, do judges selected by one method differ from those selected by others? Researchers use measurable judicial credentials, such as education and prior legal experience, as indicators of judicial quality. These studies point to two different types of conclusions.

From the standpoint of individuals who wish to become judges, methods of judicial selection make a difference, but not much. When legislators appoint judges, it is quite clear that former legislators are more likely to be selected than in other systems. Similarly, when the governor appoints, the system benefits those who have held state office (such as legislators). By contrast, elective systems elevate to the bench a higher proportion of persons who have held local political office—which typically means the district attorney. Under the Missouri Bar Plan and elective systems, former DAs are more often selected as judges. When the executive or legislature makes the selection, fewer DAs become judges. The differences between systems are pronounced. In California, for example, which governor makes the appointment has an impact on who becomes a judge (Dubois 1985).

From a broader perspective, methods of judicial selection have only a marginal influence on the types of lawyers who become judges. Whether elected by the voters, appointed by the governor, or selected through merit plans, state judges are more alike than different. In terms of personal background characteristics such as prior political experience, ties to the local community, political party affiliation, and quality of legal education, the systems of judicial selection do not appear to produce very different types of judges (Emmert and Glick 1987; 1988; Flango and Ducat 1979). In short, methods of judicial selection are not related to judges' personal characteristics in the way the debate in the literature would have us believe (Canon 1972; Nagel 1973). Thus, there is no systematic evidence that one selection system produces better judges than another selection system. But there is evidence that state supreme court judges selected in partisan elections react to public opinion, whereas those appointed by the governor are free of this constraint (Pinello 1995).

Similarities in Judges' Backgrounds

Although the United States uses a variety of methods for selecting judges, it is important to note that judges share some important similarities, which may be of even greater importance than the differences. In general, judges are males from the upper middle class, and their backgrounds reflect the attributes of that class: They are more often white and Protestant, and they are better educated than the average American.

Another similarity among judges is that most were born in the community in which they serve. Trial court judges are usually appointed from particular districts; the persons appointed were often born in that area and attended local or state colleges before going on to a law school within the state.

Finally, judges are seldom newcomers to political life. Almost three out of four state supreme court judges have held a nonjudicial political office. Trial court judges also have held prior office—most often district attorney or state legislator. Eighty percent of federal judges had prior government experience. Before becoming judges, they had some familiarity with

the range of public issues that government as well as courts must address. Because of these factors, few political mavericks survive the series of screens that precede becoming a judge. The process tends to eliminate those who hold views and exhibit behavior widely different from the mainstream of local community sentiment.

Diversity and the Judiciary

The dominant profile of judges as white males has begun to change. Since the presidency of Jimmy Carter, an increasing number of federal court vacancies have been filled with female jurists, a pattern evident during both Republican and Democratic administrations (Goldman and Slotnick 1999; Goldman and Saronson 1994). Eighteen percent of President Clinton's nomination to the federal bench were women (Spill and Bratton 2001).

The picture with regard to state judges is significantly more complicated. Until the twentieth century, the number of women judges in America was so small that they could be counted on the fingers of one hand. The twentieth century began witnessing changes, though not very quickly. By 1950, women had achieved at least token representation on the bench (Carbon 1984). Today, 21 percent of state appellate court judges are women (Hurwitz and Lanier 2001). This growth parallels increases in the number of female lawyers (Martin 1990). Thus as the number of women practicing law—now estimated at 25 percent—continues to grow, so will the number of women serving on the bench (Martin 1999).

With an increasing number of women serving on the state and federal benches, there is an understandable interest in probing the "difference" women may bring to the bench (Martin 1993). Speculation by affirmative action activists has suggested that female judges are likely to be more liberal than male jurists. Some studies report gender differences (but often the differences are at best small). For example:

■ Research on appellate courts finds that female judges tend to be stronger supporters of women's rights claims, regardless of their ideology (Palmer 2001).

■ In Pennsylvania, female judges are somewhat harsher in sentencing criminal defendants. Notably, they are particularly hard toward repeat minority offenders (Steffensmeier and Hebert 1999).

But other studies find no gender differences among judges. For example:

■ A study of Justice Sandra Day O'Connor, the first woman to serve on the U.S. Supreme Court, concludes, "Overall, the findings presented here do very little to support the assertion that O'Connor's decision making is distinct by virtue of her gender" (Davis 1993, 139).

■ Analysis of more than 2,100 written opinions from 1992 to 1995 indicated that male and female federal district court judges were not significantly different when it came to their decisions (Stidham and Carp 1997).

Perhaps the best summary is that drawing conclusions about the difference women make on the bench is still problematical (Davis, Haire, and Songer 1993).

The American Judicature Society reported in 1973 that slightly more than 1 percent of state judges were black. By the mid-1980s, the percentage had increased to 3.8 percent. Thus, Barbara Luck Graham (1990b) found 714 black state court judges in 41 states in 1986. The underrepresentation of blacks on the bench is partially a reflection of the paucity of black attorneys (25,000 out of a total pool of more than 750,000). But underrepresentation is also a product of how judges are selected. Black judges are more likely to be found in states using appointment either by the governor or the legislature; they are less likely to be selected in states using elections (Graham 1990a). In 1991 the Supreme Court held that the Voting Rights Act of 1965, as amended in 1982, applies to judicial elections (*Chisom v. Roemer* and *Houston Lawyers' Association v. Attorney General of Texas*). These rulings pave the way for major changes in the 41 states, particularly in the South, that use elections for at least some of their judges (Smith and Garmel 1992) (see Case Close-Up: *Chisom v. Roemer* and Diversity on the Bench).

JUDGING THE JUDGES

Judicial selection techniques attempt to recruit Solomon-like figures to the bench. Judicial education programs help beginning judges learn their new roles and keep veteran judges abreast of changes in the law. The troublesome problem remains, however: What should be done about unfit judges? Despite the lack of clarity in what attributes a good judge should possess, one central conclusion stands out: A few judges do not fulfill minimal standards. A few are senile, prejudiced, vindictive, tyrannical, lazy, and sometimes corrupt. Proper judicial conduct is indispensable to people's confidence in their judiciary, confidence that itself is indispensable to the rule of law. In recent years such confidence has been eroded by questions of judicial misconduct in a variety of states, including California, Illinois, Florida, New York, Oklahoma, Rhode Island, Pennsylvania, and New Hampshire.

Judicial Independence

A critical issue in judging the judges is how to devise a system for removing unfit judges while at the same time guaranteeing **judicial independence.** At times critics attempt to remove a judge from office not because of his or her misconduct, but solely because of displeasure with the substance of the judge's decisions. Clearly, protections against unpopular court rulings constitute the hallmark of an independent judiciary. Yet judicial independence is not an end in itself. As University of Chicago Law Professor Philip Kurland has put it, "The provisions for securing the independence of the judiciary were not created for the benefit of the judges, but for the benefit of the judged" (quoted in Byrd 1976, 267). Courts, Controversy, and the Administration of Justice: Is Judicial Independence Being Undermined? explores this topic in a contemporary setting.

Judicial Misconduct

Systems for removing or disciplining unfit judges must not only strike a balance between

CASE CLOSE-UP

Chisom v. Roemer and Diversity on the Bench

 Janice Clark had always wanted to be a judge. As a practicing lawyer, she seemed to possess the education and experience necessary to don the black robes, but she still faced an insurmountable barrier. The problem was not gender—after all, women were being elected to the bench on a regular basis all over the United States. Rather, the insurmountable barrier was race. White voters rarely voted for black candidates; indeed as a black candidate for a judgeship, she received only 3 percent of the white vote. So as lawyers often do, she filed suit in the U.S. District Court for the Middle District of Louisiana.

Janice Clark's lawsuit raises some deep-seated questions about who our judges are and how best to select them. Should their backgrounds matter? Is it enough to have a bench composed of fair and impartial individuals? Or does the appearance of justice also require that our judges broadly reflect the society they serve and protect?

Janice Clark's lawsuit was a class action brought by black voters and black lawyers qualified to be elected judges in Louisiana. The district court opinion stressed that only 2 of the 156 district court judgeships in Louisiana were held by blacks. The reason was that judgeships were elected from the entire judicial district, which had the effect of "diluting black voting strength," a violation of the Voting Rights Act (Engstrom 1989). This case was one of several filed in the federal courts, and the underlying legal issue was

eventually settled at the appellate level in *Chisom v. Roemer* (1991) and *Houston Lawyers' Association v. Attorney General of Texas* (1991). The Supreme Court held that judges were indeed covered by the Voting Rights Act of 1965. Crossing this important threshold means that when election districts (either for legislatures or judges) are drawn, the lines may not dilute minority voting.

The essential problem is that judges are elected from judicial districts (typically one or more counties), with multiple judgeships elected at large. These longtime practices make the remedy difficult. Several states—Arkansas, Louisiana, and Mississippi among them—have created black majority subdistricts. Some judges continue to be elected from the entire jurisdiction, but others are selected only from one area of the district (Smothers 1996). The result is that blacks win elections in these districts (Kirksey 1997).

The future of this line of decisions is cloudy. In a series of sharply divided opinions, the nation's highest court has struck down majority-minority congressional districts, ruling that the district lines were motivated primarily by race and not justified by legitimate state interests (*Bush v. Vera* 1996; *Shaw v. Hunt* 1996; *Miller v. Johnson* 1995; *Abrams et al. v. Johnson et al.* 1997) (Scruggs, Mazzola, and Zaug 1995).

Although the long-term impact of *Chisom v. Roemer* remains unclear, the outcome for Janice Clark was both immediate and positive. She ran again for the major trial court bench in Baton Rouge and won.

---

judicial accountability and judicial independence, they must also grapple with the wide range of misbehavior encompassed by the phrase *judicial misconduct* (Begue and Goldstein 1987). Most directly, judicial misconduct involves corruption. In recent years judges in big cities such as Chicago, New York, and Philadelphia have been accused of (and sometimes convicted of) such criminal offenses as taking bribes and fixing traffic tickets. But not all judicial misconduct is so venal; sometimes it involves improper or bizarre behavior on the

bench (Wice 1991). Exhibit 8-3 summarizes some recent cases that illustrate the range of behavior.

The most difficult situations involve judges of advanced years whose mental capacity has become impaired. After years of dedicated service, with exemplary conduct on the bench and no hint of scandal, a judge might become senile. Accordingly, a growing number of states impose mandatory retirement ages for judges. The Supreme Court has ruled that state laws requiring judges to retire at 70 years of age do

COURTS, CONTROVERSY, AND THE ADMINISTRATION OF JUSTICE

Is Judicial Independence Being Undermined?

 Attorney General Ashcroft's criticism of federal judges who sentence "too leniently" is but the most recent example of attacks on judges and the decisions they render. In an adversary system, a judge's decision often fails to find favor with the losing party. But some worry that in the modern era, attacks on judges seriously undermine judicial independence. In recent years, both state and federal judges have been the subject of attack.

■ Justice Penny White of the Tennessee Supreme Court was voted off the bench in a retention election because she voted in a death penalty case to allow the defendant to put on evidence in mitigation (Bright 1997).

■ Justice David Lanphier of the Nebraska Supreme Court lost a retention election when a cluster of special interest groups campaigned for his removal over displeasure with selected decisions (Reid 1999).

■ H. Lee Sarokin, U.S. Court of Appeals for the Third Circuit (based in Philadelphia), resigned. An appointee of Democratic presidents, he had been criticized by Republican presidential hopeful Robert Dole. According to Judge Sarokin, "The constant politicization of my tenure has made 'my' lifetime dream impossible" (Mauro 1996).

■ Justice Harold Baer suppressed 80 pounds of cocaine but later reversed his ruling following intense criticism from the Republican presidential candidate (Neumeister 1996).

Attacks on the federal judiciary are hardly new. President Jefferson tried to remove Justice Samuel Chase as part of a campaign to "reform" the federal judiciary. In the 1960s, a nationwide campaign was launched by the ultraconservative John Birch Society to impeach Chief Justice Earl Warren. Not surprisingly, attacks on federal judges most often occur during election years (Segal 2000). Thus, during the 1968 presidential election, candidate Richard Nixon attacked the Supreme Court, promising to remake the high court in his own image (see Chapter 17). But almost invariably, challenges to judicial independence fail (Friedman 1998).

Attacks on the judiciary, though somewhat predictable, can still exert a chilling effect on judicial independence. Chief Justice William Rehnquist has voiced concern along these lines: "There is a wrong way and right way to go about putting a popular imprint on the judiciary" (Carelli 1996). In the same vein, Law Professor Stephen Burbank (1987) reminds us that judicial independence is a means to an end rather than an end itself. Criticism is one thing; undermining judicial independence is another. "Courts are not independent when state judges are voted off the bench because of unpopular decisions by their courts, and when federal judges reverse decisions or resign from the bench after a barrage of criticism" (Bright 1997, 167).

What do you think? Where do you draw the line between fair criticism of judges and intimidation?

To continue the debate, check out the following sources:

The ABA Standing Committee on Judicial Independence http://www.abanet.org/judind/home.html

Citizens for Independent Courts http://www.constitutionproject.org/cfic.html

Brennan Center for Justice http://www.brennancenter.org/

---

not violate the federal Age Discrimination in Employment Act (*Gregory v. Ashcroft* 1991). In another widely followed case, the nation's highest court upheld the prison sentence of David Lanier, a state judge from Dyersburg, Tennessee. Judge Lanier had been convicted in federal court of sexually attacking five women in his courtroom. He had not been prosecuted in state court, nor had the state's conduct commission taken action—many said because the judge was politically well connected and his brother was the county prosecutor. The decision strengthened federal civil rights laws (Chapter 3), but the opinion stopped short of recognizing a federal right not to be raped by a state official (*U.S. v. Lanier* 1997). Exhibit 8-4

Exhibit 8-3 Examples of Errant State Judges

- Shannon Jones, a part-time judge in the Tennessee General Sessions Court, was disciplined for accepting a client for his private law practice who also had legal matters before his court ("Judge Censured," 2003).
- Rudy Montoya, a Mora County magistrate in New Mexico, agreed to a 90-day suspension without pay while contesting allegations that "he lacks fundamental integrity and honesty . . . and has intentionally disregarded the law" (Propp 2003).
- Florida Circuit Judge Michael Blackstone resigned rather than contest allegations that he abused lawyers, made arbitrary decisions, and lied under oath about these matters ("This Week in Review" 2000).
- The Maryland Judicial Commission issued a warning to a Montgomery County circuit judge who told an 11-year-old female sexual assault victim that "it takes two to tango" ("Maryland Judge Warned" 2000).
- Judge Sharon Hunter of Criminal District Court in New Orleans was removed from office for repeated failures to supervise her courtroom, resulting in numerous murder convictions' being overturned because of the absence of trial transcripts (Filosa 2002).
- Gerald Garson, a judge in Brooklyn's Supreme Court (New York's equivalent of the trial court of general jurisdiction), was indicted for taking bribes in divorce and child custody cases (Newman 2003).

Exhibit 8-4 Key Developments Concerning Judges

Judicial conduct commission	1960	California creates first judicial conduct commission.
Judicial Conduct and Disability Act	1980	Federal conduct law passed.
Gregory v. Ashcroft	1991	State laws requiring judges to retire at 70 do not violate the federal Age Discrimination in Employment Act.
Chisom v. Roemer; Houston Lawyers' Association v. Attorney General of Texas	1991	Judges are covered by the Voting Rights Act.
U.S. v. Lanier	1997	The trial court improperly ruled that state judges are not covered by federal civil rights laws, but there is no federal right not to be raped.
Republican Party v. White	2002	In campaigning for a judgeship, a candidate may discuss issues.

summarizes the Supreme Court cases affecting judges.

Formal methods for removing unfit judges—recall elections and impeachment proceedings—are generally so cumbersome that they have seldom been used. Moreover, these techniques are better directed at corrupt judges than those whose behavior is improper or whose advanced age has caught up with them. A more workable method for dealing with judicial misconduct is the judicial conduct commission.

State Judicial Conduct Commissions

In 1960 California became the first state to adopt a modern and practical system for disciplining its judges. In response to the mounting public clamor for accountability on the part of government officials, every state has followed California's pioneering lead (Brooks 1985). Under the California model, a **judicial conduct commission** is created as an arm of the state's highest court. The commission, made up of judges, lawyers, and prominent laypersons, investigates allegations of judicial misconduct and, when appropriate, hears testimony.

If the commission finds in favor of the judge, the investigation is closed and the matter is permanently concluded (Miller 1991). Confidentiality is essential, lest a judge's reputation be tarnished by a crank complaint. Many complaints are issued by disgruntled litigants, whose charges amount to simple displeasure that the judge did not rule in their favor. If the complaint has merit, the commission may recommend a sanction of private admonishment, public censure, retirement, or removal. The state supreme court retains the final power to discipline errant judges (Gardiner 1986).

Although commissions are armed with the potent weapon of a public recommendation, they prefer to act more informally. If the information gathered suggests judicial misconduct, the commission holds a confidential conference and discusses the matter with the judge, who has an opportunity to rebut the charges. The commission may try to correct the matter; a judge with a substance abuse problem, for example, is encouraged to enroll in a treatment program. If the problems are serious, continuous, or not immediately solvable, the commission usually seeks to force the judge's voluntary retirement. The informal pressures and the threat of bringing public proceedings are often powerful enough to force the judge in question off the bench. The complaints and investigations remain confidential unless the commission finds it necessary to seek a reprimand or removal before the state supreme court.

Federal Conduct and Disability Act

In 1980 Congress passed the Judicial Councils Reform and Judicial Conduct and Disability Act, which lays out a precise mechanism for acting on complaints against federal judges (Neisser 1981; Burbank 1987). Complaints are initially heard by the judicial councils (the administrative arm of each U.S. court of appeals). Most result in either a finding of no misconduct or the imposition of nonpublic sanctions. However, if there is substantial evidence of serious misconduct, the judicial council sends a written report to the Judicial Conference, which may recommend that the U.S. House of Representatives begin impeachment procedures.

Article II of the Constitution provides for the removal of the president, vice president, or civil officers of the United States—including federal judges—for crimes of "treason, bribery, or other high crimes and misdemeanors." The House must first vote articles of impeachment specifying the specific charges. **Impeachment** does not mean conviction, but rather allegations of wrongdoing—roughly equivalent to a grand jury indictment. The trial on the articles of impeachment is conducted before the Senate. Conviction requires a two-thirds vote of the senators present and carries with it **removal** from office and disqualification from holding any future office. Historically, in functioning as both judge and jury in impeachment trials, all senators observed the testimony and cross-examination of witnesses. But in the modern era, the press of legislative business makes this time-consuming process unworkable. Therefore, in 1986 the Senate made the historic decision to establish a 12-person Impeachment Committee to receive evidence and take testimony prior to the trial on the Senate floor (Heflin 1987).

An unprecedented series of allegations of misconduct against federal judges since 1981 highlights the interlocking relationships among criminal prosecutions, impeachment, and the new statutory scheme (Exhibit 8-5). The impeachment proceedings against U.S. District Judge Alcee Hastings raised the most difficult questions: Unlike Claiborne and Nixon, he was never convicted of a criminal offense. Hastings, the first black federal judge ever appointed in Florida, was indicted for soliciting a $150,000 bribe from two convicted racketeers, but the jury acquitted. Hastings argued that racial motivations lay behind the impeachment proceedings. In 1989 the Senate removed Hastings from his judicial office, but in

Exhibit 8-5 Federal Judges Who Have Faced Disciplinary Action

- **U.S. District Judge Harry Claiborne (District of Nevada)** The jury acquitted on the charge of accepting a bribe in a criminal case over which he was presiding but convicted him of income tax evasion. While he was serving a two-year sentence in federal prison, the Senate found Claiborne guilty on three of four impeachment articles by the required two-thirds vote and removed him from the bench (1986).

- **Chief Judge Walter Nixon (Southern District of Mississippi)** The jury convicted him of perjury for falsely denying before a federal grand jury that he had intervened in a state narcotics case involving the son of a friend. While he was serving his sentence at Eglin Air Force Base in Florida, the Senate removed Nixon from the federal bench (1989).

- **U.S. District Judge Alcee Hastings (Southern District of Florida)** The jury acquitted him of the charge of soliciting a $150,000 bribe from two convicted racketeers. The Eleventh Circuit and the Judicial Conference concluded that Hastings was not only guilty but had also fabricated his defense. The Senate ousted Hastings from office in 1989, but in a strange twist, Hastings was then elected to Congress.

- **U.S. District Judge Robert Aguilar (Northern District of California)** A jury convicted him of obstruction of justice for telling a friend about a government wiretap in a racketeering investigation. The Ninth Circuit reversed, but the Supreme Court reinstated the wiretap conviction (*U.S. v. Aguilar* 1995). After another conviction and yet another appellate reversal, Aguilar resigned from the bench, apparently in exchange for criminal charges' being dropped.

- **U.S. District Judge Robert Collins (Eastern District of Louisiana)** A jury convicted him of taking a $100,000 bribe from a drug smuggler. While serving a seven-year prison sentence and facing impeachment proceedings, Collins resigned from the bench before formal Senate action was taken.

- **U.S. District Judge Brian Duff (Northern District of Illinois)** Noted for a temper as black as his judicial robe and the highest rate of reversal in the Chicago courthouse, he stepped down amid reports of a Justice Department complaint filed with the Judicial Counsel for the Seventh Circuit. Judge Duff cited medical problems (Robinson 1996).

a strange twist Hastings was later elected to the U.S. House of Representatives.

The situations of these six federal judges are truly exceptional. Prior to the 1980s, only four federal judges had been removed, the most recent in 1936. But these statistics obscure the fact that many misconduct and disability problems of federal judges are resolved informally by the judiciary itself. In turn, these informal methods have been greatly strengthened by the enactment of the federal judicial discipline statute (Fitzpatrick 1988).

CONCLUSION

It is ironic that Judge Paul Cassell would be criticized for imposing lenient sentences. As a law professor, he was the leading critic of the *Miranda* decision on police interrogations (see Chapter 12) and was confirmed only after Democrats in the Senate expressed skepticism about his ability to be fair and impartial as a judge. Moreover, it has been conservative justices of the Supreme Court like Chief Justice Rehnquist who have defended fellow judges against charges of undue leniency. Thus this debate illustrates that not all criticisms of judges are ideologically based. Rather, some reflect conflicts with other branches of government. At the federal level, legislators and executives are often displeased with judicial decisions. At the state and local level, prosecutors often publicly express their displeasure when a judge suppresses evidence or imposes a "lenient" sentence. As for Judge Cassell, he has made it clear that he will not let criticism

A Virtual Tour of American Courthouses: The Judiciary

Fictional Judges

How we think about judges is greatly influenced by what we see on television. One of the most popular such shows is *Judge Judy,* who provides a no-nonsense approach to judging. Check out her Web site at **http://www.judgejudy.com/ home/home.asp**. Links about other courtroom shows are readily available at **http://dir.yahoo.com/Entertainment/ Television_Shows/Courtroom_Shows/**, which provides links to dramas ranging from *Judge Hatchet,* who offers litigants interventions to help them understand the implications of their actions, to Judge Julie Strain of *Sex Court,* who presides over a series of naughty cases. To scholars, these shows range from largely rubbish to somewhat informative.

Real-Life Judges

The work of real-life judges is much more prosaic than what one views on television. One way to judge what judges really do, at least during trial, is to watch a real trial, either in an actual courtroom or as broadcast on TV. Check out CourtTV.com at **http://www.courttv.com/index2.html** for what trials are being broadcast that day as well as what trials are available for purchase on video or DVD.

Selecting Judges

How does your state choose judges and why? When did the state last make a change? If these questions interest you, go to the American Judicature Society Web site, which provides judicial selection history for each state at **http://www.ajs. org/js/**.

   If you are confused about whom to vote for for judge, visit the League of Women Voters Web site, which offers a

Voters' Guide to Judicial Elections at **http://www.ca.lwv. org/lwvc.files/judic/**.

Judicial Education

Ever wonder what judges learn when they go back to school? If so, click on the National Judicial College Web site at **http:// www.judges.org/**. Also worth examining is the National Clearinghouse for Judicial Education Information, which features its programs at **http://jeritt.msu.edu**.

Web Sites by Judges

A variety of organizations composed of judges maintain Web sites that provide some insights into their views of the world. For example:

National Association of Women Judges **http://www.nawj.org**
American Judges Association **http://aja.ncsc.dni.us/**
National American Indian Court Judges Association **http:// www.naicja.org/**
National Council of Juvenile and Family Court Judges **http:// www.ncjfcj.org/**

Judicial Misconduct

If you are interested in how your state deals with allegations of judicial misconduct, point your browser to **http://dir.yahoo. com/Government/U_S__Government/Judicial_Branch/ State_Courts/**.

You will need to root around a little to find the Web site you want. First try the link to your state supreme court to locate your state agency. A useful comparison is the State of Illinois Judicial Inquiry Board, which provides FAQs at **http://www. state.il.us/jib/faq.htm**.

---

affect his decisions—in short, he will remain independent (Willing 2003).

   In the modern era, displeasure with judges has lead to renewed interest in how judges are selected. But no matter how we select our judges and who they are, the workaday world of the trial judge bears little resemblance to the high expectations we have about the role of the judge. The trial judge is expected to dispose of a large caseload but is often frustrated by the attorneys' lack of preparation, missing

defendants, misplaced files, little time to reflect, and probably most important, insufficient control over many vital aspects of the case. For these and other reasons, judges depend on other members of the courtroom work group. Some depend heavily on the prosecutors, defense attorneys, and probation officers, feeling content to let them make the difficult decisions. Others are much more active participants and are truly leaders of the courtroom work group.

CRITICAL THINKING QUESTIONS

1. Which method of judicial selection (election, appointment, or merit selection) do you think is best? What does your choice reveal about your personal attitudes? Stated another way, do you think the legal profession should have more say in judicial selection (merit) or less influence (elections)?

2. For your state, examine judicial selection in terms of both law on the books (formal method of judicial selection) and law in action (actual practices).

3. At what point are efforts to remove "unfit judges" really efforts to remove judges because of decisions they have made?

4. American society has high expectations for judges, yet the actions of judges are constrained by other members of the courtroom work group. To what extent is criticism of judges, whether local or national, really criticism of the actions and inactions of prosecutors and defense attorneys?

5. Does underrepresentation of women on the bench hurt justice? Would citizens' views of the fairness of courts improve if more nontraditional persons became judges?

KEY TERMS

American Bar Association (ABA) (177)
chambers (172)
gubernatorial appointment (177)
impeachment (186)
judicial conduct commission (186)
judicial election (177)
judicial independence (182)
Missouri Bar Plan (178)
removal (186)

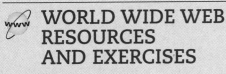

WORLD WIDE WEB RESOURCES AND EXERCISES

Web Guides

http://dir.yahoo.com/Government/Law/U_S_States/

http://dir.yahoo.com/Government/U_S__Government/ Judicial_Branch/

Web Search Terms

judges
judicial misconduct

Useful URLs

The American Judicature Society Web site is at **http://www.ajs.org**.

The National Association of Judicial Educators Web site is at **http://www.dcr.net/~aragorn/**.

The Brennan Center for Justice offers "Q and A about Judicial Independence": **http://www. brennancenter.org/resources/resources_jiqanda.html**.

The Institute for Court Management (ICM) can be found at **http://www.ncsc.dni.us/ICM/ index.html**.

The Fund for More Modern Courts is a nonpartisan, nonprofit, statewide court reform organization for New York: **http://www. moderncourts.org/**.

Visit the National Association of State Judicial Educators at **http://nasje.unm.edu/**.

Uncommon URLs

Visit the Committee to Expose Dishonest and Incompetent Attorneys and Judges at **http://www.amoralethics.com/**.

The American Judges Association is at **http://aja.ncsc.dni.us/**.

The Alliance for Justice's Judicial Selection Project stresses securing access to justice: **http://www.afj.org/jsp/home.html**.

The Center for Judicial Accountability is a national, nonpartisan organization documenting how judges break the law and get away with it: **http://www.judgewatch.org/**.

The Justice Web Collaboratory is a joint project of the Chicago–Kent College of Law and the National Center for State Courts: http://judgelink.org/.

JudicialWatch is an ethical and legal "watchdog" over our government, legal, and judicial systems, with a conservative orientation: http://www.judicialwatch.org/.

Web Exercises

1. How easy is it to find the location of your state's judicial conduct commission? Start by going to http://www.findlaw.com/, and then choose State Law Resources/State Name. The first place to look is under the state supreme court. If you are successful in locating any information, ask yourself how helpful this information is. If you were a citizen with a complaint about a judge, how easy or difficult would it be to seek remedial action?

2. Judicial selection is often a hot subject. Search for information by going to Yahoo at http://www.yahoo.com, and then choose Society and Culture/Crime. Search for "judicial selection." What types of groups appear to be involved? What arguments do they use to buttress their position that a change is needed?

3. Humor is a longtime staple of the courthouse. The following site contains some all-time favorites of what can go wrong: http://ubweb.acns.nwu.edu/~bil874/comedy/occup/lalawless.htm. Ask yourself why these situations are so humorous. Is it the lawyer or the judge who isn't thinking? Or are these situations humorous because lay citizens have such limited knowledge of law and court procedures?

INFOTRAC COLLEGE EDITION RESOURCES AND EXERCISES

Basic Searches

judges
judicial searches
judicial candidates

disqualification of judges
women judges
African American judges

Recommended Articles

Erwin Chemerinsky, "When Do Lawmakers Threaten Judicial Independence?"

Ebony, "Judges with Clout"

Jose Angel Gutierrez, "Experiences of Chicana County Judges in Texas Politics"

Richard H. Middleton, Jr., "Remembering Two Giants of Judicial Independence"

"One Man's Activist: What Republicans Really Mean When They Condemn Judicial Activism"

Stephen Williams, "Judges in the Dock"

InfoTrac College Edition Exercises

1. Using the search term "judicial selection" and/or "judges elections," locate two or more articles on the topic. What advantages and disadvantages are discussed for electing judges? How often do criticisms of current methods of judicial selection stress decisions that the writer thinks are wrong?

2. Using the search term "judicial activism," select two or more articles that discuss the U.S. Supreme Court. To what extent are discussions of judicial activism understood using the concepts of the due process and crime control models of criminal justice?

FOR FURTHER READING

Barrow, Deborah, Gary Zuk, and Gerard Gryski. *The Federal Judiciary and Institutional Change.* Ann Arbor: University of Michigan Press, 1996.

Bushnell, Eleanore. *Crimes, Follies, and Misfortunes: The Federal Impeachment Trials.* Champaign: University of Illinois Press, 1992.

Champagne, Anthony, and Judith Haydel, eds. *Judicial Reform in the States.* Lanham, MD: University Press of America, 1993.

Drachman, Virginia. *Sisters in Law: Women Lawyers in Modern American History.* Cambridge, MA: Harvard University Press, 1998.

Epstein, Cynthia. *Women in Law.* 2d ed. Urbana: University of Illinois Press, 1993.

Gerhardt, Michael. *The Federal Impeachment Process: A Constitutional and Historical Analysis.* Princeton, NJ: Princeton University Press, 1996.

Gryski, Gerard, Gary Zuk, and Deborah Barrow. "A Bench That Looks Like America? Representation of African-Americans and Latinos on the Federal Courts." *Journal of Politics* 56 (1994): 1076–1086.

Lyles, Kevin. *The Gatekeepers: Federal District Courts in the Political Process*. Westport, CT: Praeger, 1997.

Sheldon, Charles, and Linda Maule. *Choosing Justice: The Recruitment of State and Federal Judges*. Pullman: Washington State University Press, 1997.

Spohn, Cassia. "The Sentencing Decisions of Black and White Judges: Expected and Unexpected Similarities." *Law and Society Review* 24 (1990): 1197–1216.

Stidham, Ronald, Robert Carp, and Donald Songer. "The Voting Behavior of President Clinton's Judicial Appointees." *Judicature* 80 (1996): 16–28.

Van Tassel, Emily Field, and Paul Finkelman, eds. *Impeachable Offenses: A Documentary History from 1878 to the Present.* Washington, DC: Congressional Quarterly, 1999.

Washington, Linn. *Black Judges on Justice: Perspectives from the Bench.* New York: New Press, 1994.

he first officer on the scene described Pervis Tyrone Payne as looking like "he was sweating blood." The officer's partner followed the trail of blood into the kitchen, where he found Charissee Christopher and her 2-year-old daughter Lacie butchered to death. After returning a verdict of guilty of two counts of first-degree murder, the trial proceeded to the penalty phase of a capital murder prosecution. The defense called four witnesses, who testified that Payne was a very caring person but had such a low score on an IQ test that he was mentally handicapped. The prosecutor countered by calling the victim's grandmother to the stand, who testified that 3-year-old Nicholas (the lone survivor) kept asking why his mother didn't come home, and he cried for his sister. During closing argument the prosecutor made maximum use of this emotional testimony, imploring the jury to make sure that Nicholas would know later in life that justice had been done in his mother's brutal slaying. The Memphis, Tennessee, jury imposed the death penalty. ◄

The difficulty with the grandmother's testimony is that, just a couple of years before, the Supreme Court had ruled that such emotional statements are inadmissible because they tend to mislead jurors. But in the interim, the membership of the Court had changed, with the addition of two conservatives appointed by Republican presidents. By agreeing to hear the case, the Court was signaling that it might be willing to reverse itself and allow victim impact statements during sentencing.

Payne v. Tennessee directs our attention to both defendants and their victims. All too often, when we think about the criminal courts, our minds immediately focus on the members of the courtroom work group: prosecutors, defense attorneys, and judges. We are less likely to think about the other participants: victims, witnesses, or even defendants. Yet these other actors are also important.

Victims greatly influence workload. Courts are passive institutions. They do not seek out cases to decide; rather, they depend on others to bring matters to their attention. How many cases are filed, as well as what kinds of cases are brought to court, is determined by the decisions of others—police, victims, and those who violate the law in the first place. Thus, the courtroom work group has very little control over its workload. Second, victims, witnesses, and defendants are the consumers of the court process. Democratic governments are expected to be responsive to the wishes and demands of

their citizens; victims and witnesses often complain about how the courts handle their cases. Victims and defendants are both subjects and objects of the criminal justice process. Their importance for how the courtroom work group administers justice on a day-to-day basis is the subject of this chapter.

▌ DEFENDANTS

In some ways, those accused of violating the criminal law are a diverse lot. Although many defendants are economically impoverished, their numbers also include high-ranking government officials, businesspeople, and prominent local citizens. An indicator of the diversity of defendants centers on how often they are involved with the criminal justice system. At one end of the spectrum are those who are arrested once and are never involved again. At the other end are a small group of career criminals who are responsible for a disproportionate share of offenses (Moore et al. 1984). To complicate matters further, there are indications of a generational effect. Violent offenders are much more likely to have experienced abuse and violence in their families (Harlow 1999). Moreover, conviction of a parent is correlated with the likelihood of a child's being convicted (Rowe and Farrington 1997). Whether it is possible to predict who will become a career criminal, however, is subject to extensive debate.

Exhibit 9-1	Profile of State Prison Inmates		
Women	7%	High school diploma or equivalent	57%
Racial or ethnic minorities	64%	Unemployed before arrest	33%
35 or younger	57%	Non-U.S. citizen	4%
Married	18%	Offense committed under the influence of drugs	36%
Never married	55%	Offense committed under the influence of alcohol	32%
Raised primarily in single-parent home	43%		
Prior incarceration of immediate family member	36%	Violent offense conviction	49%
Prior adult incarceration	55%	Property offense conviction	20%
Prior conviction	81%	Drug conviction	21%

SOURCES: U.S. Department of Justice, Bureau of Justice Statistics, Criminal Offenders Statistics, http://www.ojp. usdoj.gov/bjs/crimoff.htm, retrieved 24 November 2003; James Lynch, Steven Smith, Helen Graziadei, and Tanutda Pittayathikhun, *Profile of Inmates in the United States and in England and Wales, 1991* (Washington, DC: U.S. Department of Justice, Bureau of Justice Statistics, 1994).

Characteristics of Defendants

Aside from certain aspects of diversity, the majority of violators conform to a definite profile. Compared to the average citizen, felony defendants are significantly younger, overwhelmingly male, disproportionately members of racial minorities, more likely to come from broken homes, less educated, more likely to be unemployed, and less likely to be married. By the time the court sorting process has ended, those sentenced to prison consist of an even higher proportion of poor, young, illiterate, minority males (see Exhibit 9-1). Three characteristics of defendants—gender, poverty, and race—figure prominently in discussions of crime and crime policy and therefore deserve expanded treatment.

Overwhelmingly Male

Defendants are overwhelmingly male. A look at Exhibit 9-1 shows that about 7 percent of prisoners are female. The male domination of crime is the subject of a book with the provocative title *Just Boys Doing Business: Men, Masculinities and Crime* (Newburn and Stanko 1994). To be sure, rates of female involvement in the justice system have been increasing in recent years, but absolute numbers still fall well below those of males. Not only are women less likely to be arrested, but when prosecuted they are charged with less serious offenses. Women in prison for crimes such as robbery, burglary, and drug dealing were likely to have had a male accomplice who played a primary role (Alarid et al. 1996).

Mostly Underclass

Typical felony defendants possess few of the skills needed to compete successfully in an increasingly technological society. They are drawn from what sociologists call the urban underclass (Jencks and Peterson 1991). The association of crime with poverty explains why the overwhelming number of crimes—primarily burglary, theft, and drug sale—are committed for economic motives. Although crimes of violence dominate the headlines, most defendants are not dangerous; they are charged with property or drug offenses.

Racial Minorities Overrepresented

Race remains a divisive issue in American politics, and nowhere is this more evident than in the area of crime. African Americans, Hispanics, and Native Americans are imprisoned at a significantly higher rate than whites. At the same time, it is important to stress that historically whites constituted the majority of those in prison, a fact conveniently ignored on some radio and TV discussions.

Why minorities are overrepresented in the criminal justice system is a topic of considerable importance (and therefore addressed in several later chapters). To some it is an indication that minorities are more likely to be poor and therefore more likely to commit crimes for economic advancement. Others counter that discrimination is the reason; minorities are more likely to be targeted by criminal justice officials and also more likely to receive a harsh sentence. Whatever the cause, the impact is enormous. One in three young black males is in trouble with the law—either in prison, on probation, or on parole (Cass 1995).

Defendants in Court

The **defendant** is supposed to stand at the center of the criminal court drama. Yet the typical felony defendant is largely powerless to control his fate—more an object to be acted upon than the key to what happens. Because most defendants are poor and uneducated, they are ill equipped to deal with the technical abstractions of the criminal court process. Many are incapable of understanding even the simplest instructions about the right to bail or the presumption of innocence. Many are too inarticulate to aid their attorneys in preparing a defense. Many hold unfavorable attitudes toward the law and the criminal justice system and thus regard the judge and all other court personnel, including their defense attorneys, with hostility and distrust. As a result, the huge majority of defendants

> submit to the painful consequences of conviction but do not know for certain whether they committed any of the crimes of which they are accused. Such defendants are so unschooled in law that they form no firm opinion about their technical innocence or guilt. (Rosett and Cressey 1976, 146)

As a result, they neither agree or disagree that it is just to punish them.

The nature of the clientele makes criminal courts a depressing place to work. Judges, prosecutors, and defense attorneys seldom come away from their day's activities with a sense of accomplishment, for many of the criminal cases involve such social problems as drug addiction, marital problems, lack of education, and mental illness, over which the court personnel have no control. Many cases stem from disputes between people who know one another. An in-depth study of felony case dispositions in New York City summed it up this way:

> The incidents that give rise to arrest are frequently not the kind that the court system is able to deal with satisfactorily. At the root of much of the crime brought to court is anger—simple or complicated anger between two or more people who know each other. Expressions of anger result in the commission of technical felonies, yet defense attorneys, judges, and prosecutors recognize that in many cases conviction and prison sentences are inappropriate responses. High rates of dismissal or charge reduction appear to be a reflection of the system's effort to carry out the intent of the law—as judges and other participants perceive it—though not necessarily the letter of the law. (Vera Institute of Justice 1981, xv)

Court personnel have little empathy with or understanding of the types of defendants whose fates they must decide. Members of the courtroom work group are essentially middle class. Little in their backgrounds or training has equipped them to deal with violations of the law committed by the poor.

COURTS THROUGH THE EYES OF VICTIMS AND WITNESSES

Traditionally, victims and witnesses have been the forgotten participants in the criminal justice system. Fictional and nonfictional treatments of

THE MURDER TRIAL OF SHAREEF COUSIN

The Anguish of the Victims

For the last several decades, the politics of victims, and not the rights of defendants, have dominated criminal justice policymaking. The anguish of the victims in the Port of Call murder case, and their alternating emotions, provide a poignant close-up.

"My life is like a black void, a hole. I can't sleep at night and I watch television until the wee hours of the morning," testified Sal Gerardi, the victim's father. His body heaving with sobs, he described roaring across Interstate 10 toward New Orleans after hearing that his son had been shot (Varney, 1996b). One can only speculate that this victim statement during the penalty phase of the Shareef Cousin murder trial had a powerful impact on the jurors. It was all the more powerful because none of Cousin's relatives would take the witness stand to offer a counter emotion to taking Cousin's life.

When the guilty verdict was announced, Sal Gerardi dropped to one knee and crossed himself. Afterwards he commented, "There still really isn't any satisfaction," and then added, "I feel sorry for their family because they've lost a son now, too" (Varney, 1996c).

The emotions of the victims were radically different two years later when DA Harry Connick announced that he would not retry Cousin. Connie Babin, now married, said the dismissal stung: "I am frustrated, I am devastated, I am angry. I am sad. I am frightened. I am all of those things." She recounted the travails of having testified. Over the past four years, vandals had struck her home, callers had harassed her on the phone, and someone had hanged her in effigy in her front yard. On the witness stand defense attorneys attacked her credibility; outside the courtroom she was branded a racist.

But overall Babin blamed herself. "I was in such a state that night. I was on a mental shutdown, and I wasn't able to express myself." She went on to say, "I am sorry. I messed up, the DA messed up, but I didn't mess up that badly." She remained adamant that Cousin was the murderer (Coyle, 1999).

● To read more about the Shareef Cousin trial, type in the search words "dead teen walking" and read the section "From Father to Son."

the court process direct attention to the criminal as victim rather than to the victim as victim (Elias 1986). Thus, although the literature on offenders is enormous, less is known about victims. In the view of many, the courts, along with the rest of the criminal justice community, have ignored the interests of victims and witnesses.

Frustrations in Coping with the Process

Crime victims once played a prominent role in the criminal process. Before the American Revolution, victims were the central figures in the criminal justice drama. Criminals' fates were closely tied to their victims' wishes. When crime became viewed as an offense against the state, the victim was assigned a subordinate role (Elias 1986). As prosecutorial dominance increased, the power of the victim declined (see Chapter 6). Victims lost control over their cases, and their role was reduced to initiating investigations by complaining to the police and testifying for the prosecution as just another piece of evidence in the state's presentation of damning facts against the accused (Karmen 2001).

Several studies have documented the hardships victims and witnesses face while participating in the criminal court process (McDonald 1976; Cannavale and Falcon 1976; Connick and Davis 1983). Although some are minor inconveniences, such as getting to the courthouse and finding a parking place, other hardships are more significant:

■ Trial delays, which result in frequent travel and wasted time

■ Long waits in uncomfortable surroundings

- Wages lost for time spent going to court
- Fear of the defendant or retaliation from the defendant's associates
- A sense that criminal justice personnel are indifferent to their plight

A Day in Court: Helping Them Bear the Pain focuses on some of the frustrations of witnesses in Philadelphia.

Travails of Testifying

Victims and witnesses also face major problems while testifying in court. Because few people are accustomed to testifying, lawyers must coach their witnesses ahead of time to answer only the question asked, to speak forcefully (but not belligerently), and not to become rattled by cross-examination. Even after such preparation, many witnesses are uncomfortable during cross-examination, as the defense attorney tests their memory, challenges their veracity, or even suggests that they were somehow responsible for their own victimization. After enduring cross-examination, some victims report feeling as though they, and not the offender, have been portrayed as the criminal.

Most of what we know about the ordeal of testifying in court comes from studies of rape victims (Resick 1984). The dominant conclusion is that the victim, rather than the defendant, is put on trial. Testifying in court provokes anxiety for several months, exacerbating psychological distress (Steketee and Austin 1989). Holmstrom and Burgess (1983), both of whom counsel rape victims in Boston City Hospital, followed the cases of 14 women who testified in court during a rape trial. They concluded that the trauma is often significant, because the victim must publicly repeat in detail how the rape occurred. The type of defense employed by the defense attorney also has an impact on the victim's adjustment to the crime. A defense claim that the woman consented to sex is injurious, because it puts the victim on trial and calls into question her discouragement of the perpetrator (Steketee and Austin 1989). Moreover, the defense often seeks to blame the victim by suggesting that she consented, did not resist, was provocatively dressed, and so on. It can take little to discredit the victim. Following the Holm-strom and Burgess study, most states have passed legislation limiting inquiry into a rape victim's past sexual conduct.

Surprising Support for the System

Somewhat surprisingly, despite the problems and frustrations experienced, victims and witnesses still express overall support for the court process (Hagan 1983). In Milwaukee, those surveyed indicated that they were satisfied or very satisfied with the handling of their case by the police (81 percent), district attorney (75 percent), and judge (66 percent). Less than 15 percent said that they were dissatisfied (Knudten et al. 1976). Favorable judgments were independent of whether a victim was satisfied with the eventual outcome of the case.

▌VICTIMS AND WITNESSES THROUGH THE EYES OF THE COURT

The criminal courts confront a double bind with regard to victims. On the one hand, victims are valued for the cases they bring to the system; their misfortunes become the raw material of the court process (Exhibit 9-2). On the other hand, individual victims represent a potential source of irrationality in the process. The personal and often emotional involvement of victims in the crime experience can generate particularized demands for case outcomes that have little to do with the public interest. Thus, at times members of the courtroom work group perceive that the victim's demands for public justice actually mask a desire for private vengeance (Hagan 1983).

Lack of Cooperation

Many victims and witnesses are reluctant to become involved in the criminal justice process. More than half of all major crimes are never reported to the police; even when they are, not all victims wish to prosecute. They may fear reprisal by the suspect, or they may

A DAY IN COURT

Helping Them Bear the Pain

When Sandy Fitzpatrick walks into a courtroom, she often heads for a box of tissue. After several years of working as a victim's advocate for the Snohomish County Prosecuting Attorney's Office, Fitzpatrick has learned the importance of tissue, as well as a hand squeeze, a good cry and listening. Like the county's eight other advocates, Fitzpatrick is the prosecutor's liaison for the victims of violent crimes, as well as their families. As prosecutors focus on winning convictions, Fitzpatrick's role is to focus on the emotional needs of those scarred by crime.

Though she is not an attorney, the 53-year-old Everett woman's job often consists of explaining the intricacies of the legal system to people whose only courtroom experience may have been watching an episode of TV's *Law & Order*. She empathizes with and consoles victims and their families, and often helps prepare them for court testimony. "I've lost three siblings suddenly and tragically, not because of crimes. I can understand that terrible empty feeling," Fitzpatrick said. "I do recognize the sting of death and what it does to families." . . .

Until her divorce in 1993, Fitzpatrick was an active member in the Church of Jesus Christ of Latter-day Saints. She said it was in the church that female parishioners talked to her about being sexually abused. Unclear of the best way to advise the women, Fitzpatrick started volunteering at Providence Everett Medical Center's sexual-assault center. As a volunteer, she was trained in how to help abuse victims. . . .

Deputy Prosecutor Lisa Paul, who oversees the special-assault unit, said Fitzpatrick and other advocates provide a buffer between prosecutors and the constant emotion that can cause attorneys to burn out. Paul said prosecutors need to stay focused on building cases against defendants and can't afford to get wrapped up in the emotional roller coaster that frequently overtakes the lives of victims and their families. It's the job of the victim's advocate to provide the ear for the victim and their family, a shoulder to cry on. They often become counselor, confidant and even friend.

"As a prosecutor, you don't want to be emotionally involved in a case," Paul said. "You really have to work not to get personally involved. You lose perspective if you do."

Though caution, sensitivity, and timing are all essential roles in Fitzpatrick's job, it sometimes can be like April 16—a mad dash from one gut-wrenching court hearing to another. Fitzpatrick began her day in court, seated between the family and ex-wife of Jerry Heimann, who in 2001 was beaten to death by a group of teens in his Everett home. She watched the family's emotion as 16-year-old defendant Kyle Boston was sentenced to 18 years in prison for his role in the slaying. . . .

Mike Shoemaker, a Philadelphia resident whose daughter Carrie was killed by a drunken driver in Everett on Oct. 26, 2001, has nothing but praise for Fitzpatrick. He said she kept him and his wife informed on the case. He said going through the court proceedings, which resulted in a three-year plea agreement for defendant Roy Gursli, would have been "frustratingly impossibly without Sandy." "Sandy, at times, had to perform the function of a counselor," said Shoemaker. "It would have worn us down to nothing without Sandy."

Fitzpatrick concedes her job can get overwhelming. She makes sure she spends time focusing on something else. Which is why she starts every day with an hourlong jog and a quick e-mail conversation with a close friend who lives in Hawaii. "I truly love what I do," Fitzpatrick said. ". . . For the most part I try to wipe my sleeves off when I walk out the back door. It will be waiting for me tomorrow."

SOURCE: Jennifer Sullivan, "Helping Them Bear the Pain," *Seattle Times*, 11 June 2003. Copyright © 2003 Seattle Times Company. Used by permission.

prefer not to go through the ordeal of the court process. Some specific witness-related problems include giving the police incorrect addresses, failing to show up in court, and offering testimony that is confused, garbled, or contradicted by other facts. Witness-related problems result in a significant number of cases in which the prosecutor refuses to file charges or the case is later dismissed (Boland et al. 1982). But when victims are cooperative

Exhibit 9-2 Major Activities of Victims in Steps of the Court Process

	Law on the Books	Law in Action
Crime	No general requirement to report crimes to the police.	Thirty-eight percent of personal and household crimes are reported to the police.
Arrest	A citizen's arrest is the taking of a person into physical custody, by a person other than a law enforcement officer, for the purpose of delivering the person to the custody of a law enforcement officer.	The vast majority of arrests are made by law enforcement officers. Citizen arrests may result in injury to the victim and may also result in civil lawsuits.
Initial appearance	Open to the public.	Very unlikely for victim to be present because unlikely to know timing of the event.
Bail	VRA provides that victims have a right to be heard if present and to submit a statement "to determine a release from custody."	Victims are very rarely present.
Charging	Victim has no role, and the VRA states that "nothing in this article shall provide grounds for the victim to challenge the charging decision."	Reluctance or refusal of victims to cooperate is a key reason for case dismissal.
Preliminary hearing	Besides the right to notice and to be present, the VRA is silent on the role of victims during this stage.	Victims rarely testify because hearsay evidence is admissible.
Grand jury	Grand jury can subpoena victim to testify.	In grand jury states, victim likely to be subpoenaed to testify.
Arraignment	VRA provides that victims of crimes have the right to notice of proceedings like this.	Victims are rarely present.
Evidence	In some jurisdictions, defense is entitled to see a copy of victim's statement to the police.	Even if not required, some DAs disclose victim's statement in hopes of inducing a guilty plea.
Plea bargaining	VRA provides that victims may be heard and may submit a statement during an acceptance of a negotiated plea.	Some jurisdictions allow victims to be heard as to the plea bargain, but few actually appear.
Trial	If they are to testify, victims generally cannot view the trial (wording in the VRA concerning public proceedings might change this law).	Victim's testimony is a key part of the trial.
Sentencing	VRA provides that victims may be heard and may submit a statement during sentencing.	Victims are unlikely to appear.
Appeal	Like other court proceedings, appellate argument is open to the public.	Victims are very unlikely to be present.

VRA = Proposed Victims' Rights Amendment to the U.S. Constitution

with the prosecution, the odds that a case will be prosecuted increase dramatically (Dawson and Dinovitzer 2001).

Not all uncooperative behavior can be blamed on victims and witnesses, however; the court process can be equally at fault. In Washington, D.C., a study focusing on what it called "noncooperative" witnesses reported that 41 percent were never told that they should contact the prosecutor, 62 percent were never notified of court appearances, and 43 percent stated that the police, prosecutor, and judge all failed to explain the witnesses' rights and duties. Other reports have found that the longer the case is delayed, the more likely it is that witnesses will not appear when summoned (Cannavale and Falcon 1976).

Characteristics of Victims

How a case is handled is determined by the identity of the victim as well as that of the offender. Prosecutors allocate their limited resources to the cases they believe constitute the most "trouble" (Hagan 1983). Not surprisingly, such judgments correlate with the desire for high conviction rates. Prosecutors assume that judges and juries will find the claims of certain kinds of victims credible and acceptable, but not the claims of others (Stanko 1981–1982). The troubles of older, white, male, employed victims are considered more worthy of public processing (Myers and Hagan 1979), but most victims of violent crime tend to be young, non-white males, divorced or never married, low income, and unemployed (Bureau of Justice Statistics 1988c; Elias 1986). For example, legal outcomes in murder cases were related to the race, gender, and conduct of victims at the time of the incident (Baumer, Messner, and Felson 2000).

Prior Relationships between Defendants and Victims

Perhaps the most important victim characteristic that influences case processing is the prior relationship between defendants and victims. The following case is illustrative.

An auxiliary police officer watched a woman approach a man as he emerged from a liquor store. It was dark. The officer thought he saw a knife flash in her hand, and the man seemed to hand her some money. She fled, and the officer went to the aid of the victim, taking him to the hospital for treatment.

The officer saw the woman on the street a few days later and arrested her for first degree robbery on the victim's sworn complaint. It was presumably a "high quality" arrest—identification of the perpetrator by an eyewitness, not from mug-shots or a lineup, but in a crowd. Yet, shortly thereafter, this apparently airtight case was dismissed on the prosecutor's motion.

What the victim had not explained to the police was that the defendant, an alcoholic, had been his girlfriend for the past five years; that they had been drinking together the night of the incident; that she had taken some money from him and got angry when he took it back; that she had flown into a fury when he then gave her only a dollar outside the liquor store; and that she had slashed at him with a pen knife in anger and run off. He had been sufficiently annoyed to have her charged with robbery, but, as the judge who dismissed the case said, "He wasn't really injured. Before it got into court they had kissed and made up." In fact, the victim actually approached the defense attorney before the hearing and asked him to prevail upon the judge and the Assistant District Attorney (ADA) to dismiss the charges against his girlfriend. (Vera Institute of Justice 1981, xxii)

This case is one of many cited by the Vera Institute that show the importance of the prior relationship between defendants and victims.

Prior relationships between defendants and victims are more common than generally assumed. In half of all felony arrests in New York, the victim had a prior relationship with the defendant. Prior relationships were frequent in cases of homicide and assault, in which they were expected, but they were also frequent in cases of robbery, in which they were not. Other studies reach a similar conclusion. Nationwide, roughly half of all violent crimes (rape, assault, and robbery) are committed by relatives, friends, or acquaintances of the victim (Bureau of Justice Statistics 2002). Homicides, in particular, are usually committed not by strangers but by someone the victim knows by sight (Hewitt 1988). Criminal court officials often regard crimes involving people who know one another as not very serious, viewing them as private disputes rather than offenses against the entire community.

Domestic Violence

The prior relationship between victims and defendants is most apparent in crimes against women. Men are more likely than women to experience violent victimization. But the nature of these events differs greatly. Women are about six times more likely than men to experience violence committed by an intimate (Bachman and Saltzman 1995). The most recent statistics indicate that about 700,000 incidents of intimate violence occur each year. In 85 percent of these incidents, women are the victims (Bureau of Justice Statistics 2003b).

The prior relationship between victim and offender causes particular problems for law enforcement officials in the area of domestic violence (Buzawa and Buzawa 1996). Many women call the police to stop the violence but later have a change of heart and refuse to sign a complaint. Historically, police officers made an arrest only as a last resort—if taking the suspect into custody seemed the only way to ensure no more violence that night. Over the past 30 years, however, advocacy groups for battered women and victims' advocacy groups have worked vigorously for policy changes designed to make the criminal justice system treat domestic violence as a serious offense. Jeffrey Fagan (1996) has given this movement a name in his aptly titled book, *The Criminalization of Domestic Violence.*

The question of what constitutes the most effective criminal justice response, however, has stirred considerable controversy (Maxwell, Garner, and Fagan 2002). The police have been urged to make more arrests and prosecutors to file charges no matter what the wishes of the victim. Whether these mandatory arrest policies are effective has been questioned, however (Hirschel et al. 1992). Researchers report that arrest reduces domestic violence in some cities but increases it in others (Schmidt and Sherman 1993). Although there is considerable debate over whether mandatory arrest policies actually work, there is little doubt that courts are now handling a higher number of these cases; 91 percent of prosecutors nationwide cite domestic violence crimes as a workload problem (McEwen 1995).

Legal sanctions against domestic violence are not limited to the criminal law. Victims of domestic violence may request a **civil protection order.** Recent legislative changes in most jurisdictions now make these court orders easier to obtain. They are no longer limited to women who have filed for divorce and may be issued on an emergency basis without the other party present. However, civil protection orders are not self-enforcing. There is even a danger that a civil protection order may induce a false sense of security among some women who are at risk of continued battery from a former intimate.

▎ AIDING VICTIMS AND WITNESSES

For decades, reformers have urged that victims and witnesses be accorded better treatment.

■ In 1931 the National Commission on Law Observance and Enforcement concluded that effective administration of public justice required willing witnesses, but testifying in court imposed unreasonable burdens on citizens.

■ A 1938 American Bar Association report found that witness fees were deplorably low, courthouse accommodations uncomfortable, and witnesses were frequently summoned to court numerous times only to have the case continued.

But it was not until the 1960s that attention was seriously devoted to the problems faced by victims and witnesses in court and to ways of improving the situation (Karmen 2001).

Exhibit 9-3 Key Developments in Law Relating to Victims

National Crime Victims' Week	1980	Annual event focusing on the plight of crime victims.
Victim and Witness Protection Act	1982	Enhance and protect the necessary role of crime victims and witnesses in the criminal justice process.
Victims' Rights Amendments	1982	California is first state to adopt.
Victim of Crimes Act	1984	Established Crime Victim Fund from fines, penalties, and bond forfeitures of convicted federal criminals.
Booth v. Maryland	1987	In capital cases, victim impact statements are unconstitutional because they introduce the risk of imposing the death penalty in an arbitrary and capricious manner.
South Carolina v. Gathers	1989	Characteristics of the victim are irrelevant during death penalty deliberations.
Payne v. Tennessee	1991	The Eighth Amendment creates no bar to the introduction of victim impact statements during sentencing.
Simon & Schuster v. New York State Crime Victims Board	1991	Declared unconstitutional New York's "Son of Sam" law, which sought to prevent criminals from profiting from their crimes.
Violence Against Women Act	1994	Comprehensive law creating a variety of programs to strengthen law enforcement, prosecution, and victim services in cases involving crimes against women.
The Antiterrorism and Effective Death Penalty Act	1996	A federal court must impose mandatory restitution, without consideration of the defendant's ability to pay.
Victims' Rights Amendment	1996	VRA proposed in the U.S. Congress.
	2000	VRA withdrawn in face of virtually certain defeat.

■ In 1967 the President's Commission on Law Enforcement and Administration of Justice highlighted a "growing concern that the average citizen identifies himself less and less with the criminal process and its officials."

In recent years, concern for victims and witnesses of crime has risen to a crescendo. Crime victims have been the subject of considerable research and have also received special attention from the White House.

■ In 1982, the President's Task Force on Victims of Crime stressed the need for achieving a balance between the needs and rights of the victim and those of the defendant.

Public and governmental concern over the plight of victims has prompted numerous pieces of legislation (Exhibit 9-3). The Victim and Witness Protection Act, a federal law passed in 1982, required greater protection of victims and witnesses and also mandated guidelines for the fair treatment of victims and witnesses in federal criminal cases. The Victims of Crime Act of 1984 authorized federal funds for state victim programs. Spurred by these concerns, every state has passed comprehensive legislation protecting the interests of victims. In short, a wide variety of programs have been adopted in recent years to improve the treatment crime victims receive from the criminal justice system. The three most common types of initiatives are (1) victim/witness assistance programs, (2) victim compensation programs, and (3) a victim's bill of rights.

Victim/Witness Assistance Programs

Victim/witness assistance programs encourage cooperation in the conviction of criminals by reducing the inconvenience citizens face when appearing in court (Finn and Lee 1988). Typical activities include providing comfortable and secure waiting areas, assisting with the prompt return of stolen property that has been recovered, and providing crisis intervention. These programs also provide victims and witnesses with a clearer understanding of the court process by distributing brochures, explaining court procedures, and notifying witnesses of upcoming court dates (Webster 1988). Of particular concern is victim and witness intimidation. Intimidation can be either case-specific—threats or violence intended to dissuade a witness from testifying in a specific case—or communitywide—acts by gangs or drug-selling groups intended to foster a general atmosphere of fear and noncooperation within a neighborhood or community (Healey 1995).

Today, virtually all jurisdictions of any size have established programs aimed at helping crime victims cope with the hardships of victimization and deal with the often troublesome demands of the criminal justice system. Most are based in criminal justice agencies (prosecutors', police, and sheriffs' offices) (Finn and Lee 1988). Often the program title is Victim Services.

Evaluations of victim/witness assistance programs have yielded mixed results. In some communities, a victim's willingness to cooperate in the future was positively associated with considerate treatment by criminal justice personnel (Norton 1983; National Institute of Justice 1982). Thus, victims and witnesses receiving help were more likely to appear when summoned than those who had not been aided. But no such impact was found in other communities (Davis 1983; Skogan and Wycoff 1987). Those helped by the program appeared at the same rate as those who were not aided, and there was no change in the rate of case dismissals.

Andrew Karmen (2001) suggests that one explanation for these research findings is that expectations of significant improvements in case outcomes were based on faulty assumptions. The presumption is that the adjudication process is characterized by an adversarial model. The reality is that the courtroom work group has a mutual interest in processing large numbers of cases expeditiously. Thus, whereas victims see their situations as unique events that deserve careful and individual consideration, judges, prosecutors, and defense attorneys see them as routine occurrences, to be disposed of based on "going rates."

Victim Compensation Programs

The criminal justice system in the United States is offender-oriented, focusing on the apprehension, prosecution, and punishment of wrongdoers. While emphasizing the rehabilitation of offenders, the system has done little to help victims recover from the financial and emotional problems that they suffer.

Civil lawsuits are of little relevance, because most criminal defendants have no money to pay monetary damages for personal injuries or damage to property. An increasingly common technique is restitution, in which the court orders the defendant to pay the victim for the losses suffered (see Chapter 15). But a major shortcoming of restitution is the fact that in many crimes no offender is convicted. Even if convicted, many defendants have little or no ability to provide adequate compensation to a victim. And once restitution is ordered, the victim's likelihood of collecting is not good (Davis, Smith, and Hillenbrand 1992).

When restitution by the offender is inadequate or impractical, compensation by a third party (an insurance company, for example) is the only alternative. But many victims, because they are poor, do not have insurance covering medical expenses or property losses. The government is another sort of third party. Victim compensation programs rest on the premise that the government should counterbalance losses suffered by victims of criminal acts. The first compensation program in the United States began in California in 1965. Similar programs quickly emerged in a few other states.

In 1984 Congress passed the Victims of Crime Act, which established a Crime Victims Fund administered by the Office for Victims of Crimes within the U.S. Department of Justice. The fund is financed primarily from fines paid by defendants in federal court (Parent, Auerbach, and Carlson 1992).

The federal backing has now spurred all states to enact legislation providing compensation for at least certain classes of crime victims.

The staffs are small, however, and relatively few claims are filed—fewer than 100,000 during a typical year. Most programs provide for recovery of medical expenses and some lost earnings; none reimburses the victim for lost or damaged property. The maximum amount that can be paid in damages ranges from $10,000 to $25,000.

Victim compensation programs appear to provide clear benefits to victims of crime, but the actual results of such programs require careful scrutiny. Preliminary evaluations of compensation programs have yielded findings disappointing for administrators (Karmen 2001). Cumbersome administrative procedures lead to added frustrations and increased alienation. Moreover, few victims of violent crimes apply for benefits, and even fewer claimants receive any money (Elias 1986). Eligibility requirements are strict. Most states require that the victim assist in the prosecution of the offender, effectively excluding many domestic violence, child abuse, and sexual assault victims (McCormack 1991). Similarly, most states also have a "family exclusion" clause, which makes victims living in the same household as the offender ineligible. Crime victims must also be "innocent" victims (those to whom no contributory fault can be ascribed). Overall, these programs are designed to spread the limited funds around, rather than to concentrate on a few badly injured victims.

Victims' Bill of Rights

Nowhere is the awakened concern about victims of crime more readily apparent than in proposals for a victims' bill of rights (see Exhibit 9-4). Apart from sharing the title, however, these proposals vary markedly, reflecting different philosophies. In 1982 the President's Task Force on Victims of Crime submitted 68 separate recommendations aimed at achieving a balance between the needs and rights of the victim and those of the defendant. Also in 1982 California voters approved Proposition 8 by a 2-to-1 margin. Known as the Victims' Bill of Rights, it added 12 controversial provisions to the state constitution and the criminal code. These versions of the victims' bill of rights reflect the rallying cry of the law-and-order movement, which accuses the courts of protecting the rights of defendants rather than those of victims. Premised on the notion that defendants escape too easily from the court process, these proposals stress substantive changes in the law, such as abolishing the exclusionary rule, limiting bail, restricting plea bargaining, and imposing stiffer sentences.

Other proposed victims' bills of rights are less ideological, emphasizing improvements in court procedures to better the lot of victims and witnesses. For example, the National Conference of the Judiciary on the Rights of Victims of Crime adopted a Statement of Recommended Judicial Practices, suggesting (1) fair treatment of victims and witnesses through better information about court procedures, (2) victim participation and input through all stages of judicial proceedings, and (3) better protection of victims and witnesses from harassment, threats, intimidation, and harm.

Most recently, discussions of the victims' bill of rights have shifted from the state to the national level (see Courts, Controversy, and Reducing Crime: Should the Victims' Rights Amendment Be Adopted?).

AIDING OR MANIPULATING VICTIMS?

After a long period of neglect, aiding victims has become good politics. These efforts are backed by a national movement for the rights of crime victims.

The Victims' Rights Movement

Organizing crime victims is a difficult task. Aside from having been harmed by criminals, victims as a group have very little in common (Karmen 2001). Despite these obstacles, victim advocacy groups have become a powerful political voice.

The emergence of the victims' rights movement reflects several parallel trends. One is the law-and-order rhetoric of the 1960s, which emphasized the harm criminals do to victims.

Exhibit 9-4 Text of Proposed Victims' Rights Amendment

105th CONGRESS
1st Session
S.J. RES. 6
IN THE SENATE OF THE UNITED STATES
JANUARY 21, 1997

Mr. KYL (for himself, Mrs. FEINSTEIN) introduced the following joint resolution; which was read twice and referred to the Committee on the Judiciary

JOINT RESOLUTION

Proposing an amendment to the Constitution of the United States to protect the rights of crime victims.

Resolved by the Senate and the House of Representatives of the United States of America in Congress assembled (two thirds of each House concurring therein), That the following article is proposed as an amendment to the Constitution of the United States, which shall be valid for all intents and purposes as part of the Constitution when ratified by the legislatures of three-fourths of the several States within seven years from the date of its submission by the Congress:

SECTION 1. Each victim of a crime of violence, and other crimes that Congress may define by law, shall have the rights to notice of, and not to be excluded from all public proceedings relating to the crime; To be heard, if present, and to submit a statement at a public pre-trial or trial proceedings to determine a release from custody, an acceptance of a negotiated plea, or a sentence; To the rights described in the proceedings portions of this section at a public parole proceedings, or at a non-public parole proceedings to the extent they are afforded to the convicted offender; To notice of a release pursuant to a public or parole proceedings or an escape; To a final disposition of the proceedings relating to the crime free from unrea-sonable delay; To an order of restitution from the convicted offender; To have the safety of the victim considered in determining any release from custody; And To notice of the rights established by this article; however, the rights to notice under this section are not violated if the proper authorities make a reasonable effort, but are unable to provide the notice, or if the failure of the victim to make a reasonable effort, to make those authorities aware of the victim's whereabouts prevents that notice.

SECTION 2. The victim shall have standing to assert the rights established by this article. However, nothing in this article shall provide grounds for the victims to challenge a charging decision or conviction; to obtain a stay of trial; or to compel a new trial. Nothing in this article shall give rise to a claim for damages against the United States, a State, a political subdivision, or a public official, nor provide grounds for the accused or convicted offender to obtain any form of relief.

SECTION 3. The Congress and the States shall have the power to enforce this article within their respective Federal and State jurisdictions by appropriate legislation, including the power to enact exceptions when required for compelling reasons for public safety or for judicial efficiency in mass victim cases.

SECTION 4. The rights established by this article shall apply to all proceedings that begin on or after the 180th day after the ratification of this article.

SECTION 5. The rights established by this article shall apply in all Federal and State proceedings, including military proceedings to the extent that Congress may provide by law, juvenile justice proceedings, and collateral proceedings such as habeas corpus, and including proceedings in any district or territory of the United States not within a State.

Another is the women's rights movement, which came to take a special interest in crimes involving women. A key feature of the feminist movement is its emphasis on grassroots activism. Thus, a logical extension of the women's movement was to form local programs to aid women who had been victims of rape or spousal abuse (Weed 1995).

The victims' rights movement involves people striking back to turn tragedy into action and rage into reform (Office for Victims of Crime 1998). The best known of these organizations is Mothers Against Drunk Driving (MADD). Founded by Candy Lightner, whose daughter was killed by a drunk driver, MADD has become the nation's largest victim advocacy group (see

COURTS, CONTROVERSY, AND REDUCING CRIME

Should the Victims' Rights Amendment Be Adopted?

 Efforts to protect the rights of victims began with the passage in most jurisdictions of victims' rights legislation. These activities soon expanded to include a demand that these protections be given even greater force of law by placing them in state constitutions, and the public has responded with overwhelming support. Thirty-four states have passed victims' rights amendments to their state constitutions, and others are considering adding similar amendments. Having achieved considerable success at the state level, victims' rights groups began pressing for an amendment to the U.S. Constitution (see Exhibit 9-4).

Proposals to amend the U.S. Constitution are frequently offered but rarely adopted. Amending the Constitution is a difficult and complicated task. Beginning in 1997, both the Senate and House judiciary committees held hearings on the resolution, but in 2000 Senate backers withdrew the legislation rather than see it defeated.

Senator Dianne Feinstein (D-California) was a cosponsor of the proposed amendment, arguing that the Constitution protects the rights of criminal defendants but "crime victims, families, survivors have no rights at all, according to the Constitution of the United States" (Cannon 1996). If the victims' rights amendment were adopted, victims of violent crimes would have the following rights:

■ Allowed to be present at major stages of a criminal case

■ Permitted to make views known during a plea of guilty and sentencing

■ Spared delays in defendants' trials

■ Notified of any release or escape of the offender

■ Guaranteed full restitution by the offender

The most fundamental concern expressed about the proposed victims' rights amendment is that its guiding assumption—that victims are being excluded from the judicial process—is patently false. Unlike many nations of the world, in the United States all steps of the criminal process (except grand jury proceedings) are mandated to be open to the public. Victims are excluded from trial only when they will be witnesses, and this is happening more often because of another facet of the victims' rights movement—victim impact statements. More substantively, critics make the following points:

■ The high volume of cases processed each year means that local courts will face enormous increases in costs.

■ Most states have already adopted similar provisions so a federal constitutional amendment is not needed.

■ Endless litigation will ensue, and appellate courts will face difficult issues in resolving potential conflicts between the rights of the accused and rights of crime victims.

■ Victims will experience more, not less, frustration because judges are not likely to impose the harsh sentence demanded by victims.

What do you think? Would adopting a victims' rights amendment to the U.S. Constitution genuinely improve the plight of crime victims, or is it another example of manipulating the plight of victims for political ends? Is this an area in which states should have great freedom to act but the national government only a limited role? In the end, would a victims' rights amendment be effective or just window dressing?

● To continue the debate, use InfoTrac College Edition to locate the following article: Marlene A. Young, Roger Pilon, "Should We Amend the Constitution to Protect Victims' Rights?"

Chapter 18). A check of the Internet reveals numerous other groups. Many of these groups are local, emphasizing various types of victims ranging from those harmed by drunk drivers to battered women. These grassroots operations function loosely under the national umbrella organization, the National Organization of Victim Assistance, which provides a larger focus for their specialized concerns.

Today the victims' rights movement involves a loose coalition of local, state, and national organizations with wide-ranging in-

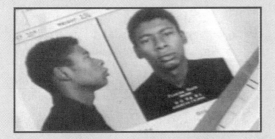

Florida v. Pitts and Lee: Death Row Deliverance

In the course of only 28 days, two young Black men were arrested, convicted, and sentenced to death. Their convictions were based on coerced confessions. After the two men had each served nine years on death row, the true killer admitted to the crime. However, the prosecutor tried the defendants a second time, with the same results. After twelve years in prison, Pitts and Lee are pardoned by the governor.

 View a video clip of this trial on your copy of the CourtTV CD-ROM. As you watch the video, keep the following questions in mind:

1. How do race relations in the South permeate the entire case?
2. Would this case have been handled differently if the prosecutor had not asked for the death penalty (see Chapter 15)?
3. What major contemporary Supreme Court decisions were not followed during the original prosecution and trial?
4. Did the court-appointed lawyer provide effective assistance of counsel (see Chapter 7)?
5. Could such a miscarriage of justice happen today? Why might blacks and whites answer this question differently?

terests. Their activities constitute a full-blown social movement that seeks to place the interests of crime victims into the mainstream of American political discourse. Although diverse in origins, the victims' rights movement shares a common ideology seeking to demonstrate the triumph of good over evil. Thus, the movement resonates with a moral view of crime held by many average citizens (Weed 1995).

Differing Goals

The victims' rights movement reflects the mutual interests of a strange set of political bedfellows, which explains why, beneath the rhetoric about aiding victims of crimes, there are important disagreements over goals and priorities (Viano 1987) (see Case Close-Up: *Payne v. Tennessee* and Victim Impact Statements). A study of a victims' rights organization in Alabama found that the membership was disproportionately white and female, with blacks excluded from potential membership. These results suggest that the victims' rights movement is becoming polarized, with some most concerned about secondary victimization and others more focused on punishment of defendants (Smith and Huff 1992). Similarly, a study in the state of Washington found that groups supporting the Community Protection Act reflected a punitive orientation toward defendants more than an effort to aid victims of sexual assault (Scheingold, Olson, and Pershing 1994). These differing goals explain why victims' rights laws and constitutional amendments are so contradictory.

Do Victims Benefit?

Everyone agrees that victims and witnesses should be treated better during the court process. But political rhetoric should not be allowed to obscure some important issues. Although enthusiasm for helping victims is clearly growing, the willingness to pay for the necessary services is not always present. Overall, legislators and other government officials find voting for victim-oriented legislation politically advantageous, but when it comes to voting money for another "welfare program," they are much more hesitant.

Moreover, it is unclear how much aid victims and witnesses receive from these programs. Once enacted, programs do not always work as intended. Elias (1993) concluded that victim compensation laws were exercises in symbolic politics. Few claimants ever received compensation; the laws provided "political placebos," with few tangible benefits for victims.

Victim/witness assistance programs appear to be important first steps in providing better services to citizens who find themselves

Payne v. Tennessee and Victim Impact Statements

 After hearing a "blood-curdling scream," a neighbor called the police, who arrived just as Pervis Tyrone Payne, covered in blood, was leaving the apartment. Inside, they encountered a horrifying scene. Blood covered the walls and floor throughout the unit. Charissee and her daughter were lying dead on the kitchen floor, stabbed numerous times with a butcher knife. Miraculously, Nicholas survived despite deep knife wounds.

Payne was convicted of two counts of first-degree murder and one count of first-degree assault. During the sentencing phase of the trial, the defense called Payne's parents, his girlfriend, and a clinical psychologist, each of whom testified as to various mitigating aspects of his background and character, including a low IQ that marked him as mentally handicapped.

The state countered with the testimony of Charissee's mother. She testified that the surviving child "cries for his mom. He doesn't seem to understand why she doesn't come home. And he cries for his sister."

During closing arguments, the prosecutor made maximum use of this emotional testimony. She acknowledged there was nothing the jury could do to ease the pain of the families involved in this case. Nor could they do anything about the victims—Charissee and her dead daughter:

> But there is something you can do for Nicholas. Somewhere down the road Nicholas is . . . going to want to know what type of justice was done. He is going to want to know what happened. With your verdict you will provide the answer.

The jury unanimously sentenced Payne to death.

Moving beyond the grisly facts of the case, the legal issue was: Should victim impact statements be admissible during the sentencing phase of capital murder trials? In two recent decisions (*Booth v. Maryland*, 1987, and *South Carolina v. Gathers*, 1989) the Court, by a 5-to-4 vote, held that victim impact statements are unconstitutional because they create an unacceptable risk that a jury may impose the death penalty in an arbitrary and capricious manner. Rehnquist swept aside these objections. The Court held that the Eighth Amendment does not prohibit the sentencing jury in a capital case from considering victim impact statements relating to the victim's personal characteristics and the emotional impact of the murder on the victim's family. Justice Thurgood Marshall thundered back in a biting dissent: "Power, not reason, is the new currency of this Court's decision making."

But are victim impact statements sound criminal justice policy? The National Victim Center and other victims' groups support giving victims a voice in the process, rather than reducing them to being a mere statistic. By venting their anger and frustrations, they are better able, proponents contend, to get on with their lives. But critics fear that the venting of frustrations can demean the judicial process. As a certain death sentence was about to be pronounced against Richard Allen Davis for sexually molesting and then killing Polly Klaas (discussed in Chapter 16), Davis told the court that Polly's father had sexually molested her, a charge that crime-victim advocates labeled outrageous and sickening.

Incidents like this one lead critics to wonder whether victim impact statements help victims; perhaps the possibility of speaking in court at a much later date unnecessarily prolongs their grieving process. Victims are not encouraged to reach a sense of closure until they testify (or in some cases until the defendant is actually executed).

To continue the debate, click on the following Web sites, which offer contrasting views on the wisdom of passing the Victims' Rights Amendment. Use the search term "victims."

National Victims' Constitutional Amendment Network: http://www.nvcan.org/

American Civil Liberties Union: http://www.aclu.org/congress/congresssearch.html

A Virtual Tour of American Courthouses: Victims

It is not always easy to view the American justice process from the perspective of the victim. A Web site that tries to explain the process to victims can be found at **http://www.ojp. usdoj.gov/BJA/html/victsguide.htm**, which provides *A Victim's Guide to the D.C. Criminal Justice System*. And to view the court process from the perspective of a victims' advocate, go to Kathy Copley's Web site at **http://cuppp. campbellsvil.edu/~victadv/**.

Governmental response to domestic violence is a hot-button issue that often focuses on individual cases. To get a better sense of how courts handle the breadth of domestic violence cases, go to any of the following court Web sites:

Delaware County (Ohio): **http://www.municipalcourt. org/dv.asp**

Family Law Court in San Diego County (California): **http://www.sandiego.courts.ca.gov/superior/ courts/domestic.html**

Palm Beach County (Florida): **http://www. pbcountyclerk.com/**

The Municipal Court of Seattle (Washington): **http://www.cityofseattle.net/courts/prob/ dvprob.htm**

In a few short years, victim/witness assistance programs have gone from experimental to mainstream. Visit the following sites to find out what types of services are being offered. As you view these sites, ask yourself whether the programs are mainly directed toward helping crime victims or toward helping government agencies gain convictions.

Victim/Witness Assistance Unit of the prosecutor's office in Golden (Colorado): **http://www.co.jefferson.co. us/dpt/da/vw.htm**

Victim Services Unit of the District 27 District Attorney (Oklahoma): **http://www.state.ok.us/~okda27/ victmser.htm**

Victim-Witness Assistance Program of the Commonwealth's Attorney for the City of Virginia Beach (Virginia): **http://www.city.virginia-beach.va.us/ courts/oca/vw.htm**

Victim-Witness Assistance Program of the Cook County (Illinois) State's Attorney: **http://www.statesattorney. org/victim/victimwi.htm**

---

thrust into the criminal court process, but not all agree that these programs actually benefit the victim. Sociologist William McDonald (1976) charges that "some projects that are billed as 'assisting victims' are more accurately described as assisting the criminal justice system and extending government control over victims. Whether the victims so controlled would regard the project as 'assisting' them is problematic" (35). Some victims do not wish to become involved.

An important question is, At whose expense should victims be compensated? Some versions emphasize protecting the rights of victims by denying privileges and benefits to suspects, defendants, and prisoners. This type of victim's bill of rights is the most recent example of the conflict between the due process model and the crime control model (highlighted in Chapter 1). Other versions emphasize improving the welfare of victims at the expense of the privileges and options enjoyed by members of the courtroom work group (Karmen 2001).

CONCLUSION

The future of both Pervis Tyrone Payne and his victim are difficult to predict. Payne sits on Tennessee's death row. Having lost on appeal to the Supreme Court, his lawyers hope to set aside the death penalty during further rounds of habeas corpus review. Meanwhile he sits in his cell, wondering whether he will die or not. Predicting Nicholas' future is even more difficult. At his young age, his mind might be able to block out the memories of seeing his mother and younger sister murdered in his presence. But there is still a good chance of flashbacks and antisocial behavior, which psychologists label post-traumatic stress disorder. It is possible that as he grows up Nicholas will himself shift from victim to defendant. As we learned in this chapter, many defendants arrested for violent crimes were themselves the victims of violent acts as children.

The perhaps troubling future of Nicholas highlights some of the contradictions still apparent in how society reacts to victims. Today there is less tendency to blame victims (particularly rape victims) for causing their own misfortune. Instead, numerous groups are ready to step forward and call for helping victims. Yet some of these same voices who are quick to champion the cause of victims are just as quick to denounce what has become popularly called the "abuse excuse."

Victims and witnesses provide the raw material for the court process. The complaints they bring, the credibility of their stories, and their willingness to participate directly affect the courtroom work group's activities. But members of the courtroom work group do not respond uncritically to the demands for their services. They find some stories more believable than others and some claims more worthy than others.

The clientele shapes the criminal court process in a less obvious way. Most defendants are young, male, illiterate, impoverished members of minority groups. Many victims share similar traits. They are also poor, unversed in the ways of the courts, and disproportionately members of minority groups. As a result, in the criminal courts, victims and witnesses often exert little influence over the disposition of the cases in which they are involved.

CRITICAL THINKING QUESTIONS

1. In what ways are victims and defendants similar? In what ways are they different? Is there any difference in the characteristics of victims and defendants when the victim is male as opposed to when the victim is female?

2. Many discussions of crime suggest that smart defendants are able to beat the rap by pleading insanity (see Chapter 14), slanting their testimony at defense counsel urging (see Chapter 7), and exploiting legal loopholes such as the exclusionary rule (see Chapter 12). Given the profile of the typical criminal defendant, how realistic are these assumptions of a smart crook?

3. To some, the victims' rights movement is more an exercise in symbolic politics than a substantive program. Thus, some critics argue that many of these programs are really more interested in severe punishment of the defendant than in helping victims adjust socially, economically, or psychologically to their new role as victim. Which dimensions of helping victims reflect the crime control model? Which dimensions reflect the due process model?

4. Would your views on victim impact statements be different if the U.S. Supreme Court had chosen a less emotional case to consider in deciding their constitutionality? Overall, do you think victim impact statements correctly allow victims a voice in the process or just add unnecessary emotionalism?

KEY TERMS

civil protection order (201)
defendant (195)

WORLD WIDE WEB RESOURCES AND EXERCISES

Web Guides

http://dir.yahoo.com/Society_and_Culture/Crime/
http://dir.yahoo.com/Society_and_Culture/Crime/
 Victims__Rights/
http://dir.yahoo.com/Society_and_Culture/Crime/
 Types_of_Crime/Domestic_Violence/
http://dir.yahoo.com/Entertainment/Humor/
 Job_Humor/Law_Enforcement/

Web Search Terms

victims　　　　　　　*victims' rights amendment*
victims' advocates　　*domestic violence*

Useful URLs

The Bureau of Justice Statistics provides up-to-date statistics on defendants and victims at http://www.ojp.usdoj.gov/bjs/; click on Criminal Offenders and Victim Characteristics.

The ABA Commission on Domestic Violence references a variety of studies and statistics: http://www.abanet.org/domviol/home.html.

The Violence Against Women Office is located in the U.S. Department of Justice: http://www.ojp.usdoj.gov/vawo/.

The Criminal Justice Legal Foundation is a nonprofit public interest law organization dedicated to restoring a balance between the rights of crime victims and the criminally accused: http://cjlf.org/.

The National Coalition against Domestic Violence is dedicated to the empowerment of battered women and their children: http://www.ncadv.org/.

The National Organization for Victim Assistance is the largest umbrella organization offering assistance to victims: http://www.try-nova.org/.

The National Association of Crime Victims Compensation Board provides information on victim compensation programs in the states: http://www.mailbag.com/users/derene/home.html.

Uncommon URLs

The Pennsylvania Coalition Against Domestic Violence is located at http://www.pcadv.org/.

The Virginia Poverty Law Center, Inc., provides legal help for victims of domestic violence or sexual assault at http://www.vplc.org/.

The Jacksonville (North Carolina) Web page on domestic violence can be seen at http://jpd.onslowonline.net/Violence/intro.htm.

Dumb Crooks offers true stories of mentally challenged criminals: http://www.dumbcrooks.com/main.htm.

The Missouri Victim Assistance Network is a good example of a state-level organization. The Web site provides lots of links useful to state citizens: http://mova.missouri.org/.

Safe Horizon offers a tour of a domestic violence shelter: http://www.dvsheltertour.org/.

Crime Victims' Rights offers a conservative perspective: http://www.victimsrights.org/.

Victim Service Council of the St. Louis Prosecuting Attorney's Office can be viewed at http://mova.missouri.org/members/vsc.htm.

Web Exercises

1. The number of victims' rights organizations is growing. You can locate many of them by using the following Yahoo search: Society and Culture/Crime/Victims' Rights/Organizations. Access several organizations, and ask yourself the following questions: Does the name of the organization provide a good description of the organization? What types of crime are mentioned? To what extent does gender play a major or minor role in the stated purpose of the organization? In terms of crime control model versus due process model, do the organizations appear to be geared to punishing defendants or providing social and psychological support for crime victims?

2. What's your favorite dumb crook joke? Check out the Dumb Crooks Web site (http://www.dumbcrooks) home page for the TV show *America's Dumbest Criminals.* Why are these tales so popular? What do they suggest about charges that smart crooks know how to beat the system using technicalities?

3. The National Victims' Constitutional Amendment Network supports amending the U.S. Constitution to recognize "the fundamental rights of crime victims to be treated with dignity, fairness, and respect by the criminal justice system." Access their home page (http://www.nvc.org) and determine who supports their efforts (both individuals and organizations). What arguments do they make in urging that "Statutes are NOT Enough"?

   Unlike many other advocacy groups, they choose to include arguments from opponents. Does this enhance their credibility as an organization? How powerful are the negative arguments they include?

   Use the Web site to determine the current status of the victims' rights amendment. The home page provides links to individual states. Click on your state to find out what type of victims' rights law and constitutional provisions affect your jurisdiction. In particular, what notification rights exist in your state? Some states are creating Web sites to notify victims and others of pending parole releases. Access one of these pages, and ask yourself how easily an average citizen would be able to locate the desired information.

INFOTRAC COLLEGE EDITION RESOURCES AND EXERCISES

Basic Search Terms

criminals
African American criminals
women criminals
recidivists
victims of crimes

victims' rights amendment
rape victims
rape victim services
victim impact statements

Recommended Articles

Julie Brienza, "Crime Victim Laws Sometimes Ignored"

Sue Carter, "Media Insensitivity to Victims of Violence"

"From a Crime Victim in Texas" (the story of a crime victim who became active in the criminal justice system)

Chester Hicks, "The Rights of Crime Victims: Does Legal Protection Make a Difference?"

Amy K. Phillips, "Thou Shalt Not Kill Any Nice People"

Nicole Walker, "Why Women Are Committing More Crimes"

Barry Yeoman, "Bad Girls"

Diane S. Young, Carrie Smith, "When Moms Are Incarcerated"

InfoTrac College Edition Exercises

1. Using the search term "victims' rights amendment," find one article that supports the passage of this law and another that opposes it. To what extent are the arguments similar to or different from those discussed in the text? To what extent do differences of opinion fall along the lines of the due process versus the crime control model of justice?

2. Using the search term "women criminals," find two or more articles that discuss why women commit fewer crimes than men but rates of female involvement in the criminal justice system have been increasing in recent years.

FOR FURTHER READING

Gender

Belknap, Joanne. *The Invisible Woman: Gender, Crime and Justice.* Belmont, CA: Wadsworth, 2001.

Frohman, Lisa. "Constituting Power in Sexual Assault Cases: Prosecutorial Strategies for

Victim Management." *Social Problems* 45 (1998): 393–427.

Greenfeld, Lawrence, and Tracy Snell. "Women Offenders." NCJ 175688. Washington, DC: Bureau of Justice Statistics, 1999.

Klein, Ethel, Jacquelyn Campbell, Esta Soler, and Marissa Ghez. *Ending Domestic Violence: Changing Public Perceptions/Halting the Epidemic.* Newbury Park, CA: Sage, 1997.

Ward, Colleen. *Attitudes Toward Rape: Feminist and Social Perspectives.* Thousand Oaks, CA: Sage, 1996.

Poverty

Backstrand, John, Don Gibbons, and Joseph Jones. "Who Is in Jail? An Examination of the Rabble Hypothesis." *Crime and Delinquency* 38 (1992): 219–229.

Dunaway, R. Gregory, Francis Cullen, Velmer Burton, and T. David Evans. "The Myth of Social Class and Crime Revisited: An Examination of Class and Adult Criminality." *Criminology* 38 (2000): 589–613.

Short, James. *Poverty, Ethnicity, and Violent Crime.* Boulder, CO: Westview Press, 1997.

Race

Cao, Liqun, Anthony Adams, and Vickie Jensen. "A Test of the Black Subculture of Violence Thesis: A Research Note." *Criminology* 34 (1997): 367–379.

Free, Marvin. *African Americans and the Criminal Justice System.* New York: Garland, 1997.

LaFree, Gary, and Katheryn Russell. "The Argument for Studying Race and Crime." *Journal of Criminal Justice Education* 4 (1993): 273–289.

Lynch, Michael, and E. Britt Patterson, eds. *Justice with Prejudice: Race and Criminal Justice in America.* Albany, NY: Harrow and Heston, 1996.

Mann, Coramae Richey. *Unequal Justice: A Question of Color.* Bloomington: Indiana University Press, 1993.

Walker, Samuel, Cassia Spohn, and Miriam DeLone. *The Color of Justice.* 3d ed. Belmont, CA: Wadsworth, 2004.

Victims

Boles, Anita, and John Patterson. *Improving Community Response to Crime Victims.* Thousand Oaks, CA: Sage, 1997.

Chermak, Steven. *Victims in the News: Crime and the American News Media.* Boulder, CO: Westview Press, 1995.

Davis, Robert, Arthur Lurigio, and Wesley Skogan. *Victims of Crime.* 2d ed. Newbury Park, CA: Sage, 1997.

Davis, Robert, and Barbara Smith. 1994. "The Effects of Victim Impact Statements on Sentencing Decisions: A Test in an Urban Setting." *Justice Quarterly* 11: 453–469.

Donahoe, Joel. "The Changing Role of Victim Impact Evidence in Capital Cases." *Western Criminology Review* 2 (1999): 1.

Feder, Lynette, and Laura Dugan. "A Test of the Efficacy of Court-Mandated Counseling for Domestic Violence Offenders: The Broward Experiment." *Justice Quarterly* 19 (2002): 343–375.

Fletcher, George. *With Justice for Some: Victims' Rights in Criminal Trials.* New York: Addison-Wesley, 1995.

Sarnoff, Susan. *Paying for Crime: The Policies and Possibilities of Crime Victim Reimbursement.* Westport, CT: Praeger, 1996.

Sebba, Leslie. *Third Parties: Victims and the Criminal Justice System.* Columbus: Ohio State University Press, 1996.

Tobolowsky, Peggy. *Crime Victim Rights and Remedies.* Durham, NC: Carolina Academic Press, 2001.

Part III Processing the Accused

The five chapters of Part III follow the steps of criminal prosecution from arrest to the determination of guilt or innocence. The central concerns are why many cases are eliminated from the process early and why most cases end not with a trial but rather with a plea of guilty.

Chapter 10 looks at case attrition. Well before trial, many cases are eliminated by actions of prosecutors, grand juries, and/or judges.

Chapter 11 focuses on the American bail system, examining why some defendants await trial in jail whereas others receive pretrial release.

Chapter 12 considers the preparation of cases for trial. The main topics are discovery and controversial Supreme Court decisions concerning the suppression of evidence.

Chapter 13 discusses plea bargaining—a much publicized but little understood part of the criminal court process. Central topics include why cases are pled out and whether plea bargaining is fair.

Chapter 14 examines the trial itself: jury selection, presentation of evidence, and the eventual jury verdict. Even though only a handful of cases go to trial, jury verdicts nonetheless have a major impact on how the courts exercise discretion.

PART III
Processing
the Accused

| **Chapter 10** | **Chapter 11** | **Chapter 12** | **Chapter 13** | **Chapter 14** |
| Arrest to Arraignment | Bail | Disclosing and Suppressing Evidence | Negotiated Justice and the Plea of Guilty | Trials and Juries |

Chapter 10 Arrest to Arraignment

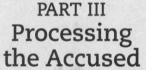

PART III
Processing the Accused

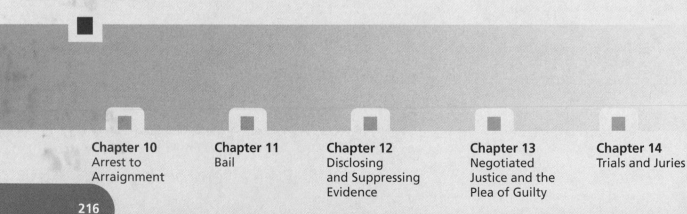

Chapter 10
Arrest to
Arraignment

Chapter 11
Bail

Chapter 12
Disclosing
and Suppressing
Evidence

Chapter 13
Negotiated
Justice and the
Plea of Guilty

Chapter 14
Trials and Juries

ike thousands of others arrested on Friday, Donald Lee McLaughlin had to wait in jail three to five days before a judge was available to conduct a probable cause hearing. The U.S. Constitution requires a more prompt hearing, argued the public defender for County of Riverside, California. Not practical, countered the lawyer for the county, stressing the realities of the contemporary criminal justice system in large urban areas—thousands of arrests, overcrowded jails, and lack of availability of judges, to say nothing of defense attorneys and prosecutors. It is in this context that the high court had to decide whether a "prompt hearing" meant 24 hours or 36 hours or 48 hours. ◄

County of Riverside v. McLaughlin highlights the importance of the early stages of a felony prosecution. At first glance, the numerous preliminary stages of a prosecution seem to be only of procedural interest, with cases moving automatically from arrest to charging through preliminary hearing and grand jury before arriving at the major trial court. But a closer look indicates that at numerous stages during these early proceedings, prosecutors, judges, police officers, and victims have the option of advancing a case to the next step, seeking an alternative disposition, or dropping the case altogether. These screening decisions result in significant case attrition, with half of all felony arrests being dropped at some point after arrest and before arraignment.

This chapter examines the early stages of a criminal case, focusing on when and why case attrition occurs. The discussion begins with crime and the arrests that sometimes follow. Our attention then shifts to events in the courthouse, including initial appearance, charging, preliminary hearing, grand jury, and (for some cases) arraignment in the trial court of general jurisdiction.

CRIME

Beginning in the early 1960s, the United States experienced a dramatic increase in crime. For almost two decades, crimes known to the police increased much faster than the growth in population. In the early 1980s, the crime rate reached a plateau, and since the early 1990s it has decreased considerably. The peaks and valleys of the official crime figures, however, are largely irrelevant to the general public. Rather, the public continues to perceive (no matter what the official figures say) that crime is on the increase. These fears are reinforced by extensive media coverage, particularly of violent crime.

The most publicized measure of crime is the Federal Bureau of Investigation's (FBI) yearly publication *Uniform Crime Reports*, which divides criminal offenses into two categories. **Type I offenses** consist of eight crimes, referred to as **index crimes.** These crimes produce headlines about rising crime rates. Note that some serious street crimes (such as sale of drugs) are not included. White-collar crimes committed primarily by the upper class—fraud and stock manipulations, for instance—are also excluded, even though their economic costs are greater than the costs of crimes committed by the poor. Contrary to public perceptions, most felony arrests are for nonviolent offenses involving burglary and larceny; property crimes outnumber violent offenses by a ratio of 7 to 1 (Federal Bureau of Investigation 2003). Type II offenses are the less serious, but more numerous, crimes ranging from theft to simple assault. Drug crimes are counted as Type II offenses.

A major weakness of the *Uniform Crime Reports* is that they are based only on crimes known to the police. But only a fraction of the number of crimes actually committed are reported to the police. Of the personal and household offenses measured in the National Crime Victimization Survey's yearly sample of

THE MURDER TRIAL OF SHAREEF COUSIN

New Orleans' Bloodiest Week in Memory

The story of the murder of Michael Gerardi was as poignant as it was brutal. He had met Connie Babin just several nights before at a Mardi Gras party. He repeatedly called her, and on their first date he gave her a red rose.

His murder at the Port of Call restaurant was but one of what the *Times-Picayune*, New Orleans' only major daily newspaper, headlined the "Bloodiest Week in Memory." In just seven days, 21 people had died and 9 others were wounded ("A Week of Violence" 1995). Some were domestic homicides. Others appeared to be drug-related—a very elastic term that the police use to encapsulate everything from attempts to rob drug dealers to fights over territory to retaliation for selling bogus drugs. Other violence occurred during the course of armed robberies.

The murder of Michael Gerardi was not the most shocking of all that took place that week. That dubious distinction went to the murder of police officer Ronald Williams and two others working in a Vietnamese restaurant in the city. They were murdered execution-style by Antoinette Frank, a New Orleans police officer who was Ronald Williams' partner. She is currently on Louisiana's death row.

The murder wave in the first week of March 1995 solidified in the citizens' minds that their city was indeed a dangerous place. Just the year before, it had been identified as the murder capital of the nation. And 1995 proved to be even worse, with a total of 421 murders. Moreover, 60 percent of the black residents reported that they heard gunfire a few times a year or even a few times a month (Howell 2000).

In high-profile murders, the police are under considerable pressure to solve the crime by making an arrest. This public pressure always produces the uncomfortable fear that the police might act in haste and arrest the wrong person. This point was made in the federal civil rights lawsuit filed by Cousin's attorneys (see Chapter 3). The complaint mentions the newspaper article with the title "Bloodiest Week" and charges that the mayor and the police chief were under political pressure to solve the crime. The complaint goes on to inject race into the discussion, arguing that Police Chief Pennington, who is African American, "voiced his desire to do more for people in the French Quarter, due to the racially biased notion that murders in that part of town are somehow more important than deaths of poorer people in other sections of the city" (*Cousin v. Small* 2000).

Since 1995, the number of murders in New Orleans has declined dramatically, dipping to a low of 162 in 1999 (Philbin 2001). In the public's mind, the reduction in crime in the Crescent City was related to major changes in the activities of the police department. Amid widespread scandal in the department and general views of ineffectiveness, the newly elected mayor hired Pennington as the city's police chief. But Pennington often complained that the city had too few police officers and that those they had were underpaid.

This situation changed dramatically after another French Quarter murder, just a few blocks from the Port of Call, in December 1996. Shortly after arriving for work on Sunday morning, a waitress at the Louisiana Pizza Kitchen found three coworkers dead in the deep freezer, gunshot victims; a fourth person was in serious condition. (The murderers were arrested shortly thereafter and later convicted.) The following Thursday, a large contingent of French Quarter residents and merchants marched on City Hall, demanding that the city council do something to shore up the police department.

Within weeks, new taxes were imposed and the police budget was increased. In the aftermath, as noted, crime in the city did go down—although not all agree that police department actions were the cause. Still, the overall impact was clear—the police were making more arrests, resulting in more cases filed in Criminal District Court (see Chapter 4) and more jail cells needed for those arrested (see Chapter 11). As stressed in this chapter, an overwhelming number of those felony arrests were for drugs—almost two-thirds of all case filings in the city.

Unfortunately, by 2003 the city's murder rate had once again increased dramatically, and the shortage of sworn police officers had become particularly acute (Young 2003).

For more information about crime and the police in New Orleans, go to http://www.nopdonline.com.

To read more about the Port of Call murder, use the search term "dead teen walking" and read the article "A Fatal Date."

households, only 49 percent of violent victimizations and 40 percent of property crimes were reported to the police (Bureau of Justice Statistics 2003a).What this means is that the official FBI crime statistics actually underestimate the total amount of crime in the United States.

No matter which set of statistics you examine and what you choose to emphasize, the United States has a much higher level of crime than any other Western industrial democracy. No wonder crime continues to be a concern of the general public and an issue in any number of contests for elective office at all levels of government.

ARREST

Of the crimes brought to the attention of the police, 21 percent result in an **arrest.** The police clearance rate by arrest varies greatly by the type of crime involved. The clearance rate for violent crimes is 50 percent, compared to 18 percent for property crimes (Federal Bureau of Investigation 2003).

Every year the police make an estimated 13.7 million arrests for nontraffic offenses—mostly minor ones such as simple assault, public drunkenness, disorderly conduct, petty theft, and possession of small amounts of illegal drugs. However, 2.2 million of these arrests are for the serious crimes of homicide, rape, arson, aggravated assault, robbery, burglary, auto theft, and larceny. Figure 10-1 displays recent arrest data by major categories of relevance to the major trial courts.

These arrests are the overwhelming source of criminal cases filed in the courts; only a handful of prosecutions begin with an indictment, for example. Exhibit 10-1 summarizes the steps of criminal procedure.

Quality of Arrests

The police have a lot to do with what happens in court after arrest. Prosecutors in particular often complain that the police tend to be sloppy in their investigations, sometimes missing important evidence and improperly seizing, marking, or storing the items they do gather. A review of more than 14,000 arrests in the District of Columbia reached the following conclusions (Forst, Lucianovic, and Cox 1977):

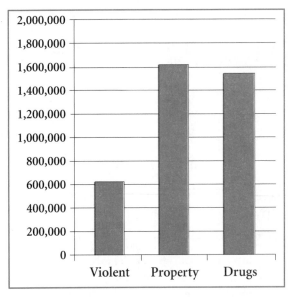

Figure 10-1
Felony Arrests

SOURCE: Federal Bureau of Investigation, *Uniform Crime Reports for the United States—2002* (Washington, DC: U.S. Government Printing Office, 2003).

■ When the arresting officer recovers tangible evidence, the prosecutor is considerably more likely to convict the defendant.

■ When the police locate cooperative witnesses for the prosecutor, the probability of conviction is significantly enhanced.

Individual police officers have varying degrees of success in providing the prosecutor with sufficient evidence for a conviction. The most important factor is the successful officers' "persistence in finding and interviewing witnesses and in supporting witnesses through the trial, as well as being particularly conscious of the gathering and maintenance of evidence" (Forst et al. 1981).

Police departments also differ in the quality of arrests referred to the district attorney. When prosecutors deal with numerous police departments, some departments often have a better record of forwarding evidence necessary for a successful conviction—in Los Angeles,

Exhibit 10-1 Steps of Criminal Procedure

	Law on the Books	Law in Action
Crime	Any violation of the criminal law.	
	Felony: The more serious of the two types of offense, bearing a possible penalty of one year or more in prison.	Property crimes outnumber violent types of criminal behavior by about 7 to 1 among Type I offenses.
	Misdemeanor: Lesser of the two basic types of crime, usually bearing a possible penalty of no more than one year in jail.	The most common misdemeanors include public drunkenness, disorderly conduct, assault, and theft.
Arrest	The physical taking into custody of a suspected law violator.	2.2 million felony arrests yearly. 11.5 million misdemeanor arrests yearly.
Initial appearance	The accused is told of the charges, advised of rights, bail is set, and a date for the preliminary hearing is set.	Occurs in lower courts. Many misdemeanor defendants plead guilty.
Charging	Formal criminal charges against defendant, stating which criminal law was violated.	From arrest to arraignment, half of felony arrests are terminated, downgraded, or diverted in some manner.
	Information: Formal accusation of a crime made by the prosecutor.	Defendant's chances of getting off are better during these private sessions in the prosecutor's office than during public trials in the courthouse.
	Complaint: Formal accusation of a crime supported by oath or affirmation of the victim.	Complaints very rarely used in felony prosecutions.
	Arrest warrant: An official document, signed by a judge, accusing an individual of a crime and authorizing law enforcement personnel to take the person into custody.	
	Prosecutor is supposed to prosecute all known criminal conduct.	Prosecutor exercises discretion in deciding which charges should be filed.
	Prosecutor controls charging decision.	Some prosecutors allow police input into the charging decision.
Preliminary hearing	A pretrial hearing to determine if there is probable cause to hold the accused for further proceedings.	In many jurisdictions the preliminary hearing is brief, with a strong probability that the case will proceed.
Grand jury	Required for felony prosecutions in 19 states and the federal courts.	Typically not a major decision maker.
	Grand juries have extensive powers, not possessed by law enforcement, to investigate crimes.	Prosecutor dominates grand jury proceedings, deciding which cases will be presented and which charges filed.
	Indictment: Formal accusation of a crime, made against a person by a grand jury, upon the request of the prosecutor.	The investigatory powers of the grand jury are most likely to be used in cases involving major drug rings, governmental corruption, and significant white-collar crime.
	Subpoena: Court order requiring a person to appear before the grand jury and/or produce documents.	
Arraignment	Stage of the criminal process in which defendant is formally informed of the charges pending and must enter a plea.	A significant milestone because it indicates that the evidence against the defendant is strong and a conviction is likely.

for example, 86 percent acceptance for sheriff's arrests, compared with 60 percent for police arrests (Brosi 1979). Such statistics support prosecutors' perceptions that some police agencies conduct more thorough investigations than others (Neubauer 1974b).

Swelling Criminal Dockets

Even though serious crime has decreased significantly during the past decade, court dockets keep growing. As stressed in Chapters 4 and 5, the workload of the criminal courts is large and growing.

■ In the federal courts, the number of suspects prosecuted by U.S. attorneys more than doubled between 1980 and 1998 (Bureau of Justice Statistics 2000).

■ In state courts, felony prosecutions increased 25 percent over the last decade and a half (Ostrom, Kauder, and LaFountain 2003).

A good deal of the growth in felony caseloads has been drug related. Police now arrest more than 1.5 million persons a year for drug-related offenses, a 125 percent increase since 1980. The massive increase in law enforcement efforts directed against drug use is clearly overloading the criminal courts. State prosecutors in large urban areas see the enormous effort against drugs as sapping resources, overloading the system, and making it difficult to respond adequately to other types of crime. The major response by courts has been the creation of drug courts (see Chapter 4).

INITIAL APPEARANCE

The **initial appearance** occurs within a few hours or a few days of arrest. It is at this stage that most misdemeanor defendants enter a plea of guilty and are sentenced immediately (see Chapter 18). For those arrested on a felony, however, a plea is not possible because the initial appearance occurs in a trial court of limited jurisdiction, which has no authority to accept a plea. Thus, the initial appearance is typically a brief affair, as little is known about the crime or the alleged criminal. At times suspects insist on

telling their side of the story, but the judge typically cautions that anything said can be used against the defendant. Lawyers provide the same advice. One author has likened the sea of humanity in initial appearance court to "Hell's Waiting Room" (see A Day in Court).

CHARGING

The criminal court process begins with the filing of a formal written accusation alleging that a specified person or persons committed a specific offense or offenses. The **charging document** includes a brief description of the date and location of the offense. All the essential elements (*corpus delicti*) of the crime must be specified. These accusations satisfy the Sixth Amendment provision that a defendant be given information upon which to prepare a defense. Applicable state and federal laws govern technical wording, procedures for making minor amendments, and similar matters.

There are four types of charging documents: complaint, information, arrest warrant, and indictment (which will be discussed later). Which one is used depends on the severity of the offense, applicable state law, and local customs. A **complaint** must be supported by oath or affirmation of either the victim or the arresting officer. It is most commonly used in prosecuting misdemeanor offenses or city ordinance violations. An **information** is virtually identical in form to the complaint, except that it is signed by the prosecutor. It is required in felony prosecutions in most states that do not use the grand jury. In grand jury states, an information is used for initiating felony charges pending grand jury action. An **arrest warrant** is issued by a judicial officer—usually a lower court judge. On rare occasions, the warrant is issued prior to arrest, but for most street crimes, the police arrest the suspect and then apply for an arrest warrant. Some states require that the prosecutor approve the request in writing before an arrest warrant can be issued. An ongoing controversy is whether police and prosecutors devote sufficient attention to white-collar crimes (see Courts, Controversy, and Economic Inequality: Are White-Collar Criminals Underprosecuted?).

A DAY IN COURT

"Hell's Waiting Room"

 It's past midnight and the bench is full. At one end of the well-worn pine slab on which new prisoners sit, a gaunt woman with a deeply lined face slumps against the wall muttering and coughing, her face covered by a gauze hospital mask. Three hookers, regular visitors to the San Francisco County Jail, are taking off their spike heels—potential weapons—and trading them in for jail-issue pale blue polyester socks tossed to them by a sheriff's deputy.

"I didn't do nothing. Nothing!" says a young man in handcuffs waiting to be booked. "All I did was not check in with my parole officer and you throw me around," he says in the general direction of a group of San Francisco cops standing at the desk.

When Randy Duane Nichols is called, a roughly handsome man with sandy red hair rises from the bench and steps forward to one of the three booking windows to be processed by a deputy. A jailhouse tattoo—a swirl of roses and his initials—adorns his neck. Nichols smirks, swaggers, and stares defiantly as his mug shot is taken. Unlike the others on the bench, Nichols has a long history of criminal activity that includes drug charges, assaults, and long stretches in state prison, a deputy notes. Captured this evening during one of the periodic police sweeps for parolees wanted back by the State Department of Corrections, Nichols is headed back to prison in a few days.

"You're on the bus, Gus," says the deputy as Nichols is led across the hall to the process tank, the cramped, fetid holding area for male prisoners awaiting assignment to a cell.

Inmates like Nichols, the hookers, the gasping drug addict, and those who loudly protest their innocence are an every hour fact of life inside the jail. From the mentally ill to homeless drunks to violent felons to parole violators returning to prison—the county jail is the processing center for anyone charged with a crime in San Francisco.

Over a three-week period spent inside County Jail One, the intake facility for San Francisco prisoners on the sixth floor of the Hall of Justice on Bryant Street, the *Examiner* was able to witness the inner workings of the lock-up. It was an education in the lives of the city's underclass, a world of petty thievery, poverty, madness, and despair.

Mostly hidden from public view, the jail is like a massive sieve for alleged wrongdoers caught by the police. The bench, where all prisoners begin their jail sojourn, could be the waiting room in hell. Gathered there are what sociologist, prison critic, and former convict John Irwin calls the rabble of society, those persons too detached, disreputable or lost to make it on the outside. Sometimes, they're just plain unlucky. . . .

The Traffic

The seemingly endless traffic of prisoners in and out of custody makes for a tense atmosphere. Dank hallways echo with the metallic clank of jail doors opening and closing, a noisy elevator creaks back and forth bringing police officers and their prisoners into the jail. The air inside is hot and close, ventilation is poor, and the rank smell of body odor and sweat is a constant.

Many of those here "are not normal," says Sheriff Hennessey. "There are a lot of drunks, sick people, and addicts. A lot of them are mad as hell at being there. It can be a stressful environment, a harsh, ugly world." For many of those dragged into the jail, it is a place to sleep, to receive a little medical care, perhaps to see a psychiatrist. For others, it is the first stop on the way to a long prison term. Sheriff Hennessey estimates that a quarter of the inmates are in need of psychiatric care and that three-quarters have a serious drug problem.

Says Alisa Riker, the director of a jail program to release misdemeanor inmates on their own recognizance: "The jail is an incredibly expensive homeless shelter, an incredibly expensive detox center, an incredibly expensive drug treatment center and it's an incredibly inept way to handle social problems. But these problems are not being dealt with in other ways."

SOURCE: A. Lin Neumann, "Hell's Waiting Room," *San Francisco Examiner,* 28 September 1998.

COURTS, CONTROVERSY, AND ECONOMIC INEQUALITY

Are White-Collar Criminals Underprosecuted?

 Normally Martha Stewart was at ease before television cameras as she demonstrated the latest in decorating and entertainment ideas, but today she was noticeably harried as cameras caught her quick entry into the New York federal courthouse. Martha Stewart became the most recognizable person to be caught up in recent high-profile white-collar crime prosecutions when she entered pleas of not guilty to a nine-count indictment alleging obstruction of justice in an insider trading scheme on the New York Stock Exchange. Other prominent persons have faced similar allegations:

- Sam Waksal, founder of ImClone, was sentenced to seven years in prison for selling stock in his company the day before a negative ruling from the Food and Drug Administration.

- Top executives of Enron have been indicted on charges of cooking the books in the wake of the nation's biggest corporate collapse.

- Officials of Worldcom have been charged with criminal activity after that company was forced into bankruptcy because of massive accounting irregularities.

The term *white-collar* is used because it suggests crimes committed by persons of higher economic status, as opposed to the typical street crimes most often associated with the social underclass. As such, the term encompasses a broad range of matters, ranging from crimes against consumers and the environment to securities fraud and governmental corruption (Rosoff, Pontell, and Tillman 2002). The public, though, remains relatively indifferent to white-collar crimes. One reason is that white-collar crimes lack the drama associated with murders and bank robberies. Another is that the defendants are respectable—they don't look like criminals (whatever that might mean). Moreover, average citizens underestimate the costs of white-collar crime. Annual losses from white-collar crime are probably 50 times greater than from ordinary property crime, but these losses are often hidden and elusive.

Allegations that white-collar crimes are underprosecuted, however, require close scrutiny. After all, a number of major prosecutions and convictions have occurred over the years. Moreover, since the Enron scandal, public attention to white-collar crimes has clearly increased. At the federal level, the Justice Department and other federal regulatory agencies such as the Securities and Exchange Commission have large staffs devoted to these matters. At the local level, though, districts attorney's office have only small staff devoted to fraud and similar crimes because the office is overwhelmed by the sheer volume of day-to-day street crimes like murder, robbery, and drug offenses. Moreover, it is hard to get juries to return guilty verdicts because the prosecutor must demonstrate not merely sloppy bookkeeping but guilty intent. Indeed, some suggest that celebrities like Martha Stewart have been singled out not so much because of their alleged criminal activity but simply because they are in the public eye (Iwata 2003).

What do you think? Are white-collar crimes underprosecuted? Would white-collar crimes be better deterred by more prosecutions or more government regulations?

To continue the debate, visit the following Web sites, which offer contradictory views on the prosecution of white-collar criminals.

Free Advice: White-Collar Crimes:
http://criminal-law.freeadvice.com/white_collar_crimes/

White-Collar Crimes FYI:
http://www.whitecollarcrimefyi.com/

FBI Denver Division White-Collar Crime Information:
http://denver.fbi.gov/white.htm/

Law on the Books: Prosecutorial Control

Through the charging decision, the prosecutor controls the doors to the courthouse. He or she can decide whether charges should be filed and what the proper charge should be. Although the law demands prosecution for "all known criminal conduct," the courts have traditionally granted prosecutors wide discretion in deciding whether to file charges (Baker 1933). For example, there are no legislative or judicial standards governing which cases merit prosecution and which should be declined. Moreover, if a prosecutor refuses to file charges, no review of this decision is possible; courts have consistently refused to order a prosecutor to proceed with a case.

Law in Action: Police Influence

Although the prosecutor has the legal authority to dominate the charging process, some choose to share this authority with the police. In some jurisdictions, prosecutors defer to the police (Miller 1969). In these communities, the police file criminal charges with minimal supervision by the prosecutor. In essence, these prosecutors have transferred their decision-making power to the police (Mellon, Jacoby, and Brewer 1981). In other jurisdictions, the prosecutor retains the formal authority to file charges, but the police influence the prosecutor's decision. In these communities, the police and prosecutor jointly discuss cases before charges are filed. The police have considerable influence during such interchanges, pressuring prosecutors to overcharge defendants or to file charges even though the evidence is weak (Skolnick 1993; Cole 1970).

In communities where prosecutors choose to control the filing of criminal charges, a substantial percentage of persons arrested are released without the filing of criminal charges. This author analyzed all nontraffic arrests for a month in a medium-sized Illinois community and found that a third of police arrests resulted in no criminal charges being filed (Neubauer 1974a). Nationwide, in communities with strong prosecutorial screening, up to half of all felony arrests do not result in criminal charges (Boland, Mahanna, and Sones 1992).

Law in Controversy: Should Prosecutors Set High Standards for Charging?

Legal reformers recommend that prosecutors, rather than the police, should control charging decision (National Advisory Commission on Criminal Justice Standards and Goals 1973). The primary justification is efficiency. Removing cases that are weak or do not warrant prosecution eliminates the need for judges and other court personnel to devote time to them.

Such recommendations, however, ignore a key element of law in action. They view prosecutorial screening as an isolated stage in the process rather than as part of a continuum in the larger process (Jacoby 1977). In this connection, the importance of the relationship between the police and the prosecutor must not be overlooked. Police departments resist prosecutorial control of the charging decision because they see case rejections as an implicit criticism of the arresting officer for making a "wrong" arrest. Prosecutorial screening can have consequences at the polls. In one jurisdiction where a DA refused to file charges in a significant number of arrests, the Fraternal Order of the Police forced the incumbent not to seek reelection (Flemming, Nardulli, and Eisenstein 1992).

PRELIMINARY HEARING

An arrested person is entitled to a timely hearing before a neutral judge to determine whether probable cause exists to detain the defendant prior to trial (*Gerstein v. Pugh* 1975). But how timely is timely? An individual may be jailed for up to 48 hours without a hearing before a magistrate to determine whether the arrest was proper. Justice O'Connor's opinion in *County of Riverside v. McLaughlin* (1991) cited burdened criminal justice systems and noted that local courts need flexibility to combine the probable cause hearing with a bail hearing or arraignment (see Case Close-up: *County of Riverside v. McLaughlin* and a Prompt Hearing before a Magistrate).

Law on the Books: Weighing Probable Cause

The **preliminary hearing** (or *preliminary examination,* as it is called in some states) represents the first time that a case is reviewed by

CASE CLOSE-UP

County of Riverside v. McLaughlin and a Prompt Hearing before a Magistrate

 Beyond the bare facts that he was arrested in Riverside County, California, little is known about Donald Lee McLaughlin. Who he was, why he was arrested, and whatever happened to his case quickly became irrelevant. For whatever reason, the public defender's office decided that the facts of his case made him an ideal candidate to be used as a plaintiff in a suit filed in federal court. The office was prepared to challenge countywide practices; a plaintiff was needed and, at the last minute, McLaughlin's name was inserted. Thus, McLaughlin's name went first in a class action lawsuit filed on behalf of McLaughlin and all other individuals in the same situation.

McLaughlin v. County of Riverside raised the difficult question of how prompt is prompt. California law mandated a probable cause hearing for all those arrested without a warrant within 48 hours of arrest, weekends and holidays excluded. Thus, an individual arrested late in the week might in some cases be held for as long as five days before appearing before a neutral judicial official; over the Thanksgiving holiday, a seven-day delay was possible. The U.S. district court agreed with part of McLaughlin's plight and ordered a probable cause hearing within 36 hours of arrest. Having lost in the trial court, the county appealed (hence the names changed place, with the county now listed as the moving party). The Ninth Circuit affirmed the district court's decision, and the county appealed to the U.S. Supreme Court, which granted cert.

Although *County of Riverside v. McLaughlin* appears to be a minor quibble over a few hours, the underlying issues are much more fundamental, centering on where to strike the balance between an individual's right to liberty and society's need for effective law enforcement. The Supreme Court has allowed police officers to make arrests, based upon their own assessment of probable cause, without first obtaining a warrant. To counterbalance this privilege, the Court established that an individual arrested without a warrant is entitled to a prompt judicial determination of probable cause afterward. In *Gerstein v. Pugh*, they wrestled with this issue and held that the defendant was entitled to a timely determination. The Court ruled that the 30-day wait in Florida was too long, but failed to be much more specific. As a result, Gerstein "created a nationwide divergence in postarrest and pretrial procedures and subjected some individuals to what numerous courts and commentators believed to be unjustifiably prolonged restraints of liberty following their arrests" (Perkins and Jamieson 1995, 535).

Justice Sandra Day O'Connor, the most centrist justice on the Court (see Chapter 17), wrote the opinion of the Court, and her opinion reflects the ability to strike a compromise. The earlier decision in *Gerstein*, she wrote, provided flexibility to law enforcement but not a blank check. She recognized that the standard of "prompt" has proven to be vague and therefore has not provided sufficient guidance. In the future, prompt shall be defined in most circumstances as 48 hours—a time period she labeled as a "practical compromise between the rights of individuals and the realities of law enforcement." A 24-hour rule would compel local governments across the nation to speed up their criminal justice mechanisms substantially, presumably by allotting local tax dollars to hire additional police officers and magistrates. What is perhaps most striking is how forthright the opinion is in recognizing that law on the books must take into account law in action.

What is most interesting about the four dissenters is their ideological mix. The three moderates agreed with the lower courts that the 36-hour standard was best. But Justice Antonin Scalia, one of the Court's most conservative members, would fix the time at 24 hours, a standard he says existed in the common law from the early 1800s.

someone other than a law enforcement official. Usually held before a lower court judge, the preliminary hearing is designed "to prevent hasty, malicious, improvident, and oppressive prosecutions, to protect the person charged from open and public accusations of crime, to avoid both for the defendant and the public the expense of a public trial, to save the defendant from the humiliation and anxiety involved in public prosecution, and to discover whether or not there are substantial grounds upon which a prosecution may be based" (*Thies v. State* 1922). In states with no grand jury, the preliminary hearing is the sole procedure for determining whether sufficient evidence exists to justify holding the defendant. In grand jury states, the preliminary hearing **binds over** the accused for possible indictment. A magistrate's ruling that there is insufficient evidence does not necessarily end the case; the prosecutor can take the case directly to the grand jury (Gilboy 1984).

During a preliminary hearing, the state does not have to prove the defendant guilty beyond a reasonable doubt, as would be required during a trial. Rather, all that is necessary is that the prosecutor establish **probable cause** that a crime has been committed and that the defendant committed it. Usually, hearsay evidence (secondhand evidence) is admissible. Generally, the defense does not have the right to cross-examine witnesses, although some states and some judges permit attorneys to ask witnesses questions (Gilboy 1984).

Law in Action: Variations in Using the Preliminary Hearing

Defense attorneys weigh several factors in deciding whether to demand a preliminary hearing or waive it (Flemming 1986b). Practices of the local prosecutor are one important consideration. If the district attorney's files are open and plea-bargaining policies are well known, it is viewed as time-consuming and redundant to hold a preliminary hearing. Second, strategic and tactical considerations are involved. Waiving the preliminary hearing may reflect an assessment that the information to be gained from holding a preliminary hearing does not outweigh the potential damage to the defen-

dant's case (for example, the publicity that may surround a rape case). A third factor is client control. Defense attorneys sometimes insist on a preliminary hearing to impress on their client the gravity of the situation. Finally, the preliminary hearing gives the defense attorney an overview of the evidence against the client and provides the opportunity for discovery (see Chapter 12).

The tactical decision of holding or waiving the preliminary hearing highlights the complexity of the preliminary hearing from the law-in-action perspective. Although the legal purpose of the preliminary hearing is simple, the actual conduct of these hearings is quite complex. In some courts, they may last an hour or more; in others, they consume only a few minutes. In some jurisdictions, preliminary hearings are an important stage in the proceedings; in others, they are a perfunctory step, in which probable cause is found to exist in virtually every case.

This variability makes it difficult to generalize about the importance of the preliminary hearing, but studies do reveal four major patterns. In some jurisdictions, preliminary hearings are almost never held. In many, they are short and routine, lasting but a few minutes with the defendant almost always bound over to the grand jury (Neubauer 1974b). In most jurisdictions, the preliminary hearing is largely ceremonial, resulting in few cases being screened out of the criminal process; but in a few courts, it is quite significant (McIntyre and Lippman 1970).

GRAND JURY

Grand juries make accusations; trial juries decide guilt or innocence. The grand jury emerged in English law in 1176, during a political struggle among King Henry II, the church, and noblemen. At first, criminal accusations originated with members of the grand jury themselves, but gradually this body came to consider accusations from outsiders as well.

After the American Revolution, the **grand jury** was included in the Fifth Amendment to the Constitution, which provides that "no person shall be held to answer for a capital, or

American Babylon: Crime in Atlantic City

Atlantic City, New Jersey, provides insight into the duality of many big cities in the United States; the glitter and glamour of gambling casinos contrasts sharply with poverty-stricken inner-city neighborhoods.

The CourtTV video clip in Chapter 4 focused on detective Jeff Fauntleroy as he made two drug busts. In this clip we again follow the detective as he patrols parts of the city that visitors rarely see. First we watch as he tries to bring calm to the streets after a knife fight. We also see him respond to a rape call and counsel the victim. In between, Fauntleroy assists a juvenile officer in arresting a 17-year-old on a fugitive warrant and observe the officer talk with the juvenile in the juvenile detention center.

 View a video clip of these police officers in action on your copy of the CourtTV CD-ROM. As you watch the video, keep the following questions in mind:

1. What contrasting images emerge about the causes of crime?
2. Will these arrests hold up in court?
3. What do these episodes suggest about the relationship between poverty, crime, and race?

otherwise infamous crime, unless on a presentment or indictment of a grand jury." The archaic phrase "otherwise infamous crime" has been interpreted to mean felonies. This provision, however, applies only to federal prosecutions. In *Hurtado v. California* (1884), the Supreme Court held that states have the option of using either an indictment or an information. In 19 states, the grand jury is the exclusive means of initiating prosecution for all felonies. In a few, it is required only for capital offenses.

In the remainder, the grand jury is an optional investigative body (Exhibit 10-2).

Grand juries are impaneled (formally created) for a set period of time—usually three months. During that time, the jurors periodically consider the cases brought to them by the prosecutor and conduct other investigations. If a grand jury is conducting a major and complex investigation, its time may be extended by the court. The size of grand juries varies greatly, from as few as 6 jurors to as many as 23, with an average size of 17. Grand jurors are normally selected randomly, in a manner similar to the selection of trial jurors. In a handful of states, however, judges, county boards, jury commissioners, or sheriffs are allowed to exercise discretion in choosing who will serve on the grand jury.

Law on the Books: Shield and Sword

The two primary functions of grand juries have been aptly summarized in the phrase "shield and sword" (Zalman and Siegel 1997). *Shield* refers to the protections the grand jury offers, serving as a buffer between the state and its citizens, preventing the government from using the criminal process against its enemies. *Sword* refers to the investigatory powers of this body (Alpert and Petersen 1985). If the grand jury believes there are grounds for holding the suspect for trial, they return an **indictment,** also termed a **true bill,** meaning that they find the charges to be true. Conversely, if they find the charges insufficient to justify trial, they return a no bill, or **no true bill.**

Many legal protections found elsewhere in the criminal court process are not applicable at the grand jury stage. One unique aspect of the grand jury is secrecy. Because the grand jury may find insufficient evidence to indict, it works in secret in order to shield those merely under investigation from adverse publicity. By contrast, the rest of the criminal court process is required to be public. Another unique aspect is that indictments are returned by a plurality vote; in most states, half to two-thirds of the votes are sufficient to hand up an indictment. Trial juries can convict only if the jurors are unanimous (or, in four states, nearly unanimous).

Exhibit 10-2 Grand Jury Requirements

Grand Jury Indictment Required	Grand Jury Indictment Optional	Grand Jury Lacks Authority to Indict
All crimes	Arizona	Pennsylvania
New Jersey	Arkansas	
South Carolina	California	
Tennessee	Colorado	
Virginia	Idaho	
All felonies	Illinois	
Alabama	Indiana	
Alaska	Iowa	
Delaware	Kansas	
District of Columbia	Maryland	
Georgia	Michigan	
Hawaii	Missouri	
Kentucky	Montana	
Maine	Nebraska	
Mississippi	Nevada	
New Hampshire	New Mexico	
New York	North Dakota	
North Carolina	Oklahoma	
Ohio	Oregon	
Texas	South Dakota	
West Virginia	Utah	
Capital crimes only	Vermont	
Connecticut	Washington	
Florida	Wisconsin	
Louisiana	Wyoming	
Massachusetts		
Minnesota		
Rhode Island		

SOURCE: Deborah Emerson, *Grand Jury Reform: A Review of Key Issues* (Washington, DC: Department of Justice, National Institute of Justice, 1983).

Finally, witnesses before the grand jury have no right to representation by an attorney, whereas defendants are entitled to have a lawyer present at all vital stages of a criminal prosecution. Nor do suspects have the right to go before the grand jury to protest their innocence or even to present their version of the facts.

In furtherance of its investigative powers, grand juries have the authority to grant **immunity** from prosecution. The Fifth Amendment protects a person against self-incrimination. In 1893 Congress passed a statute that permitted the granting of **transactional immunity.** In exchange for a witness's testimony, the prosecutor agrees not to prosecute the witness for any crimes admitted—a practice often referred to as "turning state's evidence." The Organized Crime Control Act of 1970 added a new and more limited form of immunity. Under **use immunity,** the government may not use a witness's grand jury testimony to prosecute that person. However, if the state acquires evidence of a crime independent of that testimony, the witness may be prosecuted. The Supreme Court has held that use immunity does not violate the Fifth Amendment's prohibition against self-incrimination (*Kastigar v. United States* 1972). Use immunity gives witnesses less protection than does transactional immunity. A witness may not refuse the government's offer of immunity, and failure to testify may result in a jail term for contempt of court.

The investigative powers of the grand jury to gather evidence are also seen in its **subpoena power.** Under the court's authority, the grand jury may issue a subpoena requiring an individual to appear before the grand jury to testify and/or bring papers and other evidence for its consideration. Failure to comply with a subpoena (or offer of immunity) is punishable as **contempt.** A person found in contempt of the grand jury faces a fine or being jailed until he or she complies with the grand jury request. Thus, contempt of the grand jury is potentially open ended—as long as the grand jury is in existence and as long as the person refuses to comply, the person can sit in jail. Critics contend that some prosecutors call political dissidents to testify to find out information unrelated to criminal activity.

The contempt power can also be used for punishment. A prosecutor may call a witness, knowing that he or she will refuse to testify, and then have the witness jailed. In this way, a person can be imprisoned without a trial. This has happened mainly to newspaper reporters. In *Branzburg v. Hayes* (1972), the Supreme Court ruled that journalists must testify before a grand jury. Some journalists have gone to jail rather than reveal their confidential sources, because they believe that to do so would erode the freedom of the press protected by the First Amendment.

Law in Action: Prosecutorial Domination

The work of the grand jury is shaped by its unique relationship with the prosecutor. In theory at least, the prosecutor functions only as a legal adviser to the grand jury, but in practice, the prosecutor dominates. Grand jurors hear only the witnesses summoned by the prosecutor, and, as laypersons, they are heavily influenced by the legal advice of the prosecutor. Indeed, the high court has ruled that the government is under no obligation to disclose to the grand jury evidence that would tend to clear the defendant (*U.S. v. Williams* 1992).

(This is one of a number of significant developments in the way criminal procedure has been shaped by the courts; see Exhibit 10-3.)

The net result is that grand juries often function as a rubber stamp for the prosecutor. One study found that the average time spent per case was only five minutes; in 80 percent of the cases, there was no discussion by members of the grand jury; rarely did members voice a dissent; and finally, the grand jury approved virtually all of the prosecutor's recommendations (Carp 1975). Similarly, federal grand juries rarely return no true bills. In short, grand juries generally indict whomever the prosecutor wants indicted (Gilboy 1984; Neubauer 1974b).

Law in Controversy: Reform the Grand Jury?

The grand jury system has been the object of various criticisms. In theory, the grand jury serves as a watchdog on the prosecutor, but some portray the grand jury as "the prosecutor's darling," a "puppet," or a "rubber stamp." To William Campbell (1973), U.S. District Court judge for the Northern District of Illinois, "The grand jury is the total captive of the prosecutor who, if he is candid, will concede that he can indict anybody at any time, for almost anything, before any grand jury" (174). These concerns have prompted a call for abolition of the grand jury. Early in the twentieth century, judicial reformers succeeded in abolishing grand juries in some states. More recently, such abolition efforts have not been successful, however, because they require a constitutional amendment.

Today, critics call for reforming the grand jury (Brenner 1998). Often these calls are based on concerns that grand jury proceedings have been misused to serve partisan political ends, harassing and punishing those who criticize the government. The cases most often cited include prominent opponents of the Vietnam War (Deutsch 1984). The leading advocate for federal grand jury reform is the National Association of Criminal Defense Lawyers (2000). This organization advocates a Citizens' Grand Jury Bill of Rights, which among other things would grant witnesses the right to counsel

Exhibit 10-3 Key Developments Concerning Criminal Procedure

Crime

Lanzetta v. New Jersey	1939	A law is unconstitutional if it forbids an act in terms so vague that "men of common intelligence must necessarily guess at its meaning."
U.S. v. Lopez	1995	U.S. Congress does not have the authority under the commerce clause to prohibit guns in schools.

Arrest

Chimel v. California	1969	During a search incident to arrest, the police may search only the person and the area within the immediate vicinity.
Payton v. New York	1980	Unless the suspect gives consent or an emergency exists, an arrest warrant is necessary if an arrest requires entry into a suspect's private residence.

Initial appearance

Sixth Amendment	1791	"In all criminal prosecutions, the accused shall enjoy the right . . . to be informed of the nature and cause of the accusation."
Coleman v. Alabama	1970	Defendant has a right to counsel if the initial appearance is a "critical stage" in the proceedings.

Charging

Sixth Amendment	1791	"In all criminal prosecutions, the accused shall enjoy the right . . . to be informed of the nature and cause of the accusation."
People v. Wabash, St. Louis and Pacific Railway	1882	Prosecutor has discretion in beginning prosecutions and may terminate them when, in his (or her) judgment, the ends of justice are satisfied.
Burns v. Reed	1991	Prosecutor enjoys absolute immunity to civil lawsuit for all actions involving the adversary process.

Preliminary hearing

Gerstein v. Pugh	1975	Arrested persons are entitled to a "prompt" hearing, and 30 days is too long.

during testimony, require prosecutors to disclose evidence that might exonerate the target, and allow targets of investigations to testify (Lefcourt 1998).

ARRAIGNMENT

Arraignment occurs in the trial court of general jurisdiction. During the arraignment, the defendant is formally accused of a crime (either by an information or indictment) and is called upon to enter a plea. Thus, initial appearance and **arraignment** are similar in that the defendant must be informed with some specificity about the alleged criminal actions. The major difference is that felony defendants are not allowed to enter a plea (either innocent or guilty) in a lower court because that court lacks jurisdiction to take a plea and to sentence.

Procedurally, the arraignment provides the court the opportunity to ensure that the case is on track for disposition. The judge summons the defendant, verifying his or her name and address, and the lawyer provides formal notification to the court that he or she represents the defendant in this matter. Most important, the arraignment means that the defendant must enter a plea. Typically, defendants plead not guilty and a trial date is established. In some jurisdictions, however, a significant proportion enter a plea of guilty (Neubauer 1996).

The arraignment is rarely a major decision-making stage in the process. Rather, its real importance is measured more indirectly. The

Preliminary hearing *(continued)*

County of Riverside v. McLaughlin	1991	A jurisdiction that provides judicial determinations of probable cause within 48 hours of arrest will, as a general matter, comply with the promptness requirement.
Press Enterprises v. Superior Court	1986	The preliminary hearing must be open to the public.

Grand jury

Fifth Amendment	1791	"No person shall be held to answer for a capital, or otherwise infamous crime, unless on a presentment or indictment of a grand jury."
Hurtado v. California	1884	States are not required to use a grand jury in charging felonies.
U.S. Congress	1893	Prosecutors may grant a witness transactional immunity for testimony before the grand jury.
Organized Crime Control Act	1970	Prosecutors may grant a witness use immunity for testimony before the grand jury.
Kastigar v. U.S.	1972	Use immunity does not violate the Fifth Amendment protection against self-incrimination.
Branzburg v. Hayes	1972	Journalists have no constitutional right to maintain the confidentiality of their news sources when subpoenaed before grand juries and are compelled to give testimony.
U.S. v. Williams	1992	Prosecutors are under no obligation to present exculpatory evidence to the grand jury.
Campbell v. Louisiana	1998	A white criminal defendant may challenge his conviction on grounds that blacks were discriminated against in the selection of grand jurors.

Arraignment

Sixth Amendment	1791	"In all criminal prosecutions, the accused shall enjoy the right . . . to be informed of the nature and cause of the accusation."
Hamilton v. Alabama	1961	Defendant has the right to court-appointed counsel if indigent.

arraignment is important because it signifies to all members of the courtroom work group that the defendant is in all probability guilty and that the likelihood of being found not guilty is now slim. Thus, from the perspective of law-in-action, the arraignment says something very important about case attrition.

LAW-IN-ACTION PERSPECTIVE: CASE ATTRITION

The law-on-the-books perspective suggests a mechanical process—cases move almost automatically from one pretrial stage to the next. In sharp contrast, the law-in-action perspective emphasizes a dynamic process—cases are likely to be eliminated during these early stages.

A detailed picture of case attrition emerges in the research summarized in Figure 10-2. For every 100 arrests, 24 are rejected, diverted, or referred to other jurisdictions during prosecutorial screening. Of those that survive the initial hurdle, 21 are later dismissed by the prosecutor through a **nolle prosequi** (no prosecution). When this happens, the case is said to be "nolled," "nollied," or "nol. prossed." Overall, only 55 of the 100 arrests are carried forward to the trial stage.

The high attrition rate of felony cases early in the process contrasts sharply with the small percentage of acquittals during the trial phase. Once cases reach the felony court, relatively few

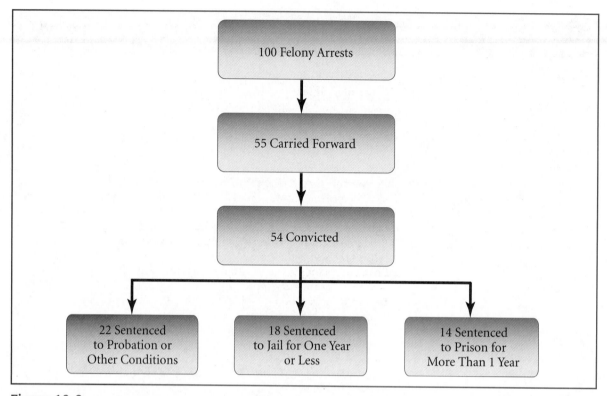

Figure 10-2
Case Attrition of Felony Arrests in 28 Urban Prosecutors' Offices

SOURCE: Barbara Boland, Paul Mahanna, and Ronald Sones, *The Prosecution of Felony Arrests, 1988* (Washington, DC: U.S. Department of Justice, Bureau of Justice Statistics, 1992).

are dismissed. Most end in either a plea or a trial (Boland, Mahanna, and Sones 1992). These statistics underscore the fact that decisions made during early steps of felony prosecutions are much more important in terminating cases than the later activities of judges and juries.

However, there are important variations among courts in the stage at which case attrition occurs. These variations reflect differences in state law, the structure of courts, and local traditions (Jacoby 1977). Thus, a critical stage for case screening and case attrition in one court may be of little importance in another jurisdiction. In some jurisdictions, for example, prosecutors make the important screening decisions, meaning that the preliminary hearing is relatively unimportant. By contrast, in other communities, prosecutors tend to defer to the police during the charging phase, resulting in significant case attrition at the preliminary hearing (McIntyre and Lippman 1970).

WHY ATTRITION OCCURS

Case attrition is the product of a complex set of factors, including the relationships among the major actors in the criminal justice system, the patterns of informal authority within the courtroom work group, the backlog of cases on the court's docket, and community standards defining serious criminal activity. We can best examine why attrition occurs by using the three facets of discretion discussed in Chapter 5: legal judgments, policy priorities, and personal standards of justice. As with other attempts to understand discretion, these categories are not mutually exclusive—some screening decisions are based on more than one criterion.

Legal Judgments

Legal judgments are the most important reason that cases drop by the wayside after arrest and before arraignment. Prosecutors, judges, and grand jurors begin with a basic question: Is there sufficient evidence to prove the elements of the offense? (Cole 1970; Feeney, Dill, and Weir 1983). One assistant district attorney phrased it this way: "When I examine the police report I have to feel that I could go to trial with the case tomorrow. All the elements of prosecution must be present before I file charges" (Neubauer 1974b, 118).

More broadly, when prosecutors in several urban jurisdictions were asked whether they would accept or decline prosecution, the legal-evidentiary strength of the case emerged as the most important factor (Jacoby et al. 1982). Witness problems (discussed in Chapter 9) constitute a specific type of legal-evidentiary problem. Three out of four prosecutors cite victim reluctance as a source of problems of felony case prosecution in their office, a percentage that reaches an astronomical 92 percent in urban areas with more than half a million people (De-Frances, Smith, and van der Does 1996).

Focusing on the strength of the state's case introduces an important change in evaluative standards. From an initial concern with *probable cause*, the emphasis shifts to whether it is a *prosecutable case*. At the preliminary hearing, the judge determines whether there is probable cause—that a crime has been committed and there are grounds to believe that the suspect committed it. From the prosecutor's perspective, however, probable cause is too gross a yardstick; even though it is present, a case may still be legally weak. Thus, a prosecutable case is not merely one that satisfies the probable cause standard required of police in making an arrest and used by the judge at the preliminary hearing. Rather, it is a case that meets the standards of proof necessary to convict.

Policy Priorities

Case attrition also results from general prosecutorial policies about priority of cases. Prosecutors devote greater resources to more serious offenses (Gilboy 1984; Jacoby et al. 1982). At times, these case priorities are reflected in office structure; district attorneys around the nation have established priority prosecution programs that focus on major narcotics dealers, organized crime, sex offenders, and the like. Just as important, prosecutors employ informal criteria that govern allocation of scarce resources. For example, some U.S. attorneys will not prosecute bank tellers who embezzle small amounts of money, get caught, and lose their jobs. The stigma of being caught and losing the job is viewed as punishment enough. Similarly, numerous local and state prosecutors have virtually decriminalized possession of small amounts of marijuana by refusing to file charges. Based on informal office policies, district attorneys are reluctant to prosecute intrafamily assaults, neighborhood squabbles, and noncommercial gambling.

Personal Standards of Justice

Personal standards of justice—attitudes of members of the courtroom work group about what actions should not be punished—constitute the third category of criteria that explain case attrition. Thus, some cases are dropped or reduced for reasons other than failure to establish guilt (McIntyre 1968). Even if the evidence is strong, defendants might not be prosecuted if their conduct and background indicate that they are not a genuine threat to society. In Detroit, among other places, a different phrase is used—but the thought is the same. Across the nation, these reasons for rejection are referred to as "Prosecution would serve no useful purpose" or "interests of justice" (Boland, Mahanna, and Sones 1992). Often personal standards of justice are based on a subjective assessment on the part of the prosecutor that the case is not as serious as the legal charge suggests. In most courthouses, officials refer to some cases as "cheap" or "garbage" cases (Rosett and Cressey 1976). Decisions not to file charges in cheap cases reflect the effort of court officials to produce substantive justice.

THE CRIMINAL JUSTICE WEDDING CAKE

The tyranny of criminal justice statistics is that they treat all cases in the same way. A homicide counts the same as a $75 theft, which under

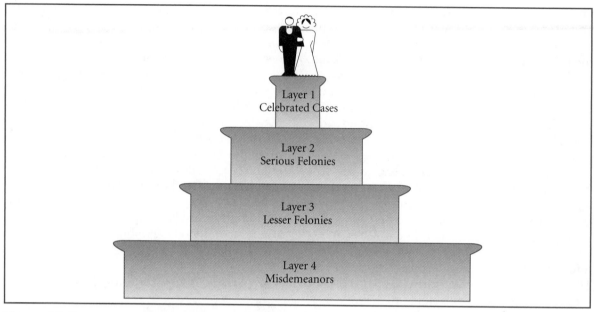

Figure 10-3
The Criminal Justice Wedding Cake

SOURCE: Samuel Walker, *Sense and Nonsense about Crime and Drugs: A Policy Guide,* 5th ed.
(Belmont, CA: Wadsworth, 2001).

state law is petty larceny but is reported as a major felony in the *Uniform Crime Reports* (adopted in the 1930s). Merely counting the number of criminal events gets in the way of understanding how and why court officials treat murder cases differently from petty thefts. To understand case attrition, Samuel Walker (2001) suggests that it is useful to view criminal justice as a wedding cake (Figure 10-3).

The wedding cake model is based on the observation that criminal justice officials handle different kinds of cases very differently. Within each layer, there is a high degree of consistency; the greatest disparities are found between cases in different layers. An examination of these layers illuminates the paradox of American criminal justice: "The problem is not that our system is too lenient, or too severe; sadly, it is both" (Zimring, O'Malley, and Eigen 1976).

Celebrated Cases

The top layer of the criminal justice wedding cake consists of a few celebrated cases. O. J. Simpson is clearly the most celebrated of the modern celebrated cases. But every year a few cases dominate media attention because of the number of persons killed, the bizarre nature of the crime, or the prominence of the defendant. Likewise, local communities may have a few celebrated cases, either because a local notable has been charged with a serious crime or because the crime itself was particularly heinous.

From the moment these cases begin, criminal justice officials treat them as exceptional, making sure that every last detail of the judicial process is followed. The cases are also extraordinary because they frequently involve the rarest of criminal court events—the full jury trial. To the fascination of the viewing and reading public, controversial matters are aired in public. As in morality plays of old and soap operas of today, public attention is focused on the battle between good and evil, although who is playing which role is not always obvious.

These celebrity cases are most likely to be broadcast on television, with the cable station Court TV providing a daily dose. Because of the publicity surrounding them, celebrated cases have a tremendous impact on public perceptions of criminal justice. On one level, these cases reinforce the textbook notion that defendants will receive their day in court, complete with a Perry Mason–type defense counsel and an attentive jury. But on another level, celebrated cases highlight the public's worst fears—the rich often get off scot-free because they can afford an expensive attorney. All too many seem to beat the rap. People assume that the court process ordinarily functions this way, but in fact it does not. Celebrated cases are atypical; they do not reflect how the courts operate on a day-to-day basis.

Serious Felonies

The second layer of the wedding cake consists of serious felonies. The courtroom work group distinguishes between this level and the next on the basis of three main criteria: the seriousness of the crime, the criminal record of the suspect, and the relationship between the victim and the offender. The guiding question is, How much is the case worth? Serious cases end up in the second layer; the "not-so-serious" ones in the third. Murders, armed robberies, and most rapes are treated by all members of the courtroom work group as serious felonies, with the result that there is less likelihood the suspect will be released on bail (see Chapter 11). In addition, at this level, there is more pretrial maneuvering (Chapter 12), with less chance that the sides can reach a plea agreement (Chapter 13), and a strong likelihood of trial (Chapter 14) and eventually an appeal (Chapter 17).

Lesser Felonies

There is, of course, no automatic formula for sorting cases into serious and not-so-serious felonies; the key is a commonsense judgment about the facts of the case. What first appears to be a serious offense might be downgraded because the victim and the offender knew one another. For example, what starts out as an armed robbery might later be viewed as essentially a private disagreement over money owed, with the criminal act a means of seeking redress outside accepted channels. On the other hand, a suspect's long criminal record might transform an otherwise ordinary felony into a serious one, at least in the eyes of the prosecuting attorney.

Analysis of the true seriousness of a case is part of the everyday language of the courthouse actors. Serious cases are routinely referred to as "heavy" cases or "real" crimes, and the less serious ones as "garbage," "bullshit," or simply not real crimes. The practical consequences are that second-layer felonies are given considerable attention, whereas third-layer crimes receive less attention and are treated in a routine and lenient manner.

The Lower Depths

The bottom layer of the criminal justice wedding cake is a world unto itself, consisting of a staggering volume of misdemeanor cases, far exceeding the number of felony cases. About half are "public order" offenses—disorderly conduct, public drunkenness, disturbing the peace, and the like. Only about a third involve crimes against property or persons, many of which are petty thefts or physical disagreements between "friends" or acquaintances. Rarely do these defendants have any social standing. In the eyes of the courtroom work group, few of these cases are worth much, and relatively little time is devoted to their processing. They are usually handled by a different court from the one that handles felony cases and processed in a strikingly different way. Dispositions are arrived at in a routine manner. Defendants are arraigned en masse. Guilt is rarely contested. Even more rarely are the punishments harsh. For these reasons, the lower courts will be treated separately in Chapter 18.

CONCLUSION

One could hardly label Donald Lee McLaughlin a bit player in the case that bears his name. He was more of a prop, no more than a convenient arrest, at least from the perspective of the public defender's office in Riverside, California. A live body was needed to challenge systematic practices; he was chosen and then promptly vanished from public awareness.

A Virtual Tour of American Courthouses: Arrest to Arraignment

Fictonal crooks are often smart and sophisticated. Reality is strikingly different. A visit to the local court will quickly drive home that point. But you can also view the reality of real defendants in criminal court by visiting the Web site of the Maricopa County Sheriff's Office (Phoenix, Arizona), which provides a live jail cam; you can view bookings at **http://www.mcso.org/**.

To view the nature of crime from a macro perspective, you can find more information about the purposes and advantages of "The Nation's Two Crime Measures," the *Uniform Crime Reports* and the *National Crime Victimization Survey,* at **http://www.ojp.usdoj.gov/bjs/abstract/ntcm.htm**.

What to do after you've been arrested is often a favorite topic of student discussion. Along those lines, the ACLU provides an online "bustcard," which discusses what to do if you are stopped by the police: **http://www.aclu.org/issues/criminal/bustcardtext.html**. In a similar vein, the Delaware Public Defender offers a useful Web site providing an overview of procedures in felony cases: **http://www.state.de.us/pubdefen/jdeffelo.htm**.

You can read about one federal grand juror's experience by going to **http://www.udayton.edu/~grandjur/recent/juror.htm**.

The debate among the nine justices over 24 hours versus 36 versus 48 seems at best arcane. But this debate illustrates the overriding reality of the modern age: At times, the rights of individuals must be considered not just on their own merits but also in the context in which they are raised. Individually providing each defendant a probable cause hearing within 24 hours would cause no disruption to the system. But providing potentially hundreds of suspects a day such a right runs smack into logistical problems—transporting prisoners from distant jails, hiring more magistrates, making sure that police reports are available quickly, and many other issues.

What is ultimately important about *County of Riverside v. McLaughlin* is that it focuses attention on what is otherwise an invisible time period in the history of a felony prosecution. The specific steps of criminal procedure are important because they help to ensure fairness in the process. But equally important is the substance of the decisions made. In statistical profile, the process resembles a funnel—wide at the top, narrow at the end. Fewer than half of all crimes are ever reported to the police. Only one in five of the crimes known to the police results in an arrest. Thus, most crimes never reach the courts. Of the small subset of criminal events referred to court officials, half are dropped following prosecutorial screening,

preliminary hearings, or grand jury deliberations. Prosecutors and judges decline to prosecute or later dismiss charges that have been filed because the case lacks sufficient evidence, falls too low on the priority list, or is viewed as a "cheap" case. The wedding cake model highlights this sorting process. Considerable resources are devoted to serious felonies. Lesser felonies receive less attention; they are more likely to be filtered out of the system.

The decisions made at these early points set the tone of cases moving through the criminal court process. Quantitatively, the volume of cases is directly related to screening decisions. In many areas, it is common for roughly half the defendants to have their charges dismissed during these early stages. Qualitatively, screening decisions greatly influence later stages in the proceedings. Most directly, plea bargaining reflects how cases were initially screened. For instance, it is a long-standing practice in many courts for prosecutors to overcharge a defendant by filing accusations more serious than the evidence indicates, in order to give themselves leverage for later offering the defendant the opportunity to plead to a less serious charge. Thus, the important decisions about innocence or guilt are made early in the process by judges and prosecutors—not, as the adversary system projects, late in the process by lay jurors.

CRITICAL THINKING QUESTIONS

1. How long can an arrested person be held before being brought before a neutral judicial official? Do you think it was proper for the Court to take into account law-in-action factors such as case volume in deciding *County of Riverside*?

2. In your community, at what stage does case attrition occur? Do you detect any public displeasure with how the process currently operates?

3. If you were the prosecutor, what arguments would you make to the police chief(s) regarding a policy of careful screening of cases soon after arrest? Conversely, what arguments do you think law enforcement officials would make?

4. To what extent do the issues of weeding out weak cases cut across ideological dimensions? In particular, the crime control model may offer contradictory advice. On the one hand, it suggests prosecution of all wrongdoers to the fullest extent of the law; on the other hand, it values efficiency, emphasizing the early elimination of weak cases so that scarce resources can be concentrated on the strong prosecutions.

5. Do you know of any local crimes that fit the celebrated cases category of the criminal justice wedding cake? Why did these cases receive such attention? Are they similar to or different from cases that receive extensive coverage in the media?

KEY TERMS

arraignment (230)
arrest (219)
arrest warrant (221)
bind over (226)
charging document (221)
complaint (221)
contempt (of court) (229)
grand jury (226)
immunity (228)
index crimes (217)
indictment (227)
information (221)

initial appearance (221)
no true bill (227)
nolle prosequi (231)
preliminary hearing (224)
probable cause (226)
subpoena (power) (229)
transactional immunity (228)
true bill (227)
Type I offenses (217)
use immunity (228)

WORLD WIDE WEB RESOURCES AND EXERCISES

Web Guides

http://dir.yahoo.com/Society_and_Culture/Crime/
http://dir.yahoo.com/Government/Law/Jury_Duty/
 Grand_Jury/

Web Search Terms

war on drugs   *preliminary hearing*
grand jury   *white-collar crimes*

Useful URLs

Federal Bureau of Investigation *Uniform Crime Reports* are available at **http://www.fbi.gov/ucr.htm**.

For the latest National Crime Victimization Survey, go to **http://www.ojp.usdoj.gov/bjs/cvict.htm**.

The Bureau of Justice Statistics provides comprehensive statistics at **http://www.ojp.usdoj. gov/bjs**.

Arrestee Drug Abuse Monitoring (ADAM) provides data on recent drug use among those arrested: **http://www.adam-nij.net/**.

Uncommon URLs

The Federal Grand Jury Web site was created by two law professors to let people know what grand juries are and what they do: **http://www. udayton.edu/~grandjur/**.

The Pacific Crest Biodiversity Project provides an activist's guide to getting arrested and going to trial: **http://www.pcbp.org/arrest.htm**.

Citizens' self-arrest form from the University of Oklahoma police department is available at **http://www.ou.edu/oupd/selfarr2.htm**.

The California Grand Jury Association can be accessed at **http://www.cgja.org/**.

To learn more about efforts at grand jury reform, go to **http://www.criminaljustice.org** and locate the Federal Grand Jury Reform report.

Web Exercises

1. Examine the latest crime victimization data summarized in the *Sourcebook of Criminal Justice Statistics* at **http://www. albany.edu/sourcebook**. How do victimization rates vary by gender, race, and size of community?

2. Do a Web search to find out where various groups stand concerning the war on drugs (discussed in Chapter 4). If you are using Yahoo, here are the commands: **http://www. yahoo.com, Society and Culture/Crime/War on Drugs**. Do these groups appear to be supportive of or hostile to the war on drugs? What arguments do they make for continuing (ending) the war on drugs? Do these groups appear to be representative of public views? If not, why not?

3. Examine the government policy on drugs as represented by the Office of National Drug Policy, located at the following Web site: **http://www.whitehousedrugpolicy.gov**. Does current drug control policy appear to reflect the crime control model or the due process model? How does current government drug policy treat the problem of court overload?

INFOTRAC COLLEGE EDITION RESOURCES AND EXERCISES

Basic Search Terms

arrest
criminal statistics
grand jury

preliminary examinations
white-collar crimes

Recommended Articles

Thomas D. Colbridge, "Protective Sweeps"

Columbia Journalism Review, "Statistics/ Crime Rates"

John C. Hall, "Police Use of Nondeadly Force to Arrest"

Bruce A. Jacobs, Jody Miller, "Crack Dealing, Gender, and Arrest Avoidance"

Daniel C. Richman, "Grand Jury Secrecy: Plugging the Leaks in an Empty Bucket"

Amanda Ripley, "A New Killing Season?"

Nicole Walker, "Why Women Are Committing More Crimes"

InfoTrac College Edition Exercises

1. Using the search term "white-collar crimes," find two or more articles on the topic. How do backers of the crime control model of criminal justice react to this issue? How do advocates of the due process model view this issue? Here are two possible articles:

   Clifton Leaf, "Enough Is Enough: White-Collar Criminals"

   Mark Taylor, "Crime and Punishment: Instead of a Slap on the Wrist . . ."

2. Using the search term "prosecution, planning," find two or more articles that deal with prosecutorial discretion to prosecute criminals. In what ways are the articles similar to or different from the perspective presented in the book.

FOR FURTHER READING

Blank, Blanche Davis. *The Not So Grand Jury: The Story of the Federal Grand Jury System*. Lanham, MD: University Press of America, 1993.

Chaiken, Jan. "Crunching Numbers: Crime and Incarceration at the End of the Millennium." *National Institute of Justice Journal* (2000): 10–17.

Felson, Richard, Steven Messner, Anthony Hoskin, and Glenn Deane. "Reasons for Reporting and Not Reporting Domestic Violence to the Police." *Criminology* 40 (2002): 617–648.

Kingsnorth, Rodney, Randall MacIntosh, and Sandra Sutherland. "Criminal Charge or Probation Violation? Prosecutorial Discretion and Implications for Research in Criminal Court Processing." *Criminology* 40 (2002): 554–578.

Meier, Robert, and Gilbert Geis. *Victimless Crimes? Prostitution, Drugs, Homosexuality, Abortion.* Los Angeles: Roxbury, 1997.

Menard, Scott. "The 'Normality' of Repeat Victimization from Adolescence through Early Adulthood." *Justice Quarterly* 17 (2000): 543–574.

Messner, Steven, and Richard Rosenfeld. *Crime and the American Dream.* 3d ed. Belmont, CA: Wadsworth, 2001.

Siegel, Larry. *Criminology: Theories, Patterns, and Typologies.* 8th ed. Belmont, CA: Wadsworth, 2004.

Weiss, Robert, Richard Berk, and Catherine Lee. "Assessing the Capriciousness of Death Penalty Charging." *Law and Society Review* 30 (1996): 607–632.

Winfree, L. Thomas, Jr., and Howard Abadinsky. *Understanding Crime: Theory and Practice.* 2d ed. Belmont, CA: Wadsworth, 2003.

Chapter 11 Bail

PART III
Processing the Accused

nthony Salerno, organized crime boss, was indicted on 29 counts of racketeering, extortion, and conspiracy to murder. Based on past practices, there
is little doubt that Salerno would have been held in jail in an indirect manner until his trial—bond would have been set so high that he would not
have been able to post the necessary cash. But Rudolph Giuliani, U.S. attorney, sought to
detain Salerno directly. A recently passed federal law allowed a judge to refuse to set
bail if the defendant might harm others while out on bail. The judge found that Salerno
met the criteria and ordered him held in jail until trial. ◀

The decision in *Salerno* represents one of the few times that the Supreme Court has wrestled with the Eighth Amendment's clause that "excessive bail shall not be required." To crime control model advocates, the historical right to bail needs to be modified in the face of pretrial releases of defendants who commit new crimes while out on bail. To due process model supporters, the original understanding that defendants merely charged with a crime shouldn't have to pay a penalty is as applicable today as when the Bill of Rights was adopted. But does this debate about law on the books really matter? From the perspective of law in action, jails are so full today that laws allowing judges to detain certain defendants prior to trial are merely toothless tigers.

The *Salerno* case underscores the importance of pretrial detention decisions. Bail represents a defendant's first major encounter with the courts. For various fees, depending on the crime, the accused can purchase freedom and return to home and family. But defendants who cannot post bond must await trial in jail, suffering many of the same penalties normally reserved only for those who have been found guilty. This chapter examines how the American system of pretrial release works, the factors that shape its operation, and the consequences of decisions about bail. Some of the key areas discussed include concerns that bail discriminates against the poor and fears that bail exposes the public to risks of being victimized.

LAW ON THE BOOKS: THE MONETARY BAIL SYSTEM

Bail is a guarantee. In return for being released from jail, the accused promises to return to court as needed. This promise is guaranteed by posting money or property with the court. If the defendant appears in court when requested, the security is returned. If he or she fails to appear, the security can be forfeited. The practice of allowing defendants to be released from jail pending trial originated centuries ago in England, largely as a convenience to local sheriffs. The colonists brought the concept of bail with them across the Atlantic. It eventually became embedded in the Eighth Amendment, which provides that "excessive bail shall not be required." The excessive bail clause establishes a right to bail (Nagel 1990). There are limitations, however. Because no security is considered large enough to deter accused persons from fleeing to save their lives, defendants accused of capital offenses have no right to bail.

Bail Procedures

Shortly after arrest, a defendant is brought before a lower court judge, who sets the conditions of release. Bail procedures vary according to the seriousness of the crime. Those arrested for minor misdemeanors can be released fairly quickly by posting bail at the police station. In most communities, the lower court judges have adopted a fixed bail schedule (also known as an emergency bail schedule), which specifies an exact amount for each offense.

Bail procedures for felony or serious misdemeanor cases are considerably more complex. The arrestee must appear before a lower court judge for the setting of bail, so those accused of serious crimes remain in police custody for a number of hours before they have the opportunity to make bail.

Forms of Bail

Once bail has been set, a defendant can gain pretrial release in four basic ways. First, the accused may post the full amount with the court in the form of a **cash bond.** All of this money will be returned when all court appearances are satisfied. Because it requires a large amount of cash, this form of bail is seldom used. If, for example, bail is set in the amount of $10,000, most persons cannot raise that much money easily and quickly.

The second method for securing pretrial release is a **property bond.** Most states allow a defendant (or friends or relatives) to use a piece of property as collateral. If the defendant fails to appear in court, the property is forfeited. Property bonds are also rare, because courts generally require that the equity in the property must be double the amount of the bond. Thus, a $10,000 bond requires equity of at least $20,000.

A third alternative for making bail is **release on recognizance (ROR** for short). Judges release a defendant from jail without monetary bail if they believe the person is not likely to flee. Such personal bonds are used most often for defendants accused of minor crimes and for those with substantial ties to the community.

Because many of those arrested lack ready cash, do not own property, or lack the needed social clout, the first three options for making bail are only abstractions. Many of those released prior to trial use the fourth method: They hire a **bail agent** (often called a **bail bondsman**), who posts the amount required and charges a fee for services rendered, usually 10 percent of the amount of the bond. Thus, a bail agent would normally collect $1,000 for writing a $10,000 bond. None of that money is refundable.

In the American system of monetary bail, those who are rich enough can buy their freedom and await trial on the streets. But the poor await trial in jail. On any given day, there are more than 665,000 persons in jail (not prison), half of whom have not been convicted of any crime. Such average daily population figures greatly underestimate the high volume of transactions that occur. Unlike prisons, where the annual turnover of the population is relatively small, large numbers of individuals pass through the revolving door of the jail, "moving into, out of, and back into, the facility during any given year" (Backstrand, Gibbons, and Jones 1992). In a typical year, there are more than 14 million entries and exits.

Conflicting Theories of Bail

Administration of bail has been greatly influenced by a long-standing disagreement over the purposes of bail. Adherents of the due process model stress that the only purpose of bail is to ensure that the defendant appears in court for trial. The basis of this view is the premise of the adversarial system that a person is innocent until proven guilty and therefore should not suffer any hardships, such as a stay in jail, while awaiting trial. According to this view, a judge should calculate bail solely on the basis of what amount will guarantee the availability of the accused for court hearings.

Supporters of the crime control model stress that bail should be used to protect society. They focus on defendants who are likely to commit further crimes while out on bail. This perspective is reflected in law in action: Informally, judges deliberately set bail so high that defendants perceived to be dangerous will be unable to post bail and therefore await trial in jail. More recently, preventive detention has been formally authorized in some jurisdictions. Exhibit 11-1 summarizes key developments in the law regarding bail.

Exhibit 11-1 Key Developments Regarding Bail

Eighth Amendment	1791	Excessive bail shall not be required.
Stack v. Boyle	1951	Bail set at a figure higher than an amount reasonably calculated to ensure the defendant's presence at trial is excessive.
Bail Reform Act	1966	Creates a presumption favoring pretrial release of federal arrestees.
Schilb v. Kuebel	1971	Illinois' bail deposit system is constitutional.
Bail Reform Act	1984	In setting bail, the judge may consider danger to the community.
U.S. v. Salerno	1987	Federal preventive detention law does not violate the Eighth Amendment.
U.S. v. Montalvo-Murillo	1990	Defendant has no "right" to freedom when a detention hearing was not held at the time of his first appearance; this failure was a minor statutory violation.
Kansas v. Henricks	1997	Upholds Kansas' Sexually Violent Predator Act, which permits the state to keep sexual offenders in a mental institution after they complete a criminal sentence.

The competing perspectives of ensuring appearance at trial and protecting society affect the daily realities of bail setting in ways that will be discussed throughout this chapter.

LAW IN ACTION: THE CONTEXT OF BAIL SETTING

Deciding whom to release and whom to detain pending trial poses critical problems for American courts. The realities of the bail system in the United States reflect an attempt to strike a balance between the legally recognized purpose of setting bail to assure reappearance for trial and the working perception that some defendants should not be allowed out of jail until their trial. As Roy Flemming (1982) argues, one can imagine two improbable extremes. On the one hand, the courts could release all defendants prior to trial. On the other, they could hold every suspect. But neither of these extremes is possible. Freeing all those accused of violent offenses is not politically feasible, no matter what the chances are of their later appearing in court. Similarly, jailing them all is not possible, because jails are simply not large enough. Thus, court officials must make decisions every day that balance these competing demands.

Legal protections such as the right to bail are meaningful only in the context of the policies that execute those protections. Only rarely do judges directly decide that a defendant should remain in jail pending trial. Rather, this important decision is made indirectly, when the amount of bail is fixed. The higher the bail, the less likely it is that the accused will be able to post the required bond. As the amount of bail increases, fewer defendants are able to secure pretrial release (Zeisel 1979).

Trial court judges have a great deal of discretion in fixing bail. Statutory law provides few specifics about how much money should be required, and appellate courts have likewise spent little time deciding what criteria should be used. Although the Eighth Amendment prohibits excessive bail, appellate courts will reduce a trial judge's bail amount only in the rare event that flagrant abuse can be proved. In practice, then, trial court judges have virtually unlimited legal discretion in determining the amount of bail.

The range of choices available to court officials is referred to as the context of bail setting. Uncertainty, risk, and jail overcrowding are the primary political and institutional

A Virtual Tour of American Courthouses: Bail and Jail

Some bail agents find that maintaining a Web site is good for business. The title of this site says it all: Bad Boyz Bail Bonds at **http://www.badboyzbailbonds.com**. This site even has the trademark of "In Jail, We Bail"™. For a Web site that promises to tell you everything about the bail bond process, go to Action Bail Bonds at **http://www.actionbail.com/**.

Not all of those released on bail actually show up for their scheduled court appearances. For 101 excuses why defendants fail to appear in court, see **http://athenabb.com/101excuses.htm**. Since excuses are plentiful, so are bounty hunters who will track down the missing—for a fee, of course. Movies have been made about bounty hunters, including *The Unforgiven* starring Clint Eastwood (**http://www.filmsite.org/unfo.html**). In the modern era, names change for better spin, so now bounty hunters are officially called "bail enforcement agencies." To learn more about how The Pacific Northwest Bail Enforcement Academy trains people to track down fugitives, go to **http://www.bailacademy.org/index1.html**. For a helpful Web site for locating bail enforcement agents across the nation, just click on **http://www.onworld.com/BHO/index.html** to view the Web site of Bounty Hunters Online.

To manage the ever growing jail populations and to provide some sort of control over those released on their own recognizance, a growing number of courts have created pretrial service agencies. The District of Columbia Pretrial Services Agency is one of the nation's most active; it can be visited at **http://www.gwu.edu/~pretrial/**. Pretrial FAQs are provided by the California Association of Pretrial Services at **http://www.napsa.org/docs/faq.htm**.

Many of the 14 million plus individuals arrested every year spend at least a few hours in jail before they are released, and some are not released at all. An increasing number of sheriffs' departments maintain Web sites that offer good insights into the realities of jails. Here are a few of my favorites:

Niagara County (New York): **http://www.ncsd.com**

Sangamon County (Springfield, Illinois): **http://www.fgi.net/sheriff/jail.html**

Chesapeake (Virginia): **http://www.chesapeake.va.us/services/depart/sheriff/sheriff/correct.htm**

factors that shape pretrial release policy in any given court.

Uncertainty

Uncertainty is a major problem facing court officials in making bail decisions. A few short hours after arrest, the defendant appears in court for bail setting. Because of this short time span, only a limited amount of information is available. The details of the alleged crime—the who, what, when, where, and especially the why—are troublingly vague. Thus, the judge must set bail on the basis of little information about the strength of the evidence against the accused (Nagel 1983).

Compounding the information void is the lack of adequate facts about the defendant's past criminal history. In many courts, police "rap sheets" (lists of prior arrests) are available but typically contain information only on prior arrests, not on how the case was eventually disposed of—dismissal, plea, or imprisonment, for example. Faced with limited information, court officials must nonetheless make a number of decisions. Is this specific defendant likely to appear in court? Is he or she dangerous to the community? In the context of the crime and the defendant, what is "reasonable" bail? Because of the scarcity of knowledge, defendants may be classified incorrectly as good or bad candidates for release.

Risk

The uncertainty court officials face during bail setting is aggravated by the risks involved. Potentially, any defendant released on bail may commit another crime. Judges fear negative publicity if they release a defendant on ROR who later injures or kills the victim. Police groups, district attorneys, and the local news-

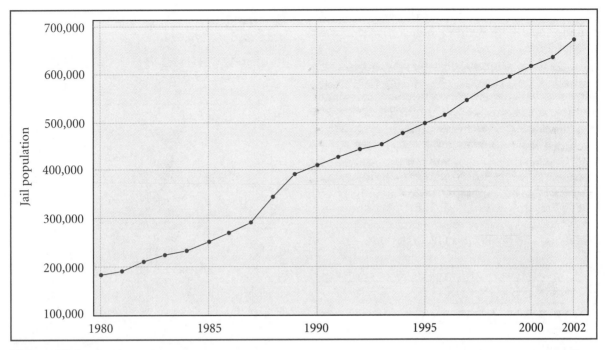

Figure 11-1
Growth in U.S. Jail Population

SOURCE: Paige Harrison and Jennifer Karberg, *Prison and Jail Inmates at Midyear 2002* (Washington, DC: Bureau of Justice Statistics, 2003). Available online: http://www.ojp.usdoj.gov/bjs

papers may criticize a judge severely for granting pretrial release to defendants. In New York City, for example, a judge was nicknamed "Turn 'Em Loose Bruce" by the Patrolman's Benevolent Association. The judge was later reassigned to civil court after a series of public controversies about his setting low bail for defendants accused of violent crimes.

It is important to recognize that in setting bail, judges and other court officials may make two types of mistakes. Type 1 errors involve releasing a defendant who later commits another crime or fails to appear in court. Type 2 errors involve detaining a suspect who should have been released. These two types of errors are inversely related; that is, the more Type 2 errors, the fewer Type 1. However, Type 2 errors are largely hidden; they appear only if a major tragedy occurs, such as a suicide in jail. Type 1 errors, on the other hand, form the stuff of which newspaper headlines are made. In short, judges face public criticism mainly for Type 1 errors. In assessing risk factors, court officials tend to err on the conservative side, preferring to make Type 2 rather than Type 1 errors.

Jail Overcrowding

The context of bail setting involves not only uncertainty and risk but also available resources. The principal limiting factor is the size of the local jail. Simply stated, jails are filled to capacity. In the decade from 1983 to 1993, the jail population more than doubled. Today there are approximately 665,000 inmates in local jails (Figure 11-1). Although construction has added thousands of new beds over the years, in some areas jail systematically operate at over capacity, meaning that there is little ability to put more arrestees in jail without releasing others (Bureau of Justice Statistics 2003c). Thus, like prisons (discussed in Chapter 15), jails face serious overcrowding problems. Indeed, prison overcrowding is a principal cause of jail overcrowding. With prisons filled to overflowing, recently sentenced defendants must often spend time in local jails awaiting a vacant cell in the state prison.

Jails filled to overcapacity force court officials to make uncomfortable decisions. Although they may believe that the defendant should be held in jail awaiting trial, they may realize that arrestees who have committed more serious offenses have already filled the jail. Thus, as jails become overcrowded or threaten to exceed their capacity, bail-setting practices become more lenient (Roth and Wice 1980; Flemming 1982). Exhibit 11-2 summarizes bail and pretrial release practices as seen by law on the books and law in action.

THE PROCESS OF BAIL SETTING

Court officials respond to the context of bail setting (uncertainty, risk, and limited jail capacity) through general guidelines concerning the proper amount of bail (shared norms in terms of the courtroom work group concept developed in Chapter 5). Judges do not ponder each case as an isolated event; rather, bail guidelines provide cues for evaluating specific cases. In essence, bail setting "involves a search by officials to establish whether or not they should follow custom" (Flemming 1982, 29). In some communities, these normal bail amounts are specified in written guidelines (Jones and Goldkamp 1991). In most communities, they operate informally but have a major impact nonetheless. Two factors are particularly important in shaping bail guidelines: the seriousness of the crime and the prior criminal record of the defendant. As will become apparent, situational justice also comes into play.

Seriousness of the Crime

By far the most important consideration in establishing bail tariffs is the seriousness of the crime: the more serious the crime, the higher the amount of bail. The underlying assumption is that the more serious the crime, the greater will be the defendant's inclination to forfeit bail, and therefore the greater the financial costs should be for such flight (Wice 1974).

COURT TV

Command and Control: Inside Rikers Island

Rikers Island is the world's largest jail, employing over 3,000 correctional officers who separate the inmates from us. Located in the Hudson river within sight of LaGuardia airport, Rikers Island is the jail for all of New York City. Its ten separate facilities house those awaiting trial as well as long-term prisoners.

Keeping drugs and guns off the Island is a major concern. Watch as the guards search visitors and occasionally arrest them for trying to smuggle in drugs and weapons. But prevention is not always foolproof. Cell searches are a daily activity, with the guards confiscating home-made weapons and razor blades. Controlling the inmate population is a difficult task. Watch and listen as several female guards describe how the strategies they use to control the male inmates differ from those used by the male guards.

 View the video clip about Rikers Island on your copy of the CourtTV CD-ROM. As you watch the video, keep the following questions in mind:

1. Jails are often described as institutions for poor people. How accurate is this assessment based on what you see in this video clip?

2. Based on what you see, compare these inmates to the profile of criminal defendants discussed in Chapter 9. Do these inmates appear to be similar or different from typical defendants awaiting trial in jail?

3. Compare the inmates you see in this clip of Rikers Island to the presentation in Chapter 10 of "A Day in Court: 'Hell's Waiting Room.'" Why do the portrayals appear to be different?

This proposition is confirmed by a Bureau of Justice Statistics report on the nation's 75 most populous counties (Reaves 2001). The mean bail amount for detained defendants ($56,900)

Exhibit 11-2 Bail and Pretrial Release

	Law on the Books	Law in Action
Right to bail	Based on the Eighth Amendment and the presumption of innocence until proven guilty, U.S. law creates a general right to bail.	The average daily jail population is approximately 650,000; more than 14 million admissions to local jails each year. Jails house about a third of all persons incarcerated in the United States.
Capital cases	Defendants awaiting trial on a murder charge that carries the death penalty have no right to bail.	
Methods of release	*Cash:* Defendant may post the full amount of the bond with clerk of court.	Most often used in minor offenses processed in the lower courts.
	Property: A piece of property with equity of twice the amount of bail posted with the clerk.	Used on rare occasions.
	Release on recognizance (ROR): Released without posting collateral.	Used in lesser felonies. Lower court defendants typically plead guilty at first appearance.
	Bail bondsmen (agents): Post bond with the court for a fee (typically 10 percent of the bond).	Prefer clients accused of less serious, nonviolent crimes.
Preventive detention	Two out of three jurisdictions allow the court to refuse to set bail if the defendant might flee and/or may be a risk to others.	Jail overcrowding is the norm, so in many jurisdictions preventive detention is never formally used. Historically, judges set high bail amounts to accomplish the same goal.
Jails	Typically funded by local governments, jails hold suspects awaiting trial, house inmates awaiting transfer to state prisons, and confine those serving short sentences.	The United States has 3,365 jails. Forty-seven jails are privately owned or operated. Annual cost per inmate is $15,000-plus.

was about five times that of defendants who secured release ($11,300). As a result, defendants charged with murder were the least likely to be granted pretrial release (16 percent), whereas those accused of drug or property crimes were released 66 percent of the time. Stated another way, the severity of the charge is inversely related to bail release.

Prior Criminal Record

A second criterion used in setting the amount of bond is the defendant's prior criminal record. Defendants with prior criminal records typi-

cally have bond set higher than normal for the offense charged (Wice 1974). For this reason, in New York City defendants with prior criminal records were more likely to await trial in jail (Nagel 1983). Nationwide, defendants with an active criminal justice status were twice as likely as those without such a status to be detained until case disposition (Reaves 2001).

Situational Justice

The use of bail tariffs enables the courts to set bail rather rapidly for most defendants. After consideration of the charge and the prior record, the judge announces the bail amount or grants a recognizance bond. However, not all bail settings are automatic. Judges often seek situational justice, in which they weigh the individual facets of the case and the defendant. Because they have so little information, judges may construct honesty tests such as the following.

> "Have you ever been arrested anywhere in the world since the day you were born to this day?" The defendant replied that he was arrested two or three years ago. "What for?"
> "I forget," the defendant answers.
> "Weren't you arrested this year? In April? Weren't you in the Wayne County jail for a day or so? On the 26th?" The judge asks the questions without giving the defendant a chance to reply. After pausing a moment, the judge informed the defendant he had a "pretty bad memory" and added, "Have to have a bondsman for people with bad memories." (Flemming 1982, 57)

The use of honesty tests is but one illustration of the fact that the demeanor of the defendant influences bail setting. Cooperative defendants are more likely to gain pretrial release (Snyder 1989).

▌BAIL BONDSMEN

Clustered around urban courthouses are the bright neon lights of the bail bondsmen. Boldly proclaiming "Bail Bonds, 24-Hour Service," they are a constant reminder that freedom is available, for a price. Bail bondsmen are as important to America's monetary bail system as they are controversial. To judicial reformers, they are parasites who prey on human misery. Abolition of bail bondsmen is a key objective of many reformers, and five states (Kentucky, Oregon, Wisconsin, Nebraska, and Illinois) have eliminated bail bonding for profit (Bureau of Justice Statistics 1988b). Despite frequent criticisms and efforts to abolish them, they continue to play an important role in the pretrial processing of defendants in many jurisdictions (Sviridoff 1986).

Published material about bail bondsmen has been strongly biased because the literature has been mostly reform-oriented. Grand jury investigations, legislative studies, journalistic exposés, and the reports of two national commissions have portrayed bondsmen as fixers of cases and corrupters of courthouses. They are viewed as essential links in the chain of official corruption. To Forrest Dill, however, these studies leave the simplistic impression that the bondsman is an isolated sore. Based on studying bail bondsmen in two California cities, he comments that their links to official corruption "contain an element of truth, of course, but it is hardly surprising that bail bondsmen in corrupt jurisdictions participate in corrupting practices" (1975, 643). To understand the role of bondsmen in the criminal justice system, one must examine two aspects of their existence: the business setting and the court setting.

The Business Setting

Bail bondsmen are businesspeople, but their business is unique. By allowing commercial intermediaries to post bond, the state has created a business operation within the criminal courts. In essence, the bondsman is a private government subcontractor; key decisions on pretrial release have been transferred from public officials to private parties, who represent neither the interests of the courts nor those of the defendant.

Bail bondsmen make money by providing a specialized form of insurance. For a nonrefundable fee, they post a bond with the court. If the defendant does not appear for trial, the bondsman is responsible for the full amount of the bond. For assuming this risk, he or she is permitted to charge a fee, usually 10 percent of the face amount of the bond.

Rarely, however, do bail bondsmen post a cash surety directly with the court. Instead, they purchase a surety bond from a major insurance company, which charges 30 percent of the bondsman's fee. Thus, if the total amount of the bail is $1,000, the bondsman receives $100 from the client and keeps $70 of it. Because the profit margin in each case is seldom large, bondsmen need to find plenty of clients willing to purchase their services, while simultaneously accepting only those who present a minimal risk of fleeing.

Competition among local bondsmen to gain "good" clients is stiff. Bondsmen use several techniques to ensure a steady supply of clients. Defendants with prior court experience know how to contact bondsmen who have provided reliable service in the past. Third parties are also a frequent (and sometimes controversial) source of referrals. Defense attorneys sometimes refer a client to a bondsman (often expecting future favors in return). Likewise, police officers, court clerks, or bailiffs may steer defendants toward bondsmen. Such referrals are sometimes an attempt to be helpful, but more often there is an expectation that the person making the referral will be compensated in some way.

Once contact has been made, bondsmen must decide whether to take the arrestee as a client. They consider the following types of defendants bad risks: first offenders (because they are likely to panic); recidivists whose new crime is more serious than previous ones; and violent defendants (they may harm the bondsman). In assessing which defendants are financially reliable, bondsmen use the very criteria ignored by the court: employment history, family situation, and roots in the community. Contrary to popular belief, bondsmen do not accept just anyone as a client. They prefer to write bonds when the bail is low, because their risks are then also low. Thus, many bondsmen make a living by posting bond for numerous defendants accused of minor crimes and an occasional large bond when repayment is assured.

As a condition of posting bail, the bondsman requires the client to sign a contract waiving any protections against extradition and allowing the bondsman to retrieve the defendant from wherever he or she may have fled. These powers exceed any possessed by law enforcement officials. For example, a bondsman can retrieve a fugitive much more easily than the police can. (See A Day in Court: "So I'm a Bounty Hunter; You Got a Problem with That, Pal?")

Bail Bondsmen and the Courtroom Work Group

Experienced bail bondsmen are on a first-name basis with such court personnel as sheriffs, bailiffs, and clerks, who represent a vital part of their business. Each of these officials can help or hinder the bondsman. As one bondsman noted, "The court clerk is probably one of the most important people I have to deal with. He moves cases, he can get information to the judge, and he has control over various calendar matters. When he's not willing to help you out, he can make life very difficult. He knows he's important, and he acts like it" (Dill 1975, 658). Bondsmen often contribute financially to judges' reelection campaigns. The relationships between bail bondsmen and the courts are reciprocal.

One way in which bondsmen help the courts is by managing the population of arrested persons. Without bail bondsmen, the courts would be faced with an intolerably large jail population. For decades, bail bondsmen have been the easiest way out of this dilemma. At the same time, bondsmen may also help the court prevent some defendants from being released. When court officials desire that a particular defendant not be released, the bondsmen usually cooperate by refusing to post bond (Dill 1975).

The major financial risk facing bondsmen is that clients will jump bail and fail to appear in court, in which case the entire amount of the bond will have to be made good. Yet in many cities, forfeited bonds regularly go uncollected. Part of this practice is legitimate. To encourage bondsmen to seek out and find those who have fled, courts allow a grace period before bonds are forfeited. But the key reason that many bonds go uncollected is the discretionary power of judges to relieve bondsmen from outstanding bonds. In many cities, bondsmen will not have to pay a bond forfeiture if they can convince the judge that they have made every effort to find the missing client (Wice 1974). These considerations cannot fully explain all of the uncollected bonds. Judges are deliberately not trying to collect. Given the help the bondsmen offer the courts, the major way the courts can reciprocate is by not trying to collect bond forfeitures.

EFFECTS OF THE BAIL SYSTEM

Even though defendants detained before trial are presumed innocent until proven guilty, they suffer many of the same disadvantages as those

"So I'm a Bounty Hunter; You Got a Problem with That, Pal?"

I wonder whether this is the best time to admit this, but shy is not my style so here goes: I'm proud to call myself a bounty hunter.

No, I'm not talking about the kind of bounty hunter who has been getting so much ink lately—the ones who kick down doors at the wrong houses, or shoot first and ask questions later, or beat up bail jumpers before handing them over to the police.

I'm talking about the bounty hunters like myself and others whose work I respect and admire—professionals who have captured dangerous fugitives after everyone else has given up, who take the time and trouble to make sure they have the right suspect, who treat bounty hunting as a job that needs to be done well and not as an opportunity to play Steve McQueen or Clint Eastwood.

And make no mistake: Like any profession, the field of bounty hunting draws its share of bad actors. I have seen bounty hunters slap people around for no reason other than to satisfy their own sadistic impulses. That's why I have no trou-

ble with those who argue that we need more regulation—perhaps a licensing system and formal training courses. As far as I'm concerned, that can only make the good bounty hunters better and get rid of the bad ones.

Bounty hunting is an accepted part of the criminal justice system. Some of my colleagues hate the term "bounty hunter" and prefer the term "bail enforcement agent." They can call themselves whatever they want. Bounty hunter is fine with me. . . .

The courts depend on us. Without bounty hunters, most bail jumpers would probably never come to trial. The police just wouldn't have the time, or the resources, to catch them all. And we can do things the police can't—something I learned early in my career. Take the case of Ricki and Dee, two women in their twenties awaiting trial on drug charges. I had traced them to a house in the nearby town of Paso Robles. I planned to arrest them, but first I told my pals in the Paso Robles police department.

Some of them were standing on the front lawn when I knocked on the door. A woman talked to

---

incarcerated after conviction. Economically, they often lose their jobs. Psychologically, they are subjected to stress, anxiety, and isolation. Physically, they are held in a violence-prone atmosphere. The President's Commission on Law Enforcement and Administration of Justice (1967) chose the following examples to dramatize the human toll that pretrial detention can exact.

- A man was jailed on a serious charge brought last Christmas Eve. He could not afford bail and spent 101 days in jail until a hearing. Then the complainant admitted the charge was false.

- A man spent two months in jail before being acquitted. In that period, he lost his job and his car, and his family was split up. He did not find another job for four months.

In a variety of ways, detained defendants are at a disadvantage during pretrial preparation, trial, and sentencing.

Case Disposition

Pretrial detention has a great impact on the legal processing of defendants.

> Viewed from the perspective of maintaining the plea-bargaining system, pretrial detention and demoralizing conditions in jails are highly functional. They discourage the defendant from bargaining too hard; they place a high price upon filing motions or demanding a trial. . . . This is not to argue that those in authority consciously plan rotten jails; clearly most are concerned about jail conditions. But it is

me through the screen door, but wouldn't open it or let me in. I sensed from her nervous behavior that one or both women were hiding inside. I went around to the side of the house, where I spotted an open window. In a flash, I leaped over the sill and landed in the kitchen.

There was Ricki. I led her out the front door to the waiting cops. I went back into the house to do a more thorough search, and I found Dee hiding in a bathroom.

My leap through the window caused quite a stir. I heard a deputy sheriff say, "Gee, I wish I could do that." He wasn't talking about my leaping ability. He was talking about entering the house without a search warrant. So why can I enter a house if the cops can't?

Because the courts long ago decided that a defendant, in accepting a bond, is agreeing to allow the bondsman to come after him if he fails to come to court.

Sound too harsh? Remember, we are dealing with accused and convicted criminals whose friends and families have put up the money for their bonds. If they don't show up for trial, their loved ones get hurt. I don't have a lot of sympathy for them.

That's also why I don't apologize for some of my tactics. When I'm trying to trace a skip, I will do anything to get information, including telling outright lies. I will even pretend I am a friend or a relative. My thinking is: They lied to me when they said they would show up for court, so I see nothing wrong with lying to bring them back. Bounty hunting is a head game, and the name of the game is scam. . . .

So when you wonder about bounty hunters and what they do, remember Mr. Rapist. Sure, we need to be careful about who does bounty hunting and how they do it. But while you're sleeping tonight, remember that bounty hunters are hiding in back alleys, crouching on rooftops and lying in muddy fields to track down fugitives who never make it to "America's Most Wanted." Let's not lose sight of who the bad guys really are.

SOURCE: Mackenzie Green, "So I'm a Bounty Hunter; You Got a Problem with That, Pal?" *The Star Tribune,* 21 September 1997, 21A.

Mackenzie Green is the owner of a San Francisco bail bond firm. Her Web site, Bounty Hunters Online, can be reached at http://www.onworld.com/BHO/index.html.

For more information, read these articles:
John Elvin, "The Strong Arm of the Law"
Thomas J. Wolf, "What United States Pretrial Services Officers Do"

to suggest that such conditions are functional, do serve the needs of the production ethic that dominates our criminal justice system. (Casper 1972, 67)

The discriminatory impact of bail has been the subject of considerable research. There is widespread agreement in the literature that jailed defendants are more likely to be convicted and (once convicted) more likely to be sentenced to prison than those who have obtained pretrial release (Reaves 2001; Ares, Rankin, and Sturz 1963). What is in dispute is the interpretation of these findings. Do these disparities result because the lack of pretrial release imposes additional burdens on the defendants? Or are these disparities a statistical artifact of a preselection process? Given that bail tariffs increase with the severity of the crime and the length of the prior record, one might reasonably expect that these defendants would end up disadvantaged, but for good reason.

John Goldkamp (1980) has attempted to answer this difficult question through a sophisticated analysis of more than 8,000 criminal cases in Philadelphia. Goldkamp found that jailed defendants did not differ from their bailed counterparts in terms of findings of guilt. At all the significant stages—dismissal, diversion, and trial—jailed defendants were as likely as bailed ones to receive a favorable disposition of their cases. When it came to sentencing, however, jailed defendants were more likely to be sentenced to prison, although the length of the sentence was not related to bail status. Another study (Eisenstein and Jacob 1977) found no uniform impact of bail status on findings of guilt or on sentencing. Does bail status negatively affect the defendant's case? Perhaps the best response is provided by Goldkamp: "It depends."

Failure to Appear

Defendants who have gained pretrial release do not always appear in court when required. Skipping bail has several consequences. First, bail is forfeited. Second, a warrant is issued for the suspect's arrest. This warrant, termed a **bench warrant** or a **capias,** authorizes the police to take the person into custody. The person must be delivered to the judge issuing the warrant and cannot be released on bail. Finally, failure to appear often subjects the defendant to a separate criminal charge of bond jumping.

How often bailed defendants fail to appear in court is subject to considerable debate (Wice 1974). A Bureau of Justice Statistics (1993) study of the nation's 75 largest jurisdictions reported that 24 percent of the released defendants missed one or more court dates. But this estimate appears to overstate the problem because it defined nonappearance as missing a single court date. Probably more accurate is the estimate of 8 percent of released defendants who failed to appear and were still fugitives at the end of the year-long study.

Defendants who fail to appear do not always intend to do so. Failure-to-appear rates are closely related to practices within the court. A number of defendants do not show up because they were not given clear notice of the next appearance date. Another way in which courts themselves contribute to nonappearances is by lengthy delay in disposing of cases. As the time from arrest to trial increases, the rate of nonappearances rises even faster (Bureau of Justice Statistics 1993).

BAIL REFORM BASED ON THE DUE PROCESS MODEL

The American system of monetary bail has been the subject of extensive debate for decades. The fairness and effectiveness of pretrial release and detention have been questioned from two conflicting perspectives. The bail reform movement of the 1960s and 1970s was largely concerned with correcting inequities. Requiring suspects to buy their freedom was viewed as unfairly discriminating against the poor. Bail reform based on the values of the due process model are reflected in the Bail Reform Act of 1966, which created a presumption favoring pretrial release. To make bail fairer, reformers advocated adopting a 10 percent bail deposit and institutionalizing pretrial service programs. These programs offered new ways to accomplish the purpose of bail: to guarantee appearance for trial.

Ten Percent Bail Deposit

Bail agents charge a nonrefundable 10 percent fee for posting bond. Since they seem to perform few services for their fee and have often been linked with corruption, bail reformers have attempted to legislate an economic end run around these third-party operators. In a handful of jurisdictions, defendants may gain pretrial release by posting 10 percent of the face amount of the bond with the court. At this point, there is no difference between what the bail agent charges and what the court requires. But when the defendant makes all scheduled court appearances, the court will refund 90 percent of the amount posted. (The remaining 10 percent covers the administrative costs of the program.) The 10 percent bail deposit program directly threatens the bail bond industry. In Illinois, the first state to adopt this program, bail agents have virtually disappeared. In other states, however, agents have been successful in defeating such proposals in the legislature.

Pretrial Service Programs

Bail reformers have been critical of traditional methods of bail setting because the court does not directly focus on whether the defendant is likely to appear in court. What were first called *bail reform projects* but are now termed *pretrial service programs* seek to remedy this deficiency by determining which defendants are good risks. First developed and tested by the Vera Institute of Justice in New York City, the program works as follows. A program worker interviews the defendant shortly after arrest about family ties, employment history, length of time in the community, prior criminal record, and (in a

THE MURDER TRIAL OF SHAREEF COUSIN

Awaiting Trial in Foti's Fortress

Because he was charged with a capital offense, Shareef Cousin was not eligible for bail. Therefore, he awaited trial (and later retrial) in what is officially known as the Orleans Parish Prison. Informally, the facility is referred to as Foti's Fortress, a tribute to one of the most powerful officials in the area, Criminal Sheriff Charles Foti, Jr. In a city in which prisons are a growth industry, Sheriff Foti is one of the most ambitious entrepreneurs in town.

When Foti was first elected in 1973, the inmate population was less than 800. Today the total number of local, state, and federal inmates is more than 7,000, making it one of the largest jail populations in the country. What is collectively referred to as the Orleans Parish Prison (OPP) is in actuality 13 separate buildings that sprawl over a 12-block area, interspersed among the New Orleans police department headquarters, the district attorney's office, criminal district court, municipal court, and traffic court.

Some of the growth in jail capacity was spurred by federal lawsuits over conditions of confinement (see Chapter 15). Old Parish Prison, for example, constructed in 1929, was in danger of being closed by the federal courts in the 1970s because of poor safety and sanitary conditions. The growth in the local jail population is also due to the increased arrest activity of the New Orleans Police Department. As the police have become more proactive (see Chapter 10), they have made more arrests, requiring more cells. Another factor is prison overcrowding at the state level (see Chapter 15). With the state prisons filled to overflowing, many prisoners are held in local jails, like Orleans Parish Prison, until they can be transferred to state prisons.

In turn, the sheriff has effectively mobilized public opinion to support building more prisons. During peak arrest periods (Mardi Gras, for instance), the sheriff constructed a tent city on vacant land near the other prisons (Cooper 1993b). These temporary facilities drew the ire of neighborhood residents and the ACLU, creating political pressures for a more permanent solution. The sheriff has likewise cleverly publicized the problem of overcrowding. In the news media it became known as the "Foti Walk." Local television stations routinely broadcast videotapes of a line of jeering criminals being released from OPP because of overcrowding.

How this prison expansion has been financed remains a persistent and mysterious issue in New Orleans politics. The sheriff takes the position that as an independently elected official he does not have to share financial information with the public, so no one knows how much money the office has or where it comes from. The city is obligated under federal court order to pay $19.65 a day per prisoner but is often late in making payments. Thus, Sheriff Foti finds it more profitable to hold prisoners for the state, which pays $22 per day, or for the federal government.

A complex of this size and magnitude has its problems. One is escapes. In 1993, for example, 15 prisoners escaped, but the sheriff did not notify the public for several weeks (Woods 1993). Another is inmate deaths. In 1999, for instance, diabetic inmate JoAnn Johnson died while in custody, prompting a protest rally in front of the jail and the filing of a federal lawsuit by the ACLU, which alleged inadequate medical care.

Despite these periodic public relations problems, Sheriff Foti is one of the most popular local officials. He has been reelected every four years with little or no opposition. This is partly due to the variety of non–law enforcement programs he sponsors, including a Halloween haunted house for teens and an annual Thanksgiving dinner for the elderly. He also takes pride in a number of programs for prisoners, including the Prison Art Program, which has literally "painted the town" by creating colorful large-scale murals on public buildings, and the About Face Program, which provides an innovative approach aimed at helping inmates learn how to redirect their lives. But critics claim that in reality Foti places a low priority on programs to assist prisoners in learning a skill or learning to read (Cooper 1993b).

In 2003 Foti successfully used his New Orleans political base to win the statewide office of Attorney General.

For a firsthand view of the Orleans Parish Criminal Sheriff's Office, visit the Web site http://www.opcso.org/.

growing number of areas) results of postarrest drug tests. Persons deemed good risks are recommended for release on recognizance. Not all defendants are eligible for the program, however; those arrested for serious charges such as murder, armed robbery, or sale of drugs are usually excluded. After release, the pretrial service agency makes follow-up contacts to ensure that the defendant knows when the court appearance is scheduled and will show up.

The guiding assumption of the Vera Project is that defendants with ties to the community are not likely to flee. By providing information about these ties (which normally is not available when bail is set), the program provides a more workable way to make sure that the wrong persons are not detained prior to trial. Research has confirmed the operating assumption. Where pretrial service programs have been tried, the rate of nonappearance for those released on recognizance has been lower than for those released through bail agents (Wice 1974). Supporters also argue that such programs save money. Because more people are being released, costs for holding defendants in jail are significantly reduced. More recently, pretrial service programs have been adopted as a means for relieving jail overcrowding (Bureau of Justice Statistics 1988b). Hundreds of such programs now operate throughout the nation.

Pretrial service agencies must operate in a very restricted political atmosphere. In an era dominated by anticrime rhetoric, programs aimed at helping people accused of crimes face an uphill battle. In an effort to head off possible negative public relations, pretrial service programs have maintained a conservative stance by selecting only the most reliable persons for pretrial release. As a result, pretrial service agencies end up concentrating government resources on those least in need. The initial concern was with truly poor defendants, many from the inner cities and ethnic minorities. But in practice, bail reform has been least able to help this group. A study of the pretrial release program in Charlotte, North Carolina, found that most of the defendants released by the program would have been released on recognizance anyway or would have been able to hire a bail agent. Thus, the pretrial release program made only a slight dent in the percentage of defendants released prior to trial

(Clarke, Freeman, and Koch 1976; Flemming, Kohfeld, and Uhlman 1980). Overall, pretrial service agencies seem to release those who would have posted cash bail anyway (Bynum 1982; Mahoney 1976).

BAIL REFORM BASED ON THE CRIME CONTROL MODEL

Beginning during the 1980s, concern shifted to the link between bail and crime. To a great extent, the demand for preventive detention reflects a backlash against the bail reform movement of the 1960s. Bail reform based on the values of the crime control model are reflected in the 1984 Bail Reform Act, which made wholesale revisions in the earlier law. Whereas release of the defendant was the primary intent of the earlier law, detention plays a prominent role in the new one. In setting bail, a federal judge may now consider danger to the community and may deny bail altogether when the accused is found to be a "grave danger to others." Bail reform based on the crime control model focuses on two topics: pretrial crimes and preventive detention.

Pretrial Crimes

Most of the attention in the contemporary discussion of bail focuses on defendants who commit additional crimes while on pretrial release. Individual occurrences are easy to find, and adherents of the crime control model are quick to highlight them in their arguments for preventive detention. But how common are such events?

Numerous studies of pretrial crime have been conducted. The dominant conclusion is that arrests of pretrial releasees for serious crimes are relatively infrequent, and convictions for such crimes are even less frequent (Jackson 1987; Walker 1989). At first glance, this does not appear to be the case. Two studies report that about 15 percent of those released were rearrested while on pretrial conditional release (Toborg 1983; Reaves and Perez 1994). But a simple measure of rearrest distorts the true picture. Many of those rearrested were initially arrested for a misde-

COURTS, CONTROVERSY, AND REDUCING CRIME

Should Defendants Be Forced to Take a Drug Test?

 The dual concerns of failure to appear and committing additional crimes while out on bail have become focused on pretrial drug-testing programs.

There is little doubt that drug use among those arrested is high; in a typical year, the percentage of male arrestees testing positive for recent illegal drug use is about 64 percent. This estimate is based on data gathered by the Arrestee Drug Abuse Monitoring (ADAM) program, which conducts urine tests on arrestees in 35 cities (Arrestee Drug Abuse Monitoring 2003). Moreover, one-fourth to one-half of all adult male arrestees are at risk for dependence on drugs.

Pretrial drug-testing programs are based on the following assumptions: First, knowledge of a defendant's drug use at the time of arrest—obtained through a drug test—provides an important predictor of pretrial misconduct. Second, monitoring drug use during the pretrial periods, coupled with sanctions, will reduce the risk of pretrial misconduct (Henry and Clark 1999).

The District of Columbia Pretrial Services Agency was the first to implement pretrial drug testing as part of the bail process. Other jurisdictions have created somewhat similar programs (Pretrial Services Resource Center 1999), and the federal courts implemented Operation Drug TEST (Testing Effective Sanctions and Treatments) in some jurisdictions.

Requiring pretrial drug testing seems commonsensical enough and therefore has become a widely used practice. But are these programs effective? Several studies find that at best they have limited success.

Requiring defendants to participate in drug testing does not reduce failure-to-appear rates (Visher 1992; Goldkamp and Jones 1992). "The lack of predictive power is not surprising from a statistical perspective because drug use is very common among arrestees and pretrial misconduct a relatively rare event" (Belenko, Mara-Drita, and McElroy 1992, 577).

Nor do pretrial drug-testing programs help predict which defendants will be rearrested while out on bail. Surprisingly, first-time arrestees who tested positive for any illicit substance were better risks for release than repeat offenders who did not test positive for recent drug use (Rhodes, Hyatt, and Scheiman 1996).

But the evidence is not all negative. Drug testing appears to be successful if used as one component of coordinated earlier intervention efforts for adult offenders (Harrell et al. 2002).

Given that evaluations have called pretrial drug testing programs into question, it is important that policymakers accurately assess the costs of these programs. They are expensive. Just as important, throughout the United States, programs to treat those addicted to alcohol and/or illicit drugs are plentiful for those covered by medical insurance but sparse for those without coverage (including most of those involved in the criminal justice system). Overall, treatment options for drug dependent arrestees are limited.

What do you think? Are pretrial drug-testing programs effective in reducing failure-to-appear rates and pretrial crimes? Or are pretrial drug-testing programs ineffective because they are based on faulty assumptions?

To continue the debate, using the search engine of your choice and the search term "pretrial drug testing," find two or more sites that provide different perspectives on the topic. In what ways do divisions of opinion on this topic mirror the debate between the crime control model and the due process model of criminal justice?

meanor and later arrested for another minor offense. A better measure is the percentage of all persons arrested for a felony, released on bail, and later arrested for another felony. Depending on the study, the pretrial crime rate ranges from 5 to 7 percent (Gottfredson 1974; Toborg 1983). The relative infrequency of serious pretrial crime makes its prediction especially difficult (Jackson 1987), not to say suspect. Nonetheless, as a tool in predicting risk, many jurisdictions are now adopting mandatory pretrial drug testing. (See Courts, Controversy, and Reducing Crime: Should Defendants Be Forced to Take a Drug Test?)

Preventive Detention

Should defendants be held in jail awaiting trial with no right to bail? Adherents of the crime control model assume that current bail practices do not successfully restrain dangerous defendants. They point to defendants who commit crimes while out of jail on pretrial release. The suggested alternative is **preventive detention,** which allows judges to hold suspects without bail if they are accused of committing a dangerous or violent crime and locking them up is deemed necessary for community safety. About three-fifths of the states have enacted laws that allow courts to consider public safety, danger to the community, jeopardy to others, or similar general reasons in setting conditions of release or in denying release altogether (Bureau of Justice Statistics 1988b; Goldkamp 1985).

The best-known example of preventive detention is the Bail Reform Act of 1984, which authorizes preventive detention for federal defendants accused of serious crimes. After a detention hearing, the defendant may be held in jail without bail for up to 90 days pending trial if the judge finds "clear and convincing evidence" that (1) there is a serious risk that the person will flee; (2) the person may obstruct justice or threaten, injure, or intimidate a prospective witness or juror; or (3) the offense is one of violence or one punishable by life imprisonment or death. The law also creates a presumption against pretrial release for major drug dealers (Berg 1985). The Supreme Court has upheld the Bail Reform Act, ruling that Congress enacted preventive detention not as a punishment for dangerous individuals but as a potential solution to the pressing social problem of crimes committed by persons on bail (see Case Close-up: *U.S. v. Salerno* and Preventive Detention).

Are preventive detention laws merely exercises in symbolic politics, or do they have substantive impact? Experience with state preventive detention statutes suggests that they are rarely implemented (Toborg and Bellassai 1986). This was certainly the case in Washington, D.C. (whose law served as the basis for the 1984 federal law). Prosecutors rarely requested detention hearings, and fewer than 2 out of every 1,000 felony defendants were formally detained (Thomas 1976). To avoid the law's elaborate procedural requirements, prosecutors relied on the traditional practice of using high monetary bail amounts as a covert form of preventive detention (Cohen 1985). It is also worth noting that, considering severe jail overcrowding at the state and local level, preventive detention laws are doomed to a symbolic status unless massively expensive efforts are undertaken to greatly increase jail capacity.

Experience at the federal level, however, suggests a more complicated pattern. The Bail Reform Act of 1984 has been implemented on a substantial scale. Detention hearings are being held and defendants detained without bail being set. In the most recent year for which data are available, more than 26,000 detention hearings were held, and 75 percent of the defendants (19,254) were ordered detained (Bureau of Justice Statistics 1999b).

Other evidence, however, suggests that the effects of the law are actually quite muted. A detailed analysis of the U.S. District Court for the Eastern District of California found that the overall detention rate, and the average detention length, remained unchanged. The greatest impact was felt by drug offenders, for whom rates of detention significantly increased (Kingsnorth et al. 1987). Similarly, a Bureau of Justice Statistics study (1988b) indicates that pretrial detention is being used as an alternative to the setting of high monetary bonds to hold defendants prior to trial. In short, the new law has changed procedures but seems to have had relatively little impact on overall detention policy.

CONCLUSION

U.S. v. Salerno marked a turning point in the lives of both participants. *Fortune* magazine once described Anthony "Fat Tony" Salerno as the richest and most powerful mobster in America. But at the age of 74, he was sentenced to 100 years in prison. The future for U.S. attorney Rudolph Giuliani was strikingly different. He resigned his office several years

U.S. v. Salerno and Preventive Detention

The 88-page federal grand jury indictment charged that Anthony Salerno, the alleged "boss of the Genovese Crime Family of La Cosa Nostra," and 14 other members described as "associates" violated 29 federal laws ranging from Racketeer Influenced and Corrupt Organizations Act (RICO) violations, mail fraud, wire fraud, and extortion to gambling and conspiracy to commit murder. The front-page article in the *New York Times* was quick to note that the indictments followed an earlier *New York Times* series detailing how the mob had infiltrated concrete companies to control construction of high-rise buildings in Manhattan, including Trump Plaza (Lubasch 1986).

In past cases like this, bond had typically been set in the millions, with the amount calculated to virtually assure that the defendant would be unable to raise the necessary funds and would therefore await trial in jail. But in this case Rudolph Giuliani, U.S. attorney for the Southern District of New York (primarily Manhattan), chose to seek preventive detention. The Bail Reform Act of 1984 allows a federal court to detain an arrestee pending trial if the government demonstrates by clear and convincing evidence that no release condition "will reasonably assure . . . the safety of any other person and the community." During the detention hearing, the U.S. attorney introduced evidence gathered through court-ordered wiretaps and also two potential trial witnesses, who asserted that Salerno had personally participated in two murder conspiracies. The district court granted the government's detention motion.

Salerno appealed, and the Second Circuit struck down the law as unconstitutional. Other circuits, though, had reached a different conclusion. An indication that the Court was anxious to hear a case like this one could be seen in the speed of the appellate process; the Court heard oral argument just 10 months after Salerno's arrest.

That the majority of the Court adheres to the crime control model on this issue is made abundantly clear in the opening paragraph of the opinion (after the statement of the facts). Written by Chief Justice William Rehnquist, the majority opinion begins by stressing the reasonable-

ness of the statute: Responding to "the alarming problem of crimes committed by persons on release . . ." Congress passed the Bail Reform Act of 1984 as the solution to a "bail crisis in the federal courts." As for the Eighth Amendment, the opinion stresses, "Nothing in the text of the Bail Clause limits permissible government considerations solely to questions of flight." Thus, Congress was justified in allowing the courts to deny bail not only if there is a danger of flight but also if the person poses a danger to others.

The three dissenting justices clearly express values of the due process model. In Thurgood Marshall's biting words, the Bail Reform Act of 1984 represents the first time Congress "declares that a person innocent of any crime may be jailed indefinitely, pending the trial of allegations which are legally presumed to be untrue." Such practices are "consistent with the usages of tyranny and excesses of bitter experience teaches us to call the police state." Likewise in dissent, John Paul Stevens argues that depriving persons of vital rights on the basis of predictions of future dangerousness is unconstitutional.

Beneath the debate over how best to reduce crime runs an important issue of how to interpret the Constitution (see Chapter 17). One theory, usually associated with conservatives, is strict constructionism: The document should be interpreted on the basis of the original intent of the framers. Another theory, usually identified with liberals, is adaptationist: The meaning of the document should be adjusted to changing conditions of society. The *Salerno* opinion dramatically illustrates that when it comes to rights of criminal defendants, these positions are reversed. Conservatives stress the need to adapt the Constitution to the pressing current problem of crime, whereas liberals emphasize that the framers were indeed correct in suspecting that the government is capable of tyranny.

The following articles provide contrasting opinions about preventive detention:

Michael Corrado, "Punishment, Quarantine, and Preventive Detention"

Michael Davis, "Preventive Detention, Corrado, and Me"

later to run successfully for mayor of New York, with crime as his lead issue. In 1997 he was overwhelmingly reelected, and in 2001 he gained international recognition as the city coped with the disaster of September 11.

Bail serves several purposes in the American court system, some legally sanctioned, others definitely extralegal. Bail is used to guarantee a defendant's appearance at trial, to protect society by holding those perceived to be dangerous, to punish those accused (but not yet convicted) of violating the law, and to lubricate the system by softening defendants up to enter a plea of guilty. These varying purposes are partially the result of the tension among conflicting principles. Although the law recognizes that the only legal purpose of bail is to guarantee a suspect's future appearance at trial, court officials perceive a need to protect society. Out of these conflicting principles arise compromises.

CRITICAL THINKING QUESTIONS

1. How do bail and bail setting illustrate the differences between law on the books and law in action?

2. In what ways do crime control model advocates approach bail differently than do backers of due process model values?

3. Examine the local papers. Have there been reports of defendants' committing crimes while out on bail? Have there been reports of poor conditions in the local jail? How might these reports affect bail setting?

4. Talk with judges, prosecutors, and defense attorneys about the relationship between pretrial release and the following two factors: jail capacity and length of time between arrest and disposition. (You may wish to review Chapter 5.)

5. Are preventive detention laws effective, or are they exercises in symbolic politics?

KEY TERMS

bail (241)
bail agent (bail bondsman) (242)
bench warrant (capias) (252)
cash bond (242)
preventive detention (256)
property bond (242)
release on recognizance (ROR) (242)

WORLD WIDE WEB RESOURCES AND EXERCISES

Web Guides

http://dir.yahoo.com/Society_and_Culture/Crime/
   Law_Enforcement/Bail_Enforcement_Agents/
http://dir.yahoo.com/Business_and_Economy/
   Shopping_and_Services/Financial_Services/
   Personal_Finance/Bail_Bonds/
http://dir.yahoo.com/Society_and_Culture/Crime/
   Law_Enforcement/Wanted/

Web Search Terms

bail	*pretrial services agency*
pretrial release	*preventive detention*
jail	*excessive bail*
bounty hunters	*pretrial drug testing*

Useful URLs

The American Jail Association is a national nonprofit organization dedicated to supporting those who work in and operate our nation's jails: **http://www.corrections.com/aja/**.

The Bureau of Justice Statistics provides up-to-date jail statistics at **http://www.ojp.usdoj. gov/bjs/jails.htm**.

Crimestoppers USA focuses on arresting fugitives: **http://www.crimestopusa.com/**.

The National Association of Pretrial Services Agencies represents professionals in the field: http://napsa.org/index.htm.

The Jail Operations Section of the National Sheriffs' Association offers correspondence courses and provides technical assistance: http://www.sheriffs.org/.

The Pretrial Services Resource Center is a clearinghouse for information on pretrial issues and a technical assistance provider: http://www.pretrial.org/.

For more than 35 years, the Vera Institute of Justice has been the pioneering organization in pretrial practices: http://www.verg.org.

Uncommon URLs

The following bail agents provide interesting and sometimes colorful Web sites:

Athena Bail Bonds: http://athenabb.com/

Bail Bond Recovery Resource Center: http://www.pimall.com/nais/bailr.html

Excalibur Bail Recovery Agency: http://www.bhunted.com/home.htm

Fort Worth Bounty Hunting Association: http://web2.airmail.net/jdt/

Jail Net: http://www.jail.net/

National Surety Services of Florida, Inc.: http://www.bailbonding.com/

Pretrial Services of the Arizona Superior Court in Pima County offers insights into a court-sponsored agency: http://www.sc.co.pima.az.us/pretrial/

The Pretrial Services Agency of the U.S. District Court for New Mexico is an example of a federal court agency: http://www.nmcourt.fed.us/ptdocs/

PX Direct sells inmate uniforms, jail cell equipment, and related items: http://www.pxdirect.com/

Pennsylvania Crimestoppers can be found at http://www.pacrimestoppers.org/.

Private Investigators Mall bills itself as "The Web's First Shopping Mall of Private Investigators": http://www.pimall.com/.

"Wanted" posters from the United States Postal Inspection Service can be found at http://www.usps.gov/websites/depart/inspect/wantmenu.htm.

Anthony Salerno died in prison in 1992. To view his grave site, go to http://www.findagrave.com and search under the name "Anthony Salerno."

Web Exercises

1. The online version of the *Sourcebook of Criminal Justice Statistics* contains the most recent data available. In particular, information on pretrial release of federal defendants can easily be found at the following URL: http://www.albany.edu/sourcebook/. Under Section 5, look for information on pretrial release to answer the following two questions: What percentage of released federal defendants had no violation? What percentage of federal defendants were held under preventive detention?

2. A growing number of bail agents have Web sites. The following Yahoo search will locate some: http://www.yahoo.com/, Business and Economy/Companies/Financial Services/Personal Finance/Bail Bonds; a search engine using the key words "bail agents" or "bail bondsmen" will yield more. From the list provided, choose three that are geographically close to you and compare their Web sites. Which one would you call if a friend or relative needed to post bond? Do the Web sites provide any information on types of clients that they prefer? Overall, how do these ads compare to ads for lawyers, doctors, insurance agents, or other personal services?

3. "Wanted: Dead or Alive" posters became the basis for nineteenth-century legendary heroes. The twenty-first-century equivalent can be found on the Internet. The bail industry's showcase to display "bond skips" can be found at http://www.bailjumpers.net/. Compare the number of fugitives who have skipped bail to those who have never been arrested. How do these lists differ from

those maintained by law enforcement (the FBI, for example)? Overall, does there appear to be a profit motive mentioned for seeking out fugitives?

INFOTRAC COLLEGE EDITION RESOURCES AND EXERCISES

Basic Search Terms

bail
pretrial release
*mandatory drug testing
 and evaluation*

bounty hunters
bail bondsmen

Recommended Articles

"Aggressive Drug-Fighting Efforts Reduce Use among Pennsylvania Inmates"

Loren Buddess, "Federal Probation and Pretrial Services—A Cost-Effective and Successful Community Connections System"

Rolando del Carmen, Maldine Beth Barnhill, "Legal Issues in Juvenile Drug Testing"

Jeffrey Fagan, Martin Guggenheim, "Preventative Detention and the Judicial Prediction of Dangerousness for Juveniles"

Barry Lester, "Drug-Addicted Mothers Need Treatment, Not Punishment"

"New Jersey Court Allows Drug Test Search, Finding Reasonable Suspicion"

Christian Parenti, "I Hunt Men"

InfoTrac College Edition Exercises

1. The debate over preventive detention offers a classic difference between advocates of the crime control and the due process model. Using the search term "preventive detention," find articles that debate this topic, and analyze their arguments.

2. Using the search term "pretrial services," find two or more articles that discuss this topic. What advantages are portrayed for these programs? Why do bail agents often oppose these government programs?

FOR FURTHER READING

Corrado, Michael. "Punishment and the Wild Beast of Prey: The Problem of Preventive Detention." *Journal of Criminal Law and Criminology* 86 (1996): 778–814.

Cushman, Robert. *Preventing Jail Crowding: A Practical Guide.* Washington, DC: National Institute of Corrections, 2002.

Devine, F. E. *Commercial Bail Bonding: A Comparison of Common Law Alternatives.* Westport, CT: Greenwood, 1991.

Haapanen, Rudy, and Lee Britton. "Drug Testing for Youthful Offenders on Parole: An Experimental Evaluation." *Criminology and Public Policy* 1 (2002): 217–244.

Katz, Charles, and Cassia Spohn. "The Effect of Race and Gender on Bail Outcomes: A Test of an Interactive Model." *Americana Journal of Criminal Justice* 19 (1995): 161–184.

Kerle, Kenneth. *American Jails: Looking to the Future.* Woburn, MA: Butterworth-Heinemann, 1998.

Mays, G. Larry, and Joel Thompson. "The Political and Organizational Context of American Jails." In *American Jails: Public Policy Issues,* edited by Joel Thompson and G. Larry Mays. Chicago: Nelson-Hall, 1991.

Mieckowski, Tom, and Kim Lersch. "Drug Testing in Criminal Justice: Evolving Uses, Emerging Technologies." *National Institute of Justice Journal* (December 1997): 9–15.

Robertson, James. *Jail Planning and Expansion: Local Officials and Their Roles.* Washington, DC: U.S. Department of Justice, National Institute of Corrections, 2003.

Robinson, Jerome, and James Jones. *Drug Testing in a Drug Court Environment: Common Issues to Address.* Washington, DC: U.S. Department of Justice, Drug Courts Program Office (NCJ 181103), 2000.

Thompson, Joel, and G. Larry Mays, eds. *American Jails: Public Policy Issues.* Chicago: Nelson-Hall, 1991.

Vance, Neil, and Ronald Stupak. "Organizational Culture and the Placement of Pretrial Agencies in the Criminal Justice System." *Justice System Journal* 19 (1997): 51–76.

Welsh, Wayne. *Counties in Court: Jail Overcrowding and Court-Ordered Reform.* Philadelphia: Temple University Press, 1995.

Chapter 12 Disclosing and Suppressing Evidence

PART III
Processing the Accused

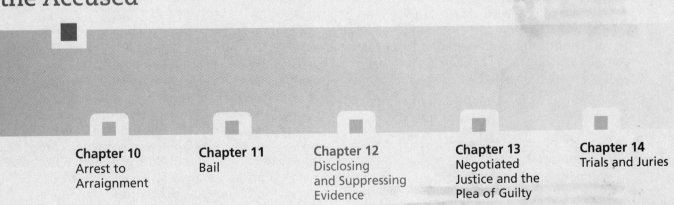

J   ust before midnight, 18-year-old Lois Ann Jameson (not her real name) left the downtown theater where she worked and walked the two blocks to her normal bus stop. A half hour later she alighted in her neighborhood for her usual short walk home. The only unusual event was a strange car, which suddenly veered in front of her. A young Hispanic man got out, grabbed her with one hand, and placed the other over her mouth while dragging her into the parked car. He drove 20 minutes into the desert, where he tore off her clothes and raped her. In a strange twist of circumstances, the assailant drove Lois Ann Jameson back to her neighborhood. Once she was home, she immediately called the police. To Detective Carroll Cooley, Jameson's story was not only somewhat contradictory but also offered few leads. Jameson couldn't provide a very good description of her attacker. The only lead was her detailed description of the car—an old model, light green, clean on the outside, and dirty brown upholstery on the inside. Moreover, in the back seat of the car was a loop of rope designed to help rear-seat passengers in pulling themselves up. This description eventually led Detective Cooley to a house on the west side of town, where he found a car exactly as described (Baker 1983). The subsequent interrogation and conviction of Ernesto Miranda was to change the landscape of American criminal justice. ◀

The *Miranda* warnings are the most controversial part of the Supreme Court's revolution in criminal justice. Responding to criticisms that police procedures were unfair and that the police were not adhering to the procedural requirements of the law, the Supreme Court imposed additional restrictions on police investigative techniques, such as searches, interrogations, and lineups. The Court's decisions produced extensive national controversy. Subsequent Courts, dominated by appointees of Republican presidents, have significantly curtailed (but not eliminated) these earlier decisions.

This chapter examines some of the diverse activities that may occur between arraignment and final disposition (either a guilty plea or a trial). The first topic will be the gathering of evidence, which is termed *discovery*. Next will be a discussion of how and why some evidence is excluded from trial.

DISCOVERY

The informal and formal exchange of information between prosecution and defense is referred to as **discovery.** Laboratory reports, statements of witnesses, defendants' confessions, and police reports are examples of information that prosecutors often gather and defense attorneys want to know about before trial.

Discovery seeks to ensure that the adversary system does not give one side an unfair advantage over the other. The guiding assumption of the adversary system is that truth will emerge after a struggle at trial. But as Justice William Brennan (1963) asked, should this struggle at trial be a sporting event or a quest for the truth? Historically, civil trials were largely sporting events, in which the outcome depended heavily on the technical skills of the lawyers. In an effort to eliminate the worst aspects of such contests, the Federal Rules of Civil Procedure were adopted in 1938, and most states have since followed the federal example. By these rules, prior to trial, every party in a civil action is entitled to the disclosure of all relevant information in the possession of any person, unless that information is privileged (Wright 1994). These discovery rules are intended to make a trial "less a game of blind man's bluff and more a fair contest with the basic issues and facts disclosed to the fullest practicable manner" (*U.S. v. Procter and Gamble Co.* 1958). There has been a long-standing

Exhibit **12-1**	Key Developments in Criminal Discovery Law	
Jencks v. U.S.	1957	Prior inconsistent statements of a witness must be made available to defense counsel.
Brady v. Maryland	1963	Due process of law is violated when prosecutors conceal evidence that might be favorable to the defense.
Williams v. Florida	1970	Requiring defense to disclose an alibi defense prior to trial does not violate the defendant's privilege against self-incrimination.
U.S. v. Agurs	1976	Under *Brady,* the prosecutor must disclose evidence only if such evidence would have been persuasive and produced reasonable doubt about guilt.
Weatherford v. Bursey	1977	No general constitutional right to discovery in criminal cases.
Kyles v. Whitley	1995	Materiality of evidence not disclosed is determined by looking at the effect of all the evidence, not simply one item.
Wood v. Bartholomew	1995	Failure of prosecutor to turn over inadmissible polygraph evidence was not a *Brady* violation.
Strickler v. Greene	1999	Even though petitioner was not given exculpatory evidence, there was no *Brady* violation because there was no prejudice.

debate, however, over the extent of pretrial discovery in criminal cases.

Law on the Books: Rules Requiring Disclosure

Although there is a very broad power of discovery in civil proceedings, there is no general constitutional right to discovery in a criminal case (*Weatherford v. Bursey* 1977). Courts have expressed concern that requiring too much prosecutorial disclosure might result in the defendant's taking undue advantage (*State v. Tune* 1953). For example, the defendant, knowing of the state's case, might procure perjured testimony or might intimidate witnesses who are likely to testify (Saltzburg 1983).

The type of information that is discoverable varies considerably from state to state. Some jurisdictions allow only limited discovery: The trial court has the discretion to order the prosecutor to disclose the defendant's confession and/or other physical documents, but that is all. Other jurisdictions take a middle ground: Discovery of confessions and physical evidence is a matter of right, but discovery of other items (witnesses' statements, for exam-

ple) is more difficult. Finally, a few states have adopted liberal discovery rules: There is a presumption strongly in favor of prosecutorial disclosure, with only certain narrow exceptions. Exhibit 12-1 summarizes significant developments in criminal discovery law.

Because of growing discontent with the discovery system, American courts have cautiously expanded mandatory disclosure by the prosecutor. In *Jencks v. U.S.* (1957), the Court ruled that prior inconsistent statements of a witness must be made available to the defense. This decision was later strengthened in *Brady v. Maryland* (1963), in which the Supreme Court held that due process of law is violated when prosecutors conceal evidence that might be favorable to the defense. Read together, these decisions stand for the proposition that, as officers of the court, prosecutors can no more suppress evidence than they can knowingly use perjured testimony.

Brady applies only to exculpatory evidence (evidence tending to show the defendant's innocence). Needless to say, this standard requires a judgment call on the part of prosecutors, and in recent years the Court has ruled that prosecutors have been too narrow in their interpretation. In *Kyles v. Whitley* (1995), the prosecutor failed to disclose statements of two of four witnesses and other evidence relating to Kyles's car. In a 5-to-4 decision, Justice David Souter wrote that the test was a cumulative one, looking at all the evidence not disclosed and not just isolated pieces. Moreover, to gain a new trial, the defense need only show a reasonable probability of a different result (not a preponderance of the evidence). (On retrial, three juries declined to convict Kyles, and charges were dropped.)

Law in Action: Informal Prosecutorial Disclosure

Discovery rules are vitally important to defense attorneys. In states that grant defense considerable discovery rights, the lawyer can go straight to the prosecutor's files and obtain the essentials of the state's case against the defendant. By learning the facts of the prosecutor's case, the defense attorney need not face the difficult task of trying to force his client to voluntarily disclose this information. Across the nation, "nearly all lawyers interviewed felt that clients' veracity is questionable and in need of thorough verification. This forces the attorney to devote extra hours, frequently wasted, verifying a client's version of the facts, which also puts a strain on their relationship— especially when the attorney is forced to confront the defendant with his prevarications" (Wice 1978, 45).

In jurisdictions that grant limited discovery rights to the defense, defense attorneys must be more resourceful in determining what actually happened. A variety of proceedings not directly designed for discovery purposes can be used for that purpose. At the preliminary hearing, intended to test the sufficiency of the evidence for holding the defendant, the defense hears at least part of the story of some critical witnesses. Similarly, during a hearing on a pretrial motion to suppress evidence, the testimony of key government witnesses may yield important new facts relevant to a trial defense. But eventually, defense attorneys may be forced to confront their clients about inconsistencies (or worse) in their statements, a confrontation that can strain lawyer–client relationships (see Chapter 7).

Some prosecutors have an office policy prohibiting assistant prosecutors from disclosing any information not required by law (see A Day in Court: Lawyers Claim DAs Exclude Evidence). But it is more usual that assistant DAs voluntarily disclose certain aspects of the state's case to defense attorneys. Such informal discovery operates within the norms of cooperation of courtroom work groups. Defense attorneys who maintain good relationships with prosecutors and are viewed as trustworthy receive selected information about the case. Conversely, defense attorneys who maintain hostile relationships with the prosecutor and/or represent clients who are viewed as troublemakers (the two frequently go together) find the prosecutors holding the cards as tightly to the vest as the law allows.

Informal prosecutorial disclosure does not stem from sympathy for the defendant, but rather from a long-held courthouse theory that an advance glimpse at the prosecutor's case encourages a plea of guilty. From the perspective of the prosecutor, defendants often tell their lawyers only part of what happened. Therefore, the defense attorney who learns what evidence the prosecutor possesses can use it to show the defendant that contesting the matter may be hopeless.

Informal prosecutorial discovery greatly encourages pleas of guilty. Paul Wice (1978) reports that in courthouses where prosecutors emphasize closed discovery, there is often a failure to plea-bargain, and a large number of cases go to trial, frequently without a jury. Overall, in courthouses where prosecutors have adopted open discovery policies, pleas of guilty are entered sooner, resulting in a significantly smaller backlog than is found in most cities with closed discovery.

Law and Controversy: Requiring Reciprocal Disclosure

Defense attorneys understandably press for broader discovery laws. A major issue in broadening discovery involves the extent to which the defense should also be required to disclose relevant materials in its possession. The guiding light, as articulated by prosecutors and law-and-order advocates, is that the trial should be a level playing field for all parties; both sides should be prevented from attempting to conduct a trial by ambush.

A DAY IN COURT

Lawyers Claim DAs Exclude Evidence

 In overturning Curtis Kyles's conviction and death penalty sentence in the 1984 murder of Gentilly housewife Delores Dye, the U.S. Supreme Court took aim squarely at Orleans Parish prosecutors, tagging them with misconduct for illegally withholding evidence that tended to undermine their case against Kyles. In a scathing 1995 opinion, the normally mild-mannered Justice David Souter said prosecutors have an "inescapable" duty to disclose such information to defense attorneys, unless the adversary system of justice is to descend to a gladiatorial level unmitigated by any prosecutorial obligation for the sake of truth.

Strong words, indeed. Among defense attorneys and courtroom junkies across the land, "Kyles" has become a household word, much as "Brady" did after the 1963 *Brady v. Maryland* decision in which the high court first asserted that a fair trial requires prosecutors to turn over evidence favorable to the defense. But if the Kyles case has resonated nationally, the public scolding has had little practical effect closer to home, defense attorneys say. Orleans Parish prosecutors still routinely withhold evidence, especially in high-profile cases, they say. "This is a pattern and a practice, and if anything, it has gotten worse," said Denise LeBoeuf, who handles capital cases throughout Louisiana. "It is worse than anywhere else in the state." [District Attorney Harry] Connick and his staff disagree. They say they turn over exculpatory evidence, evidence favorable to a defendant, and are well aware of their obligation to do so. "We are not frivolous about it and even if we know the son-of-a-bitch did it, if it is exculpatory, he is entitled to it and we turn it over," Connick said. Camille Buras, Connick's top assistant, praised the office's record and estimated only 10 convictions since 1974 have been reversed on grounds that prosecutors withheld favorable evidence.

The issue of how much information prosecutors must disclose is constantly evolving, and differences of opinion exist among judges at Criminal District Court and their counterparts on appeals courts, Buras said. . . . But local defense attorneys—who say if they gave their opponents a "Brady" test, they'd fail it—are not the only critics. . . . Increasingly, Orleans Parish Criminal Court judges are voicing their dismay. Whether prosecutors met their duty to turn over favorable information has surfaced as an issue in several recent cases:

■ "The DA's office doesn't understand it," fumed Judge Calvin Johnson from the bench during the trial of two former police officers charged with aggravated rape of a girl. Only after Johnson tacitly threatened to grant a new trial did prosecutors turn over material in dispute, including a statement in which the girl said one of the two officers asked her to have sex. The jury convicted the men of sexual battery, a significantly lesser charge. . . .

■ In a murder trial last month, Judge Frank Marullo slammed prosecutors for withholding a witness's statement. Marullo went one step farther, and, in a highly unusual move, told jurors before opening statements that prosecutors had "neglected" to give the defense attorney information that a witness had described a mustached perpetrator who was 10 years younger and at least three inches shorter than the bald, clean-shaven defendant. He was convicted of second-degree murder.

■ Two murder cases in the past six months ended in mistrials after defense attorneys complained that information that surfaced during testimony and that defense attorneys felt would have helped their cases was not made available when they asked for it before trial. Judge Denis Waldron and Julian Parker, both former prosecutors, stopped the trials.

SOURCE: Pamela Coyle, "Lawyers Claim DAs Exclude Evidence," *Times-Picayune*, 21 September 1997.

Reciprocal disclosure by the defense takes several forms. Some jurisdictions require that the defense file a notice of **alibi defense** (the crime was committed while the defendant was somewhere else), complete with a list of witnesses to be called to support the alibi (*Williams v. Florida* 1970). Such pretrial notice enables the prosecutor to investigate the backgrounds of these witnesses and thus be prepared to undermine the defendant's contention that he or she was somewhere else when the crime was committed. In the same vein, some states mandate that the defense must disclose to the prosecution prior to trial that an insanity plea will be entered or that expert witnesses will be called.

The Constitution limits reciprocal discovery, however. Unlike in civil proceedings, criminal defendants enjoy the privilege against self-incrimination (see Chapter 2). Thus, efforts in some states to require the defense to turn over to the prosecutor prior to trial statements from expert witnesses that it does not intend to call at trial are probably unconstitutional.

THE EXCLUSIONARY RULE AND THE SUPREME COURT

The most controversial of the Supreme Court's criminal justice decisions have concerned how the police gather evidence. For example, the rape conviction of Ernesto Miranda in 1966 was overturned because the police had not advised him of his constitutional right to remain silent before he confessed. In 1961, Dollree Mapp's pornography conviction was reversed because the police had illegally searched her house. In both cases, otherwise valid and trustworthy evidence was excluded from trial. These cases are applications of the exclusionary rule.

The **exclusionary rule** prohibits the prosecutor from using illegally obtained evidence during a trial. It is the Supreme Court's sole technique for enforcing several vital protections of the Bill of Rights. Its adoption has been justified on three grounds. The first is a normative argument: A court of law should not participate in or condone illegal conduct. The second reflects an empirical assessment: Excluding evidence will deter law enforcement officials from illegal behavior. The final justification is based on experience: Alternative remedies, such as civil suits for damages against police officers for misconduct, are unworkable.

The exclusionary rule is commonly associated with the search and seizure of physical evidence, but in fact there are three distinct exclusionary rules. One applies to the identification of suspects. If a police lineup is improperly conducted, the identification of the suspect must be excluded from evidence during trial. The other exclusionary rules relate to confessions and searches.

CONFESSIONS

For 70 years, the Supreme Court has struggled to place limits on how police interrogate suspects (see Exhibit 12-2). The traditional rule was that only confessions that were "free and voluntary" would be admitted at trial. Confessions obtained by physical coercion (beatings or torture, for example) were not allowed into evidence because they were not trustworthy; someone in fear of a beating is likely to say what his or her antagonists want to hear. In the 1930s, the Court rejected confessions based on physical coercion, and subsequently such practices largely ceased. The Court was then confronted with the slightly different issue of confessions obtained as a result of lengthy interrogations, psychological ploys, and the like. The Court reasoned that confessions based on psychological coercion should be rejected just as if they were based on physical coercion, because such statements were not likely to be free and voluntary. But it is not easy to define what constitutes psychological coercion. In numerous cases, the Court sought to spell out what factors the trial court should use in deciding what constitutes psychological coercion, but the standards announced were far from precise.

The Warren Court Changes the Rules

In an attempt at greater precision, the Court under the leadership of Chief Justice Earl Warren adopted specific procedures for police interrogations. In the path-breaking decision *Miranda v. Arizona* (1966), the Court imposed what are widely known as *Miranda* warnings. The police are required to tell a suspect:

Exhibit 12-2 Key Developments in Interrogation Law

Fifth Amendment	1791	"No person . . . shall be compelled in any criminal case to be a witness against himself. . . ."
English common law	19th century	Involuntary confessions are not admissible in court.
Brown v. Mississippi	1936	Use of physical coercion to obtain confessions violates the due process clause of the Fourteenth Amendment.
Ashcraft v. Tennessee	1944	Psychologically coerced confessions are not voluntary and therefore not admissible in court.
Miranda v. Arizona	1966	Suspect's due process rights were violated because he had not first been advised of his right to remain silent and to have an attorney present during a custodial interrogation.
Harris v. New York	1971	Voluntary statements made by the defendants who had not been properly warned of their constitutional rights could be used during trial to impeach their credibility when they took the witness stand in their own defense and contradicted the earlier statements.
New York v. Quarles	1984	Overriding considerations of public safety justified the police officer's failure to provide *Miranda* warnings before asking questions about the location of a weapon apparently abandoned just before arrest.
Duckworth v. Eagan	1989	Altered warnings have been upheld. Advising a suspect that counsel could be appointed only "if and when you go to court" does not render *Miranda* warnings inadequate.
Illinois v. Perkins	1990	A law enforcement officer can pose as a prison inmate and elicit a confession from an actual inmate, even though the officer gives no *Miranda* warnings about the inmate's constitutional rights.
Minnick v. Mississippi	1990	Once a suspect has invoked his or her right to counsel, police may not resume interrogation without the suspect's having his or her attorney present.
Pennsylvania v. Muniz	1990	Police officers may ask suspected drunken drivers routine questions and videotape their answers without warning them of their rights.
Arizona v. Fulminate	1991	A coerced confession does not automatically overturn a conviction.
Davis v. U.S.	1994	Police do not need to stop questioning a suspect who makes an ambiguous statement about wanting an attorney.
Dickerson v. U.S.	2000	*Miranda* has become embedded in police practices, and the Court will not overrule it.
Texas v. Cobb	2001	Defendant's confession to murder could be used at trial even though his lawyer in another case was not present when he confessed.
Chavez v. Martinez	2003	The failure of a police officer to give a suspect his *Miranda* rights may not be used in a civil case against the officer alleging police brutality.

- You have the right to remain silent.
- Anything you say can and will be used against you in a court of law.
- You have the right to talk to a lawyer and have him or her present with you while you are being questioned.

- If you cannot afford to hire a lawyer, one will be appointed to represent you before any questioning, if you wish.

In addition, the Court shifted the burden of proof from the defense, which previously had to prove that a confession was not "free and voluntary," to the police and prosecutor, who now must prove that they have advised the defendant of his or her constitutional rights (see Case Close-Up: *Miranda v. Arizona* and Limiting Police Interrogations).

The Burger and Rehnquist Courts Limit *Miranda*

The Court under the leadership of Chief Justice Warren Burger limited *Miranda*'s application by carving out exceptions. Here are the two most prominent examples:

- Voluntary statements made by defendants who had not been properly warned of their constitutional rights could be used during trial to impeach their credibility when they took the witness stand in their own defense and contradicted the earlier statements (*Harris v. New York* 1971).

- Overriding considerations of public safety justified a police officer's failure to provide *Miranda* warnings before asking questions about the location of a weapon apparently abandoned just before arrest (*New York v. Quarles* 1984).

The Rehnquist Court has likewise moved to narrow the application of *Miranda* protections, as the following cases illustrate.

- Police do not need to stop questioning a suspect who makes an ambiguous statement about wanting an attorney (*Davis v. U.S.* 1994).

- Police may question a defendant in a murder case without his lawyer in another case being present (*Texas v. Cobb* 2001).

However, the Rehnquist Court is not always unsympathetic to the plight of criminal defendants. One 6-to-2 decision seemed to take *Miranda* protections a step further. The Court overturned a capital murder conviction, holding that once a suspect has invoked his or her right to counsel, police may not resume interrogation without the suspect having his or her attorney present (*Minnick v. Mississippi* 1990). The Rehnquist Court also declined to overrule *Miranda*. Writing for seven justices, Chief Justice Rehnquist opined, "Whether or not this court would agree with *Miranda*'s reasoning and its rule in the first instance, *stare decisis* weighs heavily against overruling it now." Moreover, "*Miranda* has become embedded in routine police practice to the point where the warnings have become part of our national culture" (*Dickerson v. U.S.*, 2000).

▌SEARCH AND SEIZURE

The Fourth Amendment provides that "the right of the people to be secure in their persons, houses, papers, and effects against unreasonable searches and seizures, shall not be violated." But what constitutes an **unreasonable search and seizure**?

Historically, the gathering of physical evidence was governed by the common law rule that "if the constable blunders, the crook should not go free." This meant that if the police conducted an **illegal search and seizure** (search without probable cause), the evidence obtained could still be used. Evidence was admitted in court if it was reliable, trustworthy, and relevant. How the police obtained the evidence was considered a separate issue. Thus, there were no effective controls on search and seizure; law enforcement officials who searched illegally faced no sanctions.

Early in the twentieth century, the Supreme Court modified the common law tradition by adopting the exclusionary rule, holding that the Fourth Amendment barred the use of evidence secured through an illegal search and seizure (*Weeks v. U.S.* 1914). But this ruling was applied very narrowly. Only federal law enforcement officials were covered; state law enforcement officials were exempt.

After World War II, the Court extended the privacy component of *Weeks* to the states. But the divided Court refused to impose the exclusionary rule (*Wolf v. Colorado* 1949). Although a few states—for instance, California—did adopt it, many took no effective action to curb illegal searches. Twelve years later, the *Wolf* decision was overturned by a bare 5-to-4 vote. In a bellwether decision, the exclusionary rule was extended to the states in *Mapp v. Ohio* (1961). Evidence obtained during an illegal search

CASE CLOSE-UP

Miranda v. Arizona
and Limiting Police Interrogations

By the age of 23, Ernesto Miranda had compiled a long police record. He dropped out of Queen of Peace Grammar School in Mesa, Arizona, after the eighth grade, and shortly thereafter was arrested for car theft. By the age of 18, his police blotter showed six arrests and four prison sentences. A stint in the military to turn his life around quickly degenerated into his problems in civilian life; after going AWOL, he was given an undesirable discharge. But at 23, he appeared to have turned the corner. His boss at the produce company described him as "one of the best workers I ever had." Indeed, on Wednesday he worked from 8:00 P.M. to 8:00 A.M. and had barely slept an hour when the police knocked on the front door.

Stating that they didn't want to talk in front of his common-law wife, the police took him to a Phoenix, Arizona, police station. A lineup of three other Hispanics from the city jail was quickly assembled. Lois Ann Jameson viewed the four men but could only state that Miranda's build and features were similar to those of her assailant. In the interrogation room, Miranda asked how he did, and Detective Cooley replied, "You flunked." After two hours of questioning, he signed a written confession admitting guilt. His subsequent trial was short and perfunctory. The only prosecution exhibit was the signed confession. Needless to say, the jury quickly returned guilty verdicts for kidnapping and rape.

The interrogation of Ernesto Miranda was in most ways unremarkable. It most certainly lacked the blatant duress at the center of earlier Supreme Court decisions on the limits of police interrogation. What was missing, however, was any advice to Ernesto about his rights under the Constitution. Indeed, the police testified that they never told Miranda that he didn't have to talk to the police, nor did they advise him of his right to consult with an attorney. These facts highlighted the giant chasm between the principles of the Constitution and the realities of police stations in America.

By 1966 the Supreme Court had been grappling with the issue of confessions for three decades. Despite numerous cases, the standards for interrogating suspects were still far from clear. Chief Justice Earl Warren's opinion in *Miranda* expressed concern over the "police-dominated" atmosphere of interrogation rooms and held that warnings were required to counteract the inherently coercive nature of stationhouse questioning. But in reality *Miranda* created no new rights. Under American law, suspects have never been required to talk to the police, and the right to counsel extends to the police station as well as the courthouse. In essence, the Court held that the Fifth Amendment privilege against self-incrimination was as applicable to interrogation by the police before trial as it was to questioning by the prosecutor during trial.

Miranda v. Arizona is the Warren Court's best known and, arguably, most controversial decision extending constitutional rights to those accused of violating the criminal law. The four dissenting justices criticized the ruling on both constitutional and practical grounds. To Justice Byron White, the *Miranda* rule was "a deliberate calculus to prevent interrogation, to reduce the incidence of confessions, and to increase the number of trials." Police, prosecutors, and public officials likewise criticized the ruling, and it became a key plank in Richard Nixon's law-and-order campaign in 1968 (see Chapter 17). With four Nixon-appointed justices, the Burger Court began narrowing *Miranda*, but the holding itself has not been overturned. Indeed, *Miranda* has now become settled law, deeply imbedded in the constitutional fabric of our nation.

To learn more about this case and the debate it has sparked, read the following articles:

Richard A. Leo, "Inside the Interrogation Room"

Cathy Young, "*Miranda* Morass"

Bruce Fein and Stephen J. Schulhoffer, "Q: Should the High Court Let Police Avoid Giving the *Miranda* Warning?"

would no longer be admitted in either federal or state courts. Exhibit 12-3 describes the key developments in search-and-seizure law.

The conservative majorities of both the Burger and Rehnquist Courts have limited the application of the exclusionary rule by creating numerous exceptions.

■ A person running at the sight of a police officer could justify the police conducting a stop-and-frisk search (*Illinois v. Wardlow* 2000).

■ Police officers do not have to advise suspects that they have a right not to consent to a search (*U.S. v. Drayton* 2002).

On rare occasions, though, the Rehnquist Court does place limits on the ability of the police to search.

■ Police cannot use a thermal imagining device to scan a building to detect the presence of high-intensity lamps used to grow marijuana (*Kyllo v. U.S.* 2001).

■ Police cannot stop and search a person for a gun solely on the basis of an anonymous tip (*Florida v. J. L.* 2000).

Nonetheless, four decades later, the exclusionary rule requirements remain highly controversial (see Courts, Controversy, and Reducing Crime: Should the Exclusionary Rule Be Abolished?). Critics and supporters of the exclusionary rule agree on one central point: The grounds for a lawful search are complex and highly technical. Search and seizure is one of the most difficult areas of Supreme Court decision making, and few think that the system works particularly well (Bradley 1993). Searches fall into two broad categories: searches based on a warrant and warrantless searches.

Search Warrants

A **search warrant** is a written document, signed by a judge or magistrate, authorizing a law enforcement officer to conduct a search. The Fourth Amendment specifies that "no Warrants shall issue, but upon probable cause, supported by Oath or affirmation, and particularly describing the place to be searched and the Persons or things to be seized." A study by the National Center for State Courts provides considerable insight into how search warrants are obtained (Van Duizend, Sutton, and Carter 1984).

Once a police officer decides that a search warrant is necessary, the officer usually goes back to the station house to prepare the application, affidavit, and warrant. Three alternative procedures are used. In a few jurisdictions, search warrant applications are prepared by a deputy prosecutor on the basis of information provided by the officer. In other localities, the prosecutor systematically reviews all search warrant applications before they are presented to the magistrate. Finally, in rural areas, a significant number of warrants are obtained by telephone.

Next, the applicant goes to the courthouse or (if court is not in session) to the home of a judge. The review seldom takes long, typically consisting of a hushed conversation at the bench or a presentation in chambers after the judge has called a brief recess. Outright rejection is rare. "Most of the police officer interviewees could not remember having a search warrant application turned down" (Van Duizend, Sutton, and Carter 1984).

The final step is the execution of the warrant. The officer serves the warrant, conducts the search, and seizes evidence. Officers mainly search private residences and impound vehicles for drugs or stolen goods. Statutory law generally requires that the officer file a "return" in court, indicating what items were seized, if any. The authors of the study conclude that the warrant review process does not operate as it was intended. In many cases, the review process is largely perfunctory, and it is apparent that some judges regard themselves more as allies of law enforcement than as independent reviewers of evidence (Van Duizend, Sutton, and Carter 1984).

The Police Executive Research Forum analyzed the impact of the reasonable, good faith exception to the exclusionary rule created by the *Leon* ruling in the same cities studied by the National Center for State Courts. The study found that *Leon* had limited impact on police policies and practices. The number and content of warrants did not change. Although *Leon* gave the police added incentives to secure warrants, there was no discernible increase in the number of search warrants requested. Over-

Exhibit **12-3**	Key Developments in Search-and-Seizure Law	
Fourth Amendment	1791	"The right of the people to be secure in their persons, houses, paper, and effects against unreasonable searches and seizures, shall not be violated, and no Warrants shall issue, but upon probable cause, supported by Oath or affirmation, and particularly describing the place to be searched, and the persons or things to be seized."
Weeks v. U.S.	1914	The exclusionary rule established for federal prosecutions.
Wolf v. Colorado	1949	The exclusionary rule is applicable to the federal courts and the states that choose to adopt it.
Mapp v. Ohio	1961	The exclusionary rule applies to the states as well as the federal government (overturning *Weeks* and *Wolf*).
Terry v. Ohio	1968	Police officers may conduct a frisk of the outer clothing on the basis of reasonable suspicion that a crime is being contemplated.
Chimel v. California	1969	In a search incident to an arrest, the police may search only the defendant's person and the area within the immediate vicinity.
U.S. v. Leon	1984	Creates a limited "good faith exception."
Illinois v. Krull	1987	Good faith exception applied to a warrantless search, even when the state statute was later found to violate the Fourth Amendment.
Maryland v. Garrison	1987	Evidence is admissible even though the specifics in the search warrant were inaccurate.
Illinois v. Rodriguez	1990	Police officers were acting in good faith when the victim allowed entry into her apartment even though she no longer resided with the defendant.
Arizona v. Evans	1995	Traffic stop that led to the seizure of drugs was legal, even though the arrest warrant, which was the basis of the search, was improper because it was based on a computer error.
Knowles v. Iowa	1998	Issuing a speeding ticket does not give police authority to search the car.
Illinois v. Wardlow	2000	A person running at the sight of a police officer could, in some cases, justify the police's conducting a stop-and-frisk search.
Bond v. U.S.	2000	Bus and train passengers have an expectation of privacy when they put their luggage into an overhead rack.
Florida v. J. L.	2000	Police cannot stop and search someone solely because they have received an anonymous tip.
Kyllo v. U.S.	2001	Police cannot use a thermal imagining device to scan a building to detect the presence of high-intensity lamps used to grow marijuana.

all, the impact on judicial suppression of evidence was virtually nonexistent. Out of 2,115 applications, only 1 was rejected by a judge (Uchida et al. 1988).

Warrantless Searches

Obtaining a search warrant is still a relatively rare phenomenon. For a host of reasons, police officers and even some judges view the process of securing a search warrant as burdensome and time-consuming. It is therefore not surprising that many law enforcement officers regard the search warrant as the option of last resort. In their eyes, there are many easier ways to get the evidence or otherwise make a case against the accused.

The majority of searches are conducted without warrant. One common form of **warrantless search** is a **consent search.** The person must freely and voluntarily consent to be

COURTS, CONTROVERSY, AND REDUCING CRIME

Should the Exclusionary Rule Be Abolished?

 The exclusionary rule was controversial when it was adopted in 1961 and remains so four decades later. In a 1981 speech, President Reagan's strong words expressed the views of the crime control model in opposition to the exclusionary rule:

> The exclusionary rule rests on the absurd proposition that a law enforcement error, no matter how technical, can be used to justify throwing an entire case out of court, no matter how guilty the defendant or how heinous the crime. The plain consequence of treating the wrongs equally is a grievous miscarriage of justice: the criminal goes free; the officer receives no effective reprimand; and the only ones who really suffer are the people of the community.

But to law professor Yale Kamisar (1978), illegal conduct by the police cannot so easily be ignored. Here is how he states the due process model case for the exclusionary rule:

> A court which admits [illegally seized evidence] . . . manifests a willingness to tolerate the unconstitutional conduct which produced it.

> How can the police and the citizenry be expected to "believe that the government truly meant to forbid the conduct in the first place." A court which admits the evidence in a case involving a "run of the mill" Fourth Amendment violation demonstrates an insufficient commitment to the guarantee against unreasonable search and seizure.

While the *Mapp* decision remains controversial, the nature of the debate has changed. Initially, critics called for abolition of the exclusionary rule (Oaks 1970; Wilkey 1978); now, they just suggest modifications. This shift in thinking is reflected in the Reagan administration's Attorney General's Task Force on Violent Crime (1981). Although composed largely of long-standing critics of the exclusionary rule, the final report called only for its modification, not its abolition.

Among the alternatives proposed, former Chief Justice Warren Burger urged an "egregious violation standard" (*Brewer v. Williams* 1977). Others have proposed an exception for reasonable mistakes by the police (Fyfe 1982). To critics, modifications along these lines would reduce the number of arrests lost because of illegal searches, and the sanction would be more proportional to the seriousness of the Fourth Amendment violation. The Supreme Court, however, has recognized an "honest mistake" or a "good faith" exception to the exclusionary rule only in extremely narrow and limited circumstances (*U.S. v. Leon* 1984; *Illinois v. Krull* 1987). The high court is increasingly leaning in this direction, but only on a limited basis (*Arizona v. Evans* 1995).

When the Republican party gained control of both houses of Congress in 1995, conservatives increased their efforts to modify the exclusionary rule (Congressional Quarterly 1996). These efforts to overturn Supreme Court decisions proved unsuccessful.

The Rehnquist Court includes six justices who have publicly criticized *Mapp*. Yet this working majority has apparently been unable to agree among themselves as to how to replace *Mapp* while prohibiting truly bad-faith searches by the police. As a result, predicting the future of *Mapp* is problematical at best.

What do you think? Should the exclusionary rule be abolished outright, given "good faith" exceptions, or kept in its present form? If one admits that there are problems in its current application, what realistic alternatives might restrain law enforcement from potentially conducting blatant and flagrant searches in violation of the Fourth Amendment?

To continue the debate over the exclusionary rule, go to these sites:

American Civil Liberties Union:
http://www.aclu.org

National Center for Policy Analysis:
http://www.ncpa.org

The Cato Institute: http://www.cato.org

National Association of Criminal Defense Lawyers: http://www.criminaljustice.org

searched, but law enforcement officers indicate that consent is the easiest thing in the world to obtain. As one city detective explained, you just make an offer that cannot be refused:

> [You] tell the guy, "Let me come in and take a look at your house." And he says, "No, I don't want to." And then you tell him, "Then I'm going to leave Sam here, and he's going to live with you until we come back [with a search warrant]. Now we can do it either way." And very rarely do the people say, "Go get your search warrant then." (Van Duizend, Sutton, and Carter 1984)

The police may also lawfully search without a warrant if the search is incident to a lawful arrest or if the evidence is in **plain view.**

The precise meaning of "probable cause" remains elusive, however. The grounds for a warrantless search vary, depending on what is being searched. The Supreme Court is more likely to find a search to be reasonable if a person is searched, as opposed to a search of an area where the person has a property interest (home or business, for example) (Segal 1984). Exhibit 12-4 presents an overview of the issues surrounding disclosure and suppression of evidence discussed so far.

THE EXCLUSIONARY RULE AND THE COURTROOM WORK GROUP

The police must often make immediate decisions about searching or interrogating a suspect. In street arrests, officers do not have time to consult an attorney about the complex and constantly evolving law governing these areas. These on-the-spot decisions may later be challenged in court as violations of suspects' constitutional rights. Even though the exclusionary rule is directed at the police, its actual enforcement occurs in the courts, particularly the trial courts.

Pretrial Motions

A defense attorney who believes that his or her client was identified in a defective police lineup, gave a confession because of improper police activity, or was subjected to an illegal search can file a motion to suppress the evidence. Most states require that **suppression motions** be made prior to trial.

During the hearing on these pretrial motions, the defense attorney usually bears the burden of proving that the search was illegal or that the confession was coerced. The only exception involves an allegation that the *Miranda* warnings were not given, in which case the state has the burden of proof. The judge's ruling in the pretrial hearing is binding on the later trial.

Pretrial hearings on a motion to suppress evidence are best characterized as "swearing matches." As one defense attorney phrased it, "The real question in Supreme Court cases is what's going on at the police station" (Neubauer 1974, 167). Seldom is there unbiased, independent evidence of what happened. The only witnesses are the participants—police and defendant—and, not surprisingly, they give different versions. This dispute over the facts structures and apportions the roles that the police, defense attorneys, judges, and prosecutors play. Because they must search out the issues, defense attorneys are forced into a catalytic role. By virtue of their power as fact finders at hearings, judges become the supreme umpires that legal theory indicates they should be. Prosecutors, in contrast, play a relatively passive role. Although pretrial motions place prosecutors in a defensive posture, they are not at a major disadvantage, because the police are usually able to provide information indicating compliance.

Defense Attorney As Prime Mover

Because defense attorneys have the responsibility of protecting the constitutional rights of their clients, they are the prime movers in suppression matters. Unless the defense objects, it is assumed that law enforcement officials have behaved properly. Filing a pretrial motion to suppress evidence may produce benefits for the defense. If the motion is granted, the defense wins, because the prosecutor will usually dismiss the case for lack of evidence. Even if

Exhibit 12-4 Disclosing and Suppressing Evidence

	Law on the Books	Law in Action
Discovery	Pretrial procedure in which parties to a lawsuit ask for and receive information such as witnesses' statements, expert witnesses' reports, and lab reports.	In a number of jurisdictions, informal prosecutorial disclosure means that defense attorneys who maintain a cooperative stance toward the district attorney will be able to view most or all of the state's case prior to trial.
Brady material	Prosecutor must turn over exculpatory evidence to the defense prior to trial.	Some defense attorneys assert that some prosecutors do not always live up to their constitutional obligation.
Rules of evidence	In jurisdictions with more open discovery, defense is entitled to see witnesses' statements and lab reports before trial.	Prosecutors who maintain an open discovery policy experience quicker pleas of guilty and less case backlog.
Reciprocal discovery	Requirement that the defense disclose various materials to the prosecutor prior to trial.	In era of "get tough with criminals," an increasingly popular response by legislatures.
Lineups	The suspect has a right to have an attorney present. In addition, the lineup must represent the description given by the witness.	The police routinely take a picture of the persons in the lineup, which is typically sufficient to prove to the court that the lineup was indeed representative.
Interrogations	Method of acquiring evidence in the form of information or confessions from suspects by police.	Suspects who provide incriminating statements are more likely to be charged with a crime, more likely to be convicted, and more likely to be punished severely.
Physical coercion	Statements made to the police obtained by the use of physical force or the threatened use of physical force are not admissible because they are untrustworthy.	Historically, there is every reason to believe that physically coerced confessions were common. In contemporary practice, believable reports of physical coercion are extremely rare.
Psychological coercion	Fifth Amendment protection against self-incrimination means that any statement elicited by the police cannot be used in court if the statement is not "free and voluntary."	During the 1940s and 1950s, the Supreme Court found that a number of confessions were inadmissible because of psychological coercion. Difficulty of applying this standard on a case-by-case basis led the Court to announce *Miranda* warnings.
Miranda warnings	Prior to interrogation, the police must warn a suspect that (1) you have the right to remain silent; (2) anything you say can and will be used against you in a court of law; (3) you have the right to talk to a lawyer and have him or her present with you while you are being questioned; and (4) if you cannot afford to hire a lawyer, one will be appointed to represent you before any questioning, if you wish.	Three out of four suspects waive their *Miranda* rights (Leo 1996a). Police use advising of *Miranda* rights to gain the confidence of the suspect.

	Law on the Books	Law in Action
Search and seizure	Legal term found in the Fourth Amendment referring to the searching for and carrying away of evidence by police during a criminal investigation.	In street crimes, police officers must make quick decisions about searching a person or a car for contraband. Most often occurs in drug and weapons offenses.
Search warrant	A written order, issued by judicial authority, directing a law enforcement officer to search for property and, if found, to bring it before the court.	Judges or magistrates rarely scrutinize them closely. Police are often successful in obtaining suspect's consent for a voluntary search.
Consent search	Law enforcement officials are under no requirement to tell the suspect that they do not have the right to search.	Suspects are surprisingly willing to consent to search of person or car.
Incident to a valid arrest	After a valid arrest, police officers may search to protect themselves and to prevent the destruction of contraband.	Some officers have been known to search and then fabricate probable cause for arrest.
Plain view	Law enforcement officers may search and seize any contraband or illegal substances or items if they are in the immediate vision of the officers.	Some law enforcement officers allegedly search in hidden areas but later testify the material was in plain view.

the motion is denied, the defense may be able to discover information that may later prove valuable at trial. Moreover, filing a pretrial motion keeps options open; plea bargaining remains a possible course of action.

Despite these apparent advantages, defense attorneys face major barriers in raising objections. Possible violations of *Mapp* or *Miranda* do not come into the lawyer's office prepackaged, just awaiting a court hearing. Defense attorneys must frame the issue and determine whether enough facts exist to support the contention. According to many defense attorneys, the police follow proper procedures most of the time. Thus, the task of the lawyer is to separate the out-of-the-ordinary situation from the more numerous ones in which the police have not violated Supreme Court rulings.

In deciding whether to make a motion to suppress evidence, defense attorneys are influenced by the informal norms of the courtroom work group. Pretrial motions require extra work, not only for the defense attorney but for the judge and prosecutor as well. Defense attorneys who file too many frivolous motions or use them to harass the judge and/or prosecutor can be given a variety of sanctions. The prosecutor may refuse to plea-bargain in a given case or may insist upon a sentence harsher than normal.

The Defensive Posture of the Prosecutor

Suppression motions represent only liabilities for prosecutors. At a minimum, they must do extra work. At worst, they may lose the case entirely. Even if they win the suppression motion, they may have to expend extra effort defending that decision on appeal, where they may lose.

Despite these drawbacks, prosecutors maintain the upper hand. For once, they need only defend, because the defense attorney bears the burden of proof. Because the police control the information involved, prosecutors are generally in a favorable position to argue against excluding evidence. For example, the police are usually able to obtain the defendant's signature on the *Miranda* warning form, which indicates compliance with Supreme Court requirements (see Exhibit 12-5). Similarly, in a search-and-seizure case, the officers are familiar enough with the law to know how to testify in order to avoid suppression of evidence. Of course, the DA can dismiss a case that presents potential problems, thus avoiding a public hearing on the matter.

Trial Judges As Decision Makers

The decision to suppress evidence rests with the trial judge. After hearing the witnesses and viewing the physical evidence (if any), the judge makes a ruling based on appellate court decisions. Thus, trial court judges are key policymakers in applying and implementing Supreme Court decisions concerning confessions and search and seizure.

As noted earlier, a pretrial motion is essentially a clash over the facts. The trial court judge possesses virtually unfettered discretion in making findings of fact. Judges' backgrounds predispose them to be skeptical of defense motions to suppress. As noted in Chapter 6, many judges were once prosecutors, whose courtroom arguments supported the police. These inclinations are reinforced by the selection process. Judges are by and large appointed by governors or presidents, who are often critical of appellate court restrictions on gathering of evidence by the police, or elected by the public in campaigns that stress crime reduction. For these reasons, trial judges do not regularly grant defense motions to suppress evidence.

On appeal, higher courts examine whether the law was correctly applied by the trial judge, but they rarely scrutinize the facts to which the law was applied. Such deference is based on the trial judge's proximity to the event. Only trial judges have the opportunity to observe directly how witnesses testify—their responsiveness to questions or their attempts at concealment. Such nuances are not reflected in the trial court transcript. Moreover, when "an appeals court reverses in one of these cases they are saying that another judge abused his discretion. They are understandably reluctant to do so" (Neubauer 1974).

Police Testimony

At the center of court hearings on police practices and defendants' rights are events that happened out in the field or in the police station. Although some jurisdictions now require police to tape interrogations, many do not (Leo 1996b). What is known in court therefore is largely the product of police testimony.

Richard Leo (1996a) observed 122 interrogations in a major urban police department and reported the following. Detectives begin by cultivating the suspect, getting him to make eye contact and engage in conversation. The *Miranda* warnings are useful for this purpose because they induce suspects to respond to questions. Thus, three out of four suspects waive their *Miranda* warnings. Next, the detective states that his (occasionally her) job is to discover the truth and typically shares with the suspect some of the evidence in the case. A two-pronged approach is being used. One is the use of negative incentives, tactics that suggest the suspect should confess because there is no other plausible course of action. The other is the use of positive incentives, tactics that suggest the suspect will in some way feel better or benefit if he or she confesses. The results were as follows:

- No incriminating statement (36 percent)
- Incriminating statement (23 percent)
- Partial admission (18 percent)
- Full confession (24 percent)

A suspect's decision to provide detectives with incriminating information was fateful. Those who incriminated themselves were more likely to be charged with a crime, more likely to enter a plea of guilty, more likely to be convicted, and likely to receive more punishment than their counterparts who did not provide incriminating statements.

LAW AND CONTROVERSY: COSTS OF THE EXCLUSIONARY RULE

A key issue in the ongoing debate over the exclusionary rule centers on its costs. In a widely cited statement, Chief Justice Burger summed

Exhibit 12-5 Sample Custodial Interrogation Form

KENNER POLICE DEPARTMENT

A 47408

REV. 11/76

ADVICE OF RIGHTS

KENNER, LA.

DAY_____ DATE _____ TIME _____COMPLAINT NO. _____

LOCATION_____

NAME _____

BIRTH DATE _____ RACE_____ SEX_____ AGE_____

ADDRESS_____CITY_____ STATE_____

HIGHEST GRADE COMPLETED SCHOOL _____

ABILITY TO READ: ☐ YES ☐ NO
ABILITY TO WRITE: ☐ YES ☐ NO

☐ I am investigating -- or --
☐ You are under arrest for alleged -- Violation of _____

_____ Relative to_____

According to provisions in the Constitution of the United States and of the State of Louisiana it is my duty to inform you that:

1. You have the right to remain silent.
2. Anything you say may be used against you in court.
3. You have a right to consult with and obtain the advice of an attorney before answering any questions.
4. If you cannot afford an attorney, the court will appoint an attorney to represent and advise you.
5. You have a right to have your attorney present at the time of any questioning or giving of any statement.
6. If you decide to answer questions now without an attorney present, you will still have the right to stop answering at any time until you talk to an attorney.

DO YOU UNDERSTAND WHAT I HAVE JUST READ TO YOU? ☐ YES ☐ NO

NOTE: IF THE PERSON DOES NOT FULLY UNDERSTAND AND INTELLIGENTLY AND VOLUNTARILY WAIVE THE RIGHT OF COUNSEL, HE CANNOT BE QUESTIONED. IF THE PERSON AT ANY TIME DURING THE QUESTIONING ASKS NOT TO BE QUESTIONED FURTHER OR INDICATES IN ANY MANNER THAT HE DOES NOT WISH TO BE QUESTIONED, THEN THE QUESTIONING MUST CEASE.

ARE YOU WILLING TO ANSWER QUESTIONS AT THIS TIME WITHOUT A LAWYER? ☐ YES ☐ NO

HAVE ANY THREATS OR PROMISES BEEN MADE TO YOU OR HAS PRESSURE OF ANY KIND BEEN APPLIED TO INDUCE YOU TO ANSWER QUESTIONS OR TO GIVE UP ANY OF YOUR RIGHTS? ☐ YES ☐ NO

WITH FULL KNOWLEDGE OF MY RIGHTS I WISH TO WAIVE ALL PRIVILEGES AGAINST SELF INCRIMINATION AND MAKE A STATEMENT ABOUT MY KNOWLEDGE OF THIS CRIME. ☐ YES ☐ NO

_____
Signature of Person Receiving Rights

I have read and explained the RIGHTS OF AN ARRESTEE OR SUSPECT to the person named above, and he . . .
☐ SIGNED, WAIVING HIS RIGHTS
☐ SIGNED AS UNDERSTANDING, NOT WAIVING RIGHTS
☐ REFUSED TO SIGN
☐ WAS UNDECIDED, CONSEQUENTLY WAS ADVISED NOT TO SIGN
☐ PREFERS TO SPEAK WITH ATTORNEY BEFORE MAKING DECISION
☐ OTHER - (EXPLAIN IN REMARKS)

CONCLUDED: DAY_____ DATE _____TIME _____

RIGHTS READ BY_____

WITNESS_____

WITNESS_____

REMARKS_____

_____

KPD-122

THE MURDER TRIAL OF SHAREEF COUSIN

The DA Fails to Disclose a Witness Statement

The first police unit arrived at the Port of Call restaurant at 10:28 P.M., only two minutes after the dispatcher logged the first call for assistance. As other units also arrived, some officers secured the chaotic murder scene while others searched for witnesses. They quickly determined that Connie Babin—Michael Gerardi's date—was a witness and took her statement. She answered some questions but had trouble articulating the answers to many questions. The officers noted that she was hysterical and could not speak in complete sentences. She told the police that she did not get a good look at the gunman and probably would not be able to identify him.

Three days later, during an interview in her house, she stated that she was not wearing her glasses or contact lenses on the night of the murder and could only see patterns and shapes. Thus, she could describe the murderer only as a black male in his late teens, five feet seven or eight inches tall, with curly hair and an "old man's face," wearing colorful socks. These statements would come to dominate later proceedings but not the trial itself—because the prosecutor chose not to disclose these statements to the defense prior to trial.

When Shareef Cousin became a suspect three weeks later, Detective Anthony Small compiled a photographic lineup and Connie Babin made a positive identification of Cousin as the murderer. At trial, she repeated the positive identification. The defense learned of the existence of her statements through an anonymous tip (identified only as "an honest police officer" in Cousin's federal lawsuit). Once the existence of these witness statements became known, the defense moved for a new trial, but the judge denied the motion. Later, the issue took center stage in the appeal to the Louisiana Supreme Court.

Why didn't DA Harry Connick's office disclose these statements (Chapter 8)? The brief for the State of Louisiana offers a tortured explanation at best. According to lawyers for Connick, somewhat similar statements had been disclosed prior to trial. Therefore, "even if the transcribed statement did contain information that could be considered exculpatory, the evidence was merely cumulative and there is no reasonable probability that, had the evidence been disclosed to the defense, the result of the proceeding would have been different." On appeal, the Louisiana Supreme Court dismissed the prosecutor's argument, calling the statement "obviously exculpatory," citing *Brady* and *Kyles* (*State v. Shareef Cousin* 1998). The issue resurfaced again during preparation for the second trial. The trial judge issued what is for Louisiana a broad discovery order, requiring the prosecutor to turn over all evidence (except lawyer work product). This unusual remedy had been upheld in a previous case in which Connick's office had failed to disclose (*State v. Duc Nguyen* 1998) and the high court sanctioned its use in this case as well (*State v. Cousin* 1998).

Would the disclosure of the statements made by Connie Babin have mattered? In all likelihood, if the defense had known of these statements, the dynamics of the trial would have been fundamentally different. According to the news account (borne out by reading the actual transcript), on cross-examination Cousin's defense team "tried to pick delicately at Babin's story" (Varney 1996a). Moreover, the defense argued during later motions that they were afraid to explore the issue of eyesight, fearing that the prosecutor was laying a trap.

To most observers, the revelation of Babin's initial statement that she would never be able to identify the murderer doomed subsequent prosecutions. Essentially, the state's case was reduced to a single witness (see Chapter 14), and with that witness identification called into question, a conviction would be highly unlikely.

Jurors and laypersons give eyewitness testimony a great deal of credibility, but psychologists are more skeptical. Read Torun Lindholm and Sven-Ake Christianson, "Intergroup Biases and Eyewitness Testimony."

To find out more about the decision not to retry Shareef Cousin for murder, use the search term "follow-up (Shareef Cousin)."

COURT TV

Cliffhanger: Truthful Admission or a False Confession?

Linda Stangel's boyfriend went for a walk on the Oregon coast but never returned. Six months later his body was found amidst the rocks. Did he slip, did he commit suicide, or did his girlfriend push him over the cliff?

She denied killing him but when the police took her back up the cliff to the scene of the crime she confessed. Later she confessed again on tape. But the police had not yet given her the *Miranda* warnings. After being advised of her constitutional rights, she confessed again, but at trial she contended that the police coerced her into making a false confession.

 View a video clip of this trial on your copy of the CourtTV CD-ROM. As you watch the video, keep the following questions in mind:

1. Why didn't the police read Linda Stangel her *Miranda* rights before they began questioning her? Should all of her later admissions be inadmissible because the police and prosecutor clearly misled her?

2. How effective is Linda Stangel as a witness? Why did the defense call her to the stand (see Chapter 14)?

3. In what ways is she similar or different from the profile of criminal defendants discussed in Chapter 9?

4. What story do you think is the most believable—her confession to the police that she shoved him over the cliff by accident or her testimony at trial that she made up the story?

5. What story do you think the jury chose to believe?

up the critics' position as follows: "Some clear demonstration of the benefits and effectiveness of the exclusionary rule is required to justify it in view of the high price it exacts from soci-

ety—the release of countless guilty criminals" (*Bivens v. Six Unknown Federal Narcotics Agents* 1971).

Assessing the number of convictions lost because of the exclusionary rule is difficult, for reasons discussed in Chapter 10. Case attrition occurs at numerous stages of the proceedings and for various reasons. Several studies shed considerable light on the topic.

Exclusionary rules can lead to the freeing of apparently guilty defendants during prosecutorial screening. Prosecutors may refuse to file charges because of a search-and-seizure problem, a tainted confession, or a defective police lineup. However, this occurs very infrequently. The Comptroller General of the United States (1979) examined case rejections by U.S. attorneys and found that search and seizure was cited as the primary reason 0.4 percent of the time. Similarly, a study of seven communities reports that an average of 2 percent of the rejections were for *Mapp* or *Miranda* reasons (Boland et al. 1982). A more controversial study analyzed 86,033 felony cases rejected for prosecution in California. The National Institute of Justice (NIJ) report found that 4.8 percent were rejected for search-and-seizure reasons. The NIJ conclusion that these figures indicated a "major impact of the exclusionary rule" has been challenged as misleading and exaggerated (Davies 1983). Indeed, compared to lack of evidence and witness problems, *Mapp* and *Miranda* are minor sources of case attrition.

After charges are filed, case attrition can also occur when judges grant pretrial motions to suppress, but in actuality few pretrial motions to suppress evidence are filed (Nardulli 1983). In less than 8 percent of the cases did the defense file one or more motions to exclude evidence. Once filed, pretrial motions are rarely successful. Challenges to identifications or confessions were granted 5 percent of the time. Challenges to gathering physical evidence were somewhat more likely to be granted by the judge, but the rate was still only 17 percent (Uchida and Bynum 1991).

Piecing together the various stages of the criminal court process leads to the conclusion that the exclusionary rule has a marginal effect on the criminal court system (Nardulli 1983). Examining case attrition data from California, Davies (1983) calculated that 0.8 percent of

A Virtual Tour of American Courthouses: Disclosing and Suppressing Evidence

To learn more about Ernesto Miranda, *Miranda v. Arizona*, and the *Miranda* rights, go to **http://www.io.com/~mcapra/ miranda/rights.html**. Warren's handwritten notes on the *Miranda* decision and Brennan's responses are available through the manuscript division of the Library of Congress: **http://lcweb.loc.gov/exhibits/treasures/trr038.html**.

Several Web sites provide the perspective of practicing lawyers on *Miranda*. They include "Invoking the Miranda Right to Counsel: The Defendant's Burden" by Kimberly A. Crawford: **http://www.emergency.com/miranda.htm**.

The most direct challenge to *Miranda* came in *Dickerson v. U.S.* To read the opinion, go to **http://findlaw.com/**. Under

Laws, click on U.S. Supreme Court and then go to 2000 decisions. For contrasting views on *Dickerson*, point your browser to **http://www.aclu.org/features/f041900a.html http://www.law.utah.edu/Cassell/OverhaulMiranda?**

The following sites provide information about the Fourth Amendment:
http://www.nolo.com/encyclopedia/articles/crim/ search_seizure.html http://law.about.com/newsissues/law/cs/searchseizure/

Federal guidelines for searching and seizing computers can be seen at **http://www.web-police.org/wp_guidelines.html**.

---

arrests (8 out of 1,000) were rejected because of *Mapp* and *Miranda*. As for cases filed, Nardulli calculated that 0.57 percent of convictions (fewer than 6 out of 1,000) were lost because of exclusionary rules. Moreover, of the lost convictions, only 20 percent were for serious crimes. Weapons cases and drug cases are those most likely to involve questions about police conduct.

A special panel of the American Bar Association (1988) has likewise concluded that constitutional protections of the rights of criminal defendants do not significantly handicap police and prosecutors in their efforts to arrest, prosecute, and obtain convictions for the most serious crimes. Although many people blame the failures of the criminal justice system on judges' concern for defendants' rights, the blame is misplaced. The main problem is that the criminal justice system is stretched too thin, the ABA concluded.

▉ CONCLUSION

In many ways Ernesto Miranda fit the pattern of those arrested by the police—a young minority male with little education and few job

prospects. But the eventual outcome of his case was hardly typical. His case was heard by the nation's highest court, and he not only won the right to a new trial but also established new law in the process. Unlike most defendants, whose cases are quickly forgotten, his name became a code word for the rights of criminal defendants.

If *Miranda* the legal principle was to endure, Miranda the man was less fortunate. Initially, his chances of gaining an acquittal during retrial looked promising indeed. After all, the state's only evidence—the signed confession—had been ruled to be inadmissible evidence. It turned out, however, that while in jail Ernesto Miranda had admitted details of the crime to his common-law wife, who by now had grown afraid of him. She testified for the state, and after an hour and a half of deliberations, the jury found Miranda guilty of rape and kidnapping a second time. After serving his prison term, Ernesto Miranda was living in a Phoenix flophouse when he became involved in a barroom quarrel over small change in a poker game. A large knife normally used to harvest lettuce ended his life. It is no small irony that the Phoenix police read Miranda's killer his *Miranda* rights when they arrested him.

This chapter has examined several important aspects of what occurs while cases are being prepared for trial. One is discovery, the formal or informal exchange of information between prosecution and defense. What information is subject to discovery varies greatly. As a rule, defense attorneys who are cooperative members of the courtroom work group receive more information than others. Another important aspect of preparing for trial centers on suppression of evidence. Confessions and physical evidence that have been illegally obtained cannot be used at trial. If the defense believes that there have been illegal actions by the police, it files a pretrial motion to suppress the evidence. Prosecutors are usually in a favorable position to show that the evidence was obtained legally.

CRITICAL THINKING QUESTIONS

1. In civil cases, each party is entitled to all the information in the possession of the other side (unless that information is privileged). Why are discovery rules in criminal cases different?

2. To what extent do prosecutorial policies that restrict the sharing of information with defense attorneys other than what is legally required represent a contradiction in the crime control model? On the one hand, the crime control model suggests that criminal defendants (and their lawyers) shouldn't receive any breaks. But on the other hand, the crime control model stresses efficiency so that scarce resources can be concentrated on apprehending and convicting the guilty.

3. When the Court announced its decision in *Miranda v. Arizona* in 1966, the decision sparked massive controversy and was a major issue in the 1968 presidential campaign. Yet over time it has become much more accepted than the Court's decision in *Mapp v. Ohio* regarding search and seizure. What factors might explain this apparent shift in assessments?

4. A number of conservatives call for eliminating or restricting the exclusionary rule in street crimes. Yet some conservatives also call for a more draconian rule in white-collar crimes, suggesting that the financial records of a person or a business should be given special protections under the Fourth Amendment. Are these arguments consistent or simply a case of whose ox is being gored? How would these arguments play out if a substantial citizen in the community (whose financial records are being requested) were under investigation for major drug dealings?

5. To what extent is the continuing controversy over search-and-seizure law really a debate over the war on drugs? Recall the controversy in Chapter 8 centering on judicial independence, in which a federal judge in New York suppressed a goodly amount of illegal drugs.

KEY TERMS

alibi defense (265)
consent search (271)
discovery (262)
exclusionary rule (266)
illegal search and seizure (268)
plain view (273)
search warrant (270)
suppression motion (273)
unreasonable search and seizure (268)
warrantless search (271)

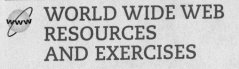 **WORLD WIDE WEB RESOURCES AND EXERCISES**

Web Guides

http://dir.yahoo.com/Government/U_S__Government/ Judicial_Branch/Supreme_Court/Court_Decisions/ Specific_Cases/Miranda_v__Arizona/

Web Search Terms

discovery + criminal   exclusionary rule
Miranda   search and seizure

Useful URLs

CNN's Legal Survival Guide discusses "What Is the Miranda Warning?" at http://www. courttv.com/legalhelp/lawguide/criminal/91.html.

Uncommon URLs

Search and Seizure Bulletin is available at http://www.policecenter.com/. And while visiting the site, you might want to take the following quiz: http://www.policecenter.com/bulletins/quiz. shtml.

Time to overhaul Miranda? University of Utah law professor Paul Cassell is the leading conservative critic of *Miranda* and *Mapp*: http://www.law.utah.edu/Cassell/.

Search and Seizure Law for New York Law Enforcement Officers can be found at http://www.gouldlaw.com/ss-toc.htm.

Judge Scott J. Silverman (Dade County Court) offers "Criminal Discovery in Florida": http://www.fl.judges.com/articles/96discov.htm.

Web Exercises

1. Access the following two cases on the Internet: *Miranda v. Arizona* at http://www.law. cornell.edu/supct/cases/ and *Terry v. Ohio* at http://www.findlaw.com/casecode/Supreme.html. Read the two decisions not so much for the specific legal issues but for the tone of the opinions. How do these opinions differ in their treatment of police investigation? Do the opinions give direct or indirect evidence of what has happened in the two years that separate the decisions—riots and protests against the Vietnam War?

2. Using the search engine of your choice, search for the phrase "exclusionary rule." Based on the articles found, what is the current status of efforts to abolish or modify the exclusionary rule?

3. Using the search engine of your choice, search using the phrase "exclusionary rule" and find two or more Web sites that discuss the topic. Web sites rarely indicate directly what political philosophy they reflect. It is important, therefore, for the student to analyze the message. Which one comes closest to the crime control model? Which more clearly reflects a due process model? Are they similar or different in the legal information provided?

INFOTRAC COLLEGE EDITION RESOURCES AND EXERCISES

Basic Search Terms

Miranda rule   discovery (laws)
police questioning   Mapp v. Ohio
exclusionary rule   Miranda v. Arizona
 (evidence)   probable cause
self-incrimination   searches and seizures

Recommended Articles

Steven D. Clymer, "Are Police Free to Disregard Miranda?"

Thomas D. Colbridge, "Search Incident to Arrest: Another Look"

Thomas Y. Davies, "Recovering the Original Fourth Amendment"

Leonard W. Levy, "Origins of the Fourth Amendment"

Timothy Lynch, "In Defense of the Exclusionary Rule"

Evan Osborne, "Is the Exclusionary Rule Worthwhile?"

John A. Wasowicz, "Exclusionary Rule: A Twentieth-Century Invention"

InfoTrac College Edition Exercises

1. Using the search term "Miranda rule" or "police questioning," find one article on each side of the issue. In what ways does this debate reflect differences between the crime control and the due process models

of criminal justice? To what extent is the debate largely symbolic? What proof is offered that defendants are really going free? Here are two possible articles:

Owen Einspahr, "The Interview Challenge"

Michael R. Napier, Susan H. Adams, "Magic Words to Obtain Confessions"

2. Using the search term "searches and seizures" or "exclusionary rule," find one article on each side of the issue. In what ways does this debate reflect differences between the crime control and the due process models of criminal justice? To what extent is the debate largely symbolic? What proof is offered that defendants are really going free? Here are two possible articles:

Guido Calabresi, "The Exclusionary Rule"

Yale Kamisar, "In Defense of the Search and Seizure Exclusionary Rule"

FOR FURTHER READING

Brandt, Charles. *The Right to Remain Silent.* New York: St. Martin's Press, 1991.

Brooks, Peter. *Troubling Confessions: Speaking Guilt in Law and Literature*. Chicago: University of Chicago Press, 2000.

Decker, John. *Revolution to the Right: Criminal Procedure Jurisprudence during the Burger–Rehnquist Court Era.* Hamden, CT: Garland, 1994.

Leo, Richard. "*Miranda's* Revenge: Police Interrogation as a Confidence Game." *Law and Society Review* 30 (1996): 259–288.

Leo, Richard, and George Thomas. *The Miranda Debate: Law, Justice, and Policing.* Boston: Northeastern University Press, 2000.

PART III
Processing
the Accused

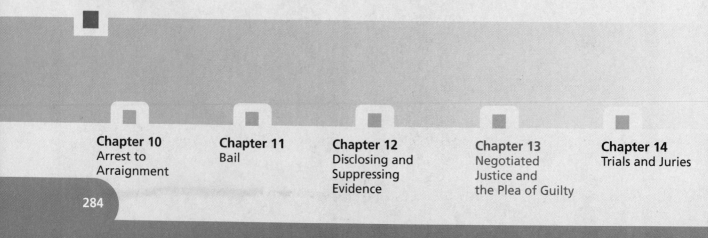

harged with two counts of felony gambling, Rudolph Santobello pled guilty to one count of a misdemeanor charge of possessing gambling records. Just as important, the prosecutor agreed to make no recommendation as to the sentence. But Santobello's sentencing hearing was delayed for several months, and in the interim the initial judge retired and another prosecutor replaced the one who had negotiated the plea of guilty. Apparently ignorant of his colleague's commitment, the new DA demanded the maximum sentence, and the new judge agreed, imposing a one-year jail term. The justices of the U.S. Supreme Court were concerned about the failure of the prosecutor's office to honor the commitment it had made to induce the guilty plea. Others were no doubt concerned whether Santobello, who had a long and serious criminal record, should have been allowed to plead guilty with such a light sentence in the first place. ◀

Santobello v. New York highlights the importance of guilty pleas. Although the average American equates criminal justice with trials, only a handful of defendants are ever tried. Instead, most convictions result not from a guilty verdict following a contested trial but rather from a voluntary plea by the accused. Views about this common practice differ. To some, it erodes the cornerstones of the adversary system: the presumption of innocence and the right to trial. To others, it enables the guilty to escape with a light penalty. To still others, it is a modern-day necessity if the courts are to dispose of their large caseloads. All agree, however, that it is the most important stage of the criminal court process.

LAW ON THE BOOKS: TYPES OF PLEA AGREEMENTS

Guilty pleas are the bread and butter of the American criminal courts. The data in Figure 13-1 demonstrate the pervasiveness of guilty pleas. Many more findings of guilt follow a plea of guilty than a trial. **Plea bargaining** can best be defined as the process through which a defendant pleads guilty to a criminal

charge with the expectation of receiving some consideration from the state.

Plea bargaining is hardly new. There is considerable evidence that it became a common practice in state courts sometime after the Civil War (Alschuler 1979; Friedman 1979; Sanborn 1986). In federal courts, the massive number of liquor cases stemming from Prohibition led to the institutionalization of plea bargaining in the first third of the twentieth century (Padgett 1990). What is new is the amount of attention plea negotiations now receive. During the early decades of this century, the issue was only sporadically discussed. The crime surveys of the 1920s reported the dominance of plea bargaining (Moley 1928), but most courts persistently denied its existence. It was not until the 1960s that plea bargaining emerged as a controversial national issue.

Plea bargaining is a general term that encompasses a wide range of practices. Indeed, court officials disagree about what is meant by plea bargaining. Some prosecutors refuse to admit that they engage in bargaining; they simply call it something else (Miller, McDonald, and Cramer 1978). Thus, any discussion of negotiated justice must start with the recognition that there are important variations both in the types of plea agreements negotiated and the process by which such agreements are reached. Typically, plea agreements take one of three

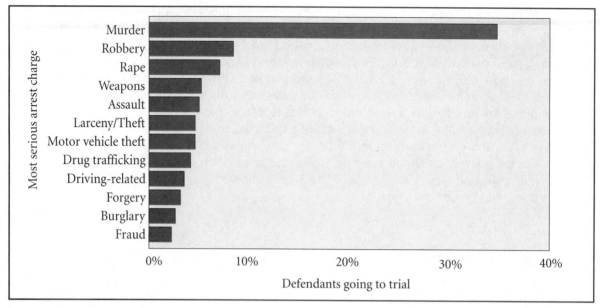

Figure 13-1
Trial Rates for Typical Felonies

SOURCE: Brian Reaves, *Felony Defendants in Large Urban Counties, 1998* (Washington, DC: Bureau of Justice Statistics, 2001).

forms: charge bargaining, count bargaining, and/or sentence bargaining. Exhibit 13-1 summarizes the different types of plea bargaining.

Charge Bargaining

One type of plea agreement is termed **charge bargaining.** In return for the defendant's plea of guilty, the prosecutor allows the defendant to plead guilty to a less serious charge than the one originally filed. For example, the defendant pleads guilty to robbery rather than the original charge of armed robbery. Or the defendant enters a plea of guilty to misdemeanor theft rather than the initial accusation of felony theft. The principal effect of a plea to a less serious charge is to reduce the potential sentence.

Some offenses carry a stiff maximum sentence. A plea to a lesser charge therefore greatly reduces the possible prison term the defendant will have to serve. Bargains for reduced charges are most commonly found in jurisdictions where the state's criminal code is rigid and/or where prosecutors routinely overcharge to begin with. Thus, some charge reductions reflect the

probability that the prosecutor would not be able to prove the original charge in a trial.

Count Bargaining

Another common type of plea agreement is called **count bargaining.** In return for the defendant's plea of guilty to one or more counts in the indictment or information, the prosecutor dismisses the remaining charges. For instance, a defendant accused of three separate burglaries pleads guilty to one burglary count, and the two remaining criminal charges are dismissed.

Like a charge reduction agreement, a count bargain reduces the defendant's potential sentence, but in a very different way. A person charged with multiple counts theoretically can receive a maximum sentence of something like 135 years, a figure arrived at by multiplying the number of charges by the maximum jail term for each charge and assuming that the judge will sentence the defendant to serve the sentences consecutively (one after another). Such figures are often unrealistic, because sentences are typically imposed concurrently (to run at

Exhibit 13-1	Forms of Plea Bargaining	
	Law on the Books	Law in Action
Plea bargaining	The process by which a defendant pleads guilty to a criminal charge with the expectation of receiving some benefit from the state.	The majority of findings of guilt occur because of plea bargaining. The proportion of pleas (as opposed to trials) varies among jurisdictions.
Charge bargaining	The defendant pleads guilty to a less serious charge than the one originally filed.	Courthouse norms control allowable reductions.
	Pleading to a less serious charge reduces the potential sentence the defendant faces.	Some prosecutors deliberately overcharge so it appears that the defendant is getting a break.
Count bargaining	The defendant pleads guilty to some, but not all, of the counts contained in the charging document. Pleading guilty to fewer counts reduces the potential sentence the defendant faces.	Some prosecutors deliberately file additional charges so they can dismiss some later on, making it appear the defendant got a good deal. In multiple-count charges, sentences are typically served concurrently (not consecutively), so the "sentence reduction" the defendant receives is largely illusionary.
Sentence bargaining	The defendant pleads guilty, knowing the sentence that will be imposed. The sentence in the sentence bargain is less than the maximum.	Sentences are based on normal penalties. Because the normal penalty for an offense is less than the maximum, defendants appear to get off lightly.

the same time). In practice, the defendant will often receive the same penalty no matter how few (or how many) charges are involved.

Sentence Bargaining

The third common form of plea agreement is called **sentence bargaining.** A plea of guilty is entered in exchange for a promise of leniency in sentencing. There may be a promise that the defendant will be placed on probation or that the prison term will be no more than a given figure—say, five years. In a sentence bargain, the defendant typically pleads to the original charge (often termed a **plea on the nose**). In some jurisdictions, however, sentence bargaining operates in conjunction with count bargaining and/ or charge reduction bargaining.

In sentence bargaining, the defendant invariably receives less than the maximum penalty. To some, this is an indication that defendants get off too easily, but in fact only defendants with long criminal records who have committed particularly heinous crimes would receive the maximum anyway. In practice, courts impose sentence on the basis of normal penalties for specific crimes involving common types of defendants. In sentence bargaining, the sentence agreed to is the one typically imposed in similar cases.

LAW IN ACTION: BARGAINING AND CASELOADS

The common explanation for plea bargaining is that the courts have too many cases. Plea bargaining is usually portrayed as a regrettable but necessary expedient for disposing of cases. In Chapter 5, it was argued that although this explanation contains some truth, it obscures too many important facets of what the courts do and why they do it. Certainly the press of cases and lack of adequate resources shape the criminal court process, plea bargaining included (Worden 1990). Certainly, because prosecutors need to move cases, they agree to more lenient pleas than they might prefer.

But the caseload hypothesis cannot explain why plea bargaining is as prevalent in courts with relatively few cases as it is in courts with heavy caseloads (Eisenstein and Jacob 1977). A comparison of plea rates in a number of courthouses across the nation found high plea rates in suburban counties with low crimes rates and below average caseloads. The vast differences among jurisdictions in the ratio of pleas to trials primarily reflect differences in the prosecution and the police, not in crime rates or court resources (Boland and Forst 1985).

A similar conclusion emerges from a study that presented the members of the courtroom work group with several hypothetical cases and asked, "Assuming that prosecution, defense, and the court have adequate resources to deal with their caseloads in a fair and expeditious manner, how do you believe this case should be resolved?" (Church 1985, 474). The responses indicated that relatively few of the cases would be disposed of by a trial. Furthermore, there was little support for the notion that practitioners considered negotiated guilty pleas a necessary but illegitimate response to inadequate court system resources (see A Day in Court: Judge's Refusal to Offer Plea Bargains Drives Up Number of Preliminary Hearings).

LAW IN ACTION: BARGAINING AND DISCRETION

The principal weakness of the excessive caseload hypothesis is that it assumes a purely mechanical process, ignoring the underlying dynamics. It seems to suggest that if there were only more judges, more prosecutors, more de-

fense attorneys, and more courtrooms, there would be many more trials, and the penalties imposed on the guilty would also increase. Such a view ignores discretion inherent in the criminal justice process. Plea bargaining is a response to some fundamental issues, the first of which centers on the question of guilt.

Presumption of Factual Guilt

The process of negotiated justice does not operate in isolation from the other stages of the criminal court process. What has gone before—for example, the setting of bail, the return of a grand jury indictment, and the prosecutor's evaluation of the strengths of a case—significantly affects how courts dispose of cases on a plea. The opposite is equally true. Throughout the history of a case, decisions on bail, indictment, and screening have been premised on the knowledge that the majority of defendants end up pleading guilty (Wright and Miller 2002).

Recall from Chapter 10 that the bulk of legally innocent defendants are removed from the criminal court process during the screening process through the preliminary hearing, grand jury, or the prosecutor's charging decision. By the time a case reaches the trial stage, the courtroom work group presumes that the defendant is probably guilty. Survival through the prior processing means that prosecutors, defense attorneys, and judges alike perceive that trial defendants are in serious trouble (Eisenstein and Jacob 1977).

One study estimated that about 50 percent of the cases in the major trial court were "hopeless" or devoid of triable issues of law (Schulhofer 1984). These cases are what some court officials term a *dead bang* or a *slam dunk* case with very strong evidence against the defendant, who has no credible explanation indicating innocence (Mather 1974a). One district attorney summarized the strong evidence of guilt in such cases: "The pervasiveness of the facts should indicate to any competent attorney that the element of prosecution is present and a successful prosecution is forthcoming" (Neubauer 1974, 200).

No two cases are ever the same, of course. Many discussions of plea bargains leave the

A DAY IN COURT

Judge's Refusal to Offer Plea Bargains Drives Up Number of Preliminary Hearings

 SANTA ANA, Calif. A dispute between a judge and the Orange County District Attorney's Office over who should offer—and be held accountable for—plea bargains is clogging parts of the court system, pulling cops off the street and bumping up police overtime pay.

District Attorney Michael Capizzi long has prohibited his attorneys from offering plea bargains, leaving it to judges to offer settlements in exchange for guilty pleas, thus avoiding the cost and time of trials. Countywide, 75 percent of all felony cases are resolved in municipal court before moving on to Superior Court for trial. In West Orange County Municipal Court, 200 cases a week usually are settled by so-called court pleas.

West Court Presiding Judge Tom Borris said West Court Judge Donald Macintyre has stopped offering settlements because he believes the district attorney's no-plea-bargain policy is a farce that leaves judges holding the bag for every settlement. . . . "The DA knows what the going rate is and if they have a weak case, they will present no objection (to the court plea) or they'll let the judge know with a wink or some sort of body language they are not averse to the sentence offered," Borris said. "Then the DA goes out (in the courtroom) and formally objects to the sentence on the record. . . . Judges thought they were helping out the DA and they end up looking light on crime." . . .

But David Himelson, the supervising deputy district attorney for West Court, said it is not the district attorney's responsibility to negotiate punishments. "It is our job to prosecute, and it is the court's job to sentence," Himelson said. . . .

The result of the standoff between Macintyre and the District Attorney's Office is felt in West Court, Superior Court and west county police departments. Instead of small cases being resolved during the first stage of the legal process, many are moving on to preliminary hearings, leaving public defenders and prosecutors scrambling to keep up.

"It means an increase in workload, in expenditures, and it drains our already limited resources," said Orange County Public Defender Carl Holmes. . . .

But the increase in preliminary hearings means witnesses, such as police officers, must be in court at 8:30 A.M. even though their case might not be called for several hours. Normally, police are summoned to court when the hearing is ready to start. "When everything is going to a preliminary hearing, it creates chaos," Holmes said. "It is impossible to determine the length of any given hearing. The unpredictability that results is that all witnesses must remain in the courthouse because as soon as you finish one (hearing), you have to start another."

Police officers are being paid time-and-a-half to be in court, and the new requirements are putting a strain on budgets, police said. "The impact is it is costing money . . . and it affects staffing levels," Garden Grove Capt. Scott Jordan said. "Many officers work nights and are just getting off when they have to go to court. If they don't get any sleep, they can't be expected to work their shift the next night. Or if they get to sleep a few hours they are not alert as they should be." . . .

The extra West Court cases have meant running two shifts of clerks on Mondays, the day West Court cases are heard. They also have meant overtime for bailiffs, who are in charge of courtroom security and monitoring prisoners who are being escorted into the courtroom for their arraignment; long hours for public defenders and deputy district attorneys assigned to Department 5; and feeding and housing in county jails some prisoners who might otherwise have been sent to state prison. . . .

SOURCE: Tiffany Montgomery, "Judge's Refusal to Offer Plea Bargains Drives Up Number of Preliminary Hearings," *Orange County Register*, 7 August 1997. Reprinted by permission of the Orange County Register. Copyright © 1997.

false impression that the attorneys haggle only over the sentence. In fact, courtroom work groups spend a lot of time discussing and analyzing how the crime was committed, the nature of the victim, the types of witnesses, and the character of the defendant (Maynard 1988). In many cases, there is little likelihood that the defendant will be acquitted outright;

there is only the possibility that he or she might be convicted of a less serious offense. The question of what charge the facts will support is an important part of plea bargaining.

Costs and Risks of Trial

The possibility of trial greatly influences negotiations. Trials are a costly and time-consuming means of establishing guilt. For example, to try a simple burglary case would take from one to four days (depending on the jurisdiction) and require the presence of the judge, bailiff, clerk, defense attorney, prosecutor, and court reporter. During this period, none of them could devote much time to the numerous other cases requiring disposition. Also, each would be forced to spend time preparing for this trial. A trial would also require the presence of numerous noncourt personnel: police officers, witnesses, victims, and jurors. For each of these persons, a trial represents an unwanted intrusion into their daily lives.

Based on these considerations, all members of the courtroom work group have a common interest in disposing of cases and avoiding unnecessary trials. Their reasons may differ. Judges and prosecutors want high disposition rates in order to prevent case backlogs and to present a public impression that the process is running smoothly. Public defenders prefer quick dispositions because they lack enough people to handle the caseload. Private defense attorneys depend on high case turnover to earn a living, because most of their clients can afford only a modest fee. In short, all members of the courtroom work group have more cases to try than time or resources to try them (Eisenstein and Jacob 1977).

To a large extent, then, a trial is a mutual penalty that all parties seek to avoid through plea bargaining. To be sure, not all trials are avoided. But through plea bargaining, scarce trial resources can be applied to the cases that need to be tried.

What to Do with the Guilty

The adversary proceedings of trial are designed to resolve conflict over guilt or innocence. In practice, however, it is not the issue of legal guilt that is most often in dispute, but rather what sentence to impose on the guilty. Sentencing decisions involve more than the verdict of guilt or innocence presented at trial; they incorporate difficult issues of judgment about the type of crime and the nature of the defendant. Moreover, because of the standards of evidence, information relevant to sentencing is not easily introduced at trial (Mather 1979). Unlike a trial, plea bargaining does focus on what to do with an offender—particularly, how much leniency is appropriate.

Criminal statutes are broad; the courtroom work group is called upon to apply these broad prohibitions to specific and variable cases. The participants are concerned with adjusting the penalties to the specifics of the crime and the defendant. In the interest of fairness, they seek to individualize justice.

Consider a case with two codefendants of unequal culpability: an armed robbery involving an experienced robber who employed a youthful accomplice as a driver. Technically, both are equally guilty, but in the interest of fairness and substantive justice, the prosecutor may legitimately decide to make a concession to the young accomplice but none to the prime mover. In short, members of the courtroom work group seek to individualize justice.

BARGAINING AND THE COURTROOM WORK GROUP

Plea bargaining is a contest involving the prosecutor, defendant, defense counsel, and at times, the judge. Each party has its own objectives. Each attempts to structure the situation to its own advantage by using tactics to improve its bargaining position. Each defines success in terms of its own objectives. Among the conflicting objectives, accommodations are possible, because each side can achieve its objectives only by making concessions on other matters. Plea bargaining is typical of "most bargaining situations which ultimately involve some range of possible outcomes within which each party would rather make a concession than fail to reach agreement at all" (Schelling

COURT TV

Florida v. Danny Rolling: Coed Serial Killer

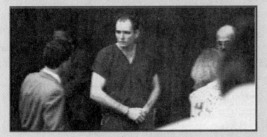

A college town is terrified by a spree of murders. Evidence at the crime scene, including DNA, points to Danny Rolling as the murderer. Rolling has previously served eight years in a Mississippi prison and blames poor prison conditions for his rage and murder spree.

By the time of trial, Danny Rolling is already serving five life sentences plus 270 years for a series of burglaries and armed robberies. Against the advice of his lawyer, Rolling pleads guilty. During the penalty phase of the murder trial, the defense mounts an insanity defense citing physical violence by the defendant's father.

View a video clip of this trial on your copy of the CourtTV CD-ROM. As you watch the video, keep the following questions in mind:

1. Why did the defense attorney advise Danny Rolling to go to trial rather than plead guilty? Are there any advantages for Rolling to plead guilty?

2. In what ways is Danny Rolling similar to other defendants in notorious crimes who insisted on acting as their own defense attorney (see Chapter 7)?

3. What does this case illustrate about the ability or inability of court-appointed lawyers to control their clients' behaviors (Chapter 7)?

4. What is Florida's standard for the insanity defense (see Chapter 14)? How does this standard affect the likelihood of the jury finding Rolling not guilty by reason of insanity?

1960, 70). Bargaining is also possible because each of the legal actors understands the realities of law in action: the presumption of guilt, the costs and uncertainties of trial, and the concern with arriving at an appropriate sentence. All these factors influence bargaining positions.

Prosecutors

To the prosecutor, a plea bargain represents the certainty of conviction without the risks of trial. Recall that prosecutors emphasize convictions. Because they value the deterrent objectives of law enforcement, they prefer that a guilty person be convicted of some charge rather than escape with no conviction at all.

The certainty and finality of a defendant's pleading guilty contrast sharply with the potential risks involved in a trial (Worden 1990). During trial, a number of unexpected events can occur, most of which work to the detriment of the prosecutor. The victim may refuse to cooperate. Witnesses' testimony may differ significantly from earlier statements made in investigative reports. There is always the possibility that a mistrial will be declared—the judge ends the trial without a verdict because of a major defect in the proceedings. Even after a jury verdict of guilty, the appellate courts may reverse, and the whole process must be repeated.

In seeking a conviction through a guilty plea, the prosecutor is in a unique position to control the negotiating process (Holmes, Daudistel, and Taggart 1992). To begin with, the prosecutor proceeds from a position of strength: In most cases, the state has sufficient evidence for conviction. If, however, the case is weak, the prosecutor can avoid the embarrassment of losing a case at trial by either dismissing it altogether or offering such a good deal that the defendant cannot refuse.

To improve their bargaining position, some prosecutors deliberately overcharge. "Sure, it's a lever," says one San Francisco prosecutor, referring to his office's practice of charging every nonautomobile homicide as murder. With unusual candor he adds, "And we charge theft, burglary, and the possession of burglar's tools, because we know that if we charged only burglary there would be a trial" (Alschuler 1968, 90).

Prosecutors, of course, control several of the forms of plea bargaining. They are in a position to offer a charge reduction or a count bargain. They can threaten to throw the book at a defendant who does not plead, or they may refuse to bargain at all. If the crime is a serious one and the defendant is viewed as very dangerous, the prosecutor may force the defendant either to plead on the nose, with no sentencing concessions, or to run the risk of trial and a harsher sentence for not having cooperated.

Defendants

If pleas give prosecutors what they want (convictions), why do defendants plead guilty? To understand plea bargaining, it is important to recognize that it is often in the defendant's best interest to give up the right to be presumed innocent at a trial. The primary benefit of a plea is the possibility of a lenient sentence.

Around the courthouse, it is a common perception that defendants who refuse to plead guilty receive harsher sentences. For example, a judge may impose a stiffer sentence because the defendant compounded the crime by lying on the witness stand or getting some friends to perjure themselves. Or a prosecutor may agree not to invoke state "career criminal" provisions, which impose higher penalties for those with a prior felony conviction. Moreover, for defendants who are unable to post bail, a guilty plea can mean an immediate release (either on probation or for time served).

Ultimately, defendants must decide whether to go along with the plea bargain or take their chances at trial. Few defendants are in a position to make a reasoned choice between the advantages of a plea and those of a trial; most are poor, inarticulate, and have little formal education. For these defendants, the experience in the courts is like their life on the streets: They learn to go along. Often softened up by the experience in jail awaiting trial, many defendants find that entering a plea is the best way to go along and avoid the possibility of even harsher penalties.

Defense Attorneys

If the prosecutor enters negotiations from a position of strength, the opposite is true of defense attorneys, who have few bargaining chips. If the chances of winning at trial are not high—and they rarely are—defense attorneys must consider the strong possibility that after a trial conviction the defendant may be penalized with a higher prison sentence.

The decision-making process for defense attorneys involves three phases. First, the defense attorney must assess the offer for a guilty plea, weighing the potential costs of delay against the likely outcome of a trial. Second, the defense attorney negotiates the terms of a plea bargain; if the initial offer is better than average, negotiations are less intense than if it is below average. Third, the defense attorney counsels the defendant, who may or may not accept the offer (Emmelman 1996).

The lawyer's main resource in negotiating a plea agreement is his or her knowledge of the courtroom work group—the types of pleas the prosecutor usually enters, the length of sentence the judge normally imposes in similar cases, and so on. Defense attorneys act as classic negotiators, trying to get the best deal possible for their clients while explaining to the clients the realistic alternatives. As noted in Chapter 7, these two roles can conflict. A defense attorney may negotiate what he or she considers the best deal under the circumstances, only to have the client refuse to go along.

Judges

Several factors limit a judge's ability to control or supervise plea bargaining. Given the division of powers in the adversary system, judges are reluctant to intrude on prosecutorial discretion. Many of the key bargaining mechanisms—specifically, the charges filed and the charges the defendant is allowed to plead to—are controlled by the prosecutor. Thus, when a prosecutor, defense attorney, and defendant have agreed either to a count bargain or a charge reduction bargain, the judge has no legal authority to refuse to accept the plea.

Even more fundamentally, the judge knows relatively little about each case. Only the prosecutor, defendant, and defense attorney know the evidence for and against the defendant. Without knowledge of why the parties agreed to plea-bargain, it is obviously difficult for a judge to reject a plea agreement. In short, the judge is dependent on the prosecutor and, to a lesser extent, the defense attorney.

Within these constraints, judges have some ability to shape the plea-bargaining process. The extent to which they are involved in the

THE MURDER TRIAL OF SHAREEF COUSIN

Pleading Guilty to Four Armed Robberies

 The defendant appeared before the bar of the court attended by Willard Hill. Through counsel, the defendant withdrew the former plea of not guilty and tendered to the court a plea of guilty as charged to R.S. 3 (Cts) 14; 64.

The legal and bureaucratic prose of this docket entry of September 28, 1995, gives little indication of the importance of the event. Shareef Cousin and his lawyer Willard Hill entered a plea of guilty to four armed robberies in other cases. (Although Cousin would not be sentenced until after the murder trial, the record indicates that a 20-year sentence had been agreed upon.) The pleas were entered while both sides were busily preparing for the upcoming murder trial and had major impacts on subsequent developments.

First, the pleas of guilty virtually guaranteed that Shareef Cousin would not testify at trial. If he had taken the stand in his own defense, the prosecution would have impeached his credibility by introducing certified copies of his four previous armed robbery convictions. Indeed, this would have provided the prosecution a back-door method of introducing what the law terms "signature crimes"—crimes committed by a criminal in a recurring and unique way.

Second, the four prior convictions were used during the penalty phase of the first-degree murder trial. Each of the four victims testified about the terror they experienced when robbed at gunpoint. One victim, for example, identified Shareef Cousin as the one who used a shotgun in a carjacking in which his 5-year-old daughter was present.

Third, the prosecution used the prior convictions to rule out mitigating circumstances during the penalty phase. One mitigating factor recognized by Louisiana law is that the defendant had no significant prior history of criminal activity. The defense now could not argue that issue to the jury.

Finally, two of the armed robberies were committed along with codefendant James Rowell.

During trial, Rowell became a turncoat prosecution witness; he was supposed to testify that Cousin had bragged of committing a murder, but he did not (see Chapter 14). The prosecution's attempt to impeach the credibility of its own witness would be the principal reason for appellate court reversal (see Chapter 17).

Two days after the jury recommended that Shareef Cousin die by lethal injection for the murder of Michael Gerardi, the defendant and his lawyers appeared before Judge Bigelow for sentencing on the four armed robbery pleas. After imposing the 20-year sentence, the judge allowed Cousin to fire his trial lawyers. The new counsel was Clive Stafford-Smith, who would later argue the appeal (see Chapter 17) and file the federal civil rights lawsuit discussed in Chapter 3.

Stafford-Smith immediately moved to set aside the four guilty pleas, arguing that Cousin had entered the pleas on "erroneous advice of counsel." Moreover, the motion argued that Cousin was factually innocent of two of the four crimes charged (Cousin admitted only to being in the car when the codefendants committed the armed robberies). The judge denied the motion, and the state's Fourth Circuit Court of Appeals agreed.

Anti–death penalty activists contend that Cousin was coerced into pleading to armed robbery, but the court record offers a different conclusion. On March 27, 1995, NOPD officer Christy Williams asked Shareef Cousin (with his mother present) what he knew about the carjacking on March 4, and he replied: "It was me, Dwayne, James, and Brent." After Dwayne committed the carjacking, "I jumped in the car." Moreover, during the penalty phase of the trial, defense attorney Willard Hill admitted that Shareef had committed some despicable acts. As for the judge, he commented, "Some of us might agree he was going to receive a relatively light sentence for the armed robberies—twenty years. I think as part of the plea, Mr. Hill may have mistakenly thought he wouldn't be convicted in the murder trial."

process varies greatly. A survey of state trial court judges (Ryan and Alfini 1979) revealed four basic patterns.

■ A few judges are actively involved in plea negotiations, offering recommendations about case disposition.

■ Some judges are indirectly involved, reviewing the recommendations made by defense and prosecutor.

■ A small percentage of judges attend plea discussions but do not participate.

■ The majority of judges do not attend plea-negotiating sessions. Thus, their role is limited to ratifying agreements reached by others.

Even judges who only ratify plea negotiations can have an important impact on the process. Regular members of the courtroom work group know the sentence the judge is likely to impose. Therefore, they negotiate case dispositions that incorporate these sentencing expectations. On rare occasions, judges may reject a plea agreement. Such rejections serve to set a baseline for future negotiations.

The extent to which a judge is actively involved in plea-bargaining negotiations is influenced by a number of factors. One is the judge's perception of his or her own negotiating skills. Judges who view themselves as effective negotiators are more likely to be active participants. Judges in large cities are also more likely to be active participants (Ryan and Alfini 1979). More stable courtroom work groups likewise tend to encourage the involvement of judges (Worden 1995). On the other hand, some states have adopted clear statements prohibiting judges from participating in plea negotiations. In these states, judicial participation is rare (Ryan and Alfini 1979).

DYNAMICS OF BARGAINING

Negotiating is a group activity, typically conducted in busy, noisy, public courtrooms. In such a courtroom, the initial impression is of constant talking and endless movement. While the judge is hearing a pretrial motion in one

case, a prosecutor and defense attorney are engaged in an animated conversation about a charge reduction in another. Meanwhile, in more hushed tones, a public defender is briefing his client about why a continuance will be requested, and nearby a mother is talking to her son who is being held in jail. These numerous conversations occur while other participants continually move in and out. Police officers leave after testifying in a motion to suppress, bail agents arrive to check on their clients, clerks bring in new files, and lawyers search for the prosecutor assigned to their case. Occasionally, the noise becomes so loud that the judge or bailiff demands silence—a request that usually produces only a temporary reduction in the decibel level.

On the surface, courtrooms appear disorganized. In fact, there is an underlying order to the diverse activities. For example, when the judge calls a case, the other participants involved in that matter are immediately expected to drop all other business and proceed to the front of the court. (Maynard 1984). Decision-making norms govern the substance of the negotiations. In particular, there are patterns to why some cases go to trial and understandings about penalties for those who do go to trial.

Decision-Making Norms

Through working together on a daily basis, the members of the courtroom work group come to understand the problems and demands of the others. They develop shared conceptions of how certain types of cases and defendants should be treated. Everyone except the outsider or the novice knows these customs of the courthouse.

As we have seen, plea bargaining is a complex process, but studies in different courts reveal important similarities in shared norms. The most important consideration is the seriousness of the offense. The more serious the crime charged, the harder the prosecutor bargains (Mather 1979; Nardulli, Flemming, and Eisenstein 1984). The next most important factor is the defendant's criminal record. Those with prior convictions receive fewer concessions during bargaining (Alschuler 1979; Nardulli 1978; Springer 1983; Smith 1986). Another key consideration is the strength of the prosecutor's case. The stronger the evidence against the defendant, the fewer concessions are offered (Adams 1983; Smith 1986).

These shared norms structure plea negotiations. In each courtroom work group, there is a well understood set of allowable reductions. Based on the way the crime was committed and the background of the defendant, nighttime burglary will be reduced to daytime burglary, drunkenness to disturbing the peace, and so on. Thus, contrary to many popular fears, defendants are not allowed to plead to just any charge (Feeley 1979). If a defendant has been charged with armed robbery, the defense attorney knows that the credibility of her bargaining position will be destroyed if she suggests a plea to disturbing the peace. Such a plea would be out of line with how things are normally done.

Courtroom work groups have similar shared norms about sentencing. On the basis of these shared norms, all parties know what is open for bargaining and what is not. The shared norms provide a baseline for disposing of specific cases. Upward or downward adjustments are made, depending on the circumstances of the individual case.

Why Cases Go to Trial

Although most cases are disposed of by a guilty plea, an important 2 percent to 10 percent of defendants are tried. Cases go to trial when the parties cannot settle a case through negotiation. In large measure, the factors that shape plea bargaining—the strength of the prosecutor's case and the severity of the penalty—are the same ones that enter into the decision to go to trial. Defense attorneys recommend a trial when the risks of trial are low and the possible gains are high.

This broad calculation leads to two very different types of trial cases. In one, the possible gains for the defendant are high because there is a chance of an acquittal. There may be reasonable doubt that the defendant committed any crime, or two sets of witnesses may tell conflicting versions of what happened (Neubauer 1974). A second category of cases going to trial involves situations in which the prison sentence will be high. Even though a judge or jury is not likely to return a verdict of not guilty, the defen-

dant may still decide that the slim possibility of an acquittal is worth the risk of the trial penalty.

However, not all trial cases are the result of such rational calculations. Some defendants insist on a trial, no matter what. Judges, prosecutors, and defense attorneys label as irrational defendants who refuse to recognize the realities of the criminal justice system and insist on a trial even when the state has a strong case (Neubauer 1974). The net effect of these considerations is that some types of cases are more likely to go to trial than others. Property offenses (burglary and larceny) are much less likely to go to trial than homicide, sexual assault, or robbery. Mather (1974) suggests that property crimes are least likely to go to trial because the state is apt to have a strong case (usually buttressed by the presence of indisputable physical evidence) and the prison sentence will not be long. Serious crimes such as murder, rape, and robbery are much more likely to be tried. In some crimes of violence, there may be reasonable doubt, because the victim may have provoked the attack. Moreover, a convicted defendant is likely to serve a long prison term and is therefore more disposed to take a chance on an outright acquittal.

Jury Trial Penalty

Although most defendants plead guilty, a significant minority of cases do go to trial. As previously indicated, it is a common assumption in courthouses around the nation that defendants who do not enter a plea of guilty can expect to receive harsher sentences. Typically called the *jury trial penalty*, the notion reflects the philosophy, "He takes some of my time, I take some of his." Here, time refers to the hours spent hearing evidence presented to a jury (Uhlman and Walker 1980; Heumann 1978).

Several studies provide empirical documentation for these courthouse perceptions (Brereton and Casper 1981–1982). In a major eastern city, "the cost of a jury trial for convicted defendants in Metro City is high: sentences are substantially more severe than for other defendants" (Uhlman and Walker 1980, 337). However, such findings have not gone unchallenged. Research on some other courts was unable to document the existence of a jury trial penalty (Rhodes 1978). In their three-city study, Eisenstein and Jacob (1977) concluded that "the effect of dispositional mode was insignificant in accounting for the variance in sentence length" (270). Read together, these various studies suggest that it is difficult to draw conclusions about nationwide practices because of the tremendous discrepancies among jurisdictions. Moreover, it appears that the jury trial penalty may be applied more selectively than earlier research indicated.

Despite the uncertainty over the extent of the jury trial penalty, the U.S. Supreme Court has clearly sanctioned the practice. A Kentucky defendant accused of forging an $88 check was offered a five-year prison sentence if he entered a plea of guilty. But the prosecutor indicated that if the defendant rejected the offer, the state would seek to impose life imprisonment because of the defendant's previous two felony convictions. Such stepped-up sentences for habitual criminals were allowed at that time by Kentucky law. The defendant rejected the plea, went to trial, was convicted, and was eventually sentenced to life imprisonment. In *Bordenkircher v. Hayes* (1978), the high court held, "The course of conduct engaged in by the prosecutor in this case, which no more than openly presented the defendant with the unpleasant alternative of forgoing trial or facing charges on which he was plainly subject to prosecution" did not violate constitutional protections. In dissent, however, Justice Powell noted that the offer of five years in prison "hardly could be characterized as a generous offer." He was clearly troubled that "persons convicted of rape and murder often are not punished so severely" as this check forger. See Exhibit 13-2 for other key legal developments involving plea bargaining.

■ COPPING A PLEA

"Your honor, my client wishes at this time to withdraw his previous plea of not guilty and wishes at this time to enter a plea of guilty." In phrases similar to this one, defense attorneys indicate that the case is about to end; the defendant is ready to plead. A plea of guilty is more than an admission of conduct; it is a conviction that also involves a defendant's waiver of the most vital rights of the court process: presumption of innocence, jury trial, and confrontation of witnesses (*Boykin v. Alabama*, 1969).

As recently as the 1960s, the process of entering a plea of guilty was usually brief and informal. Because the courts and the legal process as a whole were reluctant to recognize the existence of plea bargaining, little law guided the process. Under the leadership of Chief Justice Warren Burger, however, the U.S. Supreme Court sought to set standards for the plea-bargaining process (see Case Close-up: *Santobello v. New York* and Honoring a Plea Agreement).

Questioning the Defendant

In limited circumstances, a defendant will enter a plea of **nolo contendere**—Latin for "I will not contest it." Although a plea of nolo contendere has the same results in criminal proceedings as a plea of guilty, it cannot be used in a subsequent civil proceeding as a defendant's admission of guilt. Thus, this plea is usually entered when civil proceedings and liabilities may result. Most defendants plead guilty to one or more charges listed in the charging document. Before a defendant's plea of guilty can be accepted, the judge must question the defendant. This was not always the case; judges once merely accepted the attorney's statement that the defendant wanted to plead guilty. But in *Boykin v. Alabama* the Supreme Court ruled: "It was error, for the trial judge to accept petitioner's guilty plea without an affirmative showing that it was intelligent and voluntary."

The judge inquires whether the defendant understands the nature of the charge and the possible penalty upon conviction, whether any threats were made, if the defendant is satisfied with the services of defense counsel, and whether the defendant realizes that a plea waives the right to a jury trial. A typical *Boykin* form is shown in Exhibit 13-3. Such questioning serves to ensure that the guilty plea reflects the defendant's own choice, is made with a general understanding of the charges and consequences of conviction, and has not been improperly influenced by the prosecution, law

CASE CLOSE-UP

Santobello v. New York and

Rudolph Santobello was indicted on two counts: promoting gambling in the first degree and possession of gambling records in the first degree, both felonies under New York law. After negotiations with the prosecutor's office in the Bronx, Santobello entered a plea to the lesser included offense of possession of gambling records in the second degree, and the prosecutor also agreed to make no recommendation as to the sentence.

Months lapsed, though, before sentencing. A new defense attorney was hired, and he moved to suppress the evidence on grounds of an illegal search and seizure. The trial judge retired. Another assistant DA assumed control over the case (it is unclear whether his predecessor was promoted or resigned to take a job in private practice). Months later, when Santobello appeared for sentencing, the new prosecutor recommended the maximum one-year sentence. The judge quickly imposed this sentence, leaving no doubt of his thoughts about the defendant. Reading the probation report, he said: "I have here a history of a long, long serious criminal record. . . . He is unamenable to supervision in the community. He is a professional criminal." The judge concluded by regretting that a one-year sentence was all he was allowed to impose.

Chief Justice Warren Burger was beginning his second term on the court. Despite being a product of the law-and-order movement, his decision begins by noting the sloppiness apparent in the DA's office. "This record represents another example of an unfortunate lapse in orderly pros-

pleas fly "in the face of what crime and punishment should be all about." Thus he does not accept pleas "in cases where culpability is so obvious that the public has a right to know about it" (quoted in Steinberger 1985).

Placing the Plea Agreement on the Record

For years, plea negotiations were officially considered taboo. As a result, the taking of a plea

ORLEANS
LOUISIANA
N "J"
ANNIZZARO, JR.

CASE NO. _____

VIO:R.S. _____

L RIGHTS / PLEA OF GUILTY

ILTY to the crime of _____ ,
ch I am pleading guilty. _____
                        (Defendant's Initials)

ry and if convicted a right to appeal and by entering
rial and appeal. _____
                (Defendant's Initials)

g guilty have been explained to me as well as the fact
of _____ .
                    (Defendant's Initials)

my right to confront and cross-examine the witnesses
ry process of the court to require witnesses to appear

m, in fact, guilty of this crime. _____
                                 (Defendant's Initials)

making this plea. _____
                  (Defendant's Initials)

my attorney and the way in which my attorney has

inst self-incrimination, that at my trial I would not
ge nor the Jury could hold that against me. I also give
against my interest, such as I am doing by pleading

right to have competent counsel to represent me at
hese rights. _____
             (Defendant's Initials)

nd that no other promises which may have been made
rgain are enforceable or binding. _____
                                  (Defendant's Initials)

_____
DEFENDANT

_____
ATTORNEY FOR THE DEFENDANT

these matters and has given me the opportunity to

_____
DEFENDANT

public disclosure allows defendants and attorneys to correct any misunderstandings. Indeed, the Federal Rules of Criminal Procedure make this practice mandatory in federal courts.

To ensure fairness in negotiations between defense and prosecution, the law now gives defendants a limited right to withdraw a guilty plea. In *Santobello v. New York* (1971), Chief Justice Warren Burger wrote, "When a plea rests in any significant degree on a promise or agreement of the prosecutor, so that it can be said to be a part of the inducement or consideration, such promise must be fulfilled." Subsequent decisions likewise held that defendants must live up to their end of the plea agreement (*Ricketts v. Adamson* 1987).

LAW IN CONTROVERSY: ABOLISHING PLEA BARGAINING

Chief Justice Burger's opinion in *Santobello* supports plea bargaining because it contributes to the efficiency of the criminal justice processes. But some people find justifying plea bargaining merely on the basis of expediency to be unconvincing. What of justice? some legitimately ask. (See Courts, Controversy, and the Administration of Justice: Who Benefits from Plea Bargaining?)

Doubts about plea bargaining have resulted in attempts in some jurisdictions to abolish or reform the practice. Such efforts conform to one of the most controversial recommendations of the National Advisory Commission on Criminal Justice Standards and Goals (1973), which recommended abolishing plea bargaining altogether. This recommendation was prompted by the commission's view that plea bargaining produces undue leniency. The main weakness of the commission's recommendation to abolish plea bargaining is that it fails to recognize the importance of law in action (Rosett and Cressey 1976). The commission seemed preoccupied with an idealized criminal law that is clear and precise and that does not have to accommodate messy disagreements.

Faced with mounting public criticism and professional concern, prosecutors and judges in a number of American communities have altered traditional plea-bargaining practices. Claims that plea bargaining has been abolished or that major reforms have been instituted require critical analysis. As a result of a growing number of studies of such efforts, some important areas of interest can be highlighted.

Are the Changes Implemented?

In analyzing the impact of changes in plea-bargaining practices, a basic question is whether the changes were indeed implemented. Written policy changes do not always alter the behavior of court actors. For example, some efforts to reform plea bargaining met with resistance from defense attorneys and others. As a result, the programs did not have their intended impact and were later dropped (Nimmer and Krauthaus 1977). A similar pattern was observed in a northern California county. After the grand jury publicly criticized plea bargaining for undue leniency, the prosecutor responded by trying to eliminate plea bargaining. The defense attorneys then began to take more cases to trial. After the state lost 12 out of 16 jury verdicts, the prosecutor quietly returned to the old policies (Carter 1974). Of course, not all efforts at reform are short-lived. In some jurisdictions, efforts at reforming plea bargaining have been successfully implemented (Nimmer and Krauthaus 1977; Heumann and Loftin 1979).

Is Discretion Eliminated or Just Moved Elsewhere?

Even when programs are successfully implemented, they may not have the impact intended. Discretion in the criminal justice system (see Chapter 5) has been likened to a hydraulic process. Efforts to control discretion at one stage typically result in its displacement to another part of the process. Thus, the result of "abolishing" or "reforming" plea bargaining is often that the activity simply moves elsewhere. Such a hydraulic process occurred in California after the voters approved Proposition 8 in 1982. One of the key provisions of this victim's bill of rights (see Chapter 9) prohibits plea

COURTS, CONTROVERSY, AND THE ADMINISTRATION OF JUSTICE

Who Benefits from Plea Bargaining?

Some people within the court system are concerned that plea bargaining reduces the courthouse to a place where guilt or innocence is negotiated in the same way as one might haggle over the price of copper jugs at a Turkish bazaar (Rubin 1976). Primarily, though, opposition to plea bargaining reflects different ideological preferences. What is particularly interesting is that civil libertarians as well as spokespersons for law and order see plea bargaining as a danger, but often for different reasons.

Does Plea Bargaining Sacrifice Defendants' Rights?

Supporters of the values of the due process model are concerned that plea bargaining undercuts the protections afforded individuals, may lead to the conviction of innocent defendants, and produces few tangible benefits for defendants. This view is aptly expressed by the leading academic critic of plea bargaining, law professor Albert Alschuler (1975): "Today's guilty plea system leads even able, conscientious, and highly motivated attorneys to make decisions that are not really in their clients' interests" (1180).

A prime concern of due process adherents is that a criminal court process geared to produce guilty pleas negates the fundamental protection of the adversary system—a public trial in which the defendant is presumed innocent—because plea bargaining discourages trials by imposing a penalty on those who lose at trial. They therefore advocate abolishing bargaining and increasing the number of trials. However, such a position ignores the reality of criminal courts: In most cases, there is no substantial disagreement over the facts. Moreover, civil libertarian critics look to the jury as the proper forum for sifting guilt from innocence. Yet experienced trial attorneys often have grave doubts about such an approach. In the words of a Los Angeles public defender: "If you've got an exceptional case—one which is weak and there's a good chance that the defendant may be innocent—then you don't want to take it before a jury because you never know what they'll do" (Mather 1974a, 202).

Do the Guilty Benefit?

If advocates of due process are worried that plea bargaining jeopardizes the rights of the individual, the backers of the crime control model express the opposite concern. They believe that plea bargaining allows defendants to avoid conviction for crimes they actually committed, results in lenient sentences, and in general gives criminal wrongdoers the impression that the courts and the law are easily manipulated. In the words of the Pima County, Arizona, prosecutor, "Plea bargains send the wrong message. When criminal offenders are permitted to plead guilty to lesser charges with lesser penalties, the credibility of the entire system is corrupted" (LaWall 2001).

It is not a difficult task to single out individual cases in which these law enforcement criticisms of plea bargaining have merit. But the argument obscures too much. In particular, it confuses cause with effect. A bargained agreement on reduced charges, for example, may be the product of initial overcharging and/or of evidence problems that surface later. Moreover, such criticisms suggest that in plea bargaining anything goes— the prosecutor and judge will make any deal to dispose of a case. In reality, each court employs a more or less consistent approach to what charge or count reductions are customary, plus a set of sentencing rules of thumb.

Many of the law enforcement criticisms of plea bargaining may be reduced to an overall displeasure with the leniency of the courts. Whether sentences are too harsh or too lenient should be a separate issue from the vehicle for reaching these sentencing dispositions.

What do you think? Does plea bargaining sacrifice the rights of the defendant, or do the guilty benefit?

To continue the debate, go to the following Web sites, which offer opposing points of view:

"Should We Really 'Ban' Plea Bargaining? The Core Concerns of Plea Bargaining Critics" at **http://www. law.emory.edu/ELJ/volumes/spg98/guido.html**

Steven Silverblatt, "The Problem with Plea Bargaining" at **http://brooklyngoclub.org/jc/coercion.html**

A Virtual Tour of American Courthouses: Plea Bargaining

To learn the basics about plea bargaining, read the article "Understanding Plea Bargaining" at **http://www.lawsguide.com/mylawyer/guideview.asp?layer=2&article=147** A lawyer's self-promotion piece: George Fisher, "Plea Bargaining's Triumph."

For an article on the history of plea bargaining in one Massachusetts county, go to **http://www.yale.edu/yalelj/109/109-5ab.html**. For an up-close look at Supreme Court cases concerning plea bargaining, go to Oyez Web site at **http://www.oyez.org/oyez/portlet/directory/0/14/**.

Plea bargaining is a topic often discussed on Web sites offered by defense attorneys. The following offer both practical advice and also inducements as to why this particular lawyer should be hired. In "Heart of the Deal: Ten Suggestions for Plea Bargaining," a veteran defense attorney addresses plea bargaining in death penalty cases at **http://www.criminaljustice.org/public.nsf/0/1893d456344b3217852568230072340e?OpenDocument**. A public defender from Kentucky writes about "The Criminal Defense Lawyer As Effective Negotiator: A Systemic Approach" at **http://dpa.state.ky.us/advocate/sept98/systematic.html**. Similarly, see **http://www.hmichaelsteinberg.com/pleabargaining.htm**. For down and dirty views, go to "You Never Have to Accept an Offered Plea Bargain" at **http://www.kelattorneys.com/stages12.htm**

and "How to Beat a Speeding Ticket" at **http://www.jesbeard.com/s4.htm**.

Prosecutors approach plea bargaining from a different perspective than defense attorneys. The following sites offer a variety of prosecutorial views. See the policy statement of the Queens County, New York, DA at **http://www.queensdefense.com/annotated_policy.htm**. Andrew L. Sonner, State's Attorney for Montgomery County, Rockville, Maryland, provides a concept paper on plea bargaining at **http://www.abanet.org/ceeli/conceptpapers/CrimProcedure/crimpro1.html**.

One group noted for its opposition to plea bargaining is Mothers Against Drunk Driving (MADD). To read their views, go to **http://www3.madd.org/laws/law.cfm?LawID=ANTI**.

For a perspective on plea bargaining in other countries, visit the following sites:

Israel
http://mishpatim.mscc.huji.ac.il/ilr/ilr31_1j.htm

Australia and Canada
http://www.academon.com/lib/paper/20944.html

Philippines
http://www.mapinc.org/drugnews/v02/n1485/a07.html

---

bargaining for 25 of the most serious crimes. The ban applied only to the major trial court, however. Proposition 8 did not abolish plea bargaining but rather relocated it to the lower court, where the proportion of bargained cases increased (McCoy 1984). Indeed, the overall level of plea bargaining increased. Far from helping the victims of crime, the acceleration of plea bargaining prevented both victims and defendants from understanding the reasons for convictions and sentences (McCoy 1993).

Alaska provides another clear example. In that state, the attorney general forbade assistant prosecutors from engaging in plea bargaining or from making sentencing recommendations to the judge. Judges complained that their responsibilities increased dramatically, meaning

they had very little opportunity to give sentencing thorough consideration (Rubenstein and White 1979, 277). The hydraulic process seems to explain why a later reevaluation of Alaska's plea-bargaining ban found clear evidence of both evolution and decay in the policy. For example, charge bargaining had reemerged in most of the state (Carns and Kruse 1992).

Do Offsetting Changes Occur?

Efforts to abolish or change plea-bargaining practices may produce offsetting changes. This was the conclusion of an excellent in-depth study of a Michigan county (Church 1976). After a law-and-order antidrug campaign, the newly elected prosecuting attorney instituted a strict policy forbidding charge-reduction plea bargaining in drug sale cases. One result was an increased demand for trials, although it was not as great as some judges feared. But at the same time, outright dismissals because of insufficient evidence increased. Moreover, a much greater percentage of defendants were sentenced as juveniles rather than adults so that they would not have a felony record. Most important, plea bargaining involving defense attorneys and judges continued in drug cases, and the assistant prosecutor's ability to control the disposition of the case weakened.

Efforts to increase sentence severity by abolishing or constraining plea bargaining are not always successful. When the Coast Guard effectively eliminated plea bargains in special courts-martial, there was no increase in sentence severity (Call, England, and Talarico 1983). In short, attempts to abolish plea bargaining often produce a number of offsetting changes because overall policies fail to consider the reasons for negotiations.

CONCLUSION

Most of the Supreme Court decisions highlighted in this book deal with serious crimes—quite often murder and the death penalty. Perhaps the Court decided to rule on *Santo-*

bello because the underlying charge was a minor one. After all, establishing new rules for plea bargaining would prove less controversial if the crime was not a violent one. Nonetheless, it is still curious that Burger's opinion states so many negatives about Santobello, leaving little doubt that this small-time alleged member of one of New York's crime families was hardly a model citizen. As for Santobello, the man, little else is known. In covering the case, the *New York Times* discussed only the legal issues, not the local man whose name is now enshrined in a major Supreme Court pronouncement.

Plea bargaining vividly illustrates the difference between law on the books and law in action. The rules of criminal procedure, decisions of appellate courts, and theories of the adversary system suggest that the trial is the principal activity of the criminal courts. Instead, plea bargaining is the predominant activity. Bargaining is best understood not as a response to the press of cases but as an adaptation to the realities of the types of cases requiring court disposition. In most cases, there is little question about the defendant's legal guilt. A trial is a costly and sometimes risky method of establishing that guilt, and it cannot wrestle with the most pressing issue: what sentence to impose on the guilty. Finally, through plea bargaining, courthouse officials are able to individualize justice. In short, it is neither necessary nor desirable that every defendant have a trial.

CRITICAL THINKING QUESTIONS

1. Should a defendant be allowed to plead guilty without fully admitting guilt? Would you limit *Alford* pleas to situations in which the defendant wishes to avoid the death penalty? Would you allow white-collar defendants to enter *Alford* pleas? Some federal judges will not because they perceive that high-ranking corporate officials want to end the criminal cases without accepting full responsibility for their actions.

2. What types of plea agreements were involved in *Santobello*—charge, count, or sentence? Was the nature of the agreement implicit or explicit? How would you characterize the working relationships between defense and prosecution in *Santobello*?

3. Do defendants benefit from plea bargaining in terms of lower sentences, or is plea bargaining largely a shell game in which defendants are manipulated to think they are getting a good deal?

KEY TERMS

Boykin form (296)
charge bargaining (286)
count bargaining (286)
nolo contendere (296)
plea bargaining (285)
plea on the nose (287)
sentence bargaining (287)

WORLD WIDE WEB RESOURCES AND EXERCISES

Web Search Term

plea bargaining

Useful URLs

The most recent criminal case processing statistics are available from the Bureau of Justice Statistics at **http://www.ojp.usdoj.gov/bjs/cases.htm**.

For an update on the Alaskan plea bargaining ban, go to the Alaska Judicial Council Web site at **http://www.ajc.state.ak.us/Reports/pleafram.htm**.

This site offers a defense attorney's views on plea bargaining: **http://www.thebestdefense.com/criminal process/thecase/bargaining.html**.

Uncommon URLs

Professor Valerie Hans of the University of Delaware uses a plea-bargaining simulation in her class: **http://www.udel.edu/cte/aboutteach/fall99/hans.html**.

Web Exercises

1. Rule 11 of the Federal Rules of Criminal Procedure deals with plea bargaining. The Federal Rules can be found at **http://www.courtrules.org/frc.htm**. Select Procedure Rule 11. Why do you think the rule is so detailed? Many states also have placed their rules of procedure on the Web.

Search for the applicable rule in your state. Is it as detailed as the federal rule?

2. Using Yahoo, do a search for "plea bargain." (The use of quotation marks is important!) Find news stories of cases in which plea bargains have been accepted (or rejected). What societal reactions appear to be most important? Are the people quoted more likely or less likely to believe that the plea bargain achieved a just result?

3. Use the search engine of your choice to search for articles on plea bargaining. Read several articles. Do the materials appear to be favorable to plea bargaining or opposed to its use? Do the articles appear to reflect the due process model or the crime control model? What types of factual situations are used to advance the author's position?

4. Use a search engine to search on the phrase "plea bargaining." (Again, the use of quotation marks is important; you will find that this search yields different results from one limited to "plea bargain.") Visit several sites that discuss plea bargaining, and examine the reasons they advance for why plea bargaining should be retained or why it should be abolished.

INFOTRAC COLLEGE EDITION RESOURCES AND EXERCISES

Basic Search Term

plea bargaining

Recommended Articles

George Fisher, "Plea Bargaining's Triumph"

Michael Gorr, "The Morality of Plea Bargaining"

Gerard E. Lynch, "Screening versus Plea Bargaining: Exactly What Are We Trading Off?"

Eli Mazur, "Rational Expectations of Leniency"

Ronald Wright, Marc Miller, "The Screening/Bargaining Tradeoff"

InfoTrac College Edition Exercises

1. According to Peter Nardulli (1978), defenders of plea bargaining tend to see guilty pleas occurring when the state has a very strong case, whereas opponents tend to see them occurring most frequently when the evidence is weak. Analyze this proposition, using the search term "plea bargaining" to find two or more articles on the subject.

2. Should *Alford* pleas be allowed? Using the search term "plea bargaining," find two or more articles on the topic. Here are two articles that express opposite points of view:

   Albert Alschuler, "Straining at Gnats and Swallowing Camels: The Selective Morality of Professor Bibas"

   Stephanos Bibas, "Bringing Moral Values into a Flawed Plea-Bargaining System"

FOR FURTHER READING

Lynch, David. "The Impropriety of Plea Agreements: A Tale of Two Counties." *Law and Social Inquiry* 19 (1994): 115–136.

McCoy, Candace. *Politics and Plea Bargaining: Victim's Rights in California.* Philadelphia: University of Pennsylvania Press, 1993.

Nardulli, Peter, James Eisenstein, and Roy Flemming. *The Tenor of Justice: Criminal Courts and the Guilty Plea Process.* Champaign: University of Illinois Press, 1988.

Nasheri, Hedieh. *Betrayal of Due Process: A Comparative Assessment of Plea Bargaining in the United States and Canada.* Lanham, MD: University Press of America, 1998.

Newman, Donald. *Conviction: The Determination of Guilt or Innocence Without Trial.* Boston: Little, Brown, 1966.

Chapter **14** Trials and Juries

PART III
Processing the Accused

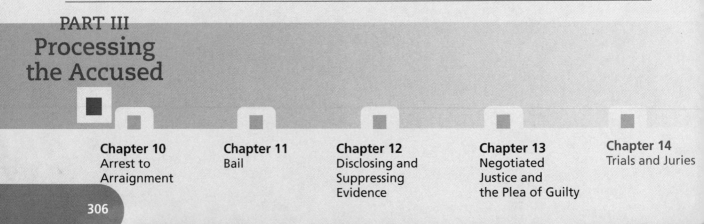

Why Isn't Sam Sheppard in Jail?" screamed the headline of a front-page editorial in a prominent Cleveland newspaper. For weeks, vivid headlines like these made it clear that the press thought the police were not pressing hard enough in arresting Dr. Samuel Sheppard—a socially prominent physician—for the brutal murder of his wife. After conviction, Sheppard served 12 years in prison before the Supreme Court reversed the conviction, likening the trial to a "Roman holiday" (*Sheppard v. Maxwell* 1966). In holding that prejudicial pretrial publicity denied Sheppard the right to a fair and impartial trial, the Court set off a long and often heated battle over where freedom of the press ends and the right to a fair trial begins. ◄

Trials attract more attention than any other step of the judicial process. The national media provide detailed accounts of the trials of celebrities like Sam Sheppard and O. J. Simpson. The local media offer extensive coverage of the trials of local notables, brazen murderers, and the like. Books, movies, and television use courtroom encounters to entertain. The importance of trials, however, extends far beyond the considerable public attention lavished on them. They are central to the entire scheme of Anglo-American law. Trials provide the ultimate forum for vindicating the innocence of the accused or the liability of the defendant. For this reason, the right to be tried by a jury of one's peers is guaranteed in several places in the Constitution.

Given the marked public interest in trials, as well as their centrality to American law, we would expect trials to be the prime ingredient in the criminal court process. They are not. Trials are relatively rare events. As Chapter 13 established, roughly 95 percent of all felony convictions result from guilty pleas. In a fundamental sense, then, a trial represents a deviant case. But at the same time, the few cases that are tried have a major impact on the operations of the entire criminal justice system. Trials are the balance wheel of the process, determining how members of the courtroom work group bargain cases.

HISTORY OF TRIAL BY JURY

The primary purpose of the jury is to prevent oppression by the government and provide the accused a "safeguard against the corrupt or overzealous prosecutor and against the compliant, biased, or eccentric judge" (*Williams v. Florida* 1970). Ideally, juries are made up of fair-minded citizens who represent a cross section of the local community. Once selected, their role is to judge the facts of the case. During trial, the judge rules on questions of law, but the jury decides the weight of the evidence and the credibility to give to the testimony of witnesses.

Trial juries are also called **petit juries,** to differentiate them from grand juries. The jury system represents a commitment to the role of laypeople in the administration of justice. The views and actions of judges and lawyers are constrained by a group of average citizens who are amateurs in the ways of the law (Kalven and Zeisel 1966).

English Roots

The trial by jury has roots deep in Western history. Used in Athens five or six centuries before the birth of Christ, juries were later employed by the Romans. They reappeared in France during the ninth century and were transferred to England from there. The concept of the jury functioning as an impartial fact-finding body was first formalized in the Magna Carta of 1215, when English noblemen forced the king to recognize limits on the power of the Crown.

No Freeman shall be taken or imprisoned, or be disseized of his Freehold, or Liberties, or free Customs, or be outlawed, or exiled or otherwise destroyed, nor will we pass upon him nor condemn him but by lawful judgment of his peers or by Law of the Land.

This protection applied only to nobility (freemen). Its extension to the average citizen occurred several centuries later. Thus in the centuries after the Magna Carta, the legal status of the jury continued to evolve. Early English juries often functioned more like modern-day grand juries. Only later did they become impartial bodies, selected from citizens who knew nothing of the alleged event.

Colonial Developments

By the time the U.S. Constitution was written, jury trials in criminal cases had been in existence in England for several centuries. This legal principle was transferred to the American colonies and later written into the Constitution. The pivotal role that the right to trial by jury plays in American law is underscored by the number of times it is mentioned in the Constitution.

Article III, Section 2, provides that "the trial of all crimes, except cases of impeachment shall be by jury and such trial shall be held in the state where the said crimes shall have been committed." This section not only guarantees the right to a trial by jury to persons accused by the national government of a crime but also specifies that such trials shall be held near the place of the offense. This prevents the government from harassing defendants by trying them far from home.

The Sixth Amendment guarantees that "in all criminal prosecutions, the accused shall enjoy the right to a speedy and public trial, by an impartial jury." The requirement of a public trial prohibits secret trials, a device commonly used by dictators to silence their opponents.

The Seventh Amendment provides: "In suits at common law . . . the right to trial by jury shall be preserved." This provision is a historical testament to the fact that the framers of the Constitution greatly distrusted the judges of the day.

LAW ON THE BOOKS: THE CONSTITUTION AND TRIAL BY JURY

Throughout most of our nation's history, the three broad constitutional provisions dealing with trial by jury had little applicability in state courts. The U.S. Constitution applied only to trials in federal courts. These practices changed dramatically, however, when the Supreme Court ruled that the jury provisions of the Sixth Amendment applied to state as well as federal courts (*Duncan v. Louisiana* 1968). (Technically, the Sixth Amendment was incorporated into the due process clause of the Fourteenth Amendment, which restricts state power.) Subsequent decisions grappled with the problem of defining the precise meaning of the right to trial by jury. (Exhibit 14-1 summarizes key decisions.) The most important issues concerned the scope of the right to a jury trial, the size of the jury, and unanimous versus nonunanimous verdicts.

Scope of the Right to a Trial by Jury

Although juries are considered "fundamental to the American scheme of justice" (*Duncan v. Louisiana* 1968), not all persons accused of violating the criminal law are entitled to a trial by jury. Youths prosecuted as juvenile offenders have no right to have their cases heard by a jury (Sanborn 1993). Similarly, adult offenders charged with **petty offenses** enjoy no right to be tried by a jury of their peers. The Sixth Amendment covers only adults charged with serious offenses. In this context, "no offense can be deemed 'petty' for the purposes of the right to trial by jury where imprisonment for more than six months is authorized" (*Baldwin v. New York* 1970). As a result, drunk drivers in five states—Louisiana, Mississippi, Nevada, New Jersey, and New Mexico—have no right to a jury trial if they face a jail term of six months or less (*Blanton v. City of North Las Vegas* 1989). Some state constitutions, however, guarantee a jury trial to anyone facing any criminal charge whatsoever, including traffic offenses.

Jury Size

During the fourteenth century, the size of English juries became fixed at twelve. Although some colonies experimented with smaller juries in less important trials, the number twelve was universally accepted by the time of the

American Revolution. However, in *Williams v. Florida* (1970), the Supreme Court declared that the number twelve was a "historical accident, wholly without significance except to mystics," and therefore not required by the Constitution. The Court concluded that the six-person jury used in Florida in noncapital cases was large enough to promote group deliberations and to provide a fair possibility of obtaining a representative cross section of the community. Attempts to use juries with even fewer than six members were struck down by *Ballew v. Georgia* (1978). The defendant's misdemeanor conviction by a five-member jury was reversed because "the purpose and functioning of the jury in a criminal trial is seriously impaired, and to a constitutional degree, by a reduction in size to below six members."

Thirty-three states have specifically authorized juries of fewer than twelve (see Exhibit 14-2), but most allow smaller juries only in misdemeanor cases. In federal courts, defendants are entitled to a twelve-person jury unless the parties agree in writing to a small jury, but six-member juries in federal civil cases are quite common.

There has been a good deal of debate over whether small juries provide the defendant with a fair trial (Saks 1996). Social science evidence suggests there are few differences in the conduct of deliberations between six- and twelve-person juries (Pabst 1973; Roper 1979). In terms of the types of verdicts reached, however, the evidence is mixed. A few studies suggest that case outcomes are about the same regardless of jury size. But other studies indicate that twelve-member juries are more likely to vote for the plaintiff in civil cases and to be more generous in their financial awards (Zeisel and Diamond 1974; Beiser 1975; Roper 1980).

Unanimity

The requirement that a jury reach a unanimous decision became a firm rule in England during the fourteenth century. An agreement by all of the jurors seemed to legitimize the verdict, giving the community a sense that the conclusion must be correct. However, the Supreme Court altered this assumption in a pair of 1972 decisions. It held that verdicts in fed-

frequently updated, and collected in districts within judicial boundaries. However, basing the master jury list on voter registration tends to exclude the poor, the young, racial minorities, and the less educated (Kairys, Kadane, and Lehorsky 1977). Because of these limitations, many jurisdictions use other sources—telephone directories, utility customer lists, or driver's license lists—in drawing up the master list. The use of multiple sources achieves a better cross section of the community on jury panels (Munstermann and Munstermann 1986; Newman 1996).

Jury panels can be challenged if they fail to include racial or other minorities. Appellate courts have ruled that the master jury list must reflect a representative and impartial cross section of the community. African Americans, Mexican Americans, and women cannot be systematically excluded from petit juries solely on the basis of race or sex. This does not mean that every jury must include African Americans, Mexican Americans (*Castenada v. Partido* 1977), or women (*Taylor v. Louisiana* 1975), but such individuals may not be denied the opportunity to be chosen for jury service equally with others in the community. The requirement of a representative cross section of the community applies only to jury pools. The Court has held that this standard does not apply to the juries chosen from the pool (*Holland v. Illinois* 1990).

Venire

The second step in jury selection is the drawing of the **venire** (or jury pool). Periodically, the clerk of court or jury commissioner determines how many jurors are needed for a given time. A sufficient number of names is then randomly selected from the master jury list, and the sheriff issues a summons for these citizens to appear at the courthouse for jury duty. The number of citizens who merely ignore their summons is increasing nationwide, however; estimates place the nonresponse rate at 20 percent (Boatright 1999; Losh, Wasserman, and Wasserman 2000).

Not all those summoned will actually serve on the venire. Virtually all states have laws that require jurors to be citizens of the United States, residents of the locality, of a certain minimum age, and able to understand English. Most states disqualify convicted felons and insane persons. Persons who fail to meet these requirements are eliminated from the venire. Others will be excused because of **statutory exemptions.** The identities of those exempted from jury duty by statute vary greatly but commonly include government officials, medical personnel, ministers, educators, and lawyers. Those not exempt by law may still be excused if they can convince the judge that jury duty would entail an undue hardship.

Although serving on a jury is a right and privilege of citizenship, many people consider it a nuisance and request to be excused (van Dyke 1977). Citizens who are not excused from jury duty eventually receive a summons, ordering them to appear at the courthouse on a given date. The clerk's office randomly selects a number of potential jurors from the venire and directs them to a specific courtroom. It is from this jury pool that a trial jury will be selected.

Voir Dire

The final step in jury selection is the **voir dire** (French legal term for "to speak the truth"), which involves the preliminary examination of a prospective juror in order to determine his or her qualifications to serve as a juror. The prospective jurors are questioned by the attorneys and/or judge about their backgrounds, familiarity with persons involved in the case (defendant, witness, or lawyer), attitudes about certain facts that may arise during trial, and any other matters that may reflect on their willingness and ability to judge the case fairly and impartially.

If it develops during the questioning that a juror cannot fairly judge the case, the juror may be **challenged for cause** by either the defense or the prosecution. The presiding judge rules on the motion and, if it is sustained, the juror is excused. In practice, few challenges for cause are made, and even fewer are sustained. **Peremptory challenge** is the second—and much more important—technique used by the prosecution and the defense in influencing who will sit on the jury. Each side has a limited number of peremptory challenges that can be used to exclude a juror. Based on hunch, prejudice, or pseudoscience, a lawyer may peremptorily exclude a juror without giving a reason.

Attorneys traditionally enjoyed unrestricted freedom to exercise peremptory challenges. But in *Batson v. Kentucky* (1986), the Court restricted the ability of prosecutors who used peremptory challenges to keep blacks off the jury in any case involving a black defendant. If a prosecutor uses peremptory challenges to exclude potential jurors solely on account of their race, the prosecutor must explain his or her actions and may be ordered to change tactics. And in a move backed by prosecutors, the Court held that the defense is also prohibited from excluding jurors based on race (*Georgia v. McCollum* 1992).

The Court extended *Batson* to cover gender jury bias, holding that lawyers may not exclude potential jurors from a trial because of their sex (*J.E.B. Petitioner v. Alabama* 1994).

Jury Duty

Every year, thousands of Americans are called to serve as jurors. Unfortunately, many jurors experience great frustration in the process. They are made to wait hours in barren courthouse rooms; the compensation is minimal, and not all employers pay for the time lost from work; and some potential jurors are apprehensive about criminals and courthouses. A Day in Court: The Verdict: Juries Work recounts the experiences of one such juror.

In spite of these hardships, most citizens express overall satisfaction with jury duty, viewing their experience as a precious opportunity of citizenship rather than an onerous obligation (Pabst 1973, 10). Just as important, there is every indication that jurors take their job seriously.

Considerable attention is being devoted to reducing the inconvenience of jury duty. Courts in all states use a juror call-in system. In these jurisdictions, jurors can dial a number to learn whether their attendance is needed on a particular day during their term of service. In addition, an increasing number of courts are reducing the number of days a person remains in the jury pool. Traditionally, jurors were asked to serve for a full 30 days.

A DAY IN COURT

The Verdict: Juries Work

 The timing couldn't have been much worse. I had been home from South Africa just a couple of hours that Wednesday night when my husband handed me the message from the jury commissioner at Criminal District Court: I had missed my first day of jury duty. Weasel out of it, a naughty voice from within said. A three-week stint out of the country, more than 20 hours in airplanes and an out-of-whack body clock that kept ticking seven hours ahead were surely a pretty good argument.

But I didn't put up much of a fight and agreed to show up with the other 200 or so men and women summoned to the courthouse basement at Tulane Avenue and Broad Street every Monday and Wednesday for the rest of May.

Justice Wheels Grind Slow

Aside from jockeying for one of the few reserved parking spaces, waiting was the worst part—hours long waits either reading outdated magazines and chatting with strangers in a crowded, stuffy basement lounge, or sitting solemnly in a freezing courtroom. Potential jurors waited in the lounge each morning until we were summoned to courtrooms to be questioned by defense attorneys and prosecutors, who both explained that they were seeking 12 "fair and impartial" people to decide the guilt or innocence of an accused person.

To the prosecutor that meant weeding out those soft hearted jurors who might waffle when it comes to issuing a guilty verdict, or be reluctant to hand down a harsh sentence. For example, the slightest pause or hint of uncertainty when a prosecutor asked, "Can you consider the death penalty," often landed unsuspecting men and women back in the basement lounge. To the defense attorneys, finding a fair and impartial juror meant just the opposite. An overly enthusiastic or confident response on the death penalty question often hastened a return downstairs.

After the questioning (called voir dire), each side is allowed by law to dismiss 12 potential jurors—known as peremptory challenges—without having to provide a reason satisfactory to the judge. It's a tricky and often discriminatory process used sometimes to purposely exclude certain kinds of jurors from certain kinds of cases—for example, African Americans in cases involving race, women in cases involving rape, and men in child support cases. For amusement, those of us waiting our turn often tried to figure out which jurors would pass those unspoken tests.

Weighing Case Seriously

Of course, news reporters rarely pass those tests. Defense attorneys often figure we may know a bit too much about the case, and prosecutors figure we're all bleeding-heart liberals. So, one or the other issues a challenge. But I passed the test once, before a no-nonsense judge who called the first 12 potential jurors then swore the same group in just minutes later. Considering the number of murder cases being heard every day at the court house, this case was minor: A man accused of making a false bomb threat. It didn't take long to reach a verdict, but I was pleasantly surprised by how seriously we all took our civic responsibility. We deliberated thoroughly, argued a few points back and forth and decided he was guilty.

All the while, we never lost sight of the fact that, no matter how insignificant the case may have seemed, a man's future hung in the balance. The jury process is imperfect. But my firsthand experience gave me more confidence that, despite its flaws, it often achieves what it seeks: justice.

SOURCE: Lisa Frazier, "The Verdict: Juries Work," *Times-Picayune*, 30 May 1994.

Although only a few jurors were needed for a particular day, the entire pool had to be present in the courthouse each and every working day. Increasingly, however, jurors are asked to serve for only a few days. An approach known as the one-day/one-trial jury system requires each juror to serve either for one day or for the duration of one trial. The person is then exempt from jury duty for a year or more (Kasunic 1983). The one-day/one-trial jury system is much more efficient than older practices because it spares many citizens the inconvenience of waiting in courthouses with no trials to hear.

LAW IN ACTION: CHOOSING A JURY BIASED IN YOUR FAVOR

The National Advisory Commission (1973) has succinctly summarized the official—that is to say, the law-on-the-books—purpose of jury selection as follows: "A defendant is entitled to an unbiased jury; he is not entitled to a jury biased in his favor" (p. 99). Members of the courtroom work group are reluctant to formally question this pious wisdom, but informally their actions are strikingly different. Particularly through selective use of peremptory challenges, lawyers for both prosecution and defense seek jurors predisposed to their side. This is the major reason why in some areas the voir dire has become a time-consuming process (Sipes 1988). Through educating jurors, trial lawyers seek decision makers who are comfortable with their approach. Through hiring jury consultants, trial lawyers aggressively seek to identify jurors who will be biased in their favor.

Educating Jurors

Attorneys use *voir dire* for purposes other than eliminating bias. The questioning of jurors develops rapport between the attorneys and the jurors. Voir dire also gives lawyers the opportunity to influence jurors' attitudes and perhaps their later vote. As the nationally recognized lawyers F. Lee Bailey and Henry Rothblat (1971, 83) have said: "As you interrogate the jurors you meet them personally for the first time. You are given a chance to start selling the defense. Your questions should educate each prospective juror to the legal principles of your defense." Defense attorneys in particular view the voir dire as necessary for ensuring that potential jurors will presume that the defendant is innocent until proven guilty.

Jury Consultants

In recent years, attorneys have employed social scientists to aid them in a more systematic use of the voir dire. By determining the social characteristics and attitudes of the local population that might be favorable to the accused, lawyers can reject some jurors while retaining others. The O. J. Simpson defense team, for example, hired Dr. Jo-Ellan Dimitrius, the head of Trial Logistics (Gollner 1995).

Consultants who offer scientific jury selection are quick to point to cases in which the winning side used their techniques. But no one has yet produced convincing evidence that advice on jury selection made the difference. Indeed, the effects of scientific jury selection are modest at best. The most valuable aid social science consultants can offer is to help attorneys develop trial presentations that are clear and convincing (Diamond 1990). Often, jury consultants advise their client not on selection but rather on deselection of jurors—avoiding potential jurors who would be adverse to their side.

OPENING STATEMENTS

Once the jury has been selected and sworn, the trial begins. (See Exhibit 14-3.) It is a common practice in many courts to select several **alternate jurors,** who will serve if one of the regular jurors must withdraw during the trial.

The prosecution and defense are allowed (but not required) to make brief **opening statements.** The purpose of an opening statement is to advise the jury of what the attorney intends to prove. Opening statements are not evidence; the attorneys offer the jurors "road maps" to guide them through the case. The lawyers are limited to statements of what they actually believe will be presented as the trial progresses (*United States v. Dinitz* 1976).

THE PROSECUTION PRESENTS ITS CASE

After the opening statements, the prosecution presents its main evidence. How the prosecutor proceeds is affected by two important aspects of the law: the burden of proof and rules of evidence.

Burden of Proof

One of the most fundamental protections recognized in the American criminal justice process is the **presumption of innocence.** The state has the burden of proving the defendant guilty of the alleged crime; the defendant is not required to prove himself or herself innocent. This difference is a fundamental one. A moment's reflection will give an idea of how hard it would be to prove that something did not happen or that a person did not commit an alleged criminal act, for it is very difficult to rule out all possibilities. Therefore, a defendant is cloaked with the legal shield of innocence throughout the criminal justice system.

In meeting the obligation to prove the defendant guilty, the prosecution is required to prove the defendant guilty beyond a reasonable doubt. **Reasonable doubt** is a legal yardstick measuring the sufficiency of the evidence. This burden of proof does not require that the state establish absolute certainty by eliminating all doubt—just reasonable doubt. In attempting to show the defendant guilty beyond a reasonable doubt, the prosecutor calls witnesses and introduces physical evidence based on the rules of evidence.

Types of Evidence

The state tries to convince the jury to return a guilty verdict by presenting **evidence.** Evidence can be classified into real evidence, testimony, direct evidence, and circumstantial evidence. **Real evidence** includes objects of any kind—guns, records, and documents, for example. The bulk of the evidence during a criminal trial consists of **testimony**—statements by competent witnesses. **Direct evidence** is eyewitness evidence. Testimony that a person was seen walking in the rain is direct evidence that a person walked in the rain. Indirect evidence is called **circumstantial evidence.** Circumstantial evidence can be used to prove the truth or falsity of a fact at issue. Testimony that the person was seen indoors with wet shoes is circumstantial evidence that the person had walked in the rain.

The presentation of evidence during trial is governed by principles called rules of evidence. A trial is an adversary proceeding in which the rules of evidence resemble the rules of a game, with the judge acting as an impartial umpire. Although they may seem to be a fixed set of legal rules, they are not. Like all other legal principles, they are general propositions that courts must apply to specific instances. During such applications, judges use a balancing test, carefully weighing whether the trial would be fairer with or without the piece of evidence in question. The basics of the rules of evidence may be briefly summarized under the headings of trustworthiness and relevance.

Rules of Evidence: Trustworthiness

The basic criterion for admissibility of evidence is **trustworthiness.** The object of the evidentiary system is to ensure that only the most reliable and credible facts, statements, and testimony are presented to the fact-finder. The **best-evidence rule** illustrates the point. Ordinarily only the original of a document or object is admissible, because a copy or facsimile may have been altered. Similarly, a judge may rule that a person of unsound mind or a very young child is not a competent witness, because he or she might not understand what was seen or heard. The mere fact that evidence is legally ruled to be competent does not, of course, mean that the jury must believe it. A wife's alibi for her husband may be competent evidence, but the jury may choose not to believe her.

Hearsay is secondhand evidence. It is testimony that is not based on personal knowledge but is a repetition of what another person has said: "My brother Bob told me he saw Jones enter the store that evening." The general rule is that hearsay evidence is not admissible because it is impossible to test its truthfulness; there is no way to cross-examine as to the truth of the matter. There are exceptions, however. In some situations, dying declarations constitute an exception to the hearsay rule.

Exhibit 14-3   Steps of the Process: Trials

	Law on the Books	Law in Action
Trial	The adversarial process of deciding a case through the presentation of evidence and arguments about the evidence.	Only a handful of felonies and even fewer misdemeanors are decided by trial.
Bench trial	Trial before a judge without a jury.	Defense prefers when the issues are either highly technical or very emotional.
Jury trial	A group of average citizens selected by law and sworn in to look at certain facts and determine the truth.	Introduces public standards of justice into the decision-making process.
Jury selection	Process of selecting a fair and impartial jury.	Each side seeks to select jurors who are biased in its favor.
Master jury list	Potential jurors are selected by chance from a list of potential jurors. List should reflect a representative cross section of the community.	Selecting only from registered voters means that the poor, the young, and minorities are less likely to be called.
Venire	A group of citizens from which jury members are chosen (jury pool).	Judges vary in their willingness to excuse potential jurors because of hardship.
Voir dire	The process by which prospective jurors are questioned to determine whether there is cause to excuse them from the jury.	Lawyers use questioning to predispose jurors in their favor.
Peremptory challenge	Each side may exclude a set number of jurors without stating a reason.	Both sides use peremptory challenges to select a jury favorable to their side.
Challenge for cause	A judge may dismiss a potential juror if the person cannot be fair and objective.	Rarely granted.
Opening statements	Lawyers discuss what the evidence will show.	Lawyers use to lead the jury to a favorable verdict.
Prosecutor's case-in-main	The main evidence offered to prove the defendant guilty beyond a reasonable doubt.	Defense suggests that the prosecution has not met its burden of proof.
Witness	A person who makes a statement under oath about the events in question.	Through cross-examination, defense undermines the credibility of the witness.
Expert witness	A person possessing special knowledge or experience who is allowed to testify not only about facts but also about conclusions he or she has drawn.	Some expert witnesses testify only for one side or the other because their conclusions are predictable.
Defense's case-in-main	Evidence that defense may present. Because the defendant is innocent until proven guilty, the defense is not required to present evidence.	Defense may rest without calling witnesses, but jurors expect to hear reasons why they shouldn't convict.

	Law on the Books	Law in Action
Witness	The defendant may waive his or her privilege against self-incrimination and testify.	Defense attorneys are reluctant to call the defendant to the stand, particularly if there is a prior conviction.
Rebuttal	Evidence that refutes or contradicts evidence given by the opposing party.	Prosecutor will call witnesses to undermine a defendant's alibi.
Closing arguments	After all the evidence has been presented, each side sums up the evidence and attempts to convince the jury why their side should win.	Many trial attorneys believe that a good closing argument will win the case. Each side attempts to convince the jury why their side should win.
Prosecution	Because the prosecution bears the burden of proof, the prosecutor goes first and last.	The district attorney's first closing argument provides an orderly summary of the evidence.
Defense	Closing argument of the defense highlights the evidence leading to a not guilty verdict.	Typically stresses that the prosecutor has failed to prove the defendant guilty beyond a reasonable doubt.
Prosecution	Rebuts defense allegations.	Impassioned statement, calling upon jurors to do their duty and convict the guilty.
Jury instructions	Explanations by the judge informing the jury of the law applicable to the case.	Legal language difficult for average citizens to follow.
Jury deliberations	Jurors are repeatedly instructed not to talk about the case.	Jurors routinely talk with other jurors about the case.
	Jurors deliberate in private.	Higher-status individuals participate more.
	Jurors select a foreperson and discuss the case.	The first vote is usually decisive.
	Jurors may request further instructions from the judge.	Such requests produce great anxiety among lawyers.
	Jurors take an oath to follow the law as instructed by the judge.	Some juries introduce popular law into the decision-making process.
Verdict	Decision that the defendant is either guilty or not guilty (acquittal).	Juries convict three out of four times.
		Jury verdicts often reflect a compromise.
Hung jury	Jury is unable to reach a verdict.	Defense attorneys consider a hung jury an important victory.
Post-verdict motions	Motions filed by the defense after conviction and before sentencing.	Judge must accept a verdict of not guilty.
Motion in arrest of judgment	Defense argues that the jury could not have reasonably convicted the defendant based on the evidence presented.	Trial judges are very reluctant to second-guess jury verdicts and almost never grant this motion.
Motion for a new trial	Defense argues that the trial judge made mistakes and therefore a new trial should be held.	On very rare occasions, trial judges admit that an error occurred and set aside a jury verdict of guilty.

Rules of Evidence: Relevance

To be admissible, evidence must not only be trustworthy but also relevant; there must be a valid reason for introducing the statement, object, or testimony. Evidence not related to an issue at trial is termed **immaterial** or **irrelevant.** If, for example, a defendant is accused of murder, the issue is whether he killed the deceased. Evidence regarding motive, intention to commit the offense, and ability to commit the offense would all be relevant. But information about the defendant's character—prior convictions or a reputation for dishonesty, for instance—would not normally be admissible, because it is not material to the issue of whether the defendant committed this crime. However, if the defendant were to testify, such evidence would be admissible during rebuttal for the sole purpose of **impeaching** (casting doubt on) his or her credibility.

Scientific Evidence

Scientific evidence analyzing materials such as blood, firearms, and fingerprints are now routinely admitted into evidence if they meet the traditional yardsticks of the rules of evidence—trustworthiness and relevance. But when the technologies for gathering and measuring these forms of evidence first emerged, their use as evidence was far from routine. Moreover, not all evidence based on "science" is necessarily admissible. Polygraph examinations and testimony gained from hypnosis are generally not admissible as evidence.

Separating science from pseudoscience is never an easy task. For 70 years, the "general acceptance" test was the dominant standard for determining the admissibility of novel scientific evidence at trial.

> Just when a scientific principle or discovery crosses the line between the experimental and demonstrable stages is difficult to define. Somewhere in this twilight zone the evidential forces of the principle must be recognized, and while courts will go a long way in admitting expert testimony deduced from a well-recognized scientific principle or discovery, the thing from which the deduction is made must be sufficiently established to have gained general acceptance in the particular field in which it belongs. (*Frye v. U.S. D.C. Cir.* 1923)

In the modern era, some courts have rejected the "general acceptance" prong of the *Frye* test, holding that this nose-counting approach is no longer adequate in the face of rapid developments in science (Labaton 1990). Following this trend, the Supreme Court has rejected the *Frye* standard. The Court has assigned federal judges an active role in screening scientific evidence. "The trial judge must ensure that any and all scientific testimony or evidence is not only relevant but reliable" (*Daubert v. Merrell Dow Pharmaceuticals Co.* 1993). *Daubert* has particular applicability in civil cases, where critics argue that "junk science" (unreliable findings by persons with questionable credentials) is producing too many civil lawsuits.

The use of DNA (deoxyribonucleic acid) as evidence has sparked considerable debate. Initially judges and lawyers debated whether such evidence was admissible, but those legal battles have now been resolved. One dimension of the contemporary debates focuses on the reliability of crime labs. In a basic sense, crime labs have become victims of their own success: Every year crime labs are called upon to analyze even more samples than the year before, resulting in significant backlogs (Steadman 2002). But to some, DNA testing has failed to live up to its potential. Evidence from tens of thousands of rapes and murders has not been analyzed. Moreover, there are significant variations among states in their abilities to match samples with suspects (Willing 2002). And as will be discussed in Chapter 17, there are demands that old cases be reopened so that DNA tests (not available at the time of the original trial) can be performed.

Objections to the Admission of Evidence

During trial, attorneys must always be alert, ready to make timely **objections** to the admission of evidence. After a question is asked but before the witness answers, the attorney may object if the evidence is irrelevant, immaterial, or hearsay. The court then rules on the objection, admitting or barring the evidence. The judge may rule immediately or may request the lawyers to argue the legal point out of the hearing of the jury (this is termed a *sidebar conference*). Occasionally, inadmissible evidence will inadvertently be heard by the jury. For example, in answering a valid question, a witness may overelaborate. When this occurs and the attorney objects, the judge will instruct the jury to disregard the evidence. If the erroneous evidence is deemed so prejudicial that a warning to disregard is not sufficient, the judge may declare a **mistrial.**

THE DEFENSE PRESENTS ITS CASE

In deciding on the defense strategy at trial, the attorney must carefully consider the strengths and weaknesses of the state's case, the character of the defendant, and how credible the defense witnesses may be. In deciding on a strategy, the defense must weigh reasonable doubt, calling the defendant as a witness, alibi defenses, affirmative defenses, and challenging scientific evidence.

Reasonable Doubt

Because the defendant is presumed innocent, the defense does not have to call any witnesses or introduce any evidence. Through cross-examination, the attorney can try to undermine the state's case and create in the jury's mind a reasonable doubt as to whether the defendant committed the crime. The key to such a strategy is the skillful use of the right to confront witnesses, one of the criminal court procedures enumerated in the Sixth Amendment: "In all criminal prosecutions, the accused shall enjoy the right . . . to be confronted with witnesses against him." One meaning of this provision is that the defendant must be present during trial—that is, the state cannot try defendants who are absent. The right to be confronted with witnesses guarantees the right to **cross-examination.** A fundamental tenet of the adversary system is the need to test evidence

COURT TV
Trouble in Paradise: Faking Insanity?

Jeffrey Wallace is a trusted employee of a popular bar in Key West, Florida, until one night he goes on a shooting spree, killing the bar manager and wounding several other people. The defense argues that Wallace is insane, pointing to his paranoia and past mental health treatments. The prosecution counters that Wallace is faking mental illness and had planned to kill. (The CourtTV video clip presented in Chapter 16 focuses on the penalty phase of this trial.)

 View a video clip of this trial on your copy of the CourtTV CD-ROM. As you watch the video, keep the following questions in mind:

1. What is the legal standard of insanity in Florida, and how might this affect the presentation of both sides of the case?

2. Knowing that the defense plans to mount an insanity defense, how does the prosecution use its case in main to rebut the defense?

3. How does the prosecutor use cross-examination of defense witnesses to undermine the insanity defense?

4. Describe how the defense uses the insanity claim during the guilt phase of the trial to anticipate the penalty phase of the trial, when it is assumed that the prosecution will ask for the death penalty.

for truthfulness, and the primary means of testing the truthfulness of witnesses is cross-examination.

If a defendant has no valid defense but will not plead guilty, the defense attorney's only choice is to force the state to prove its case and hope to create a reasonable doubt in the minds of the jury. But many experienced defense attorneys consider this to be the weakest kind of defense. They believe that to gain an acquittal, the defense must give the jury something to "hang their hat on." Thus, they must consider whether to let the defendant testify.

The Defendant As Witness

The most important part of defense strategy is the decision whether the defendant will testify. The Fifth Amendment protection against **self-incrimination** means that the defendant cannot be compelled to be a witness against himself. If the defendant chooses not to testify, no comment or inference may be drawn from this fact. The prosecutor cannot argue before the jury, "If he is innocent, why doesn't he take the stand and say so?" (*Griffin v. California* 1965). Nonetheless, jurors are curious about the defendant's version of what happened. They expect the defendant to protest innocence; in the secrecy of the jury room, they can ponder aloud why the defendant refused to testify.

Defendants may, of course, waive the privilege against self-incrimination and take the stand in their own defense. In deciding whether the defendant should testify, the defense attorney must consider whether the story is believable. If it is not, the jury will probably dismiss it, thus doing more harm to the defendant's case than if he or she had not testified at all.

Like any other witness, a defendant who takes the stand is subject to cross-examination. Because cross-examination is broader than direct examination, the defendant cannot tell only a part of the story and conceal the rest. Once the defendant chooses to testify, the state can bring out all the facts surrounding the event testified to. Just as important, once the defendant has taken the stand, the state can impeach the defendant's credibility by introducing into evidence any prior felony convic-

tions. The defense attorney must make the difficult decision whether to arouse the jury's suspicion by not letting the accused testify or letting the defendant testify and be subjected to possibly damaging cross-examination.

Alibi Defense

In an **alibi defense,** defendants argue that they were somewhere else at the time the crime was committed. Witnesses may be called to testify that during the time in question the defendant was drinking beer at Mary's or shopping downtown with some friends. Some states require that defendants provide a notice of an alibi defense prior to trial, along with a list of witnesses to be called to support this assertion. A notice of alibi defense gives the prosecution the opportunity to investigate the witnesses' story before trial. Prosecutors who suspect that witnesses have carefully rehearsed their alibi testimony can use clever cross-examination to ask questions out of sequence, hoping to catch each witness in a series of contradictions. Prosecutors can also call rebuttal witnesses to suggest that the witnesses are longtime friends of the defendant, who are likely to lie.

Affirmative Defenses

An **affirmative defense** goes beyond denying the facts of the prosecutor's case; it sets out new facts and arguments that might win for the defendant. In essence, affirmative defenses are legal excuses that should result in a finding of not guilty. Under an affirmative defense, the defense has "the burden of going forward with the evidence." From the defendant's perspective, an affirmative defense is tricky, for it often means that the defendant admits the prosecutor's case. Moreover, juries often view such a defense strategy as an attempt by the defendant to wiggle out of a guilty verdict.

There are several types of affirmative defenses. One is **self-defense,** which is the right of a person to use force upon another person in order to protect him- or herself. Another affirmative defense is **duress,** which means a person is compelled to do something he or she does not want to do. Yet another is **entrap-**

COURTS, CONTROVERSY, AND REDUCING CRIME

Should the Insanity Defense Be Abolished?

The insanity defense, one of the most hotly debated topics in criminal law, is rooted in a fundamental concept of Anglo-American law: that a person should not be punished for what he or she cannot help doing. Thus, under the concept of mens rea, an insane person is not criminally responsible for his or her acts, because he or she is incapable of having criminal intent (see Chapter 2).

But what degree of insanity, mental illness, or mental disease makes a person blameless for otherwise criminal acts? This question has been debated for centuries. At the heart of contemporary discussions are marked philosophical divergences within American society concerning an individual's responsibility for his or her own acts. The lack of agreement is reflected in major differences among states concerning the extent to which a person's mental faculties must be impaired before he or she is considered insane. The standards for insanity found in U.S. jurisdictions are shown in Exhibit 14-4.

Usually, a defendant who uses an insanity defense enters a dual plea of not guilty and not guilty by reason of insanity. The burden of proof is on the prosecution to prove that the defendant committed the crime in question, but the defense bears the burden of proof as to the defendant's insanity.

The insanity defense has sparked considerable controversy. The public perceives the insanity defense as a dodge used by tricky lawyers trying to gain sympathy for their guilty clients, who avoid punishment by pretending they are insane. When the jury acquitted would-be presidential assassin John Hinckley, Jr., as "not guilty by reason of insanity," there was a heated outcry against the verdict, even though Hinckley was then confined to a mental institution. Public and professional displeasure produced a rush to reform the insanity defense. For example, 12 states have greatly altered the traditional insanity defense and made available the verdict "guilty but mentally ill" (Klofas and Yandrasits 1989).

This debate resurfaces during trials of defendants charged with bizarre crimes. For example, Theodore Kaczynski, the alleged Unabomber, refused to allow his lawyer to plead not guilty by reason of insanity, and he was subsequently convicted. Likewise, the trial of Andrea Yates for killing her children triggered a clash between psychiatrists and prosecutors.

The often heated debate over the insanity defense is largely symbolic, however. Because the public remains skeptical about the insanity defense, defense attorneys seldom use it as a trial strategy, and jurors even more rarely find defendants not guilty by reason of insanity. One study found that of the 2 million criminal prosecution cases in one year, only 1,625 defendants were found not guilty by reason of insanity (Steadman et al. 1982). Moreover, numerous states make incarceration in a mental institution mandatory if the defendant is found not guilty by reason of insanity. Indeed, such defendants are usually held in a mental institution for a longer period of time than they might have been held in prison had they been found guilty of the crime they were charged with. For these reasons, lawyers consider insanity a defense of last resort.

What do you think? Should the insanity defense be abolished, restricted, or kept the way it is? In particular, do you think that defendants fake insanity, or are defendants really insane and therefore not responsible for their actions? If you were a juror, what types of evidence would convince you to return a verdict of not guilty by reason of insanity?

To continue the debate on this topic, read the following articles:

Richard Vatz, "Murderous Mothers: A Challenge for the Insanity Defense"

Daniel Nusbaum, "The Craziest Reform of Them All"

Timothy W. Maier, "One Flew into the Cuckoo's Nest"

Richard E. Vatz, Lee S. Weinberg, "The Unabomber's Twisted Saga"

---

ment, which is the act of a law enforcement agent inducing a person to commit a crime that the person was not otherwise disposed to commit. By far the best known and also most controversial affirmative defense is the insanity defense. (See Courts, Controversy, and Reducing Crime: Should the Insanity Defense Be Abolished?)

Exhibit 14-4 Standards for Insanity Used by the States and the U.S. Courts

Insanity Standard	Jurisdiction
McNaughton rule Oldest and most restrictive standard of insanity as legal defense, essentially requiring that the accused not be able to distinguish between right and wrong; currently applied in a modified version in 16 jurisdictions.	Arizona, Florida, Iowa, Kansas, Louisiana, Minnesota, Mississippi, Nebraska, Nevada, New Jersey, North Carolina, Oklahoma, Pennsylvania, South Carolina, South Dakota, Washington
Irresistible impulse A test of insanity under which a person is driven to commit an act by an urge that cannot be resisted or overcome because mental disease or derangement has destroyed the freedom of will, the power of self-control, and the ability to choose.	Colorado, Georgia, New Mexico, Virginia
Substantial capacity A person is not responsible for criminal conduct if at the time of such conduct and as a result of mental disease or defect he or she lacks substantial capacity either to appreciate the criminality of the conduct or to conform his or her conduct to the regiments of the law.	All federal circuits, Alabama, Alaska, Arkansas, California, Connecticut, Delaware, District of Columbia, Hawaii, Illinois, Indiana, Kentucky, Maine, Maryland, Massachusetts, Michigan, Missouri, Ohio, Oregon, Tennessee, Texas, Vermont, West Virginia, Wisconsin, Wyoming
Other	New Hampshire, New York, North Dakota, Rhode Island
No standard These states have abolished the use of the insanity defense altogether. However, psychiatric evidence is allowed on the issue of whether there is an intent to commit a crime.	Idaho, Montana, Utah

SOURCE: Adapted from Ingo Keilitz and Junius P. Fulton, *The Insanity Defense and Its Alternatives: A Guide for Policy-makers* (Williamsburg, VA: National Center for State Courts, 1984), p. 15; Bureau of Justice Statistics, *Report to the Nation on Crime and Justice*, 2d ed. (Washington, DC: U.S. Department of Justice, 1988).

Challenging Scientific Evidence

In recent years, a prominent version of the reasonable doubt defense has been a direct attack on the scientific evidence introduced by the prosecution. In particular, the way evidence was gathered, preserved, and analyzed by experts has been the centerpiece of several major trials. Most prominently, the O. J. Simpson defense team stressed the mishandling of evidence, suggesting that any subsequent analysis, no matter how precise, was not believable. This case thrust crime labs under the microscope, and the results were not always flattering. One result was a comprehensive investigation of the FBI crime lab, which highlighted numerous problems (U.S. Department of Justice 1997; Sniffen 1997). More recently, serious problems have surfaced in some state and local crime labs, resulting in some cases' being dismissed and some convictions reversed because testimony concerning scientific evidence proved unreliable.

■ REBUTTAL

After the defense rests its case, the prosecution may call rebuttal witnesses, whose purpose is either to discredit the testimony of a previous witness or to discredit the witness. The prosecutor may call a **rebuttal** witness to show that the previous witness could not have observed what she said she did because she was somewhere else at the time. Or the prosecutor may call witnesses or otherwise present evidence to show that the previous witnesses have dishonorable reputations. The rules of evidence regarding rebuttal witnesses are complex. In general, evidence may be presented in rebuttal that could not have been used during the prosecution's main case. For example, the prosecution may legitimately inform the jury of the previous convictions of defendants who take the stand, in an attempt to impeach their credibility.

CLOSING ARGUMENTS

After the prosecution and defense have rested (that is, completed the introduction of evidence), each side has the opportunity to make a closing argument to the jury. **Closing arguments** allow each side to sum up the facts in its favor and indicate why it believes a verdict of guilty or not guilty is in order.

The prosecutor goes first, carefully summing up the facts of the case and tying together into a coherent pattern what appeared during the trial to be isolated or unimportant matters. The prosecutor calls upon the jurors to do their duty and punish the defendant, who has committed the crime. The defense attorney goes next, highlighting the evidence favorable to the defendant, criticizing the witnesses for the state, and showing why they should not be believed. The defense also calls upon the jurors to do their sworn duty and return a not guilty verdict. Because the prosecutor bears the burden of proof, he or she has the opportunity to make one last statement to the jury, refuting the defense arguments.

Closing arguments are often the most dramatic parts of the trial. However, there is a fine line between persuasiveness and unnecessary emotionalism. Jury verdicts have been reversed on appeal because the prosecutor interjected prejudicial statements into the closing argument.

JURY INSTRUCTIONS

Although the jury is the sole judge of the facts of the case, the judge alone determines the law. Therefore, the court instructs the jury as to the meaning of the law applicable to the facts of the case. These **jury instructions** begin with discussions of general legal principles (innocent until proven guilty, guilty beyond a reasonable doubt, and so forth). They follow with specific instructions on the elements of the crime in the case and what specific actions the government must prove before there can be a conviction. If the defendant has raised a defense such as insanity or duress, the judge instructs the jury as to the meaning of the defense according to the law in that jurisdiction. Finally, the judge instructs the jury on possible verdicts in the case and provides a written form for each verdict of guilty and not guilty. Often juries have the option of choosing alternative forms of guilty verdicts, called *lesser included offenses*. In a murder case, for example, the jury may find the defendant guilty of murder in the first degree, murder in the second degree, or manslaughter—or they may acquit on all charges.

The judge and the trial attorneys prepare the jury instructions during a special **charging conference** that precedes jury deliberations. Each side drafts suggested instructions, and the judge chooses the ones most appropriate. If the judge rejects a given instruction, the lawyer enters an objection on the record, thus preserving the issue for later appeal. The instructions are written out, signed by the judge, and then read to the jury. Some judges allow the jurors to take a copy of the instructions into the jury room as a guide.

Jury instructions represent a formal, detailed lecture on the law. Because faulty jury instructions are a principal basis for appellate court reversal, judges are careful in their wordings. Unfortunately, the result is a pitifully low rate of juror comprehension (Severance and Loftus 1982). For example, given jury instructions stressing that a defendant is presumed innocent until proven guilty by the evidence beyond any reasonable doubt, only 50 percent of the jurors understood that the defendant did not have to present any evidence of innocence, and 10 percent were still uncertain what the

A Virtual Tour of American Courthouses: Juries

Watching real trials no longer requires a trek to the court-house—instead, you can turn on your TV. To see which trials are being broadcast today, go to **http://www.courttv.com/**. The following jurisdictions make their rules for cameras in the courtroom available on the Web:

Arizona
http://www.supreme.state.az.us/media/cameras.htm

California
http://www.courtinfo.ca.gov/reference/cameras-sectionf.htm

Missouri
http://www.courtrules.org/camera.htm

Second U.S. Circuit Court of Appeals
http://www.nylj.com/rules/scpf.html

As for famous trials of the past, law professor Doug Linder offers a fascinating view of many of the trials that have shaped our nation's history: **http://www.law.umkc.edu/faculty/projects/ftrials/ftrials.htm**.

It is also helpful to view yourself in the shoes of being a juror. For FAQs on the jury selection process from the Cook County (Illinois) court, see **http://www.cookcountycourt.org/jury/faq-selection.html**.

As for the evidence that will be admitted or not admitted, the Legal Information Institute provides an excellent overview of evidence at **http://www.law.cornell.edu/topics/evidence.html**. The Federal Rules of Evidence can be found at **http://www.law.cornell.edu/rules/fre/overview.html**. A growing number of states place their rules of evidence on-line, including

Pennsylvania
http://www.pennlegal.com/

Texas
http://tarlton.law.utexas.edu/texas/rcve_toc.htm

For actual case histories of how forensics solves crimes, go to **http://www.forensic-lab.com/casehist/index.html**.

---

presumption of innocence was (Strawn and Buchanan 1976). The major difficulty in improving jury comprehension is the complexity of the law itself; it is difficult to translate into plain English the subtleties of meaning of certain legal terms and the intentional vagueness of the law ("reasonable person" and "preponderance of the evidence" come quickly to mind) (Steele and Thornburg 1991).

JURY DELIBERATIONS

How juries decide has long fascinated lawyers and laypeople alike. There is a great deal of curiosity about what goes on behind the locked jury room door. During the trial, jurors are passive observers who are not allowed to ask questions and are usually prohibited from taking notes. But after the judge reads the jury instructions, the lawyers, judges, and defendants must wait passively, often in tense anticipa-

tion, for the jury to reach a verdict. The only hints of what is occurring during **jury deliberations** occur on the rare occasions when the jurors request further instructions from the judge about the applicable law or ask to have portions of the testimony read in open court.

What Motivates a Jury?

Rates of participation by jurors vary with social status: Men talk more than women, better-educated jurors participate more frequently, and persons with high-status occupations are more likely to be chosen as foremen (Strodtbeck, James, and Hawkins 1957; Simon 1967). Discussions among jurors mostly concern court procedures, opinions about the trial, and personal reminiscences; there is far less discussion of the testimony or the judge's instructions to the jury (James 1958).

Juries usually reach a verdict after short deliberations. Typically, juries take an initial vote as soon as they retire to the jury room, and 90 percent of the time the majority on the first ballot eventually wins out (Broeder 1959). Most important, a lone juror rarely produced a hung jury. The psychological pressures associated with small-group discussions are so great that a single juror can buck predominant sentiment only if he or she can find at least one ally. Thus, jury deliberations "do not so much decide the case as bring about a consensus" (Kalven and Zeisel 1966, 488). If the jury does become deadlocked and cannot reach a verdict, the trial ends with a **hung jury.** The prosecutor then has the option of trying the defendant again. Despite recent concerns, the rate of hung juries is low and has been stable for years (Hannaford, Hans, and Munsterman 1999). Nationwide, juries are unable to reach a decision only 6 percent of the time (National Center for State Courts 2003).

Are Juries Biased?

But what of jury bias? Do different groups of jurors decide differently? In terms of gender, race, age, and education, jurors who vote to convict are not very different as a group from jurors who vote to acquit (Mills and Bohannon 1980). Even in trials involving emotional issues like sexual assault, evidence is the primary factor in decision making. Jurors were influenced by extralegal factors, but these effects were largely limited to weak cases in which the state presented little hard evidence (Reskin and Visher 1986). Although there is some evidence that extralegal factors play a role, American juries appear to perform remarkably well on the whole, deciding primarily on the basis of legal factors (Ford 1986).

▌ THE VERDICT

Once the jury informs the judge that a decision has been reached, the lawyers and the defendant gather in the courtroom. Typically, the foreman announces the **verdict.** How often do juries convict? Given that the vast majority of cases have already been dismissed or disposed of by a plea of guilty, one might expect that the defendant's chances of winning at trial are roughly 50-50, but the real odds against acquit-

tal are significantly higher. In federal courts, juries convict 82 percent of the time in nondrug cases. Data from various states point in the same direction; juries convict two-thirds of the time in criminal cases (Roper and Flango 1983; Vidmar et al. 1997).

Do juries view cases differently than judges? Harry Kalven and Hans Zeisel (1966) found that judges and juries agree more than three out of four times. When judge and jury disagree, the judge is more likely to convict and the jury to acquit. But this pattern is tied to the severity of the charge. Juries convict felons at a higher rate than judges do, but judges convict nonfelons at a higher rate (Roper and Flango 1983; Levine 1983).

▌ POST-VERDICT MOTIONS

A trial verdict of **acquittal** (not guilty) ends the case; the defendant can leave the courthouse a free person. A verdict of guilty, however, means that further proceedings will occur; the defendant must be sentenced (see Chapters 15 and 16) and in all likelihood will appeal (see Chapter 17).

If the jury returns a verdict of guilty, the defendant still has certain legal options remaining. A guilty defendant may file **post-verdict motions,** which are heard prior to sentencing. These motions give the defense attorney the opportunity to reargue alleged mistakes made at trial. The trial judge may have a change of mind and become convinced that some ruling made against the defendant was erroneous. The most common post-verdict motion is a *motion for a new trial.* It asserts that serious errors were made at trial (either by the trial judge or by the prosecutor), so the guilty verdict should be set aside and a new trial granted. Post-verdict motions are largely a formality; few are ever granted.

▌ LAW IN ACTION: TRIALS AS BALANCING WHEELS

Trials exert a major influence on the operation of the entire criminal court process. This process resembles a balance. A balance wheel

THE MURDER TRIAL OF SHAREEF COUSIN

Two Trial-Day Surprises

In fictional courtrooms, trials proceed in an orderly manner with predictable outcomes. In real-world courtrooms, however, trials are sometimes disjointed, with unexpected developments. During the murder trial of Shareef Cousin, both sides experienced trial-day surprises. For the prosecution, a key witness became a turncoat. For the defense, a few frames of a videotape blurred the much-heralded alibi defense.

During its case-in-main, the prosecution called a variety of law enforcement officers who testified about the crime scene, provided diagrams of the crime scene, and so on. The coroner was also called to the stand to testify as to the cause of death. But establishing that a crime had been committed was the easy part; tying the crime to Shareef Cousin proved much more difficult. Several witnesses testified that they were only "reasonably certain" that Cousin was the killer. Thus, for the prosecution, the trial hinged on one and only one witness—the victim's date. Connie Babin forcefully identified Shareef Cousin as the murderer. As discussed in Chapter 12, the defense could not vigorously cross-examine her because they did not know of her previous statements about being unable to identify any suspect.

To bolster the credibility of Connie Babin's eyewitness identification, the prosecution called James Rowell, a 16-year-old friend of the defendant, who had earlier admitted to committing several armed robberies with Cousin (see Chapter 13). During opening arguments, the DA had promised jurors that Rowel would testify that Shareef Cousin had bragged that he had shot a man outside a French Quarter restaurant during a botched robbery. But when Rowell took the stand, he would only say that that was the story the DA wanted him to testify to. Faced with a turncoat witness, prosecutor Roger Jordan asked Judge Bigelow to declare him a hostile witness and now tried to rehabilitate his own witness. Thus the prosecution called Rowell's attorney, who testified that his client overheard Cousin boasting that he had killed someone. Indeed, Cousin was reputed to have said that after killing someone he would find killing easier the next time. But was this hearsay testimony solely to impeach the credibility of the witness, or did the prosecution offer this testimony as proof of the crime? The appeal (see Chapter 17) would center on this question.

For the defense, the trial hinged on the jury's believing that Shareef Cousin had an alibi for the time of the crime. According to Eric White, a basketball coach with the New Orleans Recreation Department, Shareef Cousin had been his star player the night of March 2, 1995, coming off the bench to score 10 points in a come-from-behind victory. Because the game ran late, he didn't drop Cousin off at his house until about 10:45 (some 20 minutes after the murder occurred). On cross-examination, however, the prosecution introduced a videotape of the game, and under hard questioning the coach was forced to admit that the quarters were actually six minutes long, not the eight he had testified to. Moreover, a clock in the gym seemed to suggest the game ended much earlier than his testimony indicated. The prosecution also pressed hard on a previous statement in which White had said the game ended about 9:20 or 9:25. In short, the prosecution used cross-examination to shred the alibi defense. Although the defense had stressed Cousin's alibi throughout the five-day trial, Hill only mentioned it briefly during his 30-minute closing argument.

The defense rested without calling Cousin to the stand, probably because of his previous convictions for four armed robberies.

At 11:30 on Friday night, the jury returned a unanimous verdict of guilty of first-degree murder. Their next task would be to decide whether Shareef Cousin would spend the rest of his life in prison or die by lethal injection (see Chapter 16).

regulates or stabilizes the motion of a mechanism. Although only a handful of cases go to trial, the possibility of trial operates as a balancing wheel on all other cases. Most important, the likelihood of conviction determines the negotiating position of lawyers during plea bargaining. Thus, jury trials must be measured not only in terms of their impact on specific cases but also on how the decisions reached affect similar cases in the future.

Popular Standards of Justice

Juries introduce the community's common-sense judgments into judicial decisions. The University of Chicago jury project (Broeder 1959) found that popular standards of justice are by far the major reason for disagreement between judge and jury. The result is jury legislation—a jury's deliberate modification of the law to make it conform to community views of what the law ought to be (Kalven and Zeisel 1966).

One example of how juries introduce popular standards into the criminal court process involve prosecutions for hunting violations. Rural juries are dubious about laws that restrict hunting privileges. Thus, federal defendants accused of shooting too many birds (and the like) have a good chance of finding friendly juries ready to come to their rescue (Levine 1983). Similarly, juries are less likely to convict if they perceive that the potential sentence is too severe. Thus a defendant charged with drunken driving, but who caused no injury, has a chance of being acquitted because jurors think that the loss of the driver's license is too severe for the crime. In ways like this, jury verdicts establish boundaries on what actions the local community believes should and should not be punished.

In recent years, the importance of juries' introducing popular standards into the justice system has been associated with the concept of **jury nullification**—the right of juries to nullify or refuse to apply law in criminal cases despite facts that leave no reasonable doubt that the law was violated (Brown 1997). Some advocates of jury nullification base their ideas on a perceived need to reduce government intrusion into citizens' lives. Others are motivated by concern over racial injustice (Butler 1995). Judges are quick to denounce jury nullification because they feel that the rule of law is undermined. But others counter that juries have been refusing to follow the law for centuries, and they have every right to send a message by not following a law they find, for whatever reason, to be flawed. Contemporary discussions focus on whether juries should be told they have the right to disregard the judge's jury instructions and substitute their own views (Galiber et al. 1993).

Uncertainty

Jury trials also affect the criminal court system by introducing uncertainty into the process. Stories about irrational juries form part of the folklore of any courthouse. Here are two examples. During jury deliberations in a drug case, two jurors announced that "only God can judge" and hung the jury by refusing to vote. After an acquittal in a burglary case, a juror put her arm around the defendant and said, "Bob, we were sure happy to find you not guilty, but don't do it again" (Neubauer 1974, 228). Legal professionals resent such intrusions into their otherwise ordered world; they seek to reduce such uncertainties by developing the norms of cooperation discussed throughout this book. Viewed in this light, plea bargaining serves to shield the system from a great deal of the uncertainty that results when lay citizens are involved in deciding important legal matters.

PREJUDICIAL PRETRIAL PUBLICITY

The conviction of Dr. Sam Sheppard for bludgeoning his wife to death in her bedroom and later reversal by the Supreme Court (see Case Close-Up: *Sheppard v. Maxwell* and Prejudicial Pretrial Publicity) raised the issue of **prejudicial pretrial publicity.** The Court, in holding that Sheppard had been denied a fair and impartial trial, set off a long and heated battle over fair trial versus freedom of the press. Defendants have a right to a fair and impartial trial, but at the same time, press coverage of the crime and the trial are protected by the First Amendment of the Constitution (*Times-Picayune v. Schulingkamp* 1975). Similar concerns have led some courts to ban cameras in the courthouse (see Courts, Controversy, and the Administration of Justice: Should Cameras Be Allowed in the Courtroom?).

Pretrial publicity does affect juries. A team of researchers provided one set of "jurors" with prejudicial news coverage of a case and a control group with "nonprejudicial" information. After listening to an identical trial involving a case in which the guilt of the defendant was

CASE CLOSE-UP

Sheppard v. Maxwell and Prejudicial Pretrial Publicity

On July 4, 1954, Marilyn Sheppard—the pregnant wife of Dr. Samuel Sheppard—was bludgeoned to death in the upstairs bedroom of the couple's home in a fashionable Cleveland suburb. The case produced some of the most sensational press coverage the country had witnessed. Sheppard told the police that he was asleep on a sofa when he was awakened by his wife's screams. Rushing upstairs, he grappled with the intruder, only to be struck unconscious by a blow to the head. From the outset, officials focused suspicion on Sheppard.

The official investigation was prodded by extensive media coverage, which was critical of how the police handled the case. Day after day, vivid headlines called for the arrest of Dr. Sheppard and implied that the police were going easy because he and his family were socially prominent. To add fuel to the fire, the paper published a front-page editorial headlined "Why Don't Police Quiz Top Suspect," claiming somebody "was getting away with murder." At the coroner's inquest, Dr. Sheppard's attorney was present but not allowed to participate. Live radio broadcast the six-hour questioning of Sheppard about his activities the night of the murder and about his lovers before that night. Six weeks after the murder, Sheppard was indicted.

The case came to trial two weeks before a general election in which the judge was seeking re-election and the prosecutor was running for municipal court judge. The names and addresses of potential jurors were published in the paper, resulting in letters and phone calls concerning the trial. The courtroom was so packed that reporters were allowed to sit behind the defense table, meaning that Sheppard could not converse privately with his lawyer. Every day, newspapers printed trial testimony verbatim; no effort was made to prevent the jury from reading these accounts, even when evidence was ruled inadmissible. Not surprisingly, after a nine-week trial in which jurors were free to return home every night, Sheppard was convicted of second-degree murder.

Sheppard spent 12 years in prison. A string of appeals and habeas corpus petitions were denied. Eventually the family hired a young Boston lawyer, F. Lee Bailey, who would go on to become one of the most famous and controversial lawyers in the United States. Indeed, Bailey figured prominently in a trial that later received extensive media coverage—the murder trial of former football star and TV commentator O. J. Simpson. Bailey convinced the high court to hear the Sheppard case and won a stunning victory.

Justice Tom Clark held that prejudicial pretrial publicity denied Sheppard the right to a fair and impartial trial (*Sheppard v. Maxwell* 1966). But finding that pretrial publicity can be prejudicial is a far easier task than deciding how to control it. The essential problem underlying the issue of prejudicial pretrial publicity is that two key protections of the Bill of Rights are on a collision course. The Sixth Amendment guarantees defendants the right to a trial before an impartial jury; decisions about guilt or innocence must be based on what jurors hear during the trial, not what they have heard or read outside the courtroom. At the same time, the First Amendment protects freedom of the press; what reporters print, say on radio, or broadcast on television is not subject to prior censorship. Without the First Amendment, there would be no problem; courts could simply forbid the press from reporting anything but the bare essentials of a crime. Although this is the practice in England, such prior restraints are not allowed in the United States.

To the Supreme Court, the answer to this dilemma lay in controlling the flow of information. "The carnival atmosphere at trial could easily have been avoided since the courtroom and courthouse premises are subject to the control of the court." But decades later, trial courts still struggle to strike the balance between freedom of the press and the rights of criminal defendants. Perhaps the biggest difference is that television (which was in its infancy when Sheppard was first tried) is now a dominating presence.

To learn more about the Sam Sheppard trial, go to http://dir.yahoo.com/Government/Law/Cases/Sam_Sheppard_Case/.

COURTS, CONTROVERSY, AND THE ADMINISTRATION OF JUSTICE

Should Cameras Be Allowed in the Courtroom?

 The rise of electronic media has added a new dimension to the defendant's right to a fair trial. Trials, of course, are open to the public, and journalists are free to observe and report on courtroom proceedings. However, since the sensational Lindbergh trial of the 1930s, radio and television coverage of the judicial process has been limited. In that case, German immigrant Bruno Hauptman was accused of kidnapping and murdering the son of the famous aviator Charles Lindbergh. Because it was perceived that the daily press coverage of the trial was excessive, rules of court came to forbid cameras or recording devices in the courthouse.

Restrictions on cameras in the courtroom are changing, however. The Supreme Court unanimously held that electronic media and still photographic coverage of public judicial proceedings do not violate a defendant's right to a fair trial; states are therefore free to set their own guidelines (*Chandler et al. v. Florida* 1981). Since then, the barriers against cameras in the courtroom have fallen in state after state. The U.S. Judicial Conference adopted a resolution allowing each court of appeals to decide whether cameras should be allowed (but only a few circuits have acted favorably). Just as important, only two states still prohibit all forms of electronic coverage of criminal court proceedings. Most states allow electronic coverage of criminal trials (Alexander 1996a). State rules and guidelines include many specific restrictions designed to prevent disruptions of the proceedings—limiting the number of cameras in the courtroom and prohibiting camera operators from moving around the courtroom while the trial is in session. The scope of permissible coverage varies greatly, though. In some states, the consent of the parties is required, meaning either side can veto coverage of the proceedings. In others, the news media need only receive permission from the trial judge to broadcast the proceedings.

Some people complain that televising trials distorts the process by encouraging the participants to play to the camera (Thaler 1994). They also argue that by covering only sensational trials and presenting only the most dramatic moments of hours of testimony, television stations fail to portray the trial process accurately. Others argue that cameras in the courtroom have a valuable educating role, providing the public with a firsthand view of how court proceedings operate. Law professor Donna Demac argues that televising court proceedings ultimately leads to greater trust in government: "Many people suspect that the legal system dispenses a different standard of justice for the wealthy," but the more the people see the system firsthand, the greater the chance that the system will be fair (quoted in Scardino 1989). Indeed, two separate studies found that viewers of a television trial of moderate interest became more knowledgeable about the judicial process (Alexander 1991; Raymond, 1992). As to the possibility of the camera's disrupting judicial proceedings, a detailed study of Florida, where the guidelines are the most liberal of any state allowing camera coverage, concluded: "Broadcast journalists who follow state guidelines present coverage which, upon close examination by presiding judges, participating attorneys and jurors, is perceived as undistorted" (Alexander 1991).

The widely televised trial of O. J. Simpson clearly caused some rethinking about cameras in the courtroom. Perceptions that lawyers were playing to the cameras apparently had an impact in several highly publicized cases that followed. Thus, some trial judges have refused to allow broadcasts of their trials.

What do you think? Should cameras be allowed in the courtroom, or should the nation return to its former ban on electronic media in the courthouse? Does the educative role of watching real trials outweigh the possibility that lawyers will play to the cameras?

 To continue the debate on whether cameras should be allowed in courtrooms, point your browser to:

http://www.nysda.org/Hot_Topics/Cameras_in_the_Court/cameras_in_the_court.html
http://www.mediastudies.org/courts/mauro.html
http://www.ibiblio.org/nppa/sherer/npp3.html

greatly in doubt, the study found that the "prejudiced jurors" were more likely to convict than the "nonprejudiced jurors" (Padawer-Singer and Barton 1975). Indeed, even modest pretrial publicity can prejudice potential jurors against a defendant (Moran and Cutler 1991).

Very few criminal trials, however, involve prejudicial pretrial publicity; news reports seldom extend beyond police blotter coverage. Indeed, the conditions necessary for media coverage to prejudice jurors to the extent that they are unable to decide a case based on courtroom evidence are likely to occur in only 1 of every 10,000 cases (Frasca 1988). But when there is extensive pretrial publicity, the jury selection process is greatly strained. Voir dire is geared to ferreting out ordinary instances of unfairness or prejudice, not to correcting the possibility of a systematic pattern of bias. For example, if an attorney excuses all jurors who have heard something about the case at hand, he or she runs the risk of selecting a jury solely from the least attentive, least literate members of the general public. On the other hand, if an attorney accepts jurors who assert that they will judge the case solely on the basis of testimony in open court, he or she is still not certain that the juror—no matter how well-intentioned—can hear the case with a truly open mind.

In trying to reconcile conflicting principles of a fair trial and freedom of the press, trial courts employ (singly or in combination) three techniques: limited gag orders, change of venue, and sequestering of the jury. Each of these methods suffers from admitted drawbacks (Kramer, Kerr, and Carroll 1990).

Limited Gag Order

The First Amendment forbids the court from censoring what the press writes about a criminal case, but it says nothing about restricting the flow of information to the media. Thus, in notorious cases in which it seems likely that selecting a jury may be difficult, judges now routinely issue a limited **gag order** forbidding those involved in the case—police, prosecutor, defense attorney, and defendant—from talking to the press. Violations are punishable as **contempt of court** (disobeying a judge's order). Since these people know the most about the

case (and often have the most to gain from pretrial publicity), the net effect is to dry up news leaks. However, consistent with the First Amendment, the press is free to publish any information it discovers. The greatest difficulty is that one of the people involved in the case may secretly provide information, in violation of the judge's order. The judge can then subpoena the reporter and order disclosure of the source. Reporters believe that identifying their sources will dry up the flow of information, so they refuse to testify. They are cited for contempt and go to jail. Thus, the court may infringe on freedom of the press when its intent is simply to guarantee another Bill of Rights protection—the right to a fair trial.

Change of Venue

The term **venue** refers to the place where a case is tried. If the court is convinced that a case has received such extensive publicity that picking an impartial jury is impossible, the trial may be shifted to another part of the state. If a case has received statewide coverage, however, such a change is of limited use. Defense attorneys face a difficult tactical decision in deciding whether to request a **change of venue.** They must weigh the effects of prejudicial publicity against the disadvantages of having a trial in a more rural and conservative area, where citizens are hostile to big-city defendants (particularly if they are black). Prosecutors generally oppose such moves because they believe that the chances of conviction are greater in the local community. To justify this position, prosecutors cite the expense of moving witnesses, documents, and staff to a distant city for a long trial.

Sequestering the Jury

A prime defect in the trial of Dr. Sheppard was the failure to shield the jury from press coverage of the ongoing trial. Indeed, jurors read newspaper stories of the trial, which included inadmissible evidence. One remedy that is common in trials involving extensive media coverage is to **sequester** the jury. The jurors live in a hotel, take their meals together, and participate in weekend recreation together. Sheriff deputies censor newspapers and shut off television news. The possibility of being in virtual quarantine for a number of weeks makes many citizens reluctant to serve. When sequestering is probable, the jury selected runs the risk of including only those citizens who are willing to be separated for long periods of time from friends and family, who can afford to be off work, or who look forward to a Spartan existence. At a minimum, sequestration is a trying experience for the jurors and may result in an unfair verdict (Levine 1996).

■ CONCLUSION

After 12 years in prison, Sheppard was retried. The prosecution put on essentially the same case, but they now faced one of the top defense attorneys in the nation. F. Lee Bailey tore into the prosecutor's witnesses and in closing argument likened the prosecution's case to "ten pounds of hogwash in a five-pound bag." After deliberating for less than 12 hours, the jury returned a verdict of not guilty. But for Sam Sheppard, liberty proved short-lived. He died in 1970, probably sent to an early grave by journalistic excess.

The Sheppard murder trial has been called the "first trial of the century," second only in celebrity status to the trial of O. J. Simpson. The legacy of the Sheppard case lived on not only in the important Supreme Court decision that it spawned but also in fiction—the TV series and later movie *The Fugitive*. More recently, the family has again sought to clear Dr. Sheppard's name. They blame the murder on a former gardener and argue that DNA evidence conclusively proves that an innocent man was convicted amid a media spectacle. However, in 2000 a Cleveland jury refused to find Sam Sheppard innocent, thus dealing a fatal legal blow to his son's efforts to clear his father's name.

In many ways, highly publicized jury trials for defendants—whether well known like Sam Sheppard and O. J. Simpson or hardly known at all—are the high point of the judicial process. Indeed, along with Lady Justice, jury trials stand as the primary symbol of justice. In turn, many Supreme Court decisions emphasize the importance of adversarial procedures at trial. Yet in examining the realities of trial, we are presented with two contradictory perspectives: Full-fledged trials are relatively rare, yet trials are an important dimension of the court process. Every year, 2 million jurors serve in some 200,000 civil and criminal cases. Although only a relative smattering of cases are ever tried, the possibility of trial shapes the entire process. Thus, long after trials have declined to minimal importance in other Western nations, the institution of the jury trial remains a vital part of the American judicial process.

CRITICAL THINKING QUESTIONS

1. What impact does the jury system have on the rest of the criminal justice system? How would criminal justice function differently if defendants had no right to a trial by a jury of their peers, which is the situation in virtually all of the non–common law nations of the world?

2. If you are in a federal courthouse and observe a six-member jury, what type of case is being tried? Why?

3. Compare two recent trials in your community. What were the similarities and differences in terms of jury selection, the prosecutor's case-in-main, the defense strategy, and the verdict? If possible, compare a murder trial to one involving another major felony. In what ways are murder trials different from, say, a trial for armed robbery or rape?

4. In the wake of the O. J. Simpson verdict of not guilty, many commentators spoke about the collapse of the jury system. Were these sentiments driven by the one verdict, or were there other reasons?

5. Why are some jury verdicts popular and others not? To what extent do differences of opinion over the fairness of a jury verdict reinforce notions that equate justice with winning (see Chapter 2)?

KEY TERMS

acquittal (325)
affirmative defense (320)
alibi defense (320)
alternate jurors (314)
best-evidence rule (315)
challenge for cause (312)
change of venue (330)
charging conference (323)
circumstantial evidence (315)
closing argument (323)
contempt of court (330)
cross-examination (319)
direct evidence (315)
duress (320)
entrapment (320)
evidence (315)
gag order (330)
hearsay (315)
hung jury (325)
immaterial (318)
impeach (318)
irrelevant (318)
jury deliberations (324)
jury instructions (323)
jury nullification (327)
master jury list (311)
mistrial (319)
objection (318)
opening statement (314)
peremptory challenge (312)
petit jury (307)
petty offense (308)
post-verdict motions (325)
prejudicial pretrial publicity (327)
presumption of innocence (315)
real evidence (315)
reasonable doubt (315)
rebuttal (323)
self-defense (320)
self-incrimination (320)
sequester (330)
statutory exemptions (312)
testimony (315)
trustworthiness (315)
venire (311)
venue (320)
verdict (325)
voir dire (312)

WORLD WIDE WEB RESOURCES AND EXERCISES

Web Guides

http://dir.yahoo.com/Government/Law/Jury_Duty/
http://dir.yahoo.com/Government/Law/Cases/
http://dir.yahoo.com/Society_and_Culture/Crime/
  Evidence/

Web Search Terms

jury
jury consultants
DNA
evidence

cameras in the courtroom
insanity defense
jury nullification
DNA testing

Useful URLs

The American Academy of Forensic Sciences is a professional society dedicated to the application of science to the law: **http://www. aafs.org/**.

Crime scene investigation can be found at **http://police2.ucr.edu/csi.html**.

Read jury news from the research division of the National Center for State Courts at **http:// www.ncsc.dni.us/research/jurors/Jurynews.htm**.

The Jury Research Institute provides trial consulting services: **http://www.jri-inc.com/**.

The National Court Reports Association is a trade association with a Web page at **http:// www.verbatimreporters.com/**.

Uncommon URLs

The Fully Informed Jury Association seeks to restore the political function of government: **http://www.fija.org/**.

Visit the Juror's Web Site: **http://members.tripod. com/~jctMac/jurynull.html**.

The Jury Rights Project educates jurors about their right to acquit people who have been accused of victimless crimes and thereby veto bad laws: **http://www.levellers.org/jrp/**.

The following Web site provides background and information about the insanity defense: **http://www.psych.org/public_info/insanity.cfm**.

To find out more about jury consultant Dr. Jo-Ellan Dimitrius and her consulting firm, go to **http://www.vindim.com/**.

Web Exercises

1. Watch a criminal trial on Court TV. How do prosecutors use the rules of evidence to prove the defendant guilty? What type of strategy does the defense use? A listing of current trials can be found at **http://www.courttv.com**.

2. Using the search engine of your choice, use the term "DNA testing" or "scientific evidence" to locate articles on the latest developments in scientific evidence. What issues are presented? To what extent does the discussion of these issues parallel differences of opinion embodied in the due process versus crime control models of justice?

3. Using the search engine of your choice, search for the term "jury nullification" to locate information on the topic. Do supporters of jury nullification form a full-fledged movement, or are they isolated groups of one or two people? To what extent do opinions about jury nullification reflect ideological differences between the due process model and the crime control model? To what extent do the views instead reflect a form of populist protest against the justice system?

INFOTRAC COLLEGE EDITION RESOURCES AND EXERCISES

Basic Searches

jury	*right to trial by jury*
cameras in the	*jury nullification*
courtroom	*DNA testing*
insanity defense	

Recommended Articles

Clay S. Conrad, "Jury Nullification"

Paul Jackson, "Jurors Flex Their Muscles"

Dan Johnson, "Witness: A Weak Link in the Judicial System"

Harper's, "Fear of a Black Jury"

Erick J. Haynie, "Populism, Free Speech, and the Rule of Law: The 'Fully Informed' Jury Movement and Its Implications"

Jet, "Lawyer's Comments about Race Leads to Mistrial in Murder Case"

Jeffrey Robert White, "The Civil Jury: 200 Years Under Siege"

InfoTrac College Edition Exercises

1. Using the search term "jury members," select two or more articles that discuss jury bias and/or jury diversity. What problems do these articles discuss, and what reforms are recommended?

2. Using the search term "jury," select two or more articles that discuss jury reform. What problems do these articles identify, and why? What solutions do they recommend? Do the articles represent similar or different social and/or political agendas?

3. Using the search term "DNA testing, evidence" or "DNA testing, laws," select two or more articles that discuss the advantages and/or drawbacks of expanding the use of DNA evidence in criminal trials. To what extent do these articles reflect concerns associated with the due process or the crime control model of justice?

FOR FURTHER READING

Abramson, Jeffrey. *We, the Jury: The Jury System and the Ideal of Democracy*. New York: Basic Books, 1994.

Boatright, Robert. "The 21st-Century American Jury: Reflections from the Cantigny Conference." *Judicature* 83 (2000): 288–297.

Burns, Robert. *A Theory of the Trial.* Princeton, NJ: Princeton University Press, 1999.

Chiasoon, Lloyd. *The Press on Trial: Crimes and Trials as Media Events.* Westport, CT: Praeger, 1997.

Fahringer, Herald. "The Peremptory Challenge: An Endangered Species?" *Criminal Law Bulletin* 31 (1995): 400–463.

Gardner, Thomas, and Terry Anderson. *Criminal Evidence: Principles and Cases*, 5th ed. Belmont, CA: Wadsworth, 2004.

Giles, Robert, and Robert Snyder, eds. *Covering the Courts: Free Press, Fair Trials and Journalistic Performance.* New Brunswick, NJ: Transaction Publishers, 1999.

Goldfarb, Ronald. *TV or Not TV: Television, Justice, and the Courts.* New York: New York University Press, 1998.

Munsterman, G. Thomas, Paula Hannaford, and G. Marc Whitehead, eds. *Jury Trial Innovations.* Williamsburg, VA: National Center for State Courts, 1997.

National Institute of Justice. *Eyewitness Evidence: A Guide for Law Enforcement.* Washington, DC: U.S. Department of Justice, 1999.

Insanity and Other Affirmative Defenses

Bonnie, Richard, Norman Poythress, Steven Hoge, John Monahan, and Marlene Eisenberg. "Decision-Making in Criminal Defense: An Empirical Study of Insanity Pleas and the Impact of Doubted Client Competence." *Journal of Criminal Law and Criminology* 87 (1996): 48–76.

Caplan, Lincoln. *The Insanity Defense and the Trial of John W. Hinckley, Jr.* Boston: D. R. Godine, 1984.

Miller, Kent, and Michael Radelet. *Executing the Mentally Ill: The Criminal Justice System and the Case of Alvin Ford.* Newbury Park, CA: Sage, 1993.

Morris, Norval. *The Brothel Boy and Other Parables of the Law.* New York: Oxford University Press, 1992.

Scientific Evidence and DNA

Champagne, Anthony, Danny Easterling, Daniel Shuman, Alan Tomkins, and Elizabeth Whitaker. "Are Court-Appointed Experts the Solution to the Problems of Expert Testimony?" *Judicature* 84 (2001): 178.

Foster, Kenneth, and Peter Huber. *Judging Science: Scientific Knowledge and the Federal Courts.* Cambridge, MA: MIT Press, 1999.

Freeman, Michael, and Helen Reece, eds. *Science in Court.* Brookfield, VT: Ashgate, 1998.

Huber, Peter. *Galileo's Revenge: Junk Science in the Courtroom.* New York: Basic Books, 1991.

Ragle, Larry. *Crime Scene.* New York: Avon Books, 1995.

Part IV Sentencing the Guilty

Sentences are the currency of the realm. Reformers, law professors, and appellate courts spend most of their time debating and analyzing how courts determine guilt or innocence. But judges, prosecutors, defense attorneys, and defendants focus much of their attention on sentencing. Will the defendant be granted probation? If not, how many years in prison will be imposed? These are the main topics that fuel the dynamics of courthouse justice.

Sentencing is involved in both the beginning and the end of the criminal justice system. For society, sentencing is the starting point; the reasons for punishing law violators establish the very purpose of the criminal justice system. For the defendant, sentencing is the last step in the process; whether he or she will be sentenced to prison or placed on probation will be decided. The courts stand in the middle; they must wrestle with a host of conflicting considerations, some of which have no easy answers. Dissatisfaction with how the courts perform these tasks is widespread and long-standing.

Chapter 15 considers the legal basis of judicial discretion in sentencing. Of particular interest are the why, the who, and the what of sentencing. Asking *why* we sentence provokes fundamental disagreement. Asking *who* sentences highlights the important role that legislative and executive agencies play in sentencing. Asking *what* sentences may be imposed draws our attention to the limited options available for punishing wrongdoers—typically prison or probation.

Chapter 16 examines how courtroom work groups choose between prison and probation. The choices judges actually make are criticized from both sides: To some, sentences are too harsh; others argue that sentences are too lenient. Still others are concerned that sentencing is unfair.

Chapter 15 Sentencing Options

I t was two o'clock in the morning and William Furman, a seventh-grade dropout, was intent on burglary. Awakened by a strange noise, William Micke, father of five, went downstairs to investigate. In his haste to flee, Furman tripped over a washing machine cord on the back porch, discharging his gun and hitting Micke through a closed solid plywood door. Although the killing was accidental, Georgia law authorized the death penalty. Judge and jury agreed with this policy, and William Furman was sentenced to death. ◀

Like so many other capital cases, the Furman conviction was appealed to the U.S. Supreme Court. Indeed, 118 cases were on the Court's docket that day. Like the rest of the nation, the highest court had been wrestling with the moral issue of who deserves to die in the electric chair, and like the rest of the nation, it was badly divided over the matter. In an unexpected move, however, Furman's appeal was granted certiorari. The Supreme Court agreed for the first time to hear arguments on whether the imposition of the death penalty constitutes "cruel and unusual punishment," as prohibited by the Eighth Amendment. The Court's first, tentative, groping answer came a year later. By the slimmest of margins, the Court declared all existing death penalty laws unconstitutional, and in the process irrevocably altered the debate over what punishments are appropriate for those who violate the criminal law.

The debate over the death penalty is the most obvious example of the unprecedented attention the nation has devoted over the last decades to crime. In large measure, the public holds judges, from the Supreme Court on down, responsible for high rates of crime and points to decisions such as *Furman* as examples. Understanding the dissatisfaction with sentencing and the sentencing reforms that have resulted requires an understanding of the legal basis of sentencing. This chapter focuses on the why, the who, and the what of sentencing. Punishments are shaped by philosophical and moral considerations. Asking *why* we sentence focuses attention on the competing justifications for sentencing. Probing *who* should make these choices reveals the complex sentencing structure in the United States. Although the public associates the judge with sentencing, closer scrutiny indicates that other branches of gov-

ernment share sentencing responsibility as well. Finally, examining the *what* of sentencing shows that a variety of sentences may be imposed on the guilty, including prison, probation, intermediate sanctions, fines, and restitution. And most controversial of all, a penalty of death may be imposed on a select number of defendants found guilty at trial.

WHY DO WE SENTENCE?

"An eye for an eye, a tooth for a tooth."

"Lock them up and throw away the key."

"Let this sentence be a warning to others."

"Sentencing should rehabilitate the offender."

These statements—variously drawn from the Bible, newspaper headlines, casual conversations, and statements by court officials—demonstrate that there is no consensus on how the courts should punish the guilty. Retribution, incapacitation, deterrence, and rehabilitation are the four principal justifications offered. These sentencing philosophies differ in important ways. Some focus on past behavior, whereas others are future-oriented. Some stress that the punishment should fit the crime, whereas others emphasize that punishment should fit the criminal. These issues influence contemporary thinking about sentencing.

Retribution

"An eye for an eye, a tooth for a tooth." This Old Testament phrase expresses the oldest of sentencing philosophies (see Exhibit 15-1).

Exhibit 15-1 Old Testament View of Sentencing

When one man strikes another and kills him, he shall be put to death. Whoever strikes a beast and kills it shall make restitution, life for life. When one man injures and disfigures his fellow-countryman, it shall be done to him as he has done; fracture for fracture, eye for eye, tooth for tooth; the injury and disfigurement that he has inflicted upon another shall in turn be inflicted upon him.

—Leviticus 24:17–22

What is most distinctive about **retribution** is its focus on past behavior; the severity of the punishment is directly tied to the seriousness of the crime. This concept is based on strongly held moral principles: Individuals are held responsible for their own actions. Because they have disregarded the rights of others, criminals are wicked people and therefore deserve to be punished. Punishing wrongdoers also reflects a basic human emotion, the desire for revenge: Because the victim has suffered, the criminal should suffer as well.

The concept of retribution clearly stands for punitive sentencing, but a closer probing reveals important subtleties involving limits on sentencing. Because society as a whole is punishing the criminal, individuals are not justified in taking the law into their own hands. Moreover, in applying sanctions, the severity of the punishment is limited to the severity of the injury of the victim. This is how Leviticus 24:20 differs from other ancient notions about punishment.

From biblical times through the eighteenth century, retribution provided the dominant justification for punishment. Beginning with the Enlightenment, however, retribution lost much of its influence. Criminal penalties based on revenge began to be viewed as barbaric, and more utilitarian reasons for sentencing were preferred. In recent times, however, retribution has once again attracted the interest of scholars and criminal justice reformers, who use a more humane phrasing: deserved punishment or **just deserts**. "Someone who infringes the rights of others . . . does wrong and deserves blame for his conduct. It is because he deserves blame that the sanctioning authority is entitled to choose a response that expresses moral disapproval; namely punishment" (von Hirsch 1976). In short, the severity of the sanction should be proportionate to the gravity of the defendant's criminal conduct.

As a sentencing philosophy, retribution suffers from several limitations. Its focus on crimes of violence offers little apparent guidance for sentencing the far more numerous defendants who have committed property violations. Its moralistic emphasis on individual responsibility does not fit well with modern explanations of human behavior based on social, physical, and psychological factors. Its emphasis on vengeance does not easily square with constitutional limits on government power (individual rights) that are fundamental to a representative democracy. Most important, though, it emphasizes the past behavior of the defendant and exhibits no concern for future criminal activity. Some studies demonstrate that extended periods of custody may actually increase the likelihood that an inmate will commit future criminal acts. Thus, sentencing on the basis of retribution may prove to be contrary to the goal of crime reduction.

Incapacitation

"Lock them up and throw away the key." Average citizens, outraged by a recent, shocking crime, often express sentiments like this. The assumption of **incapacitation** is that crime can be prevented if criminals are physically restrained. The theory of isolating current or potential criminals differs from the theory of retribution in two important ways. First, it is future-oriented; the goal is to prevent future crimes, not punish past ones. Second, it focuses on the personal characteristics of the offender; the type of person committing the crime is more important than the crime committed. Unlike rehabilitation, however, incapacitation has no intention of reforming the offender.

Since ancient times, societies have banished persons who have disobeyed the rules. England transported criminals to penal colonies, such as Georgia and Australia. Russia exiled dissidents to cold, distant Siberia, where they could not threaten the government. More commonly, nations have used prisons to isolate guilty offenders, preventing them from committing additional crimes in the community. Some people likewise justify the death penalty on the basis that it prevents future crimes.

Incapacitation is probably the most straightforward justification offered for punishing wrongdoers. As a sentencing philosophy, however, it suffers from important limitations. It cannot provide any standards about how long a sentence should be. Indeed, the goal of crime prevention may be used to justify severe sanctions for both trivial and serious offenses. Moreover, isolation without efforts directed toward rehabilitation may produce more severe criminal behavior once the offender is released. Prisons protect the community, but that protection is only temporary. Applying the incapacitation theory to the fullest would require the building of many more prisons, at great expense.

The incapacitation theory of sentencing has never been well articulated. Its assumptions about crime and criminals are simplistic. But in recent years a more focused variant, **selective incapacitation,** has received considerable attention. Research has shown that a relatively small number of criminals are responsible for a large number of crimes (Haapanen 1989). These findings have led to an interest in targeting dangerous offenders (Chaiken and Chaiken 1990). Some studies estimate that sending serious offenders to prison for longer periods of time will result in a significant reduction in crime (Shinnar and Shinnar 1975). Not all researchers agree, however, that selective incapacitation will greatly reduce crime (Van Dine, Conrad, and Dinitz 1979). Critics argue that even though some offenders may be imprisoned, others on the verge of criminality are ready to take their places (Visher 1987; Auerhahn 1999).

Deterrence

"Let this sentence be a warning to others." Phrases like this reflect one of the more modern and also most widely held justifications for punishment. According to **deterrence theory,** the purpose of punishment is the prevention of future crimes. Deterrence is not content to punish the given wrongdoer; rather, it seeks to prevent other potential offenders from committing crimes. Deterrence, however, does not propose to change offenders—just deter them. Much like rehabilitation, deterrence argues that the punishment should fit the criminal. Note that this is a different concern from that of retribution theory, in which the punishment should fit the crime.

A nineteenth-century British lawyer, reformer, and criminologist, Jeremy Bentham, first articulated the deterrence theory. To Bentham, punishment based on retribution was pointless and counterproductive. Instead, sanctions should be used to further society's goal of preventing crime. Bentham believed that human behavior is governed by individual calculation: People seek to maximize pleasure and minimize pain. Under this utilitarian theory, the basic objective of punishment is to discourage crime by making it painful. Because people seek to minimize pain, they will refrain from activities, such as crimes, that result in painful sanctions.

Notions of deterrence form the core of contemporary discussions about sentencing. In a general sense, many people refrain from committing illegal acts because they fear the consequences of being convicted. After a party, for example, an intoxicated guest may take a taxi home rather than run the risk of being arrested and disgraced by a drunken driving conviction. In this situation, one can easily argue that the threat of punishment does deter. In terms of other applications, however, the picture becomes much cloudier.

The exact nature of the role that deterrence plays and the extent to which sentencing policies affect crime and criminals is unclear. An extensive literature examines deterrence but reaches no firm conclusions. Some studies find a deterrent effect, and others do not (Nagin 1998). Although discussions of deterrence are usually coupled with calls for increasing the severity of sentences, some research suggests that certainty of punishment is more of a deterrent than the severity of punishment (Wilson 1983). Moreover, deterrence rests on the assumption of rational, calculating behavior. Many crimes (particularly crimes of violence) are committed on the spur of the moment. Other offenses are committed while the defendant is under the influence of drugs or alcohol. For these reasons, many observers question whether court sentences—particularly severe ones—do indeed deter.

Rehabilitation

The most appealing modern justification for imposing punishment is to restore a convicted offender to a constructive place in society through vocational, educational, or therapeutic treatment. The idea of **rehabilitation** assumes that criminal behavior is the result of social or psychological disorders, and that the treatment of such disorders should be the primary goal of corrections. Success means assessing the needs of the individual and providing a program to meet those needs. Ultimately, then, offenders are not being punished but treated, not only for their own good but also for the benefit of society. Under rehabilitation, sentences should fit the offender rather than the offense.

The concept of rehabilitation dominated thinking about sentencing throughout the twentieth century, providing the intellectual linchpin for such important developments as probation and parole. Most court personnel and correctional officials have strongly favored rehabilitation. It has also enjoyed widespread public support; almost three out of four persons favor the idea that the main emphasis in prisons should be to help the offender become a productive citizen.

During recent decades, the rehabilitative ideal has been challenged on both empirical and normative grounds. Growing evidence shows that rehabilitative programs do not substantially reduce the later criminality of their clients (Blumstein et al. 1983). California, for example, where the rehabilitative model had been most completely incorporated, was also marked by high rates of recidivism (repeat criminal behavior). To some, the key weakness of rehabilitation is that people cannot be coerced to change. Some prisoners participate in prison rehabilitation programs, such as counseling, job training, and religious services, in order to gain an early release—not because they wish to change their behavior.

Apart from the empirical question of whether rehabilitation programs have been successful, concern has also been voiced that sentencing structures based on the rehabilitative ideal grant too much discretion to judges and parole boards. As a result of this discretion, the humanitarian goal of rehabilitation can serve to mask punishment. In most prisons, rehabilitation programs are minimal or nonexistent. Yet judges often sentence in the hope of rehabilitating the offender, which may result in lengthier prison sentences. Thus, to critics, sentencing an offender according to the rehabilitative ideal may be more punitive than sentencing for the sake of punishment alone.

Competing Sentencing Philosophies

Justifications for punishing wrongdoers are based on religious and moral views of right and wrong as well as empirical perceptions of human behavior (see Exhibit 15-2). Of the four philosophies—retribution, incapacitation, deterrence, and rehabilitation—none alone is adequate; the various goals must be balanced. Therefore, elements of each of these four philosophies have been incorporated into society's efforts to control crime. As a result, sentencing decisions reflect ambivalent expectations about the causes of crime, the nature of criminals, and the role of the courts in reducing crime. The limitations of historical sentencing philosophies have led a small band of adherents to pioneer a new way of thinking about criminals and their victims (see Courts, Controversy, and Reducing Crime: Should Restorative Justice Replace Revenge-Based Sentencing?).

Since the late 1970s, the reasons for sentencing have been the subject of intense debate. After three-quarters of a century, the intellectual dominance of the rehabilitative ideal began to crumble and then collapse. This has resulted in widespread sentencing reforms, many of which focus on who should have the authority to impose a sentence and what limits should be placed on that authority.

WHO SHOULD DECIDE THE SENTENCE?

From the inside looking out, sentencing is a judicial function. With a few exceptions, only the judge has the legal authority to send the guilty

Exhibit 15-2 Contrasting Sentencing Philosophies

	Law on the Books	Law in Action
Retribution	Punishment inflicted on a person who has infringed on the rights of others and so deserves to be penalized to a degree commensurate with the crime.	Focuses on the crime committed (not on the defendant). Limits punishment to the harm done to the offender.
Incapacitation	Deprives a convicted person of the capacity to commit crimes against society by detention in prison.	Focuses on defendant's past history. Can lead to very unequal sentences because minor offenses can be punished more severely than major ones.
Deterrence	Punishment of criminals to prevent future crimes.	Based on Bentham's utilitarian theory. General deterrence (directed toward the general populace) differs from special deterrence (the specific defendant).
Rehabilitation	The process of restoring a convicted offender to a constructive place in society through some form of vocational, educational, or therapeutic treatment.	Focuses on the defendant rather than the crime committed. Dominant sentencing philosophy for most of the twentieth century. Under what conditions defendants can be rehabilitated is subject to extensive debate.

to prison or grant probation. From the outside looking in, however, sentencing responsibility involves all three branches of government—legislative, executive, and judicial. The result is a varied and complex sentencing structure that has changed greatly over the past 30 years (Tonry 1999).

Throughout most of the twentieth century, sentencing was exercised within broad limits set by the legislature, which prescribed maximum sentences. The judicial branch of government had primary authority over who went to prison, and an executive agency—parole boards—controlled the length of the prison term. Since the mid-1970s, dramatic changes have been made in the laws under which offenders are sent to prison and in the mechanisms that control how long they stay there. Legislatures have increased their control over the sentencing process, and the judiciary and the parole boards have taken steps to formalize and regularize their exercise of discretion in applying sanctions. The result has been a significant narrowing of sentencing discretion in most states (see Exhibit 15-3).

Legislative Sentencing Responsibility

Legislatures are initially responsible for creating sentencing options. Recall from Chapter 2 that there can be no crime and no punishment without law. Legislative sentencing responsibility is expressed in the criminal codes enacted by legislative bodies. Legislatures specify terms of imprisonment in two different ways. Consistent with the goal of rehabilitation, which dominated correctional thinking through most of the twentieth century, state legislatures adopted **indeterminate** (often called *indefinite*) **sentences,** based on the idea that correctional personnel must have discretion to release an offender when treatment has been successful. States with indeterminate sentences stipulate a minimum and maximum amount of time to be served in prison—1 to 5 years, 3 to 10 years, 20 years to life, and so on. At the time of sentencing, the offender knows the range of the sentence and knows that parole is a possibility after the minimum sentence, minus good time, has been served.

COURTS, CONTROVERSY, AND REDUCING CRIME

Should Restorative Justice Replace Revenge-Based Sentencing?

After imposing a prison sentence on a rapist, Justice John Kelly observed that the victim was no less distraught than she had been throughout the court proceedings. So before he called the next case, he asked the victim to approach the bench. Speaking briefly and quietly, he concluded with these words: "You understand that what I have done here demonstrates conclusively that *what happened was not your fault.*" Hearing these words, she began to weep and ran from the courtroom. Several days later, the Australian judge called the family and learned that his words had been words of vindication for the woman; they marked the beginning of her psychological healing. Her tears had been tears of healing. In *Restoring Justice,* Daniel Van Ness and Karen Strong (1997) use this example to emphasize their central theme—that sentencing should promote healing. The restorative justice movement seeks to replace retribution with restoration. In essence, the failures of the contemporary criminal justice system are traced to the historical emphasis on vengeance.

Restorative justice is based on three distinct elements (Galaway and Hudson 1996):

- Crime is primarily a conflict between individuals, which results in injuries (physical and/or psychological) to victims, the community, and the offender as well. Therefore, crime is only secondarily a violation of governmental laws.

- The principal aim of the criminal justice system should be to repair these injuries. Therefore, promoting peace and reconciling parties is much more important than punishing the guilty.

- The criminal justice system should facilitate involvement of victims, offenders, and the community. Therefore, lay citizens should play a central role in the criminal justice system, and professionals (police, prosecutors, and probation officers, for example) should play less of a role.

Clearly, proponents of restorative justice reject the crime control model's emphasis on punishment. In their view, vengeance is counterproductive. But at the same time, they view the due process model as not going far enough. The rehabilitative model targets offenders but provides no healing for victims and fails to address the trauma they have experienced.

Skeptics voice concern that restorative justice means considerably different things to different people. Indeed, by stressing abstract concepts rather than pointing to specific programs, proponents make it somewhat difficult to discuss restorative justice because many of the examples singled out as demonstrating successful implementation are drawn from other countries.

If skeptics seem somewhat receptive to this new idea, critics express open hostility about subjecting a victim to another, possibly equally damaging, encounter with the defendant. Typical was the person on an Internet discussion list who wanted to know why victims should be forced to bargain with a person who has caused them harm. Perhaps victims do not want to go through the process because of legitimate concerns (unnecessarily revisiting the original trauma) or out of shortsightedness (holding onto the role of victim is comfortable). Overall, it is clear that the restorative justice understanding of victims is far different from those views that stress punishment and not forgiveness (discussed in Chapter 9).

What do you think? Should our current criminal justice system, which is often characterized as a revenge-based system, be replaced by restorative justice? What types of victims might be most amenable to conferencing? What types of defendants are most likely to express remorse? What elements of the community would be most supportive of restorative justice?

To continue the debate, use the search term "restorative justice" to locate an article on either side of the debate. Here are two possibilities:

The Economist, "Really Really Sorry: Restorative Justice"

Russell S. Harrison, "Community-Based Mediation Programs . . ."

Exhibit **15-3** Changing Sentencing Structures in the United States		
	Most of Twentieth Century	Since the Mid-1970s
Legislative responsibility	Legislators provided wide parameters for possible sentences. Little guidance provided about who should be placed on probation. Little guidance offered on how long a prison sentence should be.	Perceiving judges as unduly lenient, legislatures have adopted sentencing guidelines, mandatory minimums, and three-strikes laws (see Chapter 16).
Judicial responsibility	Judges had wide discretion in deciding on a specific sentence. Actual sentences imposed could vary significantly from judge to judge.	Judges' sentencing discretion has been greatly curtailed. Judges complain that they are unable to shape sentences to real crimes committed by real criminals.
Executive responsibility	Correction officials enjoyed wide discretion in awarding good time and deciding when to place a convict on parole.	Good time and parole have been abolished or greatly restricted in most jurisdictions. Prison overcrowding has resulted in even wider discretion for correction officials.

How long the person actually remains in prison is determined by the parole authority, based on its assessment of the offender's progress toward rehabilitation.

Because of growing disillusionment with the rehabilitative model, determinate sentences have become more popular. **Determinate sentences** (sometimes called *fixed sentences*) consist of a specified number of years rather than a range of years. For example, the judge must sentence the defendant to imprisonment for 5 years, or 10 years, or whatever the legislature specifies for a particular offense.

In waging wars on crime and wars on drugs, legislative bodies have adopted the deterrent theory of sentencing, opting to mandate harsher sentences for criminal violations. In furtherance of this goal, numerous legislative bodies have enacted major changes in sentencing laws, aiming to reduce the amount of discretion exercised by actors in the other branches of government. A number of states have restricted the carte blanche authority historically granted judges and have also limited (and in some cases abolished) the discretion of executive agencies as well (Griset 1991). Chapter 16 will explore in more detail issues related to

mandatory minimums, sentencing guidelines, and the like.

Judicial Sentencing Responsibility

Only judges have the authority to choose among the sentencing options provided by the legislature. Other members of the work group may recommend, but only the judge can decide. Of course, there are some minor exceptions to this general proposition, but these minor exceptions aside, American judges traditionally have enjoyed virtually unlimited judicial sentencing responsibility.

Wide judicial discretion in sentencing reflected the rehabilitative model, which stressed that punishment should fit the criminal. No two crimes or criminals are exactly alike; sentences should therefore be individualized, with judges taking these differences into account. But there is no agreement on what factors should increase the penalty or reduce it. By the mid-1970s, wide judicial discretion had come under attack from both ends of the political spectrum. Advocates of the due process model of criminal justice expressed concern that judicial sentencing discretion was too broad, resulting in inequities such as racial discrimination (Frankel 1972). Conversely, proponents of the crime control model expressed concern that too much judicial discretion led to unduly lenient sentences. These twin political movements, although contradictory, led legislatures to greatly reduce judicial sentencing discretion. Thus, an increasing number of jurisdictions are narrowing judicial discretion over sentencing in some manner.

Executive Sentencing Responsibility

Sentences imposed by judges are typically carried out by officials of the executive branch. Of particular importance is the impact of executive officials on prison populations. How long an offender will be imprisoned depends not only on the length of the sentence imposed by the judge but also on the decisions made by governors, parole boards, and departments of corrections. Few prisoners serve their maximum terms of imprisonment. Each year, more than 700,000 inmates are released from prison to serve the remainder of their sentences in the community (Bureau of Justice Statistics 1998). The most common forms of early release are parole, good time, and (to a lesser extent) executive clemency.

Parole is the conditional release of an inmate from incarceration, under supervision, after a portion of the prison sentence has been served. A parole officer supervises the conditions of release, and any rule violations or new crimes can result in a return to prison for the balance of the unexpired term. **Parole boards,** which are usually appointed by the governor, vary greatly in their discretionary authority. More than 750,000 persons are currently on parole in the United States (Bureau of Justice Statistics 2003f).

There is another way in which decisions made by the executive branch affect how long an inmate must stay in prison. In many states, prisoners are awarded **good time**—days off their minimum or maximum terms as a reward for good behavior or for participation in various vocational, educational, and treatment programs. The amount of good time that can be earned varies from 5 days a month to 45 days a month in some states. Correctional officials find these sentence-reduction provisions necessary for the maintenance of institutional order and as a mechanism to reduce overcrowding. They usually have discretion in awarding good time.

State governors, as well as the president of the United States, have the power to pardon any prisoner in their jurisdiction, reduce the sentence, or make the prisoner eligible for parole (Moore 1989; Ruckman 1997). **Pardons** are not a common method of prisoner release, however; only a small group of inmates receive executive clemency each year.

The early release of prisoners through the use of parole and good time has come under heavy political attack in recent years. The result has been significant changes in some jurisdictions. Sixteen states and the federal government have abolished parole board authority to release offenders, and another four have abolished parole board authority for releasing violent offenders. Similarly, legislatures in many states have reduced or eliminated good time for certain types of prisoners. Despite efforts to reduce the use of parole and curb the awarding of good time, burgeoning prison populations increasingly force correctional officials to use parole as a backdoor solution to prison overcrowding (Kelly and Ekland-Olson 1991).

▌WHAT SENTENCE SHOULD BE IMPOSED?

What types of sentences should be imposed upon the guilty? Today answers center on prison and probation, with a hot debate over the death penalty. But throughout history sentences were very different. Flogging, the stocks, exile, chopping off a hand, and branding are just a few examples of punishments historically inflicted on the guilty. Today such sanctions are viewed as violating the Constitution's prohibition against **cruel and unusual pun-**

COURT TV

Punishment: Cruel and Unusual

Prisons, through the ages, have been thought of as barbaric and inhumane institutions. They were typically places where people went to await punishment, not institutions for correction. The persons leaving were typically worse off than when they entered.

The prison system, as we think of it today, emerged about 200 years ago. In the United States, the Quaker movement pioneered the idea that prisons should be places where criminals were corrected not punished. Based on these ideas, Eastern State Penitentiary in Philadelphia opened in 1820. Punishment was now administered in private, not in public. But the good intentions of the reformers did not produce the results intended. Prisoners were more likely to be driven insane than to be reformed.

Some people wonder whether the faulty assumptions of the past are being repeated today, only in a different form.

View a video clip of the Eastern State Prison on your copy of the CourtTV CD-ROM. As you watch the video, keep the following questions in mind:

1. In what ways have contemporary theories of punishment—retribution, incapacitation, deterrence, and rehabilitation—been influenced by early American prison reforms as reflected in the Eastern State Penitentiary?

2. Punishment in early American life was often public. Today it is more private. But in what ways might removing punishment from public eye mask inhumanity?

3. What do the visual images of Eastern State Penitentiary suggest about contemporary standards reflected in condition-of-confinement lawsuits?

4. Do you agree with the concluding narration that suggests "perhaps we haven't changed at all"?

ishment. In their place, we use imprisonment, probation, intermediate sanctions, fines, and restitution. Many states also make formal provisions for capital punishment, but the death penalty is rarely used. In essence, these forms of punishment are tools created under the sentencing structure to advance society's theories of punishment. They are the options from which the sentencing judge must choose (see Exhibit 15-4).

One can approach the question of which penalty should be imposed upon the guilty from either a micro or a macro perspective. The micro perspective focuses on a specific defendant convicted of a crime. It is from this perspective that victims often view sentencing, and from this vantage point they are often critical of the judge's (or sometimes the legislature's) choice, arguing that the sentence is too lenient. It is vitally important, however, to assess such criticisms from a macro perspective. From this vantage point, prisons are already overcrowded, the caseloads of probation officers overwhelming. It is for this reason that judges occasionally address crime victims and explain the painfully obvious—to send this defendant to prison will require correctional officials to release someone who is possibly an even greater threat to the community.

The next chapter will examine how the courtroom work group decides on the specific penalty for a convict. For now, we will examine the various options available, beginning with that most distinctly American institution, the prison.

IMPRISONMENT

Although it has been used from time to time throughout history, **imprisonment** (incarceration) has become the dominant form of punishment only during the last two centuries. The United States imprisons a larger share of its population than any other nation. More than 2 million inmates are currently housed in prisons and jails. One reason for this high rate of imprisonment is the length of sentences; prison sentences in the United States are quite long compared to those imposed in Europe,

Exhibit 15-4 Sentencing Options

	Law on the Books	Law in Action
Prison	A correctional facility for housing adults convicted of felony offenses, usually under the control of state government.	Almost 1.4 million U.S. adults are in prison. Seven percent of inmates are female. Forty-five percent of prison inmates are black.
Parole	Adults conditionally released to community supervision after serving part of a prison term. The parolee is subject to being returned to prison for rule violations or other offenses.	More than 700,000 are on parole from state or federal prison. Twelve percent of parolees are women. Fifty-three percent of parolees are white.
Probation	Punishment for a crime that allows the offender to remain in the community without incarceration but subject to certain conditions.	More than 4 million adults are under federal, state, or local jurisdiction on probation. Half of all offenders on probation are on probation for a felony.
Intermediate sanctions	A variety of punishments that are more restrictive than traditional probation but less stringent than incarceration.	Much less costly than imprisonment. Community service requires offender to perform public service such as street cleaning or hospital volunteer work.
Fines	A sum of money to be paid to the government by a convicted person as punishment for an offense.	Often used in misdemeanors. Recent research shows that it can be effectively used in select felonies.
Restitution	Requirement that the offender pay to the victim a sum of money to make good the loss.	Most defendants are so poor that they cannot reasonably be expected to make restitution.
Capital punishment	The use of the death penalty (execution) as the punishment for the commission of a particular crime.	More than 3,500 prisoners are on death row. Seventy-one executions during 2002. Fifty-five percent of death row inmates are white.

where it is rare for a defendant to be sentenced to more than five years.

Prison Overcrowding

The political rhetoric of getting tough on criminals (see Chapter 1) clearly has had an impact—prisons are filled to overflowing. Prison overcrowding has become the dominant reality of criminal justice policy. Figure 15-1 shows how the size of the prison population has skyrocketed in recent years, more than tripling from the 1970s to today. And the trend continues; record high numbers of prisoners are reported every year, with increases averaging from 8 percent to 12 percent. It is worth noting that skyrocketing prison populations occurred during

a period when crime rates (see Chapter 10) were largely constant and now are falling.

Conditions of Confinement Lawsuits

Numbers of prisoners provide only part of the picture. Rapid increases in the size of the prison population occurred during the same time that federal courts began to demand improvements in prison conditions that have often been described as substandard.

Traditionally, courts followed a hands-off policy regarding prisons, choosing not to interfere in their internal administration. But this policy began to change in 1964 (*Cooper v.*

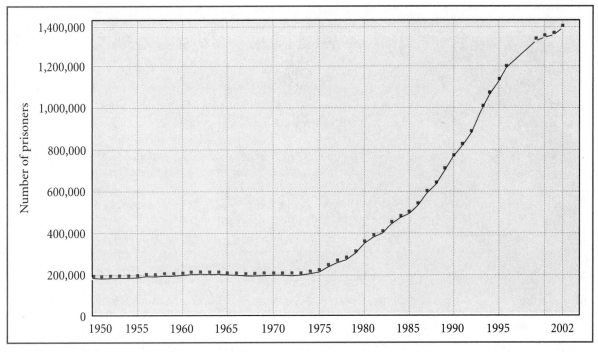

Figure 15-1
Growing Prison Population

SOURCE: Paige Harrison and Allen Beck, *Prisoners in 2002* (Washington, DC:
U.S. Department of Justice, Bureau of Justice Statistics, 2003).

Pate). By the 1970s, the federal courts began to scrutinize the operations of correctional institutions to ensure compliance with the Eighth Amendment's protection against cruel and unusual punishment (DiIulio 1990). Prisoners have sued, in what are often termed **conditions of confinement lawsuits,** contending that state officials have deprived them of their constitutional rights, such as adequate medical treatment and protection against excessive force by correctional officers and violence by other inmates (Hanson and Daley 1995). Exhibit 15-5 summarizes key developments in the law concerning imprisonment.

The entire prison systems of at least nine states were declared unconstitutional, and individual prisons were found constitutionally defective in many others. The net effect was that for many years most states operated all or part of their correctional systems under a federal court order. Federal judges in virtually all states ordered state governments to alter dramatically the way in which they operate their prisons and jails. These court orders specified a maximum prison population, required phys-

ical conditions to be upgraded, increased the number of prison guards, and mandated minimal medical facilities (Chilton 1991; Crouch and Marquart 1990; Taggart 1989). These federal court orders have had a significant effect in transforming prison conditions, particularly in the South (Feeley and Rubin 1998).

It is now harder to challenge prison conditions in federal court, however. The Rehnquist Court created a new standard under the Eighth Amendment, holding that the prisoner must show "deliberate indifference" on the part of prison officials (*Wilson v. Seiter* 1991). And in 1996, Congress passed the Prison Litigation Reform Act, which terminated federal court supervision of state prisons. Nonetheless, state correctional officials are aware that slipping back to old practices will result in future litigation.

High Costs

Getting tough on criminals is popular, yet public opinion polls show that spending money for

Exhibit 15-5 Key Developments Concerning Imprisonment

Eighth Amendment	1791	Excessive bail shall not be required, nor excessive fines imposed, nor cruel and unusual punishments inflicted.
Cooper v. Pate	1964	Prisoners can sue prison officials in federal court.
Ruiz v. Estelle	1980	U.S. District Court declares that conditions of confinement in the Texas prison system are unconstitutional.
Estelle v. Gamble	1976	Deliberate indifference to serious medical needs of prisoners constitutes the unnecessary and wanton infliction of pain, and thus violates the Eighth Amendment.
Rhodes v. Chapman	1981	Double-celling and crowding do not necessarily constitute cruel and unusual punishment.
Whitley v. Albers	1986	A prisoner shot in the leg during a riot does not suffer cruel and unusual punishment if the action was taken in good faith to maintain discipline rather than for the mere purpose of causing harm.
Wilson v. Seiter	1991	Prisoners contesting conditions of confinement in federal court must show that prison officials acted with "deliberate indifference" to prisoner needs and living conditions.
Prison Litigation Reform Act	1996	Congress limits the authority of federal courts to supervise the operations of correctional institutions.
Miller v. French	2000	Upheld the Prison Litigation Reform Act, saying Congress could lawfully impose a 90-day time limit to rule on prison condition lawsuits.

more prisons is not a high priority for the general public. Prisons are costly to build and even more costly to maintain. Estimates of the costs of constructing a single cell for a prisoner range from $75,000 to $100,000 (Clear and Cole 2003). The costs of incarcerating a prisoner (clothes, food, and guards, primarily) depend on the level of confinement and also vary from state to state, ranging from $20,000 to $30,000 per prisoner per year. Exhibit 15-6 shows the total cost of building and maintaining a 500-cell prison over 30 years as $337.5 million.

Faced with swelling prison populations and federal court orders over conditions of confinement, state legislatures have been faced with spending enormous sums of money to build new prisons and upgrade existing ones. Prison construction during the 1990s was a growth industry, with 213 state and federal prisons built during the first five years at an estimated cost of $30 billion ("In '90s, Prison" 1997). Despite large expenditures, no state has been able to build prisons fast enough to keep ahead of surging prison admissions. On December 31, 2002, half of the states were operating prisons at between 1 percent and 16 percent above capacity, and federal prisons were operating at 33 percent above capacity (Bureau of Justice Statistics 2003d).

Some states have declared an emergency situation, thus triggering the early release of certain types of prisoners. States that fail to take such action face sanctions from federal judges. Contempt of court, hefty fines, and judicially mandated release of prisoners are some of the remedies federal judges have imposed on state and local officials who have failed to take action to solve prison overcrowding (Clear and Cole 2003).

The long-standing political debate over sentencing has now given way to the overriding reality of a severe shortage of prison cells. State after state is discovering that the political rhetoric of the late twentieth century

THE MURDER TRIAL OF SHAREEF COUSIN

Doing Time on the Farm

After denying defense motions for a new trial, Judge Bigelow officially ordered that Shareef Cousin die by lethal injection. Soon after, Cousin was transported to Louisiana's death row, featured in the movie *Dead Man Walking*. After the district attorney decided not to try Cousin a second time for murder, he was returned to the Louisiana State Penitentiary (LSP) at Angola, the largest maximum security prison in the United States. It houses some 5,100 men, three-quarters of whom are black and 85 percent of whom will die within its walls.

Angola has been a prison since the end of the Civil War. The prison is divided into six self-contained units, many of which are called camps. Camp F is death row. Each has its own warden, kitchen, and other facilities. According to the Louisiana State Penitentiary Museum Web site, "LSP consists of 18,000 acres of the finest farmland in the south. It is ideally situated for the prison as it is located in a rural area, surrounded on three sides by the Mississippi River, and bordered on the fourth side by the rugged Tunica Hills." The location is "ideal" in the sense that it is virtually escape-proof because it is so isolated. But this isolation also symbolizes one of the oldest of American traditions—NIMBY (Not In My Back Yard).

The rural area has embraced the prison because it provides employment for 1,517 correctional officers plus a host of medical and support staff. Many of these are third- or fourth-generation employees, some of them living right on the prison grounds. At Angola, the principal activity is farming. The majority of medium and maximum security inmates work eight hours a day, five days per week, growing corn, soybeans, cotton, and food for the prison. The rural nature of the prison was featured in the 1998 documentary film *The Farm: Angola USA*. It is also famous for its annual prison rodeo, held every October. The rural focus of Angola is in stark contrast to its principal inhabitants—inmates from big cities. LSP provides some rehabilitation programs—education and self-help groups, primarily—but these programs are limited.

At one time Angola was one of the most violent prisons in the United States, notorious for beatings, rapes, and murder. In 1973, for example, there were 40 prison murders. In 1971 the first lawsuit protesting conditions of confinement was filed. In 1975 the federal courts took over the entire prison system, finding that conditions at Angola "shock the conscience of any right-thinking person" and "flagrantly violate basic constitutional requirements" (*Williams v. Edwards*). In the words of U.S. District Judge Frank Polozola, who has been overseeing the state prison system since 1973, when he first visited Angola "he couldn't tell the difference between guards and inmates," partly because guards did not wear uniforms and some "trusties" carried guns (Wardlaw 1998). The state has been forced to spend massive amounts of money to improve conditions. Improvement in conditions have been major. For example, inmate murder is now a rarity. Finally, in 1999, the federal court order was dissolved.

Shareef Cousin was later transferred to the Washington Correctional Institute, another Louisiana prison. On at least one occasion he was placed in administrative segregation, and he has filed a prisoner petition in federal court contending that the prison officials acted illegally. According to his handwritten petition, he is prisoner #363553 in Sleet 4, 4s, cell #8.

For some views of life inside Angola, go to

The Louisiana State Penitentiary Museum:
http://www.angolamuseum.org/

"Fixin' to Die": The Louisiana Prison Hospice:
http://www.npha.org/fixin.html

Prison art by Kevin Seward, inmate at Louisiana State Prison: http://prisonart.virtualave.net/

to get tough on criminals by sending more people to prison for longer periods must give way to the fiscal realities of the twenty-first century—adjusting sentencing policies to fit prison capacity. Almost out of desperation, states are now turning to alternative penalty programs that resemble ideas that were tried and largely discarded a decade ago.

Exhibit **15-6**	Financial Projections over 30 Years for Building a New 500-Cell Prison		
	Cells	1-Year Total	30-Year Total
Construction costs	500 × $75,000	$37.5 million	$ 37.5 million
Incarceration costs	500 × $20,000	$10.0 million	$300.0 million
Totals		$47.5 million	$337.5 million

PROBATION

Probation is the principal alternative to imprisonment. It is also the most commonly used sanction in the United States; about four times as many offenders are placed on probation every year as are sent to prison. Altogether, about 4 million adults are on probation, a number that represents a doubling in less that two decades. The increasing use of probation is a direct reflection of the serious problem of prison overcrowding. Ironically, it has resulted in a significant amount of "probation crowding" (overload of the probation system equivalent to prison overcrowding) (Byrne, Lurigio, and Baird 1989). Figure 15-2 shows that probation crowding is rising almost as dramatically as prison overcrowding. As a result, probation officers often must handle excessive caseloads.

Unlike incarceration, **probation** is designed as a means of maintaining control over offenders while permitting them to live in the community (under supervision). The major justification for probation is that prisons are inappropriate places for some defendants and limited supervision is a better way to rehabilitate criminals. Youthful or first-time offenders may only become embittered if mixed in prison with hardened criminals; they may end up learning more sophisticated criminal techniques. But most important, probation is significantly less expensive than imprisonment.

State and federal laws grant judges wide discretion in deciding whether to place a defendant on probation. Generally, statutes allow probation when it appears that

1. The defendant is not likely to commit another offense.

2. The public interest does not require that the defendant receive the penalty provided for the offense.

3. The rehabilitation of the defendant does not require that he or she receive the penalty provided for the offense.

Legislative provisions regarding who may be placed on probation vary considerably from state to state. Some states have statutes prohibiting certain types of offenders—typically violent offenders—from receiving probation.

Offenders placed on probation must agree to abide by certain rules and regulations prescribed by the sentencing judge. Termed *conditions of probation*, these rules typically include keeping a job, supporting the family, avoiding places where alcoholic beverages are sold, reporting periodically to the probation officer (see Chapter 16), and not violating any law. Because probation is a judicial act, the judge can revoke probation and send the defendant to prison if the conditions of probation are violated.

One topic of particular interest is the effectiveness of probation. Some studies report high rates of recidivism (the repetition of criminal behavior) among probationers (Langan and Cunniff 1992). Such high failure rates seem to suggest limited or cautious use of probation for felons. But these conclusions concerning rampant recidivism have been challenged by other studies that report much lower rates of recidivism. These findings suggest

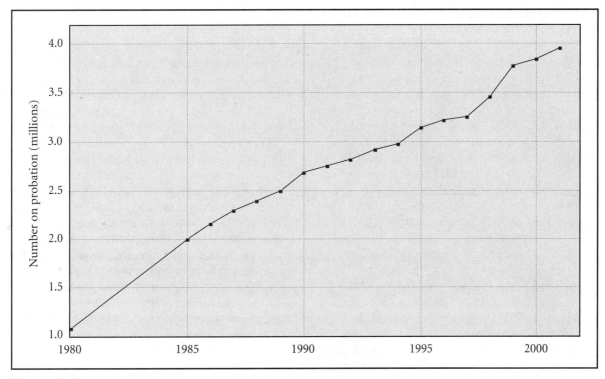

Figure 15-2
Growth in Probation Population

SOURCE: Lauren Glaze, *Probation and Parole in the United States, 2001* (Washington, DC: U.S. Department of Justice, Bureau of Justice Statistics, 2002).

that probation is not an unreasonable option for some felony offenders, especially drug offenders, who tend to have low rates of recidivism (Whitehead 1991).

INTERMEDIATE SANCTIONS

There is growing concern that the United States relies much too heavily on imprisonment and probation. Prison is viewed as too harsh (as well as unavailable) for many defendants, while probation is really unsupervised. Alternative sentences that lie somewhere between prison and probation are often referred to as **intermediate sanctions.** Intermediate sanctions begin with probation with limited supervision, move along a continuum of intrusiveness and control, and end with penal incarceration. Punishments of this type include

community-based penalties such as substantial fines, community service, restitution, intensive probation, electronic monitoring, house arrests, shock incarceration, boot camp, and treatment (Parent et al. 1997; Clear and Cole 2003).

FINES

The imposition of a **fine** is one of the oldest and also one of the most widely used forms of punishment. Fines are used extensively for traffic offenses and minor ordinance violations, generating well over $1 billion annually for local governments. Judges in the lower courts impose a fine alone or in combination with other sanctions in about 86 percent of their cases. But the imposition of fines is not confined to the lower courts. In the major trial courts, a fine, either alone or together with other sanctions, is imposed in almost 45 percent of the cases. First offenders with a known ability to pay are most likely to be sentenced in this way (Cole et al. 1988).

The limited use of fines as punishment in felony cases contrasts sharply with practices in some Western European countries. Some countries have adopted sentencing policies that explicitly make fines the sentence of choice for many offenses, including some crimes of violence that would result in jail sentences in many American courts. In Germany, for example, a major legislative goal is to minimize the imposition of jail terms of less than six months. Instead, German courts make extensive use of "day fines," which enable judges to set fines at amounts reflecting the gravity of the offense but also taking into account the financial means of the offender (Hillsman and Mahoney 1988). In the United States, the day fine concept has been relabeled "structured fines" and is being recommended as a less costly sentencing option than imprisonment (Bureau of Justice Statistics 1996).

American judges frequently cite the poverty of offenders as an obstacle to the broader use of fines as sanctions (Gillespie 1988–1989). Nonetheless, some courts regularly impose fines on persons whose financial resources are extremely limited and are successful in collecting those fines. Recent research suggests that fines can be collected. Performance can be improved substantially if administrators systematically apply collection and enforcement techniques that already exist and have been proven effective (Cole 1992; Turner and Greene 1999).

RESTITUTION

Restitution is the requirement that the offender provide reparation to the victim for the harm caused by the criminal offense. Requiring defendants to compensate victims (giving something back) for their losses was customary in ancient civilizations, particularly for the people in the time of the Old Testament. But as the government replaced the victim as the principal party in criminal prosecution, restitution fell into decline; offenders paid fines to the government rather than restitution to the victim (Tobolowsky 1993). Beginning in the mid-1960s, the idea of restitution became the focus of renewed interest and is now being touted as one of the criminal justice system's more creative responses to crime (McCarthy, McCarthy, and Leone 2001). Nearly all states have enacted laws providing for the collection and distribution of restitution funds. Restitution efforts generally take one of two forms—direct or symbolic (Galaway 1988).

In **direct restitution,** the offender is required, as a condition of probation, to make monetary payments to the victim. As a criminal sanction, it is largely restricted to property crimes, since it has little relevance if violence figured in the commission of the offense. As we saw in Chapter 9, the 1996 Congressional Act requires the federal court to impose mandatory restitution, without consideration of the defendant's ability to pay. Thus, there is a danger that court-imposed restitution can only increase victim dissatisfaction when the offender fails to pay. Nonetheless, close program monitoring of offenders, coupled with greater program attention to victims, can increase offenders' compliance with restitution orders (Davis and Bannister 1995).

In **symbolic restitution,** the offender makes reparation for the harm done in the form of good works benefiting the entire community rather than the particular individual harmed. Such work is often called *community service*. The offender is required to perform a specified number of hours of public service work, such as collecting trash in parks or working in a social service agency. This sanction is most often used when there is no direct victim of the offense—for example, in convictions for drunk driving.

THE DEATH PENALTY

Of all the forms of punishment, the **death penalty** is by far the most controversial, but it is also the least used; only a handful of offenders potentially face the ultimate sanction society can impose on the guilty.

Capital punishment was once almost the only penalty applied to convicted felons. By the

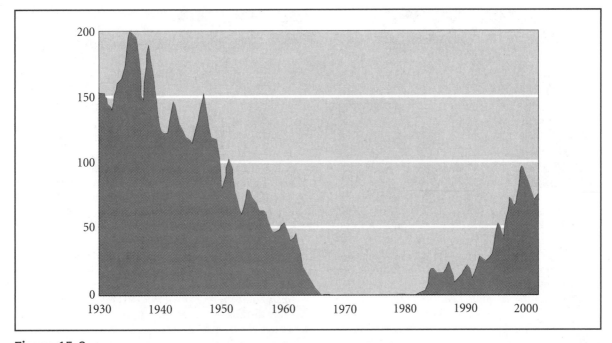

Figure 15-3
Persons Executed in the United States, 1930–2002

SOURCE: Tracy Snell and Laura Maruschak, *Capital Punishment 2001* (Washington, DC: U.S. Department of Justice, Bureau of Justice Statistics, 2002).

time of the American Revolution, the English courts had defined more than 200 felonies, all of which were **capital offenses.** However, many death penalties were not carried out; instead, offenders were pardoned or banished to penal colonies. Over time, courts and legislatures began to recognize other forms of punishment, such as imprisonment and probation.

From the 1930s to the 1970s, the number of executions in the United States fell steadily (see Figure 15-3). Between 1930 and 1967, nearly 3,800 persons were put to death. During the peak years of 1935 and 1936, nearly 200 executions occurred each year, but executions declined substantially thereafter. From 1967 to 1972, an unofficial moratorium on executions existed. Since 1976, the numbers have steadily increased once again, reaching a peak of 98 in 1998.

Abolition of the death penalty has been a hot political issue. Opponents contend that it is morally wrong for the state to take a life; it has no deterrent value and is inherently discriminatory. These arguments have led all Western democracies except the United States to abolish the death penalty. Supporters counter that retribution justifies the taking of a life and that the death penalty does deter; they are generally unconcerned or unconvinced about allegations of discriminatory impact. (See Courts, Controversy, and Judicial Administration: Should a Moratorium on the Death Penalty Be Imposed?)

Eighth Amendment Standards

Is capital punishment consistent with the Eighth Amendment's prohibition against cruel and unusual punishment? The Supreme Court first addressed this question in its 1972 landmark decision in *Furman v. Georgia,* which invalidated all 37 state death penalty statutes (see Case Close-Up: *Furman v. Georgia* and Cruel and Unusual Punishment). The Court was deeply divided, however, with every justice writing a separate opinion.

Furman v. Georgia raised more questions than it answered, and state legislatures attempted to write new capital punishment laws

Should a Moratorium on the Death Penalty Be Imposed?

Anthony Porter was two days away from dying by lethal injection when the Illinois Supreme Court intervened, holding that his IQ of 51 dictated that his mental competency be examined. Northwestern University Professor David Protess and his journalism students delved into Porter's case and found that he had not committed the pair of 1982 murders (McCormick 1999). Another suspect later confessed.

In the wake of the Porter case, Illinois Governor George Ryan, a Republican, declared a temporary halt to executions in his state, saying "I now favor a moratorium, because I have grave concerns about our state's shameful record of convicting innocent people and putting them on death row." The thoroughgoing review of the death penalty in Illinois would result in some death row prisoners' being freed altogether because DNA evidence, witnesses who recanted, or independent investigations showed their innocence. Moreover, according to the *Chicago Tribune*, 33 death row inmates were defended by attorneys who were later disbarred or suspended, and 46 convictions were obtained through questionable testimony of jailhouse informants (Stern 2000). Just days before stepping down as governor, Ryan commuted the sentences of the remaining 167 inmates on death row to life imprisonment.

Over the past several years, different groups—most notably, the American Bar Association—have called for moratoriums on the death penalty. Illinois, however, has been the only state to actually implement a moratorium. Indeed, governors in other states have shown little inclination to follow the lead of the Land of Lincoln.

The focus on innocents on death row represents the latest round in a long-running debate over the death penalty. Not surprisingly, there are profound ideological differences on the three central issues in the death penalty debate: morality, deterrence, and fairness (see Chapter 17). To advocates of the due process model of criminal justice, the death penalty is immoral because the state should not take a life. To proponents of the

crime control model, the death penalty is moral because the defendant has already taken a life. To advocates of the due process model, the death penalty is not a deterrent because many of those who commit murder are incapable of rational calculation. To proponents of the crime control model, the death penalty is a deterrent because some who might murder refrain from doing so because they know they might themselves die.

To advocates of the due process model, the death penalty is unfairly administered. They stress that members of racial minorities are more likely than whites to be executed (see Chapter 16). They also believe that in too many cases, people on death row are innocent or their trials involved procedural irregularities (see Chapter 17). To this the proponents of the crime control model respond that the fairness of the death penalty is unimportant or unproven. They believe that blacks are no more likely to be executed than whites. They also argue that the review process works because appeals have freed the few innocents who were wrongfully convicted.

What do you think? Of the three main issues in the death penalty debate—morality, deterrence, and fairness—which provides the best argument for abolishing the death penalty? Which one offers the best grounds for keeping the death penalty? Do you think that the issue of innocents on death row justifies a moratorium on the death penalty?

To continue the debate, point your browser to these sites:

Pro Death Penalty:
http://www.prodeathpenalty.com
Campaign to End the Death Penalty:
http://www.ncadp.org/

Will Manning, Jacqueline Rhoden-Trader, "Rethinking the Death Penalty"
William Tucker, "The Chair Deters"
Carl M. Cannon, "The Problem with the Chair"

CASE CLOSE-UP

Furman v. Georgia and Cruel and Unusual Punishment

William Furman, a seventh-grade dropout, was 26 at the time he broke into William Micke's home and accidentally killed him. Before trial, Furman was committed to the Georgia Central State Hospital for a psychiatric examination. The unanimous conclusion of the hospital staff was that William Furman had a mild to moderate mental deficiency and was legally insane. After several months of psychiatric treatment, the hospital determined that Furman was still mentally ill but that he now knew the difference between right and wrong (Georgia's insanity test) and was also able to cooperate with his counsel. Furman was convicted of murder and sentenced to death. The U.S. Supreme Court consolidated Furman's appeal with three others. These four cases had little in common except that all the victims were white, all the defendants were black, and all four had been sentenced to death following conviction (Meltsner 1973).

The Court clearly signaled the importance of the issue by allotting a full four hours for oral argument. The lawyers argued over what the somewhat archaic eighteenth-century phrase "cruel and unusual punishment" meant in the twentieth century. To Stanford law professor Tony Amsterdam, the standard should be whether a punishment, if evenhandedly applied, would be unacceptable to contemporary standards of decency. University of Texas Law School professor Charles Alan Wright (representing the state of Texas) set out to refute Professor Amsterdam, arguing that executing only 1 out of 100 rapists did not violate the Eighth Amendment.

On the morning of June 29, 1972, the last day of the term, the nine justices issued their opinion, striking down all state death penalty laws. But like the American public, the justices of the Supreme Court proved to be deeply divided over who should die and who should live. Each justice penned a separate opinion. Among the five justices in the majority, two argued that capital punishment constituted cruel and unusual punishment under all circumstances. But the other three justices in the majority wrote more narrowly, expressing concern that the death penalty was selectively applied. Justice Potter Stewart likened the randomness of the death penalty to being struck by lightning. The three justices believed the death penalty violated the Eighth Amendment because existing death penalty laws allowed too much discretion and therefore opened the door to discriminatory practices.

The four dissenting justices likewise expressed divergent views about why they believed capital punishment was consistent with the Eighth Amendment. Chief Justice Burger clearly favored the use of the death penalty and argued that legislatures should be able to retain capital punishment if they chose to do so. Justice Harry Blackmun, on the other hand, expressed his "distaste, antipathy, and indeed, abhorrence, for the death penalty" but concluded that abolition should be left to elected legislatures. (Just before his retirement, Blackmun reversed this position.)

Within minutes, the story began to appear on the major wire-service tickers. A few governors and correctional officials supported the decision, but most reactions were negative. Indeed, by the time the evening papers went to press, a few members of Congress had already proposed a constitutional amendment to overturn *Furman*. Soon after the initial shock subsided, lawyers in state capitals across the nation began to write new laws.

The divergent approaches adopted by the five justices in the majority meant that *Furman v. Georgia* set no precedent. Although the Court ruled that existing laws did not pass constitutional muster, the wording left open the possibility that future laws, more narrowly drafted, might comply with the Eighth Amendment to the Constitution. The second time around, the Court would provide a different answer to the question of who deserves to die.

consistent with the Eighth Amendment. By 1976, 37 states had enacted new legislation designed to avoid the arbitrary application of capital punishment. These laws took two forms.

Some states passed mandatory death penalty laws, which removed all discretion from the process by requiring that anyone convicted of a capital offense be sentenced to death. Other states enacted guided discretion statutes, which required judges and juries to weigh various aggravating and mitigating circumstances in deciding whether or not a particular defendant should receive the death penalty (Blankenship et al. 1997).

These new laws were tested in a series of five companion cases, collectively known as the death penalty cases (**Gregg v. Georgia** 1976). Again, the Court was badly divided, but a seven-justice majority agreed that the death penalty did not constitute cruel and unusual punishment under all circumstances. Next, the Court considered under what circumstances the death penalty was unconstitutional. Mandatory death penalty laws in 21 states were struck down because they failed to focus on the circumstances of the case. Guided discretion death penalty laws, on the other hand, were upheld: "The concerns expressed in *Furman* that the penalty of death not be imposed in an arbitrary or capricious manner can be met by a carefully drafted statute that ensures that the sentencing authority is given adequate information and guidance."

For a death penalty law to be constitutional, the high court ruled, it must provide for a bifurcated process. During the first, or guilt, phase of the trial, the jury considers only the issue of guilt or innocence. If the jury unanimously convicts for a crime carrying the death penalty, then the jury reconvenes. During the second, or penalty, phase of the trial, the jury considers aggravating and mitigating circumstances and then decides whether to impose the death penalty. If the death penalty is not imposed, the defendant is usually sentenced to life imprisonment (see Exhibit 15-7).

Contemporary Death Penalty Laws

Many state legislatures, citing public opinion polls showing that a majority of citizens favor the death penalty for murder, quickly revised their laws to conform with those upheld in the death penalty cases. Today, 38 states and the federal government (covering roughly 90 percent of the nation's population) have death penalty laws on the books. All death penalty laws apply to murder; the death penalty for crimes other than murder has been struck down. According to the Supreme Court, rape is not a grave enough offense to justify the imposition of the death penalty (*Coker v. Georgia* 1977). Twelve states and the District of Columbia do not have capital punishment statutes (Exhibit 15-8).

State death penalty laws have some differences (Acker 1993b). For one, they vary in the specific types of homicide cases that are death-eligible. They also differ in the minimum age at which the death penalty may be imposed. The minimum age varies from 12 to 18, with a few states not specifying a minimum age. Defendants who were 15 or younger at the time they committed murder may not be executed (*Thompson v. Oklahoma* 1988). But the Supreme Court refused to set aside the death penalty for defendants who were 17 at the time of the crime (*Stanford v. Kentucky* 1989).

Important variations also exist in how often states use their death penalty laws. One state has no one on death row, and some states rarely impose the death penalty. A few jurisdictions, particularly in the South and West, regularly use capital punishment (Figure 15-4).

Appeals and Evolving Standards

Like all defendants found guilty, those sentenced to death are entitled to appellate court review. In death penalty cases, however, special provisions govern appeal. Except for Arkansas, all jurisdictions with death penalty statutes provide for automatic review after a sentence of death is imposed. This review is undertaken regardless of the defendant's wishes and is conducted by the state's highest appellate court, bypassing any intermediate courts of appeals. Next, a writ of certiorari may be filed with the U.S. Supreme Court. Even though the chances of four justices' voting to hear the case are not high, they are much higher than for ordinary criminal appeals. Having exhausted these appellate remedies, defendants sentenced to death often file numerous writs of habeas corpus in the state and federal courts, although this practice changed greatly in 1996 (see Chapter 17).

The review process in death penalty cases is quite lengthy. The 66 prisoners executed during

Exhibit 15-7 Key Developments Concerning Capital Punishment

Eighth Amendment	1791	Excessive bail shall not be required, nor excessive fines imposed, nor cruel and unusual punishments inflicted.
Witherspoon v. Illinois	1968	Prospective jurors cannot be excluded because they oppose the death penalty.
Furman v. Georgia	1972	All existing death penalty laws invalidated; five-judge majority expresses different reasons for this action.
Gregg v. Georgia	1976	Death penalty laws do not constitute cruel and unusual punishment under all circumstances. Mandatory death penalty laws struck down.
Coker v. Georgia	1977	Rape is not a grave enough offense to justify the imposition of the death penalty.
Pulley v. Harris	1984	The Eighth Amendment does not require states to assess whether a sentence of death is compared to other cases to determine whether the sentence is proportional.
Lockhart v. McCree	1986	Potential jurors may be excluded if they oppose the death penalty. Thus, a death-qualified jury was upheld (overturning *Witherspoon v. Illinois*).
Thompson v. Oklahoma	1988	Defendants who were 15 or younger at the time they committed murder may not be executed.
Stanford v. Kentucky	1989	It is not unconstitutional to apply the death penalty to persons who are convicted of murder when they were 17.
Penry v. Lynaugh	1989	It is constitutional to execute mentally retarded persons.
Simmons v. South Carolina	1994	Defense may tell jurors that the only alternative to a death sentence is life without parole.
Harris v. Alabama	1995	States may give judges the power to sentence a capital defendant to death even if the jury votes not to impose the death penalty.
Ramdass v. Angelone	2000	Upheld sentence of death even though jurors were not told that defendant would not be eligible for parole if sentenced to life in prison.
Williams v. Taylor	2000	Upheld a section of the Anti-Terrorism and Effective Death Penalty Act intended to shorten time between sentencing and execution.
Atkins v. Virginia	2002	Convicted defendants with an IQ of 70 or less may not be executed (*Penry* overturned).

2001 had been under sentence of death an average of seven years and three months—less than that for inmates executed during earlier years (Snell and Maruschak 2002). Critics objected to the old habeas corpus system because it allowed condemned prisoners constant opportunities for review and resulted in lengthy delays.

The lengthy appellate process is partly due to evolving standards concerning the application of the death penalty. The Supreme Court has become America's life-and-death tribunal.

No other Supreme Court in history has been as preoccupied with the questions of when life begins and when a state may snuff one out. The following two issues illustrate some of the questions the Court has faced in the aftermath of the *Gregg* decision.

One long-standing issue has been the exclusion of persons opposed to the death penalty from juries in capital cases. The Warren Court rejected the classic "hanging jury," holding in *Witherspoon v. Illinois* (1968) that states cannot

Exhibit 15-8 Jurisdictions without a Death Penalty

Alaska	Minnesota
District of Columbia	North Dakota
Hawaii	Rhode Island
Iowa	Vermont
Maine	West Virginia
Massachusetts	Wisconsin
Michigan	

SOURCE: Tracy Snell and Laura Maruschak, *Capital Punishment 2001* (Washington, DC: U.S. Department of Justice, Bureau of Justice Statistics, 2002).

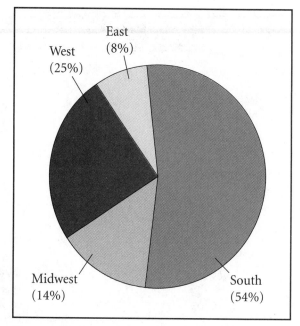

Figure 15-4
Prisoners under Sentence of Death, by Region

SOURCE: Tracy Snell and Laura Maruschak, *Capital Punishment 2001* (Washington, DC: U.S. Department of Justice, Bureau of Justice Statistics, 2002).

exclude from juries in capital cases any persons who voice general objections to the death penalty or express religious scruples against its imposition. However, the more conservative Rehnquist Court has limited *Witherspoon* (*Wainwright v. Witt* 1985), ruling that the Constitution does not prohibit the removal for cause of prospective jurors whose opposition to the death penalty is so strong that it would prevent or substantially impair the performance of their duties as jurors at the sentencing phase of the trial (*Lockhart v. McCree* 1986). The erosion of *Witherspoon* clearly works to the advantage of the prosecution, which can use voir dire to select a "death-qualified" jury.

A second issue relates to Eighth Amendment concerns about the execution of the mentally retarded. The Court provided conflicting answers in an opinion written by Justice Sandra Day O'Connor (who has been the swing vote in many death penalty cases). The Court concluded that mentally retarded people convicted of capital murder can be executed (*Penry v. Lynaugh* 1989). In 2001, however, the court reversed *Penry*, holding that persons with an IQ of 70 or lower cannot be executed (*Atkins v. Virginia* 2002).

Death Row Inmates

As a result of post-*Gregg* statutes, more than 3,500 prisoners are under a sentence of death. Death row inmates are predominantly male (a scant 1 percent are female) and disproportionately nonwhite (45 percent); most have never completed high school (62 percent) and have a prior felony conviction (60 percent). The median age is 27 at the time of arrest. Figure 15-4 highlights the regional pattern of the use of the death penalty, with the highest percentage of those awaiting execution in the South.

On January 16, 1977, convicted murderer Gary Gilmore's execution by a Utah firing squad attracted considerable national and international attention, not only because he was the first person executed in the United States since the unofficial moratorium began in 1967, but also because Gilmore had opposed all attempts to delay the execution. From the time the Supreme Court reinstated the death penalty in 1976 through the end of 2002, a total of 749 persons were executed. The most common methods of execution are lethal injection, electrocution, and lethal gas.

A sentence of death does not necessarily mean that the offender will be executed. From 1976, when the death penalty was upheld,

A Virtual Tour of American Courthouses: Corrections

The details of sentencing structure vary in important ways from jurisdiction to jurisdiction. To determine the sentencing structure in your state, examine the Bureau of Justice Statistics Report, *1996 National Survey of State Sentencing Structures,* available online at **http://www.ncjrs.org/courdocs. htm#169270.**

Many jurisdictions now maintain Web sites that offer useful information about their operations. Among them are

Georgia Board of Pardons and Paroles: **http://www.pap. state.ga.us/**

Missouri Board of Probation and Parole: **http://www. corrections.state.mo.us/division/prob/prob.htm**

U.S. Parole Commission: **http://www.usdoj.gov/uspc/**

Pennsylvania Board of Probation and Parole: **http://www. pbpp.state.pa.us/**

South Carolina Department of Probation, Parole, and Pardon Services: **http://www.state.sc.us/ppp/**

For an interesting view of how expensive it is to build a modern prison, you can watch the SuperMax prison in Wisconsin being built: **http://supermax.jobsight.net/public/ sitepic.stm.**

To learn more about prisoners' rights, go to these sites:

> **http://www.aclu.org/issues/prisons/ hmprisons. html**
>
> **http://www.wehelpyou.cc/**

For a sense of what it is like to be a prisoner, go to The Black People's Prison Survival Guide: **http://www.cs.oberlin.edu/ students/pjaques/etext/prison-guide.html**. See also Prison Life Inside the California Department of Corrections: **http://www.inmate.com/inmates/davidcdc.htm**.

To take a virtual tour of a death row cell, go to **http:// www.dc.state.fl.us/oth/vtour/index.html**. Look at Texas Death Row Statistics: **http://www.tdcj.state.tx.us/statistics/ stats-home.htm**. Read the Death Row Book: **http://www. editionnine.deathrowbook.com/deathrow.htm**.

---

through the end of 2001, a total of 6,754 prisoners were under a sentence of death. Of those, 11 percent were executed. An additional 32 percent had their death sentences vacated on appeal or commuted by the governor, or else they died in prison. The others remain on death row pending the outcome of their appeals (Snell and Maruschak 2002).

CONCLUSION

The issues raised in *Furman v. Georgia* more than 30 years ago are still with us. Although public support for the death penalty has increased, we as a nation execute very few defendants. Often unrecognized is the fact that murder (the only crime for which the death penalty is allowed) constitutes only a tiny percentage of crime.

The public's demands that something be done about "rising" crime rates has directly and indirectly affected the why, who, and what of sentencing.

During the last three decades, there has been an unprecedented public debate over *why* we sentence. The previously dominant goal of rehabilitation has come under sharp attack, and many voices urge that punishment should instead be based on the principle of just deserts. After nearly 40 years of stability, the indeterminate sentencing system has been rejected in state after state.

Intense interest in crime has also produced major alterations in *who* has the authority to sentence. The mix of sentencing responsibilities has changed in major ways. Legislators have inserted themselves more directly in the sentencing process, reducing the sentencing discretion of judges in many jurisdictions. Legislatures have also restricted parole board authority over early release in some jurisdictions and abolished parole altogether in a few areas.

The *what* of punishment has likewise come under intense scrutiny. Prison overcrowding has become the dominant issue. Probation overcrowding is an equally pressing, if less visible, problem. Perhaps more pressing than the debate over capital punishment is the lack of a national debate over prison overcrowding. Our nation's emphasis on getting tough on criminals is apparently a policy without costs, until we total the bill for building and maintaining prisons. Although citizens and public officials want to send even more offenders to prison, they are unwilling to expend large sums of tax dollars to build the needed facilities. Thus, sentencing is likely to remain an important public policy issue for the foreseeable future.

CRITICAL THINKING QUESTIONS

1. In what ways is restorative justice similar to the four dominant sentencing philosophies of retribution, incapacitation, deterrence, and rehabilitation? In what ways is restorative justice different from these four sentencing philosophies?

2. Should the punishment fit the crime, or should the punishment fit the criminal? In what ways do the four sentencing philosophies provide different answers to this question?

3. What is the mix of legislative, judicial, and executive sentencing responsibilities in your state? What changes, if any, have occurred over the last decade in the balance of sentencing responsibilities?

4. Under contemporary standards, would the *Furman* case be considered a death-eligible case?

5. Public criticism of lenient sentencing tends to occur in a select number of violent crimes or highly unusual circumstances. In what ways do such discussions deflect attention from the question of what the appropriate sentence should be for the bulk of defendants convicted of nonviolent crimes (burglary and theft, for example) and drug-related crimes?

KEY TERMS

capital offense (353)
capital punishment (352)
conditions of confinement lawsuit (347)
cruel and unusual punishment (344)
death penalty (352)
determinate sentence (343)
deterrence theory (339)
direct restitution (352)
fine (351)
Furman v. Georgia (353)
good time (344)
Gregg v. Georgia (356)
imprisonment (345)
incapacitation (338)
indeterminate sentence (341)
intermediate sanctions (351)
just deserts (338)
pardon (344)
parole (344)
parole board (344)
probation (350)
rehabilitation (340)
restitution (352)
retribution (338)
selective incapacitation (339)
symbolic restitution (352)

WORLD WIDE WEB RESOURCES AND EXERCISES

Web Guides

http://dir.yahoo.com/Society_and_Culture/Crime/
   Correction_and_Rehabilitation/
http://dir.yahoo.com/Society_and_Culture/Crime/
   Correction_and_Rehabilitation/Sentencing/
http://dir.yahoo.com/Society_and_Culture/Crime/
   Correction_and_Rehabilitation/Death_Penalty/
http://dir.yahoo.com/Government/Law/Criminal_
   Justice/Restorative_Justice/

Web Search Terms

prison *restorative justice*
probation *death penalty*

Useful URLs

The American Correction Association is a multidisciplinary organization of professionals representing all facets of corrections and criminal justice, including federal, state, and military: **http://www.corrections.com/aca/**.

Visit these related sites:

Bureau of Justice Statistics Corrections Statistics: **http://www.ojp.usdoj.gov/bjs/correct.htm**

Federal Bureau of Prisons: **http://www.bop.gov/**

National Institute of Corrections: **http://www. nicic.org/**

The Corrections Connection: **http://www.corrections.com/**

Focus on the Death Penalty is a comprehensive resource that includes history, U.S. Supreme Court cases, and statistics: **http://www.uaa.alaska.edu/just/death/**.

Uncommon URLs

The Civil Rights Lawyers Defense Team handles parole matters: **http://www.parole.cc/**.

Restitution Incorporated promotes healing between victim and offender: **http://www. restitutioninc.org/**.

The Center for Restorative Justice and Mediation provides current information: **http://ssw. che.umn.edu/rjp/default.html**.

Visit the Restorative Justice Project: **http:// www.fresno.edu/dept/pacs/rjp.html**.

The Other Side of the Wall offers news about prison issues: **http://www.prisonwall.org/**.

Visit the Anamosa State Penitentiary (formerly the Iowa Men's Reformatory) at **http://www.geocities.com/Heartland/2201/ oldphoto.htm**.

Look at the famous Alcatraz Island: **http:// www.alcatrazhistory.com/**.

Ken Light Texas Death Row offers photos and articles about life on death row: **http:// sightphoto.com/sightphoto/Light/light_texas.html**.

The Victim-Offender Mediation Center is at **http://www.voma.org/**.

Web Exercises

1. If your state department of corrections has a Web page, access it and ask yourself the following questions: Does it discuss costs (and increases in costs) of incarcerating prisoners? Does it indicate whether any or all prisons have been under federal court order? Overall, what image does the information project?

2. Using the data provided by your state department of corrections, chart the growth in the prison population in your state over the last decade. Is the rate of increase similar to, or different from, the rate of increase nationwide (Figure 15-1)?

3. Two of the groups most active in advocating restorative justice are Restorative Justice: Healing the Effects of Crime (**http:// www.restorativejustice.com/**) and the Mennonite Central Committee (**http://www.mcc. org/programs/crime/restorative-justice.html**). Examine their home pages, and answer the following questions: In what ways do their arguments appear to be working within dominant American thought patterns about victims? In what ways are they challenging dominant thought patterns about punishment?

INFOTRAC COLLEGE EDITION RESOURCES AND EXERCISES

Basic Searches

punishment *probation*
prisons *fines (penalties)*
pardon *restorative justice*
imprisonment *Prison Litigation*
capital punishment *Reform Act of 1966*
cruel and unusual *executions*
  punishment

Recommended Articles

Alcoholism & Drug Abuse Weekly, "California Alternative-Sentencing Program Seeks Greater Participation"

William C. Collins, Darlene C. Grant, "The Prison Litigation Reform Act"

David Dolinko, "Justice in the Age of Sentencing Guidelines"

Mario A. Paparozzi, "Reinventing Probation from the Top Down"

James Turpin, "Restorative Justice Challenges Corrections"

Emilio C. Viano, "Restorative Justice for Victims Offenders: A Return to American Traditions"

InfoTrac College Edition Exercises

1. Using the search term "prisons" or "imprisonment," find two or more articles that discuss the problem of prison overcrowding. Why do the authors think that prison overcrowding is a problem, and what solutions do they suggest?

2. Using the search term "restorative justice," find two or more articles that discuss the topic, and answer the following questions: Do the authors support restorative justice? If so, what benefits do they cite? If not, what downside do they see? What types of crimes would restorative justice be most suited for? What types of defendants? What types of victims?

FOR FURTHER READING

Christianson, Scott. *With Liberty for Some: 500 Years of Imprisonment in America*. Boston: Northeastern University Press, 1998.

Crouch, Ben, and James Marquart. *Appeal to Justice: Litigated Reform of Texas Prisons*. Austin: University of Texas Press, 1989.

DiIulio, John. *No Escape: The Future of American Corrections*. New York: Basic Books, 1991.

Hudson, Joe, and Burt Galaway. *Introduction to Restorative Justice: International Perspectives*, edited by Burt Galaway and Joe Hud-

son. Monsey, NY: Criminal Justice Press, 1996.

Lin, Ann Chih. *Reform in the Making: The Implementation of Social Policy in Prison*. Princeton, NJ: Princeton University Press, 2000.

Mauer, Marc. *The Race to Incarcerate*. New York: New Press, 1999.

Simon, Jonathan. *Poor Disciple: Parole and the Social Control of the Underclass, 1890–1990*. Chicago: University of Chicago Press, 1994.

Welch, Michael. *Punishment in America: Social Control and the Ironies of Imprisonment*. Thousand Oaks, CA: Sage, 1999.

Death Penalty

Abbott, Geoffrey. *Lords of the Scaffold: A History of the Executioner*. New York: St. Martin's Press, 1991.

Baldus, David, George Woodworth, and Charles Pulaski. *Equal Justice and the Death Penalty: A Legal and Empirical Analysis*. Boston: Northeastern University Press, 1990.

Bedau, Hugo Adam, ed. *The Death Penalty in America: Current Controversies*. New York: Oxford University Press, 1996.

Borg, Marian. "The Southern Subculture of Punitiveness? Regional Variation in Support for Capital Punishment." *Journal of Research in Crime and Delinquency* 34 (1997): 24–45.

Haines, Herbert. *Against Capital Punishment: The Anti–Death Penalty Movement in America, 1972–1994*. New York: Oxford University Press, 1996.

Latzer, Barry. 1998. *Death Penalty Cases*. Boston: Butterworth-Heineman, 1988.

Paternoster, Raymond. *Capital Punishment in America*. New York: Lexington, 1992.

Radelet, Michael, Hugo Adam Bedau, and Constance Putnam. *In Spite of Innocence: Erroneous Convictions in Capital Cases*. Boston: Northeastern University Press, 1993.

Streib, Victor. *A Capital Punishment Anthology*. Cincinnati: Anderson, 1996.

Wright, Harold, Robert Bohm, and Katherine Jamieson. "A Comparison of Uninformed and Informed Death Penalty Opinions: A Replication and Expansion." *American Journal of Criminal Justice* 20 (1995): 57–87.

Chapter 16 Sentencing Decisions

T welve-year-old Polly Klaas was kidnapped from a slumber party in her home while her mother and little sister slept in the next room. Her two friends were found a short time later, bound and gagged, and were able to provide a general description of the bearded intruder. For nine weeks, hundreds of law enforcement officers and thousands of volunteers attempted to find the girl, but to no avail. Just before Christmas, the bad news came. Polly had been killed shortly after her abduction. ◀

The police arrest of parolee Richard Allen Davis did little to calm an angry public. The kidnapping and murder of Polly Klaas was blamed on a badly flawed criminal justice system that failed to keep a dangerous person like Davis behind bars. The murder of Polly Klaas, and the extensive national media coverage that surrounded it, sparked another round of get-tough-with-crooks legislation. Whereas earlier laws resulted in mandatory minimums, abolition of parole, and sentencing guidelines, the focus now shifted to "three strikes and you're out" laws.

While public attention focuses on the sentences handed out in the handful of sensational cases such as the Polly Klaas murder (refer to the wedding cake analogy used in Chapter 10), judges must wrestle with the sentence to impose on the almost 900,000 felons convicted each year. The problems members of the courtroom work group face in reaching these sentencing decisions are captured by the powerful symbol of Lady Justice. Held high in her right hand are the scales of justice, symbolizing fairness in the administration of justice. Draped across her eyes is a blindfold, suggesting that all who come before her will receive impartial justice. Grasped low in her left hand is a sword, standing for the power and might of law. Replicas of Lady Justice adorn the exteriors of many American courthouses, but whether the sentencing process inside the courtrooms lives up to those high ideals is open to question.

The scales of justice are the starting point in examining sentencing. This chapter begins by focusing on who is and who is not sentenced to prison, granted probation, or executed. First, we need to know what factors judges and other members of the courtroom work group weigh in deciding between prison and probation. Normal penalties are the most important consideration in sentencing. Based on the seriousness of the offense and the defendant's prior record, courthouses have developed going rates, which are used as parameters in fine-tuning a sentence for a given offender.

The blindfold is the next major topic. Sentences imposed on the guilty are expected to be fair and just. Many observers argue that they are not; disparities and discrimination in sentencing are major topics of concern. Numerous studies probe the extent to which economic status, age, gender, and race improperly pierce the judicial blindfold when sentences are imposed.

The sword of justice will also be discussed. Whereas some worry that the scales of justice are tipped, others are concerned that the sword of justice is sheathed. Frustration over rising crime rates has given rise to charges that judges are too lenient. Demands that sentences be more certain as well as more severe have become a staple of American politics. Legislators have responded by increasing the severity of some punishments and altering sentencing structures in hopes of producing greater predictability in sentencing. Sentencing guidelines are now the centerpiece in discussions of increasing the predictability of sentencing as well as increasing the severity of the penalty.

COURTROOM WORK GROUPS AND SENTENCING DECISIONS

Sentencing is a joint decision-making process. Although only judges possess the legal authority to impose sentence, other members of the

Exhibit 16-1 The Courtroom Work Group and Sentencing

	Law on the Books	Law in Action
Probation officer	Conducts pre-sentence investigation (PSI).	Judges most often follow the recommendation in PSI. Studies disagree whether the sentencing decision is guided by PSI or provides a paper rationale for an already agreed-upon sentence.
Prosecutor	In most jurisdictions, the DA makes a sentencing recommendation to the judge.	Judges are more likely to impose the sentence recommended by the DA than by the defense attorney.
Defense attorney	During the sentencing hearing, defense attorney argues for the court to show leniency to the defendant.	Pleas for leniency are viewed as efforts to impress the client and the client's family and therefore are often ignored. Defense attorneys with good working relationships with the other members of the courtroom work group are influential in achieving lenient sentences in selected instances.
Judge	By law, the only person who can impose sentence. Mandatory sentences and sentencing guidelines restrict the judges' discretion in a growing number of jurisdictions.	Judges most often sentence within the normal penalty structure. Judges often criticize legislatures for restricting judicial sentencing discretion.

courtroom work group are also influential (Exhibit 16-1). The extent of this influence varies from jurisdiction to jurisdiction and from judge to judge. Where sentence bargaining predominates, for example, the judge almost invariably imposes the sentence that the prosecutor and defense attorney have already agreed upon. Where count and charge bargaining is used, the actors reach agreements based on past sentencing patterns of the judge. The most significant actors in sentencing are probation officers, prosecutors, defense attorneys, and (of course) judges.

Probation Officers

Probation officers perform two major functions in the sentencing process. One is the supervision of offenders after a sentence of probation has been imposed (Clear and Cole 2003). The other is investigation prior to sentencing.

The primary purpose of a **pre-sentence investigation** (PSI) is to help the judge select an appropriate sentence by providing information about the crime and the criminal. Most often, the PSI is ordered by the court following the defendant's conviction. A date is set for sentencing the offender, and meanwhile the probation officer conducts the investigation (see A Day in Court: Probation Officers Classify Defendants). The report is based on police reports, prosecutor's records, an interview with the offender, and perhaps a talk with the defendant's family as well. A typical pre-sentence report contains a description of the offense, the defendant's version of the crime, the person's prior criminal record and social history, and a psychological evaluation (if needed). The pre-sentence report gives the judge, who must select the proper sentence, an appropriate database. This is particularly important when the defendant has entered a plea of guilty, because then the judge knows little

A DAY IN COURT

Probation Officers Classify Defendants

PO [probation officers] did not so much process individuals as they processed types of individuals who had been labeled in particular ways. . . . [They] used a three-fold typology of criminal defendants which was based on the defendant's risk of recidivism.

1. Low-risk defendants were usually in trouble with the criminal justice system for the first time, were between the ages of 18 and 25, and were either attending university or had a steady job. These defendants, therefore, had much to lose by possessing a criminal record and they took their current involvement with the courts seriously. As one PO put it, "These people have made one screwy mistake and it's shaken them up so much we'll probably never see them again." For example, one defendant had been convicted of attempted theft after he had altered a sales receipt to obtain items he hadn't paid for. This defendant was unusually cooperative during the interview and expressed concern about the fact that business associates and local bankers would find out about the criminal record he now possessed. His PO told me, "I don't think we'll see him come through here again. This was his first offense and I think it really made an impression on him."

2. High-risk defendants usually had at least two prior arrests and convictions, little formal education, and were seen as unwilling or unable to hold a steady job. Often, they were perceived as not taking their involvement with the courts seriously. For these reasons, POs saw these defendants as likely to be in and out of trouble for much of their adult lives. For example, a defendant had been convicted of burglary and had several other theft related convictions. In addition, he had never held a job for more than three months at a time. The PO who handled the case told me: "This [defendant] is just too lazy to work. . . . He commits these burglaries because of that. I'll bet ya we see this guy again. He's definitely [high-risk] material."

3. The final category of defendants consisted of individuals whose risk of recidivism was neither definitely high or low, but was seen as problematic. Some of these defendants had been in trouble with the law before, generally involving minor offenses such as shoplifting. Others possessed characteristics of alcoholism or a "bad attitude," which POs considered likely to be related to future criminal behavior. While there was no specific set of characteristics which defined this category of defendants, POs pointed out that what they did share was the potential for "heading for trouble." For example, a defendant had been convicted of theft and had two prior theft-related convictions. However, he also was working two jobs to pay off a student loan and return to the university. The PO described the defendant's risk of recidivism in the following way: "It is hard to tell with him. He's got these [prior offenses], but he's got these things [two jobs, a car] going for him. If he was in a situation where he could steal, I don't know."

What was important for POs was that, whatever the problem, these defendants were "workable." As one PO put it: "I spend the most time with these [defendants]. I try to make them aware of alternatives . . . or refer them for heavy-duty counseling, or do some things myself so hopefully they won't get in trouble again."

SOURCE: Jack Spencer, "Accounts, Attitudes, and Solutions: Probation Officer Defendant Negotiations of Subjective Orientations," *Social Problems* 30 (1983): 570–581. Reprinted by permission.

---

about the particulars of the crime or the background of the offender.

Beyond providing background information, many pre-sentence reports also include a recommendation of an appropriate sentence. However, some judges will not allow a recommendation, claiming that this is the prerogative solely of the court. Even if there is no explicit recommendation, most PSIs leave little room for doubt about what the probation officer thinks the sentence should be. If probation is recommended, the report usually includes a suggested level of supervision (ranging from intensive through regular to minimal), a listing of special conditions of probation, a plan for treatment, and an assessment of community resources available to facilitate rehabilitation.

Probation officers clearly play a significant role in the sentencing process. Judges are very likely to impose the sentence recommended in the PSI. Indeed one study found a 95 percent rate of agreement between the judge and the probation report when probation was recommended and an 88 percent rate of agreement when the report opposed probation (Carter and Wilkins 1967). Thus, although sentencing judges are not required to follow such recommendations, they usually do (Campbell, McCoy, and Osigweh 1990; Hagan 1977).

There is considerable disagreement, however, over the actual influence of probation officers in the sentencing process. Some studies suggest that judges seriously consider the recommendations and use them to guide their decisions—that judges lean heavily on the professional advice of probation officers (Walsh 1985). Other researchers argue that probation officers have little real influence on the sentencing process—that probation recommendations have been supplanted by plea bargaining. Prosecutors and defense attorneys usually talk to the probation officer before the PSI is submitted to the court. The conversation indicates what information should be stressed to justify the sentence already agreed upon (Kingsnorth and Rizzo 1979). The probation report then provides a rationale after the fact. Overall, the probation officer's role in sentencing is largely ceremonial (Hagan, Hewitt, and Alwin 1979). By and large, recommendations by probation officers "do not influence judicial sentencing significantly but serve to maintain the myth that criminal courts dispense individual justice" (Rosencrance 1988, 236).

Prosecutors

Prosecutors can influence the sentencing decision in several important ways. By agreeing to a count or charge bargain, prosecutors limit the maximum penalty the judge may impose. During the sentencing hearing, prosecutors can bring to the court's attention factors that are likely to increase the penalty—for example, that the victim was particularly vulnerable or that the defendant inflicted great harm on the victim. Alternatively, prosecutors can bring out factors that would lessen the penalty—for example, the defendant's cooperation with the police.

Finally, prosecutors may make a specific sentencing recommendation. If, for example, there has been a sentence bargain, the prosecutor will indicate the penalty agreed on, and the judge will usually adopt that recommendation as the sentence. When such prosecutorial recommendations are based on office policy, they can have the positive effect of muting sentencing disparities among the different judges. In some courts, however, prosecutors are not allowed to make sentencing recommendations, because sentencing is viewed solely as a judicial responsibility.

Defense Attorneys

The defense attorney's role in sentencing begins early in the history of a case. The decision whether to go to trial or to enter a guilty plea is partially based on the attorney's assessment of the sentence likely to be imposed. Based on the knowledge of what sentences have been handed out to past defendants accused of similar crimes and with similar backgrounds, the attorney must advise the client as to the probable sentence.

At the same time, the defense attorney seeks to obtain the lightest sentence possible. One way to accomplish this goal is to maneuver the case before a judge with a lenient sentencing record. Another way is to discuss the case with the prosecutor in hopes that he or she will agree to (or at least not oppose) a recommendation of probation in the pre-sentence investigation. Defense attorneys also try to emphasize certain circumstances that make the defendant look better in the eyes of the judge, prosecutor, and probation officer. They may try to downplay the severity of the offense by stressing the defendant's minor role in the crime or the fact that the victim was not without blame; or they may have friends or employers testify about the defendant's general good character and regular employment.

Overall, though, defense attorneys are less influential than prosecutors. Judges and prosecutors typically view defense attorneys' arguments for leniency as efforts to impress their clients with the fact that they tried as hard as they could.

Judges

Courtroom work groups impose informal limits on how judges exercise their formal legal authority to impose sentences. Judges are well aware that the disposition of cases is related to plea bargaining, which in turn depends on being able to anticipate the sentencing tendencies of judges. Judges share in a framework of understandings, expectations, and agreements that are relied upon to dispose of most criminal cases. If a judge strays too far from expectations by imposing a sentence substantially more lenient or more severe than the one agreed on by defendant, defense lawyer, and prosecutor, it becomes more difficult for the prosecutor and defense counsel to negotiate future agreements (Rosett and Cressey 1976).

In working within the limits established by the consensus of the courtroom work group, judges are also constrained because the other members of the work group have more thorough knowledge of the details of the defendant and the nature of the crime. In particular, a judge's sentencing decision is restricted by the bargains struck between prosecution and defense. Indeed, judges who enjoy stable relationships with the prosecutors who practice before them are more likely to defer to those prosecutors' sentencing recommendations (Worden 1995).

Judges, though, are not without influence. They are the most experienced members of the courtroom team, so their views carry more weight than those of relatively inexperienced prosecutors or defense attorneys. The particular judge's attitudes on sentencing are reflected in the courtroom work group's common understanding of what sentences are appropriate.

▌ NORMAL PENALTIES AND SENTENCING DECISIONS

Sentencing involves a two-stage decision-making process. After conviction, the first decision is whether to grant probation or to incarcerate the defendant. If incarceration is chosen, the second decision is determining how long the sentence should be. Exhibit 16-2 indicates that of the more than 900,000 adults found guilty of a felony in state courts every year, 68 percent are incarcerated (either in prison or jail), with the remaining 32 percent sentenced to probation. Thus, for every 100 felons sentenced, 32 are granted probation and 68 are incarcerated (44 in prison and 24 in jail) (Durose, Levin, and Langan 2001).

Making these sentencing decisions is not an easy task; most judges say that sentencing is the most difficult part of their job. The frustrations of sentencing stem in part from the need to weigh the possibility of rehabilitation, the need to protect the public, popular demands for retribution, and any potential deterrent value in the sentence (see Chapter 15). Of course, courtroom work groups do not consider these competing perspectives in the abstract. They must sentence real defendants found guilty of actual crimes. Each defendant and crime is somewhat different. Sentences are expected to be individualized—to fit the penalty to the crime and the defendant.

In seeking individualized sentences, courtroom work groups use **normal penalties** (Sudnow 1965). Based on the usual manner in which crimes are committed and the typical backgrounds of the defendants who commit them, courtroom work groups develop norms of what penalties are appropriate for given categories. The normal sentences are not used mechanically; rather, they guide sentencing. It is within the context of these normal penalties that individualization occurs. Upward and downward adjustments are made. Normal penalties governing appropriate sentences for defendants take into account the seriousness of the crime, the prior criminal record, and any aggravating or mitigating circumstances.

Seriousness of the Offense

The most important factor in setting normal penalties is the seriousness of the offense. The more serious the offense, the less likely the defendant will be granted probation (see Exhibit 16-2). Also, the more serious the offense, the longer the prison sentence. These conclusions

Exhibit 16-2	Types of Sentences Imposed by Conviction Offense		
	Prison (%)	Jail (%)	Probation (%)
All offenses	44	24	32
Violent offenses	59	19	22
Murder	94	2	4
Sexual assault	67	15	18
Robbery	76	12	12
Aggravated assault	46	26	28
Other violent	41	26	33
Property offenses	43	22	35
Burglary	54	21	25
Larceny	40	24	36
Fraud	35	20	45
Drug offenses	42	26	32
Possession	36	29	35
Trafficking	45	26	29
Weapons offenses	42	24	34
Other offenses	35	28	37

SOURCE: Durose, Matthew, David Levin, and Patrick Langan, *Felony Sentences in State Courts, 1998* (Washington, DC: U.S. Department of Justice, Bureau of Justice Statistics, 2001).

This information is provided either in the pre-sentence report or by the police arrest report. By focusing on the real offense, judges can counteract charge bargaining. For example, pre-sentence reports for simple robbery cases sometimes include the type of weapon used. Thus, the defendant who has been found guilty only of unarmed robbery may often be sentenced on the basis that he really committed an armed robbery. The opposite also happens. By examining the prior relationship between the defendant and the victim, the courtroom work group may perceive that the underlying crime is a squabble among friends and therefore less serious than the official charge indicates (Vera Institute of Justice 1977).

Sentencing on the basis of seriousness is one of the principal ways courts attempt to arrive at consistent sentences. Most courts use a rank ordering that incorporates the full range of offenses—from the most serious crimes of armed robbery and rape, through middle-level crimes of domestic violence, to the lowest level of forgery, theft, and burglary. One reason that sentences appear to critics to be lenient is that most cases are distributed at the lowest level of this ranking.

Prior Record

After the seriousness of the offense, the next most important factor in sentencing is the defendant's prior record. As the prior record increases, so does the sentence. In choosing between probation and imprisonment, the courtroom work group carefully considers the defendant's previous criminal involvement. If the decision has been made to sentence the offender to prison, the prior record also plays a role in setting the length of incarceration. Overall, a previous incarceration increases the length of the sentence (Welch and Spohn 1986).

How courts assess prior records varies. Some consider only previous convictions, whereas others look at arrests as well. In addition, courtroom work groups often consider the length of time between the current offense and the previous one. If there has been a significant gap, the defendant will often receive a sentence more lenient than normal. On the other hand, if the previous conviction is a

are hardly surprising. Society expects that convicted murderers will be punished more severely than defendants found guilty of theft. What is important is how courtroom work groups go about the task of deciding what offenses are serious.

When weighing the seriousness of the offense, courtroom work groups examine the harm or loss suffered by the crime victim in what they perceive to be the "real offense" (what really happened, not the official charge).

recent one, this is often taken as an indication that the defendant is a "bad actor," and the severity of the punishment will increase. Finally, the prior record is assessed within the context of the severity of the crime itself. A study of federal defendants found that prior record had its greatest impact on less serious offenses. When the crime is perceived as being less serious, individual factors such as prior record seem to be given relatively more weight than when the crime is more serious (Tiffany, Avichai, and Peters 1975).

Aggravating or Mitigating Circumstances

In passing sentence, judges and other members of the courtroom work group consider not only the formal charge but also the way the crime was committed. Prosecutors and defense counsel engage in a careful calculation of moral turpitude, examining the nature of the crime and the role of the victim (McDonald, Rossman, and Cramer 1979). Some of the aggravating circumstances that lead to a higher penalty are the use of a weapon and personal injury to the victim.

Mitigating factors include youth of the defendant, lack of mental capacity, and role (principal or secondary actor) in the crime. One of the most important mitigating factors is the perceived social stability of the defendant. Marital status, relationship with the family, length of employment, and prior alcohol or drug abuse are considered to be indicators of social stability or instability. Social stability is a particularly important predictor of judges' sentencing, especially when probation is under consideration.

Law in Controversy: Uncertainty and Public Opinion

Sentencing is more art than science. Judges, prosecutors, probation officers, and defense attorneys are well aware that they will make mistakes in considering the seriousness of the offense, the prior record of the defendant, aggravating or mitigating circumstances, and the stability of the defendant. Uncertainty is ingrained in the process. They may send someone to prison who should not be there or impose a prison sentence longer than necessary. Or they may err in the opposite direction: A defendant recently granted probation may commit a serious and well-publicized crime. Note that only the second type of error will reach public attention; mistakes of the first kind may appear, but only well after the fact.

The uncertainties inherent in sentencing are particularly important at a time when public opinion is critical of the courts and sentencing. The majority of Americans feel that sentences are too lenient. In response, courts are sentencing a higher proportion of defendants to prison. Prisons are overcrowded, adding further complexity to the difficult task of arriving at a fair and appropriate sentence.

▌ DISCRIMINATION AND SENTENCING

The ideal of equal justice under the law means that all persons convicted of the same offense should receive identical sentences. But not all deviations from equality are unwarranted. The law also strives for individualized dispositions, sometimes reflecting varying degrees of seriousness of the offense, sometimes reflecting varying characteristics of the offender.

What one person may perceive as unfairness, another may see as justifiable variation. Discussions about unwarranted variation in sentencing involve two widely used terms: *discrimination* and *disparity*. Although widely used, these terms are rarely defined consistently. Moreover, the concepts overlap somewhat. Nonetheless, for our purposes they should be treated as involving distinct phenomena.

Disparity, discussed in more detail later in the chapter, refers to inconsistencies in sentencing; the decision-making process is the principal topic of interest. **Discrimination,** on the other hand, refers to illegitimate influences on the sentencing process; defendants' attributes are the primary focus. Legal factors such as the seriousness of the offense and the prior criminal record of the defendant are considered legitimate factors. Sentencing discrimination exists when some illegitimate attribute is associated with sentence outcomes after all

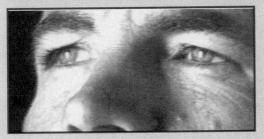

COURT TV

Trouble in Paradise: Should the Defendant Die?

Jeffrey Wallace is a trusted employee of a popular bar in Key West, Florida, until one night he goes on a shooting spree, killing the bar manager and wounding several other people. The defense argues that Wallace is insane, pointing to his paranoia and past mental health treatments. The prosecution counters that Wallace is faking mental illness and had purposely planned to kill.

The jury finds Wallace guilty. In the words of one juror—his confession indicates he knew the difference between right and wrong. But now the jury must decide if he is to die or is to be sentenced to life imprisonment without the possibility of parole.

During the sentencing phase, the prosecution calls friends and family members of the victim, who offer emotional testimony about how the death has affected their lives. The defense counters with some equally emotional testimony that pleads for Wallace's life to be spared.

 View the video clip of the sentencing phase of this trial on your copy of the CourtTV CD-ROM. As you watch the video, keep the following questions in mind:

1. What testimony from family and friends of the victim provides the best justification for putting Jeffrey Wallace to death? What testimony provides the least justification? What testimony from family and friends of the defendant provides the best justification for sparing his life? What testimony provides the least justification?

2. The Supreme Court has allowed victim impact statements in death penalty cases (Chapter 9). Based on the testimony you see in this case, do victim impact statements provide jurors with useful and necessary information in reaching a decision? Or does the highly emotional testimony merely cause confusion about the real issues?

3. During the guilt phase of the trial, the defense presents an insanity defense. Although the jury finds Jeffrey Wallace guilty, do you think the insanity defense may have saved his life?

other relevant variables are adequately controlled. These objectionable influences are referred to as *extralegal variables* (Walker, Spohn, and DeLone 2004).

Imbalance versus Discrimination

No one doubts that the criminal justice system reflects an imbalance in terms of the types of people caught in its web. Whether we examine arrests, prosecutions, convictions, and/or sentences, the statistical profile highlights the same imbalance—poor, young minority males are disproportionately represented.

Evidence of imbalance in outcomes, however, is not proof of discrimination. Imbalance could be the result of legally relevant factors discussed earlier in this chapter (such as seriousness of the offense and prior record). In making claims about discrimination, researchers want to make sure they are comparing cases that are truly similar. By way of illustration, consider two defendants of different races who have received different sentences. One of the defendants is a first offender who pled guilty to burglary and received one year probation. The other has two prior felony convictions and was convicted by a jury of simple robbery and sentenced to three years in prison. Irrespective of which offender was white or black, we would not conclude solely on this evidence that the sentences were discriminatory. Rather, we would want to compare a number of cases involving similar crimes and defendants with similar backgrounds.

In trying to ensure that like cases are being compared, researchers use statistical controls. A variety of statistical procedures allow researchers to compare first offenders to other first offenders, and burglars to other burglars. Only after legally relevant variables have been held constant can claims about the existence (or absence) of discrimination be made.

Earlier studies often failed to incorporate appropriate statistical controls. They considered only the single variables of race and sentencing, for example, and found racial discrimination in the sentencing. When these studies were reanalyzed, Hagan (1974) found that claims of racial discrimination were not supported by the data.

Conflicting Findings

Numerous studies have probed the extent to which a defendant's attributes, such as economic status, gender, and race, pierce the judicial blindfold when sentences are imposed. The results are provocative, not only because they raise important issues of equality before the law but also because they frequently appear to contradict one another. For example, Eisenstein and Jacob (1977) concluded from a study of sentencing in Baltimore, Chicago, and Detroit that "blacks are not treated worse than whites"; but Lizotte (1978) used some of the same data from Chicago to calculate that "the 'cost' of being a black laborer is an additional 8.06 months of prison sentence."

Some studies find patterns of discrimination, and others do not. Clearly, sentencing discrimination involves complex issues, and researchers disagree over how best to study it. The discussion that follows examines the research concerning discrimination under the headings of economic status, gender, race in sentencing, and race in capital punishment.

DISCRIMINATION AND ECONOMIC STATUS

The courts are a sorting process. At several stages during the process, it is obvious that access to economic resources makes a difference, with the poor receiving less preferential treatment. For example, the poor are less likely to be released on bail prior to trial and also are less likely to be able to hire a private attorney. These differences during processing carry over to sentencing: Defendants who are not released on bail or represented by a court-appointed attorney are granted probation less often and are given longer prison sentences.

Outcome differences based on economic status are, therefore, readily apparent in sentencing. The provocative title of a recent book by Jeffrey Reiman (2001), *The Rich Get Richer and the Poor Get Prison*, reflects this fact. Prisons are indeed the modern equivalent of the poorhouse. Do these patterns indicate that courts discriminate against the poor in sentencing, or are they the product of other, legally permissible, factors? A number of studies yield conflicting and complex answers.

Some studies conclude that unemployment affects sentencing decisions (Chiricos and Bales 1991; Walsh 1987). Other studies find that unemployment has no significant influence on sentencing (Clarke and Koch 1976; Myers and Talarico 1986a).

A comprehensive study comparing two cities highlights the complexity of the relationship between economic status and sentencing. In Kansas City, unemployment had a direct effect on the decision to grant probation but none on the length of imprisonment. In Chicago, on the other hand, unemployment had no effect on the decision to grant probation but directly affected sentence length. Perhaps most important, unemployment interacted with race and ethnicity. If the offender was white, unemployment status had no effect. For black or Hispanic young males, though, unemployment was related to harsher sentencing. Nobiling, Spohn, and DeLone (1998) conclude that certain types of unemployed offenders are perceived as "social dynamite." The term *social dynamite* is used to characterize the segment of the deviant population seen as particularly threatening and dangerous. Viewed from this perspective, economic status appears to be a dimension of social stability considered by the courtroom work group during sentencing.

DISCRIMINATION AND GENDER

Crime, as Chapter 9 emphasized, is predominantly (but not exclusively) a male enterprise. Sixteen percent of adults convicted each year are women (Levin, Langan, and Brown 2000), and 6 percent of the prison population are women. The marked imbalance between male and female defendants complicates efforts to examine gender-based differences in sentencing outcomes. Researchers, nonetheless, focus on two key questions: Why are women increasingly being sentenced to prison, and why are women sentenced more leniently than men? The results of research on gender and sentencing reveal a complex sentencing process.

Why Are Women Increasingly Being Sentenced to Prison?

In recent years the number of women incarcerated in state and federal prisons has increased dramatically. The almost 100,000 women under the jurisdiction of state and federal authorities stands in sharp contrast to the 23,000-plus held in 1985 (Bureau of Justice Statistics 2003e). This increase of more than 300 percent in the number of female prisoners outpaces the increase in male inmates.

Much of this growth in the number (and rate) of women imprisoned is attributed to the war on drugs. The number of women incarcerated for drug offenses increased 432 percent from 1986 to 1991 (Bureau of Justice Statistics 1997). Citing evidence like this, Meda Chesney-Lind (1997) concludes that the war on drugs has translated into a war on women. In other words, women have been the silent targets of punitive responses against drug use, coupled with get-tough sentencing policies such as sentencing guidelines, mandatory minimums, and three-strikes laws. As a result, the criminal justice system now seems more willing to incarcerate women.

Are Women Sentenced More Leniently Than Men?

A variety of studies document the more lenient sentencing of women compared to men. That is, compared to male defendants, women are more likely to be granted probation and also more likely to receive shorter prison sentences. In *The Invisible Woman*, Joanne Belknap (2001) aptly summarizes the three competing hypotheses concerning the treatment of women by the criminal justice system: (1) chivalry or paternalistic treatment, (2) the evil woman, and (3) equal treatment.

The chivalry/paternalism hypothesis stresses that men are unwilling to punish women because they don't believe that a woman could really be a criminal (Moulds 1978). Paternalism emphasizes the notion that women are childlike, and therefore "women are incapable of achieving, nor are they in fact held to, the same standards of personal responsibility as are men" (Rapaport 1991, 368). In essence, gender stereotypes lead predominantly male criminal justice officials to treat women in a protective manner.

The evil woman hypothesis focuses on traditional sex-role expectations. This hypothesis emphasizes that women lose the advantages normally provided by chivalry and paternalism when they are convicted of "manly" crimes such as robbery or assault. This evil woman view argues that women might actually be treated more harshly than men when they deviate from stereotypical sex-role expectations (Weisheit and Mahan 1988).

The third hypothesis is that men and women are actually treated equally during sentencing. Pennsylvania sentencing data indicate that "when men and women appear in (contemporary) criminal court in similar circumstances and are charged with similar offenses, they receive similar treatment" (Steffensmeier, Kramer, and Streifel 1993). Studies in other jurisdictions likewise report no significant gender-based differences (Crew 1991; Spohn and Spears 1997; Steury and Frank 1990). Boritch (1992, 293) writes that "some of the less severe treatment of women is attributable to the fact that women usually are less serious offenders than men," and therefore studies using appropriate statistical controls for legally relevant variables find less evidence of differential leniency in the severity of sanctions.

In *Gender, Crime, and Punishment*, Kathleen Daly (1994) fleshes out this argument. She selected 40 male–female pairs of apparently similar crimes and then analyzed transcripts of the court proceedings. She concludes that women were involved in less serious crimes, and this factor (not gender) explains "lenient" treatment.

Contemporary researchers now explicitly reject the chivalry/paternalism and evil woman explanations. Nonetheless, concern remains that different criteria influence the legal processing of male and female offenders. Some studies report that gender role expectations and stereotypes guide parole decision making

(Erez 1992), and there is a form of gender bias in capital punishment laws (Rapaport 1991).

DISCRIMINATION AND RACE

Critics of the criminal justice system view the high rates of arrest and imprisonment for blacks and other minorities as evidence of racial discrimination. Although the law contains no racial bias, these critics claim that, because criminal justice officials exercise discretion, discrimination can and often does occur. (See Courts, Controversy, and Equal Justice: Should Federal Penalties for Crack Be Lowered to Remove Racial Disparities?)

There are more studies of racial discrimination at the sentencing stage than at any other decision point in the criminal justice system. Studies conducted from the 1930s through the 1960s often reported that extralegal factors such as race were responsible for differences in sanctions. These original findings, however, have not stood up to further analysis, because they failed to use appropriate statistical techniques. When Hagan (1974) reexamined the data from early studies, he found that the relationship between the race of the offender and the sentence handed out was not statistically significant.

Contemporary research using appropriate statistical techniques has produced conflicting findings. Some researchers conclude that blacks are sentenced more harshly than whites, others that there are no differences, and still others that blacks are sentenced more leniently (Walker, Spohn, and DeLone 2004).

One group of studies reports that blacks are sentenced more harshly than whites (Spohn and Holleran 2000; Zatz 1984; Steffensmeier, Ulmer, and Kramer 1998). A prominent example of this type of conclusion is based on a study of six American cities. In three Southern cities, blacks were sentenced to prison more often than whites. No such differences were found in Northern jurisdictions, however (Welch, Spohn, and Gruhl 1985). Overall, these studies report modest levels of racial discrimination (Spohn and Cederblom 1991).

A second group of studies fails to find a link between race and sentencing (Klein, Pe-

tersilia, and Turner 1990; Myers and Talarico 1986a; Kramer and Steffensmeier 1993). Research in diverse geographical locations reports the absence of consistent evidence of systematic racial discrimination in sentencing. Perhaps typical is a study of sentencing in federal courts, which found that from 1986 to 1988 "white, black, and Hispanic offenders received similar sentences, on average, in Federal district courts." After sentencing guidelines were imposed in 1989, Hispanic and black offenders were slightly more likely than white offenders to be sentenced to prison, but these apparent racial differences were directly attributable to characteristics of offenses and offenders (McDonald and Carlson 1993).

Finally, a few studies conclude that blacks are sentenced more leniently than whites (Bernstein, Kelly, and Doyle 1977). For example, research in Atlanta found that black defendants received the same sentences as whites after taking into account seriousness of the offense, prior record, and so on. In analyzing sentences handed down by individual judges, however, a more complex pattern emerged. Some judges were clearly anti-black, others pro-black, and some nondiscriminatory (Gibson 1978).

Given these inconsistent findings, it is difficult to draw firm conclusions. A prominent summary of the literature argues that the contemporary sentencing process, while not racially neutral, is not characterized by "a widespread systematic pattern of discrimination" (Blumstein et al. 1983, 93). Thus, although a few studies suggest overt racial discrimination, most find more subtle and indirect racial effects (Zatz 1987; Spohn and Spears 1996).

DISCRIMINATION AND CAPITAL PUNISHMENT

Capital punishment has figured prominently in studies of racial discrimination in sentencing. Marked racial differences in the application of the death penalty in the South provide the most obvious historical evidence of racial discrimination in sentencing. From 1930 to 1966, 72 percent of the prisoners executed in the South were black. This proportion is dramatically

COURTS, CONTROVERSY, AND EQUAL JUSTICE

Should Federal Penalties for Crack Be Lowered to Remove Racial Disparities?

 Crack is a cheap, smokable form of cocaine that provides a quick high, and carries a long federal prison term. Powder cocaine, on the other hand, carries a significantly lesser sentence. Under federal law, 5 grams of crack triggers the same mandatory five-year prison term for first offenders as does 500 grams of powder cocaine. (Most state codes make no such distinction.)

The difficulty is that the sentences are based on the weight of the drug and not the weight of the active ingredient in the drug. Through the years, sentencing disparities like this have been common but have rarely entered public discussion. In this case, the debate centers on who uses these drugs. Crack cocaine is more likely to be used by blacks and powder by whites. The undeniable result is a racial imbalance—88 percent of all people prosecuted in federal courts for trafficking in crack cocaine are black.

Some in law enforcement believe that such sentencing disparities are justified because crack is a more serious problem than powder cocaine. Crack is more often sold by gangs and used by poor people who, in their desperation to repeat the quick high that crack affords, commit robbery or worse to get the money to buy more. Indeed, law enforcement officials often insist that crack is behind a large percentage of the crime they see (Hodges 1997).

When faced with crime issues, Congress increasingly asks the U.S. Sentencing Commission to study the matter, and study they did. The Sentencing Commission concluded that crack is somewhat more addictive and more closely associated with other crime than is powder cocaine. But the analysis of federal sentencing decisions also documents racial imbalance. The Commission therefore recommended narrowing the sentencing disparity significantly, arguing that a 2-to-1 disparity would be more fitting. But so far Congress has failed to act.

The U.S. Supreme Court has likewise shown no enthusiasm for tackling this divisive issue. The justices rejected, without comment, the argument that federal sentencing laws are racially discriminatory in treating crack cocaine dealers more severely than traffickers of powder cocaine ("Court: Sentences for Crack" 1997).

The Clinton administration also handled the issue ever so cautiously. Initially the administration opposed any changes in the penalty for crack cocaine (clearly fearing to make it a Republican election issue). But in 1997 the administration softened its stance, proposing to reduce the current 100-to-1 ratio to 10-to-1 by *increasing* the penalties for possession of powder cocaine. This proposal drew negative comments from the Congressional Black Caucus, which argues there should be no racial disparity. The Bush administration has made no effort to reduce apparent racial disparities in this area.

What do you think? Are the differences in cocaine sentencing fair? Should the apparent racial discrepancy in sentencing drug offenders be a matter of concern? Is crack cocaine more addictive than powder cocaine, and therefore more likely to be linked with crime? If you favor reducing the disparity in sentencing between crack and powder cocaine, would you do so by reducing the penalty for crack cocaine or raising the sanction for powder cocaine? Overall, do you think Congress is justified in imposing a mandatory minimum for drug crimes, or do mandatory minimums end up producing an irrational sentencing structure, with minor offenders being punished more severely than major ones?

To continue the debate, go to the following sites and search for "crack cocaine":

The Sentencing Project: http://www.sentencingproject.org/ (go to Publications)

Policy.com: http://www.policy.com/

Office of National Drug Court Policy: http://www.whitehousedrugpolicy.gov/

National Institute of Drug Abuse: http://www.nida.nih.gov/

Families Against Mandatory Minimums: http://www.famm.org/

Alcoholism & Drug Abuse Weekly, "Drop in Violent Crime Linked to Crack Decline"

Alcoholism & Drug Abuse Weekly, "Senate Supports Tougher Penalties for Powder Cocaine Offenses"

higher than the ratio of blacks in the overall population or the ratio of blacks convicted of capital offenses. The racial gap was even more pronounced in rape cases. Only the South executed rapists, and 90 percent of those executed for rape were black. Those most likely to be executed were blacks who had raped white women (Wolfgang and Riedel 1973).

Offender–Victim Dyad

The executions in the South clearly show major racial differences. As indicated earlier, however, racial imbalances in outcomes do not necessarily prove discrimination. Interestingly, many studies found that the most obvious factor—race of the defendant—was not as important as the race of the offender in combination with the race of the victim. The offender–victim dyad, ordered according to the perceived seriousness of the offense, is

1. Black offender, white victim
2. White offender, white victim
3. Black offender, black victim
4. White offender, black victim

Research on the offender–victim dyad established that blacks killing or raping whites were the most likely to be executed; conversely, whites killing or raping blacks were least likely to receive the death penalty. These findings have been interpreted as indicating that severe punishments were motivated by a desire to protect the white social order. Some also argue that black lives were not valued as much as white lives. A variety of studies indicate that the use of the death penalty in the South was racially discriminatory (Hindelang 1972; Baldus, Pulaski, and Woodworth 1983; Ralph, Sorensen, and Marquart 1992). A different conclusion emerges for the North. Studies of the death penalty in Northern states find no evidence of racial discrimination (Kleck 1981).

Evidence of Discrimination since *Gregg*

Major racial differences in execution rates, together with studies finding racial discrimination in the application of the death penalty, figured prominently in the opinions of several justices when the Supreme Court struck down state death penalty laws in 1972 (*Furman v. Georgia*). The Court later upheld guided discretion statutes designed to reduce or eliminate the arbitrariness with which the death penalty is imposed. Since *Gregg v. Georgia* in 1976, several studies have reported evidence of racial discrimination in the application of post-*Gregg* death penalty laws (Keil and Vito 1990).

The prosecution of homicide cases involves several discretionary decisions that can affect the use of capital punishment (Weiss, Berk, and Lee 1996). Several studies find that racial discrimination exists from the time the police classify a homicide until the case is presented in court (Sorensen and Wallace 1999). For example, a study of more than 1,000 homicide defendants in Florida compared original police classifications with the charges later filed by the prosecutor. Blacks accused of killing whites were the most likely to have the charges upgraded to a death-eligible charge and least likely to be downgraded (Radelet and Pierce 1985). Similarly, in South Carolina, the race of the victim was found to be a significant factor structuring the district attorney's decision to request capital punishment. For black offenders who killed white victims, the prosecutor was 40 times more likely to request the death penalty than in the case of black defendants accused of killing other blacks (Paternoster 1984).

Evidence of No Discrimination since *Gregg*

Findings that the application of the death penalty remain racially biased despite the apparent protections required by *Gregg* have been challenged by a study of all death-eligible cases appealed to the Louisiana Supreme Court (Klemm 1986). The initial analysis revealed the impact of extralegal variables. The chance of receiving a death sentence steadily decreased as one moved down the scale of offender–victim dyads. These findings clearly paralleled earlier ones in other states. More sophisticated analysis, however, highlighted the importance of legal variables.

Unlike previous researchers, Klemm also examined how the crime was committed. The prior relationship of the offender to the victim emerged as an important factor. Primary homicides are crimes of passion involving persons who knew each other. Nonprimary homicides occur during the commission of another felony (most typically, armed robbery), and the victim is a total stranger. Those convicted of nonprimary homicides were more likely to receive a sentence of death, regardless of the race of the offender or the race of the victim. Thus, the chances of receiving a death sentence were greater if the victim was a stranger.

Overall, the race of the victim had only an indirect effect in Louisiana. Likewise, a study of the use of the death penalty in Texas prior to *Furman* finds some remarkable parallels to the findings from Louisiana. In particular, nonprimary homicides were more likely to result in the imposition of the death penalty (Ralph, Sorensen, and Marquart 1992).

McCleskey v. Kemp Bars Social Science Evidence

The Supreme Court squarely addressed the issue of racial discrimination in capital punishment in a controversial 1987 decision (*McCleskey v. Kemp*). At issue was a study in Georgia that the application of capital punishment was related to the offender–victim dyad. Defendants convicted of killing a white victim were four times more likely to receive a sentence of death than those found guilty of slaying a black victim. These racial differences remained even after controls for such relevant factors as prior record and type of homicide were introduced. The authors conclude that Georgia had a dual system of capital punishment, based on the race of the victim (Baldus, Pulaski, and Woodworth 1983).

By a 5-to-4 vote, the majority rejected claims that statistical studies indicated that the state's death penalty law was "wanton and freakish" in application. To Justice Lewis Powell, "Disparities are an inevitable part of our criminal justice system." The opinion argued that the statistics do not prove that race enters into any capital sentencing decisions or that race was a factor in McCleskey's case.

Overall, as the Court has become more supportive of the death penalty, it has become

| Exhibit **16-3** | Justice Blackmun's Dissent |

From this day forward, I no longer shall tinker with the machinery of death. For more than 20 years I have endeavored—indeed, I have struggled, along with a majority of this Court—to develop procedural and substantive rules that would lend more than the mere appearance of fairness to the death penalty endeavor. . . .

Rather than continue to coddle the Court's delusion that the desired level of fairness has been achieved and the need for regulation eviscerated, I feel morally and intellectually obligated simply to concede that the death penalty experiment has failed. It is virtually self-evident to me now that no combination of procedural rules or substantive regulations ever can save the death penalty from its inherent constitutional deficiencies. The basic question—does the system accurately and consistently determine which defendants "deserve" to die?—cannot be answered in the affirmative. . . .

The problem is that the inevitability of factual, legal and moral error gives us a system that we know must wrongly kill some defendants, a system that fails to deliver the fair, consistent and reliable sentences of death required by the Constitution.

—Justice Harry Blackmun dissenting in *Callins v. James,* 1994

less inclined to consider social science evidence that might show patterns of racial discrimination (Acker 1993a). Nonetheless, critics continue to point to patterns of discrimination in the application of the death penalty. These concerns motivated Justice Harry Blackmun to shift his position on the death penalty just before his retirement (Exhibit 16-3).

DISPARITIES AND SENTENCING

Unlike discrimination, which focuses on attributes of defendants, disparity centers on the process that sentences defendants. Thus, **disparity** refers to inconsistencies in sentencing resulting from the decision-making process.

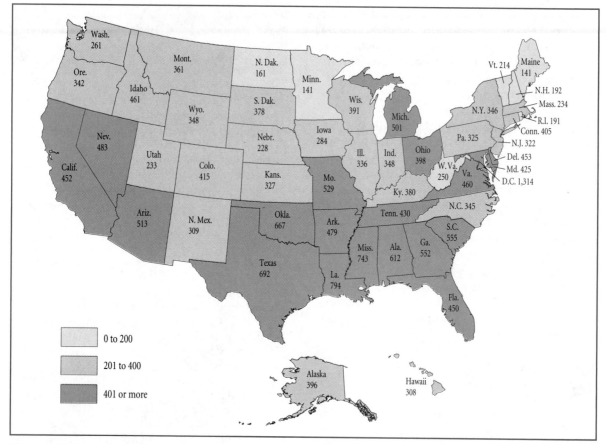

Figure 16-1

Number of Prisoners in State Institutions per 100,000 Civilian Population

SOURCE: U.S. Department of Justice, Bureau of Justice Statistics, *Prisoners in 2002* (Washington, DC: U.S. Government Printing Office, 2003).

The most commonly cited types of sentencing disparity involve geography (variations across jurisdictions) and judicial backgrounds and attitudes (variations among judges within the same jurisdiction).

The Geography of Justice

What counts against defendants is not only what they do but also where they do it. Significant variations in the sentencing patterns of judges in different judicial districts within the same political jurisdiction is referred to as the *geography of justice*. The frequency of fines, probation, or imprisonment varies from county to county. Similar differences occur among the

states in convicts imprisoned per 100,000 people (Figure 16-1).

Geographical differences in justice are the product of a number of factors, including the amount of crime, the effectiveness of the police in apprehending offenders, and the types of screening employed by the court. Also, some courts deal with more serious offenses, as well as with a greater number of defendants having prior records. But even after controlling for such factors, it is apparent that important geographic differences remain (Kautt 2002; Rengert 1989; Gertz and Price 1985; Myers and Talarico 1987).

Overall, it appears that the South imposes harsher sentences than other regions. Executions, for example, are concentrated in this region. Similarly, urban courts make greater use of probation and shorter prison terms than their rural counterparts (Austin 1981). Such geographic patterns demonstrate that court officials, drawn as they are from the local communities, vary in their views of what offenses are the most serious as well as what penalty is appropriate (Myers and Talarico 1986b; Myers and Reid 1995).

Judges' Backgrounds and Attitudes

What counts against defendants is not only what they do and where they do it, but also which judge imposes the sentence. Sentencing disparities among judges have fascinated social scientists for decades. A study of women's court in Chicago is typical of this interest. The proportion of shoplifting defendants placed on probation ranged from a low of 10 percent for one judge to a high of 62 percent for another (Cameron 1964). Although such sentencing disparities may be due to variations in the seriousness of the cases heard, differences in judges' backgrounds and attitudes are a more likely cause.

Judges come to the bench from a variety of backgrounds. We might reasonably expect these differences to be reflected in varying patterns of judicial behavior, and studies of judicial decision making support this proposition. U.S. district court judges appointed by Democratic presidents are more likely to decide for the defendant than those appointed by Republican presidents (Carp and Rowland 1983).

Variations in judges' backgrounds are associated with different perceptions of what crimes are serious as well as the relative weights to be assigned to conflicting sentencing goals. Several studies have directly examined judicial attitudes and sentences imposed (Green 1961; Gibson 1980). In Ontario, Canada, judges who stressed deterrence were more likely to favor prison sentences over other forms of sentencing. Conversely, judges who were more treatment-oriented were more likely to impose suspended sentences or relatively short jail sentences (Hogarth 1971).

Although the public views judges as either harsh or lenient sentencers, detailed studies indicate that the pattern is far more complex (Myers and Talarico 1987). It is an accepted fact that judges have different sentencing tendencies. Some have reputations for handing out stiff sentences. "Maximum Max" or "Mean Geraldine" are examples of the colorful labels used by members of the courtroom work group to characterize such judges. Others are known for lenient sentences. "Cut 'em Loose Bruce" is one name given such a judge by courthouse regulars. The sentences of most judges fall somewhere in between these extremes (Partridge and Eldridge 1974). Because they are less distinctive, these courtroom actors seldom get colorful nicknames.

CHANGING SENTENCING STRUCTURES

During the late 1960s and early 1970s, an unusual (and temporary) political coalition developed between liberals and conservatives. Both sides found considerable fault in existing sentencing practices. Although their reasons reflected fundamentally different concerns, liberals and conservatives defined the problem in similar terms: The criminal laws permitted too much latitude in sentencing, providing judges with little or no guidance on how to determine the proper sentence for each individual case. This coalition therefore sought greater predictability in sentencing (Griset 1991). The result was a fundamental change in how defendants are sentenced (see Chapter 15).

Law in Controversy: Reducing Judicial Discretion

Adherents of the due process model were concerned that excessive discretion resulted in a lack of fairness in sentencing. They perceived that criminal justice officials, ranging from police officers to parole boards, were making decisions in a discriminatory manner, especially on the basis of race. They were also concerned that judges' sentencing discretion resulted in sentencing disparities. Thus, the political left saw determinate sentences as a means of reducing individual discretion and thereby (presumably) reducing disparity and discrimination.

THE MURDER TRIAL OF SHAREEF COUSIN

The Jury Chooses Death

"Today we focus on the character of the man that you found guilty as charged of first-degree murder. That's the character of Shareef Cousin." With these words, Assistant DA Roger Jordan began the penalty phase of the murder trial. In urging the jury to recommend the death penalty, Jordan emphasized two aggravating circumstances: (1) the killer was perpetrating, or attempting to perpetrate, an armed robbery, and (2) the especially heinous, atrocious, and cruel manner of the crime.

Toward those ends, the prosecution called six witnesses. The first was Sal Gerardi, who tearfully offered a victim impact statement (see Chapter 9) about how empty his life had become since his son's murder. Next, the state called the four victims of the armed robberies (see Chapter 13), who testified about the terror they experienced. Donald Rhodes, for example, was walking a few blocks from the Port of Call restaurant when Shareef Cousin pointed a gun in his face. After Rhodes gave him his wallet and watch, Shareef walked a few steps and then turned around, pointing his gun at Rhodes in the

firing position. Finally, the prosecution called detective Christy Williams, who introduced into evidence Cousin's confession to the four armed robberies. (Since Cousin did not take the witness stand in his own defense, the jury had not known of the previous armed robbery convictions.)

The defense countered with only three witnesses who offered substantive testimony. The first was Richard Collins from Worcester, Massachusetts, where Shareef Cousin had lived for a while with his older brother. Collins testified that the boy "was like a son to me" and was doing well in school until he left for New Orleans in the spring of 1994. Two New Orleans teachers were also called to testify that Cousin did well in their math classes (although under cross-examination one admitted that at times he had been a discipline problem).

Perhaps what was most significant about the defense during the penalty phase was who was not called. Outside the hearing of the jury, attorney Willard Hill informed the court of an ongoing problem during the trial: "But it has become more acute as a result of the verdict rendered on Friday. I am referring to the reluctance of his

Adherents of the crime control model were far more concerned that excessive discretion resulted in a lack of effective crime control. They perceived that criminal justice officials were making decisions that produced undue leniency. Concern about disparity or discrimination was not part of the agenda. In particular, they viewed trial judges as all too ready to impose sentences well below the statutory maximum. They perceived that parole boards were too willing to release prisoners early; they were shocked that prisoners were back on the streets on parole well before the maximum sentence had expired. To conservatives, the essential problem was that sentencing was not reducing crime. In an effort to make sentencing more effective, a "justice" model of sentencing came into increasing prominence. Wrongdoers should be punished on the principle of just deserts, which implies a certainty and uniformity of punishment (see Chapter 15).

Law on the Books: Determinate Sentencing Returns

In response to criticisms of the rehabilitation model, with its emphasis on indeterminate sentences and discretionary parole release, a number of states have adopted determinate or fixed sentencing laws (see Chapter 15). These new sentencing laws are based on the assumption that judges should give offenders a specific amount of time to serve rather than a minimum and a maximum. The change to determinate sentencing is usually accompanied by a move to abolish release on parole as well. Under determinate sentencing, the prisoner is automatically released to community supervision at the end of the term. (See Exhibit 16-4 for a summary of key developments concerning sentencing.)

The statutory systems in these states vary widely. At one end of the continuum is Maine's

family members, for whatever reason, to testify in this case. . . . We have spent many hours with the family trying to convince them to testify in this case. It has been our advice—our strong recommendation to the family that they do so. They have refused."

Events outside the courtroom (and therefore not observed by the jury) flesh out what Hill alluded to. Family members orchestrated a demonstration on the courthouse steps, claiming that authorities vigorously pressed their case against Cousin because "white people consider themselves superior to black people" (Varney 1996b).

In short, the jury never heard the other family members plead for mercy, imploring the jury to spare Shareef Cousin's life. During closing arguments, Hill tried to highlight the good aspects of Cousin's short life. He seemed to do well when a positive male role model was present, Hill asserted, but seemed to fall off the wagon when he returned from living with his brother near Boston.

During closing arguments, the prosecution pressed home the brazen nature of the armed robberies. Referring to Cousin's character witnesses, the DA drove home his point: "They didn't see the face that was pointing a gun. . . ." In mid-sentence, Shareef Cousin exploded, jumping from his seat and shouting "I wasn't out there.

I'm innocent." His attorney ordered him to sit down, and the judge threatened to remove him from court. But the damage had been done. Seizing the opportunity, Roger Jordan pointed at Cousin and argued "that is the face that Michael Gerardi saw. That's the face that he saw and the anger in his eyes, with a gun in his hand."

Several hours later the jury returned, and Judge Bigelow read into the record their verdict:

Having found the below listed statutory aggravating circumstance or circumstances, and after consideration of the mitigating circumstances offered, the jury unanimously determines that the defendant should be sentenced to death. The aggravating circumstance: That the victim in this murder was killed when the offender was engaged in the perpetration or attempted perpetration of an armed robbery.

On July 2, 1996, Judge Bigelow formally imposed sentence, writing on the standard court form that the sentence for Shareef Cousin was "death by lethal injection."

Helen Prejean, "Letter from Death Row"

For more about age and the death penalty, type in the search term "dead teen walking" and read the section "The Kids on Row."

---

law, which retains the broad discretion of judges to determine the time to be served in prison. Because of the abolition of parole, however, prisoners can predict at sentencing when they will be released. At the other end of the continuum is California's Uniform Determinate Sentencing Law, which abolished parole release for most prisoners and enacted detailed statutory sentencing standards. The determinate sentencing laws of other states fall in between those of Maine and California; they provide more guidance to judges than the former but less than the latter.

Law in Action: Diverse Impacts

Whether determinate sentencing laws are seen as successful depends somewhat on one's political vantage point. Some adherents hoped that these laws would increase the certainty of pun-

ishment; others feared that prison populations would swell. A number of studies have investigated the impact of determinate sentencing laws. The findings indicate that the impacts are diverse.

An offender's chance of receiving probation declined in California (McCoy 1984), but there was no change in Colorado (Covey and Mande 1985). Analysis of sentence length yields a slightly different pattern. In Indiana (Clear, Hewitt, and Regoli 1979) there was a projected 50 percent increase in the actual length of sentence for first offenders, yet in North Carolina (Clarke 1984) increase in sentence length was less severe. Finally, researchers have examined overall prison population. In California (Casper, Brereton, and Neal 1982), as in other states (Carroll and Cornell 1985), there have been significant increases in the prison population following the passage of determinate sentencing legislation (Marvell and Moody 1996). The lack

Exhibit 16-4 Key Developments in Sentencing

Determinate sentencing	Early twentieth century	In most jurisdictions, the judge imposes a specific number of years of imprisonment.
Indeterminate sentencing	Through 1970s	Based on the rehabilitation model, many jurisdictions allow judge to impose a sentencing range. Corrections officials and parole boards decide the actual length of time served.
Mandatory minimums	1960s	Most jurisdictions require that a defendant serve a minimum prison sentence for selected offenses.
Maine	1976	First state in modern era to return to determinate sentencing.
California, Illinois, and Indiana	1977	Determinate sentencing laws enacted.
Minnesota	1980	First state to create a sentencing commission and adopt sentencing guidelines.
Sentencing Reform Act	1984	Federal sentencing guidelines adopted and parole abolished in federal courts, effective 1987.
McCleskey v. Kemp	1987	Court rejects use of statistical information to prove racial discrimination in the use of the death penalty.
Mistretta v. U.S.	1989	Federal sentencing guidelines and Sentencing Commission do not violate constitutional separation of powers.
Megan's Law	1994	Following the rape and murder of 7-year-old Megan Kanka, New Jersey passes law requiring convicted sex offenders to register with local police departments.
Polly's Law	1994	California passes three-strikes law, named after murder victim Polly Klaas.
"Three Strikes and You're Out"	1993–1995	Twenty-four states and the federal government pass three-strikes laws.
Truth in Sentencing Laws	1990s	First enacted in 1984, Truth in Sentencing Laws require offenders to serve a substantial portion of their prison sentence. Most often applied for violent offenses.
San Diego County v. Romero	1996	California Supreme Court holds that judges have discretion in counting prior convictions.
Edwards v. U.S.	1997	Court refuses to hear challenge that federal sentencing laws dealing with crack are racially discriminatory.
Aimee's Law	1999	Proposed federal law named after murder victim Aimee Willard, a college athlete killed by a parolee. Law would encourage states to incarcerate individuals convicted of murder, rape, or child molestation.
Ewing v. California	2002	Three-strikes laws do not violate the Eighth Amendment prohibition against cruel and unusual punishment.
Connecticut v. Doe	2002	Affirmed Connecticut's "Megan law" requiring convicted sex offenders to register and have their names published in a registry.

of clear findings is not surprising. The American legal system consists of numerous independent units, and the laws in question vary in important ways.

SENTENCING GUIDELINES

Early efforts to impose determinate sentencing suffered from a serious weakness: Legislative bodies had neither the time nor the skills to enact detailed sentencing rules. Therefore, since the 1980s, efforts to provide certainty and consistency in sentencing have taken a different form. Legislatures have created commissions to devise detailed sentencing rules, and the legislatures have then enacted these guidelines into law.

At the national level, Congress created the U.S. Sentencing Commission in 1984 to develop guidelines for sentencing federal offenders. Over strong objections, the federal sentencing guidelines went into effect on November 1, 1987. By an 8-to-1 vote, the Supreme Court upheld the guidelines (see Case Close-up: *Mistretta v. U.S.* and Sentencing Guidelines).

At the state level, sentencing guidelines operate in 17 states, and 5 more have appointed commissions to implement or study this approach (Frase 1995). There are, however, important differences in how guidelines are written.

Law on the Books: Voluntary versus Presumptive Guidelines

Sentencing guidelines provide a recommended sentencing range based on the seriousness of the offense and the criminal history of the offender. In arriving at a sentence, judges first calculate the severity of the crime. Next, with the help of probation officers, the judge computes a criminal history score (the lower the number, the better for the defendant). The recommended sentence is then located in the appropriate grid. The sentencing grid used in Minnesota illustrates how sentencing guidelines operate (Exhibit 16-5).

The impact of the recommended sentence depends on whether the jurisdiction has adopted voluntary or presumptive sentencing guidelines. Voluntary sentencing guidelines are most commonly used. Recommended sentencing ranges are derived by analyzing the types of sanctions judges in the jurisdiction have imposed in various types of cases in the past. Once adopted, these guidelines may be used voluntarily by judges, but they are advisory only. Voluntary sentencing guidelines do not have the force of law, and noncompliance by a judge creates no right to appeal the sentence.

Presumptive sentencing guidelines, on the other hand, are prescriptive because they express what sentence should be imposed, regardless of existing practices (Kramer, Lubitz, and Kempinen 1989). Once adopted, these guidelines must be followed by the sentencing judges. If a sentence is imposed outside of the guidelines, the judge must provide reasons for the deviation. Both defendants and prosecutors have the right to have the sufficiency of that explanation reviewed by an appellate court. Thus presumptive, or prescriptive, guidelines have substantial legal authority.

Law in Action: Varied Impacts

The impact of sentencing guidelines varies according to the type of guidelines used. In jurisdictions with voluntary sentencing guidelines, not all judges actually use the guidelines when imposing sentence, and even fewer judges provide reasons for sentences outside the guidelines. As a result, in Florida the guidelines did not reduce sentencing disparity. In Maryland the findings were somewhat more ambiguous, with reports of modest decreases in disparity in at least some of the four test sites (Carrow 1984).

Presumptive sentencing guidelines, as you might expect, achieve a much higher rate of judicial compliance. As a result, they have helped reduce sentencing disparity. Overall, racial, ethnic, and gender differences in sentencing generally decline (Parent et al. 1996; Kramer and Ulmer 1996). Disparity reductions, though, tend to erode somewhat over time.

Minnesota's sentencing guidelines provide a case in point. They appear to have achieved their goals of more predictable and more uniform sentencing. During the first year of operation, the law achieved significant increases in

CASE CLOSE-UP

Mistretta v. U.S. and Sentencing Guidelines

 The opinion of the Court is remarkably silent about the background of John Mistretta. All that is known is that he sold cocaine (probably a small amount) to an undercover federal narcotics agent. Like countless other federal drug charges, Mistretta's indictment would probably have resulted in a plea of guilty and a minor sentence. But Mistretta had the misfortune of being charged a month after the federal sentencing guidelines became effective. Thus, through happenstance, Mistretta's name became forever linked to the bold sentencing experiment of the 1980s—sentencing guidelines.

Defense attorneys across the nation vehemently opposed the new scheme, arguing the guidelines would send a lot more people to prison for a lot longer periods of time. A number of federal judges likewise opposed the guidelines, believing that the congressional legislation represented a slap in the face, an indication that judges' discretion could no longer be trusted. Indeed, the judges of the Western District of Missouri (where Mistretta was indicted) were divided over the matter. The majority of trial judges in the district, though, rejected legal challenges to the new sentencing scheme.

Mistretta pled guilty and was sentenced to 18 months in prison. But before his appeal could be heard by the Court of Appeals for the Eighth Circuit, the U.S. Supreme Court, citing the "imperative public importance" of the issue, granted certiorari.

In an 8-to-1 decision written by Justice Harry Blackmun (a Nixon appointee who was nonetheless known for a moderate-to-liberal bent on the Court), the Court upheld the law. At the center of the controversy was the composition of the seven-member commission, which by law must include three federal judges. Blackmun wrote that the independent commission "unquestionably is a peculiar institution within the framework of our government." Nonetheless, merely because it is an anomaly or innovation does not mean that the federal sentencing law violated constitutional requirements of separation of powers among the branches of government or delegated excessive authority to the sentencing commission.

The lone dissenter was Justice Antonin Scalia (the Court's most conservative member). He rejected arguments that this case was about comingling of the branches of government. Rather, in his opinion, this case was about "the creation of a new branch altogether, a sort of junior-varsity Congress." In short, Article I, which deals with Congress, was at stake and not Article III, which hinges on judicial independence.

Many federal judges firmly opposed the federal sentencing guidelines, with somewhere between 100 to 150 declaring the law unconstitutional. Numerous others found the law defective on statutory grounds or found ways to avoid its application. Thus *Mistretta* is important because the high court chose not to confront Congress. Although on many issues the Rehnquist Court is deferential to Congress, when it comes to deciding the proper role of the federal judiciary under Article III, the Court has challenged Congress at times. But in *Mistretta* the Court decided that this was not an issue worthy of a confrontation.

 To learn more about the pros and cons of sentencing guidelines, point your browser to:

United States Sentencing Commission
http://www.ussc.gov/

Crack Cocaine Sentencing Guidelines: Pros and Cons http://www.lectlaw.com/files/leg15.htm

Association of Americans for Constitutional Laws and Justice "The Truth about Sentencing Guidelines" http://www.pixi.com/~itmc/Sentencing.html

 Jeffrey T. Ulmer, John H. Kramer, "The Use and Transformation of Formal Decision-Making Criteria: Sentencing Guidelines"

Joseph S. Hall, "Guided to Injustice? The Effect of the Sentencing Guidelines on Indigent Defendants and Public Defense"

both uniformity and neutrality. But not all judicial discretion was eliminated; the law allowed judges some leeway. Over time, judges came to follow the guidelines less faithfully, but uniformity of sentencing remained well above pre-guideline levels (Miethe and Moore 1989). Overall, the Minnesota sentencing guideline law has been more successful than other

Exhibit 16-5 Minnesota Sentencing Guidelines

Severity Level of Conviction Offense		Criminal History Score						
		0	1	2	3	4	5	6 or more
Murder, 2nd degree (intentional murder, drive-by-shootings)	X	306 299–313	326 319–333	346 339–353	366 359–373	386 379–393	406 399–413	426 419–433
Murder, 3rd degree Murder, 2nd degree (unintentional murder)	IX	150 144–156	165 159–171	180 174–186	195 189–201	210 204–216	225 219–231	240 234–246
Criminal sexual conduct, 1st degree Assault, 1st degree	VIII	86 81–91	98 93–103	110 105–115	122 117–127	134 129–139	146 141–151	158 153–163
Aggravated robbery, 1st degree	VII	48 44–52	58 54–62	68 64–72	78 74–82	88 84–92	98 94–102	108 104–112
Criminal sexual conduct, 2nd degree (a) & (b)	VI	21	27	33	39 37–41	45 43–47	51 49–53	57 55–59
Residential burglary, Simple robbery	V	18	23	28	33 31–35	38 36–40	43 41–45	48 46–50
Nonresidential burglary	IV	12*	15	18	21	24 23–25	27 26–28	30 29–31
Theft crimes (over $2,500)	III	12*	13	15	17	19 18–20	21 20–22	23 22–24
Theft crimes ($2,500 or less) Check forgery ($200–$2,500)	II	12*	12*	13	15	17	19	21 20–22
Sale of controlled substance	I	12*	12*	12*	13	15	17	19 18–20

Note: The left-hand column ranks the seriousness of the offense according to ten categories. The upper rows provide a seven-category criminal history score, calculated by summing the points allocated to such factors as the number of previous convictions, the total times incarcerated, whether the offender was on probation or parole, employment status or educational achievement, and the offender's history of drug and/or alcohol abuse. After calculating the offense severity ranking and the criminal history score, the judge determines the recommended sentence by finding the cell of the sentencing grid in the applicable row and column. The cells below the bold line call for sentences other than imprisonment; these numbers specify months of supervision. The cells above the bold line contain the guideline sentence expressed in months of imprisonment. The single number is the recommended sentence. The range extends plus or minus 5 to 8 percent from the guideline sentence. By law first-degree murder is excluded from the guidelines and continues to have a mandatory life sentence.

*One year and one day.

SOURCE: Minnesota Sentencing Guidelines Commission, 1981, p. 23.

sentencing reforms. The chief reason for this success, at least in the areas governed by the guidelines, is that the state's sentencing guidelines were backed by the weight of law (Moore and Miethe 1986).

Sentencing guideline laws are associated with increases in sentencing severity (Tonry 1987; Kramer and Lubitz 1985; Holten and Handberg 1990). There is, however, a debate in the literature whether increasing prison populations are attributable to sentencing guidelines or simply reflect long-term trends (D'Alessio and Stolzenberg 1995; Moody and Marvell 1996).

Law in Controversy: Has Too Much Discretion Been Removed?

Federal sentencing guidelines remain highly controversial (Stith and Cabranes, 1998). Indeed, many federal judges, defense attorneys, and even some prosecutors resent and resist the guidelines. According to Michael Tonry (1993), the federal sentencing guidelines "are a failure and should be radically revised or repealed." In support of this conclusion, he offers the following arguments. First, the guidelines are unduly harsh, as reflected in the dramatic increase in the federal prison population. Second, the guidelines have failed to reduce disparities in federal sentencing. Finally, the guidelines contribute to unfairness in sentencing because they are rigid and complex. Judges are specifically forbidden to consider the defendant's employment status or family life in passing sentence.

State guidelines are not as controversial, mainly because they are more diverse and often allow greater discretion to judges. But this greater flexibility has also lessened their impact. Moreover, not all efforts to develop sentencing guidelines have been successful. Some efforts foundered because legislatures were unwilling to devote sufficient resources to the task. But mainly the political culture of the state was not conducive to generating the consensus needed to develop and implement guidelines (Tonry 1991).

Consider New York (Griset 1995). The members of the New York commission reflected the same political divisions as were found in the state's criminal justice policymaking circles. Unlike Minnesota, where the commission members were all committed to sentencing reform and shared a vision for sentencing guidelines, the New York commissioners were torn by internal factionalism and saw themselves as representing the partisan interests of their background (Gizzi 1992). Thus, New York and other states have been unsuccessful in developing and implementing sentencing guidelines.

INCREASING THE SEVERITY OF THE PENALTY

The majority of Americans believe that prison sentences are too lenient (Krisberg 1988), and elected officials often express these views (Thomson and Ragona 1987). Thus, when confronted with a crime problem, legislators respond by sounding a clarion call to get tough with criminals. Such actions reflect the notion that increasing the severity of the penalty will deter criminals and reduce crime. These ideas are more often justified by moral claims than supported by valid scientific evidence. Researchers are skeptical that this type of deterrent effect actually exists.

Law on the Books: Mandatory Minimum Sentences

Mandatory minimum sentencing laws are one method legislatures use to increase the severity of sentencing. These types of laws are typically enacted in response to allegations that lenient judges are allowing many serious offenders (particularly violent ones) to go free. (The "proof" of this proposition is often limited to one or two highly publicized cases.) Virtually all states have passed mandatory minimum sentencing laws.

Typically, **mandatory minimum sentencing** laws require that offenders convicted of certain offenses must be sentenced to a prison term of not less than a specified period of years, and nonprison sentences (such as probation) are expressly precluded. In short, a term of imprisonment is mandated regardless of the circumstances of the offense or the background of the individual.

In recent years, the most popular mandatory minimum laws have supposedly targeted violent offenders with previous felony convictions (see Courts, Controversy, and Reducing Crime: Should "Three Strikes and You're Out" Laws Be Passed?). Through the years, legislative bodies have also enacted mandatory minimums for crimes that are particularly unpopular at the moment, including convicted felons in possession of a firearm, repeat drunk drivers (Chapter 18), and those in possession of certain drugs (such as cocaine) with intent to sell. Most recently, mandatory minimum legislation has been called Truth in Sentencing laws, which require offenders to a serve a substantial portion of their prison term (often 85 percent) before release (Ditton and Wilson 1999).

Law in Action: Nullification by Discretion

Mandatory minimum sentencing laws have proven popular because they promise certainty of punishment. "If Every Criminal Knew He Would Be Punished If Caught" is the title of an article by neoconservative James Q. Wilson (1973). But researchers caution that administering the law is seldom that automatic.

Sharp increases in formal penalties tend to be sidestepped by those who apply the law. At a variety of points in the application of legal sanctions—police arrest, prosecutorial discretion, jury conviction, and judicial sentencing—discretion may be exercised to offset the severity of the penalty (McCoy 1984).

A reduction in the number of arrests is one type of discretionary reaction that may occur when the severity of the penalty is increased. This clearly occurred when Connecticut's governor tried to crack down on speeders by imposing a mandatory loss of the driver's license; arrests for speeding decreased after the severe penalties were announced, because the police and other legal officials perceived that the penalty was too severe for the offense (Campbell and Ross 1968).

An increase in prosecutorial discretion may also compensate for an increase in the harshness of sentencing. Prosecutors often respond to new legislative actions by reducing the number of charges for that category. In 1973, the New York legislature enacted a tough new antidrug law that provided stiff mandatory sentences and sought to prevent plea bargaining. As a result, indictments for drug violations in New York State fell by 14 percent the next year (Association of the Bar of the City of New York Drug Abuse Council 1976). Thus, prosecutors may choose to file charges for an offense that does not carry the most severe penalties when they anticipate that judges and juries will be reluctant to convict.

A decrease in the number of convictions may also occur when legislators increase the severity of punishment. The most commonly cited example is capital punishment in late eighteenth- and early nineteenth-century England, when most felonies were punishable by death. Judges often strained to avoid convicting defendants by inventing legal technicalities (Hall 1952). Similarly, in New York State, after the tough drug law was passed, the number of convictions dropped.

After conviction, judges are reluctant to apply the severe penalty (Ross and Foley 1987). When Chicago traffic court judges sought to crack down on drunk drivers by voluntarily agreeing to impose a seven-day jail term, the penalty was rarely applied (Robertson, Rich, and Ross 1973).

There is clearly a relationship between punishment policy and the system that administers it. Through the discretionary actions of police, prosecutors, judges, and juries, harsh penalties are nullified. The more severe the penalty, the less likely it will be imposed when its severity exceeds what is viewed as appropriate. The final result is that more produces less. Stepping up the severity of the punishment does not increase the threat of punishment; it reduces it.

Law in Controversy: Negative Side Effects

One reason legislators find raising penalties so attractive is that they appear to be fighting crime without having to increase appropriations. It is a policy apparently without costs; the

COURTS, CONTROVERSY, AND REDUCING CRIME

Should "Three Strikes and You're Out" Laws Be Passed?

The kidnapping and murder of Polly Klaas focused the nation's attention on violent, predatory criminals. The man convicted of the crime, Richard Allen Davis, was an ex-con who had recently been released from prison on parole. The news coverage of the kidnapping and eventually the arrest fed the nation's fears that no one was safe, not even those who lived in a tranquil small town like Petaluma, California. At fault were not only societal outcasts like Richard Allen Davis, but also a criminal justice system that was a failure (Surette 1996).

Faced with an unsettled public, elected officials sought to reassure them by taking dramatic action. Thus, the murder of Polly Klaas became the reference event for passing "three strikes and you're out" legislation.

The basic arguments advanced by proponents of the three-strikes concept parallel the crime control model. Incapacitating chronic offenders who have demonstrated by their acts that they are both dangerous and unwilling to reform will protect the public. Moreover, repeat offenders will be deterred because they will be off the streets.

Critics counter that substantial increases in the use of imprisonment over the past decade have had little if any effect on violent crime rates. Life terms for three-time losers will require the allotment of expensive prison cells to offenders who are well past the peak age of criminal conduct. These adherents of the due process model argue that spending the same amount of money in other areas would produce a much greater reduction in crime than three-strikes laws (Greenwood et al. 1996).

Court arguments aside, public support for three-strikes laws was overwhelming, and in quick order elected officials in 24 states and the federal government enacted new laws using the "three-strikes" moniker. What was left largely unspoken during the debate was the fact that for many years most states have had provisions in their laws for enhanced sentencing of repeat offenders (Clark, Austin, and Henry 1998). Thus, outside of California, three-strikes provisions rarely applied. These laws have had minimal impacts because they were drafted to apply to only the most violent repeat offenders, the very defendants already covered by habitual offender laws and also the very offenders who fare the worst under existing normal penalties (Clark, Austin, and Henry 1997).

California's law potentially has greater impact because it was more loosely drafted. Because any felony can be a third strike, life sentences can be imposed for relatively nonviolent crimes. Thus, the California law applies to criminals with a record of one or more violent or serious felonies. After one such crime ("strike"), the sentence for any new felony is doubled. After two strikes, a new felony requires a term of 25 years to life (Criminal Justice Consortium 1997).

Three-strikes laws are the most recent example of spasmodic attempts by the public, and the politicians they elect, to respond in an extreme manner to what is perceived as skyrocketing crime rates and an unduly lenient criminal justice system. These outbursts are followed by adaptation by members of the courtroom work group (Feeley and Kamin 1996; Harris and Jesilow 2000). Adaptive behavior is readily apparent in the California Supreme Court's decision holding that judges do not have to impose life sentences on repeat criminals if they think the punishment is too harsh (*San Diego County v. Romero* 1996). Later the court held that juvenile convictions likewise need not be counted (*San Diego County v. Garcia* 1999). In essence, the California high court held that the law went too far and judges should use discretion.

What do you think? Are three-strikes laws an appropriate and effective response to violent crimes by predators? Or do you think that these laws are overreactions? Given that adaptation by the courtroom work group seems inevitable, why do legislatures periodically pass such laws?

To continue debating the topic, read the following articles:

Robert N. Scola, Jr., H. Scott Fingerhut, "Tough Times in the Sunshine State"

John R. Schafer, "The Deterrent Effect of Three-Strikes Laws"

John J. Dilulio, Jr., "Against Mandatory Minimums"

A Virtual Tour of American Courthouses: Sentencing Issues

The following Web sites provide information on sentencing in their jurisdictions:

United States Sentencing Commission http://www.ussc.gov/

Minnesota Sentencing Commission http://www.msgc.state.mn.us/

North Carolina Sentencing Commission http://www.aoc.state.nc.us/www/copyright/commissions/sentcom/index.htm

State of Washington Sentencing Guidelines Commission http://www.sgc.wa.gov/

The Pennsylvania Commission on Sentencing http://pcs.la.psu.edu/

New Jersey Sentencing Guidelines http://www.judiciary.state.nj.us/sentguid.htm

For an insider's view of what probation officers do, go to any of the following sites:

Federal http://www.uic.edu/~jmaghan/intern/postperm.html

Santa Clara County (California) http://claraweb.co.santa-clara.ca.us/probation/Adult.htm

Suffolk County (New York) http://www.co.suffolk.ny.us/probation/

Pima County (Arizona) http://www.sc.co.pima.az.us/apo/

Marion County (Indiana) http://www.ci.indianapolis.in.us/probation/

The National Association of Sentencing Advocates is a professional membership organization of sentencing advocates and defense-based mitigation specialists:

http://www.sentencingproject.org/nasa/index.html.

The following advocacy groups identify race and the death penalty as a significant problem:

Amnesty International: "Race Drives Use of Death Penalty" http://amnestyusa.org/news/1999/usa05181999.html

American Civil Liberties Union (ACLU): "Double Justice: Race and the Death Penalty" http://www.aclu.org/issues/death/death5.html

National Association for the Advancement of Colored People (NAACP) http://www.naacp.org/

For discussions about race and the death penalty from a variety of perspectives, go to the following:

ABA Focus on Law Studies http://www.abanet.org/publiced/focus/spr97rac.html

Policy.com http://www.policy.com

National Center for Policy Analysis http://www.ncpa.org/

Visit the Web site of Families Against Mandatory Minimums (FAMM), a national organization of citizens working to repeal statutory mandatory minimum sentences: http://www.famm.org/.

public will be appeased without the painful necessity of voting for higher taxes. But a number of studies suggest that increasing the severity of the punishment produces negative side effects (referred to by economists as *hidden costs* and others as *unanticipated consequences*). That is, harsher laws have impacts, but often not the ones intended.

One negative side effect of increasing the severity of punishments centers on the greater time, effort, and money courts must expend. Faced with severe sanctions, defendants de-

mand more trials, which consumes more court time. This clearly happened in New York State. Before the 1973 drug law, 6.5 percent of the drug cases went to trial; after it, 13.5 percent did (Association of the Bar 1976). As a result, a backlog of cases developed, delays increased, and the certainty and speed of conviction declined. Moreover, the courts were forced to spend considerably more money to comply with the law.

Critics are also concerned that mandatory minimum sentencing legislation results in a rigid and inflexible overreaction to problems of judicial discretion. By requiring every single defendant convicted under the same statute to serve the identical sentence, it threatens to create a system so automatic that it may operate in practice like a poorly programmed robot. In the words of U.S. District Court Judge Vincent Broderick, "The most frustrating aspect of mandatory minimum prison sentences is that they require routinely imposing long prison terms based on a single circumstance, when other circumstances in the case cry out for a significantly different result. The same sentence is mandated for offenders with very different criminal backgrounds and whose roles differ widely one from another" (Vincent and Hofer 1994).

■ CONCLUSION

Richard Allen Davis was convicted of first-degree murder and sentenced to death. But as mentioned in Chapter 9, he used the sentencing hearing to make yet another dramatic statement, accusing the father of sexual misconduct with his daughter.

Whether the "three strikes and you're out" laws passed in the aftermath of the Polly Klaas kidnapping and murder will have a lasting impact is open to question. The essential difficulty is that the criminals who figure prominently in the media bear little resemblance to the ones who appear before U.S. judges every day. While the replica of Lady Justice on the outside of the courthouse contemplates justice in the abstract, judges inside the courthouse must pass judgment on real-life defendants, not the stereotypical villains who dominate the rhetoric of elected officials. In deciding whether to send an offender to prison or grant him or her probation, the scales of justice require the judge (and other members of the courtroom work group) to weigh the normal penalty for the offense, the seriousness of the crime, and the defendant's prior record and social stability. The resulting decisions have become the focus of heated public debate.

To some, American courthouses do not mete out fair and impartial justice. These critics find that the blindfold is improperly pierced by sentences that are discriminatory and/or disparate. To others, American courthouses hand out sentences that are too lenient. These critics argue that wielding the sword of justice will protect the public from crime. These dual concerns have prompted numerous changes since the mid-1970s. Determinate sentencing laws, mandatory minimum sentencing provisions, and sentencing guidelines are the most prominent changes undertaken.

Sentencing is likely to remain on the nation's political agenda. All too often, members of the public, as well as elected officials, have ignored an important reality: Prison populations are swelling. The United States sends more people to prison than any other Western nation, and the rate of incarceration is growing steadily. The result is severe prison overcrowding, compounded by federal court orders requiring major improvements in prison conditions. Limitations on the capacity and quality of prisons create a political dilemma. Although citizens and public officials want to send even more offenders to prison for longer periods of time, they are unwilling to spend large sums of tax dollars to build the needed facilities. Sentencing is thus likely to remain an important public policy issue for the foreseeable future. Alas, in the end, Lady Justice appears to cost more than the public is able or willing to spend.

CRITICAL THINKING QUESTIONS

1. Within the courtroom work group, which actor is the most influential in sentencing decisions? Why? How might influence vary from one courtroom to the next?

2. In what ways do the crime control model and the due process model differ over the issues of disparity and discrimination in sentencing?

3. In what ways do sentencing guidelines reflect normal penalties? In what ways do they differ?

4. To what extent can slight variations in the defendant's background produce markedly different sentences? In Exhibit 16-5, calculate the recommended sentence for a defendant convicted of second-degree assault. How much does the sentence change if the criminal history score is a 2 or a 3? Do you think this is too much variation to be determined by a mathematical calculation?

5. How have public demands to "get tough with crooks" changed the sentencing process in the last two decades? Why do courtroom work groups resist such efforts and often subvert them?

KEY TERMS

discrimination (370)
disparity (377)
mandatory minimum sentencing (386)
normal penalties (368)
pre-sentence investigation (365)

 ## WORLD WIDE WEB RESOURCES AND EXERCISES

Web Guides

http://dir.yahoo.com/Society_and_Culture/Crime/
  Correction_and_Rehabilitation/
http://dir.yahoo.com/Society_and_Culture/Crime/
  Correction_and_Rehabilitation/Sentencing/
http://dir.yahoo.com/Society_and_Culture/Crime/
  Correction_and_Rehabilitation/Sentencing/
  Mandatory_Minimum_Sentences/
http://dir.yahoo.com/Society_and_Culture/Crime/
  Correction_and_Rehabilitation/Death_Penalty/

Web Search Terms

sentencing   *sentencing guidelines*
sentencing commission   *mandatory minimums*

Useful URLs

The Sentencing Project is a source for criminal justice policy analysis, data, and program information for policymakers and the public: http://www.sentencingproject.org/.

Bureau of Justice Statistics sentencing statistics are available at http://www.ojp.usdoj.gov/bjs/sent.htm.

Bureau of Justice Statistics death penalty statistics are available at http://www.ojp.usdoj.gov/bjs/cp.htm.

Uncommon URLs

The Coalition for Federal Sentencing Reform is united by a concern that the federal sentencing guidelines are not fulfilling their promise: http://www.sentencing.org/.

Citizens for Effective Justice is working toward changes that would reduce crime and prison overcrowding through an alternative sentencing program that combines punishment and rehabilitation: http://www.reducecrime.org/.

The National Association of Sentencing Advocates is a professional membership organization of sentencing advocates and defense-based mitigation specialists: http://www.sentencingproject.org/nasa/index.html.

Davrie Communications asserts that, although the current federal sentencing regime leaves little room to maneuver, steps can be taken to position defendants for the most advantageous programs allowed by the Bureau of Prisons: http://www.davrie.com/PreSentencing.htm.

The Criminal Justice Division of the Alteo Group provides advocacy services under the federal sentencing guidelines: http://www.alteo.com/cj/.

Web Exercises

1. The Bureau of Justice Statistics publishes a variety of statistics on sentencing, which can be found at http://www.ojp.usdoj.gov/bjs/welcome.html. Access the site, and under Courts and Sentencing, find the most recent report "Felony Sentences in State Courts." Use these data to update the information in Exhibit 16-2.

    At the same site, under the heading Corrections, examine the summary statistics provided. Compare this information to the discussion of normal penalties. What evidence do you find to support the discussion that seriousness of the crime and prior record of the defendant are key factors in sentencing?

2. Several Web sites are devoted to capital punishment and represent a broad array of views buttressed by facts. Using the search engine of your choice, locate these pages. If you are using Yahoo, the commands are as follows: **http://www.yahoo.com/Society_Culture/ Crime/Death_Penalty**.

   Select one group from "Opposing Views" and another from "Supporting Views." Compare these Web sites, asking yourself the following questions: What arguments do the two sides make, and what evidence do they use to support their positions? It is also important to analyze issues that are not addressed. What do opponents of the death penalty have to say about deterring crime? What do supporters have to say about the death penalty being fairly (or unfairly) applied?

3. To monitor the latest discussions on sentencing guidelines, do a subject search with the search engine of your choice using the search term "sentencing guidelines." Pick out three Web pages, and see how their discussions relate to topics discussed in the chapter—particularly, whether the guidelines produce injustice by removing too much discretion from the judge. Overall, do the Web sites support or oppose sentencing guidelines?

INFOTRAC COLLEGE EDITION RESOURCES AND EXERCISES

Basic Searches

sentences
mandatory sentences
pre-sentence investigation reports

sentencing guidelines
discrimination in criminal justice administration
prison sentences

Recommended Articles

Ian F. Haney Lopez, "Institutional Racism: Judicial Conduct and a New Theory of Racial Discrimination"

Celia C. Lo, Richard C. Stephens, "Drugs and Prisoners: Treatment Needs on Entering Prison"

InfoTrac College Edition Exercises

1. Using the search term "discrimination in criminal justice administration," find two or more articles that discuss racial discrimination in sentencing. To what extent do they make the distinction between imbalance and discrimination?

2. Using the search term "sentences," locate two or more articles that research the sentencing process. What information do they provide about the operation of normal penalties?

FOR FURTHER READING

Alozie, Nicholas, and C. Wayne Johnson. "Probing the Limits of the Female Advantage in Criminal Processing: Pretrial Diversion of Drug Offenders in an Urban County." *Justice System Journal* 21 (2000): 239–259.

Austin, James, and John Irwin. *It's About Time: America's Imprisonment Binge*, 3d ed. Belmont, CA: Wadsworth, 2001.

Caulkins, Jonathan, C. Peter Rydell, William Schwabe, and James Chiesa. *Mandatory Minimum Drug Sentences: Throwing Away the Key or the Taxpayers' Money?* Santa Monica, CA: Rand Corporation, 1997.

Christianson, Scott. *With Liberty for Some: 500 Years of Imprisonment in America.* Boston: Northeastern University Press, 1998.

Cole, David. *No Equal Justice.* New York: New Press, 1999.

Diaz-Cotto, Juanita. *Gender, Ethnicity, and the State: Latina and Latino Prison Politics.* Albany: State University of New York Press, 1996.

Foglia, Wanda. "They Know Not What They Do: Unguided and Misguided Discretion in Pennsylvania Capital Cases." *Justice Quarterly* 20 (2003): 103–107.

Free, Marvin. *African Americans and the Criminal Justice System.* New York: Garland, 1997.

Grana, Sheryl. *Women and (In)Justice.* Boston: Allyn and Bacon, 2002.

Kempf-Leonard, Kimberly, and Lisa Sample. "Disparity Based on Sex: Is Gender-Specific Treatment Warranted?" *Justice Quarterly* 17 (2000): 89–128.

Lynch, Michael, and E. Britt Patterson. *Race and Criminal Justice.* Fairfax, VA: Harrow and Heston, 1996.

Mann, Coramae Richey, and Marjorie Zatz. *Images of Color, Images of Crime.* Los Angeles: Roxbury, 1998.

Marquart, James, Sheldon Edland-Olson, and Jonathan Sorensen. *The Rope, the Chair, and the Needle: Capital Punishment in Texas, 1923–1990.* Austin: University of Texas, 1994.

Mays, G. Larry, and L. Thomas Winfree. *Contemporary Corrections,* 2d ed. Belmont, CA: Wadsworth, 2002.

Morris, Norval, and David Rotman, eds. *The Oxford History of the Prison.* New York: Oxford University Press, 1996.

Myers, Martha. *Race, Labor and Punishment in the New South.* Columbus: Ohio State University Press, 1998.

National Council on Crime and Delinquency. *National Assessment of Structured Sentencing.* Washington, DC: Bureau of Justice Assistance, 1996.

Parent, Dale, Terence Dunworth, Douglas McDonald, and William Rhodes. *Mandatory Sentencing.* Washington, DC: National Institute of Justice, 1997.

Pollock, Jocelyn. *Women, Prison, and Crime,* 2d ed. Belmont, CA: Wadsworth, 2002.

Russell, Gregory. *The Death Penalty and Racial Bias: Overturning Supreme Court Assumptions.* New York: Greenwood, 1994.

Tarver, Marsha, Steve Walker, and Harvey Wallace. *Multicultural Issues in the Criminal Justice System.* Boston: Allyn and Bacon, 2002.

Ulmer, Jeffrey. *Social Worlds of Sentencing: Court Communities Under Sentencing Guidelines.* Albany: State University of New York Press, 1997.

Wicharaya, Tamasak. *Simple Theory, Hard Reality: The Impact of Sentencing Reforms on Courts, Prisons, and Crime.* Albany: State University of New York Press, 1995.

Part V

Appellate, Lower, and Juvenile Courts

art V examines several specialized courts that are important for the criminal justice system. Some of these judicial bodies are separate and distinct from other courts—appellate courts, for example. Others are considered special courts whether they are separate and distinct or not. They are special courts because they handle a specific type of case. Juvenile courts differ from those that process adults accused of violating the criminal law because juvenile law is distinctive.

Chapter 17 focuses on appellate courts, which are designed to provide a second look at how the case was handled in the lower courts. Although few guilty defendants successfully challenge their convictions, the public is convinced that courts are releasing countless guilty defendants on technicalities.

Chapter 18 discusses the nation's lower courts, which process literally millions of less serious offenses each year. Increasingly, however, these minor matters loom large in terms of criminal justice policymaking. Clearly, domestic violence and drunk driving are two topics that criminal justice officials cannot dismiss as unimportant.

Chapter 19 considers juvenile courts, which deal with millions of children each year. The cases that attract the most attention are those in which children are accused of adult crimes involving violence. But these are relatively few compared to the millions of juveniles who appear in these courts each year because of less serious adult violations as well as "crimes" that only juveniles can commit. To complicate matters further, some of these juveniles have not committed any criminal act; rather, they are before the court because their parents have abused or neglected them.

Chapter 17 Appellate Courts

oger Coleman, an Appalachian coal miner, was convicted of rape and murder in the small town of Grundy, Virginia, and sentenced to death. After his first appeal was unsuccessful, Coleman sought further review by filing a writ of habeas corpus in federal court. Alas, his lawyer filed the notice of appeal with the Virginia Supreme Court one day late, and the case was dismissed. ◀

Should this error by his lawyer prevent Coleman from having federal courts also review his case? Proponents of the crime control model argue that Coleman is a textbook example of endless appeals, and therefore he should not be allowed yet one more review. Supporters of the due process model, on the other hand, counter that basic fairness is far more important than failure to comply with a narrow technical requirement.

Coleman v. Thompson highlights the importance of appellate court decisions. To be sure, appellate courts decide far fewer cases than the trial courts. Nonetheless, the relative handful of cases decided by the appellate courts are critically important for the entire judicial process. Appellate courts subject the trial court's action to a second look, examining not a raw dispute in the course of being presented, but rather a controversy already decided. This second look provides a degree of detachment, by a group of judges who can examine the process to see if mistakes were made. Appellate courts are important for a second reason: Through written opinions, appellate judges engage in significant policymaking. Ultimately, the decisions of a group of judges not only determine the results of specific cases (the fate of individual defendants like Roger Coleman) but also, and more important, shape the law by providing the reasons for the decisions reached. *Coleman v. Thompson* also symbolizes how the relative handful of death penalty decisions receive a disproportionate share of appellate court time and attention.

NATURE OF THE APPELLATE PROCESS

One of the few aspects of the American judicial process about which there is a consensus is that every loser in a trial court should have

the right to appeal to a higher court. Appellate courts were created partly because of the belief that several heads are better than one. In essence, the decisions of a single judge are subjected to review by a panel of judges who are removed from the heat engendered by the trial and are consequently in a position to take a more objective view of the questions raised. They operate as multimember or collegial bodies, with decisions made by a group of judges. In the courts of last resort, all judges typically participate in all cases. On intermediate appellate courts, decisions are typically made using rotating three-judge panels, but in important cases all judges may participate (this is termed an **en banc** hearing).

In unraveling the complexities of the review process, it is helpful to begin by asking why appellate courts exist and why dissatisfied litigants are permitted to appeal.

The Purposes of Appeal

The most obvious function of appellate courts is **error correction.** During trial, a significant portion of the decision making is spur of the moment. As one trial judge phrased it, "We're where the action is. We often have to 'shoot from the hip' and hope you're doing the right thing. You can't ruminate forever every time you have to make a ruling. We'd be spending months on each case if we ever did that" (quoted in Carp and Stidham 1990, 256). As reviewing bodies, appellate courts oversee the work of the lower courts, ensuring that the law was correctly interpreted. Thus, the error correction function of appellate review protects against arbitrary, capricious, or mistaken decisions by a trial court judge.

The other primary function of appellate courts is **policy formulation.** The lawmaking function focuses on situations in which appellate courts fill in the gaps in existing law, clarify old doctrines, extend existing precedent to new situations, and on occasion even overrule previous decisions. Thus, through policy formulation, appellate courts shape the law in response to changing conditions in society. Stated another way, error correction is concerned primarily with the effect of the judicial process on individual litigants, whereas policy formulation involves the impact of the appellate court decision on other cases.

Scope of Appellate Review

A basic principle of American law is that the losing party has the **right to one appeal.** But at the same time, it is important to stress that the defendant has now lost his or her legal shield of innocence. The individual is no longer considered innocent until proven guilty but rather now stands, in the eyes of the law, guilty. This has important implications for bail. Guilty defendants no longer have a right to bail; courts may set a bail amount (typically in higher amounts than prior to trial), but many defendants wait out their appeal in prison.

Although American law recognizes the right to one appeal, the scope of appellate review is subject to several important limits and exceptions. Appeals, for example, may be filed only by parties who have lost in the lower court. But prosecutors may not appeal a finding of not guilty. The Fifth Amendment guarantees, "Nor shall any person be subject for the same offense to be twice put in jeopardy of life or limb." This provision protects citizens from **double jeopardy** (a second prosecution of the same person for the same crime by the same sovereign after the first trial). Thus, once a not guilty verdict is returned in a criminal case, jeopardy is said to attach, and the prosecutor cannot appeal.

Appeals are also discretionary; that is, the losing party is not required to seek appellate court review. The lone exception involves capital punishment cases. When a jury imposes a sentence of death, the case must be appealed regardless of the defendant's wishes. Typically, this automatic review is heard directly by the state supreme court, thus bypassing any intermediate courts of appeals. The mandatory appeal requirements in capital punishment cases

aside, in all other cases, civil and criminal, appeal is discretionary.

There are also limits on when cases may be appealed. As a general rule, the losing party may only appeal from a final judgment of the lower court. In this context, a judgment is considered final when a final decision has been reached in the lower court. In very limited situations, however, litigants may appeal certain types of **interlocutory** (nonfinal) orders. Prosecutors may file an interlocutory appeal on certain pretrial rulings that substantially hinder the state's ability to proceed to trial. For example, if the trial court suppresses a defendant's confession or excludes physical evidence because of an illegal search and seizure, the prosecution may file an interlocutory appeal arguing that the judge's ruling was in error.

Appeals are also restricted to questions of law; findings of fact are not appealable. Because they have not been directly exposed to the evidence, appellate courts are reluctant to second-guess findings of fact made by lower tribunals. Thus, appellate courts hear no new testimony and consider no new evidence. Rather, they focus on how decisions were made in the trial court, basing their review on the appellate court record. Questions of law that are commonly raised on appeal include defects in jury selection, improper admission of evidence during the trial, and mistaken interpretations of the law. The appellant may also claim constitutional violations, including illegal search and seizure or improper questioning of the defendant by the police (see Chapter 12). Finally, some defendants who have pled guilty may seek to set aside the guilty plea because of ineffective assistance of counsel or because the plea was not voluntary.

Appeals are also confined to issues properly raised in the trial court. Recall from Chapter 14 that during trial attorneys must make timely objections to the judge's rulings on points of law. When an attorney makes such an objection, and the trial judge overrules it, there is a disagreement over a point of law and the issue has been preserved for appeal.

Appeals in criminal cases have also historically been limited in the United States to findings of guilt. That is, a defendant cannot appeal the sentence imposed as being too harsh (nor can the prosecutor appeal a sentence as too

Exhibit 17-1 State Appellate Court Structure

Court of Last Resort Only	Court of Last Resort and One Intermediate Appellate Court		One Court of Last Resort and Two Intermediate Appellate Courts	Two Courts of Last Resort and One Intermediate Appellate Court
Delaware	Alaska	Massachusetts	Alabama	Oklahoma*
Maine	Arizona	Michigan	New York	Texas
Montana	Arkansas	Minnesota	Pennsylvania	
Nevada	California	Mississippi	Tennessee	
New Hampshire	Colorado	Missouri		
Rhode Island	Connecticut	Nebraska		
South Dakota	Florida	New Jersey		
Vermont	Georgia	New Mexico		
West Virginia	Hawaii*	North Carolina		
Wyoming	Idaho*	North Dakota*		
	Illinois	Ohio		
	Indiana	Oregon		
	Iowa*	South Carolina*		
	Kansas	Utah		
	Kentucky	Virginia		
	Louisiana	Washington		
	Maryland	Wisconsin		

*Court of last resort assigns cases to intermediate appellate court.

SOURCE: David Rottman, Carol Flango, Melissa Cantrell, Randall Hansen, and Neil La Fountain, *State Court Organization 1998* (Williamsburg, VA: National Center for State Courts, 2000).

lenient). This restriction is changing, however, in a few states. In recent years, a handful of states have allowed defendants to appeal the sentence imposed by the trial judge (Williams 1992).

Finally, the right to appeal is limited to a single appeal, within which all appealable issues have to be raised. Appeals from U.S. district courts and most appeals from state courts of general jurisdiction are heard by intermediate courts of appeals. In the less populous states, which do not have intermediate appellate bodies, the initial appeal is filed with the court of last resort (see Chapter 4). These courts have **mandatory appellate jurisdiction,** which means they must hear all properly filed appeals. But after the first reviewing body has reached a decision, the right to one appeal has been exhausted. The party that loses the appeal may request that a higher court review the case again, but such appeals are discretionary; the higher court does not have to hear the appeal. The U.S.

Supreme Court and most state supreme courts have largely **discretionary appellate jurisdiction,** which means that they can pick and choose which cases they will hear. The bulk of appeals are decided by intermediate courts of appeals and are never heard by state or national supreme courts. Exhibit 17-1 shows the appellate court structure of the states.

APPELLATE COURT PROCEDURES

Appellate court procedures reflect numerous variations among the nation's 51 legal systems. Nonetheless, each judicial system utilizes essentially the same six steps (Meador 1974). Exhibit 17-2 summarizes the appeals process.

In recent years, however, traditional appellate court procedures have been modified

Exhibit 17-2 Steps of Criminal Procedure: Appeal and Post-Conviction Remedies

	Law on the Books	Law in Action
Appeal	Legal challenge to a decision by a lower court.	Virtually certain if the defendant is convicted at trial.
Mandatory	Appellate court must hear the case.	Many appeals are "routine," which means they have little likelihood of succeeding.
Discretionary	Appellate court may accept or reject.	Appellate courts hear a very small percentage of discretionary appeal cases.
Notice of appeal	Written statement notifying the court that the defendant plans to appeal.	Standards for indigent defenders mandate that an appeal must be filed.
Appellate court record	The transcript of the trial along with relevant court documents.	Some appellate courts prefer a focused record of contested matters, whereas others want the entire record.
Briefing the case	Written statement submitted by the attorney arguing a case in court.	Defense lawyers make numerous arguments in hopes that one will be successful.
Oral argument	Lawyers for both sides argue their cases before appellate court justices, who have the opportunity to question lawyers.	Judges often complain that they learn little during oral argument. To expedite decision making, some courts limit oral argument to select cases.
Written opinion	Reasons given by appellate courts for the results they have reached.	Only appellate court opinions are considered precedent.
Disposition		
Affirmed	Appellate court decision that agrees with the lower court decision.	Seven out of eight criminal appeals are affirmed.
Remanded	Case is sent back to the lower court for a hearing on a specific issue.	Often an indication that the appellate court is troubled by the judge's action but doesn't wish to reverse.
Reversed	The lower court decision is set aside, and further proceedings may be held.	Defendants are very often remanded and reconvicted following retrial.

because of exponential increases in appellate court filings. Appellate court caseloads have been increasing more rapidly than those of the trial courts. By way of illustration, appeals filed in the U.S. courts of appeals increased by a whopping 705 percent from 1961 to 1983. Today, federal appellate courts hear more than 57,000 cases a year. Appeals heard by state courts have likewise grown rapidly. Today, state appellate courts hear about 275,000 appeals every year (Ostrom, Kauder, and LaFountain 2003). To accommodate the steadily rising volume of appeals, reviewing bodies now often use expedited processing for some cases (Hanson 1996).

Notice of Appeal

An appeal does not follow automatically from an adverse trial court judgment. Rather, the **appellant** (the losing party in the lower court) must take affirmative action to set an appeal in motion. The first step consists of filing a **notice of appeal.** Rules of appellate procedure fix a precise time—usually 30 or 60 days—within which this short written statement must be filed.

Appellate Court Record

After the notice of appeal has been filed, the next step is preparing and transmitting the record. The **appellate court record** consists of the materials that advance to the appellate court. Many of these items—papers and exhibits—are already in the case file. A major item not in the clerk's office is the transcript of the testimony given at the trial. To include this in the record, the court reporter prepares a typewritten copy and files it with the court.

Briefing the Case

The third step in the appeal process consists of writing briefs. A **brief** is a written argument that sets forth the party's view of the facts of the case, the issues raised on appeal, and the precedents supporting their position. First, the appellant's brief is filed, which lists alleged errors on questions of law that were made at trial. Next, the winning party in the lower court (termed the **appellee,** or **respondent**) files a brief setting forth arguments as to why the original decision of the lower court is legally correct and should stand. The appellant then has the option of filing a reply brief.

Oral Argument

The lawyers for both parties are allotted a limited time to argue their side of the case before the appellate court panel. The appellant's oral argument, for example, briefly discusses the facts on which the cause of action is based, traces the history of the case through the lower courts, and presents legal arguments as to why the decision of the trial court was erroneous. **Oral argument** provides the opportunity for face-to-face contact between judges and lawyers. In this phase, judges typically ask lawyers questions about particular issues in the case.

Eliminating oral argument is one type of expedited procedure. Many judges view oral arguments as not particularly helpful in deciding routine cases (Wasby 1982). Thus, some courts have eliminated oral argument altogether in straightforward cases. By ruling solely on the basis of the appellate court record, judges conserve some of their time.

Written Opinion

After the case has been argued, the court recesses to engage in group deliberations. Decisions are made in private conference, with one judge in the majority assigned the task of writing the opinion, which summarizes the facts of the case and discusses the legal issues raised on appeal. If the case is an easy one, the **opinion** of the court may be short, perhaps no more than a page or two. But if the legal issues are important or complex, the court's opinion may run dozens of pages. Judges who disagree with the majority often write **dissenting opinions,** explaining why they believe their fellow judges reached the wrong conclusions.

Opinion preparation consumes more of appellate judges' time than any other activity, and for this reason the opinion-writing process is a prime candidate for increasing the efficiency of appellate courts. Some appellate courts are therefore deciding some cases by summary affirmation, in which the court affirms the decision of the lower court without providing a written opinion and often without granting oral argument as well (Neubauer 1985; Douglas 1985).

Many courts are reluctant to take the drastic step of not writing opinions, even in selected cases. Therefore, a more common practice is curtailing opinion publication; the litigants are given written reasons for the decision reached, but the opinion is not published and therefore may not be cited as precedent. Unpublished opinions are used in error correction cases when the court is applying existing law (Songer 1990). They save considerable judicial time because unpublished opinions need not be as polished as published opinions.

Disposition

The court's opinion ends with a disposition of the case. The appellate court may **affirm** (uphold) the judgment of the lower court. Or the court may modify the lower court ruling by changing it in part but not totally reversing it. Alternatively, the previous decision may be **reversed** (set aside) with no further court action required. A disposition of **reversed and remanded** means that the decision of the lower court is overturned and the case is sent back to the lower court for further proceedings, which may include holding a hearing or conducting a new trial. Often the defendant is tried a second time, but not always. Finally, the case may be **remanded** to the lower court with instructions for further proceedings (Neubauer 1992).

Appellate courts modify, reverse, remand, or reverse and remand only if they find **error**—that is, a mistake made by a judge during the trial. If the error is substantial, it is called **reversible error** by the higher court. If the error is minor, it is called **harmless error** (Traynor 1970). The appellate court may find error but affirm the lower court anyway.

CRIMINAL APPEALS

The bulk of trial court filings are never appealed because the case is settled without a trial—civil cases are negotiated and criminal cases are plea-bargained. As a result, only a small percentage of state trial court cases are reviewed by higher courts. The majority of appeals involve civil cases, but the number of criminal appeals has increased dramatically since the 1960s.

Law on the Books: Expanded Opportunity to Appeal Criminal Convictions

For decades, most defendants found guilty by judge or jury did not appeal because they could not afford the expense. This pattern changed significantly in the early 1960s. A series of important Warren Court decisions held that economically impoverished defendants cannot be barred from effective appellate review. Indigent defendants, therefore, are entitled to a free trial court transcript (*Griffin v. Illinois* 1956) and a court-appointed lawyer (*Douglas v. California* 1963). Indigents, however, are not normally provided free legal service to pursue discretionary appeals (*Ross v. Moffitt* 1974).

As a result of these rulings, it is now rare for a convicted defendant not to appeal from a trial verdict of guilty. Indeed, indigent defendants have everything to gain and nothing to lose by filing an appeal. For example, if the appeal is successful but the defendant is reconvicted following a new trial, the sentencing judge cannot increase the sentence out of vindictiveness (*North Carolina v. Pearce* 1969; *Texas v. McCullough* 1986). See Exhibit 17-3 for a summary of key developments concerning appeals.

The Warren Court decisions expanding the opportunity for indigent defendants to appeal produced an exponential increase in the number of criminal appeals filed. Whereas criminal appeals composed only 10 to 15 percent of total appeals before 1963, two decades later they constituted about 45 percent of total appellate volume (Bureau of Justice Statistics 1985).

Law in Action: Defendants Rarely Win on Appeal

Criminal appeals are drawn from a fairly narrow stratum of the most serious criminal convictions in the trial courts (Davies 1982). For example, more than half the criminal appeals contest convictions for crimes of violence (primarily homicides and armed robberies). Moreover, these appeals cases often involve substantial sentences (Chapper and Hanson 1990). In short, criminal appeals are atypical of crimes prosecuted in the trial courts.

Criminal appeals are also by and large routine because they seldom raise meritorious issues (Wold and Caldeira 1980). Current standards of effective assistance of counsel force lawyers to appeal, no matter how slight the odds of appellate court reversal. As a result, a significant number of criminal appeals lack substantial merit. According to one intermediate appellate court judge, "If 90 percent of this stuff were in the United States Post Office, it would be classified as junk mail" (Wold 1978).

Criminal appeals rarely succeed; appellate courts often find that no reversible error was committed during the trial court proceedings. Thus, the vast majority of criminal appeals affirm the conviction. Roughly speaking, de-

A Reversal on Narrow Grounds

 Because the jury had imposed the death penalty, the conviction of Shareef Cousin was appealed directly to the Louisiana Supreme Court. The fact that it took longer for the appellate court to review the case (22 months) than it took to get the case to trial (10 months) is a reflection of how seriously these matters are treated. Some of this time lapse occurred because both sides requested additional time to prepare their briefs. In addition, the state's highest court found that the original trial court record was defective and ordered the clerk of court for Criminal District Court to resubmit the entire record.

The final record is nothing if not voluminous. Besides the briefs and the filings, there are 22 volumes of trial court transcripts. Stacked one atop the other, the complete record (without the cardboard box) stands 26 inches tall. The brief on appeal for the appellant runs 81 pages and argues that 49 errors occurred during the trial proceedings. By contrast, the brief of the State of Louisiana, the appellee, provides 45 pages of refutation.

The court heard oral argument in December 1997, with a total of 80 minutes allotted to both sides. To ensure that the workload is distributed equally, the Louisiana Supreme Court assigns opinion writing on a rotating basis. Thus, by rotation, the opinion was assigned to Justice Harry Lemmon. After working as a chemist for four years and serving in the army for two years, Lemmon graduated cum laude from Loyola University School of Law. He practiced law for several years before being elected to the state's intermediate court of appeals in 1970. Ten years later, he was elected to the Louisiana Supreme Court.

Justice Lemmon's 17-page opinion focuses primarily on the evidence introduced by the prosecution to impeach the credibility of James Rowell, their turncoat witness (see Chapter 14). His prior statements were hearsay but nonetheless admissible for the purposes of establishing a prior inconsistent statement—he had indeed earlier stated that he had a conversation with Sha-

reef Cousin two days after the murder. But the prosecutor went too far when he introduced that evidence to show the substantive guilt of the defendant, the opinion noted. Moreover, the prosecutor compounded the error by "flagrant misuse" of hearsay evidence during closing arguments.

As for the prosecutor's failure to disclose the key statements from Connie Babin, the opinion largely ducks the issue. At one point the court says that the evidence was clearly exculpatory (and therefore should have been given to the defense), but in a footnote says it does not reach the issue because the defense now knew about the statement.

But if the court thought it could duck the contentious issue of prosecutorial misconduct, it was mistaken. For the next year and a half, the lawyers battled over the scope of discovery. Eventually, the state's high court granted broad discovery rights to the defense (see Chapter 12).

While examining the voluminous appellate court record, I made a surprise finding—a 10 × 12 × 4-inch box. Inside are hundreds of letters addressed to the Justice of the Supreme Court, Louisiana Supreme Court. I sampled a few that had been opened. Although handwritten, the letters were similar, urging the court to reverse Cousin's conviction because he was too young to die and also because his alibi showed that he was innocent. Clearly, the murder trial of Shareef Cousin had become a national and in some cases an international cause célèbre, with anti–death penalty groups urging concerned citizens to write the court. There was no indication, however, that the letters had been read by any of the justices; indeed, most had never been read at all—they were still sealed, taking up space in the clerk of court's office.

To view how anti–death penalty groups tried to rally support for Shareef Cousin, go to http://www.ncadp.org/motivate.html.

To read national coverage of the reversal, search for "New Trial Granted to Shareef Cousin."

fendants win on appeal only 1 out of 8 times. A closer look, though, indicates that even an appellate court reversal produces only minor victories for many criminal defendants. For

example, some "reversals" produce a modification but do not otherwise disturb the conviction (Neubauer 1992). Moreover, if the appellate court reverses and remands the case to the

Exhibit 17-3   Key Developments Concerning Appeal

U.S. Constitution, Article I	1789	The Privilege of the Writ of Habeas Corpus shall not be suspended unless when in Cases of Rebellion or Invasion the public Safety may require it.
Fifth Amendment	1791	Prohibits double jeopardy.
Griffin v. Illinois	1956	Indigents are entitled to a free trial court transcript.
Douglas v. California	1963	Indigents are entitled to a court-appointed attorney during first appeal.
Fay v. Noia	1963	Warren Court decision greatly expanded the right of state prisoners to file habeas corpus petitions in federal court.
North Carolina v. Pearce	1969	If the appeal is successful, the sentencing judge cannot increase the sentence if the defendant is later reconvicted.
Ross v. Moffitt	1974	Indigent defendants are not entitled to a court-appointed lawyer for discretionary appeals.
Stone v. Powell	1976	Burger Court decision held that federal courts cannot consider Fourth Amendment search-and-seizure questions in habeas corpus proceedings.
Coleman v. Thompson	1992	Death row inmate whose lawyers filed papers late has no further right to federal court review.
Antiterrorism and Effective Death Penalty Act	1996	State inmates are typically limited to only one review of their prisoner petition in federal courts.
Felker v. Turpin	1996	Upheld the Antiterrorism and Effective Death Penalty Act.
Roe v. Flores-Ortega	2000	A lawyer's failure to file an appeal does not necessarily violate the right to counsel.
Williams v. Taylor	2000	Under the Antiterrorism and Effective Death Penalty Act, a federal judge can reject an inmate's claim only if the state court used an unreasonable interpretation of federal law.
Edwards v. Carpenter	2000	Limited state prisoner access to federal courts based on claims that their lawyers gave them inadequate help.

lower court for a new trial, half of the defendants are convicted a second time (Roper and Melone 1981). Although the public perceives that many criminals are freed on technicalities, in reality appellate court reversals are relatively rare. Overall, only about 1 out of every 16 criminal appeals produces a tangible victory for the defendant (Neubauer 1991).

What is even more interesting is the types of cases in which reversals occur. Defendants convicted of nonviolent offenses and who received a relatively lenient sentence are the most likely to win on appeal. Conversely, defendants convicted of violent offenses and sentenced to lengthy prison terms are the least likely to win on appeal. Reading the court's opinions sug-

gests that this pattern of winners and losers is far from random. Rather, the appellate court justices strain to find ways to affirm convictions in crimes such as murder and armed robbery when the defendant has a long criminal record.

POST-CONVICTION REVIEW

After the appellate process has been exhausted, state as well as federal prisoners may challenge their convictions in federal courts on certain limited grounds. These post-conviction remedies are termed *collateral attacks,* because they

CASE CLOSE-UP

Coleman v. Thompson and Federal Court Scrutiny of State Court Convictions

Roger Coleman was convicted of rape and murder in the small coal-mining town of Grundy, Virginia. The Virginia Supreme Court affirmed both the conviction and the imposition of the death penalty. Coleman then filed a habeas corpus action, which raised numerous federal constitutional claims that had not been raised on direct appeal. After a two-day hearing, the County Circuit Court again ruled against Coleman. The volunteer attorneys who argued the appeals were unfamiliar with Virginia rules of appellate procedure, some of the most complicated in the nation. Thus, they filed the notice of appeal with the Virginia Supreme Court one day late, and the case was dismissed for this procedural reason.

Some observers thought there were solid grounds for further review, including evidence that a local juror told friends he wanted to hear the case to nail the defendant. But when the habeas corpus petition was filed in U.S. district court, it was rejected without a hearing. The federal judge ruled that Coleman had procedurally defaulted his claims in state court and therefore also waived his right to review in federal courts.

The opinion of the Supreme Court was delivered by Justice Sandra Day O'Connor. It begins, "This is a case about federalism. It concerns the respect that federal courts owe the States. . . ." Her opinion stresses that federal courts will not review a question of federal law decided by a state court if the decision of that court rests on an independent and adequate aspect of state law. The Court was also unconcerned about attorney error. O'Connor wrote that after the first appeal, Coleman had no right to counsel, and therefore "any attorney error that led to the default of Coleman's claims in state court cannot constitute cause to excuse the default in federal habeas."

In a forceful dissent, Justice Harry Blackmun wrote, "One searches the majority's opinion in vain . . . for any mention of petitioner Coleman's right to a criminal proceeding free from constitutional defect or his interest in finding a forum for his constitutional challenge to his conviction and sentence of death." The dissent terms the majority opinion's emphasis on federalism as cavalier, arguing, "The form of Federalism embraced by today's majority bears little resemblance to that adopted by the Framers of the Constitution."

The decision in *Coleman* sparked a debate over whether it is fair to penalize the prisoner for his lawyer's mistake. Calling the conclusion "bizarre," the editorial writers of the *New York Times* argued that the Court's opinion reflects "a cramped distortion of federalism's scheme of justice under the Constitution. In the name of states' rights, the Court has produced a terrible injustice" ("Federalism Despoiled" 1991). Others, however, applauded the Court's decision, hailing it as another effort to reduce federal review of state death penalty decisions.

Virginia executed Coleman in 1992. But the controversy over his guilt resurfaced eight years later. Three newspapers have filed suit seeking new DNA testing in the case (Masters 2000). But the Virginia courts rejected the request (Farrell 2001). Thus, even in death, Roger Coleman became enmeshed in yet another controversy surrounding the death penalty: Should death row inmates have the right to new DNA testing that might show their innocence? To law professor Samuel Gross (2002), it is troubling that the evidence will be destroyed, thus preventing us from knowing if Coleman was indeed the first person in the United States who was innocent but executed anyway.

---

are attempts to avoid the effects of a court decision by bringing a different court proceeding. Although they are filed by prisoners who have been convicted of a criminal offense, they are civil matters. Thus, they are filed against the prison warden. The Case Close-up in this chapter illustrates this point. When Roger Coleman appealed, the case title was *Coleman v. Commonwealth of Virginia*. But after the right to appeal had been exhausted, he later filed a habeas petition in federal court, and the case was captioned *Coleman v. Thompson*. The warden, Thompson, is considered a nominal respondent because no actions on his part are at issue. Thompson is merely a stand-in; the defendant contends he is being illegally detained because of the actions of the trial judge.

How Post-Conviction Remedies Differ from Appeals

Post-conviction remedies differ from appeals in several ways that have important implications for the criminal justice system. First, they may be filed only by those actually in prison. Second, they may raise only constitutional defects, not technical ones. Third, they may be somewhat broader than appeals, which are limited to objections made by the defense during the trial. Post-conviction petitions can bring up issues not raised during trial, assert constitutional protections that have developed since the original trial, and contest conditions of confinement. Finally, post-conviction remedies in state courts are unlimited in number; a prisoner can file numerous petitions at all levels of the court system.

Coleman v. Thompson illustrates these factors. Coleman was eligible to file because he was in prison. His petition listed six different constitutional violations of his rights, many of which had not been argued on appeal. Finally, the petition had been filed in two state courts and the U.S. District Court for the Western District of Virginia, had been reviewed by the Fourth Circuit Court of Appeals, and was now being considered by yet another federal court— the U.S. Supreme Court.

The most common type of post-conviction relief is **habeas corpus** (Latin for "you have the body"). Protected by the U.S. Constitution, it is a judicial order to someone holding a person to bring that person immediately before the court. Article I provides that "the Privilege of the Writ of Habeas Corpus shall not be suspended unless when in Cases of Rebellion or Invasion the public Safety may require it." This provision traces its roots to seventeenth-century England, when the king's officers often detained citizens without ever filing charges. The writ of habeas corpus has been described as the "great writ," because it prevents the government from jailing citizens without ever filing charges. Many total-

COURT TV

Michigan v. Budzyn: Appeal

Two white Detroit police officers were convicted of beating to death an African-American outside a crack house (see the CourtTV video clip in Chapter 6 of the trial). The officers were sentenced to prison. But convinced they had done nothing wrong, the two appealed their convictions.

The intermediate appellate court affirmed both the convictions, but the Michigan Supreme Court ordered a new trial for one of the officers but not for the other. A writ of habeas corpus was successful, however, in the U.S. District Court, which ordered a new trial.

 View a video clip of this appeal on your copy of the CourtTV CD-ROM. As you watch the video, keep the following questions in mind:

1. In terms of appellate court procedures, what steps are shown on this video clip? Which steps have been omitted?

2. In what ways are these cases similar to outcomes of appeals in typical felony cases? In what ways are these outcomes atypical?

3. What do these cases suggest about the long-standing debate over federal court overview of state court convictions? Is this a situation where the federal courts should be able to oversee state court proceedings? Or is this an example of a federal court unnecessarily intruding into areas reserved for the states?

4. In what ways were the judicial proceedings influenced by public opinion? Do you think the trial courts or the appellate courts were more or less likely to be affected by public passions in this case?

itarian regimes have no such protections; even some Western democracies allow the police or prosecutors to detain a person suspected of a crime for up to a year without formally accusing the person of any wrongdoing.

Originally, habeas corpus was regarded as an extraordinary means to determine the legality of detention prior to trial. But the great writ of liberty has undergone considerable transformation in recent decades. See Courts, Controversy, and the Administration of Justice: Should Federal Courthouse Doors Be Closed to State Prisoners?

Expansion under the Warren Court

In three 1963 decisions, the Warren Court greatly expanded the application of habeas corpus, making it much easier for state prisoners to seek judicial relief in the federal courts (*Fay v. Noia* 1963; *Towsend v. Sain* 1963; *Sanders v. U.S.* 1963). These decisions opened the floodgate for federal review. The annual number of habeas corpus petitions jumped from 2,000 in 1960 to more than 68,000 in 1996.

How often prisoners actually win depends on the time period being considered. In 1970, more than 12,000 petitions were granted—an indication that state courts were slowly adopting the new procedural requirements of the Warren Court revolution in criminal justice. By the 1980s, however, prisoners were rarely successful; fewer than 2 percent gained release.

Contraction under the Burger and Rehnquist Courts

Warren Court decisions expanding habeas corpus relief have been steadily cut back in recent years by a more conservative Supreme Court. The Burger Court restricted the grounds for prisoner petitions, ruling that if state courts provide a fair hearing, federal courts cannot consider Fourth Amendment search-and-seizure questions in habeas corpus proceedings (*Stone v. Powell* 1976). The Rehnquist Court repeatedly tightened restrictions on prisoner petitions (*Butler v. McKeller* 1990; *Saffle v. Parks* 1990; *McClesky v. Zant* 1991; *Keeney v. Tamayo-Reyes* 1992).

Congress Greatly Restricts Federal Habeas

For more than two decades Congress considered proposed changes in habeas corpus proceedings (Smith 1995). This inconclusive debate was shattered by the Oklahoma City bombing in 1995. Victims were anxious to channel their grief into tangible reform, and one avenue was habeas corpus reform (Gest 1996). Thus, as the 1996 elections loomed, Congress passed the Antiterrorism and Effective Death Penalty Act. In terms of habeas corpus actions filed in federal courts, the act does the following:

■ Creates one-year deadlines for filing habeas petitions

■ Limits successive petitions

■ Restricts the review of state prisoner petitions if the claim was adjudicated on the merits in state courts

■ Requires a "certificate of appealability" before a habeas petition may be appealed to a federal court of appeals

■ Provides that decisions of a federal appellate panel are not appealable by writ of certiorari to the Supreme Court

Moving with unusual speed, the Court agreed to hear a challenge to the new law within two months of passage. A unanimous court held that the law was constitutional (*Felker v. Turpin* 1996). The decision was predicted to speed up the pace of executions. This ruling and others principally affect death penalty cases. (See A Day in Court: A Self-Appointed Lawyer for the Nation's Condemned.)

■ STATE SUPREME COURTS

There is no typical state supreme court. Indeed some are not even called supreme court but rather court of appeals, supreme judicial court, court of criminal appeals, or supreme court of appeals. More important, the role that state supreme courts play is affected by the control these judicial bodies exercise over their dockets. Perhaps just as important is the exact wording of the state constitution. But these legal factors only partially explain the policymaking

COURTS, CONTROVERSY, AND THE ADMINISTRATION OF JUSTICE

Should Federal Courthouse Doors Be Closed to State Prisoners?

The right of convicted offenders to seek virtually unlimited review through habeas corpus proceedings has sparked a heated debate. Some people would keep the doors of the federal courts wide open to state prisoners; others would slam the doors firmly shut in most cases.

Some proposals to restrict habeas corpus relief are based on problems of judicial administration. Post-conviction petitions contribute to the heavy caseload of the federal courts, are sometimes frivolous, and undermine the value of a final determination of guilt. But most restrictive efforts are anticrime proposals. Typical is the letter President Reagan wrote Congress urging passage of remedial legislation: "As a result of judicial expansion of the habeas corpus remedy, state prisoners are now free to relitigate their convictions and sentences endlessly in the lower federal courts" (quoted in Remington 1988). Conservatives stress that a criminal trial is a procedure that determines the defendant's guilt or innocence, not a game in which the accused may elude justice for any imperfection (Fein 1994).

Writs of habeas corpus play a particularly important role in capital punishment cases. After exhausting appellate remedies, defendants engage in lengthy challenges to the sentence of death by filing multiple writs of habeas corpus in various state and federal courts. Chief Justice William Rehnquist has criticized his colleagues for providing capital offenders with "numerous procedural protections unheard of for other crimes" and "for allowing endlessly drawn out legal proceedings."

Others counter that the death penalty is qualitatively different from other types of sanctions, so multiple scrutiny of such cases is more than justified. The argument for keeping the federal courthouse doors open is forcefully stated by Justice John Paul Stevens, who notes that federal habeas proceedings reveal deficiencies in 60 to 70 percent of the capital cases (*Murray v. Giarratano* 1989). Advocates of this policy also argue that not only should there be no rush to judgment, but death row inmates should have access to legal assistance, yet often do not. The majority of post-conviction cases are pro se—the prisoner is appearing on his or her own behalf. Recall from Chapter 7 that the Court has held that there is no right to counsel after the first appeal has been exhausted. Many death row defendants must rely on overworked volunteer attorneys (Applebome 1992).

Since the passage of the Antiterrorism and Effective Death Penalty Act, the number of habeas corpus petitions filed in federal court has increased (not decreased), rising to 31,556 in 2000 (Scalia 2002). Moreover, the law took effect just as national attention began to focus on innocents on death row. Thus, some now question whether the law went too far in denying federal court access to inmates—particularly death row inmates—who may be innocent (see Courts, Controversy, and the Administration of Justice: Innocent on Death Row).

What do you think? Should the federal courthouse doors be reopened to state prisoners, particularly those on death row, to ensure that justice is not short-circuited? Or should the federal courthouse doors remain as they are now, with only one federal review (unless the case presents an extraordinary issue)? Asked another way, where should the line be drawn between the interests of justice (ensuring that only the truly guilty are executed) and the need for finality (many of the habeas petitions raise issues that are very unlikely to succeed)?

To continue the debate, go to the following sites:

Southern Center for Human Rights: http://www.schr.org/reports/report.html

National Center for Policy Analysis: http://www.ncpa.org/crime (search for "habeas corpus")

Burke W. Kappler, "Small Favors: Chapter 154 of the Antiterrorism and Effective Death Penalty Act, the States, and the Right to Counsel"

Dwight Aarons, "Getting Out of This Mess: Steps Toward Addressing and Avoiding Inordinate Delay in Capital Cases"

A DAY IN COURT

A Self-Appointed Lawyer for the Nation's Condemned

 On Elisabeth Semel's bulletin board is a *New Yorker* cartoon that shows a man with a thick briefcase walking into an empty prison cell: "Hi, I'm your court-appointed lawyer," he announces. "Whoa! Don't tell me you've been executed already." While it may have been a mordant joke for *New Yorker* readers, for Ms. Semel it defines, in a fundamental way, the parameters of her life. Death row. Incompetent, court-appointed lawyers. Speeded-up executions.

"You're in crisis mode all the time," said Ms. Semel, who was at her desk in her office on Capitol Hill, talking between phone calls, existing, it seemed, on mineral water, lattes, and passion for her work as the director of the American Bar Association's Death Penalty Representation Project. Right now she needs to find volunteer lawyers for dozens of death row inmates in Texas, Virginia, Alabama, and Georgia who are without representation and are facing strict deadlines for filing state and federal appeals. At the same time, two men on federal death row in Indiana are several weeks from execution.

Ms. Semel has been a criminal defense lawyer for 25 years. Three years ago, she left the highly successful San Diego law firm she had helped found and, taking a pay cut of more than 50 percent, moved across the country to revive the bar association's death penalty project. California has executed only eight people since capital punishment was reinstated in 1976, and it provides better counsel and more resources than most other states for those charged with capital murder. Ms. Semel wanted to work on behalf of death row inmates in states like Texas, which has executed 232 people since 1976, and Virginia, which has executed 76, that provide the fewest legal resources.

"I wanted closer proximity to death," she said, paraphrasing the title of a book about a group of crusading lawyers in Atlanta who represent death row inmates. The obstacles were enormous. The federal government had eliminated all financing to help states with capital appeals, and Congress had passed a bill to speed up review of these cases in federal court. And she would be trying to recruit big law firms to take cases pro bono at a time when they were increasingly focused on profits.

She has on a wall a photograph of Calvin E. Swann, the first Virginia inmate to have his scheduled execution halted by Gov. James S. Gilmore III, who commuted the sentence to life in prison. One of Mr. Swann's relatives has inscribed it to his lawyers: "The Family!!!! With deepest gratitude." Ms. Semel helped find the New York law firm that took the case.

These days she worries about Juan Garza and David Hammer, the first federal prisoners scheduled to be executed since 1963. Both have clemency petitions before President Clinton. The combination of recent Justice Department findings of geographic and racial disparities in the federal system and the public's growing doubts about the fairness of the administration of the death penalty, Ms. Semel said, "call on the president to refuse to permit these executions to go forward." Mr. Garza, whose case she has been actively involved in, was convicted of three drug-related murders. But Ms. Semel never refers to him, or any of her former clients, as a murderer. "That's not how you define a human being," she said. "A human being is always more than the worst thing he's ever done. Do you deny the crime an individual has been convicted of, or the fact that he's guilty? No. But that's not who he is." . . .

She was probably destined to be a lawyer, she said. "The law is the greatest opportunity if you have a passion for advocacy," she said. "The death penalty is my civil rights issue," she added. "It's the ultimate expression of the legal system's unequal treatment of people who are poor, and people of color." She gets to her office most days by 7:30. She has one lawyer on staff and one assistant. By 11 P.M., she is still working, returning e-mail messages. This is not the sort of schedule that leaves much room for a personal life. Running is how she relaxes. . . .

Update: Juan Garza was executed on June 19, 2001. As of October 2003, the U.S. Bureau of Prisons lists Hammer as awaiting execution.

SOURCE: Sara Rimer, "A Self-Appointed Lawyer for the Nation's Condemned," *New York Times,* 30 October 2000. Copyright © 2000 by The New York Times Co. Reprinted by permission.

role of state supreme courts. Perhaps nowhere is this more obvious than in death penalty appeals.

Law on the Books: State Supreme Courts and Discretionary Dockets

In states that have not created intermediate courts of appeals, the responsibility for appellate review falls directly on the state supreme court. In such circumstances, the state's highest court finds itself relegated to dealing with a succession of relatively minor disputes, devoting its energies to error correction rather than to more time-consuming efforts to shape the law of the state.

By contrast, in the 40 states and the District of Columbia that have created intermediate courts of appeals, it is the lower appellate courts that are primarily concerned with error correction. This leaves the state's highest court free to devote more attention to cases that raise important policy questions (Tarr and Porter 1988). Discretionary review at the highest level transforms the nature of the judicial process. The high court is no longer merely reacting to disputes brought to it by disgruntled litigants; rather, it is selecting those disputes in which it chooses to participate. In sum, the architecture of the system tells the judges of the top court to be creative (Carrington, Meador, and Rosenberg 1976). In states with intermediate courts of appeals, the court of last resort is characterized by high discretion and low caseloads. A substantial portion of their work consists of reviewing petitions and then deciding the petitions granted.

Law in Action: State Supreme Courts as Policymakers

In recent years, state supreme courts have become important policymakers in a number of contentious areas such as tort reform, same-sex marriages, and parental rights in divorce cases. No wonder that elections for state supreme court judgeships have become nastier, noisier, and costlier (Neubauer and Meinhold 2004).

Applications of U.S. Supreme Court decisions is one way that state supreme courts participate in policymaking. Although in theory federal law is supreme over conflicting state law, in practice state supreme courts do not invariably follow authoritative pronouncements of the nation's highest court (Tarr 1982). Noncompliance was pronounced in race relation cases, with southern state supreme courts often aiding and abetting their state's massive resistance to desegregation (Tarr and Porter 1988). Noncompliance has also occurred in a variety of states in areas such as police interrogations and search and seizure. Some state supreme courts have, on occasion, refused to accept the constitutional principles enunciated by the Supreme Court (Johnson and Canon 1984). Moreover, some state supreme courts have eroded constitutional standards adopted by the nation's highest court. This clearly occurred in the area of police interrogations, with most state supreme courts carving out exceptions to *Miranda* (Gruhl 1981).

Interpretation of state constitutional provisions is another way that state supreme courts act as important government policymakers. The phrase **new judicial federalism** refers to the movement in the state supreme courts to reinvigorate state constitutions as sources of individual rights over and above the rights granted by the federal Constitution. New judicial federalism occurred partially as a response to the Burger Court's unwillingness to continue the Warren Court's understanding of civil liberties (Galie 1987). Just as important, though, new judicial federalism reflects the growing understanding that the federal Constitution establishes minimum guarantees of individual rights rather than maximum protections (Emmert and Traut 1992). In some instances, for example, state supreme courts have interpreted state bill of rights provisions regarding criminal procedures more expansively than the equivalent sections of the U.S. Bill of Rights. Researchers have identified hundreds of state supreme court decisions that interpret state charters as more rights-generous than their federal counterpart (Fino 1987).

The image of the new judicial federalism is that of a wholly liberal legal movement, but recent research suggests a more complex pattern. An examination of all 50 state supreme courts' criminal procedure decisions based on state constitutional law decided from the late

1960s to the end of 1989 found a "hidden conservatism." Two-thirds of the criminal rulings endorsed—"not repudiated"—the conservative holdings of the U.S. Supreme Court (Latzer 1991). Indeed, in some states, conservatives have succeeded in changing the thrust of new judicial federalism.

Law in Controversy: State Supreme Courts and Death Penalty Cases

State supreme courts reveal pronounced differences in their handling of death penalty cases. In California (Emmert and Traut 1996) and New Jersey, for example, the state supreme courts are openly hostile to the imposition of the death penalty. New Jersey's highest court has thrown out all but one of the 29 death sentences it has reviewed (Sullivan 1991). At the other extreme is Georgia, whose supreme court is very likely to uphold the imposition of a sentence of death. Other states fit somewhere in between. The Louisiana Supreme Court, for example, has through the years thrown out roughly half of the sentences of death it has reviewed, but has upheld the rest. (See Courts, Controversy, and the Administration of Justice: Innocent on Death Row?)

Differences in how state courts of last resort respond to death penalty appeals is not random. Supreme court justices in states with competitive judicial elections are more likely to uphold death sentences (Brace and Hall 1997). In particular, liberal justices facing reelection with possibly close margins of victory are more likely to conceal their opposition to the death penalty; they cast votes reflecting their constituents' opinions.

THE U.S. SUPREME COURT AND CRIMINAL JUSTICE POLICY

"I'll appeal all the way to the Supreme Court" is a familiar phrase. Alas, it is not very realistic. The jurisdiction of the U.S. Supreme Court is almost exclusively discretionary; that is, it can pick and choose the cases it wishes to decide. Most of the time it decides not to decide. Of the roughly 92 million lawsuits filed in the United States every year, only about 7,000 will ever be appealed to the nation's highest court; and from this small number, the justices will select a mere handful, about 90 in recent years, for briefing, argument, and written decision. Moreover, of this small number, criminal cases constitute an even smaller percentage; in a typical year, only 26 criminal decisions are reviewed by the Supreme Court with full opinion.

The importance of the Supreme Court, then, is measured not in terms of quantity but quality. Presidents Ronald Reagan and George Bush made five appointments to the nation's highest court; their choices were intended to move the court in a more conservative direction. Have the Republican presidents been successful? Figure 17-1 charts Supreme Court support for the rights of criminal defendants, showing a major decline over the last two decades. To fully understand today's practices, it is helpful to place the Rehnquist Court in historical perspective. Competing claims that a Court is "too conservative" or "too liberal" can be understood only on the basis of the Court's performance in other periods (Wasby 1993).

Informally, scholars refer to Court eras according to the chief justice. Thus, the Warren Court refers to the period from 1953 to 1969, when Earl Warren (a former Republican governor of California appointed by President Eisenhower) was chief justice. Because the associate justices change, however, these references provide only informal guides to the dominant thinking of the court. Nonetheless, an examination of the Warren Court, Burger Court, and now the Rehnquist Court offers a useful summary of major differences in the direction of criminal justice policy.

The Warren Court (1953–1969)

Although it is now more than 30 years since Chief Justice Earl Warren stepped down, the **Warren Court** (1953–1969) commands our attention because in the areas of civil liberties and civil rights it remains the benchmark against which subsequent periods of the Supreme Court will be measured. The Warren

COURTS, CONTROVERSY, AND THE ADMINISTRATION OF JUSTICE

Innocent on Death Row?

For six weeks, Ron Williamson sat in his cell next to the Oklahoma electric chair screaming, "I am an innocent man!" Just five days before his scheduled execution, his public defender persuaded a U.S. district judge that his state trial had serious constitutional flaws. Before the former professional baseball player was retried, however, the Innocence Project at the Benjamin Cardozo Law School arranged for new DNA testing. The results conclusively showed that Williamson was indeed innocent of the rape and murder of Debra Sue Carter.

In *Actual Innocence*, Barry Scheck, Peter Neufeld, and Jim Dwyer (2000) use the Williamson case and others to argue that many convicts are wrongly on death row. According to their most recent count, 138 death row prisoners have been exonerated (Innocence Project 2003). Similarly, an influential article, "A Broken System: Error Rates in Capital Cases," examines 5,760 capital verdicts imposed between 1973 and 1995 (Liebman, Fagan, and West 2000a). The authors report that 68 percent of all verdicts fully reviewed were found to be so seriously flawed that they had to be scrapped and retried. And where retrials were known, only 18 percent resulted in the reimposition of the death penalty (Liebman, Fagan, and West 2000b). Studies like these lead proponents of the due process model to argue that "for every seven people executed in this country since 1976, when the Supreme Court reinstated capital punishment, an eighth person—completely innocent—has been condemned to die and later exonerated" (American Civil Liberties Union 2000).

But not all are convinced that the capital appeals process is broken. Barry Latzer and James Cauthen (2000) argue that the statistical conclusions cited above are flawed. They distinguish between two types of errors: conviction errors and sentencing errors. Their analysis shows that conviction errors constitute only a small percentage of appellate court reversals in capital cases. It is sentencing errors, then, that dominate reversals and this is to be expected because capital cases receive much closer scrutiny than noncapital appeals. Overall, advocates of the crime control model argue that the process is working—the few wrong trial court verdicts are indeed identified and corrected on appeal.

In recent years, the debate over innocents on death row has focused on DNA testing (see Chapter 14). To be sure, some who have been freed from death row or life imprisonment were later found to be innocent because of witnesses who lied at trial. But some like Williamson have been freed after reexamination of trial evidence using advanced DNA testing techniques that were not available during the original trial. Barry Sheck, for one, argues that all convicts on death row should be legally entitled to have the original evidence retested. In 2003, Colorado, Georgia, New Mexico, and Nevada enacted legislation giving convicted death row inmates access to post-conviction DNA testing. Conservatives quickly counter that calls for retesting are yet another delaying tactic for defendants who were convicted on the basis of overwhelming physical and testimonial evidence.

What do you think? Does the number of innocent persons released from death row or life imprisonment indicate that the capital appeals process is broken or that it is actually working as it should? Do you think that all convicts on death row should have the right to have physical evidence retested using more advanced DNA techniques, or should such requests be granted only upon a strong showing that the suspect might indeed be innocent?

For contrasting views about innocents on death row, go to "Innocence" Critique:
http://www.prodeathpenalty.com/Innocence.htm

The Innocence Project:
http://www.innocenceproject.org/

Peter Vilbig, "Innocent on Death Row"
"Wrong Guy, Good Cause" (protesting the death penalty)

John Leo, "An Innocent Martyr?" (media bias against capital punishment)

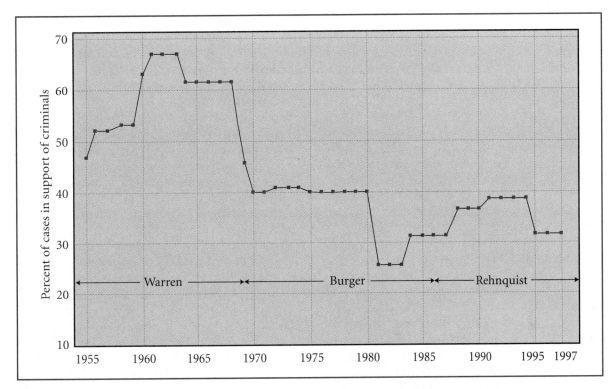

Figure 17-1
Declining Support by the Supreme Court for Rights of Criminals

Note: The data were smoothed using a running median using 53R'H (Frederick Hartwig with Brian Dearing, *Exploratory Data Analysis,* Beverly Hills, CA: Sage, 1979).

SOURCE: Adapted from Lee Epstein, Thomas Walker, and William Dixon, "The Supreme Court and Criminal Justice Disputes: A Neo-Institutional Perspective," *American Journal of Political Science* 33 (1989): 834. Updated by Harold Spaeth, *United States Supreme Court Judicial Data Base, 1953–1997 Terms* (Ann Arbor, MI: Inter-University Consortium for Political and Social Research, 2001).

Court revolutionized constitutional law and American society as well, giving to minorities victories they had not been able to obtain from reluctant legislatures and recalcitrant executives. Thus, the Warren Court revolution reflects a distinct departure from earlier Courts, which were often characterized as conservative.

The Warren Court first captured national attention with its highly controversial 1954 decision invalidating racial segregation in the public schools (*Brown v. Board of Education* 1954). In addition, the Court first confronted the difficult problem of defining obscenity and considerably narrowed the grounds for prosecution of obscene material (*Roth v. U.S.* 1957). What produced the greatest controversy, however, was the adoption of a series of broad rules protecting criminal defendants.

During the 1960s, the Supreme Court for the first time attempted to exercise strong policy control over the administration of criminal justice. The nation's highest court began to apply to state courts some of the more specific requirements of the Bill of Rights. Earlier opinions enunciating vague standards of "due process" were replaced by decisions specifying precise rules. The Bill of Rights was seemingly transformed from a collection of general constitutional principles into a code of criminal procedure. These sweeping changes in constitutional interpretation have been called the "due process revolution."

Listing the significant Warren Court criminal justice decisions virtually constitutes a review of the major chapters of this book. The right to counsel was expanded (*Gideon v.*

Wainwright 1963, discussed in Chapter 7); limits were placed on prosecutorial power (Chapter 6); courts were compelled to bring defendants before a judge without unnecessary delay (Chapter 10); restrictions were placed on police searches (*Mapp v. Ohio* 1961, Chapter 12); limits on police interrogations were mandated (*Miranda v. Arizona* 1966, Chapter 12); jury selection was significantly changed to ensure equality and fairness (Chapter 14); the death penalty was declared unconstitutional (Chapters 15 and 16); the ability of the guilty to appeal their convictions was made easier (this chapter); and the right of convicts to file habeas corpus petitions was also greatly expanded (also this chapter).

If nothing else, the Warren Court put the issues of criminal justice on its docket and eventually on the nation's agenda as well. The Warren Court revolution in areas as diverse as segregation, pornography, school prayer, and reapportionment greatly changed American society. But many of these changes were far from popular. The Supreme Court's attempt to nationalize, rationalize, and constitutionalize the criminal justice system came at a time of increasing crime in the streets, riots in big cities, political violence protesting the Vietnam War, and most tragically of all, assassinations of American leaders. To the public, there appeared to be a connection between the new trends of what was seen as judicial permissiveness and the breakdown of law and order. Supreme Court justices were accused of "coddling criminals" and "handcuffing the police." This controversy became the focus of national debate.

The Burger Court (1969–1986)

During the 1968 presidential campaign, Republican candidate Richard Nixon made the Warren Court's decisions on criminal procedure a major issue. He promised to appoint "strict constructionists" to the Court, and after his election he made good on this promise. With his four appointments, Nixon achieved remarkable success in remodeling the Court. After Warren Burger, Harry Blackmun, Lewis Powell, and William Rehnquist took the bench,

support for civil liberties quickly began to diminish (Segal and Spaeth 1989).

The Nixon Court was named after the new Chief Justice, Warren Burger. Although on balance the **Burger Court** (1969–1986) was more conservative than its predecessor, there was no constitutional counterrevolution, only modest adjustment. The withdrawal from Warren Court decisions was most apparent in criminal justice. *Miranda* was weakened but not overturned. Similarly, despite clamor by conservatives, *Mapp* was not overruled, although the Court began creating "good faith" exceptions to the exclusionary rule (see Chapter 12). To be sure, the death penalty was reinstated, but overall the Burger Court did not cut back on Warren Court criminal procedure rulings as much as had been expected.

Just as important, the Burger Court began to tackle new sets of issues not previously treated. In sex discrimination, women were not given as complete protection as had been given to racial minorities, but the tone was moderate to liberal, not conservative (Wasby 1993). Plea bargaining was openly discussed, and rather than abolishing it (as some conservatives urged), the Burger Court sought to regularize its practice (see Chapter 13). And in one of the most controversial decisions ever issued, the Burger Court struck down a variety of requirements that interfered with a woman's right to obtain an abortion (*Roe v. Wade* 1973).

Amid this diversity, it is hard to capture the essence of the Burger Court. Indeed, it is probably best characterized by the headline "Pragmatism, Compromise Marks Courts: Tricky Track Record Harder to Categorize than Pundits Predicted" (Wasby 1993, 17). Overall, the Burger Court was composed of seven justices appointed by Republican presidents. Yet President Reagan sought to remake this Republican body in his even more conservative image.

The Rehnquist Court (1986–)

Presidents Ronald Reagan and George Bush continued the Republican policy of appointing conservatives to the court. The **Rehnquist Court** (1986–) officially began when William Rehnquist was elevated from associate justice

Exhibit 17-4	Supreme Court Justices in Order of Seniority				
Name	Year of Birth	Home State	Year of Appointment	President	Senate Vote
William Rehnquist*	1924	Arizona	1971	Nixon	65–33
John Paul Stevens	1920	Illinois	1975	Ford	78–0
Sandra Day O'Connor	1930	Arizona	1981	Reagan	99–0
Antonin Scalia	1936	New York	1986	Reagan	98–0
Anthony Kennedy	1936	California	1988	Reagan	97–0
David Souter	1940	New Hampshire	1990	Bush	90–9
Clarence Thomas	1948	Georgia	1991	Bush	52–48
Ruth Bader Ginsburg	1933	New York	1993	Clinton	96–3
Stephen Breyer	1938	Massachusetts	1994	Clinton	87–9

*William Rehnquist was promoted from associate justice to chief justice in 1986 by President Reagan.

to chief justice. Unofficially, it can be dated from the 1988 appointment of Anthony Kennedy, who provided a conservative vote far more dependably than did his predecessor Lewis Powell. Thus, it was during the 1988 term that the Rehnquist Court seemed to come of conservative age by cutting back abortion rights, condoning mandatory drug testing, and permitting capital punishment for juveniles and retarded persons convicted of murder. And as we have emphasized in this chapter, it virtually eliminated the right of convicts to seek habeas corpus relief.

But other Rehnquist Court decisions cannot be so easily categorized as conservative; for example, the high court upheld flag burning and unanimously ruled that mistaken jury instructions can never be considered harmless error. And most interesting, the Court announced a new constitutional right grounded in the Eighth Amendment's prohibitions against excessive fines; these limits place brakes on the government's aggressive use of its authority under the drug forfeiture laws (see Chapter 3).

The Court's conservative justices have been criticized for their activist inclination to disregard precedent (Smith and Hensley 1993). For example, the 1991 decision permitting victim impact testimony in capital sentencing hearings (*Payne v. Tennessee* discussed in Chapter 9) directly overturned precedents that were merely two and four years old (*Booth v. Maryland* 1987; *South Carolina v. Gathers* 1989).

There is little doubt that the Rehnquist Court is more conservative on many issues than its predecessors. Perhaps Law Professor Yale Kamisar said it best in his comment that the Rehnquist Court "gives weight to the needs, convenience, and practical problems of law enforcement" (quoted in Wicker 1991). Overall, the Court is increasingly pragmatic but still very conservative.

With the retirement of Byron White, President Clinton became the first Democratic president in 26 years to make an appointment to the high court. He chose Ruth Bader Ginsburg. With his second appointment, he elevated Stephen Breyer to the high court (Exhibit 17-4). Both have been moderates who on some cases forge an alliance with the centrist justices.

Decisions reflect shifting alliances of the justices. Firmly on the right are Antonin Scalia, Clarence Thomas, and William Rehnquist, with Anthony Kennedy often joining them. Arrayed more to the left are John Paul Stevens, Ruth Bader Ginsburg, Stephen Breyer, and David Souter. It is Sandra Day O'Connor who often holds the balance of power. These shifting alliances are reflected in two controversial 2003 decisions in which the court declared unconstitutional a state law prohibiting intimate sexual conduct between persons of the same sex (*Lawrence v. Texas*) and upheld some types of diversity programs in university admissions (*Grutter v. Bollinger*).

The Post-Rehnquist Court

During the 2000 presidential campaign, the future composition of the Court was a minor issue. Amid rumors that at least three justices (Rehnquist among them) wished to retire, the two major candidates offered contrasting views about how they would fill potential vacancies: Democratic nominee Al Gore suggested he would nominate middle-of-the-road justices, whereas Republican George W. Bush expressed strong preferences for justices on the far right.

Following the election, the current membership of the Court became the dominating topic. With ballot problems in Florida, the five conservatives on the Court ruled that the vote counting should end, thus ensuring that George W. Bush would become the nation's forty-third president (*Bush v. Gore* 2000). The sharp division on the nation's highest judicial body has muddied the waters of future appointments to the Court. If George W. Bush attempts to appease the right wing of the Republican Party by nominating justices in the mold of Scalia and Thomas, then he risks defeat in the U.S. Senate. If, on the other hand, he chooses to nominate more moderate justices, he risks alienating a key political base and risks defeat in the 2004 presidential election. Either way, the direction he attempts to lead the Supreme Court might become the defining domestic issue of his presidency.

The Supreme Court in Broad Perspective

Newspaper coverage of the Supreme Court tends to resemble the play-by-play of an athletic event, with each decision in the term described as a "victory" or "defeat" for conservatives or liberals. Unfortunately, what gets lost in this commentary is the broader perspective.

Overall, the decisions of the Supreme Court swing back and forth much like a pendulum on a clock. Far from being random, however, these swings reflect major political movements in the nation. Most directly, this occurs because of the swing of electoral politics; presidential appointments control the composition of the bench and may temper the speed, if not shift the direction, of the Court. More indirectly, public opinion also affects the justices' lives and may serve to curb them when they threaten to go too far or too fast in their rulings. "But changes in the direction of the Court are ultimately moderated by its functioning as a collegial body, in which all nine justices share power and compete for influence" (O'Brien 1988, 13). The Court thus generally shifts direction gradually, incorporating and accommodating the views of new appointees. Ultimately these long-term trends, more than individual decisions, have the most influence.

▌CONCLUSION

Roger Coleman died in the Virginia electric chair, but the controversy over the Supreme Court decision continues. To some observers, it represented a much-needed step toward reducing a long, drawn-out review process. To others, it reflected a hollow formalism devoid of considerations of justice. Ultimately, though, it was a law passed by Congress, more than any decisions by the Supreme Court, that has recently altered post-conviction reviews in federal courts.

The right to one appeal is being increasingly used. Appellate court caseloads have grown dramatically in recent years. The explosive growth in appellate court caseloads not only reflects the greater willingness of litigants to ask reviewing bodies to correct errors but also represents the greater role appellate courts play in policymaking. U.S. Supreme Court decisions have important impacts on the criminal justice system. But the nine justices are often as divided over the correct answer to a legal problem as is society. Thus, predicting specific case outcomes is difficult; indeed, the conservative Rehnquist Court has not always ruled in a predictably conservative manner.

A Virtual Tour of American Courthouses: Appellate Courts

For starters I recommend sites that focus on the nation's most visible and also most important court, the United States Supreme Court. The Oyez Project at Northwestern University provides a comprehensive view of our nation's highest court at **http://oyez.itcs.northwestern.edu/oyez/tour/**. One unique feature is that the site provides links to oral arguments in many of the Supreme Court's most important decisions: **http://oyez.nwu.edu/**. The recently redesigned U.S. Supreme Court Web site provides easy access to current cases and past ones as well: **http://www.supremecourtus.gov/**. Finally, CourtTV offers an innovative Web site, The Supreme Court: A Journey Through Time, at **http://www.courttv.com/ multimedia/supremecourt/index.html**.

All of the U.S. Courts of Appeals have Web sites. As a start, go to these:

http://www.tourolaw.edu/2ndcircuit/
http://www.ca5.uscourts.gov/
http://www.ca7.uscourts.gov/
http://www.ca9.uscourts.gov/

A growing number of state supreme courts offer virtual tours. You are just a click away from viewing the courtrooms where some of the nation's most important legal matters are argued, including:

Alabama **http://www.judicial.state.al.us/tour.cfm**

Arizona **http://www.supreme.state.az.us/azsupreme/**

New Jersey **http://www.judiciary.state.nj.us/ supreme/index.htm**

North Dakota **http://www.court.state.nd.us/Court/ VirtualTour/**

Ohio **http://www.sconet.state.oh.us**

Virginia **http://www.courts.state.va.us/scv/home.html**

For those with an interest in history, I recommend taking a tour of the U.S. Supreme Court's former courtroom in the nation's Capitol at **http://www.senate.gov/vtour/ 1main.htm**. Another interesting historical site is the Philadelphia City Hall, which once housed the state supreme court: **http://www.ajaxelectric.com/cityhall/tour11.htm**.

CRITICAL THINKING QUESTIONS

1. Do you think the Supreme Court was correct in ruling that Roger Coleman should not have his murder conviction reviewed in federal court because his lawyer filed the notice of appeal one day late? Would your answer be the same or different if this was not a death penalty case? Would your answer be the same or different if the basis of the review would be procedural as opposed to the substance of the evidence?

2. In the public's mind, at least, appeals drag on endlessly and result in a lack of finality in the process. Do you think this is a significant problem, or is it merely one of appearance?

3. How does the appeal and review process in a capital murder case differ from the appeal and review process in a serious felony?

4. Why are most findings of guilt at the trial level not appealed? In what ways are appellate cases unrepresentative of trial court cases?

5. Based on material in this chapter and earlier ones, what have been the significant differences in decisions between the Warren Court, the Burger Court, and the Rehnquist Court? In particular, consider Court decisions related to right to counsel (Chapter 7), bail (Chapter 11), right to trial (Chapter 14), the death penalty (Chapter 15), and habeas corpus.

KEY TERMS

affirm (401)
appellant (400)
appellate court record (401)
appellee (respondent) (401)

brief (401)
Burger Court (414)
discretionary appellate jurisdiction (399)
dissenting opinion (401)
double jeopardy (398)
en banc (397)
error (402)
error correction (397)
habeas corpus (406)
harmless error (402)
interlocutory (398)
mandatory appellate jurisdiction (399)
new judicial federalism (410)
notice of appeal (400)
opinion (401)
oral argument (401)
policy formulation (397)
Rehnquist Court (414)
remand (402)
reverse (402)
reversed and remanded (402)
reversible error (402)
right to one appeal (398)
Warren Court (411)

WORLD WIDE WEB RESOURCES AND EXERCISES

Web Guides

http://dir.yahoo.com/Government/Law/U_S__States/
(select State, then Judicial Branch)
http://dir.yahoo.com/Government/U_S__Government/
Judicial_Branch/Federal_Courts/Appeals_Courts/

Web Search Terms

habeas corpus
Anti-Terrorism and Effective Death Penalty Act

Useful URLs

The official Web site of the U.S. Supreme Court is http://www.supremecourtus.gov.

Visit CNN'S Supreme Court Center: http://www.cnn.com/LAW/scotus/.

See the Supreme Court Resource Center at Findlaw.com: http://supreme.lp.findlaw.com/supreme_court/.

See the Supreme Court at *USA Today*: http://usatoday.com/news/court/courtfront.htm.

The Legal Information Institute at Cornell University includes lots of information about the Supreme Court as well as the full text of many opinions in a searchable format: http://supct.law.cornell.edu/supct.

Uncommon URLs

The Virtual Supreme Court is a teaching tool to explore the role of the judiciary in deciding how to interpret the words of the Constitution: http://www.law.upenn.edu/fac/bwoodhou/vsc/.

The Georgia Association of Criminal Defense Lawyers disseminates information about the Anti-Terrorism and Effective Death Penalty Act: http://www.gacdl.org/habeas.htm.

The Supreme Court Historical Society offers insights into the Court's history and also provides an online gift service: http://www.supremecourthistory.org.

The Colorado State Public Defender provides an appellate brief online at http://www.state.co.us/gov_dir/pdef_dir/library/e_garcia/garcia%20toc.htm.

The State Appellate Defender Organization (Michigan) provides lots of information about appeals on its Web site: http://www.sado.org. Of special interest is "How to Seek Judicial Review of Your Felony Conviction and Sentence" at http://www.sado.org/fbull.htm.

The Center on Wrongful Convictions of Northwestern University has freed several falsely accused convicts from death row: http://www.law.nwu.edu/depts/clinic/wrongful/.

The DNA Testing Program of the Oklahoma Indigent Defense System can be accessed at http://www.state.ok.us/~oids/.

The National Committee to Prevent Wrongful Executions is a bipartisan committee of death penalty supporters and opponents who are concerned about the risk of wrongful executions: http://www.constitutionproject.org/.

Web Exercises

1. Read press accounts of recent U.S. Supreme Court decisions to see if the Court continues to give limited support to the rights of criminal defendants. One of the most comprehensive Web sites is provided by CNN at **http://www.cnn.com/LAW/scotus/archive/**.

2. Jerry Goldman at Northwestern University has created an award-winning Web site, Oyez Oyez Oyez, which provides access to oral argument and the Court's opinion announcement: **http://oyez.nwu.edu/**. Many of the cases highlighted in this book are now available (you will need RealAudio, however). Once on the site, you can access specific opinions either by title, case citation, subject, or decision date. Tune in to *Felker v. Turpin* to hear the lawyers argue the case and the justices ask questions.

3. Biographies of Supreme Court justices, past and present, are readily available on the Web through **http://www.yahoo.com/Government/U_S__Government/Judicial_Branch-Supreme_Court/Justices/**. Pick a justice from the conservative camp and one from the moderate wing. Compare their careers. Besides the appointing president, are there any differences in background related to law school attended, type of law practiced, governmental service, and the like?

4. One of the most hotly contested death penalty cases centers on Mumia Abu-Jamal, who was convicted of murdering a Philadelphia police officer. The battle to free him revolves around habeas corpus filings. Using the search term "Mumia Abu-Jamal," find one Web site on each side of the issue. Two possibilities are Mumia Abu-Jamal's Freedom Journal (**http://www.mumia.org/**) and Justice for Police Officer Daniel Faulkner (**http://www.danielfaulkner.com/**). In examining these sites, ask yourself what is more important, the procedures in the case or the substance of the matter. Moreover, how does this case relate to Courts, Controversy, and the Administration of Justice: Should Federal Courthouse Doors Be Closed to State Prisoners?

INFOTRAC COLLEGE EDITION RESOURCES AND EXERCISES

Basic Searches

appellate courts
appellate procedure
courts of appeal
briefs
certiorari
waiver of appeal
court of last resort
Supreme Court, United States
supreme court
Antiterrorism and Effective Death Penalty Act of 1996
habeas corpus
Warren, Earl
Burger, Warren
Rehnquist, William

Recommended Articles

Jennifer S. Carroll, "Appellate Specialization and the Art of Appellate Advocacy"

The Christian Century, "States Review Death Penalty"

Raymond T. Elligett, Jr., "Top 10 Appellate Mistakes"

"Legal Malpractice in the Criminal Context: Is Postconviction Relief Required?"

Andrew Phillips, "The Long Needle of Justice"

Speedy Rice, "Preserving Your Evidence and Record for Appeal"

"'Serious Error' Found in Death Penalty System"

Andrew Peyton Thomas, "Penalty Box: A Much-Needed Reform Seemed Poised to Hasten Executions"

InfoTrac College Edition Exercises

1. Using the search term "Supreme Court, United States," locate two or more articles that discuss the current decisions of the Court relating to criminal justice. To what extent do the authors think that the decisions are too liberal or too conservative?

2. Using the search term "capital punishment," "capital punishment, cases," or

"capital punishment, law regulations," locate two or more articles that discuss the length of time from a sentence of death to execution. To what extent do the authors think that delay is good or bad? Why?

3. Using the search term "habeas corpus," find articles that relate to contemporary practices. To what extent are discussions of habeas corpus practices dominated by death penalty cases? In discussing habeas corpus, to what extent do the authors come closer to the crime control model or the due process model of criminal justice?

FOR FURTHER READING

Amar, Akhil Reed. *The Constitution and Criminal Procedure: First Principles.* New Haven, CT: Yale University Press, 1997.

Biskupic, Joan, and Elder Witt. *The Supreme Court at Work.* Washington, DC: CQ Publishing, 1996.

Hanson, Robert, and Henry Daley. *Federal Habeas Corpus Review.* Williamsburg, VA: National Center for State Courts, 1995.

Hickey, Thomas. "A Double Jeopardy Analysis of the Medgar Evers Murder Case." *Journal of Criminal Justice* 23 (1995): 41–51.

Hoffman, Joseph, and Lauren Robel. "Federal Court Supervision of State Criminal Justice Administration." *Annals of the American Academy* 543 (1996): 154–166.

Kincaid, John. "The New Federalism Context of the New Judicial Federalism." *Rutgers Law Journal* 26 (1995): 913–979.

Latzer, Barry. *State Constitutions and Criminal Justice.* Westport, CT: Greenwood, 1991.

Lopeman, Charles. *The Activist Advocate: Policy Making in State Supreme Courts.* Westport, CT: Praeger, 1999.

Marvell, Thomas. "The Effectiveness of Flexible Assignment of Appeals Between Supreme and Intermediate Courts." *Judicature* 78 (1995): 292–298.

Matthew, Jonathan. *Inside Appellate Courts: The Impact of Court Organization on Judicial Decision Making in the United States Courts of Appeals.* Ann Arbor: University of Michigan Press, 2002.

McCoy, Candace, and Illya Lichtenberg. "Providing Effective Habeas Counsel for Indigents in Capital Cases." *Justice System Journal* 21 (1999): 81–87.

O'Brien, David. *Storm Center: The Supreme Court in American Politics.* 6th ed. New York: W.W. Norton, 2003.

Perry, Barbara. *The Priestly Tribe: The Supreme Court's Image in the American Mind.* Westport, CT: Praeger, 1999.

Schwartz, Bernard. *The Warren Court: A Retrospective.* New York: Oxford University Press, 1996.

Tarr, G. Alan, ed. *Constitutional Politics in the States: Contemporary Controversies and Historical Patterns.* Westport, CT: Greenwood, 1996.

Williams, Jimmy. "Type of Counsel and the Outcome of Criminal Appeals: A Research Note." *American Journal of Criminal Justice* 19 (1995): 275–285.

Chapter 18 The Lower Courts

he Lynch City Police Court meets every Thursday night, Judge C. B. Russell presiding. Like many others born and raised in the small towns of Kentucky's coal-mining region, Russell dropped out of high school and worked in the coal mines. Later he was elected judge. During one session, Judge Russell found Lonnie North guilty of drunk driving and sentenced him to 30 days in jail. But Kentucky law allows only a fine for Lonnie North's charge. It seems that the nonlawyer judge had exceeded his legal authority.

On appeal, North's lawyers argued that defendants cannot receive due process of law when the judge is not a lawyer. Chief Justice Warren Burger's majority opinion disagreed, arguing that rural courts, with nonlawyer judges, were convenient to the citizens, providing simple and speedy justice. But critics wonder if convenient and speedy may not equate all too often to rough justice. ◄

North v. Russell is a rare case—the nation's highest court almost never hears appeals from the trial courts of limited jurisdiction, preferring instead to concentrate on the more intellectually challenging legal issues raised by murderers and drug dealers who have been found guilty in the major trial courts. Nonetheless, countless Lonnie Norths appear in the nation's lowest courts every day. These are the courts that process the millions of Americans accused each year of disturbing the peace, shoplifting, being drunk, and driving too fast. Individually, these cases may appear to be minor—almost petty—but collectively, the work of the lower courts is quite important.

This chapter discusses the rapid, rough justice dispensed by the lower courts. We begin with an examination of the scope of the lower courts and then consider their problems. As we shall see, lower courts exhibit immense variation; big-city courts function very differently from their counterparts in rural areas. Therefore, we consider the different issues presented in rural justice of the peace courts as opposed to the big-city municipal courts. Finally, we examine alternative dispute resolution (ADR), which is designed to reduce the caseloads of the courts by providing nonadversarial alternatives to traditional courtroom procedures.

SCOPE OF THE LOWER COURTS

At the first level of state courts are **trial courts of limited jurisdiction,** sometimes referred to as **inferior courts** or, more simply, **lower**

courts. Although these minor courts stand at the bottom of the judicial hierarchy, the base is much larger than the typical pyramid diagram suggests. Indeed, when we count up the number of courts, judges, and cases filed in courts all across the nation, the numbers are dominated by the nation's lowest judiciary. The 17,943 lower courts constitute 60 percent of all judicial bodies. Exhibit 18-1 highlights the large volume of cases heard by the lower courts: The more than 61 million case filings represent about two-thirds of yearly state court filings.

The precise jurisdiction of lower courts varies from place to place. In some states, major trial courts in rural areas hear traffic cases and the like because there are few lower courts. Moreover, in six states and the District of Columbia, the lower courts have been consolidated with the major trial courts; as a result, statistical comparisons between these jurisdictions and the other 44 states are difficult at best. Nonetheless, the workload of the lower courts can usefully be examined in terms of felony criminal cases, nonfelony criminal cases, and civil cases.

Felony Criminal Cases

Lower court jurisdiction typically includes the preliminary stages of felony cases (see Chapter 4). Thus, after an arrest, a judge in a trial court of limited jurisdiction will hold the initial appearance, appoint counsel for indigents, and conduct the preliminary hearing. Later the case is transferred to a trial court of general jurisdiction for trial (or plea) and sentencing.

Exhibit 18-1	Volume of Cases Filed in Lower Courts and Major Trial Courts in a Year (millions)	
	Lower Courts	Major Trial Courts
Criminal	9.2	4.8
Juvenile	.7	1.3
Traffic/ordinance violations	41.6	14.1
Domestic relations	1.5	3.8
Civil	8.4	7.4
Total	61.4	31.4

SOURCE: Brian Ostrom, Neal Kauder, and Robert LaFountain, *Examining the Work of State Courts, 2002* (Williamsburg, VA: National Center for State Courts, 2003).

Note also, from Exhibit 18-2, that lower court judges typically sign search warrants—a decision that may prove crucial for decisions in the major trial court.

Nonfelony Criminal Cases

Typically, criminal cases are divided into felony and misdemeanor, a distinction that fits nicely with the work of the trial courts of general jurisdiction. But for the lower courts, a broader concept of nonfelony cases is better. Nonfelony includes not only misdemeanors but also ordinance violations and traffic cases.

A **misdemeanor** is a crime punishable by fine and/or imprisonment, usually in a local jail, for a period of less than one year. Misdemeanors are enacted by state legislative bodies and cover the entire state. **Ordinances,** on the other hand, are laws passed by a local governing body such as a city council. They are similar in effect to a legislative statute, but they apply only to the locality, and any fine that is assessed for violations goes to the local government, not to the state. It is typical for ordinances to prohibit the same types of conduct (for example, disorderly conduct, public drunkenness) as state misdemeanors. Ordinance

violations are technically noncriminal, which means that they are easier to prosecute. At times, police prefer to arrest a suspect for an ordinance violation because it presents fewer legal obstacles to gaining a conviction.

Traffic offenses refer to a group of offenses involving self-propelled motor vehicles. These violations range from parking violations to improper equipment. Speeding is the most common traffic offense, along with driving without a license and driving while a license is suspended or revoked. Traffic offenses are typically punishable by a small fine. But because the volume of these cases is quite large, traffic tickets can be big moneymakers for local governments.

Traffic cases are one area in which court caseloads have actually declined in recent years, while the rest of state court caseloads continue to grow. From 1987 to 2001, traffic cases declined by 14 percent because, increasingly, less serious traffic cases are being decriminalized or transferred to an executive branch hearing for what is essentially an administrative (rather than a judicial) proceeding (Ostrom, Kauder, and LaFountain 2003). Overall, traffic constitutes 68 percent of lower court caseloads. The most watched aspects of traffic cases are prosecutions for drunk driving.

Civil Cases

On the civil side, the lower courts decide disputes under a set dollar amount, often referred to as *small claims*. The term *small claims* refers not to a substance but to a process. **Small claims courts** handle cases involving maximum amounts that range from a low of $1,000 in some states to a high of $10,000 in others. The trend is clearly in an upward direction. The largest number of cases falling under these dollar amounts are debt collection, primarily involving nonpayment for goods purchased or services rendered. Another major category includes landlord–tenant disputes—mostly claims by landlords against tenants concerning past-due rent, evictions, and property damage. A smaller number of small claims cases involve alleged property damage, largely stemming from automobile accidents.

In most states, streamlined procedures have been adopted to provide quick, inexpensive

Exhibit 18-2 Steps of Criminal Procedure in Lower Courts for Nonfelony Cases

	Law on the Books	Law in Action
Crime	*Misdemeanor:* Crime punishable by fine or local jail for less than one year. *Ordinance violation:* Law passed by local government similar to a misdemeanor. *Traffic offense:* Relating to motor vehicle.	With the exception of drunk driving and domestic violence, the criminal law has changed little in the last decades.
Arrest	*Arrest:* Taking of a person into custody for the purpose of charging him or her with a crime. *Citation:* Written order issued by a law enforcement officer notifying a defendant to appear in court. *Complaint:* Sworn statement by victim alleging that a specific person has committed a specified crime.	Drunkenness and other liquor law: 1,225,000. Disorderly conduct: 670,000. Driving under the influence: 1,460,000. Weapons: 165,000. Vandalism: 275,000.
Initial appearance	Suspects are told the charges pending; lower court judges can take a plea in nonfelony cases.	Often held within 24 hours of arrest. Two out of three defendants plead guilty during the first appearance.
Bail	Money posted for bail or for a citation may be forfeited as an alternative to appearance in court.	Many suspects plead guilty immediately, so bail release doesn't come into play.
Preliminary hearing	Preliminary hearings are not applicable in nonfelony cases.	
Charging	Charges are filed by police (based on an arrest or citation) or directly by the victim (complaint).	Prosecutor and judge typically proceed on the basis of the police arrest.
Grand jury	Grand juries are not applicable to nonfelony cases.	
Arraignment	Arraignments in trial courts of general jurisdiction are not applicable in nonfelony cases.	
Evidence	Lower court judges have authority to sign search warrants.	Search warrants are very rare in nonfelony cases.
Plea negotiations	Misdemeanor defendants sentenced to jail have a right to counsel (*Argersinger v. Hamlin*).	Few defendants have an attorney, so defendants must negotiate on their own.
Trial	Defendants have a constitutional right to a trial by jury only if the offense is punishable by imprisonment for more than six months (*Baldwin v. New York*).	Trials are rare indeed. Defendants charged with drunk driving may demand a trial, particularly if they have a previous drunk driving conviction.
Sentencing	Defendants may not be jailed because they are unable to pay a fine (*Tate v. Short*).	Fines predominate. Jail sentences (short) sometimes imposed.
Appeal	Appeals from lower courts are heard by trial court of general jurisdiction or intermediate court of appeals.	Very few defendants appeal. Appeals may occur following drunk driving convictions.

COURT TV
Sex for Sale

Every year the police make about 100,000 prostitution arrests, yet the "world's oldest profession" continues to thrive, netting $15 billion a year by some estimates.

"Sex for Sale" explores the many faces of prostitution in the United States. You will see Clara, an admitted drug addict as she works the streets every night. The video also takes you along on a ride with two San Francisco cops, who provide a travel guide to the various layers of prostitution in the City by the Bay.

The justice system finds itself caught in the middle of a societal debate over how to respond to prostitution. Views vary from outright legalization to implementing an even stronger ban, with some opting for a middle ground of greater health regulations.

View this video clip on your copy of the CourtTV CD-ROM. As you watch the video, keep the following questions in mind:

1. What solutions to prostitution would advocates of the crime control model of criminal justice favor? How would these solutions differ from those offered by supporters of the due process model of criminal justice?

2. In what ways does police enforcement of laws against prostitution and other victimless crimes contribute to the problems of the lower courts?

3. Should efforts to respond to prostitution shift away from individual case adjudication and come to reflect court–community collaboration?

4. Prosecution in the lower courts has often resembled a revolving door. In what ways is prostitution enforcement similar to other revolving-door prosecutions such as public drunkenness? In what ways does it differ?

processing by dispensing with strict rules of evidence and the right to trial by jury (Goerdt 1992). Accordingly, small claims cases are less formal and less protracted than other civil cases.

PROBLEMS OF THE LOWER COURTS

It is the quantity of caseload that makes the trial courts of general jurisdiction so qualitatively important. Individually the cases may be minor, but collectively they are of critical importance because these are the matters that bring typical citizens to court. Jury duty aside, an appearance in lower court is for many citizens their only direct encounter with the judiciary, and these encounters in turn shape citizens' perceptions of the quality of justice meted out by all courts, whether state or federal, trial or appellate.

For decades, reformers have criticized the lower courts, highlighting a variety of problems. Only a shadow of the adversary model of criminal justice can be found in these courts. Few defendants are represented by an attorney. Trials are rare. Informality, rather than the rules of courtroom procedure, predominates. Jail sentences are imposed, sometimes with lightning speed. In short, practices that would be condemned if they occurred in higher courts are commonplace in the lower courts. Is this justice? The President's Commission on Law Enforcement and Administration of Justice (1967, 128) found the conditions of the lower courts disquieting.

> The commission has been shocked by what it has seen in some lower courts. It has seen cramped and noisy courtrooms, undignified and perfunctory procedures, and badly trained personnel. It has seen dedicated people who are frustrated by huge case loads, by the lack of opportunity to examine cases carefully, and by the impossibility of devising constructive solutions to the problems of offenders. It has seen assembly-line justice.

An observer's most lasting impression of such courts is the nonjudicial atmosphere of the proceedings. The process instills little respect for the criminal justice system in defendants, witnesses, or court officials. To identify the most pressing problems of the trial courts of limited jurisdiction, the American Judicature Society surveyed six states: Colorado, Illinois, Louisiana, New Hampshire, New Jersey, and Texas. They found the problems confronting the lower courts to be as varied as the courts themselves, but four are particularly important: inadequate financing, inadequate facilities, lax procedures, and unbalanced caseloads (Ashman 1975).

Inadequate Financing

Generally, lower courts are funded locally. Sparsely populated counties and small municipalities often lack funds to staff and equip their courts adequately. Even when funds are available, there is no guarantee that local governments will spend money on the lower courts. In many cities, these courts are expected to produce revenue for local governments. Indeed, some court officials have come to realize that monitoring financial reports on a regular basis, coupled with a systematic collection program, can net considerable additional revenue (Burrell 1997). Even though they may generate a fairly large amount of income by assessing fines and imposing court costs, the local courts have no control over how these funds are spent. Indeed, some lower courts generate revenues five times greater than their operating expenses, yet they still lack adequate courtrooms and other facilities (Ashman 1975). The remainder of the funds go to pay for city services.

Inadequate Facilities

Lower court courtrooms are often crowded and noisy, with 100 or more people forced to spend hours waiting for their minute before the judge. Some are makeshift, hastily created in the side of a store or the back of a garage. Such courtroom conditions lack dignity and leave a bad impression, suggesting that the judiciary is more interested in collecting the fine for speeding than in bothering to do justice. Such inadequate facilities are detrimental to the attitudes of the defendant, prosecutor, judge, and all others involved in the justice process.

Lax Court Procedures

Besides singling out inadequate facilities, critics of lower courts often cite lax procedures in the day-to-day administration of these courts. Many trial courts of limited jurisdiction do not have written rules for the conduct of cases. Conventional bookkeeping methods are often ignored. How much fine money was collected and how it was spent is often impossible to determine. You can find some information in the city budget but not the court records; this frustrates any attempts to assess the effectiveness of these courts.

Unbalanced Caseloads

Many lower courts are characterized by moderate to heavy caseloads, but others appear to have little to do. Because of unbalanced caseloads, some courts have huge backlogs for which they are unequipped. But because these courts are locally controlled, there is no way to equalize the workload.

Unbalanced caseloads are the clearest indication that any generalizations about the problems of the lower courts must be coupled with the observation that the nation's lowest tribunals are tremendously varied. From state to state, between one county and its neighboring county, and even within a city, wide discrepancies exist in the quality of justice rendered. There is no easy way to determine what is wrong (or even what is right) about these courts. Because of the wide disparity, it is best to examine rural justice of the peace courts separately from urban municipal courts. Although they share many problems, they are also sufficiently different to warrant separate treatment.

■ RURAL JUSTICE

More than 60 million Americans get their justice off the main road. Although the United States is increasingly a nation where most people live in big cities and surrounding suburbs, roughly 25 percent of the population still live and work in small towns and rural areas. For them, the law is meted out in rural courthouses that are more numerous than usually imagined: Approximately 80 percent of the courts of general jurisdiction in the United States are in rural areas. These rural courthouses are often presided over by part-time judges and administered by overworked and underpaid court clerks. It is clear that there are marked differences between urban and rural criminal justice. Compared to their big-city counterparts, rural courts exhibit three special features: lower caseload, lack of resources, and greater familiarity (Bartol 1996).

Lower Caseloads

Caseloads in rural courts are lighter than those in suburban or urban courts. Moreover, in rural areas serious crimes are exceptional—less than 1 percent of all arrests in rural counties are for homicide, robbery, and rape (Thompson 1996). But this does not mean that rural citizens do not experience crime. To be sure, urban crime is roughly three times higher than rural crime, but over the last decades rural crimes have increased at the same rate as big-city crimes. And some types of crime—drunk driving and fraud, for example—are more prevalent in rural areas. In addition, in recent years the use of illegal drugs like methamphetamines has spread to rural areas (Herz 2000). Law enforcement officials also recognize that rural areas may be attractive because their settings are fairly insulated from government and citizen monitoring. Rural settings may harbor hate groups, militia, and others who bill themselves as antigovernment. In recent years, the United States has experienced a series of unrelated standoffs between law enforcement and private citizens in Ruby Ridge (1992), Waco (1993), and the Republic of Texas (1997), several of which ended with violent confrontations.

Lack of Resources

Although rural courts have lower caseloads, this does not mean that they don't face problems processing the workload. Rural courts receive less federal money and have a lower local tax base than larger counties (McDonald, Wood, and Pflug 1996). As a consequence, court facilities are often outmoded and salaries are low. Lack of resources is a particular problem in criminal cases in which defendants are indigent (Chapter 7). Because few attorneys practice law in rural areas, the defense pool is limited. These built-in limitations have been compounded in recent years by cutbacks in federal funding. Rural areas have been hardest hit by drastic reductions in publicly funded legal services to the poor, resulting in ever less access to justice for nonurban residents.

Familiarity

Justice in rural areas involves fewer agencies and also fewer personnel than in urban or suburban systems. Whereas big-city courts are characterized by the interface of numerous bureaucracies, in rural areas contacts are invariably one-on-one (Weisheit, Wells, and Falcone 1995). The active bar consists of a dozen or fewer members, including the prosecutor, the judge, and the lawyer who represents the local government. Often, there are five or fewer sheriff's deputies and a single probation officer, each of whom is known to the judge. The clerk's office typically consists of two or three long-term employees. In short, "fewer than 30 people routinely work together, a group about the size of a small family reunion" (Fahnestock 1991, 14).

Not only is the number of actors in rural courts small, but their interactions are frequent and long-term. By and large, justice is administered by those who grew up in the community, and they are bound together by long-standing social and family networks. As a result, rural courts place greater emphasis on informal mechanisms of social control, whereas urban courts are more legalistic and formal (Weisheit, Wells, and Falcone 1995).

Assessing Rural Justice

The most commonly mentioned aspect of rural justice is comity. Generally, it speaks of a friendly social atmosphere and group harmony. But in this context, it also can mean "You scratch my back, and I'll scratch yours." It's not always a conscious thing. The judge and the prosecutor are friends. Sometimes they're related. Thus, some point to a lack of an independent judiciary and a weak adversary process in many parts of rural America. The danger is that community knowledge is substituted for the Constitution. Some specific type of injustices include capricious arrests, unduly high bonds, rubber-stamping prosecutorial decisions, and pressuring defendants into pleading guilty (Sitomer 1985).

To Albert Barney, longtime chief justice of Vermont's Supreme Court, local mores and loyalty tend to work against an effective justice system in small towns. In Barney's words, "It's all in the name of protecting the community" (Sitomer 1985). Consequently, the process is sometimes more convenient than constitutional, more community-oriented than concerned with individual rights. In many places, lack of funds, lack of expertise, inadequate knowledge about proper procedures, and even unfamiliarity with constitutional mandates have often resulted in an uneven, unequal, unresponsive judicial process. Defendants who are not part of the community (either socially or geographically) may be at a disadvantage. According to the Rural Justice Center, "What they want to do is preserve the peace and traditional community values" at the expense of minorities, the poor, and those considered "outsiders" (Sitomer 1985).

Citizens of small towns and rural areas beg to differ with their often urban-based critics. They are fearful of trying to impose urban solutions on rural problems. In the context of rural America, discussions of court reform typically center on the justice of the peace.

JUSTICE OF THE PEACE COURTS

In rural areas, the lower courts are collectively called **justice of the peace** courts. The office-holder is usually referred to simply as a **JP.** This system of local justice traces its origins to fourteenth-century England, when towns were small and isolated. The JP system developed as a way to dispense simple and speedy justice for minor civil and criminal cases. The emphasis was decidedly on the ability of local landowners, who served as part-time JPs, to decide disputes on the basis of their knowledge of the local community.

The small-town flavor of the JP system persists today. By and large, present-day JPs are part-time nonlawyers who conduct court at their regular place of business—the back of the undertaker's parlor, the front counter of the general store, or next to the grease rack in the garage. The nation has more than 15,000 JPs, most of whom are locally elected officials serving short terms. Some serve *ex officio*—many small-town mayors also serve as judges in city court. Although a few earn a comfortable income from the job, the salaries are low for the most part. Moreover, support personnel are often limited. In the smaller courts, the JP's spouse may serve as clerk, but many courts have no clerk at all.

Critics argue that the JP system has outlived its purpose. It may have met the needs of the small, isolated towns of a century ago, but it is out of step with the modern era. Some lower courts administer fair and evenhanded justice, but all too many do not. Critics doubt whether the current diversified and fragmented JP system can ever deliver fair, impartial, and evenhanded justice. Efforts at improving the quality of justice dispensed by the rural lower courts focus on abolishing the JP courts and upgrading the quality of the personnel.

Abolition of the JP System

The ultimate goal of judicial reformers is to abolish the JP system altogether. A major defect is that JP courts are not part of the state judiciary; they are controlled only by the local government bodies that create them and fund them. Only recently have judicial conduct commissions (see Chapter 8) been granted the authority to discipline or remove local judges who abuse their office.

Nor are the activities of the lower courts subject to appellate scrutiny. Rarely are trial courts of limited jurisdiction courts of record; no stenographic record is kept of the witnesses' testimony or the judges' rulings. When a defendant appeals, the appeal is heard by a trial court of general jurisdiction. This court must conduct an entirely new trial, taking the testimony of the same witnesses and hearing the same attorneys' arguments as the lower court did. This is called a *trial de novo.* By far the major weakness of the trial de novo system is that it insulates the lower court from scrutiny. No opportunity exists for higher courts

A DAY IN COURT

(Traffic) Crime and Punishment

 Guy tries to prove that the '97 sticker on his license plate belongs there and was not, say, lifted from some other car. Here's a registration, he says.

"Sir," O'Flaherty says, "I'm reading it. It says it expires 10/31/96. I can't do a lot of things, but I can read." Same guy produces another registration card. It's for a '98 sticker. Zero for 2. "Any other paper you'd like to show me?" O'Flaherty says.

"No, sir," the guy says. "That's all I have."

Can't blame a guy for trying.

"Guilty."

How can you not laugh? "My job is not to laugh," O'Flaherty says back in his chambers. And he doesn't, at least not while sitting on the bench, listening with a blank face, exuding courtesy, giving the Traffic Court defendants every chance to explain, buying a fair number of their stories, but not most.

O'Flaherty, 50, . . . [has] been a General District Court judge in Fairfax County for nearly seven years, a job that requires him to spend every other month hearing the traffic cases that fill at least four courtrooms at the judicial center in Fairfax City every workday.

His domain this day is Courtroom 1B, a modern, windowless arena that takes on the aura of church during Traffic Court, because the alleged sinners are arrayed in rows of long pews, awaiting redemption or punishment. The accusers, the cops, sit in the first two rows, clutching paperwork from the days and nights in dispute. . . .

It would seem to be one of life's more satisfying, well-positioned jobs. Unlike the rest of us, who can't do a thing about the macho cases and airheads who infest our roadways, O'Flaherty controls the fate of hundreds of alleged miscreants, the ones who've opted not to prepay a ticket but to try to find mercy, the ones charged with DUI, the ones charged with driving without a valid license. There being no jury in Traffic Court, O'Flaherty is the trier of fact and deliverer of sentence. You can nail those puppies, right, judge? "I can't feel like I'm a vigilante," O'Flaherty says. "My job is to sit there as detached as possible."

Most of the [traffic offenses are] being committed by basically good people who have screwed up with their cars. "There are too few roads and too many cars around here, and under the right circumstances, they boil over," O'Flaherty says. . . .

Because most violators aren't career maniacs, O'Flaherty doesn't speechify or condemn to Hell. Many defendants are harder on themselves than he is. Most have never been to court, and their nervousness is tangible. If the defendant is contrite, made a simple mistake, or was just absentminded, the punishment isn't much, because merely being there is enough to make most think twice down the road, literally.

At one point, a defendant apologizes for causing an accident. "I've seen only a few people in my life deliberately run into someone," O'Flaherty replies. "The rest is just a mistake." He makes two exceptions. If you've driven really fast—more than 90 mph—he'll make you miserable. As an assistant commonwealth's attorney, he went to accident scenes in which sheets covered bodies. What worries him is that the mass of traffic is moving ever faster, so the really aggressive have to move faster still, to be able to do what they do best: bob and weave. O'Flaherty will make you spend a night in jail for every mile per hour above 90 you go.

Lying is the other exception. If he thinks you're making it up as you go, you're toast. Better to promptly plead guilty than try to shovel.

"I love this job," he says. Of course, he does have to drive to and from it.

SOURCE: Steve Twomey, "(Traffic) Crime and Punishment," *Washington Post*, 9 June 1997. Reprinted by permission of the Washington Post Writer's Group.

---

to correct errors in court procedure, the denial of defendants' constitutional rights, or erroneous interpretations of criminal law (Bing and Rosenfeld 1974).

Some reformers would unify state courts into a three-tier system, consisting of a single trial court, an intermediate appellate court, and a supreme court (see Chapter 4). This reform would abolish the justice of the peace, require all judges to be lawyers, and eliminate the trial de novo system. Reformers have had only limited success in their efforts to abolish the JP system. One major obstacle is the powerful influence of nonlawyer judges, who do not want their jobs abolished. Another is some people's belief that JPs are easily accessible, whereas more formal courts are miles away. For example, JPs are readily available to sign arrest warrants for the police or to try a motorist accused of driving too fast. Supporters of the current system contend that a knowledge of the local community better prepares JPs to solve minor disputes than does a law degree, mainly because few minor disputes involve any complex legal issues. Thus, JP courts are often viewed as people's courts, forums where people without much money can go to resolve their problems without the necessity of having a lawyer.

Upgrading the Quality of the Personnel

The low pay and equally low status of the JP have not attracted highly qualified personnel. One survey found that only 5 percent of the JPs in Virginia were college graduates. Another showed that between a third and a half of California's lower court judges were not even high school graduates (Ashman and Chapin 1976). Perhaps most shocking of all, the assistant attorney general of Mississippi estimated that "33 percent of the justices of the peace are limited in educational background to the extent that they are not capable of learning the necessary elements of law" (North v. Russell 1976).

High on the judicial reformers' list of priorities is upgrading the quality of lower court judges. Some states have instituted training programs for lay judges, but only a few of the judges have yet received any training in basic legal concepts or the duties and responsibilities of the office. But to many reformers the ultimate goal remains the elimination of nonlawyer judges (see Case Close-Up: North v. Russell and Nonlawyer Judges).

▌ MUNICIPAL COURTS

The urban counterparts of the justice of the peace courts are **municipal courts.** Decades ago, the increasing volume of cases in the big

cities overwhelmed the ability of the rurally conceived JP system to dispense justice. The forerunner of the municipal court was the police magistrate, who had strong ties to local police departments. Municipal courts were also shaped by political machines, which viewed the lower courts as opportunities for patronage. Party bosses controlled the selection of judges. Similarly, the positions of bailiff and clerk were reserved for the party faithful. It is not surprising that municipal courts were often tainted by corruption. Charges would be dropped, or files would mysteriously disappear, in return for political favors or cash. No wonder the judicial reformers of the 1920s and 1930s sought to clean up the courts by removing them from politics (see Chapter 4).

The Assembly Line

"The Sausage Factories" (1974) was the title of a *Time* article on municipal courts. "Hurricanes of Humanity" was the term used by the American Judicature Society in the first national survey of the lower courts. Both phrases draw our attention to the overriding reality of municipal courts in the nation's big cities: the press of cases (Ashman 1975). The major concern is moving cases; any "obstacles" to speedy disposition—constitutional rights, lawyers, trials—are neutralized. In a process some have labeled an assembly line, shortcuts are routinely taken to keep the docket moving. Thus, the municipal courts more closely resemble a bureaucracy geared to mass processing of cases than an adjudicative body providing consideration for each case.

The emphasis on moving cases begins when the defendant is arraigned. Instead of addressing defendants individually—a time-consuming process—municipal court judges often open court by advising defendants of their constitutional rights as a group. Notification of rights is treated by the court as a clerical detail to be dispensed with before the taking of guilty pleas can begin (Mileski 1971).

Defense attorneys constitute another potential obstacle to the speedy disposition of cases. Although defendants have a theoretical right to be represented by an attorney, in practice the presence of an attorney in the lower

CASE CLOSE-UP

North v. Russell and Nonlawyer Judges

 Judge C. B. Russell made a number of legal errors in the Lynch City Police Court the night he sentenced Lonnie North to jail for drunk driving. Judge Russell refused the defendant's request for a jury trial, did not inform him of his right to a court-appointed lawyer, and failed to advise him of his right to an appeal. Perhaps most glaring of all, Judge Russell listened only to the arresting officer's story and did not allow the defendant to tell his version of events.

The facts of *North v. Russell* (1976) highlight the long-standing issue confronting the American judiciary: Should lower court judges be attorneys? Although judges in the major trial and appellate courts are required to be lawyers, many states impose no such requirement for lower court judges. Nonlawyer judges are more numerous than is usually realized (Bronstein 1981). A disproportionate number of these part-time, nonlawyer judges are located in New York and Texas (Alfini and Passuth 1981).

The U.S. Supreme Court considered the question of nonlawyer judges in *North v. Russell*. Chief Justice Warren Burger's majority opinion argued that nonlawyer judges do not violate the due process clause of the Fourteenth Amendment, nor do they deny equal protection. He described the JP system as courts of convenience for citizens in small towns and spoke favorably of the fact that "the inferior courts are simple and speedy." Burger argued that any defects in the proceedings (which were numerous in this case) could be corrected by the availability of defense attorneys, the right to a jury trial, and a trial de novo. Significantly, though, these were the specific legal matters that Judge Russell failed to inform defendant North about.

In a dissenting opinion, Justice Potter Stewart stated the case for requiring judges to be lawyers. He found it constitutionally intolerable that nonlawyer judges can sentence defendants to jail. He further noted that a defendant's right to a lawyer is eroded if the judge is not capable of understanding a lawyer's argument on the law. Indeed, a later study found that lay judges in New York tended to be slightly more favorable toward police officers and prosecutors than were legally trained officials (Ryan and Guterman 1977).

States are beginning to eliminate nonlawyer judges. The California Supreme Court has ruled that the nonlawyer magistrate violates the state's constitution. Moreover, when states adopt court reorganization, they invariably abolish the nonlawyer JP, although incumbents typically are retained.

Does the elimination of nonlawyer judges alter the decisions reached? After Iowa amended its constitution to require legally trained lower court judges, small claims proceedings became more formal, which frightened away the individual civil plaintiffs. Moreover, decisions in small claims increasingly benefited the merchants (Green, Russell, and Schmidhauser 1975). A handful of other studies, however, have found few, if any, differences between the behavior of lay and lawyer judges (Provine 1981). A survey in New York concluded that nonlawyer judges are as competent as lawyer judges in carrying out judicial duties in courts of limited jurisdiction (Provine 1986).

James Dignan, Arnold Wynne, "A Microcosm of the Local Community?"

courts is rare (Mileski 1971). This is partly because of the minor nature of most municipal court cases; some defendants believe the charge is too minor to justify the expense of hiring a lawyer (Bing and Rosenfeld 1974). The general absence of defense attorneys reinforces the informality of the lower courts and the lack of attention to legal rules and procedures.

What of those too poor to hire a lawyer? In *Argersinger v. Hamlin* (1972), the Supreme Court ruled that "absent a knowing and intelligent waiver, no person may be imprisoned for any offense, whether classified as petty, misdemeanor, or felony unless he was represented by counsel." Thus, an indigent defendant may be fined without having a lawyer, but a judge considering imposing a jail term must give the impoverished defendant the opportunity to have a court-appointed counsel at state expense. Compliance, however, has generally been token in nature, meaning that the legal right to counsel in lower courts remains "an empty right for many defendants" (Krantz et al. 1976). (See Exhibit 18-3 for key developments in the law concerning the lower courts.)

In municipal courts, the defendant's initial appearance is usually the final one. Most people charged with a traffic violation or minor misdemeanor plead guilty immediately. The quick plea represents the fatalistic view of most defendants: "I did it—let's get it over with." Realistically, a defendant charged with such crimes as public drunkenness and disorderly conduct probably cannot raise a valid legal defense. What has struck all observers of the lower courts is the speed with which the pleas are processed:

> The Court generally disposes of between 50 and 100 cases per day, but on any Monday there are 200 to 250 and on Monday mornings after holiday weekends the Court may handle as many as 350 cases. I would estimate that, on the average, cases take between 45 seconds and one minute to dispose of. (Wiseman 1976, 235)

Other studies likewise report that the median time to accept a defendant's plea and impose sentence is less than a minute (Mileski 1971).

Few trials are held in the lower courts. A defendant has a right to a jury trial only if the offense can be punished by imprisonment for more than six months (*Baldwin v. New York* 1970). The absence of attorneys and the minor nature of the offenses combine to make requests for jury trials rare. If there is a trial, it is a bench trial often conducted in an informal manner.

The Courtroom Work Group

It is no accident that most defendants waive their rights to counsel and trial before quickly entering a plea of guilty. The courtroom work group tries to encourage such behavior by controlling the flow of defendants. Some courts manipulate bail to pressure defendants into an immediate disposition. During arraignment, each defendant is informed of the right to a full hearing with a court-appointed attorney. But the hearing cannot be held for two or three weeks, which the defendant will have to spend in jail (Wice 1974). Not surprisingly, the majority of defendants choose to waive their right to counsel in favor of a speedy disposition.

Above all, the routines of the lower courts may be threatened by uncooperative defendants. Judges and prosecutors dislike defendants who "talk too much." Those accused who unreasonably take up too much of the court's time can expect sanctions. Consider the case of a young middle-class white man who made a detailed inquiry into his rights and then gave a relatively lengthy account (roughly two minutes) of his alleged offense of vagrancy. Although the defendant was polite, the judge interrupted him with "That will be all, Mr. Jones" and ordered him to jail. Other defendants who "talked too much" received sentences that were longer than normal (Mileski 1971).

Sentencing

In a sense, municipal courts are not trial courts, because few defendants contest their guilt. In actuality, they are a sentencing institution. The courtroom encounter is geared to making rapid decisions about which sentence to impose. The punishments imposed by lower court judges include many of those found in the major trial courts—fines, probation, and jail. In the misdemeanor courts, however, judges can choose alternative sanctions, including community service, victim restitution, placement in substance abuse treatment programs, mandatory counseling, and required attendance in education programs (driver clinics, for example) (Meyer and Jesilow 1997). Despite the diversity of potential sanctions, fines play a predominant role. Few misdemeanor defendants are sentenced to jail. Instead, approximately two-thirds of all defendants pay a fine of some amount (Ragona and Ryan 1983).

The sentencing process in the lower courts involves elements of both routinization and individualization. Lower court judges define their role as "doing justice"; rather than merely being bound by rules of law, judges use their discretion to achieve what they believe to be a fair and just result (Meyer and Jesilow 1997). In attempting to achieve justice, lower court judges use readily identifiable characteristics

Exhibit **18-3**		Key Developments Concerning the Lower Courts
Tumey v. Ohio	1927	Paying a justice of the peace a fee only if the defendant is found guilty denies a defendant the right to trial before an impartial judge.
Baldwin v. New York	1970	Defendants have a constitutional right to a trial by jury only if the offense is punishable by imprisonment for more than six months.
Tate v. Short	1971	Defendants may not be jailed because they are unable to pay a fine.
Argersinger v. Hamlin	1972	Misdemeanor defendants sentenced to jail have a right to counsel.
North v. Russell	1976	Nonlawyer judges do not violate the rights to due process or equal protection of the U.S. Constitution.

to sort defendants into categories. In the lower courts, sentencing involves a process of quickly determining group averages. The result is a high degree of uniformity; by and large, a defendant gets the same sentence as all others in the same category. To the casual observer, the process appears to be an assembly line, but sentences can also be fitted to the specific defendant. During plea negotiations, there is some individual attention to cases. Despite sentencing consistencies, exceptions are made (Ragona and Ryan 1983). The most important factors in both the routinization and the individualization of sentencing in the lower courts are the nature of the event and the defendant's criminal record.

How defendants are pigeonholed according to their offense emerges in a four-city study (Ragona and Ryan 1983). Drunk driving and traffic cases nearly always resulted in a fine, sometimes combined with a short jail term or probation. By contrast, theft and other miscellaneous criminal offenses resulted much less often in a fine; more commonly, these defendants were sentenced to jail or placed on probation. The basis for a decision not to fine in minor criminal cases may be either that such crimes are too serious to be treated merely with a fine—and that the offenders are in need of ongoing counseling or supervision—or the practical realization that many defendants cannot afford to pay a fine, or some combination of the two.

A key factor in sentencing is the defendant's prior criminal record. First offenders rarely receive a jail term. Indeed, for petty offenses, first offenders may be released without any penalty whatsoever. Repeaters are given more severe

sanctions. For example, the jailing of defendants for public intoxication increases strikingly as prior arrests become more numerous and more recent. The importance of a prior criminal record in sentencing partially explains an otherwise unaccountable pattern: Serious misdemeanants are fined, while minor misdemeanants are jailed. The explanation is that few of the serious misdemeanor defendants had prior records, whereas more of the minor misdemeanor defendants did (Mileski 1971).

A study of drunk driving dispositions in Sacramento, California, highlights the importance of prior record and the nature of the event (Kingsnorth, Barnes, and Coonley 1990). For defendants with no prior convictions, the likelihood of a charge reduction to reckless driving increased three to four times. Similarly, the probability of receiving a jail sentence increased dramatically for those with a prior record. The nature of the event (measured by the level of blood alcohol) also played a role. A low level of blood alcohol was of primary importance in the decision to reduce charges from drunk driving to reckless driving. Similarly, defendants with a high level of alcohol in their systems (.25 and over) were much more likely not only to receive jail but also a lengthy jail term. These two factors, of course, operate together. Defendants with no priors and low levels of blood alcohol fared much better than those with prior convictions and high levels of alcohol in their system. Studies like this one, however, rarely enter the public discourse. (See Courts, Controversy, and Reducing Crime: Should Drunk Driving Prosecutions Be Increased?)

Should Drunk Driving Prosecutions Be Increased?

"Drunk Driver Kills Mother of Two"
"Motorist Arrested for Fifth Drunk Driving Offense"

Headlines like these have become all too familiar to readers of the local papers. In a recent year, more than 17,000 persons were killed in alcohol-related automobile accidents (40 percent of all traffic fatalities). Moreover, the police make more arrests—more than 1.5 million annually—for drunk driving than for any other crime. Public concern over drunk driving has focused attention on the otherwise virtually invisible activities of the nation's lowest (and often forgotten) courts.

Depending on the state, drunk driving is termed driving under the influence (DUI) or driving while intoxicated (DWI). Drinking and driving has been a problem since the invention of the automobile but did not gain recognition as a prominent social concern until the early 1980s (Applegate et al. 1996). The group most responsible for focusing public attention on drunk driving is Mothers Against Drunk Driving (MADD). MADD is not neo-Prohibitionist, recognizing that trying to eliminate alcohol would hamper the organization's ability to recruit members. Rather, MADD is victim-oriented, with many leaders having themselves experienced a family death due to drunk driving. They are closely related to the victims' rights movement (see Chapter 9).

Today, MADD has more than 600 chapters and community action teams nationwide. Their efforts include victim services; a hotline provides emotional support and guidance to bereaved families and injured victims of drunk driving. But publicly they are recognized as the leading proponents of increasing the criminal penalties for drunk driving (Jacobs 1989; Reinarman 1988).

Getting Tough with Drunk Drivers

In the last two decades, legislatures—under considerable pressure from MADD and other groups like it—have passed a variety of "get tough with drunk drivers" laws, including

- Increasing the drinking age to 21
- Lowering from .15 to .08 the blood alcohol content (BAC) level at which a person is presumed legally intoxicated
- Increasing jail penalties for DWI, particularly for repeat offenders

But somehow the get-tough laws recently passed never seem to be harsh enough, so in subsequent years legislatures are called upon to crack down even harder on drunk drivers. New legislative agendas are crucial for organizations like MADD because they need to constantly motivate their constituents lest the organization lose momentum and also lose members (Jacobs 1989). Among the new sanctions currently mentioned are

- Confiscation of the automobile for repeat offenders
- Mandatory minimum prison sentence for persons convicted of vehicular homicide while intoxicated

Societal Ambivalence toward Drinking and Driving

To sociologist Joseph Gusfield, groups like MADD engage in symbolic politics, portraying drunk drivers as villains. The difficulty with this approach is that DWI arrestees reflect a range of social backgrounds, including ordinary citizens and at times even prominent members of the community. Moreover, the range of behavior varies greatly from a person barely at .08 and

Is the Process the Punishment?

Some researchers have challenged the image of the lower courts as assembly-line operations. To some, the standard picture of lower courts as wholesale, mechanical processors of a high volume of cases is only partially correct. The operations of the misdemeanor courts are not as chaotic, or disordered, as they may first appear (Silbey 1981). A second

having caused no accident to those measuring near .30 (comatose for most people) who have killed several people.

The absence of criminal stereotypes is compounded by the pervasive role of alcoholic beverages in American social and economic life. As a result, there is considerable societal ambivalence toward drinking and driving (Homel 1988). Society is quick to condemn drunk drivers involved in serious accidents, but those who drive after a few drinks often evoke the attitude of "There but for the grace of God go I" (Gusfield 1981).

Adjudicating Drunk Driving Cases

The contradictions in societal attitudes toward drinking and driving (which is different from drunk driving) explain why the enforcement of drunk driving laws is riddled with loopholes. These contradictions help us understand why actual enforcement of drunk driving laws blunts the cutting edge of the harsh penalties. Law on the books treats driving and drinking as a serious problem, but law in action (the activities of police, prosecutors, judges, juries, and defense attorneys) sees drunk driving not as a criminal offense but a traffic violation. The end product is not a series of absolutes propounded by MADD but a negotiated reality (Homel 1988).With the imposition of tougher laws:

■ Police do not necessarily make more arrests. Faced with serious crime problems, big-city police forces assign higher priority to violent offenders than to drunk drivers (Mastrofski and Ritti 1996).

■ Prosecutors are pressured to plea-bargain. Given that local jails are already overcrowded and most defendants are not as villainous as public images suggest, pleas to lesser charges such as reckless driving are often arranged.

■ Juries are reluctant to convict. As discussed in Chapter 14, if jurors think the penalty is too harsh for the crime, they are less likely to convict.

■ As more people go to jail, for longer, following DUI convictions, the prisons become overcrowded, which necessitates shortening actual sentences (Vermont Center for Justice Research 1995).

■ Those who lose their license may continue to drive, and those previously convicted may continue to drive drunk. Indeed, one survey found that more than half the persons in local jails charged with DWI had prior sentences for DWI offenses (Cohen 1992).

Overall, studies of drunk driving laws tend to be skeptical of a deterrent effect of get-tough legislation. Typically, new, tougher laws are ushered in with announcements of a major crackdown followed by increased arrests for DWI. But over time, levels of drinking and driving return to previous levels as the perceived certainty of punishment declines with experience (Homel 1988; Ross 1992). Finally, increasing the penalty for DWI makes it more likely that the defendant will fight the charge, resulting in longer delays and fewer convictions; in the long run, DWI laws become even harder to enforce.

What do you think? Should there be tougher punishments for drunk driving, or are current punishment levels about right? Should more efforts be made to arrest and prosecute drunk drivers, or is the current level of effort about right? Overall, how do punishment and enforcement levels of drunk driving compare to other social problems like domestic violence and drug abuse?

To continue the debate, go to
Mothers Against Drunk Driving:
http://www.madd.org

The American Beverage Institute:
http://www.abionline.org

The National Commission Against Drunk Driving:
http://www.ncadd.com

The National College for DUI Defense, Inc.:
http://www.ncdd.com

consideration is that the lower courts do try to provide justice, but they do so by responding to problems rather than crimes, concentrating their efforts on producing substantive justice rather than focusing on purely formal (due process) justice. Separate studies in New Haven, Connecticut (Feeley 1979) and Columbus, Ohio (Ryan 1980–1981) have assessed the disparate functions served by the lower courts.

To Malcolm Feeley, *the process is the punishment*. This finding is based on several years of studying the lower court in New Haven first-hand. The main punishment of defendants occurs during the processing of cases, not after a finding of guilt. Feeley contends that the pretrial process imposes a series of punishments ("price tags") on the accused. These price tags often include staying in jail (briefly), paying a bail agent, and losing time and perhaps wages because of repeated court appearances. These costs far outweigh any punishment imposed after the defendant pleads guilty. These price tags also affect the roughly 40 percent of the defendants eventually found not guilty. In short, the pretrial process itself is the primary punishment, according to Feeley.

To John Paul Ryan, *the outcome is the punishment*. This contrasting finding is based on statistical analysis of actual court sentences in Columbus, Ohio. Unlike those in New Haven, lower court judges in Columbus routinely impose fines on convicted defendants. Often these fines are substantial. Further, 35 percent of the guilty in Columbus are sentenced to jail—six times as many as in New Haven. Finally, defendants in traffic cases often have their driver's licenses suspended and/or are ordered to attend drunk driver schools. In short, Columbus defendants are more likely to be fined, to pay heavier fines, to go to jail, and to be required to participate in some sort of treatment program than their counterparts in New Haven.

These sharply contrasting conclusions about New Haven and Columbus accentuate the point made earlier in the chapter: Misdemeanor courts are very diverse in their operations and procedures. In short, any assessment of the activities of the lower courts requires an awareness of their diversity.

COURT–COMMUNITY COLLABORATION

Lower courts have dwindled substantially in number and importance since 1960. Court reform efforts have consolidated the diverse minor courts into more centralized units. In the process, most of the justice of the peace and magistrate courts have been eliminated.

These reforms have had unintended consequences. Court activities have been consolidated and streamlined for good reasons, but in the process, some of the qualities of locally dispensed justice have been lost. Today there is a concerned effort to reestablish court–community cooperation (Efkeman and Rottman 1996–1997).

The central target of these community justice efforts is minor disputes between parties in ongoing relationships (domestic partners, neighbors, consumers–merchants, landlords–tenants, employees–employers). Examples include unruly children who annoy neighbors, dogs who defecate on the wrong lawns, owners who neglect their property, and acquaintances who dispute small debts. It is not clear what role the criminal justice system can play in resolving such private disputes. Yet private disagreements between friends, neighbors, or significant others are the steady diet of the police and the lower courts. A trial would only obscure the underlying issues because the problem is either irrelevant or immaterial to the legal action. In such interpersonal disputes, the person who files a complaint may be as "guilty" as the defendant. Many of these private disputes are essentially civil matters, yet criminal justice agencies must deal with them to head off the commission of a more serious crime—murder or battery, for example. In addressing problems such as these, mediation programs seek solutions not in terms of a formal finding by a judge but through compromise and bargaining. The goal is to seek long-term solutions in hopes the disputants will not return.

Efforts at court–community collaboration are but one example of a broader movement termed **alternative dispute resolution (ADR),** which seeks to settle disputes by less adversarial means than traditional legal processes. Many ADR programs function as alternatives to going to court. Others involve efforts to settle court cases after they have been filed but before they are tried by a judge. ADR efforts most often focus on civil matters, but nonserious criminal matters may also be included.

Alternatives to the formal judicial processes, of course, are hardly new. Juvenile courts, small claims courts, and family courts are a few examples of long-standing activities that were established because it was felt they would be more effective than traditional court operations. Today, drug courts and community courts have joined the list (see Chapter 4). In recent years, however, there has been a new wave of concern about court congestion and cost, and a new set of alternatives has appeared in response.

Beyond a core concern over essentially minor private disputes, however, community justice programs are diverse in goals and orientations. Some programs, for example, are motivated by concerns that the formal procedures of the lower courts discourage individuals from taking their disputes to these institutions. Thus, community dispute settlement centers stress increasing the accessibility of justice to individuals. By contrast, criminal justice officials are often concerned with making the justice system more efficient by reducing caseloads. In essence, the first envisions more cases, whereas the second wants fewer.

Community justice approaches are diverse and ongoing. We will examine two broad types: community dispute settlement centers (which operate outside of the judicial system) and community courts (which operate within the judicial system).

Community Dispute Settlement Centers

Community dispute settlement centers provide mediation programs for a range of minor civil and criminal matters in nonjudicial settings. These programs go by a variety of names, including citizen dispute resolution programs and community mediation. They were in the vanguard of the ADR movement, serving a catalytic role in rethinking the court-dominated model of dispute resolution.

Community-oriented mediation programs rest on the philosophy that the winner-takes-all approach of adjudication is poorly suited to resolving many minor disputes typically brought to court. Although minor compared to felonies and major civil litigation, these matters are nonetheless major events in the daily lives of the disputants.

Community mediation programs are typically sponsored by private organizations and receive the bulk of their cases from walk-ins or referrals from other community-based organizations. These programs are not particularly concerned with reducing the caseload of courts but instead place a heavy emphasis on providing a more sensible means of settling disputes. They are motivated by the notion that they can offer a dispute resolution process that is superior to the one provided in courts with their stress on legal rights. They place less emphasis on any efficiency advantages to the court (McGillis 1997).

Perhaps the best-known example of the community mediation approach is the San Francisco Community Boards Program, which is extensively probed in a book edited by Sally Engle Merry and Neal Milner (1993). The book's title, *The Possibility of Popular Justice*, highlights the philosophy of the founding director, Raymond Shonholtz, who defined the underlying problem as alienation and based the solution on empowerment. The principal task, therefore, was transforming society by bringing people together. The long-term goal was "not so much the settlement of disagreements, but the long-term rebuilding of community capacities" (Adler, Lovass, and Milner 1988, 321). Popular justice was to be found among the people, not in the corridors of government buildings. In essence, the San Francisco program was created in opposition to the formal legal system, and therefore often faced problems of attracting enough cases to keep itself in operation.

A more recent effort is the Dispute Settlement Center of Durham, North Carolina. Originally the program accepted only minor criminal cases referred by the local court but later greatly expanded to include numerous other services such as family and divorce mediation, school conflict resolution programs, and corporate workplace training. It has also recently added court-referred mediation cases involving juveniles (McGillis 1998). Unlike the San Francisco program, the one in Durham tries to work actively with government officials.

Community Courts

Courts across the nation are searching for ways to reach out in order to be more responsive to the needs of specific communities within their geographical jurisdiction. The phrase "justice community" refers to the range of organizations and people within any specific locale who have a stake in the justice system. It includes judges, court personnel, district attorneys, public defenders, private attorneys, probation departments, law enforcement personnel, community organizers, business groups, and others (Borys, Banks, and Parker 1999).

Often these outreach efforts lead to an emphasis on mediation of minor disputes. There are important organizational differences, though, between court-based mediation and community mediation programs. For one, they are government-sponsored (either court or prosecutor); as a result, these programs receive the bulk of their cases as referrals from criminal justice agencies (something community programs object to). A second difference centers on goals: The dominant goal is to improve the justice system by removing minor cases from the court. In their view, cases such as simple assault, petty theft, and criminal trespass are prime candidates for mediation and not formal processing in the lower courts.

Initially, what today are called community courts were termed criminal justice–based mediation programs, also known as multidoor courthouses or neighborhood justice centers (Adler, Lovass, and Milner 1988). Many of these dispute resolution programs began with a primary emphasis on misdemeanor criminal cases and later added civil matters from the local small claims court and other sources. In a sense, they convert criminal matters to civil ones by treating the cases as matters for discussion between the individual disputants and not for processing between the state and the defendant.

The best-known community court in the nation is the Midtown Community Court in New York City. The Midtown experience was born of a profound frustration with quality-of-life crime in the neighborhood, particularly prostitution, vandalism, and low-level drug offenses. Offenders are sentenced to make restitution to the community through work projects in the neighborhood: removing graffiti, cleaning subway stations, and sorting cans and bottles for recycling. But at the same time the court attempts to link offenders with drug treatment, health care, education, and other social services. Perhaps one of the most distinctive features is that the courthouse includes an entire floor of office space for social workers to assist offenders referred by the judge in the courtroom a few floors below (Feinblatt and Berman 1997). Thus, instead of sending an offender to a distant bureaucracy, the courthouse now incorporates helping institutions within its midst. The Midtown Community Court is serving as a prototype for other jurisdictions as well (Goldkamp, Weiland, and Irons-Guynn 2001; Clear and Cadora 2003).

■ CONCLUSION

North v. Russell is a reminder that one out of four Americans get their justice off the main road. Here they often find that justice is dispensed by part-time, nonlawyer justices of the peace who may or may not have much training in the law. Moreover, the justice officials are not only few in number but also bound by long-term social relationships. Thus, compared to their big-city brethren, citizens in rural courthouses experience justice that is convenient and informal, but critics wonder if a little more of the Constitution might better serve outsiders.

The problems of the lower courts in urban areas are fundamentally different from those of rural courts. Courthouse officials are numerous and often knowledgeable about their tasks. Moreover, although the relationships are cordial, it is obvious that the courtroom is merely a place where representatives of many bureaucracies meet to do their work. Thus, compared to their brethren in more rural settings, citizens in municipal court experience justice that is quick and in many ways certain; sentences are arrived at by applying the group average. Critics argue the process all too often resembles an assembly line geared to rapid dispositions, and the process is the punishment.

Whether lower courts are found in small towns or big cities, they share an important denominator: For most Americans, their only firsthand experience with real courtroom justice (as opposed to the courthouse justice they see on TV or read about in newspapers) will be

A Virtual Tour of American Courthouses: Lower Courts

Perhaps nowhere is the old saying "Fact is stranger than fiction" more true than on reality television. A number of these shows use the lower courts as their setting. Two of the most popular are *People's Court* (**http://peoplescourt.warnerbros.com/**) and *Judge Judy* (**http://www.judgejudy.com/home/main.asp**).

To learn more about the unique problems of rural justice, point your browser to the Small Town and Rural Crime Page maintained by Dr. Ralph Weisheit of Illinois State University: **http://www.ilstu.edu/~raweish/rural/**. A few justices of the peace maintain Web sites, including these:

Denton (Texas): **http://www.co.denton.tx.us/dept/JP6/jp6.htm**

Spring (Texas): **http://nashforjp.com/**

Swanzey (New Hampshire): **http://top.monad.net/~shamrockrlestate/**

The Massachusetts Justice of the Peace Association offers educational programs to enable justices of the peace to fulfill the duties and responsibilities of their office in a professional and efficient manner: **http://www.mjpa.org/**.

A growing number of municipal courts maintain Web sites, providing information on matters ranging from court calendars to how to pay fines:

Bernalillo County (New Mexico) Metropolitan Court: **http://www.metrocourt.state.nm.us/**

Hamilton County (Cincinnati): **http://www.hamilton-co.org/MunicipalCourt/**

Milwaukee: **http://www.ci.mil.wi.us/citygov/court/index.html**

Seattle: **http://www.ci.seattle.wa.us/courts/house.htm**

Sylvania (Ohio): **http://www.sylvaniacourt.com/**

The Austin (Texas) Municipal Court provides its schedule of fines online: **http://www.ci.austin.tx.us/court/fine_sch.htm**. The Delaware (Ohio) Municipal Court offers daily court proceedings streamed live on the Internet at **http://www.municipalcourt.org/**.

You can visit some community dispute settlement centers on the Web:

Cambridge Community Dispute Settlement Center: **http://www.cambridgedispute.org/**

Mountain Dispute Settlement Center (North Carolina): **http://www.dnet.net/mtndsc/**.

To take an Internet tour of the Midtown Community Court or other community courts around the nation, go to **http://www.communityjustice.org/**, click on Best Practices, then National Scene.

---

the brief encounter before a lower court judge. The lower courts come into contact with more citizens every year than virtually any other government institution. All too often, the average citizen comes away from such encounters with a poor impression, pondering whether the judge was really interested in justice or merely in a hurry to feed the cash register.

The cases processed by the lower courts are indeed minor and have often been referred to as petty. The legal problems of drunks and drunk drivers, vagrants and vagabonds, used to be dismissed as of no interest, something for beat cops and low-level judges to deal with, but certainly not important enough for the real criminal justice system to be concerned about.

Until recently, judicial reformers baldly suggested that these cases shouldn't even be in court. No longer. These cases are increasingly important to the public and, therefore, are now important to criminal justice officials as well. As discussed in Chapter 9, spousal abuse is the subject of serious debate, and no elected official dares dismiss these events as petty. The same holds true for drunk driving, which has catapulted to center stage in national attention. Moreover, some scholars and police officials see confronting minor crimes as an important way to reduce crime, arguing that cracking down on drunks and punks, thereby allowing good citizens to reclaim their community, will reduce major crimes.

CRITICAL THINKING QUESTIONS

1. The justice of the peace system provides quick and convenient access to the courts, but does it cheapen the notion of justice? Or are the critics off-base, seemingly suggesting that every speeding motorist deserves a high-priced lawyer to defend his or her actions?

2. To some, the shorthand used in the lower courts best achieves justice because sentences tend to be uniform. To others, relying on group averages violates a defendant's right to have his or her case considered on its own merits. What do you think?

3. Are the lower courts really courts? With few defense attorneys and even fewer trials, maybe we should label activities in lower courts as hearings, not trials. What are your views on this?

4. Each legislative session, laws are passed getting tougher with drunk drivers. How long do you think this trend will continue?

5. The municipal court studied by Meyer and Jesilow (1997) processed relatively few traditional misdemeanors—assaults and thefts, for example. Instead, much of the court's time was taken up with victimless crimes such as homeless drug addicts, drunks, careless motorists driving on suspended licenses, or streetwalkers plying their trade on busy avenues. Do these cases belong in the courts? Would society be better served by taking many of these types of cases and handling them in social institutions?

KEY TERMS

alternative dispute resolution (ADR) (436)
inferior court (lower court) (422)
justice of the peace (JP) (428)
misdemeanor (423)
municipal court (430)
ordinance (423)
small claims court (423)
traffic offenses (423)
trial courts of limited jurisdiction (422)

WORLD WIDE WEB RESOURCES AND EXERCISES

Web Guides

http://dir.yahoo.com/Society_and_Culture/Crime/
  Types_of_Crime/Drunk_Driving/
http://dir.yahoo.com/Recreation/Automotive/
  Driving/Red_Light_Running/
http://dir.yahoo.com/Recreation/Automotive/
  Driving/ Speeding/
http://dir.yahoo.com/News_and_Media/Television/
  Shows/Reality_Television/Courtroom/
http://dir.yahoo.com/Government/Law/Alternative_
  Dispute_Resolution/

Web Search Terms

municipal court
justice of the peace
drunk driving
rural crimes

neighborhood justice
  centers
community justice

Useful URLs

The National Highway Traffic and Safety Institute makes the case for lowering the BAC to .08: http://www.nhtsa.dot.gov/people/injury/alcohol/limit.08/.

Visit the Texas Municipal Courts Education Center: http://www.tmcec.com/.

The Community Justice Exchange offers information and assistance to help bring together criminal justice agencies and ordinary citizens to make communities safer: http://www.communityjustice.org/.

The National Traffic Law Center of the American Prosecutors Research Institute provides information on topics ranging from blood alcohol level to vehicular homicide: http://www.ndaa.org/apri/NTLC/Index.htm.

The Center for Court Innovation works for court reform in New York and offers challenging new ideas and technology at http://www.courtinnovation.org.

The Community Courts Forum provides practical tools and advice for creating a community court at http://www.communityjustice.org/.

Uncommon URLs

Don't Go to Municipal Court Alone is presented by the law office of Ronald P. Mondello: http://www.municipalcourt.com/.

Speedtrap.com bills itself as information for efficiency: http://www.speedtrap.com.

Trafficschool.com is a commercial site that allows local courts to sentence traffic offenders to online traffic safety school: http://www.trafficschool.com.

The Definitive Guide to Speeding Tickets offers lots of advice on how to beat speeding tickets: http://home.att.net/~speeding/.

See Businesses Against Drunk Driving: http://www.baddpage.com.

Visit the San Francisco Community Courts Initiative: http://www.ci.sf.ca.us/da/comcourts.htm.

See the National Center for State Courts, Courts and Communities: http://www.ncsc.dni.us/research/cfc.htm.

The Center for Court Innovation is a public–private partnership located in New York City that works to improve public confidence in justice: http://www.courtinnovation.org/.

Web Exercises

1. The home page for Mothers Against Drunk Driving (MADD) can be found at http://www.madd.org. Critically examine statements made by this organization. Do they document sources? Do they discuss counter-arguments? Next, under the heading "Public Policy," examine the policy objectives of MADD. In what ways are their objectives similar to the ones discussed in the text? In what ways are they different?

2. Drunk driving remains a controversial issue. Use this Yahoo guide—http://dir.yahoo.com/Society_and_Culture/Crime/Types_of_Crime/Drunk_Driving/—to find at least one organi-

zation on either side of the issue. How do the groups differ in terms of organization and membership? Do they address the same arguments or different ones?

3. A handful of lower courts have Web sites. Choose the search engine of your choice and use the search term "municipal courts." Examine two of these Web sites, first from the perspective of a layperson who is contemplating filing a small claims lawsuit. What types of helpful information does the Web site provide? What additional types of information would you find useful? Next, examine the sites from the perspective of a defendant who must go to court in response to a misdemeanor arrest or traffic ticket. Does the site provide useful information to defendants? What additional information might you suggest? Overall, do the municipal court Web pages that you examined seem more oriented toward lawyers or lay citizens?

4. Find two or more Web sites that provide legal advice to those who might be arrested for drunk driving or those who already have been. In what ways does the tone of these home pages differ from those of organizations against drunk driving? What practical advice do they provide? Overall, do these home pages suggest a high or low probability of being convicted once arrested? In what ways do these home pages try to avoid offending the dominant social culture, which views drunk driving in very negative terms?

INFOTRAC COLLEGE EDITION RESOURCES AND EXERCISES

Basic Searches

municipal courts	drunk driving
neighborhood justice centers	Mothers Against Drunk Driving
small claims courts	dispute resolution (laws)
rural crimes	traffic regulations

Recommended Articles

James J. Baxter, "The Mythology of Setting Low Speed Limits"

Julie Brienza, "ADR: Doing Two Things at Once Can Be Problematic"

Julie Brienza, "Community Courts Reach Out to Put a Dent in Petty Crime"

Cheryl J. Cherpitel, Tammy W. Tam, "Variables Associated with DUI Offender Status among Whites and Mexican Americans"

Christina Couret, "Courthouse Cameras Save Police Time"

Ralph W. Hingson, Timothy Heeren, Michael R. Winter, "Preventing Impaired Driving"

Patrick C. Jobes, "Residential Stability and Crime in Small Rural Agricultural and Recreational Towns"

"Liability Laws Effective in Reducing Harmful Alcohol-Related Behaviors"

Jeanne Mejeur, "Drunk Drivers Beware"

"Report: More Drunk Drivers Are in Correctional System"

InfoTrac College Edition Exercises

1. Using the search term "drunk driving, laws, regulations," find two or more articles that discuss drunk driving enforcement. To what extent do the articles emphasize a law-on-the-books approach as opposed to a law-in-action perspective? To what extent do the policy recommendations fall along the lines of the crime control or due process model of justice?

2. Using the search term "rural crimes," find two or more articles that discuss rural justice. To what extent are the problems in small towns similar to those in big cities? To what extent are they different, and why?

FOR FURTHER READING

Chermak, Steven, Edmund McGarrell, and Alexander Weiss. "Citizens' Perceptions of Aggressive Traffic Enforcement Strategies." *Justice Quarterly* 18 (2001): 365–391.

Clear, Todd, and Eric Cadora. *Community Justice*. Belmont, CA: Wadsworth, 2003.

Jamieson, Katherine, and Anita Neuberger Blowers. "A Structural Examination of Misdemeanor Court Disposition Patterns." *Criminology* 31 (1993): 243–262.

Katz, Charles, Vincent Webb, and David Schaefer. "An Assessment of the Impact of Quality-of-Life Policing on Crime and Disorder." *Justice Quarterly* 18 (2001): 825–876.

Kelling, George, and Catherine Coles. *Fixing Broken Windows: Restoring Order and Reducing Crime in Our Communities*. New York: Martin Kessler, 1997.

Lindquist, John. *Misdemeanor Crime: Trivial Criminal Pursuit*. Newbury Park, CA: Sage, 1988.

Perkins, David. "Indigent or Immune? Constitutional Standards for Incarceration of the Poor in Fine-Only Cases." *Criminal Law Bulletin* 32 (1996): 3–24.

Thurman, Quint, and Edmund McGarrell. *Community Policing in a Rural Setting*. Cincinnati: Anderson, 1996.

Chapter 19 Juvenile Courts

G erald Gault was charged with making a lewd phone call. If he had been an adult, the maximum sentence was on the lenient side—a fine of $50 and two months in jail. But because he was 15 years old, the sentence was potentially much stiffer—up to six years in the state industrial school. These substantive differences mirrored important procedural contrasts as well. If he had been an adult, Gerald Gault would have had the right to confront the witness making the accusation and also the right to have a lawyer present. But because he was a juvenile, none of these basic legal protections applied. ◄

In re Gault highlights the duality of juvenile court, which is part court of law and part social welfare agency. It sometimes operates formally, but more often its procedures are informal. These contrasts produce a series of contradictions, which are highlighted in the words of a former judge of the Denver Juvenile Court:

> It is law, and it is social work; it is control, and it is help; it is the good parent and, also, the stern parent; it is both formal and informal. It is concerned not only with the delinquent, but also with the battered child, the runaway, and many others. . . . The juvenile court has been all things to all people. (Rubin 1984, 79–80)

The historic mandate of juvenile court was to rescue children from a criminal life by providing the care and protection normally afforded by the natural parents. Thus, helping a child was far more important than protecting constitutional rights. But in certain instances, helpful benevolence has been replaced by harsh punishments. In deciding *In re Gault,* the Supreme Court confronted the difficult task of determining the relationship between the social welfare functions of juvenile court and basic due process so important to the American court system.

The best starting point in unraveling these dualities is an examination of the last 100 years of juvenile court.

JUVENILE COURTS 100 YEARS AGO

Juvenile courts are a distinctly twentieth-century development. The major economic and social changes of the late nineteenth century prompted a rethinking of the role of youth. The result was the creation of specialized courts to deal with what were thought to be distinctly youth-oriented problems. Many of the issues that arose 100 years ago remain with us today, shaping the thinking that will affect juvenile courts for the next 100 years.

Industrialization, Cities, and Crime

By the last third of the nineteenth century, the United States was well on its way to becoming the world's greatest industrial nation. What had once been a nation of small farmers was rapidly becoming a nation of city dwellers. The factories were located in the cities, and the workers for these factories were partially drawn from those who wished to escape the hard work of farming. But most of the new jobs were filled by immigrants from foreign lands who sought freedom from political oppression or economic want in their home countries. The result was a tremendous growth in cities. Indeed, the population of the nation almost doubled, growing from 40 million in 1870 to 76 million in 1900.

America's emerging big cities were truly diverse. The residents spoke different languages, ate strange foods, dressed differently, and worshiped in a variety of churches. The white Anglo-Saxon Protestants who controlled the institutions of the United States at the time did not extend a cordial welcome to these new immigrants. On the contrary, the immigrant urban masses were associated with the poverty, social disorder, and crime of the emerging big cities. Protecting society from the "dangerous poor" became a pressing social concern.

Then, as now, there was confusion over what was poverty and what was crime.

The Child Savers and the Progressive Movement

Beginning around 1890, members of the Progressive movement advocated a variety of political, economic, and social reforms. They were genuinely concerned about the economic disparities, social disorders, and excesses of industrialization, particularly as they affected children.

Progressives denounced the evils of child labor and pushed for legislation banning the practice. They were likewise appalled by the violent and exploitive conditions of reform schools. The fact that orphans were thrown into reform schools for the uncontrollable circumstance of having no parents shocked the Progressives' moral values. Taking up the plight of the children of the urban immigrant poor, they argued that these children were not bad, but were corrupted by the environment in which they grew up.

The Progressives' concern for the plight of the urban masses was also motivated by self-interest. They were largely middle class, and their position in society was threatened by the growth of a competing urban class composed of the poor and the working poor. These Anglo-Saxon Protestants found the culture of the Southern European Catholics shocking. Anthony Platt's (1969) classic study, *The Child Savers*, notes the types of behavior the Progressives sought to punish—drinking, fighting, begging, frequenting dance halls, staying out late at night, and sexual license. Within a generation, many of the social forces unleashed by the Progressive movement would lead to Prohibition, which was directed squarely at the growing political power of big-city Catholic immigrants, whose power base was the neighborhood tavern.

Thus from its origins, the juvenile court movement reflected class distinctions: The children of the poor were processed through the system, but those of the more well-to-do were handled informally. These class differences would mark juvenile court activities throughout the century.

Then, as now, there was confusion over what was genuine social concern and what was self-serving class interest.

Parens Patriae

The Progressives' efforts to save the children of the urban masses reflected a major shift in thinking about children. Historically, children had been viewed as miniature adults. Children under the age of 7 were presumed to be incapable of criminal intent and were therefore exempt from prosecution. Those 8 and older were considered adults in the eyes of the law, prosecuted as adults, convicted as adults, and served their sentences in the same prison cells as adults.

By the end of the nineteenth century, the notion of children as miniature adults was giving way to a very different conceptualization—children as persons with less than fully developed moral and cognitive capacities. This shift in thinking was reflected in the emerging legal doctrine of **parens patriae** (state as parent). No longer were parents considered to have sole and exclusive legal responsibility over their children. If the parents failed in their responsibility to raise a child properly, the state could intervene to protect children's welfare. This doctrine also meant that in extreme circumstances parental rights over their children could be terminated altogether.

Then, as now, there was confusion over the right of parents to raise their children in their own image and the need of the state to limit social disorder.

▎ HOW JUVENILE COURTS DIFFER FROM ADULT COURTS

The juvenile court is a continuing legacy of the Progressive movement. Not content to tinker with existing procedures, the Progressives insisted upon a radical departure from past practices. Adopting the legal doctrine of *parens patriae* resulted in juvenile judicial proceedings that differed greatly from those used in adult courts.

The unique legal dimensions of **juvenile court** are reflected in the legal terms employed. Whereas adults are arrested, tried, and sentenced to prison, juveniles are summoned, have a hearing, and are committed to residential placement. Juvenile courts differ from adult courts in five important ways: They emphasize helping the child, they are informal, they are based on civil law, they are secret, and they rarely involve a jury.

Emphasis on Helping the Child

Prosecution of adults at the turn of the twentieth century sought to achieve punishment. By contrast, the newly created juvenile courts emphasized helping the child. Benevolence, not punishment, was of paramount importance.

The doctrine of parens patriae became the underlying philosophy of juvenile court; the state should deal with a child who broke the law much as a wise parent would deal with a wayward child (Platt 1969). The Progressives sought to use the power of the state to save children from a life of crime. Juvenile courts would provide flexible procedures for the treatment of the underlying social problems that were seen as the basis of juvenile crime. Guidance would be the norm.

Informal Proceedings

Criminal prosecutions involving adults are formal and adversarial in nature. By contrast, juvenile court proceedings emphasize informality. Although key elements of due process have been integrated into juvenile court in recent years, juvenile proceedings nonetheless retain their informal nature. As a result, rules of evidence and rules of procedure, so important in adult criminal courts, have little relevance in juvenile proceedings.

Flowing from the premise that juvenile courts are meant to help the child, the creators of juvenile court viewed procedural safeguards not only as unnecessary but also as harmful. The concern was that a legal technicality might allow a child to avoid help (Sanborn 1993). In essence, the substance of the decision (helping the child) was more important than the procedures used to reach that decision.

Proceedings Based on Civil Law

Prosecutions of adults are based on the criminal law (see Chapter 2). By contrast, juvenile court proceedings are based on the civil law (see Chapter 2). This is why the legal terminology used in adult and juvenile courts differs so greatly. The terms *summons* and *commitment*, for example, are borrowed directly from civil practice.

Using civil rather than criminal law reinforced the key notion that juvenile courts were intended to rehabilitate, not punish. It is for this reason, for example, that a child's juvenile court record is not admissible in adult court. Regardless of the frequency or severity of the offenses committed by a juvenile, once he or she becomes an adult in the eyes of the criminal law, the person starts over with no prior record.

Over the years, the Supreme Court, state courts, and legislatures have added some procedural due process features of adult courts to juvenile proceedings. Thus, today it is probably best to view juvenile proceedings as a blend of civil and criminal law.

Secret Proceedings

Criminal proceedings involving adults are open to the public (except grand jury proceedings, and, on the rarest of rare occasions, jury selection in ultrasensitive cases). By contrast, juvenile court proceedings are secret. This means that crime victims who are interested in what happens in their case, or ordinary citizens who are simply curious about what goes on in the courthouse, may freely attend sessions involving adults but not involving juveniles. In most jurisdictions it is illegal for law enforcement personnel or juvenile court officials to release the names of juveniles to the media. Moreover, even if the media are able to find out the names, journalistic ethics prohibit that information from being printed or broadcast.

To its supporters, the secrecy of juvenile court proceedings is essential in meeting the key goal of working with children in trouble to prevent future criminal behavior. To critics, this secrecy merely reinforces the informality of the process and prevents much-needed public scrutiny.

Absence of Jury Trials

Adults accused of violating the criminal law have the right to a trial by a jury of their peers. By contrast, juveniles have no such constitutional right. To be sure, a few states have created, often by statute, an extremely limited right to a trial by jury in some matters concerning juveniles. Nonetheless, the central point is clear: Whereas the possibility of a jury trial structures the disposition of adult offenders, the likelihood of a jury trial almost never enters into the discussion in juvenile court.

The absence of jury trials reinforces the informal nature of the proceedings. It also strengthens the control of juvenile court personnel—both judges and probation officers. In adult courts the views of ordinary citizens may prove to differ from those of judge or prosecutor, but there is no such possibility in juvenile court.

THE ORGANIZATION OF JUVENILE COURTS

Today, all states have juvenile courts, but their organizational relationship to other judicial bodies varies greatly. In some ways the term *juvenile court* is a misnomer. Only a few states have created juvenile courts that are completely separate from other judicial bodies.

As Chapter 4 emphasized, important variations exist in state court organization. Nowhere is this diversity more apparent than in the organization of juvenile courts. Along a continuum from the most to the least distinctive, juvenile courts are organized in one of three ways: a separate court, part of family court, or a unit of the trial court.

Juvenile Court as a Separate Court

In a few jurisdictions, juvenile court is completely separate from other judicial bodies. This is the case in the states of Connecticut, Rhode Island, and Utah. A juvenile court as a separate statewide entity means that it has its own administration, judges, probation officers,

COURT TV

The Interrogation of Michael Crowe

Michael Crowe's younger sister is stabbed to death in their parents' home and the police believe that Michael is the killer. The 14-year-old is interrogated by the police without a lawyer or a parent present. During the lengthy interrogation, the police have Michael Crowe undergo a voice-stress analysis, and from the results they claim he is lying.

The juvenile seemingly confesses to the crime, and police later arrest and interrogate two of his friends. All three are charged with murder, even though the confessions are devoid of any details of the crime.

During jury selection, however, DNA evidence emerges that shows that the victim's blood is on the shirt of a mentally ill drifter. Once the false confessions are discredited, all charges against the three juveniles are dismissed.

 View a video clip of the investigation on your copy of the CourtTV CD-ROM. As you watch the video, keep the following questions in mind:

1. Does Michael Crowe understand his *Miranda* rights? Should special *Miranda* rules govern interrogations of juveniles?

2. The police appear to be complying with the letter of *In re Gault* but are they complying with the spirit of the case?

3. Was the trial judge correct in ruling that the confession was psychologically coerced and therefore should be suppressed? In thinking about this question you may wish to review the material discussed in Chapter 12 on *Miranda* and the interrogation process.

4. Would the outcome of this case have been different if the interrogation had not been videotaped?

clerks of court, and other employees. Stated another way, matters concerning juveniles are its exclusive jurisdiction. A few large cities, such as Boston and Denver, also separate juvenile courts from other judicial bodies.

Juvenile Court as Part of Family Court

A second organizational arrangement is for juvenile court to be a part of family court, which has broad responsibility over family matters. One major type of case is divorce and related issues, including child custody, child support, alimony, and property settlement. In addition, jurisdiction of family courts encompasses paternity matters and adoption of children. Most important for our purposes, family court jurisdiction also typically includes matters concerning juveniles (delinquency, status offenses, and child-victim cases).

Six states and the District of Columbia have authorized family courts on a statewide basis. In Delaware, New York, Rhode Island, and South Carolina, family courts are separately organized. In the District of Columbia, Hawaii, and New Jersey, family courts are a separate division of the trial court of general jurisdiction.

Juvenile Court as a Unit of Trial Court

The third place that juvenile courts are housed organizationally is as part of a trial court. Typically, juvenile court is part of the jurisdiction of the major trial court, but on occasion it is in the minor trial court.

Beyond the legal considerations of jurisdiction, the question of where matters concerning juveniles are heard is largely a function of case volume. In rural areas with few cases, they most often are a type of case on the judge's calendar much like tort and contract. But most areas have sufficient cases to justify one or more judges who devote themselves full-time to matters concerning juveniles. This specialization is dictated partly by case volume, but also by the requirement that juvenile proceedings be conducted in secret. Administratively, therefore, a separate section of court (sometimes in a different courthouse) makes it easier to keep juvenile proceedings closed to the public.

Law in Action: The Impact of Structure

Since juvenile courts were first established, there has been a debate over the appropriate place in the judicial hierarchy for this new judicial body. Where a state ended up placing its juvenile court was largely determined by broader debates over court organization.

Court reformers recommend that juvenile court be part of family court. But whether this structural arrangement results in "better" justice is at best hard to document. There is some evidence, for example, that the more the judge is a juvenile court specialist, the more likely the judge will handle cases informally rather than conduct a full hearing (Sosin 1978). Similarly, specialists are less likely to find a youth to be a delinquent (Johnson and Secret 1995). The structural differences, however, appear to be far less important than the social environment in which the juvenile court operates; juvenile courts in big cities march to a different drummer than those in rural or suburban areas (Sanborn 1994).

▌JUVENILE COURT JURISDICTION: AGE

For adults, court jurisdiction is largely determined by the nature of the criminal offense. For **juveniles,** on the other hand, jurisdiction is normally determined by their age. Different states provide complex sets of criteria relating to the **upper age of jurisdiction,** when a child becomes an adult (at least in the eyes of the criminal law), as well as the **lower age of jurisdiction,** when a juvenile may be prosecuted as an adult in court.

No Consensus on Age of Juveniles

Most states consider children to be juveniles until they reach their eighteenth birthday. However, 18 hardly constitutes a consensus among

A Virtual Tour of American Courthouses: Juvenile Justice

For a look at a juvenile court, go to **http://www.lawforkids. org/DetTour/PicturePages/p14p3.htm**. Likewise, the National Center for Juvenile Justice provides a dynamic interactive resource called Juvenile Justice State Profiles at **http:// www.ncjj.org/**. For the latest facts and figures about juveniles and crime, go to the *Statistical Briefing Book* of the Office of Juvenile Justice and Delinquency at **http://ojjdp.ncjrs. org/ojstatbb/index.html**.

A few juvenile courts offer Web sites, including these:

Boston (Massachusetts) **http://www.state.ma.us/ courtsandjudges/courts/juvenilecourt**

Hamilton (Ohio) **http://www.hamilton-co.org/ juvenilecourt/**

Iowa **http://www.judicial.state.ia.us/families/ juvcourt/**

Ninth Judicial Circuit (Florida) **http://www.ninja9.net/ courts/juvenile/juvcrt.htm**

Northampton (Pennsylvania) **http://www.nccpa.org/ divs/juvcourtprob.html**

Pierce County (Washington) **http://www.co.pierce. wa.us/abtus/ourorg/supct/abtusjuv.htm**

Pima County (Arizona) **http://www.sc.co.pima.az.us/ Juvenile/**

Virginia Beach (Virginia) **http://www.virginiabeach. va.us/courts/jdrcourt/jdrintak.htm**

The Florida Department of Juvenile Justice includes information on prevention and delinquency trends, community-based efforts, innovative sanctions, treatment, and getting involved on its Web site: **http://www.djj.state.fl.us/**. The Virginia

Department of Juvenile Justice develops policies, programs, and institutions to assist the courts in holding juveniles accountable for their actions and affording them opportunities for reform: **http://www.dcjs.state.va.us/juvenile/ index.htm**.

For a look at juvenile detention centers, click on any of the following:

Southwest Idaho **http://www.canyoncounty.org/ juvdet/swijdc.htm**

Oklahoma City **http://www.oklahomacounty.org/ jjc/OCJDC.html**

Rankin County (Mississippi) **http://rankincounty.org/ SO/RCSOJDC.htm**

Fairfax County (Virginia) **http://www.co.fairfax.va.us/ courts/jdr/jdc/Geninfo.htm**

Northwestern Louisiana **http://www.ghpc.org/cases/ cs0062.htm**

For contrasting views on juvenile court reform, go to

Illinois Juvenile Court Improvement Project Assessment: **http://www.chapin.uchicago.edu/ProjectsGuide/ JuvenileCourt.html**

Amnesty International: **http://www.amnesty-usa.org/** (search for "Juvenile")

Familycourts.com: **http://www.familycourts.com/**

The Coalition for Family Court Reform: **http:// courtreform.hypermart.net/**

ACLU Fact Sheet on the Juvenile Justice System: **http:// aclu.org/library/fctsht.html**

---

the states. Three states establish the upper age of juvenile court jurisdiction at 15, eight others at age 16, and the remaining states at 17 (see Figure19-1).

The adjoining states of New York and Pennsylvania illustrate this complex national pattern. In New York, a 16-year-old is considered an adult and is prosecuted in the adult criminal justice system. But move across the border, and Pennsylvania treats that same 16-year-old as a juvenile to be processed in the juvenile court

system (DeFrances and Strom 1997). This difference in laws of jurisdictions sometimes no more than a few feet apart illustrates the tremendous diversity of American law, which is highlighted in Chapter 4.

Transfer to Adult Court

Although a fairly uniform upper age limit for juveniles has been established in the United

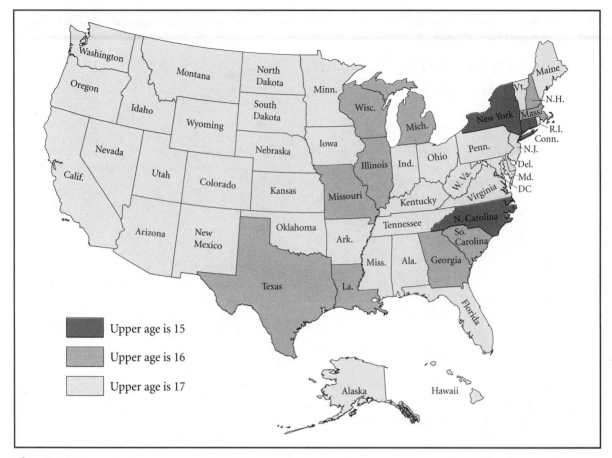

Figure 19-1
Upper Age of Juvenile Court Jurisdiction in States

SOURCE: Adapted from material compiled by P. Griffin in 2000 for the National Center for Juvenile Justice's State Juvenile Justice Profiles Web site: http://www.ncjj.org/stateprofiles/; *OJJDP Statistical Briefing Book:* http://ojjdp.ncjrs.org/ojstatbb/html/qa085.html (accessed 25 April 2002).

States, there is far less uniformity involving lower age limits (see Figure 19-2). Juveniles charged with serious offenses, or who have a history of repeated offenses, may be tried as adults (Singer 1993). **Transfer to criminal court** (alternatively referred to as *certification* or *waiver*) refers to the process whereby the jurisdiction over a juvenile delinquent is moved to adult court. Many states have no lower age for transfer. For those stating a lower age limit, 14 to 16 is the most common.

The procedures surrounding the decision to transfer juveniles to adult court also vary. In some jurisdictions the juvenile court judge makes the decision, but in the majority the prosecutor has the discretionary authority to decide which juveniles above the lower age will be tried as adults.

In the most recent year for which statistics are available, only a very small proportion of juveniles (1 percent, or approximately 12,000 cases) were transferred to adult court (Puzzanchera et al. 2000). Juveniles transferred to criminal court were generally violent felony offenders. Two-thirds were charged with a violent offense, including about 11 percent with murder, 34 percent with robbery, and 15 percent with felony assault (Strom, Smith, and Snyder 1998). A disproportionate number of juveniles transferred to adult criminal court were black males (63 percent). Figures like these lead youth advocacy groups like Build-

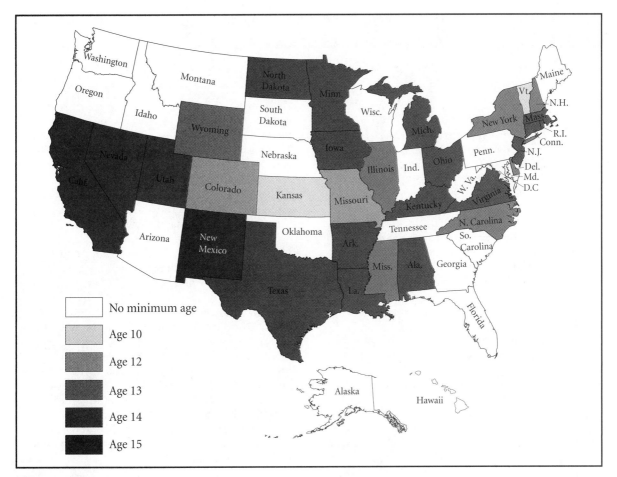

Figure 19-2
Youngest Age at Which Juvenile May Be Transferred to Criminal Court by Judicial Waiver

SOURCE: Adapted from material compiled by P. Griffin in 2000 for the National Center for Juvenile Justice's State Juvenile Justice Profiles Web site: http://www.ncjj.org/stateprofiles/; *OJJDP Statistical Briefing Book:* http://ojjdp.ncjrs.org/ojstatbb/html/qa089.html (accessed 25 April 2002).

ing Blocks for Youth (2000) to conclude that the juvenile justice system is not "racially neutral" and that states have not done enough to address racial disparities.

Public pressure to try juveniles as adults is spawned by concerns over violent juvenile crimes. Reality, though, does not match the expectations of elected officials or the public. (See Courts, Controversy, and Reducing Crime: Should Juveniles Be Tried As Adults?) Moreover, once transferred, juveniles do not always receive longer sentences than they would have in juvenile court, because they are appearing in court for the first time and at a relatively young age (Snyder and Sickmund 2000).

The Office of Juvenile Justice and Delinquency Prevention recently evaluated changes in Wisconsin, New Mexico, and Minnesota (Torbet et al. 2000). The final report highlights the following lessons learned:

■ A disconnect exists between legislative intent and the actual implementation of new laws.

■ The new sentencing laws encourage plea bargaining.

COURTS, CONTROVERSY, AND REDUCING CRIME

Should Juveniles Be Tried As Adults?

During the mid-1990s the nation's focus on crime began to shift from drugs to juvenile crime, particularly violent juvenile crime. Public concern with crimes committed by juveniles often takes the form of efforts to lower the age at which a juvenile may be prosecuted as an adult.

Beginning in the mid-1980s the juvenile crime rate increased, with juvenile arrests more than doubling from 197 teen arrests per 100,000 teenagers to 465 per 100,000 (Cannon 1997). What has attracted the most public attention is the increase in violent juvenile crime, which shot up 93 percent (compared with 22 percent in property cases).

To some observers, a juvenile crime wave was on the horizon. Newspaper headlines proclaimed, "Youth Violence Explosion Likely to Worsen" (Bass 1995) and "Violent Children Straining Limit of Justice System" (Hallinan 1993). These concerns were bolstered by the realization that the juvenile population would increase from 27 million to 39 million in 2010. But these dire predictions failed to materialize. Beginning in 1995, arrests for violent juvenile crimes declined significantly. Thus, what some had predicted to be a juvenile crime wave now appears to have been only a ripple (Johnson and Fields 1996).

The commonly held belief that juvenile delinquents are becoming younger as a group and committing more serious crimes at earlier ages than in the past does not hold up to scrutiny. The Office of Juvenile Justice and Delinquency Prevention (1996) compared the characteristics of young offenders arrested in the 1990s with those arrested in 1980 and concluded that serious and violent juvenile offenders were not significantly younger than those of 10 or 15 years earlier. But downward trends in juvenile crime have apparently had little impact on the public dialogue. The U.S. Congress has been considering a juvenile crime bill that would encourage states to become harsher in prosecuting young offenders.

Numerous states are likewise responding to public perceptions that violent juvenile crime is a growing menace and making it easier to transfer juveniles. Since the late 1970s, for example, 44 states have changed their laws affecting the transfer of juveniles to adult courts. Some of these efforts involve lowering the age of transfer. Others involve increasing the list of crimes for which juveniles may be transferred. Others seek to mandate transfers in certain situations. Today, at least 24 states have laws that automatically send violent kids to adult courts, and several others are considering enacting such laws.

Efforts to greatly increase the number of juveniles tried as adults has prompted tremendous concern in the juvenile justice community. One possibility is that juveniles will be incarcerated with adult offenders. "It is likely that the number of young inmates sentenced to confinement will increase and . . . placing juveniles in adult facilities raises issues such as their risk of being raped or assaulted by the older inmates. If kept in isolation for protection they are then at increased risk for suicide" (Snyder 2000). Advocates of restorative justice (see Chapter 15) in particular emphasize that juvenile matters are the prime example of where efforts at reconciliation are likely to yield more positive results than punitive measures.

What do you think? Should juveniles be prosecuted as adults? If you answer yes, under what conditions should juveniles be prosecuted as adults, and for what crimes? In what ways are your standards similar to or different from existing practices? If you answer no, what would you suggest to strengthen rehabilitative efforts in juvenile court? In what ways are your recommendations similar to or different from existing practices? In forming your answer, also consider the following question: Do you think that the recent decrease in juvenile crime, particularly violent crime, is temporary or long-term?

John Thomas, Dorothy E. Stubbe, Geraldine Pearson, "Race, Juvenile Justice, and Mental Health: New Dimensions in Measuring Pervasive Bias"

"Juveniles Facing Criminal Sanctions: Three States That Changed the Rules"

Richard E. Redding, "Examining Legal Issues: Juvenile Offenders in Criminal Court and Adult Prison"

- Judicial and prosecutorial discretion expand.
- Local application of new laws varies widely.
- New sentencing laws have a disproportionate impact on minorities.

Stated another way, alterations of laws on the books do not necessarily produce the intended changes in law in action.

JUVENILE COURT JURISDICTION: SUBJECT MATTER

Of those children brought before juvenile court because of their age, there is enormous variation in the types of cases. Felons and misdemeanants, petty offenders and truants are all under the jurisdiction of the juvenile court because of their age. And to complicate matters even further, some juveniles are before the court because of neglect or abuse by their parents.

Juvenile court matters fall into three major categories: delinquency, status offenses, and child-victim.

Juvenile Delinquency

Delinquency is a violation of a criminal law that would be a crime if the act were committed by an adult. Common examples include theft, burglary, sale or possession of drugs, and criminal damage to property. Thus, in a juvenile delinquency matter, there is no age difference in the substance of the criminal law, but the procedures are considerably different.

A juvenile delinquent may be placed on probation or committed to a juvenile institution. The period of confinement may exceed that of an adult. These criminal-type juvenile cases constitute 64 percent of all matters concerning juveniles.

Status Offenses

Status offenses involve acts that are illegal only for juveniles. Common examples include running away from home, truancy, possession of alcohol, ungovernability, and curfew violations. Each year juvenile courts handle almost 100,000 such cases. Traditionally, juveniles found to be status offenders could be sent to the same juvenile correctional institutions as those found to be delinquent, but this is changing. In recent years, some states have decriminalized some of these behaviors; offenders are now treated as dependent children, and child protective service agencies are given the primary responsibility for addressing the problem.

Child-Victim

Juvenile courts also deal with **child-victim** petitions involving neglect or dependency. Thus, the child is before the court for no fault of his or her own. Common examples include battered children, children abandoned by their parents, and children who are not receiving proper education or medical care. Neglected or dependent children cannot be sentenced to juvenile institutions. Rather, the court has a broad mandate to order social services, foster home or group home care, or medical or mental health services.

Clearly, neglected or dependent children present strikingly different issues from those who are before the court because of their own actions. Child-victim cases are also the ones that evoke considerable public emotion over the child's condition. Because of the complexities inherent in the distinctive nature of these cases, space does not permit further discussion.

Law in Action: One-Pot Jurisdiction

The broad subject matter jurisdiction of juvenile courts complicates the task of addressing the problems facing juvenile justice. At any given time in juvenile court, the judge, prosecutor, probation officer, and police officer are simultaneously dealing with a wide variety of problems. This has been called the one-pot jurisdictional approach, in which youths who commit serious crimes, status offenders, and deprived children are put into the same "pot" (Springer 1986).

Consider the following three hypothetical cases, all of which would meet a given state's age criteria:

■ A juvenile who has burglarized a liquor store

■ A juvenile who has been stopped by the police for possessing liquor

■ A juvenile whose parents drink so heavily that they have given up any efforts to raise their child

The first is a delinquent, the second a status offender, and the third a child-victim. Yet,

> all three kinds of kids were thought to be the products or victims of bad family and social environments; consequently it was thought, they should be subject, as the wards of the court, to the same kind of solicitous, helpful care. (Springer 1986, 62–63)

It is this broad diversity of juvenile problems that members of the courtroom work group must confront in trying to dispense juvenile court's version of justice.

DUE PROCESS IN JUVENILE COURTS

Juvenile court statutes set forth two standards for deciding the appropriate disposition for a child: the best interests of the child and the best interests of the community. Because the concept of the juvenile court was to aid—not punish—children, the due process guarantees of the adult criminal court were absent. Procedures were more administrative than adversarial, stressing the informal, private, and noncombative handling of cases. It is for this reason that juvenile cases are often captioned *In re*, a Latin phrase meaning "in the matter of." But at what point do juveniles obtain benefits from the special procedures applicable to them that offset the disadvantage of denial of due process?

Key Court Decisions

The nature of the juvenile court process remained unchanged until the 1960s. When the Warren Court began to scrutinize procedures in adult criminal courts, its attention turned also to juvenile courts. In a groundbreaking decision, the Supreme Court held in *In re Gault* (1967) that the due process clause of the Fourteenth Amendment applied to juvenile court proceedings. The court emphasized that "under our Constitution the condition of being a boy does not justify a kangaroo court." The opinion specified that juveniles have (1) the right to notice, (2) the right to counsel, (3) the right to confront witnesses, and (4) privilege against self-incrimination. (See Case Close-up: *In re Gault* and Due Process in Juvenile Courts.)

The *Gault* decision points to the constant tension within the juvenile court system between those who think that children should be given all the due process guarantees accorded adults and those who reason that children must be handled in a less adversarial, more treatment-oriented manner so that legal procedures will not interfere with efforts to secure the justice that is in the children's best interests.

Gault signaled that the juvenile court must become a real court and its procedures must be regularized in accordance with constitutional requirements (Rubin 1984). Juvenile courts, however, afford far fewer due process rights than their adult counterparts. Following *Gault*, the more conservative Burger and Rehnquist Courts have been less enthusiastic about extending due process (see Exhibit 19-1). Juvenile delinquents, for example, have no constitutional right to a trial by jury (*McKeiver v. Pennsylvania* 1971), and preventive detention is allowed (*Schall v. Martin* 1984).

Important Congressional Acts

Congress has also imposed key mandates on the juvenile justice process. The Juvenile Justice and Delinquency Prevention Act of 1974 mandated deinstitutionalization of status offenders by stating that juveniles not charged with acts that would be crimes for adults shall not be jailed. Similarly, the law specifies that juveniles charged with criminal acts shall not be detained in any institution in which they have contact with adult inmates (Snyder and Sickmund 2000). There is little doubt that this law has fundamentally changed the way our nation deals with troubled youth (Holden and Kapler 1995).

THE MURDER TRIAL OF SHAREEF COUSIN

Few Options or Safeguards in a City's Juvenile Courts

 We have no way of knowing for certain whether Shareef Cousin was ever before juvenile court in New Orleans, because juvenile court records are sealed. But if he had ever been in juvenile court, and his troubled record certainly suggests that this was likely, this is some of what he would have experienced.

Clarence Richardson, the public defender appointed to represent a 12-year-old boy charged with driving a stolen car, met his client for the first time only a few minutes before the trial began. They talked in the packed waiting area outside the courtroom because Mr. Richardson, like other public defenders here, has no office. Nor does he have a file cabinet, a telephone to contact defendants, or a clerk or secretary to help him draw up motions or conduct investigations.

As Judge Lawrence Lagarde Jr. recited the evidence against his client and swiftly pronounced a two-year sentence in juvenile prison, Mr. Richardson sat largely silent. His defense table was conspicuously bare: no case files, law books, or even the police report on the defendant, to use to challenge the prosecutor.

Welcome to the Orleans Parish Juvenile Court, considered by many lawyers and children's rights advocates to be the most troubled juvenile court system in the country. Juvenile courts nationwide are in crisis, with the public and elected officials denouncing them as overwhelmed and ineffective, a revolving door for young predators. Congress, in fact, may soon pass legislation that would weaken the role of the juvenile courts by pushing large numbers of young people into the adult criminal system. But even as critics clamor for tougher laws dealing with crime by juveniles, an examination of the New Orleans juvenile court reveals another problem with the current system: a lack of constitutional protections like the right to adequate legal representation and due process for young people, an overwhelming majority of whom are poor and black.

In the tradition-bound world of New Orleans, public defenders are expected to play a subservient role, and prosecutors routinely rack up by far the highest conviction rate of any big-city juvenile court in the country. Some young defendants remain in detention centers for up to eight months, without coming to trial, much longer than the 10- to 30-day limits imposed by most state laws. . . .

But even the judges here are concerned about the system. "The juvenile court is the stepchild of the criminal justice system," said Ernestine Gray, the administrative judge of the New Orleans juvenile court, "and everything about how this court works suggests this is not a place that believes in innocent till proven guilty."

There are about a half-dozen public defenders, one for each courtroom, to handle the 2,200 delinquency cases brought here each year. Others who have worked in the New Orleans court were even blunter than Judge Gray. "It's medieval," said Anne Turissini, who spent five years as a public defender in juvenile court here until she gave up in disgust and moved to a similar job in suburban Jefferson Parish. Her salary, Ms. Turissini said, was $18,000 a year, and with more than 100 cases at a time each, she and her colleagues were "overworked, underpaid, burned out, and demoralized." "You are supposed to go along and get along with your judge," Ms. Turissini said, "and if you object too often in court, they will have you fired."

"All this has an effect on the kids, because they can sense the court is not serious, so they don't take it seriously," she added. "It is absolutely the worst situation, because these are kids with no self-esteem anyway, with parents and teachers telling them they have no value, which is why they shoot people for sneakers."

The ineffectiveness of the public defender system for juveniles here is forcing more and more poor young people to spend unnecessarily long periods in the city's youth detention centers before they are brought to trial or even charged, said James Bell, a lawyer with the Youth Law Center, an advocacy group for children, in San Francisco.

SOURCE: Fox Butterfield, "Few Options or Safeguards in a City's Juvenile Courts," *New York Times,* 22 July 1997.

CASE CLOSE-UP

In re Gault and Due Process in Juvenile Courts

 The Sheriff of Gila County, Arizona, took 15-year-old Gerald Francis Gault into custody for making a lewd phone call to a neighbor. As to what was actually said, the Supreme Court would only say, "It will suffice for purposes of this opinion to say that the remarks or questions put to her were of the irritatingly offensive, adolescent, sex variety."

Gault was transported to the Children's Detention Home, and no effort was made to contact his parents. Over the next couple of weeks, several brief hearings were held, but no record exists of what happened. What is known, though, is that there is some dispute whether Gerald Gault actually made the phone call. According to one version, he dialed the number, but his friend did the talking. Whatever may have transpired, the hearing would not be able to determine, because the witness was never present.

After another brief hearing, Gerald was found to be a juvenile delinquent and committed to the State Industrial School "for the period of his minority [that is, until 21] unless sooner discharged by due process of law." This harsh sentence was probably influenced by the fact that at the time he was on six months' probation as a result of having been in the company of another boy who had stolen a woman's purse.

It was the lack of procedural regularity in cases like this one that concerned the American Civil Liberties Union (ACLU) (Manfredi 1998). Through a series of complex maneuvers, the ACLU was able to get the case before the Arizona Supreme Court and then the U.S. Supreme Court.

In deciding *Gault*, the Court was essentially writing on a blank slate concerning juveniles. A year earlier, the Court had ever so tentatively imposed some due process requirements for juveniles accused of serious felonies (*Kent v. U.S.* 1966). But now the Court was ready to confront head-on the basic question about juvenile courts: Does the Bill of Rights apply to juveniles, or are

children's best interests protected by informal and paternalistic hearings? Justice Abe Fortas's opinion underscored the lack of procedural regularity, stressing that "Due process of law is the primary and indispensable foundation of individual freedom."

At the same time, the opinion in *Gault* supports the purposes of the juvenile court: A juvenile court proceeding is one "in which a fatherly judge touched the heart and conscience of the erring youth by talking over his problems, by paternal advice and admonition" to save him from a downward career. The goodwill and compassion of the juvenile court will not, however, be diminished by due process of law. In one bold stroke, *In re Gault* carved out the following four new constitutional rights in juvenile proceedings:

■ Juveniles have the right to timely notice of charges. In the future, parents must be informed that their child has been taken into custody, and written charges must be filed.

■ Juveniles have the right to counsel. Following *Gideon*, the Court held that juveniles, like adults, have the right to have an attorney present during the proceedings, and if they are indigent, to have a lawyer appointed.

■ Juveniles have the right against self-incrimination. *Miranda*, decided by the Court just a year before, greatly extended the right for adults, and many of the same strictures were now extended to juveniles.

■ Juveniles have the right to confront and cross-examine complainants and other witnesses.

The Court's opinion in *Gault* was supported by seven justices and partially by an eighth. Only Justice Potter Stewart dissented outright. He viewed the decision as "a long step backwards into the nineteenth century." The danger he saw was that abolishing the flexibility and informality of the juvenile courts would cause children to be treated as adults in courts.

Congressional mandates, coupled with *Gault* and other Supreme Court rulings, have had a marked effect on juvenile court procedures. "Today's juvenile court is constantly discarding many of its traditional and fundamental characteristics, and it is adopting many of the features customarily associated with criminal court" (Sanborn 1993).

Exhibit 19-1 Key Developments Concerning Juvenile Courts

Ex parte Crouse	1839	Philadelphia Supreme Court uses term *parens patriae*.
Illinois Juvenile Court Act	1899	First juvenile court created in Cook County, Illinois.
Juvenile Court Act	1938	Federal government adopts principles of juvenile court movement.
Wyoming	1945	Last state to create a juvenile court.
Kent v. U.S.	1966	Court establishes conditions of waiver to criminal court.
In re Gault	1967	Juveniles are entitled to due process guarantees.
In re Winship	1970	Proof must be established "beyond a reasonable doubt" in classifying juveniles as delinquent.
McKeiver v. Pennsylvania	1971	Juvenile delinquents are not entitled to a jury trial.
Juvenile Delinquency and Prevention Act	1974	Mandates deinstitutionalization of status offenders.
Schall v. Martin	1984	Court departs from trend of increasing juvenile rights, upholding the general notion of parens patriae.
Thompson v. Oklahoma	1988	Execution of a person under the age of 16 at the time of his or her crime is unconstitutional.

Some observers see the future of juvenile courts as more formal institutions of law, and they advocate replacing discretion with due process. These critics would open hearings to the public and make juvenile court records accessible. Along the same lines, they would make trials more important. Thus, Joseph Sanborn (1993) concludes that it is time for juvenile courts to provide defendants whom the court seeks to punish the right to a public jury trial.

Another proposal would go even further, stripping juvenile courts of their secrecy. The "seemingly hidden juvenile court operations have contributed to the public perception that the court is overly lenient. When open hearings have been tried there have been few negative consequences" (Krisberg and Austin 1993, 184). There seems little doubt that the juvenile courts over the next 100 years will increase the amount of due process provided juveniles, but how much (and how fast) is an open question.

COURTROOM WORK GROUP

At first glance, members of juvenile courtroom work groups are similar to those found in adult courts—prosecutors bring charges, de-fense attorneys attempt to get the best deal possible for their clients, and judges decide matters that others have not successfully negotiated. These parallels, though, can be deceiving because the tasks of juvenile and adult courts are not the same. More so than courts dealing with adults accused of violating the law, juvenile courts grant judges and other officials unusually wide latitude in making discretionary decisions intended to "individualize justice" (Bazemore 1994). Moreover, although the Supreme Court has imposed minimal due process requirements, juvenile courts remain judicial bodies where informal processing still dominates.

Shared norms are the hallmark of courtroom work groups, Chapter 5 argued. In assessing the worth of a case, members of the juvenile court work group incorporate many of the same factors as those in adult courts—the severity of the offense and the prior record of the offender. The juvenile court tradition of individualized treatment, though, encourages the consideration of another important factor—the characteristics of the family (Matza 1964). The control the parent or parents have over the youth is a major consideration in deciding the disposition of the case (Fader et al. 2001). Similarly, members of the juvenile court work group also consider family structure, including the number of parents in the household and patterns of criminality among other family members (Corley, Bynum, and Wordes 1995).

The legally trained members of the courtroom work group rely heavily on professional judgments of nonlawyers in assessing both the background of the youth and the characteristics of the family. This affects the juvenile court work group in a critical way. Whereas in adult court the skills of lawyers are of fundamental importance, in juvenile court they are secondary. Judges, lawyers, and defense attorneys have been trained to interpret and apply the law, but these skills provide little help in making the key decisions in juvenile court cases. Instead, social workers, psychologists, and counselors have been trained to assess the child's problem and devise a treatment plan.

Judges

Judges are the central authority in the juvenile court system. More so than their counterparts in criminal court, they have wide discretion over detention, the adjudicatory hearing, disposition, and other matters. Depending on the size of the court and the rotation system, an individual judge may spend only a little time or a great deal of time in juvenile court (Bazemore and Feder 1997).

In many jurisdictions, assignment to the juvenile court is not a highly sought-after appointment. Although some judges like the challenges of juvenile court, to others it is a dead-end assignment. Judges who specialize in juvenile court matters are often those who enjoy the challenges of working with people rather than those who are intrigued by nuances of legal interpretations (see A Day in Court: Juvenile Court Judge Finds Peace of Mind). But even judges deeply committed to the juvenile system may seek rotation to other sections to advance their judicial careers (Krisberg and Austin 1993).

Hearing Officers

In many jurisdictions, judges are assisted by *hearing officers* (sometimes known as *referees*, *masters*, or *commissioners*). Typically, hearing officers are attorneys appointed by the court to serve on a full- or part-time basis to hear a range of juvenile court matters. These hearing officers enter findings and recommendations that require confirmation by the judge to become an order (Rubin 1989).

Prosecutors

Over the past several decades, the power and influence of the prosecutor have grown in U.S. courthouses (see Chapter 6). Rising crime rates, coupled with Supreme Court decisions requiring more due process, have contributed to the growing role of the prosecutor in juvenile courts (Shine and Price 1992).

Prosecutors now dominate the intake processing stage in most jurisdictions. At times, intake officers make the initial decision and the prosecutor later reviews that determination. At other times, the prosecutor is the chief decision maker (with input from others, of course). This prosecutorial dominance does not necessarily mean that DAs prefer formal processing. For status offenses and misdemeanor allegations, prosecutors are more likely to opt for informal, rather than formal, processing (Rubin 1989). Similarly, prosecutors, more so than judges, are typically the ones who negotiate the disposition of all but the most serious juvenile delinquency cases.

Although the role of the prosecutor's office has increased in juvenile court, an assignment to a section of juvenile court is not a sought-after promotion. On the contrary, it is the newly hired assistant DAs fresh out of law school who tend to be assigned to juvenile court. Thus, much like judges, assistant DAs typically hope for a promotion to a felony unit, where they can practice "real law," trying and convicting "real criminals."

Defense Attorneys

Defense attorneys play very much a secondary role in the juvenile court (Burruss and Kempf-Leonard 2002). One study found that only half of juveniles had a lawyer (Feld 1988), and another reported a lawyer present during only one-third of formal hearings (Walker and Ostrander 1982). The American Bar Association

Juvenile Court Judge Finds Peace of Mind

 Just across the Trinity River, miles away from downtown Dallas' legal epicenter, is a government building where most of the city's heartbreaking cases are heard. On a daily basis, lawyers, judges, and caseworkers inside the Henry Wade Juvenile Justice Center examine the details of unfathomable crimes, from 15-year-old murderers who kill for a few dollars to parents who sexually abuse their children.

Since 1987, 304th District Judge Hal Gaither has sat in judgment of both parents and children accused of mind-numbing depravity as one of Dallas County's two juvenile court judges. Somehow, he's managed to be at peace with himself. "You learn to leave it all at the office," Gaither says. "If you don't it will kill you." It's easy to see why.

Juvenile judges have incredible power over other people's lives. But with that power comes a mandate to make some rather unpleasant decisions. Juvenile judges decide whether a child accused of a crime will be adjudicated in the juvenile system where rehabilitation is the focus, or sent through the adult system where hope is usually abandoned at the penitentiary gates.

And they decide whether children taken from their parents by Child Protective Services will remain with the family or be placed elsewhere, sometimes in state care—an option few concede is the best place to raise a child.

The easiest way to sleep at night, Gaither says, is to keep one thing in mind while making decisions on matters such as CPS removals. "You've got to focus on who is the most important person in the courtroom," he says. "And that's the kid." . . .

Gaither was Gov. George W. Bush's chief adviser during the 1996 rewrite of the juvenile code, an effort that dropped the age a juvenile can be certified as an adult to 14. But it also expanded the determinate sentencing statutes (offenses that usually involve violent crime) to keep minors in juvenile detention for longer periods of time instead of sending them to adult prison.

Gaither sticks by the tenets of the law he helped create. Very few juveniles are certified as adults in Gaither's court—about 30 per year by his estimation. Although the prosecution decides whether to seek adult certification, Gaither says prosecutors know what he'll certify, so they don't ask unless it's a worthy case.

But as a former juvenile prosecutor with nearly 10 years' experience, Gaither is quick to certify a juvenile as an adult in cases involving violent offenses—especially if the juvenile poses a danger to society, lawyers say. However, Gaither listens to lawyers' suggestions on sentencing matters in unusual cases. . . .

In CPS removal cases, it doesn't matter if the parents are from high-toned North Dallas or impoverished South Dallas, they will be treated the same by Gaither, lawyers say. . . . "He gives folks the benefit of the doubt," says Allison Sartin, a former Dallas juvenile prosecutor who is now in private practice. . . . But there are some types of parents that Gaither has no patience for, Sartin says. "I think he has a firm conviction that you can't be a drug user and an effective parent at the same time. He doesn't have much tolerance for parents who are drug abusers," Sartin says. . . .

On Dec. 31, 2002, Gaither will hang up his robe for the last time and walk out of the juvenile courthouse for good. Gaither says he figures 15 years is a long enough time to be a judge. And he says he told his political supporters that his fourth campaign would be his last. "I just let everybody know this is it," Gaither says. "It's time to smell the roses, I've had a good life." . . .

SOURCE: John Council, "Juvenile Court Judge Finds Peace of Mind," *Texas Lawyer,* 25 September 2000. Copyright 2000 American Lawyer Newspapers Group, Inc.

and other juvenile advocacy groups are concerned that the legal interests of many young people in juvenile court are compromised because of a lack of legal representation (Young 2000; Puritz et al. 1995).

Lack of representation by a lawyer partially reflects the nature of the caseload—many of the cases are minor. As we saw with adults in misdemeanor court, few have lawyers because the penalties are so light. The same holds true for juveniles—most cases will receive some form of probation, supervision, and/or restitution irrespective of whether a lawyer is, or is not, present.

The role of the defense attorney is further limited by the informality of juvenile courts. In contrast to adult court, juvenile court proceedings place little emphasis on the privilege against self-incrimination. From the initial police contact (and often arrest) through the intake proceedings, juveniles are urged to tell the truth. It should be no surprise, therefore, to learn that fewer than 10 percent of juveniles assert their right to remain silent (Grisso 1981).

Defense attorneys, when they are present at all, become involved after their client has cooperated with police and prosecutor, and perhaps the probation officer and judge as well. For the cases where there is only weak evidence, the defense strategy is to seek a dismissal. For the vast majority of cases where there is strong evidence, defense attorneys negotiate, based on the norms of the work group, the best possible deal for their client. Since most of the cases are, by adult standards, relatively minor, the dispositions reached tend to be on the lenient side—primarily probation, restitution, and community service.

Probation Officers

From the beginning, probation and **probation officers** were a key part of juvenile court. In fact, probation in adult court traces its heritage to these developments. Juvenile probation takes several forms. In some states, probation officers are part of the judicial branch (either locally or statewide); in other jurisdictions, they are part of the executive branch (either locally or statewide) (Rubin 1989).

As in adult court, probation officers in juvenile court conduct background reports and supervise those placed on probation. What is strikingly different, though, is the stage at which they become involved. In adult courts, probation officers are brought into the process after the defendant has entered a plea of guilty or been found guilty. In juvenile courts, they become involved from the early stages of the process on. Thus, the probation officer, not a judge or prosecutor, is often the first court offi-

cial to have contact with the child. Indeed, it is often the probation officer who recommends an informal disposition to the case. Moreover, in more serious cases, the probation officer's recommendation, along with the social worker's, most often becomes the order of the court.

▌STEPS OF THE JUVENILE COURT PROCESS

From the perspective of law on the books, the steps of the juvenile court process resemble those for adult courts. Although the terminology is slightly different, juveniles accused of violating the law appear to be treated the same as adults in the same situation (see Exhibit 19-2).

From the perspective of law in action, however, the steps of the juvenile court process are strikingly different from their adult counterparts. More than merely differences in terminology, what makes the processing of juveniles so distinctive is the heavy emphasis on informal decision making. The vast majority of decisions are reached not by lawyers and defendants standing before a judge in open court but rather by a juvenile, a parent, and a probation officer sitting around a desk discussing what will happen next.

Delinquency (Crime)

How many crimes are committed by juveniles (as opposed to adults) is impossible to determine with any great precision. As discussed in Chapter 10, the FBI's *Uniform Crime Reports* are based on crimes reported to the police, and most crime victims have no way of knowing the age of the person responsible. Juvenile crime increased steadily beginning in 1985, but this increase declined dramatically after 1995. Two important features related to juvenile crime are worth noting:

■ Crimes against juveniles are less likely to be reported to the police.

■ Juveniles are twice as likely as adults to be victims of serious violent crime and three times as likely to be victims of assault (Snyder and Sickmund 2000).

Summons (Arrest)

A **summons** is a legal document requiring an individual (in this case, a juvenile) to appear in court at a certain time and on a certain date. Although the summons is the official term used in juvenile court, it is informally referred to as an arrest. In 2002, law enforcement agencies in the United States made an estimated 2.5 million arrests of persons under 18. Overall, juveniles were involved in 16 percent of all violent crime index arrests and 32 percent of all property crime index arrests. Juvenile arrest statistics include two noteworthy features:

■ One in four juvenile arrests were of females, and the female proportion of arrests has grown in recent years.

■ Juvenile arrests disproportionately involve minorities.

Intake (Initial Hearing)

Delinquency cases begin with a **referral.** Arrests by law enforcement personnel are by far the biggest source of these referrals—85 percent in a typical year. Referrals, though, may originate from several other sources; for example, some juvenile court cases stem from petitions filed by teachers, neighbors, merchants, or even parents unable to control their children. But mainly they follow after a juvenile has been arrested by the police.

These arrests and other referrals produce 1.67 million juvenile court delinquency cases every year. Best estimates indicate that 61 percent of juvenile filings involve delinquency, with the remainder evenly split between status offenses and child-victim cases.

Juvenile court cases have leveled off in recent years after a period of marked growth. From 1988 to 1997, the total number of filings increased 48 percent. Similar to domestic relations caseloads, juvenile court filings have increased much more rapidly than criminal and civil caseloads (Ostrom and Kauder 1996).

Soon after referral to juvenile court, an **initial hearing** (sometimes called a *preliminary inquiry*) is held. As with much of the terminology of juvenile court, *hearing* is often a misnomer. A hearing implies a formal setting in front of a judge, but more typically it is an informal exchange among the police officer, probation officer, child, and parent.

Detention Hearing

Police make the first **detention** decision shortly after taking the juvenile into custody. Typically, the police release the youth to the custody of his or her parents (or guardians). If the crime is serious, however, the police may detain the youth in a police lockup or local jail. In an earlier era, juveniles were held in the same facilities as adult offenders, but no longer. Federal law mandates that juveniles be held in facilities separated by sight and sound from detention facilities for adults. In many communities the number of cells is limited, so even serious violators may be returned to the streets.

A second detention decision may occur after the juvenile has been referred to the juvenile court. Intake personnel review the case and determine whether the youth should be released to parents or detained. Juveniles may be detained if they are thought dangerous to themselves or others if released. Statutes in most states now mandate that, if the juvenile is to be detained, a detention hearing must be held before a judge or other hearing officer within 24 to 72 hours of arrest.

In a typical year, one out of five juveniles are detained prior to the adjudicatory hearing. On any given day, 100,000 youths are held in public and private juvenile detention facilities (Perkins, Stephan, and Beck 1995).

Petition

During the initial hearing, a decision is made not only about detention but also about whether the case will be handled formally (petition) or informally (nonpetitioned). This decision is most often referred to as the **intake decision** (the juvenile equivalent of the charging decision for adults accused of violating the criminal law).

As Figure 19-3 shows, 42.5 percent of delinquency cases are handled informally (termed **nonpetitioned**). An informal process is used when the decision makers (police, probation

Exhibit 19-2 Steps of the Juvenile Court Process

Law on the Books		Law in Action
Adult	Juvenile	
Crime	*Delinquency:* Acts or conduct in violation of criminal laws.	Juveniles are more likely than adults to be victims of violent crime.
	Status offense: Behavior that is considered an offense only when committed by a juvenile.	Poor, young, minority males are disproportionately at risk of being victims of violent crime.
Arrest	*Summons:* A legal document ordering an individual to appear in court at a certain time on a certain date.	Some 2.9 million juveniles are arrested yearly. Juveniles are arrested primarily for property offenses.
Initial appearance	*Initial hearing:* An often informal hearing during which an intake decision is made.	There are 1.9 million juvenile cases a year. Sixty-five percent of juvenile filings involve delinquency.
Bail	*Detention:* Holding a youth in custody before case disposition.	There are 100,000 offenders in public and private juvenile detention facilities.
Charging	*Intake decision:* The decision made by juvenile court that results in the case being handled either informally at the intake level or more formally and scheduled for an adjudicatory hearing.	Intake decisions are often informal. Courtroom work group norms govern decision making.
	Nonpetitioned: Cases handled informally by duly authorized court personnel.	Forty-five percent of juvenile delinquency cases are handled informally (nonpetitioned).
	Petition: A document filed in juvenile court alleging that a juvenile is delinquent or a status offender and asking that the court assume jurisdiction over the juvenile.	Fifty-five percent of juvenile delinquency court cases are handled formally. Older juveniles with more serious charges are more likely to be handled formally.
Preliminary hearing	*Conference:* Proceeding during which the suspect is informed of rights and a disposition decision may be reached.	In the vast majority of petitioned cases, the juvenile admits guilt during the conference.
Grand jury	Not applicable.	One percent (12,300) of juvenile cases are transferred to adult court.

officers, intake workers, and prosecutors) believe that accountability and rehabilitation can be achieved without the use of formal court intervention. Informal sanctions are voluntary. At times they involve no more than a warning and counseling, but more often they consist of voluntary probation, restitution, and community service.

Juvenile cases that are handled formally are referred to as **petition** cases (or petitioned). Figure 19-3 indicates that 57 percent of cases each year receive such treatment. Intake officers are more likely to petition if

■ Juveniles are older and have longer court histories
■ The delinquency is serious (involves violence, for example)

Fifty-eight percent of all formally processed delinquency cases result in a finding of delinquency. The sanction may be probation, with the juvenile released into the custody of a parent or guardian and ordered to undergo some form of training, education, or counseling. But in 24 percent of adjudicated cases, the juvenile is ordered by the court to residential place-

	Law on the Books	Law in Action
Adult	Juvenile	
Arraignment	Occurs during the conference.	Fifty-five percent of juvenile delinquency cases are handled formally (petitioned).
Evidence	Juveniles have the same constitutional protections as adults with regard to interrogation and unreasonable search and seizure.	Police gathering of evidence is very rarely contested.
Plea bargaining	*Plea bargaining:* Formal and informal discussions resulting in juvenile's admitting guilt.	Even more than in adult court, dispositions in juvenile court are the product of negotiations.
Trial	*Adjudicatory hearing:* Hearing to determine whether a youth is guilty or not guilty.	Adjudicatory hearings are more informal than adult trials.
Sentencing	*Disposition:* A court decision on what will happen to a youth who has not been found innocent.	The disposition is often referred to as a treatment plan.
	Placement: Cases in which juveniles are placed in a residential facility or otherwise removed from their homes.	More than 150,000 juveniles are placed in residential facilities each year.
	Probation: Cases in which youths are placed under informal/voluntary or formal/court-ordered supervision.	More than 500,000 youths each year receive court supervision.
	Dismissal: Cases dismissed (including those warned, counseled, and released) with no further disposition anticipated.	Even case dismissals may include a treatment plan or restitution.
	Other: Miscellaneous dispositions including fines, restitution, and community service.	Teen courts are a modern version of other dispositions.
Appeal	*Appeal:* Request that a higher court review the decision of the lower court.	Appeals are very rare in juvenile proceedings.

ment, such as training school, camp, ranch, or group home. Every year, about 100,000 juveniles are committed to long-term facilities (primarily training schools).

Conference

The **conference** is roughly equivalent to a preliminary hearing in an adult proceeding. The more minor the transgression, the more likely the conference will be held at the same time as the initial hearing and the detention hearing. In more serious matters, particularly if the decision has been made to file a petition, the conference is more likely to be held in closed court.

During the conference, the judge informs the respondent of the charges in the petition. The person is also informed of constitutional protections, including the right to counsel, the right to free counsel, the right to subpoena witnesses for the defense, and the opportunity to cross-examine prosecution witnesses.

Vast numbers of juveniles admit to their offense during the conference, waiving the

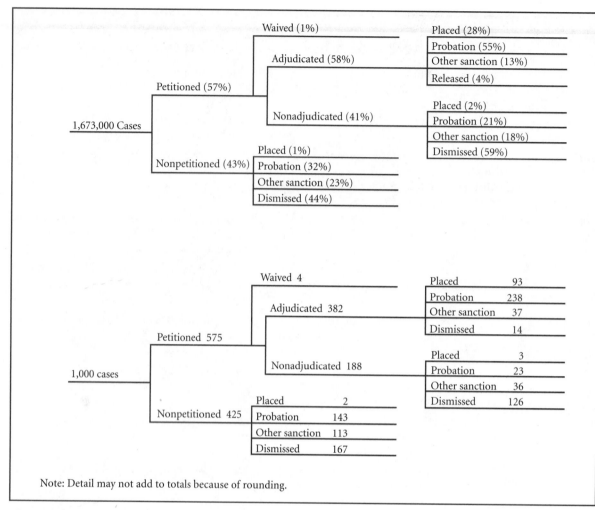

Figure 19-3

Juvenile Court Processing of a Typical 1,000 Delinquency Cases, 1999

SOURCE: Office of Juvenile Justice and Delinquency Prevention, *Statistical Briefing Book* (Washington, DC: U.S. Department of Justice), http://ojjdp.ncjrs.org/ojstatbb/html/ COURT.html (accessed 16 October 2003).

right to counsel and the right to trial. Others request counsel, adjourn to the hallway of the courthouse, and after five or ten minutes with an attorney come back before the judge and admit their offense (Rubin 1989).

Evidence: Gathering and Suppressing

Challenges to how the police gathered evidence play a very minor role in juvenile cases. The presumption is that the child is in trouble (with the juvenile delinquency charge an indicator of that trouble). This presumption makes it difficult to challenge evidence gathering— the judge might conclude that there is insufficient evidence to find the child a delinquent, but still enough to conclude that the child is in need of supervision. Moreover, the informal nature of the entire proceeding discourages legal challenges. The general absence of defense attorneys likewise discourages raising issues associated with *Mapp* and *Miranda*.

Plea Bargaining

The informality of juvenile court makes it somewhat difficult to focus on plea bargaining as a distinct phase, because often it is not. Rather, the discretion that runs throughout the juvenile court process is really plea bargaining by a different name (Dougherty 1988).

Efforts to negotiate the matter typically begin during the intake process. Parent, child, and probation officer discuss the matter and often arrive at a solution satisfactory to all parties. Thus, the 43 percent of juvenile delinquency cases that are nonpetitioned clearly represent what in adult court would be labeled plea bargaining.

Efforts to negotiate a settlement continue after a petition is filed. As Figure 19-3 underscores, 33 percent of petitioned cases are in the "nonadjudicated" category. As we shall discuss shortly, even the adjudicatory hearing resembles an informal exchange of settlement possibilities more than a formal, combative trial.

Adjudicatory Hearing

The **adjudicatory hearing** is equivalent to the trial in adult court. The purpose is to determine whether the allegations contained in the petition are supported by a "preponderance of the evidence" (for status offenses) or "beyond a legal doubt" (for juvenile delinquency).

One of the key changes growing out of the due process revolution associated with *In re Gault* is that juveniles have the right to present evidence in favor, which includes cross-examining the government's witnesses and subpoenaing defense witnesses. The juvenile also maintains the privilege against self-incrimination.

Statistics provided by the Office of Juvenile Justice and Delinquency Prevention indicate that 58 percent of petitioned cases are **adjudicated.** This seems like a high "trial" rate, but a closer look indicates that this is not the case. Adjudicatory hearings are much less formal than adult trials. This is due in part to the lack of juries (except in a few exceptional cases in a handful of states). The rules of evidence (see Chapter 14) are designed to keep certain information from lay jurors lest they place undue emphasis on some information. But since there are no juries, these rules have considerably less applicability.

Disposition

The more serious the crime and/or the longer the juvenile has been in trouble with the law, the more likely it is that a formal probation report will be prepared. Like its adult counterpart, the probation report (sometimes called the predisposition report) is prepared by the probation officer; it is based on interviews with the juvenile, the parents, school officials, and others. The report chronicles the juvenile's prior history with the court and also may estimate the economic harm suffered by the victim. Finally, the report makes a **disposition** recommendation.

The most common disposition is a **dismissal.** Cases dismissed (including those warned, counseled, and released), with no further disposition anticipated, are most likely to occur among cases that are handled informally.

The second most common disposition is **probation.** Probation cases are those in which youths were placed under informal/voluntary or formal/court-ordered supervision.

Another common disposition is **placement.** Placement cases are those in which youth are placed in a residential facility for delinquents or status offenders, or otherwise removed from their homes and placed elsewhere. Consistent with the nonpunishment orientation of the juvenile process, juveniles are not sentenced to prison, but rather are placed in residential treatment facilities called training institutes and the like.

Finally, a significant number of dispositions that do not fall under the previous three categories are referred to simply as **other dispositions.** These include fines, restitution, community service, and referrals outside the court for services with minimal or no further court involvement anticipated.

In making disposition decisions, juvenile court judges focus primarily on offense characteristics and are influenced only marginally by the offender's social characteristics. These findings are more consistent with the view that juvenile courts are becoming more like adult criminal courts than with the view that individualized justice is the goal (Applegate et al. 2000).

Juvenile courts in urban areas tend to send proportionally fewer delinquents to state detention facilities than do courts serving less populous areas (Rubin 1989). Officials in rural areas are sometimes quicker to "pull the string" and send less serious delinquency cases to state placement—partially because they have fewer institutional resources to deal with these youths, but also because the equivalent event is viewed as more harmful in small towns than in big cities.

Appeal

Juveniles have a constitutional right to appeal. The opinion in *Gault* discussed the importance of appeals for due process rights but declined to make it a constitutional requirement. Prompted, however, by the possibility that the Supreme Court might indeed make it a constitutional right, state legislatures have passed laws granting juveniles the right to appeal. Thus, today the common practice is to give juveniles the same rights to appeal that apply to adults (Davis 1984). By statute, juveniles also have the right to a transcript and a right to counsel for the first appeal.

The right to appeal is primarily limited to juveniles (and their parents). The state may appeal only in limited circumstances, and this right is seldom exercised.

JUVENILE COURTS: THE NEXT 100 YEARS

Juvenile courts, which were once virtually invisible judicial bodies, have in recent years become the central focus in the debate over crime. The war on crime, Chapter 1 argued, is constantly evolving, and as the twenty-first century begins, there are pressures to change the nature of juvenile court justice. A century after the founding of juvenile courts, it is appropriate to ask, what will juvenile courts be like 100 years from now? Indeed, some critics argue that this grand experiment has been a failure and should be scrapped.

The debate over the future reflects basic disagreements along the lines of the crime control versus due process models.

Crime Control Model: More Adult Penalties

The crime control model begins with the premise that crime is the product of moral breakdown. This is clearly the theme sounded by Darlene Kennedy (1997) of the National Center for Public Policy Research. "Let's hold juveniles responsible for their crimes," she argues, blaming undue leniency of juvenile court for violent juvenile crimes.

One version of more adult penalties for juvenile offenders involves increasing the number of transfers to adult court. Other proposals include merging adult and juvenile records into one. Argues Marvin Wolfgang: "The dual system of juvenile and criminal justice that prevents the sharing of information and permits a serious, chronic violent juvenile to become a virgin offender after his 19th birthday is a strange cultural invention" (quoted in Bureau of Justice Statistics 1990, 18).

Some go so far as to argue that it is time to abolish juvenile court altogether. Peter Reinharz, chief of New York City's juvenile prosecution unit, argues, "It's time to sell everything off and start over" (quoted in Butterfield 1997). Chronic overcrowding is one problem often mentioned, but it is unclear how merely shuffling the overcrowding problems of juvenile facilities to already overcrowded adult courts and adult prisons will alleviate the problem.

In short, a sharp increase in the public's fear of juvenile crime, particularly gangs, drugs, and violence, has added impetus to a get-tough attitude toward juvenile criminals.

Due Process Model: More Youth Crime Prevention

The due process model starts with the premise that crime is a reflection of social problems. Punishment alone, therefore, is not necessarily the answer and might even be counterproductive. Placing juveniles in the same prisons as adults, for example, might simply make the youths more hardened and more accomplished crooks.

Amidst numerous voices arguing that the juvenile court created 100 years ago is now

A DAY IN COURT

Teen Court

 Serving as a juror for the Holland (Michigan) Teen Court has its perks—sometimes after the teen jurors have finished a case, the police department kicks in and buys a pizza. Founded in 1991, the Holland Teen Court assigns a punishment appropriate to the defendant's attitude and crime. For level one violations (curfew infractions and cigarette possession, for example), the usual penalty is 8 to 12 hours of community service. For level two violations (shoplifting and disorderly conduct, for example), the typical penalty is 13 to 24 hours of community service (Sager 2000).

The Holland Teen Court is but one example of how local government officials are experimenting with a variety of new approaches to juvenile offenders. *Teen courts*, or *youth courts*, as they are sometimes called, have been established in 675 local jurisdictions nationwide as an alternative to traditional juvenile courts (Butts and Buck 2000). The programs target juvenile first offenders accused of committing minor crimes. Teen court is designed not only to give these first offenders a second chance but also to provide an educational experience to the offender and to its other volunteer participants. The ultimate goal is to increase participants' self-esteem and instill respect for the legal system (*Official Teen Court Homepage* 1998).

Teen court has also been referred to as *peer court*. This is most appropriate, considering that teenagers assume the roles of prosecuting and defense attorneys, jury members, and even judge in some jurisdictions. The young officers of the court are volunteers who are trained and supervised by professional volunteers. The structure of teen court varies by jurisdictions. The jury panel usually includes a combination of volunteers from the community and former teen court defendants for whom jury duty is part of the punishment for their offense (Zehner 1997).

Most teen court juries do not deliberate the guilt or innocence of a defendant. A prerequisite of being accepted into the program is an admission of guilt by the defendant. Instead, the jury decides the nature of the offender's noninstitutionalized punishment based on preestablished guidelines. The focus of the sentence is on rehabilitation. In addition to jury duty, offenders may be ordered to pay restitution and formally apologize to victims, perform community service, obtain counseling, attend educational seminars, or participate in any other activities the jury finds warranted by the facts of the individual case (Shiff and Wexler 1996).

What is responsible for the growing popularity of teen court programs nationwide is their apparent success in controlling teenage criminal recidivism. In 1995 the Bend, Oregon, teen court reported statistics indicating that 95 percent of its teen participants avoided being rearrested in the first ten years of the court's existence (Oregon Peer 1998). Other jurisdictions report similar success rates. But experts are concerned over the lack of rigorous and comprehensive research evaluations of the effectiveness of teen courts in the prevention of teenage criminal recidivism. It is entirely possible that the statistics look so good because only juveniles viewed as "good risks" are initially selected for the programs.

To view firsthand what teen courts do, click on any of these sites:

Holland (Michigan) Teen Court http://www.teen-court.org/

Charlotte County (Florida) http://www.charlotte-florida.com/community/teen.htm

Knox County (Illinois) http://library.thinkquest.org/2640/

Irving (Texas) http://www.ci.irving.tx.us/Courts/welcomet.htm

outmoded, some respond that the nation should return to those roots. The Progressive movement was concerned about mistreatment of juveniles at the turn of the last century, and we should have the same concern today, argues the American Civil Liberties Union (1996) in a policy statement about "Whatever happened to prevention?"

The core of the argument is that crime prevention works. Instead of pouring increasing amounts of public dollars into prisons (both adult and juvenile), we need to put more into education and prevention. Perhaps most needed are programs that work with youth in new and creative ways. Teen Court is but one example (see A Day in Court: Teen Court).

▌CONCLUSION

The charge against Gerald Gault—making a lewd telephone call—seems tame compared with today's concerns about preteens committing violent crimes. Nonetheless, this irritating but hardly life-threatening behavior was to usher in a new era. Whereas the Progressives saw procedural rights as an impediment to helping children in need, a later generation viewed due process as providing an important safety net against high-handed behavior by government officials.

Court decisions like *In re Gault* and changing patterns of youthful behavior—to say nothing of the types of crimes committed by youths today—could not have been foreseen by the Progressive movement. Whether the founders of juvenile court would recognize their innovation 100 years later is debatable. Initially, juvenile court was supposed to make decisions based on the "best interests" of the child. Today, a get-tough attitude has come to dominate discussions of juvenile court. Holding the youth accountable to community standards now plays a major role in the dispositions reached (Sanborn 1994).

The future of juvenile courts is rapidly unfolding. To some observers, juvenile courts need to provide more adultlike due process. To others, juvenile courts need to provide more adultlike sentences. Still others would stress the need for new and creative ways of dealing with contemporary problems of American youth. The Progressive movement, after all, responded to changing conditions in society produced by the Industrial Revolution. To many, the current challenge is to respond to the changing conditions of society produced by the information age.

CRITICAL THINKING QUESTIONS

1. In what ways do juvenile courts differ from courts that process adults accused of violating the criminal law? In what ways are juvenile courts similar?

2. What are the key features of the juvenile courts in your state? How are they organized, what is the upper age limit, and what is the lower age limit?

3. What advantages do you see in adding due process rights to juvenile court? What disadvantages do you see? To what extent are discussions over this matter influenced by atypical cases?

4. Compare the courtroom work group of adult court and juvenile court. Which actors are the same? Which actors are different? Do the members of the courtroom work group function the same in juvenile court as in adult court?

5. Compare the steps of the adult court process with the steps of juvenile court. In what ways are they similar? In what ways are they different?

6. What do you think juvenile courts will look like 100 years from now? Will they incorporate more adult due process? Will they stress more adult penalties? Or will they develop more innovative helping programs?

KEY TERMS

adjudicated (465)
adjudicatory hearing (465)
child-victim (453)
conference (463)
delinquency (453)
detention (461)
dismissal (465)
disposition (465)
initial hearing (461)
intake decision (461)
juvenile (448)
juvenile court (446)
lower age of jurisdiction (448)
nonpetitioned case (461)
other dispositions (465)
parens patriae (445)
petition (462)
placement (465)

probation (465)
probation officer (460)
referral (461)
status offense (453)
summons (461)
transfer to criminal court (450)
upper age of jurisdiction (448)

WORLD WIDE WEB RESOURCES AND EXERCISES

Web Guides
http://dir.yahoo.com/Society_and_Culture/Crime/
   Juvenile/
http://dir.yahoo.com/Society_and_Culture/Crime/
   Correction_and_Rehabilitation/
   Juvenile_Detention_Centers/
http://dir.yahoo.com/Society_and_Culture/Crime/
   Juvenile/Teen_Court/

Web Search Terms
juvenile courts   *juvenile justice*
teen courts

Useful URLs
The American Bar Association Juvenile Justice Center works in partnership with other ABA entities, bar associations, and local and state advocacy groups to monitor and influence juvenile justice policy and practice: http://www.abanet.org/crimjust/juvjus/home.html.

The Center for Community Alternatives provides services, training, and technical assistance to professionals in the criminal and juvenile justice systems: http://www.communityalternatives.org/.

The National Center for Juvenile Justice is the leading source of statistics on juvenile delinquency and the operation of juvenile and family courts: http://www.ncjj.org/.

The U.S. Department of Justice, Office of Juvenile Justice and Delinquency Prevention, is charged with leading the fight against juvenile violence and victimization and promoting practical solutions to the problems challenging the nation's juveniles: http://ojjdp.ncjrs.org/.

Visit the National Council of Juvenile and Family Court Judges: http://www.ncjfcj.unr.edu/.

Visit the National Juvenile Detention Association: http://www.njda.com/.

Uncommon URLs
Building Blocks for Youth is an advocacy group particularly concerned about racial disparities: http://www.buildingblocksforyouth.org/.

Juvenile Justice is an online magazine serving juvenile justice professionals in all 50 states involved in youth and human services, law enforcement, probation, and parole: http://www.juvenilejustice.com/.

For a close-up view of juvenile court, visit the Criminon Program in Los Angeles Central Juvenile Hall: http://www.criminon.org/html/juvenile.htm.

New Jersey Juvenile Detention Association offers a model Web page: http://www.njjda.org/.

Cook County Juvenile Detention Center 4-H and Urban Gardening stresses innovative programs: http://www.urbanext.uiuc.edu/ptw/03cookjdc.html.

Web Exercises
1. Update statistics on the number of juvenile arrests and the number of juveniles in placement facilities, using the National Criminal Justice Reference Center home page, http://www.ncjrs.org. Look under Juvenile Justice to find the latest government reports.
2. Do a search for home pages dealing with teen courts. Here is an example of how to do the search: http://yahoo.com/Society_and_Culture/Crime/Juvenile/TeenCourt. Select one home page that is geographically close to you and another one more distant. In what ways are the programs similar? In what ways are they different? What goals do these programs articulate? What claims do they make for success? Which program would you

recommend to your local court? Why? If you wish, also use a search engine such as google.com.

3. Policies affecting juvenile courts are under intense scrutiny. The American Bar Association's Juvenile Justice Center provides a quick overview of changing legislation. The URL is **http://www.abanet.org/crimjust/juvjus**. Click on Hill Watch to monitor the progress of pending national legislation. Also click on State Watch. What current proposals are under consideration in your state?

4. Using the search engine of your choice and the search term "juvenile court" + "reform," choose two or more sites. Are the proposed reforms more representative of the crime control model or the due process model?

INFOTRAC COLLEGE EDITION RESOURCES AND EXERCISES

Basic Searches

juvenile courts	*teen courts*
juvenile justice, administration of	*juvenile probation*
	In re Gault

Recommended Articles

"Comprehensive Juvenile Justice: A Legislator's Guide"

Thomas F. Geraghty, Steven A. Drizin, "Charting a New Course for Juvenile Justice: Listening to Outsiders"

Dan Johnson, "Rehabilitating Criminals Before They Grow Up"

Sharon Mihalic, "Blueprints for Violence Prevention"

Judge David B. Mitchell, "Congress Needs to Consult Profession before Enacting Juvenile Justice Reform"

Denise Casamento Musser, "Kansas' Grassroots Juvenile Justice Reform"

Steven H. Rosenbaum, "Civil Rights Issues in Juvenile Detention and Correctional Systems"

Bobbie Wilbur, Colleen Murphy, Kaye Caulkins, "Making a Difference in Juvenile Justice"

InfoTrac College Edition Exercises

1. Using the search term "juvenile courts, waiver of jurisdiction of," find two or more articles that discuss the topic. What factors influence decisions to transfer some juvenile offenders to adult court? Are juveniles transferred to adult court sanctioned more severely compared to the punishment they would have received in juvenile court?

2. Using the search term "juvenile courts" or "juvenile justice, administration of," find two or more articles that discuss juvenile court reform. Analyze the articles. Are the recommendations more consistent with the crime control or the due process model of criminal justice?

FOR FURTHER READING

Bazemore, Gordon. "Judges in the Punitive Juvenile Court: Organizational, Career and Ideological Influences on Sanctioning Orientation." *Justice Quarterly* 14 (1997): 87–114.

Chesney-Lind, Meda, and Randall Shelden. *Girls, Delinquency, and Juvenile Justice.* Belmont, CA: Wadsworth, 2004.

Dean, Charles, J. David Hirschel, and Robert Brame. "Minorities and Juvenile Case Dispositions." *Justice System Journal* 18 (1996): 267–285.

Feld, Barry. *Bad Kids: Race and the Transformation of the Juvenile Court.* New York: Oxford University Press, 1999.

———. *Justice for Children: The Right to Counsel and the Juvenile Courts.* Boston: Northeastern University Press, 1993.

Fisher, Margaret. *Youth Courts: Young People Delivering Justice.* Chicago: American Bar Association, 2002.

Gaarder, Emily, and Joanne Belknap. "Tenuous Borders: Girls Transferred to Adult Court." *Criminology* 40 (2002): 481–518.

Gramckow, Heike, and Elena Tompkins. *Enhancing Prosecutors' Ability to Combat and*

Prevent Juvenile Crime in Their Jurisdictions. Washington, DC: Office of Juvenile Justice and Delinquency Prevention, 1999.

Guarino-Ghezzi, Susan, and Edward Loughran. *Balancing Juvenile Justice.* New Brunswick, NJ: Transaction, 1996.

Jacobs, Mark. *Screwing the System and Making It Work: Juvenile Justice in the No-Fault Society.* Chicago: University of Chicago Press, 1990.

Kurlychek, Megan, Patricia Torbet, and Melanie Bozynski. *Focus on Accountability: Best Practices for Juvenile Court and Probation.* Washington, DC: Office of Juvenile Justice and Delinquency Prevention, 1999.

Mears, Daniel, and Samuel Field. "Theorizing Sanctioning in a Criminalized Juvenile Court." *Criminology* 38 (2000): 983–1020.

Moon, Melissa, John Wright, Francis Cullen, and Jennifer Pealer. "Putting Kids to Death: Specifying Public Support for Juvenile Capital Punishment." *Justice Quarterly* 17 (2000): 663–684.

Parent, Dale, Terence Dunworth, Douglas McDonald, and William Rhodes. *Key Legislative Issues in Criminal Justice: Transferring Serious Juvenile Offenders to Adult Courts.* Washington, DC: U.S. Department of Justice, National Institute of Justice, 1997.

Scalia, John. *Juvenile Delinquents in the Federal Justice System.* Washington, DC: Bureau of Justice Statistics, 1997.

Schwartz, Ira. *(In)Justice for Juveniles: Rethinking the Best Interests of the Child.* New York: Lexington Books, 1989.

Siegel, Larry, Brandon Welsh, and Joseph J. Senna. *Juvenile Delinquency: Theory, Practice, and Law,* 8th ed. Belmont, CA: Wadsworth, 2003.

Torbet, Patricia, Richard Gable, Hunter Hurst, Imogene Montgomery, Linda Szymanski, and Douglas Thomas. *State Responses to Serious and Violent Juvenile Crime.* Pittsburgh: National Center for Juvenile Justice, 1996.

Wright, Linda. "Juvenile Crime in Rural Areas." *Justice System Journal* 19 (1997): 355–364.

Chapter 1 began by noting that crime has been a pressing national concern for more than three decades. This epilogue will return to that initial theme and discuss why crime is a political issue and how the persistence of crime as a political issue influences the judicial process.

CRIME AS AN EMPTY VESSEL

Crime has persisted as a political issue for more than 30 years because it is a vague term, and purposefully so. Indeed, the political dimension of crime has been likened to an empty vessel (Heinz, Jacob, and Lineberry 1983); mention the word, and the listener is free to pour in whatever content he or she prefers.

Viewing crime as an empty vessel helps explain why the content changes so much over time. Crime as a political issue has tremendous advantages (political, social, and moral) for entrepreneurs because it is so readily transformed into new and yet more alarming images. To a public that perceives that society is going to hell in a handbasket, the ever-changing nature of the crime problem provides reinforcement. As soon as the public becomes bored or jaded about one issue, a new one can quickly take its place. There is a continuous need to find new types of deviance because the public loses interest in denunciations of sin and degradation that have been around for a while. Consequently, analyzing crime is equivalent to diagnosing illness in a hypochondriac; as soon as the doctor rules out a specific malady, the patient discovers he or she suffers from another illness (which by some mysterious process is closely tied to media attention to that illness).

Thus, crime persists as a political issue because it comes close to being all things to all people at all times. As an empty vessel, it is a convenient surrogate for the two persistent underlying political issues of contemporary America: poverty and race.

Poverty and Crime

Crime remains a persistent political issue because it is intimately intertwined with poverty. To quote the old adage: "The law in all its infinite majesty prohibits the rich as well as the poor from sleeping under bridges." In the words of Lawrence Friedman (1993), criminal justice "has always fallen more heavily on the underclass, on the deviants, on the 'outs.' Criminal justice was the strong arm of the stratification system." Not that all the poor are swept up in the net of the criminal justice system, nor are the nonpoor immune to its sting, but as Jonathan Simon (1994) argues, prisons and parole are replacing welfare as forms of controlling the poor.

Race and Crime

Crime also remains a persistent political issue because it is intimately related in the public's mind to race. Race is the major fault line of American politics. Today, overt racism is rare in American politics, but race is nevertheless part of a hidden agenda underlying many domestic issues. Depending on where you live, the specific "out" group varies but includes blacks, Hispanics, Asians, and Native Americans. There is little doubt that when some politicians denounce the ravages of crime, voters fill in the gaps and single out racial groups as the primary cause.

The tragic reality is that for most Americans, crime has a black face (Marby and Thomas 1992). What gets lost in the discussion is the overriding fact that most crime is intraracial. But some elected officials couch the issue in terms that listeners understand as interracial. Thus, white and black Americans view crime in very different terms (Browning and Cao 1992).

CONSEQUENCES OF POLITICAL RHETORIC FOR THE CRIMINAL COURTS

The continuing political rhetoric of crime has important consequences for the courts. In trying to construct a realistic assessment of the troubled courthouse, one must attempt to walk the fine line between two extremes: the rhetoric of crisis and endorsement of the status quo.

Increased Expectations

One way in which political rhetoric about crime affects the courts is to increase expectations. The problems of the courthouse are real and should be acknowledged. But this does not mean that the courts are on the brink of collapse. Public perceptions of these problems are often exaggerated, as this book frequently points out. Exaggerated assertions distract attention from realistic assessments of what the problems are and what can be done to solve them. The primary problems of the courts are not the result of external calamities, such as high crime rates and expanded caseloads. Rather, these problems are due to increased attention and raised standards (Feeley 1983).

This tide of rising expectations is clearly legitimate. What is of concern is that some of these increased expectations are unrealistic, and frustration results when lofty goals are not met. We need to ask the right questions. How much delay is too much? How much due process can the lower courts reasonably expect to provide?

The troubled history of the Law Enforcement Assistance Administration (LEAA) is a case in point (Feeley and Sarat 1980). Congress had no clear idea about what needed to be done—only a general sense that change was necessary. Instead of providing policy direction, the act created a planning process. But this left unclear what was to be planned. Overall, the stated goals were overly ambitious. The

LEAA did foster important changes and some much-needed improvements. But unrealistic expectations distracted attention from these achievements and contributed to a sense of frustration about reform. Eventually LEAA was disbanded, but some components, including the Bureau of Justice Assistance and the National Institute of Justice, remain in the Justice Department.

Disagreement over Goals

The political rhetoric of crime also has the unfortunate consequence of papering over a lack of agreement on the fundamental goals of the courts. The value of court reform often lies in the eyes of the beholder. What one person applauds as progress, another denounces as a step backward. The essential difficulty is that reform efforts mask these areas of disagreement.

All too often, the emphasis on procedural improvements comes at the expense of substantive policy issues. Government reform movements that purport to be neutral ways of doing things better may actually disguise policy alternatives. Thus, it is necessary to separate the reformers' rhetoric from their underlying and sometimes unarticulated concerns. The emphasis on procedure not only masks substantive policy issues but also diverts attention from questions about the fairness of the system and protection of defendants' rights (Cole and Neubauer 1979). Efforts to improve court efficiency must be considered in substantive terms.

The Dynamics of Courthouse Justice

A flawed understanding of the court process contributes to unrealistic expectations (Feeley 1983). Reformers focus on individual problems in isolation from the broader process. They stress the formal dimensions of the process (law on the books), neglecting the informal ways that discretionary power is controlled and channeled (law in action).

The courts are a community of actors. Throughout this book, the central role of the courtroom work group has been stressed.

THE MURDER TRIAL OF SHAREEF COUSIN

Uncertainties and Contradictions

Trials, Americans have come to expect, finally decide matters. After the evidence has been presented and the lawyers have argued about the meaning of that evidence, the public expects an answer to the most basic question: Did he (or she) commit the crime or not? But after trial some cases still seem to be unresolved. To some, unanswered questions remain after the trials of Sacco and Vanzetti and of Julius and Ethel Rosenberg. These cases linger in the national consciousness because of doubts about whether the verdict was correct. In New Orleans, the murder trial of Shareef Cousin likewise remains unsettled, offering uncertainties and contradictions.

One of the most fundamental unanswered questions centers on the defendant himself. The official court records and the unofficial media reports paint two contradictory images of Shareef Cousin. From one vantage point, he appears to be a teenager who was in a little more trouble than most, but not much. In school he seemed to excel in math (when he wanted to), and he seemed to experience no major problems while living in the Boston area. From another vantage point, however, Shareef Cousin appears to have been a young man whose life was rapidly spinning out of control. He ran with the wrong crowd, most likely was abusing drugs, and committed four armed robberies in a few short months. Perhaps the answers to some of these questions could be found in Shareef Cousin's medical records, which remain under court seal.

The puzzle of who Shareef Cousin was interacts with one of the dominant issues of American society: race. Newspaper coverage of the trial clearly highlighted the importance of race—for example, by reporting on protests outside the courthouse. By contrast, the official court record shows little if any evidence of race—for example, in the absence of an appeal based on race by the defense during closing arguments. But the reality that a white person was murdered by an African American is bound to fuel the racial divide so prominent in big U.S. cities like New Orleans.

Also striking is the contradictory publicity the case received nationally as opposed to locally. On the national scene, the case was, for a while, prominently featured. For example, Bianca Jagger (ex-wife of rock star Mick Jagger) was to visit New Orleans to lend moral support (but canceled after the district attorney chose not to retry the boy). Locally, however, the case generated only passing attention, perhaps because Shareef Cousin failed to strike a sympathetic chord (probably because he is serving a 20-year prison sentence for four armed robberies).

Another set of contradictions relates to how national groups have stated (or misstated) the facts in the case. Anti–death penalty groups, for example, unequivocally proclaim Shareef Cousin innocent. For example, the National Coalition to Abolish the Death Penalty (2001) boldly declares that "Shareef couldn't have killed Michael Gerardi." They support this position by restating the alibi defense, which Chapter 14 stressed was effectively shredded by the prosecutor during cross-examination. Conversely, pro–death penalty groups seem equally convinced that Cousin was a guilty murderer released on a technicality. For example, Pro-Death Penalty.com (2001) states without reservation that the conviction was reversed because the prosecutor improperly impeached a witness with prior inconsistent statements: "Other jurisdictions would not necessarily find this evidence inadmissible." This seems a dubious legal interpretation of the case if for no other reason than that the national group completely ignores the key issue of the prosecutor's hiding exculpatory evidence from the defense. If their interpretation was correct, the DA would have retried the case. In short, both sides appear guilty of making absolute statements about matters that are in reality ambiguous.

The contradictions and uncertainties underlay the basic question in the trial of Shareef Cousin: Did he murder Michael Gerardi? I will let readers form their own conclusion. Was Shareef Cousin a brutal murderer whose conviction was overturned on legal technicalities, or an innocent on death row falsely convicted because of prosecutorial misconduct and police incompetence?

Judges, prosecutors, defense attorneys, juries, and the police are tied together by more than a shared workplace. Because these actors appear daily on the same judicial stage, their interactions combine to create what is best described as a social organization. Limited knowledge about the dynamics of courthouse justice explains why numerous reform efforts have not been successful. Efforts to limit or control discretion at one point in the process typically result in increased discretion elsewhere. To be successful, reforms must recognize the fundamental role of the courtroom work group.

CONCLUSION

In the final analysis, crime is a persistent political issue because the crime problem is insoluble. The public is concerned about crime. Needless to say, politicians respond; it would be strange indeed for politicians not to promise to do something. Alas, once in office, public officials discover there is little agreement on the specifics of solving the crime problem and even less money to fund any promising ideas. Thus, elected officials discover that the voters are fearful of crime but often even more fearful of rising taxes (Heinz, Jacob, and Lineberry 1983).

Crime as a political issue often forces government officials to take action for action's sake, and in the end, the politics of promise deteriorate into the politics of scapegoating. Throughout this book we have examined why the most often mentioned areas for change have little if anything to do with the crime rate.

The political rhetoric of crime ignores the basic reality: The courts cannot be expected to solve the problem of crime. This perspective stands in sharp contrast to political rhetoric that lashes out at the criminal courts for their failure to protect the community. For those who want to take advantage of it, crime as a political issue is ideal because it can be associated with action for action's sake. Everyone demands that something be done. What can be done, of course, is unclear to politicians and court officials alike. It is unrealistic to expect that the courts can have much impact on the crime rate.

The elastic nature of crime as a persistent political issue explains why this book repeatedly suggests that a number of major reform efforts should be regarded with a healthy dose of skepticism. However, it should also be noted that in a number of important ways the court process is fairer and more focused than in earlier times. Future efforts require the establishment of realistic expectations about the nature of the court process, how change occurs, and what can be done to make courts better.

Some reform efforts resemble thunderbolts from far-off Mount Olympus. Outsiders proclaim that a problem exists and reform is needed to correct the problem. But those on the working level either fail to see the problem or find that the proposed solution bears little resemblance to how the court system actually operates. When the reform fails because it was poorly tailored to local conditions, the sense that nothing works gains greater momentum. Reform efforts need to refocus by taking into account legitimate practices reflected in the courtroom work group.

Glossary

A

acquittal The decision of the judge or jury that the defendant is not guilty.

adjudicated Judicial determination (judgment) that a youth is a delinquent or status offender.

adjudicatory hearing Court hearing to determine whether a youth is guilty or not guilty.

administrative regulations Rules and regulations adopted by administrative agencies that have the force of law.

adversary system A proceeding in which the opposing sides have the opportunity to present their evidence and arguments.

affirm In an appellate court, to reach a decision that agrees with the result reached in the case by the lower court.

affirmative defense Without denying the charge, defendant raises extenuating or mitigating circumstances, such as insanity, self-defense, or entrapment.

alibi defense A defense alleging that the defendant was elsewhere at the time of the crime he or she is charged with.

alternate jurors Jurors chosen in excess of the minimum number needed, in case one or more jurors is unable to serve for the entire trial.

alternative dispute resolution (ADR) Less adversarial means of settling disputes that may or may not involve a court.

American Bar Association (ABA) The largest voluntary organization of lawyers in the United States.

Anglo-American law The American legal system (see *common law*).

appellant The party, usually the losing one, that seeks to overturn the decision of a lower court by appealing to a higher court.

appellate court A court that hears appeals from trial courts on points of law.

appellate court record Papers, documents, and exhibits, as well as the transcript of the trial, that are submitted to the appellate court for review.

appellate jurisdiction The authority of a court to hear, determine, and render judgment in an action on appeal from an inferior court.

appellee (respondent) A party, usually the winning party, against whom a case is appealed

arraignment The stage of the criminal process in which the defendant is formally told the charges and allowed to enter a plea.

arrest The physical taking into custody of a suspected law violator or juvenile.

arrest warrant A document issued by a judicial officer authorizing the arrest of a specific person.

Article I Section of the U.S. Constitution concerning the legislative branch of the national government.

Article III Section of the U.S. Constitution concerning the judicial branch of the national government.

assembly-line justice The operation of any segment of the criminal justice system in which excessive workload results in decisions being made with such speed and impersonality that defendants are treated as objects to be processed rather than as individuals.

assigned counsel system Arrangement that provides attorneys for persons who are accused of crimes and are unable to hire their own lawyers. The judge assigns a member of the bar to provide counsel to a particular defendant.

attempt An act done with the intent to commit a crime, an overt act toward its commission, the failure to complete the crime, and the apparent possibility of committing it.

attendant (accompanying) circumstances Conditions surrounding a criminal act—for example, the amount of money stolen in a theft.

B

bail The security (money or bail bond) given as a guarantee that a released prisoner will appear at trial.

bail agent (bail bondsman) A person whose business it is to effect release on bail for persons held in custody by pledging to pay a sum of money if a defendant fails to appear in court as required.

bankruptcy judge Judicial officer who presides over the legal procedure under federal law by which a person is relieved of all debts after placing all property under the court's authority. An organization may be reorganized or terminated by the court in order to pay off creditors.

bench warrant (capias) An order issued by the court itself, or from the bench, for the arrest of a person; it is not based, as is an arrest warrant, on a probable cause showing that a person has committed a crime, but only on the person's failure to appear in court as directed.

best-evidence rule Rule requiring that someone coming into court must bring the best available original evidence to prove the questions involved in the case.

beyond a reasonable doubt Burden of proof required by law to convict a defendant in a criminal case.

Bill of Rights The first ten amendments to the U.S. Constitution, guaranteeing certain rights and liberties to the people.

bind over If at the preliminary hearing the judge believes that sufficient probable cause exists to hold a criminal defendant, the accused is said to be bound over for trial.

***Boykin* form** Document intended to show that the defendant entered a guilty plea voluntarily and intelligently, understanding the charges and consequences of conviction (*Boykin v. Alabama* 1969).

brief A written statement submitted by the attorney arguing a case in court. It states the facts of the case, presents legal arguments in support of the moving party, and cites applicable law.

Burger Court The Supreme Court under the leadership of Chief Justice Warren Burger (1969–1986).

C

capital offense Any crime punishable by death.

capital punishment Use of the death penalty as the punishment for the commission of a particular crime.

cash bond   Requirement that money be posted to secure pretrial release.

challenge for cause   Method for excusing a potential juror because of specific reasons such as bias or prejudgment; can be granted only by the judge.

chambers   The private office of a judge.

change of venue   The removal of a case from one jurisdiction to another. It is usually granted if the court believes that, due to prejudice, a defendant cannot receive a fair trial in the area where the crime occurred.

charge bargaining   In return for the defendant's plea of guilty, the prosecutor allows the defendant to plead guilty to a less serious charge than the one originally filed.

charging conference   Meeting attended by judge, prosecutor, and defense attorney during which the judge's instructions to the jury are discussed.

charging document   An information, indictment, or complaint that states the formal criminal charge against a named defendant.

child-victim   Juvenile court case involving a child who has been neglected and/or abused by the parents.

circumstantial evidence   An indirect method of proving the material facts of a case; testimony that is not based on the witness's personal observation of the material events.

civil law   Law governing private parties; other than criminal law.

civil protection order   Court order requiring a person to stay away from another person.

clerk of court   An elected or appointed court officer responsible for maintaining the written records of the court and for supervising or performing the clerical tasks necessary to conduct judicial business.

closing argument   Statement made by an attorney at the end of the presentation of evidence in which the attorney summarizes the case for the jury.

common law   Law developed in England by judges who made legal decisions in the absence of written law. Such decisions served as precedents and became "common" to all of England. Common law is judge-made, it uses precedent, and it is found in multiple sources.

complaint   In civil law, the first paper filed in a lawsuit. In criminal law, a charge signed by the victim that a person named has committed a specified offense.

conditions of confinement lawsuit   Lawsuit brought by a prisoner contesting prison conditions.

conference   Juvenile court proceeding roughly equivalent to a preliminary hearing, in which the suspect is informed of his or her rights and a disposition decision may be reached.

consent search   A person, place, or movables may be lawfully searched by an officer of the law if the owner gives free and voluntary consent.

constitution   The fundamental rules that determine how those who govern are selected, the procedures by which they operate, and the limits to their powers.

constitutional courts   Federal courts created by Congress by virtue of its power under Article III of the Constitution to create courts inferior to the Supreme Court.

contempt of court   The failure or refusal to obey a court order; may be punished by a fine or imprisonment.

contract   A legally enforceable agreement between two or more parties.

contract system   Method of providing counsel for indigents under which the government contracts with a law firm to represent all indigents for the year in return for a set fee.

corpus delicti   The body or substance of a crime, composed of two elements—the act and the criminal agency producing it.

count bargaining   The defendant pleads guilty to some, but not all, of the counts contained in the charging document, which reduces the potential sentence.

courtroom work group   The regular participants in the day-to-day activities of a particular courtroom; judge, prosecutor, and defense attorney interacting on the basis of shared norms.

crime control model   A perspective on the criminal justice process based on the proposition that the most important function of criminal justice is the repression of crime, focusing on efficiency as a principal measure.

criminal justice system   Agencies and institutions directly involved in the implementation of public policy concerning crime, mainly the law enforcement agencies, courts, and corrections.

criminal law   Laws passed by government that define and prohibit antisocial behavior.

cross-examination   At trial, the questions of one attorney put to a witness called by the opposing attorney.

cruel and unusual punishment   Governmental punishment that is prohibited by the Eighth Amendment.

D

death penalty   Capital punishment, or executions by the state for purposes of social defense.

declaratory judgment   Judicial pronouncement declaring the legal rights of parties involved in an actual case or controversy.

defendant   The person or party against whom a lawsuit or prosecution is brought.

delay   Postponement or adjournment of proceedings in a case; lag in case-processing time.

delinquency   An act committed by a juvenile that would require an adult to be prosecuted in a criminal court. Because the act is committed by a juvenile, it falls within the jurisdiction of the juvenile court. Delinquent acts include crimes against persons or property, drug offenses, and crimes against public order.

detention   Holding a youth in custody before case disposition.

determinate sentence   A term of imprisonment, imposed by a judge, that has a specific number of years.

deterrence theory   The view that sure and swift punishment will discourage others from similar illegal acts.

direct evidence   Evidence derived from one or more of the five senses.

direct restitution   The defendant pays money directly to the victim of the crime.

discovery   Pretrial procedure in which parties to a lawsuit ask for and receive information such as testimony, records, or other evidence from each other.

discretion   The lawful ability of an agent of government to exercise choice in making a decision.

discretionary appellate jurisdiction   Jurisdiction that a court may accept or reject in particular cases. The Supreme Court has discretionary jurisdiction over most cases that come to it.

discrimination   Illegitimate influences in the sentencing process based on the characteristics of the defendants.

dismissal   Cases terminated (including those warned, counseled, and released) with no further disposition anticipated.

disparity   Unequal sentences resulting from the sentencing process itself.

disposition   A court decision on what will happen to a youth who has not been found innocent.

dissenting opinion   An opinion written by a judge of an appellate court in which the judge states the reasons for disagreeing with the majority decision.

district courts   U.S. trial courts established in the respective judicial districts into which the whole United States is divided. These courts are established for the purpose of hearing and deciding cases in limited districts to which their jurisdiction is confined.

diversity of citizenship   When parties on the opposite sides of a federal lawsuit come from different states, the jurisdiction of the U.S. district courts can be invoked if the case involves a controversy concerning $75,000 or more in value.

domestic relations   Relating to the home; the law of divorce, custody, support, adoption, and so on.

double jeopardy   Fifth Amendment prohibition against a second prosecution after a first trial for the same offense.

drug courts   Specialty courts with jurisdiction over cases involving illegal substances. Drug courts typically stress treatment rather than punishment.

dual court system   A court system consisting of a separate judicial structure for each state in addition to a national structure. Each case is tried in a court of the same jurisdiction as that of the law or laws involved.

due process model   A philosophy of criminal justice based on the assumption that an individual is innocent until proven guilty and has a right to protection from arbitrary power of the state.

due process of law   A right guaranteed in the Fifth, Sixth, and Fourteenth Amendments of the U.S. Constitution and generally understood to mean the due course of legal proceedings according to the rules and forms established for the protection of private rights.

duress   Unlawful pressure on a person to do what he or she would not otherwise have done.

E

elements of a crime   Five principles of a crime that are critical to the statutory definition of crimes: guilty act, guilty intent, relationship between guilty act and guilty intent, attendant circumstances, and results.

en banc   French term referring to the session of an appellate court in which all the judges of the court participate, as opposed to a session presided over by three judges.

entrapment   The act of a government official or agent inducing a person to commit a crime that the person would not have committed without the inducement.

error   A mistake made by a judge in the procedures used at trial, or in making legal rulings during the trial, that allows one side in a lawsuit to ask a higher court to review the case.

error correction   Appellate courts seek to correct legal errors made in lower courts.

estate   The interest a person has in property; a person's right or title to property.

evidence   Any kind of proof offered to establish the existence or nonexistence of a fact in dispute—for example, testimony, writings, other material objects, demonstrations.

exclusionary rule   A rule created by judicial decisions holding that evidence obtained through violations of the constitutional rights of the criminal defendant must be excluded from the trial.

extradition   Legal process whereby officials of one state surrender an alleged criminal offender to officials of the state in which the crime is alleged to have been committed.

F

federal question   Case that contains a major issue involving the U.S. Constitution or U.S. laws or treaties.

felony   The more serious of the two basic types of criminal behavior, usually bearing a possible penalty of one year or more in prison.

fine   A sum of money to be paid to the state by a convicted person as punishment for an offense.

Furman v. Georgia   Supreme Court ruling that statutes leaving arbitrary and discriminatory discretion to juries in imposing death sentences are in violation of the Eighth Amendment.

fusion of the guilty act and guilty intent   One of the components of a crime (see *elements of a crime*). Criminal law requires that the guilty intent and the guilty act occur together.

G

gag order   A judge's order that lawyers and witnesses not discuss the trial with outsiders.

geographical jurisdiction   Geographical area over which courts can hear and decide disputes.

good time   A reduction of the time served in prison as a reward for not violating prison rules.

grand jury   A group of citizens who decide whether persons accused of crimes should be indicted (true bill) or not (no true bill).

Gregg v. Georgia   Supreme Court ruling that (1) the death penalty is not, in itself, cruel and unusual punishment, and (2) a two-part proceeding—one for the determination of innocence or guilt and the other for determination of the sentence—is constitutional and meets the objections noted in *Furman v. Georgia*.

gubernatorial appointment   Method of judicial selection in which the governor appoints a person to a judicial vacancy without an election.

guilty act (actus reus)   Requirement that, for an act to be considered criminal, the individual must have committed an overt act that resulted in criminal harm (see *elements of a crime*).

guilty intent (mens rea)   Mental state required for a crime.

H

habeas corpus   Latin phrase meaning "you have the body"; a writ inquiring of an official who has custody of a person whether that person is being lawfully imprisoned or detained.

harmless error   An error made at trial that is insufficient grounds for reversing a judgment.

hearsay   An out-of-court assertion or statement, made by someone other than the testifying witness, which is offered to prove the truth of testimony. Hearsay evidence is excluded from trials unless it falls within one of the recognized exceptions.

hierarchical jurisdiction   Refers to differences in the functions of courts and involves original as opposed to appellate jurisdiction.

hung jury   A jury that is unable to reach a verdict.

I

illegal search and seizure   An act in violation of the Fourth Amendment of the U.S. Constitution.

immaterial   Evidence that neither proves nor disproves the issue of a trial.

immunity   A grant of exemption from prosecution in return for evidence or testimony.

impeach   To question the truthfulness of a witness's testimony.

impeachment   Official accusation against a public official brought by a legislative body seeking his or her removal.

imprisonment   Placing a person in a prison, jail, or similar correctional facility as punishment for committing a crime.

in rem   Against a thing; a legal proceeding instituted to obtain decrees or judgments against property.

incapacitation   Sentencing philosophy that stresses crime prevention through isolating wrongdoers from society.

incorporation   The theory that the Bill of Rights has been incorporated or absorbed into the due process clause of the Fourteenth Amendment, thereby making it applicable to the states.

indeterminate sentence   A sentence that has both a minimum and maximum term of imprisonment, the actual length to be determined by a parole board.

index crimes   The specific crimes used by the FBI when reporting the incidence of crime in the United States in the *Uniform Crime Reports*.

indictment   A formal accusation of a criminal offense made against a person by a grand jury.

indigents   Defendants who are too poor to pay a lawyer and therefore are entitled to a lawyer for free.

inferior court (lower court)   Term for a trial court of limited jurisdiction; also may refer to any court lower in the judicial hierarchy.

information   A formal accusation charging someone with the commission of a crime, signed by a prosecuting attorney, which has the effect of bringing the person to trial.

inheritance   Property received from a dead person, either by effect of intestacy or through a will.

initial appearance   Shortly after arrest, the suspect is brought before a judicial official who informs the per-son of the reason for the arrest and, in the case of a felony, sets bond.

initial hearing   In juvenile court, an often informal hearing during which an intake decision is made.

injunction   A court order directing someone to do something or to refrain from doing something.

intake decision   The decision made by juvenile court that results in the case being handled either informally at the intake level or more formally by petition and scheduled for an adjudicatory or transfer hearing.

interlocutory   Provisional; temporary; while a lawsuit is still going on.

intermediate courts of appeals (ICAs)   Judicial bodies falling between the highest, or supreme, tribunal and the trial court; created to relieve the jurisdiction's highest court of hearing a large number of cases.

intermediate sanctions   Variety of sanctions that lie somewhere between prison and probation.

irrelevant   Testimony that has no bearing on the issue of a trial.

J

judge-made law   The common law as developed in form and content by judges or judicial decisions.

judgment   The official decision of a court concerning a legal matter.

judicial conduct commission   An official body whose function is to investigate allegations of misconduct by judges.

judicial election   Method of judicial selection in which the voters choose judicial candidates in a partisan or nonpartisan election.

judicial independence   Normative value that stresses a judge should be free from outside pressure in making a decision.

jurisdiction   The power of a court to hear a case in question.

jury deliberations   The action of a jury in determining the guilt or innocence, or the sentence, of a defendant.

jury instructions   Directions given by a judge to the members of the jury informing them of the law applicable to the case.

jury nullification   Idea that juries have the right to refuse to apply the law in criminal cases despite facts that leave no reasonable doubt that the law was violated.

just deserts   Punishment for criminal wrongdoing should be proportionate to the severity of the offense.

justice of the peace (JP)   A low-level judge, sometimes without legal training, typically found in rural areas of some states, empowered to try petty civil and criminal cases and to conduct the preliminary stages of felony cases.

juvenile   Youth at or below the upper age of juvenile court jurisdiction.

juvenile court   Any court that has jurisdiction over matters involving juveniles.

juvenile delinquency   An act committed by a juvenile for which an adult could be prosecuted in a criminal court.

L

law   Body of rules enacted by public officials in a legitimate manner and backed by the force of the state.

legal defense   Legally recognized justification for illegal actions, or acceptance that individuals were not legally responsible for their actions.

legislative courts   Judicial bodies created by Congress under Article I (legislative article) and not Article III (judicial article).

local prosecutors   General term for lawyers who represent local governments (cities and counties, for example) in the lower courts; often called *city attorneys* or *solicitors*.

lower age of jurisdiction   Minimum age at which a youth may be transferred to adult court.

M

mandatory appellate jurisdiction   Jurisdiction that a court must accept. Cases falling under a court's mandatory jurisdiction must be decided officially on their merits, though a court may avoid giving them full consideration.

mandatory minimum sentencing   Minimum required penalty specified for a certain crime.

master jury list   A list of potential jurors in a court's district, from which a representative cross section of the community in which a crime allegedly was committed can be selected for a trial. It is usually compiled from multiple sources, such as voter registration lists, driver's license lists, utility customer lists, and telephone directories. Also called *jury wheel* or *master wheel*.

misdemeanor Lesser of the two basic types of crime, usually punishable by no more than one year in prison.

Missouri Bar Plan The name given to a method of judicial selection combining merit selection and popular control in retention elections.

mistrial Invalid trial.

monetary damage Compensatory damages—payment for actual losses suffered by a plaintiff. Punitive damages—money awarded by a court to a person who has been harmed in a malicious or willful way.

municipal court A trial court of limited jurisdiction created by a local unit of government.

municipal ordinance Law passed by a local unit of government.

N

new judicial federalism Movement in state supreme courts to reinvigorate states' constitutions as sources of individual rights over and above the rights granted by the U.S. Constitution.

no true bill The decision of a grand jury not to indict a person for a crime.

nolle prosequi The ending of a criminal case because the prosecutor decides or agrees to stop prosecuting. When this happens, the case is "nollied," "nolled," or "nol. prossed."

nolo contendere Latin phrase meaning "I will not contest it." A plea of "no contest" in a criminal case means that the defendant does not directly admit guilt but submits to sentencing or other punishment.

nonpetitioned case A case handled informally by duly authorized court personnel.

normal crime Categorization of crime based on the typical manner in which it is committed, the type of defendant who typically commits it, and the typical penalty to be applied.

normal penalties Norms for proper sentencing based on the crime committed and the defendant's prior record.

notice of appeal Written document filed with the clerk of court stating that the defendant in the criminal case plans to appeal.

O

objection The act of taking exception to a statement or procedure during a trial.

officer of the court Lawyers are officers of the court and, as such, must obey court rules, be truthful in court, and generally serve the needs of justice.

opening statement Address made by attorneys for both parties at the beginning of a trial in which they outline for the jury what they intend to prove in their case.

opinion The reasons given for the decision reached by an appellate court.

oral argument The part of the appellate court decision-making process in which lawyers for both parties plead their case in person before the court.

ordinance A law enacted by a local government body for the regulation of some activity within the community.

original jurisdiction Jurisdiction in the first instance; commonly used to refer to trial jurisdiction as opposed to appellate jurisdiction. Appellate courts, however, have limited original jurisdiction.

other dispositions Miscellaneous dispositions, including fines, restitution, community service, and referrals outside the court for services, with minimal or no further court involvement anticipated.

P

pardon An act of executive clemency that has the effect of releasing an inmate from prison and/or removing certain legal disabilities from persons convicted of crimes.

parens patriae The state as parent; the state as guardian and protector of all citizens (such as juveniles) who are unable to protect themselves.

parole Early release from prison on the condition of good behavior.

parole board An administrative body whose members are chosen by the governor to review the cases of prisoners eligible for release on parole. The board has the authority to release such persons and to return them to prison for violating the conditions of parole.

peremptory challenge Method for excusing a potential juror without specifying the reason.

personal injury Negligence lawsuits, often involving automobile accidents.

petit jury A trial jury as distinguished from a grand jury.

petition A document filed in juvenile court alleging that a juvenile is a delinquent or a status offender and asking that the court assume jurisdiction over the juvenile or that an alleged delinquent be transferred to criminal court for prosecution as an adult.

petty offense A minor criminal offense that does not entitle the defendant to a trial by jury.

placement Cases in which youths are placed in a residential facility or otherwise removed from their homes and placed elsewhere.

plain view If police happen to come across something while acting within their lawful duty, that item may be used as evidence in a criminal trial even if the police did not have a search warrant.

plaintiff The person or party who initiates a lawsuit.

plea bargaining The process by which a defendant pleads guilty to a criminal charge with the expectation of receiving some benefit from the state.

plea on the nose The defendant pleads guilty to the charges contained in the indictment or bill of information.

policy formulation Function of appellate courts to make new law and adjust existing law to changing circumstances.

post-verdict motions Various motions made by the defense after a jury conviction in hopes of gaining a new trial.

precedent A case previously decided that serves as a legal guide for the resolution of subsequent cases.

prejudicial pretrial publicity Prejudicial information, often inadmissible at trial, that is circulated by the news media before a trial and that reduces the defendant's chances of a trial before an impartial jury.

preliminary hearing A pretrial hearing to determine whether there is probable cause to hold the accused for the grand jury.

preponderance of the evidence In civil law, the standard of proof required to prevail at trial. To win, the plaintiff must show that the greater weight, or preponderance, of the evidence supports his or her version of the facts.

pre-sentence investigation Investigation by a probation department into circumstances surrounding a crime in order to help judges make appropriate sentencing decisions.

presumption of innocence Assumption that whenever a person is charged with a crime, he or she is innocent until proved guilty. The defendant is presumed to be innocent, and the burden is on the state to prove guilt beyond a reasonable doubt.

preventive detention   Holding a defendant in custody pending trial in the belief that he or she is likely to commit further criminal acts or flee the jurisdiction.

prisoner petition   Civil lawsuit filed by a prisoner alleging violations of his or her rights during trial or while in prison.

privileged communication   A recognized right to keep certain communications confidential or private.

probable cause   Standard used to determine whether a crime has been committed and whether there is sufficient evidence to believe a specific individual committed it.

probation   Punishment for a crime that allows the offender to remain in the community without incarceration but subject to certain conditions.

probation officer   Employee of probation agency, responsible for supervision of convicted offenders who have been released to the community under certain conditions of good behavior.

procedural law   Law that outlines the legal processes to be followed in starting, conducting, and finishing a lawsuit.

property   Legal right to use or dispose of particular things or subjects.

property bond   Use of property as collateral for pretrial release.

prosecutor   A public official who represents the state in a criminal action.

public defender   An attorney employed by the government to represent indigent defendants.

R

real evidence   Objects, such as fingerprints, seen by the jury.

reasonable doubt   The state of mind of jurors when they do not feel a moral certainty about the truth of the charges and when the evidence does not exclude every other reasonable hypothesis except that the defendant is guilty as charged.

rebuttal   The introduction of contradictory evidence.

referral   A request by a law enforcement agency, governmental agency, parent, or individual that a juvenile court take jurisdiction of a youth. A referral initiates court processing.

rehabilitation   The notion that punishment is intended to restore offenders to a constructive role in society; based on the assumption that criminal behavior is a treatable disorder caused by social or psychological ailments.

Rehnquist Court   The Supreme Court under the leadership of Chief Justice William Rehnquist (1986–).

release on recognizance (ROR)   The release of an accused person from jail on his or her own obligation rather than on a monetary bond.

remand   In an appellate court, to send a case back to the court from which it came for further action.

remedy   Vindication of a claim of right; a legal procedure by which a right is enforced or the violation of a right is prevented or compensated.

removal   To dismiss a person from holding office.

restitution   To restore or to make good on something—for example, to return or pay for a stolen item.

result   A consequence; an outcome.

retribution   A concept that implies the payment of a debt to society and thus the expiration of one's offense.

reverse   In an appellate court, to reach a decision that disagrees with the result reached in the case by the lower court.

reversed and remanded   Decision of an appellate court that the guilty verdict of the lower court be set aside and the case be retried.

reversible error   An error made at trial serious enough to warrant a new trial.

right to counsel   Right of the accused to the services of a lawyer paid for by the government, established by the Sixth Amendment and extended by the Warren Court (*Gideon v. Wainwright*) to indigent defendants in felony cases.

right to one appeal   U.S. law generally grants the loser in trial court the right to a single appeal, which the upper court must hear.

routine administration   A matter that presents the court with no disputes over law or fact.

S

search warrant   A written order, issued by judicial authority, directing a law enforcement officer to search for personal property and, if found, to bring it before the court.

selective incapacitation   Sentencing philosophy that stresses targeting dangerous offenders for lengthy prison sentences.

self-defense   The right to use physical force against another person who is committing a felony, threatening the use of physical force, or using physical force.

self-incrimination   Forcing a suspect to provide evidence against him- or herself; prohibited by the Fifth Amendment.

sentence bargaining   The defendant pleads guilty knowing the sentence that will be imposed; the sentence in the sentence bargain is less than the maximum.

sequester   To isolate members of a jury from the community until they have reached a final verdict.

small claims court   A lower-level court whose jurisdiction is limited to a specific dollar amount—for example, damages not exceeding $1,500.

solicitor general   Third-ranking official in the U.S. Department of Justice who conducts and supervises government litigation before the Supreme Court.

stare decisis   Latin phrase meaning "let the decision stand." The doctrine that principles of law established in earlier judicial decisions should be accepted as authoritative in similar subsequent cases.

state attorney general   The chief legal officer of a state, representing that state in civil and, under certain circumstances, criminal cases.

state supreme court   General term for the highest court in a state.

status offense   Behavior that is considered an offense only when committed by a juvenile—for example, running away from home.

statute   A written law enacted by a legislature.

statutory exemptions   Rules adopted by legislatures exempting certain types of persons or occupations from jury duty.

subject matter jurisdiction   Types of cases courts have been authorized to hear and decide.

subpoena (power)   An order from a court directing a person to appear before the court and to give testimony about a cause of action pending before it.

substantive law   Law that deals with the content or substance of the law—for example, the legal grounds for divorce.

summons   A legal document ordering an individual to appear in court at a certain time on a certain date.

suppression motion Request that a court of law prohibit specific statements, documents, or objects from being introduced into evidence in a trial.

symbolic restitution The defendant performs community service.

T

testimony The giving of evidence by a witness under oath.

therapeutic jurisprudence Judicial bodies such as drug courts that stress helping defendants in trouble through nonadversarial proceedings.

tort A private or civil wrong, not arising as the result of a breach of contract, in which the defendant's actions cause injury to the plaintiff or to property.

traffic offenses A group of offenses, including infractions and minor misdemeanors, relating to the operation of self-propelled motor vehicles.

transactional immunity Absolute protection against prosecution for any event or transaction about which a witness is compelled to give testimony or furnish evidence.

transfer to criminal court A case is moved to a criminal court because of a waiver or transfer hearing in the juvenile court.

trial court Judicial body with primarily original jurisdiction in civil or criminal cases. Juries are used, and evidence is presented.

trial court of general jurisdiction A trial court responsible for major criminal and civil cases.

trial court of limited jurisdiction A lower-level state court, such as a justice of the peace court, whose jurisdiction is limited to minor civil disputes or misdemeanors.

true bill A bill of indictment by a grand jury.

trustworthiness Basic criterion for the admissibility of evidence, which seeks to ensure that only the most reliable and credible facts, statements, and testimony are presented to the fact-finder.

Type I offenses Serious crimes of homicide, rape, arson, aggravated assault, robbery, burglary, auto theft, and larceny, according to the FBI's *Uniform Crime Reports;* also called *index crimes.*

U

U.S. attorney general Head of the Department of Justice; nominated by the president and confirmed by the Senate.

U.S. attorneys Officials responsible for the prosecution of crimes that violate the laws of the United States; appointed by the president and assigned to a U.S. district court.

U.S. magistrate judges Judicial officers appointed by the U.S. district courts to perform the duties formerly performed by U.S. commissioners and to assist the court by serving as special masters in civil actions, conducting pretrial or discovery proceedings, and conducting preliminary review of applications for post-trial relief made by individuals convicted of criminal offenses.

unified court system A simplified state trial court structure with rule making centered in the supreme court, system governance authority vested in the chief justice of the supreme court, and state funding of the judicial system under a statewide judicial budget.

unreasonable search and seizure The Fourth Amendment provides for protection against unreasonable searches and seizures, or the illegal gathering of evidence, but was not very effective until the adoption of the exclusionary rule, barring the use of evidence so obtained (*Mapp v. Ohio* 1961).

upper age of jurisdiction The oldest age at which a juvenile court has original jurisdiction over an individual for behavior that violates the law.

use immunity A witness may not be prosecuted based on grand jury testimony he or she provides but may be prosecuted based on evidence acquired independently from that testimony.

V

venire A group of citizens from which members of the jury are chosen.

venue The geographic location of a trial, which is determined by constitutional or statutory provisions.

verdict The decision of a trial court.

voir dire French legal phrase meaning "to speak the truth." The process by which prospective jurors are questioned to determine whether there is cause to excuse them from the jury.

W

warrantless search Search without a search warrant.

Warren Court The Supreme Court under the leadership of Chief Justice Earl Warren (1953–1969).

writ of certiorari Order issued by an appellate court for the purpose of obtaining from a lower court the record of its proceedings in a particular case.

References

Acker, James. 1993a. "A Different Agenda: The Supreme Court, Empirical Research Evidence, and Capital Punishment Decisions, 1986–1989." *Law and Society Review* 27: 65–86.

Acker, James. 1993b. "Doing the Devil's Work: Toward Model Death Penalty Legislation." *Criminal Law Bulletin* 29: 219–247.

Adams, Kenneth. 1983. "The Effect of Evidentiary Factors on Charge Reduction." *Journal of Criminal Justice* 11: 525–538.

Adler, Peter, Karen Lovass, and Neal Milner. 1988. "The Ideologies of Mediation: The Movement's Own Story." *Law and Policy* 10: 317–339.

Alarid, Leanne, James Marquart, Velmer Burton, Francis Cullen, and Steven Cuvelier. 1996. "Women's Roles in Serious Offenses: A Study of Adult Felons." *Justice Quarterly* 13: 431–454.

Albonetti, Celesta. 1987. "Prosecutorial Discretion: The Effects of Uncertainty." *Law and Society Review* 21: 291–313.

Alexander, S. L. 1991. "Cameras in the Courtroom: A Case Study." *Judicature* 74: 307–313.

Alexander, S. L. 1996a. "The Impact of *California v. Simpson* on Cameras in the Courtroom." *Judicature* 79: 169–175.

Alexander, S. L. 1996b. "The Impact of Sequestration on Juries." *Judicature* 79: 266–272.

Alfini, James, and Patricia Passuth. 1981. "Case Processing in State Misdemeanor Courts: The Effect of Defense Attorney Presence." *Justice System Journal* 6: 100–116.

Alpert, Geoffrey, and Thomas Petersen. 1985. "The Grand Jury Report: A Magic Lantern or an Agent of Social Control?" *Justice Quarterly* 2: 23–50.

Alschuler, Albert. 1968. "The Prosecutor's Role in Plea Bargaining." *University of Chicago Law Review* 36: 50–112.

Alschuler, Albert. 1975. "The Defense Attorney's Role in Plea Bargaining." *Yale Law Journal* 84: 1179–1314.

Alschuler, Albert. 1979. "Plea Bargaining and Its History." *Law and Society Review* 13: 211–246.

American Bar Association. 1988. *Criminal Justice in Crisis*. Chicago: Author.

American Bar Association Commission on Minimum Standards for Criminal Justice. 1968. *Standards Relating to Speedy Trial*. Chicago: American Bar Association.

American Civil Liberties Union. 1996. *ACLU Fact Sheet on Juvenile Crime*. Available online: http://www.aclu.org/congress/juvenile.htm

American Civil Liberties Union. 2000. "Act Now to Stop the Execution of the Innocent." Available online: http://www.aclu.org/death-penalty/

Applebome, Peter. 1992. "Indigent Defendants, Overworked Lawyers." *New York Times*, 18 September.

Applegate, Brandon, Francis Cullen, Bruce Link, Pamela Richards, and Lonn Lanza-Kaduce. 1996. "Determinants of Public Punitiveness Toward Drunk Driving: A Factorial Survey Approach." *Justice Quarterly* 13: 57–79.

Applegate, Brandon, Michael Turner, Joseph Sanborn, Edward Latessa, and Melissa Moon. 2000. "Individualization, Criminalization, or Problem Resolution: A Factorial Survey of Juvenile Court Judges' Decisions to Incarcerate Youthful Felony Offenders." *Justice Quarterly* 17: 309–332.

Ares, Charles, Ann Rankin, and Herbert Sturz. 1963. "The Manhattan Bail Project: An Interim Report on the Use of Pretrial Parole." *New York University Law Review* 38: 67–92.

Arrestee Drug Abuse Monitoring Program. 2003. *Preliminary Data on Drug Use & Related Matters Among Adult Arrestees & Juvenile Detainees 2002*. Washington, DC: National Institute of Justice. Available online: http://www.adam-nij.net/ (viewed 9 September 2003).

Ashman, Allan. 1975. *Courts of Limited Jurisdiction: A National Survey*. Chicago: American Judicature Society.

Ashman, Allan, and Pat Chapin. 1976. "Is the Bell Tolling for Nonlawyer Judges?" *Judicature* 59: 417–421.

Aspin, Larry, William Hall, Jean Bax, and Celeste Montoya. 2000. "Thirty Years of Judicial Retention Elections: An Update." *Social Science Journal* 37: 1.

Associated Press, "Judge Censured by Court of Judiciary." 2003, 31 March.

Associated Press, "Maryland Judge Warned for Scolding Sex Victim." 2000, 22 June.

Association of the Bar of the City of New York Drug Abuse Council. 1976. *The Effects of the 1973 Drug Laws on the New York State Courts*. New York: Author.

Attorney General's Task Force on Violent Crime. 1981. *Final Report*. Washington, DC: U.S. Department of Justice.

Auerhahn, Kathleen. 1999. "Selective Incapacitation and the Problem of Prediction." *Criminology* 37: 703–734.

Austin, Thomas. 1981. "The Influence of Court Location on Types of Criminal Sentences: The Rural-Urban Factor." *Journal of Criminal Justice* 9: 305–316.

Baar, Carl. 1980. "The Scope and Limits of Court Reform." *Justice System Journal* 5: 274–290.

Baca, Kim. 2001. "The Changing Federal Role in Indian Country." *National Institute of Justice Journal* (April): 8–13.

Bachman, Ronet, and Linda Saltzman. 1995. *Violence Against Women: Estimates from the Redesigned Survey.* Washington, DC: U.S. Department of Justice, Bureau of Justice Statistics.

Backstrand, John, Don Gibbons, and Joseph Jones. 1992. "Who Is in Jail? An Examination of the Rabble Hypothesis." *Crime and Delinquency* 38: 219–229.

Bailey, F. Lee, and Henry Rothblat. 1971. *Successful Techniques for Criminal Trials.* New York: Lawyers Cooperative.

Baker, Liva. 1983. *Miranda: Crime, Law and Politics.* New York: Atheneum.

Baker, Newman. 1933. "The Prosecutor: Initiation of Prosecution." *Journal of Criminal Law, Criminology and Police Science* 23: 770–796.

Baldus, David, Charles Pulaski, and George Woodworth. 1983. "Comparative Review of Death Sentences: An Empirical Study of the Georgia Experience." *Journal of Criminal Law and Criminology* 74: 661–753.

Barrineau, H. E. 1994. *Civil Liability in Criminal Justice.* Cincinnati: Anderson.

Bartol, Anne. 1996. "Structures and Roles of Rural Courts." Pp. 79–92 in *Rural Criminal Justice: Conditions, Constraints, and Challenges,* edited by Thomas McDonald, Robert Wood, and Melissa Pflug. Salem, WI: Sheffield.

Bass, Alison. 1995. "Youth Violence Explosion Likely to Worsen." *Times-Picayune,* 2 July, p. A14.

Baum, Lawrence. 1991. "Specializing the Federal Courts: Neutral Reforms or Efforts to Shape Judicial Policy?" *Judicature* 74: 217–224.

Baumer, Eric, Steven Messner, and Richard Felson. 2000. "The Role of Victim Characteristics in the Disposition of Murder Cases." *Justice Quarterly* 17: 281–308.

Bazemore, Gordon. 1994. "Understanding the Response to Reforms Limiting Discretion: Judges' Views of Restrictions on Detention Intake." *Justice Quarterly* 11: 429–452.

Bazemore, Gordon, and Lynette Feder. 1997. "Judges in the Punitive Juvenile Court: Organizational, Career and Ideological Influences on Sanctioning Orientation." *Justice Quarterly* 14: 87–114.

Beerhalter, Susan, and James Gainey. 1974. *Minnesota District Court Survey.* Denver: National Center for State Courts.

Begue, Yvette, and Candace Goldstein. 1987. "How Judges Get into Trouble." *Judges Journal* 26: 8.

Beiser, Edward. 1975. "Six-Member Juries in the Federal Courts." *Judicature* 58: 424.

Belenko, Steven, Iona Mara-Drita, and Jerome McElroy. 1992. "Drug Tests and the Prediction of Pretrial Misconduct: Findings and Policy Issues." *Crime and Delinquency* 38: 557–582.

Belknap, Joanne. 2001. *The Invisible Woman: Gender, Crime, and Justice.* 2d ed. Belmont, CA: Wadsworth.

Bell, Griffin. 1993. "Appointing United States Attorneys." *Journal of Law and Politics* 9: 247–256.

Bell, Rhonda. 2001. "Evidence Flap Has DA on Defensive: Connick Insists Case an Aberration." *Times-Picayune,* 31 May, A1.

Berg, Kenneth. 1985. "The Bail Reform Act of 1984." *Emory Law Journal* 34: 687–740.

Berkson, Larry, and Susan Carbon. 1978. *Court Unification: History, Politics, and Implementation.* Washington, DC: National Institute of Law Enforcement and Criminal Justice.

Bernstein, Ilene Nagel, William Kelly, and Patricia Doyle. 1977. "Societal Reaction to Deviants: The Case of Criminal Defendants." *American Sociological Review* 42: 743–795.

Bertram, Eva, et al. 1996. *Drug War Politics: The Price of Denial.* Berkeley: University of California Press.

Bing, Stephen, and Stephen Rosenfeld. 1974. "The Quality of Justice in the Lower Criminal Courts of Metropolitan Boston." Pp. 259–285 in *Rough Justice: Perspectives on Lower Criminal Courts,* edited by John Robertson. Boston: Little, Brown.

Biskupic, Joan. 1993. "Congress Cool to Proposals to Ease Load on Courts." *Congressional Quarterly* (7 April): 1073–1075.

Blankenship, Michael, James Luginbuhl, Francis Cullen, and William Redick. 1997. "Juror Comprehension of Sentencing Instructions: A Test of Tennessee's Death Penalty Process." *Justice Quarterly* 14: 325–357.

Blumberg, Abraham. 1967a. *Criminal Justice.* Chicago: Quadrangle Books.

Blumberg, Abraham. 1967b. "The Practice of Law as a Confidence Game." *Law and Society Review* 1: 15–39.

Blumberg, Abraham. 1970. *Criminal Justice.* New York: Quadrangle Books.

Blumstein, Alfred, Jacqueline Cohen, Susan Martin, and Michael Tonry, eds. 1983. *Research on Sentencing: The Search for Reform.* Washington, DC: National Academy Press.

Boatright, Robert. 1999. "Why Citizens Don't Respond to Jury Summonses, and What Courts Can Do about It." *Judicature* 82: 156–165.

Boland, Barbara. 1996. "What Is Community Prosecution?" *National Institute of Justice Journal* 231 (August): 35–40.

Boland, Barbara, Elizabeth Brady, Herbert Tyson, and John Bassler. 1982. *The Prosecution of Felony Arrests.* Washington, DC: Institute for Law and Social Research.

Boland, Barbara, and Brian Forst. 1985. "Prosecutors Don't Always Aim to Pleas." *Federal Probation* 49: 10–15.

Boland, Barbara, Paul Mahanna, and Ronald Sones. 1992. *The Prosecution of Felony Arrests, 1988.* Washington, DC: U.S. Department of Justice, Bureau of Justice Statistics.

Bonnie, Richard, Norman Poythress, Steven Hoge, John Monahan, and Marlene Eisenberg. 1996. "Decision-Making in Criminal Defense: An Empirical Study of Insanity Pleas and the Impact of Doubted Client Competence." *Journal of Criminal Law and Criminology* 87: 48–77.

Boritch, Helen. 1992. "Gender and Criminal Court Outcomes: An Historical Analysis." *Criminology* 30: 293–317.

Borys, Bryan, Cynthia Banks, and Darrel Parker. 1999. "Enlisting the Justice Community in Court Improvement." *Judicature* 82: 176–185.

Brace, Paul, and Melinda Gann Hall. 1997. "The Interplay of Preferences, Case Facts, Context, and Rules in the Politics of Judicial Choice." *Journal of Politics* 59: 1206–1241.

Bradley, Craig. 1993. *The Failure of the Criminal Procedure Revolution*. Philadelphia: University of Pennsylvania Press.

Brennan, William. 1963. "The Criminal Prosecution: Sporting Event or Quest for Truth?" *Washington University Law Quarterly*: 279–294.

Brenner, Susan. 1998. "Is the Grand Jury Worth Keeping?" *Judicature* 81: 190–199.

Brereton, David, and Jonathan Casper. 1981–1982. "Does it Pay to Plead Guilty? Differential Sentencing and the Functioning of Criminal Courts." *Law and Society Review* 16: 45–70.

Bright, Stephen. 1997. "Political Attacks on the Judiciary." *Judicature* 80: 165–173.

Broeder, D. W. 1959. "The University of Chicago Jury Project." *Nebraska Law Review* 38: 744–760.

Bronstein, Julie. 1981. *Survey of State Mandatory Judicial Education Requirements*. Washington, DC: American University.

Brooks, Daniel. 1985. "Penalizing Judges Who Appeal Disciplinary Sanctions: The Unconstitutionality of 'Upping the Ante.'" *Judicature* 69: 95–102.

Brosi, Kathleen. 1979. *A Cross-City Comparison of Felony Case Processing*. Washington, DC: Institute for Law and Social Research.

Brown, Darryl. 1997. "Jury Nullification Within the Rule of Law." *Minnesota Law Review* 81: 1149–1200.

Browning, Sandra Lee, and Liqun Cao. 1992. "The Impact of Race on Criminal Justice Ideology." *Justice Quarterly* 9: 685–701.

Buchanan, John. 1989. "Police–Prosecutor Teams: Innovations in Several Jurisdictions." *NIJ Reports* 214 (May/June): 2–8.

Building Blocks for Youth. 2000. *Youth Crime/Adult Time: Is Justice Served?* Available online: http://www.buildingblocksforyouth.org/

Burbank, Stephen. 1987. "Politics and Progress in Implementing the Federal Judicial Discipline Act." *Judicature* 71: 13–28.

Bureau of Justice Statistics. 1985. *Bulletin: The Growth of Appeals, 1973–83 Trends*. Washington, DC: U.S. Department of Justice.

Bureau of Justice Statistics. 1987. *State Felony Courts and Felony Laws*. Washington, DC: U.S. Department of Justice.

Bureau of Justice Statistics. 1988a. *Criminal Defense for the Poor, 1986*. Washington, DC: U.S. Department of Justice.

Bureau of Justice Statistics. 1988b. *Pretrial Release and Detention: The Bail Reform Act of 1984*. Washington, DC: U.S. Department of Justice.

Bureau of Justice Statistics. 1988c. *Report to the Nation on Crime and Justice: The Data*. 2d ed. Washington, DC: U.S. Department of Justice.

Bureau of Justice Statistics. 1990. *Juvenile and Adult Records: One System, One Record?* Washington, DC: Author.

Bureau of Justice Statistics. 1993. *Jail Inmates 1992*. Washington, DC: U.S. Department of Justice.

Bureau of Justice Statistics. 1995. *Violence Against Women: Estimates from the Redesigned Survey*. Washington, DC: U.S. Department of Justice.

Bureau of Justice Statistics. 1996. *How to Use Structured Fines (Day Fines) as an Intermediate Sanction*. Washington, DC: U.S. Government Printing Office.

Bureau of Justice Statistics. 1997. *Correctional Populations in the United States, 1995*. Washington, DC: U.S. Department of Justice.

Bureau of Justice Statistics. 1998. *1996 National Survey of State Sentencing Structures*. Washington, DC: U.S. Department of Justice.

Bureau of Justice Statistics. 1999a. *American Indians and Crime*. Washington, DC: U.S. Department of Justice.

Bureau of Justice Statistics. 1999b. *Federal Pretrial Release and Detention, 1996*. Washington, DC: U.S. Department of Justice.

Bureau of Justice Statistics. 2000. *Federal Criminal Case Processing, 1998*. Washington, DC: U.S. Department of Justice.

Bureau of Justice Statistics. 2002. "Criminal Victimization 2001: Changes 2000–2001 with Trends." Available online: http://www.ojp.usdoj.gov/bjs/abstract/cv01.htm

Bureau of Justice Statistics. 2003a. *Criminal Victimization, 2002*. Washington, DC: U.S. Department of Justice.

Bureau of Justice Statistics. 2003b. *Intimate Partner Violence, 1993–2001*. Washington, DC: U.S. Department of Justice, Bureau of Justice Statistics.

Bureau of Justice Statistics. 2003c. *Jail Statistics*. Bureau of Justice Statistics. Available online: http://www.ojp.usdoj.gov/bjs/jails.htm (viewed 9 September 2003).

Bureau of Justice Statistics. 2003d. "Prison Statistics." Available online: http://www.ojp.usdoj.gov/bjs/prisons.htm (accessed 27 September 2003).

Bureau of Justice Statistics. 2003e. *Prisoners in 2002*. Available online: http://www.ojp.usdoj.gov/bjs/prisons.htm (accessed 22 October 2003).

Bureau of Justice Statistics. 2003f. "Probation and Parole Statistics." Available online:

http://www.ojp.usdoj.gov/bjs/pandp.htm (accessed 27 September 2003).

Bureau of Justice Statistics. 2004. *Expenditure and Employment Statistics.* http://www.ojp.usdoj.gov/bjs/eande.htm. Washington, DC: U.S. Department of Justice.

Burrell, Diane. 1997. "Financial Analysis of Traffic Court Collections in Ada County, Idaho." *Justice System Journal* 19: 101–116.

Burruss, George, and Kimberly Kempf-Leonard. 2002. "The Questionable Advantage of Defense Counsel in Juvenile Court." *Justice Quarterly* 19: 37–68.

Butler, Paul. 1995. "Racially Based Jury Nullification: Black Power in the Criminal Justice System." *Yale Law Journal* 105: 677–725.

Butterfield, Fox. 1997. "Justice Besieged: With Juvenile Courts in Chaos, Critics Propose Their Demise." *New York Times,* 21 July.

Butts, Jeffrey, and Janeen Buck. 2000. *Teen Courts: A Focus on Research.* Washington, DC: U.S. Department of Justice, Juvenile Justice Bulletin.

Buzawa, Eve, and Carl Buzawa. 1996. *Domestic Violence: The Criminal Justice Response.* 2d ed. Thousand Oaks, CA: Sage.

Bynum, Tim. 1982. "Release on Recognizance: Substantive or Superficial Reform?" *Criminology* 20: 67–82.

Byrd, Harry. 1976. "Has Life Tenure Outlived Its Time?" *Judicature* 59: 266–277.

Byrne, James, Arthur Lurigio, and Christopher Baird. 1989. "The Effectiveness of the New Intensive Supervision Programs." *Research in Corrections* 2: 1–15.

Call, Jack, David England, and Susette Talarico. 1983. "Abolition of Plea Bargaining in the Coast Guard." *Journal of Criminal Justice* 11: 351–358.

Cameron, Mary. 1964. *The Booster and the Snitch.* Glencoe, IL: Free Press.

Campbell, Curtis, Candace McCoy, and Chimezie Osigweh. 1990. "The Influence of Probation Recommendations on Sentencing Decisions and Their Predictive Accuracy." *Federal Probation* 54: 13–21.

Campbell, Donald, and H. Laurence Ross. 1968. "The Connecticut Crackdown on Speeding: Time-Series Data in Quasi-Experimental Analysis." *Law and Society Review* 3: 33–54.

Campbell, Linda. 1990. "Court Urged to Protect Prosecutors." *Chicago Tribune,* 29 November.

Campbell, Linda. 1991. "High Court Reduces Prosecutor Immunity." *Chicago Tribune,* 31 May.

Campbell, William. 1973. "Eliminate the Grand Jury." *Journal of Criminal Law and Criminology* 64: 174–182.

Cannavale, F., and W. Falcon. 1976. *Witness Cooperation.* Lexington, MA: D. C. Heath.

Cannon, Angie. 1996. "Bill Spells Out Rights of Victims." *Times-Picayune,* 23 April.

Cannon, Angie. 1997. "Violent Teen Crime Rate Drops Two Years in a Row." *Times-Picayune,* 3 October.

Canon, Bradley. 1972. "The Impact of Formal Selection Processes on the Characteristics of Judges—Reconsidered." *Law & Society Review* 6: 579–594.

Caplan, Lincoln. 1988. *The Tenth Justice: The Solicitor General and the Rule of Law.* New York: Vintage.

Carbon, Susan. 1984. "Women in the Judiciary." *Judicature* 65: 285.

Carelli, Richard. 1996. "Independent Judiciary Vital, Rehnquist Says." *Times-Picayune,* 27 April.

Carns, Teresa White, and John Kruse. 1992. "Alaska's Ban on Plea Bargaining Reevaluated." *Judicature* 75: 310–317.

Carp, Robert. 1975. "The Behavior of Grand Juries: Acquiescence or Justice?" *Social Science Quarterly:* 853–870.

Carp, Robert, and C. K. Rowland. 1983. *Policymaking and Politics in the Federal District Courts.* Knoxville: University of Tennessee Press.

Carp, Robert, and Ronald Stidham. 1990. *Judicial Process in America.* Washington, DC: Congressional Quarterly Press.

Carrington, Paul, Daniel Meador, and Maurice Rosenberg. 1976. *Justice on Appeal.* St. Paul, MN: West.

Carroll, Leo, and Claire Cornell. 1985. "Racial Composition, Sentencing Reforms, and Rates of Incarceration, 1970–1980." *Justice Quarterly* 2: 473–490.

Carrow, Deborah. 1984. "Judicial Sentencing Guidelines: Hazards of the Middle Ground." *Judicature* 68: 161–171.

Carter, Lief. 1974. *The Limits of Order.* Lexington, MA: D. C. Heath.

Carter, Robert, and Leslie Wilkins. 1967. "Some Factors in Sentencing Policy." *Journal of Criminal Law, Criminology and Police Science* 58: 503–514.

Casper, Jonathan. 1972. *American Criminal Justice: The Defendant's Perspective.* Englewood Cliffs, NJ: Prentice-Hall.

Casper, Jonathan, David Brereton, and David Neal. 1982. *The Implementation of the California Determinate Sentencing Law.* Washington, DC: U.S. Department of Justice.

Cass, Connie. 1995. "1 in 3 Young Black Men Run Afoul of Law." *Times-Picayune,* 5 October.

Cassella, Stefan. 1996. "Third-Party Rights in Criminal Forfeiture Cases." *Criminal Law Bulletin* 32: 499–537.

Cauchon, Dennis. 1999. "Indigents' Lawyers: Low Pay Hurts Justice?" *USA Today,* 3 February.

Chaiken, Marcia, and Jan Chaiken. 1990. *Redefining the Career Criminal: Priority Prosecution of High-Rate Dangerous Offenders.* Washington, DC: U.S. Department of Justice.

Champagne, Anthony, and Greg Thielemann. 1991. "Awareness of Trial Court Judges." *Judicature* 74: 271–277.

Chapper, Joy, and Roger Hanson. 1990. "Understanding Reversible Error in Criminal Appeals." *State Court Journal* 14: 16–24.

Charles, Alfred. 1996. "Teen Denied Murder Retrial." *Times-Picayune,* 2 July.

Chesney-Lind, Meda. 1997. *The Female Offender: Girls, Women and Crime.* Thousand Oaks, CA: Sage.

Chicago Tribune, "Paying for Justice." 2000, 16 January.

Chilton, Bradley. 1991. *Prisons under the Gavel: The Federal Takeover of Georgia Prisons*. Columbus: Ohio State University Press.

Chiricos, Theodore, and William Bales. 1991. "Unemployment and Punishment: An Empirical Assessment." *Criminology* 29: 701–724.

Church, Thomas. 1976. "Plea Bargains, Concessions and the Courts: Analysis of a Quasi-Experiment." *Law and Society Review* 10: 377–389.

Church, Thomas. 1982. "The 'Old' and the 'New' Conventional Wisdom of Court Delay." *Justice System Journal* 7: 395–412.

Church, Thomas. 1985. "Examining Local Legal Culture." *American Bar Foundation Research Journal:* 449–518.

Church, Thomas, Alan Carlson, Jo-Lynne Lee, and Teresa Tan. 1978. *Justice Delayed: The Pace of Litigation in Urban Trial Courts*. Williamsburg, VA: National Center for State Courts.

Church, Thomas, and Virginia McConnell. 1978. *Pretrial Delay: A Review and Bibliography*. Williamsburg, VA: National Center for State Courts.

Clark, John, James Austin, and D. Alan Henry. 1997. *"Three Strikes and You're Out": A Review of State Legislation*. Washington, DC: National Institute of Justice.

Clark, John, James Austin, and D. Alan Henry. 1998. "'Three Strikes and You're Out': Are Repeat Offender Laws Having Their Anticipated Effects?" *Judicature* 81: 144–154.

Clarke, Stevens. 1984. "North Carolina's Determinate Sentencing Legislation." *Judicature* 68: 140–152.

Clarke, Stevens, Jean Freeman, and Gary Koch. 1976. *The Effectiveness of Bail Systems: An Analysis of Failure to Appear in Court and Rearrest While on Bail*. Chapel Hill: University of North Carolina, Institute of Government.

Clarke, Stevens, and Gary Koch. 1976. "The Influence of Income and Other Factors on Whether Criminal Defendants Go to Prison." *Law and Society Review* 11: 57–92.

Clear, Todd, and Eric Cadora. 2003. *Community Justice*. Belmont, CA: Wadsworth.

Clear, Todd, and George Cole. 2003. *American Corrections*. 6th ed. Belmont, CA: Wadsworth.

Clear, Todd, John Hewitt, and Robert Regoli. 1979. "Discretion and the Determinate Sentence: Its Distribution, Control and Effect on Time Served." *Crime and Delinquency* 24: 428–445.

Clynch, Edward, and David Neubauer. 1981. "Trial Courts as Organizations: A Critique and Synthesis." *Law and Policy Quarterly* 3: 69–94.

Cohen, Fred. 1985. "Special Feature: An Introduction to the New Federal Crime Control Act." *Criminal Law Bulletin* 21: 330–337.

Cohen, Robyn. 1992. *Drunk Driving: 1989 Survey of Inmates of Local Jails*. Washington, DC: Bureau of Justice Statistics.

Cole, George. 1970. "The Decision to Prosecute." *Law and Society Review* 4: 313–343.

Cole, George. 1992. "Using Civil and Administrative Remedies to Collect Fines and Fees." *State Court Journal* 16: 4–10.

Cole, George, Barry Mahoney, Marlene Thornton, and Roger Hanson. 1988. "The Use of Fines by Trial Court Judges." *Judicature* 71: 325–333.

Cole, George, and David Neubauer. 1979. "The Living Courtroom: A Critique of the National Advisory Commission Recommendations." *Judicature* 59: 293–299.

Coles, Catherine, and Ronald Earle. 1996. *The Evolution of Problem-Oriented Prosecution*. Paper presented at the annual meeting of the American Criminological Association, Chicago, November.

Coles, Catherine, and George Kelling. 1999. "Prevention Through Community Prosecution." *The Public Interest* 36: 69.

Comptroller General of the United States. 1979. *Impact of the Exclusionary Rule on Federal Criminal Prosecutions*. Washington, DC: General Accounting Office.

Congressional Quarterly. 1996. "House Republicans Advance Six Anti-Crime Bills." *1995 Congressional Quarterly Almanac*. Washington, DC: Author.

Connick, Elizabeth, and Robert Davis. 1983. "Examining the Problems of Witness Intimidation." *Judicature* 66: 438–447.

Cooper, Christopher. 1993a. "Bench Hopefuls: Educate Offenders." *Times-Picayune*, 14 October.

Cooper, Christopher. 1993b. "Wish Comes True: Prison Space for 7,140." *Times-Picayune*, 20 October.

Corley, Charles, Timothy Bynum, and Madeline Wordes. 1995. "Conceptions of Family and Juvenile Court Process: A Qualitative Assessment." *Justice System Journal* 18: 157–172.

Covey, Herbert, and Mary Mande. 1985. "Determinate Sentencing in Colorado." *Justice Quarterly* 2: 259–270.

Cox, Gail. 1993. "Hellish Clients, Big Trouble." *National Law Journal* 15 (15 February): 1.

Coyle, Pamela. 1999. "Murder Victim's Date Sticks to Story." *Times-Picayune*, 9 January.

Coyle, Pamela. 2000a. "Court to Tackle Issue of Paying Innocent Convicts: N.O. Fighting Damages Awarded to Ex-Inmate." *Times-Picayune*, 16 January.

Coyle, Pamela. 2000b. "One-Time Murder Suspect Suing City; Inmate Claims Cops Framed Him in Killing." *Times-Picayune*, 11 January.

Crew, B. Keith. 1991. "Sex Differences in Criminal Sentencing: Chivalry or Patriarchy?" *Justice Quarterly* 8: 59–84.

Criminal Justice Consortium. 1997. "Count of Prisoners Sentenced for Third and Second Strike Cases." Available online: http://www.cjc

Crouch, Ben, and James Marquart. 1990. "Resolving the Paradox of Reform: Litigation, Prisoner Violence, and Perceptions of Risk." *Justice Quarterly* 7: 103–123.

Currie, Elliot. 1985. *Confronting Crime: An American Challenge*. New York: Pantheon.

Currie, Elliot. 1989. "Confronting Crime: Looking Toward the Twenty-First Century." *Justice Quarterly* 6: 5–15.

Currie, Elliott. 1993. *Reckoning: Drugs, the Cities, and the American Future.* New York: Hill and Wang.

D'Alessio, Stewart, and Lisa Stolzenberg. 1995. "The Impact of Sentencing Guidelines on Jail Incarceration in Minnesota." *Criminology* 33: 283–302.

Daly, Kathleen. 1994. *Gender, Crime, and Punishment.* New Haven, CT: Yale University Press.

Davies, Thomas. 1982. "Affirmed: A Study of Criminal Appeals and Decision-Making Norms in a California Court of Appeal." *American Bar Foundation Research Journal:* 543–648.

Davies, Thomas. 1983. "A Hard Look at What We Know (and Still Need to Learn) About the 'Costs' of the Exclusionary Rule: The NIJ Study and Other Studies of 'Lost Arrests.'" *American Bar Foundation Research Journal:* 611–690.

Davis, Robert. 1983. "Victim/Witness Noncooperation: A Second Look at a Persistent Phenomenon." *Journal of Criminal Justice* 11: 287–299.

Davis, Robert, and Tanya Bannister. 1995. "Improving Collection of Court-Ordered Restitution." *Judicature* 79: 30–33.

Davis, Robert, Barbara Smith, and Susan Hillenbrand. 1992. "Restitution: The Victim's Viewpoint." *Justice System Journal* 15: 746–758.

Davis, Samuel. 1984. *Rights of Juveniles.* 2d ed. New York: Clark Boardman.

Davis, Sue. 1993. "The Voice of Sandra Day O'Connor." *Judicature* 77: 134–139.

Davis, Sue, Susan Haire, and Donald Songer. 1993. "Voting Behavior and Gender on the U.S. Court of Appeals." *Judicature* 77: 129–133.

Dawson, Myrna, and Ronit Dinovitzer. 2001. "Victim Cooperation and the Prosecution of Domestic Violence in a Specialized Court." *Justice Quarterly* 18: 593–649.

DeFrances, Carol. 2001. *State-Funded Indigent Defense Services, 1999.* Washington, DC: Bureau of Justice Statistics.

DeFrances, Carol. 2002. "Prosecutors in State Courts, 2001." *Bulletin.* Washington, DC: Bureau of Justice Statistics, National Institute of Justice.

DeFrances, Carol, and Marika Litras. 2000. *Indigent Defense Services in Large Counties, 1999.* Washington, DC: Bureau of Justice Statistics.

DeFrances, Carol, Steven Smith, and Louise van der Does. 1996. "Prosecutors in State Courts, 1994." *Bulletin.* Washington, DC: Bureau of Justice Statistics.

DeFrances, Carol, and Kevin Strom. 1997. "Juveniles Prosecuted in State Criminal Courts." Washington, DC: Bureau of Justice Statistics.

Deutsch, Michael. 1984. "The Improper Use of the Federal Grand Jury: An Instrument for the Internment of Political Activists." *Journal of Criminal Law and Criminology* 75: 1159–1189.

Diamond, Shari. 1990. "Scientific Jury Selection: What Social Scientists Know and Do Not Know." *Judicature* 73: 178–183.

DiIulio, John, ed. 1990. *Courts, Corrections, and the Constitution: The Impact of Judicial Intervention on Prisons and Jails.* New York: Oxford University Press.

Dill, Forrest. 1975. "Discretion, Exchange and Social Control: Bail Bondsmen in Criminal Courts." *Law and Society Review* 9: 639–674.

Ditton, Paula, and Doris Wilson. 1999. *Truth in Sentencing in State Prisons.* Washington, DC: Bureau of Justice Statistics.

Dooley, Jeanne, and Erica Wood. 1992. "Opening the Courthouse Door: The Americans with Disabilities Act's Impact on the Courts." *Judicature* 76: 39–41.

Dougherty, Joyce. 1988. "Negotiating Justice in the Juvenile Justice System: A Comparison of Adult Plea Bargaining and Juvenile Intake." *Federal Probation* 52: 72–80.

Douglas, Charles. 1985. "Innovative Appellate Court Processing: New Hampshire's Experience with Summary Affirmance." *Judicature* 69: 147–156.

Dubois, Philip. 1980. *From Ballot to Bench: Judicial Elections and the Quest for Accountability.* Austin: University of Texas Press.

Dubois, Philip. 1984. "Voting Cues in Nonpartisan Trial Court Elections: A Multivariate Assessment." *Law & Society Review* 18: 395–436.

Dubois, Philip. 1985. "State Trial Court Appointments: Does the Governor Make a Difference?" *Judicature* 70: 20–28.

Durose, Matthew, David Levin, and Patrick Langan. 2001. *Felony Sentences in State Courts, 1998.* Washington, DC: U.S. Department of Justice, Bureau of Justice Statistics.

Efkeman, Hillery, and David Rottman. 1996–1997. "Community-Focused Courts: Progress on a Developmental Initiative." *State Court Journal* 20: 10–16.

Eisenstein, James. 1978. *Counsel for the United States: U.S. Attorneys in the Political and Legal System.* Baltimore: Johns Hopkins University Press.

Eisenstein, James, Roy Flemming, and Peter Nardulli. 1988. *The Contours of Justice: Communities and Their Courts.* Boston: Little, Brown.

Eisenstein, James, and Herbert Jacob. 1977. *Felony Justice: An Organizational Analysis of Criminal Courts.* Boston: Little, Brown.

Elias, Robert. 1986. *The Politics of Victimization: Victims, Victimology and Human Rights.* New York: Oxford University Press.

Elias, Robert. 1993. *Victims Still: The Political Manipulation of Crime Victims.* Thousand Oaks, CA: Sage.

Emmelman, Debra. 1996. "Trial by Plea Bargain: Case Settlement as a Product of Recursive Decisionmaking." *Law and Society Review* 30: 335–360.

Emmert, Craig, and Henry Glick. 1987. "Selection Systems and Judicial Characteristics: The Recruitment of State Supreme Court Judges." *Judicature* 70: 228–235.

Emmert, Craig, and Henry Glick. 1988. "The Selection of State Supreme Court Justices." *American Politics Quarterly* 16: 445–465.

Emmert, Craig, and Carol Ann Traut. 1992. "State Supreme Courts, State Constitutions, and Judicial Policymaking." *Justice System Journal* 16: 37–48.

Emmert, Craig, and Carol Ann Traut. 1996. *An Integrated Model of Judicial Decisonmaking: The California Justices and Capital Punishment.* Paper presented at the annual meeting of the Midwest Political Science Association, Chicago.

Engstrom, Richard. 1971. "Political Ambitions and the Prosecutorial Office." *Journal of Politics* 33: 190.

Engstrom, Richard. 1989. "When Blacks Run for Judge: Racial Divisions in the Candidate Preferences of Louisiana Voters." *Judicature* 73: 87–89.

Erez, Edna. 1992. "Dangerous Men, Evil Women: Gender and Parole Decision-Making." *Justice Quarterly* 9: 105–126.

Fader, Jamie, Philip Harris, Peter Jones, and Mary Poulin. 2001. "Factors Involved in Decisions on Commitment to Delinquency Programs for First-Time Juvenile Offenders." *Justice Quarterly* 18: 323–341.

Fagan, Jeffrey. 1996. *The Criminalization of Domestic Violence: Promises and Limits.* Washington, DC: National Institute of Justice.

Fahnestock, Kathryn. 1991. "The Loneliness of Command: One Perspective on Judicial Isolation." *Judges' Journal* 30: 13–19.

Farrell, John. 2001. "Judge Denies Bid for DNA Test to Verify Guilt of Executed Man." *Boston Globe,* 2 June.

Federal Bureau of Investigation. 2003. *Uniform Crime Reports for the United States—2002.* Washington, DC: U.S. Government Printing Office.

Feeley, Malcolm. 1979. *The Process Is the Punishment: Handling Cases in a Lower Criminal Court.* New York: Russell Sage Foundation.

Feeley, Malcolm. 1983. *Court Reform on Trial: Why Simple Solutions Fail.* New York: Basic Books.

Feeley, Malcolm, and Sam Kamin. 1996. "The Effect of 'Three Strikes and You're Out' on the Courts: Looking Back to See the Future." In *Three Strikes and You're Out: Vengeance as Public Policy,* edited by David Shichor and Dale Sechrest. Thousand Oaks, CA: Sage.

Feeley, Malcolm, and Edward Rubin. 1998. *Judicial Policy Making and the Modern State: How the Courts Reformed America's Prisons.* New York: Cambridge University Press.

Feeley, Malcolm, and Austin Sarat. 1980. *The Policy Dilemma: Federal Crime Policy and the Law Enforcement Assistance Administration, 1968–1978.* Minneapolis: University of Minnesota Press.

Feeney, Floyd, Forrest Dill, and Adrianne Weir. 1983. *Arrests Without Conviction: How Often They Occur and Why.* Washington, DC: U.S. Department of Justice, National Institute of Justice.

Fein, Bruce. 1994. "Don't Play Criminals' Game." *USA Today,* 15 April, p. 11.

Feinblatt, John, and Greg Berman. 1997. *Responding to the Community: Principles for Planning and Creating a Community Court.* Washington, DC: U.S. Department of Justice, Bureau of Justice Assistance.

Feld, Barry. 1988. "*In re Gault* Revisited: A Cross-State Comparison of the Right to Counsel in Juvenile Court." *Crime and Delinquency* 34: 379–392.

Filosa, Gwen. 2002. "N.O. Judge Is Taken Off the Bench: Justices Question Hunter's Competence." *Times-Picayune,* 20 August.

Finch, Susan. 1998. "Former Inmate Wins Millions: N.O. Owes Money to Innocent Man." *Times-Picayune,* 20 February.

Finn, Peter, and Beverley Lee. 1988. *Establishing and Expanding Victim-Witness Assistance Programs.* Washington, DC: National Institute of Justice.

Fino, Susan. 1987. *The Role of State Supreme Courts in the New Judicial Federalism.* Westport, CT: Greenwood.

Fish, Peter. 1973. *The Politics of Federal Judicial Administration.* Princeton, NJ: Princeton University Press.

Fitzpatrick, Collins. 1988. "Misconduct and Disability of Federal Judges: The Unreported Informal Responses." *Judicature* 71: 282–283.

Flanders, Steven. 1977. *Case Management and Court Management in United States District Courts.* Washington, DC: Federal Judicial Center.

Flanders, Steven. 1991. "Court Administration and Diverse Judiciaries: Complementarities and Conflicts." *Justice System Journal* 15: 640–651.

Flango, Victor. 1991. "Did Increasing the Federal Jurisdictional Amount Have the Predicted Impact on State Courts?" *State Court Journal* (Spring): 21–24.

Flango, Victor. 1994. "Court Unification and Quality of State Courts." *Justice System Journal* 16: 33–56.

Flango, Victor Eugene, and Craig Ducat. 1979. "What Differences Does Method of Judicial Selection Make? Selection Procedures in State Courts of Last Resort." *Justice System Journal* 5: 25–44.

Flemming, Roy. 1982. *Punishment Before Trial: An Organizational Perspective on Felony Bail Process.* New York: Longman.

Flemming, Roy. 1986a. "Client Games: Defense Attorney Perspectives on Their Relations with Criminal Clients." *American Bar Foundation Research Journal:* 253–277.

Flemming, Roy. 1986b. "Elements of the Defense Attorney's Craft: An Adaptive Expectations Model of the Preliminary Hearing Decision." *Law and Policy* 8: 33–57.

Flemming, Roy. 1989. "If You Pay the Piper, Do You Call the Tune? Public Defenders in America's Criminal Courts." *Law and Social Inquiry* 14: 393–405.

Flemming, Roy. 1990. "The Political Styles and Organizational Strategies of American Prosecutors: Examples from Nine Courthouse Communities." *Law and Policy* 12: 25.

Flemming, Roy, C. Kohfeld, and Thomas Uhlman. 1980. "The Limits of Bail Reform: A Quasi Experimental Analysis." *Law and Society Review* 14: 947–976.

Flemming, Roy, Peter Nardulli, and James Eisenstein. 1987. "The Timing of Justice in Felony Trial Courts." *Law and Policy* 9: 179–206.

Flemming, Roy, Peter Nardulli, and James Eisenstein. 1992. *The Craft of Justice: Politics and Work in Criminal Court Communities.* Philadelphia: University of Pennsylvania Press.

Ford, Marilyn. 1986. "The Role of Extralegal Factors in Jury Verdicts." *Justice System Journal* 11: 16–39.

Forst, Brian, Frank Leahy, Jean Shirhall, Herbert Tyson, and John Bartolomeo. 1981. *Arrest Convictability as a Measure of Police Performance.* Washington, DC: U.S. Department of Justice, National Institute of Justice.

Forst, Brian, J. Lucianovic, and S. Cox. 1977. *What Happens After Arrest? A Court Perspective of Police Operations in the District of Columbia.* Washington, DC: Law Enforcement Assistance Administration.

Frankel, Marvin. 1972. *Criminal Sentences: Law Without Order.* New York: Hill and Wang.

Frasca, Ralph. 1988. "Estimating the Occurrence of Trials Prejudiced by Press Coverage." *Judicature* 72: 162–169.

Frase, Richard. 1995. "State Sentencing Guidelines: Still Going Strong." *Judicature* 78: 173–179.

Friedman, Barry. 1998. "Attacks on Judges: Why They Fail." *Judicature* 81: 150–156.

Friedman, Lawrence. 1979. "Plea Bargaining in Historical Perspective." *Law and Society Review* 13: 247–259.

Friedman, Lawrence. 1984. *American Law: An Introduction.* New York: Norton.

Friedman, Lawrence. 1985. *A History of American Law.* 2d ed. New York: Simon & Schuster.

Friedman, Lawrence. 1993. *Crime and Punishment in American History.* New York: Basic Books.

Friedman, Lawrence, and Robert Percival. 1976. "A Tale of Two Courts: Litigation in Alameda and San Benito Counties." *Law and Society Review* 10: 267–302.

Fukurai, Hiroshi, Edgar Butler, and Richard Krooth. 1991. "Cross-Sectional Jury Representation or Systematic Jury Representation? Simple Random and Cluster Sampling Strategies in Jury Selection." *Journal of Criminal Justice* 19: 31–48.

Fyfe, James. 1982. "In Search of the 'Bad Faith' Search." *Criminal Law Bulletin* 18: 260–265.

Galanter, Marc. 1988. *The Life and Times of the Big Six: or, The Federal Courts Since the Good Old Days.* Working Paper 9:2. Madison: University of Wisconsin, Institute for Legal Studies.

Galaway, Burt. 1988. "Restitution As Innovation or Unfilled Promise?" *Federal Probation* 52: 3–14.

Galaway, Burt, and Joe Hudson, eds. 1996. *Restorative Justice: International Perspectives.* Monsey, NY: Criminal Justice Press.

Galiber, Joseph, Barry Latzer, Mark Dwyer, Jack Litman, H. Richard Uviller, and G. Roger McDonald.

1993. "Law, Justice, and Jury Nullification: A Debate." *Criminal Law Bulletin* 29: 40–69.

Galie, Peter. 1987. "State Supreme Courts, Judicial Federalism and the Other Constitutions." *Judicature* 71: 100–110.

Gallas, Geoff. 1976. "The Conventional Wisdom of State Court Administration: A Critical Assessment and an Alternative Approach." *Justice System Journal* 2: 35.

Gardiner, John. 1986. "Preventing Judicial Misconduct: Defining the Role of Conduct Organizations." *Judicature* 70: 113–121.

Garner, Joel. 1987. "Delay Reduction in the Federal Courts: Rule 50(b) and the Federal Speedy Trial Act of 1974." *Journal of Quantitative Criminology* 3: 229–250.

Gershman, Bennett. 1993. "Defending the Poor." *Trial* 29: 47–51.

Gertz, Marc. 1977. "Influence in Court Systems: The Clerk as Interface." *Justice System Journal* 3: 30–37.

Gertz, Marc, and Albert Price. 1985. "Variables Influencing Sentencing Severity: Intercourt Differences in Connecticut." *Journal of Criminal Justice* 13: 131–139.

Gest, Ted. 1996. "The Law That Grief Built." *U.S. News and World Report,* 29 April, p. 58.

Gibson, James. 1978. "Race as a Determinant of Criminal Sentences: A Methodological Critique and a Case Study." *Law and Society Review* 12: 455–478.

Gibson, James. 1980. "Environmental Restraints on the Behavior of Judges: A Representational Model of Judicial Decision Making." *Law and Society Review* 14: 343–370.

Giffuni, Matthew. 1995. "Civil Forfeiture and the Excessive Fines Clause Following *Austin v. United States.*" *Criminal Law Bulletin* 31: 502–533.

Gilboy, Janet. 1984. "Prosecutors' Discretionary Use of the Grand Jury to Initiate or to Reinitiate Prosecution." *American Bar Foundation Research Journal:* 1–81.

Gillespie, Robert. 1988–1989. "Criminal Fines: Do They Pay?" *Justice System Journal* 13: 365–378.

Gizzi, Michael. 1992. *Thinking about Sentencing Reform: What Makes Sentencing Commissions Work?* Paper presented at the annual meeting of the American Political Science Association, September 3–6.

Glaberson, William. 2003. "Family Seeks Longer Term for Stabbing in Crown Hts." *New York Times,* 2 August.

Glick, Henry, and Kenneth Vines. 1973. *State Court Systems.* Englewood Cliffs, NJ: Prentice-Hall.

Goerdt, John. 1992. *Small Claims and Traffic Courts: Case Management Procedures, Case Characteristics, and Outcomes in 12 Urban Jurisdictions.* Williamsburg, VA: National Center for State Courts.

Goldberg, Deborah, Craig Holman, and Samantha Sanchez. 2002. "The New Politics of Judicial Elections." Available online: http://www.justiceatstake.org/files/JASMoneyReport.pdf

Goldberg-Ambrose, Carole. 1994. "Of Native Americans and Tribal Members: The Impact of Law on Indian Group Life." *Law and Society Review* 28: 1123–1148.

Goldkamp, John. 1980. "The Effects of Detention on Judicial Decisions: A Closer Look." *Justice System Journal* 5: 234–257.

Goldkamp, John. 1985. "Danger and Detention: A Second Generation of Bail Reform." *Journal of Criminal Law and Criminology* 76: 1–74.

Goldkamp, John. 2002. *The Importance of Drug Courts: Lessons from Measuring Impact.* Paper presented at the American Society of Criminology, Chicago.

Goldkamp, John, Cheryl Irons-Guynn, and Doris Weiland. 2002. *Community Prosecution Strategies: Measuring Impact.* Washington, DC: Bureau of Justice Assistance.

Goldkamp, John, and Peter Jones. 1992. "Pre-Trial Drug-Testing Experiments in Milwaukee and Prince George's County: The Context of Implementation." *Journal of Research in Crime and Delinquency* 29: 430–465.

Goldkamp, John, and Doris Weiland. 1993. "Assessing the Impact of Dade County's Felony Drug Court." *National Institute of Justice Research in Brief.* Washington, DC: U.S. Department of Justice, December.

Goldkamp, John, Doris Weiland, and Cheryl Irons-Guynn. 2001. *Developing an Evaluation Plan for Community Courts: Assessing the Hartford Community Court Model.* Washington, DC: Bureau of Justice Assistance.

Goldman, Sheldon. 1997. *Picking Federal Judges: Lower Court Selection from Roosevelt through Reagan.* New Haven, CT: Yale University Press.

Goldman, Sheldon, and Matthew Saronson. 1994. "Clinton's Nontraditional Judges: Creating a More Representative Bench." *Judicature* 78: 68–73.

Goldman, Sheldon, and Elliot Slotnick. 1999. "Clinton's Second Term Judiciary: Picking Judges Under Fire." *Judicature* 82: 264–285.

Gollner, Phillip. 1995. "Consulting by Peering into Minds of Jurors." *New York Times,* 7 January, A25.

Gordon, Corey, and William Brill. 1996. *The Expanding Role of Crime Prevention Through Environmental Design in Premises Liability.* Washington, DC: National Institute of Justice.

Gottfredson, Michael. 1974. "Empirical Analysis of Pretrial Release Decisions." *Journal of Criminal Justice* 2: 287.

Graham, Barbara Luck. 1990a. "Do Judicial Selection Systems Matter? A Study of Black Representation on State Courts." *American Politics Quarterly* 18: 316–336.

Graham, Barbara Luck. 1990b. "Judicial Recruitment and Racial Diversity on State Courts: An Overview." *Judicature* 74: 28–34.

Green, Edward. 1961. *Judicial Attitudes in Sentencing.* New York: St. Martin's Press.

Green, Justin, Ross Russell, and John Schmidhauser. 1975. "Iowa's Magistrate System: The Aftermath of Reform." *Judicature* 58: 380–389.

Greenwood, Peter, C. Peter Rydell, Allan Abrahamse, Jonathan Caulkins, James Chiesa, Karyn Model, and Stephen Klein. 1996. "Estimated Benefits and Costs of California's New Mandatory Sentencing Law." In *Three Strikes and You're Out: Vengeance as Public Policy,* edited by David Shichor and Dale Sechrest. Thousand Oaks, CA: Sage.

Griset, Pamala. 1991. *Determinate Sentencing: The Promise and the Reality of Retributive Justice.* Albany: State University of New York Press.

Griset, Pamala. 1995. "Determinate Sentencing and Agenda Building: A Case Study of the Failure of a Reform." *Journal of Criminal Justice* 23: 349–362.

Grisso, Thomas. 1981. *Juveniles' Waiver of Rights.* New York: Plenum.

Gross, Samuel. 2002. "For Some, the Evidence Doesn't Matter." *Times-Picayune,* 17 November.

Gruhl, John. 1981. "State Supreme Courts and the U.S. Supreme Court's Post-*Miranda* Rulings." *Journal of Criminal Law and Criminology* 72: 886–913.

Gusfield, Joseph. 1981. *The Culture of Public Problems: Drinking-Driving and the Symbolic Order.* Chicago: University of Chicago Press.

Gyan, Joe. 1997. "Judge Has Tight Grip on Trial." *Times-Picayune,* 18 May.

Haapanen, Rudy. 1989. *Selective Incapacitation and the Serious Offender: A Longitudinal Study of Criminal Career Patterns.* New York: Springer-Verlag.

Hagan, John. 1974. "Extra-Legal Attributes and Criminal Sentencing: An Assessment of a Sociological Viewpoint." *Law and Society Review* 8: 357–381.

Hagan, John. 1977. "Criminal Justice in Rural and Urban Communities: A Study of the Bureaucratization of Justice." *Social Forces* 55: 597–612.

Hagan, John. 1983. *Victims Before the Law: The Organizational Domination of Criminal Law.* Toronto: Butterworth's.

Hagan, John, John Hewitt, and Duane Alwin. 1979. "Ceremonial Justice: Crime and Punishment in a Loosely Coupled System." *Social Forces* 58: 506–527.

Hakim, Simon, George Rengert, and Yochanan Shachmurove. 1996. "Estimation of Net Social Benefits of Electronic Security." *Justice Quarterly* 13: 153–170.

Hall, Jerome. 1952. *Theft, Law and Society.* Indianapolis: Bobbs-Merrill.

Hall, William, and Larry Aspin. 1992. "Distance from the Bench and Retention Voting Behavior: A Comparison of Trial Court and Appellate Court Retention Elections." *Justice System Journal* 15: 801–813.

Haller, Mark. 1979. "Plea Bargaining: The Nineteenth-Century Context." *Law and Society Review* 13: 273–280.

Hallinan, Joe. 1993. "Violent Children Straining Limit of Justice System." *Times-Picayune,* 31 October, p. A24.

Hannaford, Paula, Valerie Hans, and G. Thomas Munsterman. 1999. "How Much Justice Hangs in the Balance? A New Look at Hung Jury Rates." *Judicature* 83: 59–67.

Hanson, Roger. 1996. *Time on Appeal.* Williamsburg, VA: National Center for State Courts.

Hanson, Roger, and Henry Daley. 1995. *Challenging the Conditions of Prisons and Jails.* Washington, DC: U.S. Department of Justice, Bureau of Justice Statistics.

Hanson, Roger, William Hewitt, and Brian Ostrom. 1992. "Are the Critics of Indigent Defense Counsel Correct?" *State Court Journal* (Summer): 20–29.

Harlow, Caroline. 1999. *Prior Abuse Reported by Inmates and Probationers.* NCJ 172879. Washington, DC: U.S. Department of Justice, Office of Justice Programs.

Harrell, Adele, Shannon Cavanagh, and John Roman. 2000. "Evaluation of the D.C. Superior Court Drug Intervention Programs." Washington, DC: National Institute of Justice.

Harrell, Adele, Ojmarrh Mitchell, Alexa Hirst, Douglas Marlowe, and Jeffrey Merrill. 2002. "Breaking the Cycle of Drugs and Crime: Findings from the Birmingham BTC Demonstration." *Criminology and Public Policy* 1: 189–216.

Harris, John, and Paul Jesilow. 2000. "It's Not the Old Ball Game: Three Strikes and the Courtroom Workgroup." *Justice Quarterly* 17: 185–204.

Hastie, Reid, Steven Penrod, and Nancy Pennington. 1984. *Inside the Jury.* Cambridge, MA: Harvard University Press.

Healey, Kerry. 1995. *Victim and Witness Intimidation: New Developments and Emerging Responses.* Washington, DC: National Institute of Justice.

Heflin, Howell. 1987. "The Impeachment Process: Modernizing an Archaic System." *Judicature* 71: 123–125.

Heinz, Anne, Herbert Jacob, and Robert Lineberry, eds. 1983. *Crime in City Politics.* New York: Longman.

Heinz, John, and Edward Laumann. 1982. *Chicago Lawyers: The Social Structure of the Bar.* New York: Russell Sage Foundation.

Hemmens, Craig, Kristin Strom, and Elicia Schlegel. 1997. *Gender Bias in the Courts: A Review of the Literature.* Paper presented at the Academy of Criminal Justice Sciences, Louisville, KY.

Henry, D. Alan, and John Clark. 1999. "Pretrial Drug Testing: An Overview of Issues and Practices." *Bulletin,* Bureau of Justice Assistance (NCJ 176341).

Henschen, Beth, Robert Moog, and Steven Davis. 1990. "Judicial Nominating Commissioners: A National Profile." *Judicature* 73: 328–334.

Herz, Denise. 2000. "Drugs in the Heartland: Methamphetamine Use in Rural Nebraska." Washington, DC: National Institute of Justice.

Heumann, Milton. 1975. "A Note on Plea Bargaining and Case Pressure." *Law and Society Review* 9: 515–528.

Heumann, Milton. 1978. *Plea Bargaining: The Experience of Prosecutors, Judges, and Defense Attorneys.* Chicago: University of Chicago Press.

Heumann, Milton, and Colin Loftin. 1979. "Mandatory Sentencing and the Abolition of Plea Bargaining: The Michigan Felony Firearm Statute." *Law and Society Review* 13: 393–430.

Hewitt, John. 1988. "The Victim-Offender Relationship in Convicted Homicide Cases: 1960–1984." *Journal of Criminal Justice* 16: 25–33.

Hillsman, Sally, and Barry Mahoney. 1988. "Collecting and Enforcing Criminal Fines: A Review of Court Processes, Practices, and Problems." *Justice System Journal* 13: 17–36.

Hindelang, Michael. 1972. "Equality Under the Law." Pp. 312–323 in *Race, Crime and Justice,* edited by Charles Reasons and Jack Kuykendall. Pacific Palisades, CA: Goodyear.

Hirschel, J. David, Ira Hutchison, Charles Dean, and Anne-Marie Mills. 1992. "Review Essay on the Law Enforcement Response to Spouse Abuse: Past, Present and Future." *Justice Quarterly* 9: 247–284.

Hodges, Sam. 1997. "Should Federal Punishments for Crack, Powder Be Closer?" *Mobile Register,* 22 June, A-20.

Hoffman, Richard. 1991. "Beyond the Team: Renegotiating the Judge-Administrator Partnership." *Justice System Journal* 15: 652–666.

Hogarth, John. 1971. *Sentencing as a Human Process.* Toronto: University of Toronto Press.

Hojnacki, Marie, and Lawrence Baum. 1992. "Choosing Judicial Candidates: How Voters Explain Their Decisions." *Judicature* 75: 300–309.

Holden, Gwen, and Robert Kapler. 1995. "Deinstitutionalizing Status Offenders: A Record of Progress." *Juvenile Justice* 2 (Fall/Winter): 3–10.

Holmes, Lisa, and Elisha Savchak. 2003. "Judicial Appointment Politics in the 107th Congress." *Judicature* 86: 240–250.

Holmes, Malcolm, Howard Daudistel, and William Taggart. 1992. "Plea Bargaining and State District Court Caseloads: An Interrupted Time Series Analysis." *Law and Society Review* 26: 139–160.

Holmes, Oliver Wendell. 1920. *Collected Legal Papers.* Boston: Harcourt.

Holmstrom, Lynda, and Ana Burgess. 1983. *The Victim of Rape: Institutional Reactions.* New Brunswick, NJ: Transaction Publishers.

Holten, N., and R. Handberg. 1990. "Florida's Sentencing Guidelines: Surviving—But Just Barely." *Judicature* 73: 259–267.

Homel, Ross. 1988. *Policing and Punishing the Drinking Driver: A Study of General and Specific Deterrence.* New York: Springer-Verlag.

Horney, Julie, and Cassia Spohn. 1996. "The Influence of Blame and Believability Factors on the Processing of Simple versus Aggravated Rape Cases." *Criminology* 34: 135–162.

Houlden, Pauline, and Steven Balkin. 1985. "Costs and Quality of Indigent Defense: Ad Hoc vs. Coordinated Assignments of the Private Bar Within a Mixed System." *Justice System Journal* 10: 159–172.

Howell, Susan. 2000. *1998 Quality of Life Survey: Orleans and Jefferson Parishes.* Unpublished manuscript, Department of Political Science, University of New Orleans.

Hurwitz, Mark, and Drew Noble Lanier. 2001. "Women and Minorities on State and Federal

Appellate Benches, 1985 and 1999." *Judicature* 85: 84–92.

Innocence Project. 2003. Available online: http://www.innocenceproject.org/ (accessed 14 October 2003).

Iwata, Edward. 2003. "Has Hunt for Corporate Criminals Gone too Far?" *USA Today*, 22 July.

Jackson, Donald. 1974. *Judges*. New York: Atheneum.

Jackson, Patrick. 1987. "The Impact of Pretrial Preventive Detention." *Justice System Journal* 12: 305–334.

Jacob, Herbert. 1966. "Judicial Insulation: Elections, Direct Participation, and Public Attention to the Courts in Wisconsin." *Wisconsin Law Review:* 812.

Jacob, Herbert. 1984. *Justice in America*. 4th ed. Boston: Little, Brown.

Jacob, Herbert. 1991. "Decision Making in Trial Courts." Pp. 211–233 in *The American Courts: A Critical Assessment,* edited by John Gates and Charles Johnson. Washington, DC: CQ Press.

Jacob, Herbert. 1997. "Governance by Trial Court Judges." *Law and Science Review* 31: 3–37.

Jacobs, James. 1989. *Drunk Driving: An American Dilemma*. Chicago: University of Chicago Press.

Jacoby, Joan. 1977. *The Prosecutor's Charging Decision: A Policy Perspective*. Washington, DC: U.S. Government Printing Office.

Jacoby, Joan. 1980. *The American Prosecutor: A Search for Identity*. Lexington, MA: D. C. Heath.

Jacoby, Joan. 1995. "Pushing the Envelope: Leadership in Prosecution." *Justice System Journal* 17: 291–308.

Jacoby, Joan, Leonard Mellon, Edward Ratledge, and Stanley Turner. 1982. *Prosecutorial Decisionmaking: A National Study*. Washington, DC: U.S. Department of Justice, National Institute of Justice.

James, Rita. 1958. "Status and Competence of Jurors." *American Journal of Sociology* 69: 563–570.

Jencks, Christopher, and Paul Peterson, eds. 1991. *The Urban Underclass*. Washington, DC: Brookings Institution.

Jensen, Eric, and Jurg Gerber. 1996. "The Civil Forfeiture of Assets and the War on Drugs: Expanding Criminal Sanctions While Reducing Due Process Protections." *Crime and Delinquency* 42: 421–434.

Johnson, Charles, and Bradley Canon. 1984. *Judicial Policies: Implementation and Impact*. Washington, DC: Congressional Quarterly Press.

Johnson, James, and Philip Secret. 1995. "The Effects of Court Structure on Juvenile Court Decisonmaking." *Journal of Criminal Justice* 23: 63–82.

Johnson, Kevin, and Gary Fields. 1996. "Juvenile Crime 'Wave' May Be Just a Ripple." *USA Today*, 13 December, p. 3.

Jones, David. 1994. *Prosecutorial Tenure in Wisconsin*. Paper presented at the Midwest Criminal Justice Association Meeting, Chicago, September.

Jones, David. 2001. *Toward a Prosecutorial "Civil Service": A Wisconsin Case Study*. Paper presented at the Annual Meeting of the American Society of Criminology, Atlanta.

Jones, Peter, and John Goldkamp. 1991. "The Bail Guidelines Experiment in Dade County, Miami: A Case Study in the Development and Implementation of Policy Innovation." *Justice System Journal* 14: 445–476.

Kairys, David, Joseph Kadane, and John Lehorsky. 1977. "Jury Representativeness: A Mandate for Multiple Source Lists." *California Law Review* 65: 776–827.

Kalven, Harry, and Hans Zeisel. 1966. *The American Jury*. Boston: Little, Brown.

Kamisar, Yale. 1978. "Is the Exclusionary Rule an 'Illogical' or 'Unnatural' Interpretation of the Fourth Amendment?" *Judicature* 78: 83–84.

Kaplan, John. 1973. *Criminal Justice: Introductory Cases and Materials*. Mineola, NY: Foundation Press.

Kappeler, Victor, Michael Vaughn, and Rolando Del Carmen. 1991. "Death in Detention: An Analysis of Police Liability for Negligent Failure to Prevent Suicide." *Journal of Criminal Justice* 19: 381–393.

Karmen, Andrew. 2001. *Crime Victims: An Introduction to Victimology*. 4th ed. Belmont, CA: Wadsworth.

Kasunic, David. 1983. "One Day/One Trial: A Major Improvement in the Jury System." *Judicature* 67: 78–86.

Kautt, Paula. 2002. "Location, Location, Location: Interdistrict and Intercircuit Variations in Sentencing Outcomes for Federal Drug-Trafficking Offenses." *Justice Quarterly* 19: 633–669.

Keil, Thomas, and Gennaro Vito. 1990. "Race and the Death Penalty in Kentucky Murder Trials: An Analysis of Post-*Gregg* Outcomes." *Justice Quarterly* 7: 189–207.

Kelly, William, and Sheldon Ekland-Olson. 1991. "The Response of the Criminal Justice System to Prison Overcrowding: Recidivism Patterns among Four Successive Parolee Cohorts." *Law and Society Review* 25: 601–620.

Kennedy, Darlene. 1997. "Let's Hold Juveniles Responsible for Their Crimes." National Center for Public Policy Research. Available online at http://www.nationalcenter.inter.net/NPA166.html

Kingsnorth, Rodney, Carole Barnes, and Paul Coonley. 1990. *Driving Under the Influence: The Role of Legal and Extralegal Factors in Court Processing and Sentencing Practices*. Unpublished manuscript, Department of Sociology, California State University, Sacramento.

Kingsnorth, Rodney, Carole Barnes, Cynthia Davis, Tina Hodgins, and Camille Nicholes. 1987. "Preventive Detention: The Impact of the 1984 Bail Reform Act in the Eastern Federal District of California." *Criminal Justice Policy Review* 2: 150–173.

Kingsnorth, Rodney, and Louis Rizzo. 1979. "Decision-Making in the Criminal Courts: Continuities and Discontinuities." *Criminology* 17: 3–14.

Kirksey, Jason. 1997. *Sentencing Behavior of Judges Elected from Subdistrict*. Unpublished Ph.D. dissertation, Department of Political Science, University of New Orleans.

Kleck, Gary. 1981. "Racial Discrimination in Criminal Sentencing: A Critical Evaluation of the Evidence with Additional Data on the Death Penalty." *American Sociological Review* 46: 783–805.

Klein, Stephen, Joan Petersilia, and Susan Turner. 1990. "Race and Imprisonment Decisions in California." *Science* 247: 812–816.

Klemm, Margaret. 1986. *The Determinants of Capital Sentencing in Louisiana, 1979–1984.* Unpublished doctoral dissertation, University of New Orleans.

Klofas, John, and Janette Yandrasits. 1989. "'Guilty but Mentally Ill' and the Jury Trial: A Case Study." *Criminal Law Bulletin* 24: 424.

Knudten, Richard, Anthony Meader, Mary Knudten, and William Doerner. 1976. "The Victim in the Administration of Criminal Justice: Problems and Perceptions." Pp. 115–146 in *Criminal Justice and the Victim,* edited by William McDonald. Newbury Park, CA: Sage.

Kramer, Geoffrey, Norbert Kerr, and John Carroll. 1990. "Pretrial Publicity, Judicial Remedies, and Jury Bias." *Law and Human Behavior* 14: 409–438.

Kramer, John, and Robin Lubitz. 1985. "Pennsylvania Sentencing Reform: The Impact of Commission-Established Guidelines." *Crime and Delinquency* 31: 481–500.

Kramer, John, Robin Lubitz, and Cynthia Kempinen. 1989. "Sentencing Guidelines: A Quantitative Comparison of Sentencing Politics in Minnesota, Pennsylvania, and Washington." *Justice Quarterly* 6: 565–587.

Kramer, John, and Darrell Steffensmeier. 1993. "Race and Imprisonment Decisions." *Sociological Quarterly* 34: 357–376.

Kramer, John, and Jeffrey Ulmer. 1996. "Sentencing Disparity and Departures from Guidelines." *Justice Quarterly* 13: 81–106.

Kramer, Larry. 1990. "Diversity Jurisdiction." *Brigham Young University Law Review:* 3–66.

Krantz, Sheldon, Charles Smith, David Rossman, Paul Froyd, and Janis Hoffman. 1976. *Right to Counsel in Criminal Cases: The Mandate of Argersinger v. Hamlin.* Cambridge, MA: Ballinger.

Krisberg, Barry. 1988. "Public Attitudes About Criminal Sanctions." *Criminologist* 13: 1–21.

Krisberg, Barry, and James Austin. 1993. *Reinventing Juvenile Justice.* Newbury Park, CA: Sage.

Labaton, Stephen. 1990. "DNA Fingerprinting Is Facing Showdown at an Ohio Hearing." *New York Times,* 22 June.

LaFave, Wayne. 1965. *Arrest: The Decision to Take a Suspect into Custody.* Boston: Little, Brown.

Lamber, Julia, and Mary Luskin. 1992. "Court Reform: A View from the Bottom." *Judicature* 75: 295–299.

Landsberg, Brian. 1993. "The Role of Civil Service Attorneys and Political Appointees in Making Policy in the Civil Rights Division of the U.S. Department of Justice." *Journal of Law and Politics* 9: 275–289.

Langan, Patrick, and Mark Cunniff. 1992. *Recidivism of Felons on Probation, 1986–89.* Washington, DC: U.S. Department of Justice, National Institute of Justice.

Latzer, Barry. 1991. "The Hidden Conservatism of the State Court 'Revolution.'" *Judicature* 74: 190–197.

Latzer, Barry, and James Cauthen. 2000. "Capital Appeals Revisited." *Judicature* 84: 64–71.

LaWall, Barbara. 2001. "Should Plea Bargaining Be Banned in Pima County?" Pima County (Arizona) Attorney's Office. Available online: http://www.pcao.co.pima.az.us/Newsletters/Summer%202001.pdf (viewed 16 September 2003).

Lawson, Harry, and Dennis Howard. 1991. "Development of the Profession of Court Management: A History with Commentary." *Justice System Journal* 15: 580–605.

Lee, Monica. 1992. "Indigent Defense: Determination of Indigency in the Nation's State Courts." *State Court Journal* (Spring): 16–23.

Lefcourt, Gerald. 1998. "Curbing the Abuse of the Grand Jury." *Judicature* 81: 196–197.

Leo, Richard. 1996a. "Inside the Interrogation Room." *Journal of Criminal Law and Criminology* 86: 266–303.

Leo, Richard. 1996b. "The Impact of *Miranda* Revisited." *Journal of Criminal Law and Criminology* 86: 621–692.

Levin, David, Patrick Langan, and Jodi Brown. 2000. *State Court Sentencing of Convicted Felons, 1996.* Washington, DC: U.S. Department of Justice, Bureau of Justice Statistics.

Levine, James. 1983. "Using Jury Verdict Forecasts in Criminal Defense Strategy." *Judicature* 66: 448–461.

Levy, Leonard. 1996. *A License to Steal: Forfeiture of Property.* Chapel Hill: University of North Carolina Press.

Lewis, Anthony. 1972. *Clarence Earl Gideon and the Supreme Court.* New York: Random House.

Lichtenstein, Michael. 1984. "Public Defenders: Dimensions of Cooperation." *Justice System Journal* 9: 102–110.

Liebman, James, Jeffrey Fagan, and Valerie West. 2000a. "A Broken System: Error Rates in Capital Cases, 1973–1999." *Texas Law Review* 73: 1862.

Liebman, James, Jeffrey Fagan, and Valerie West. 2000b. "Death Matters: A Reply to Professors Latzer and Cauthen." *Judicature* 84: 72–77.

Lipscher, Robert. 1989. "The Judicial Response to the Drug Crisis." *State Court Journal* 13: 13.

Liptak, Adam. 2003. "County Says It's Too Poor to Defend the Poor." *New York Times,* 15 April.

Litman, Harry, and Mark Greenberg. 1996. "Dual Prosecutions: A Model for Concurrent Federal Jurisdiction." *Annals of the American Academy of Political and Social Science* 543: 72–86.

Lizotte, Alan. 1978. "Extra-Legal Factors in Chicago's Criminal Courts: Testing the Conflict Model of Criminal Justice." *Social Problems* 25: 564–580.

Lochner, Todd. 2002. "Strategic Behavior and Prosecutorial Agenda Setting in United States Attorneys' Offices: The Role of U.S. Attorneys and Their Assistants." *Justice System Journal* 23: 271–294.

Losh, Susan, Adina Wasserman, and Michael Wasserman. 2000. "Reluctant Jurors: What Summons Responses Reveal about Jury Duty Attitudes." *Judicature* 83: 304–311.

Lubasch, Arnold. 1986. "Reputed Mob Leader Among 15 Indicted on Racketeering Counts." *New York Times*, 21 March.

Lushing, Peter. 1992. "The Fall and Rise of the Criminal Contingent Fee." *Journal of Criminal Law and Criminology* 82: 498–568.

Mahoney, Barry. 1976. *Evaluating Pretrial Release Programs.* Paper presented at the annual meeting of the American Political Science Association, Chicago.

Mahoney, Barry. 1994. "Drug Courts: What Have We Learned So Far?" *Justice System Journal* 17: 127–133.

Mahoney, Barry, with Alexander Aikman, Pamela Casey, Victor Flango, Geoff Gallas, Thomas Henderson, Jeanne Ito, David Steelman, and Steven Weller. 1988. *Changing Times in Trial Courts.* Williamsburg, VA: National Center for State Courts.

Manfredi, Christopher. 1998. *The Supreme Court and Juvenile Justice.* Lawrence: University Press of Kansas.

Marby, Marcus, and Evan Thomas. 1992. "Crime: A Conspiracy of Silences." *Time* (18 May): 37.

Marion, Nancy. 1995. *A Primer in the Politics of Criminal Justice.* New York: Harrow and Heston.

Martin, Elaine. 1990. "Men and Women on the Bench: Vive la Difference?" *Judicature* 73: 204–208.

Martin, Elaine. 1993. "Women on the Bench: A Different Voice?" *Judicature* 77: 126–128.

Martin, Elaine. 1999. "Women Judges: The Next Generation." In *Women in Politics: Outsiders or Insiders? A Collection of Readings,* edited by Lois Duke Whitaker. Upper Saddle River, NJ: Prentice Hall.

Marvell, Thomas, and Mary Luskin. 1991. "The Impact of Speedy Trial Laws in Connecticut and North Carolina." *Justice System Journal* 14: 343–357.

Marvell, Thomas, and Carlisle Moody. 1996. "Determinate Sentencing and Abolishing Parole: The Long-Term Impacts on Prisons and Crime." *Criminology* 34: 107–128.

Masters, Brooke. 2000. "Another Look at '92 Execution Backed." *Washington Post*, 11 November.

Mastrofski, Stephen, and R. Richard Ritti. 1996. "Police Training and the Effects of Organization on Drunk Driving Enforcement." *Justice Quarterly* 13: 291–320.

Mather, Lynn. 1974a. "Some Determinants of the Method of Case Disposition: Decision-Making by Public Defenders in Los Angeles." *Law and Society Review* 8: 187–216.

Mather, Lynn. 1974b. "The Outsider in the Courtroom: An Alternative Role for the Defense." In *The Potential for Reform of Criminal Justice,* edited by Herbert Jacob. Newbury Park, CA: Sage.

Mather, Lynn. 1979. *Plea Bargaining or Trial?* Lexington, MA: D. C. Heath.

Matza, David. 1964. *Delinquency and Drift.* New York: Wiley.

Mauro, Tony. 1996. "Appeals Judge Steps Down After Dole Attacks." *USA Today*, 5 June.

Maxwell, Christopher, Joel Garner, and Jeffrey Fagan. 2002. "The Preventive Effects of Arrest on Intimate Partner Violence: Research, Policy, and Theory." *Criminology and Public Policy* 2: 51–80.

Maynard, Douglas. 1984. *Inside Plea Bargaining: The Language of Negotiation.* New York: Plenum Press.

Maynard, Douglas. 1988. "Narratives and Narrative Structure in Plea Bargaining." *Law and Society Review* 22: 449–481.

Mays, G. Larry, and William Taggart. 1986. "Court Clerks, Court Administrators, and Judges: Conflict in Managing the Courts." *Journal of Criminal Justice* 14: 1–7.

McCampbell, Robert. 1995. "Parallel Civil and Criminal Proceedings: Six Legal Pitfalls." *Criminal Law Bulletin* 31: 483–501.

McCarthy, Belinda, Bernard McCarthy, and Matthew Leone. 2001. *Community-Based Corrections.* 4th ed. Belmont, CA: Wadsworth.

McCormack, Robert. 1991. "Compensating Victims of Violent Crime." *Justice Quarterly* 8: 329–346.

McCormick, John. 1999. "Coming Two Days Shy of Martyrdom." *Newsweek*, 15 February.

McCoy, Candace. 1984. "Determinate Sentencing, Plea Bargaining Bans, and Hydraulic Discretion in California." *Justice System Journal* 9: 256–275.

McCoy, Candace. 1993. *Politics and Plea Bargaining: Victim's Rights in California.* Philadelphia: University of Pennsylvania Press.

McDonald, Douglas, and Kenneth Carlson. 1993. *Sentencing in the Federal Courts: Does Race Matter? The Transition to Sentencing Guidelines, 1986–1990.* Washington, DC: Bureau of Justice Statistics.

McDonald, Thomas, Robert Wood, and Melissa Pflug, eds. 1996. *Rural Criminal Justice: Conditions, Constraints, and Challenges.* Salem, WI: Sheffield.

McDonald, William, ed. 1976. *Criminal Justice and the Victim.* Newbury Park, CA: Sage.

McDonald, William. 1979. "The Prosecutor's Domain." In *The Prosecutor,* edited by William McDonald. Newbury Park, CA: Sage.

McDonald, William, Henry Rossman, and James Cramer. 1979. "The Prosecutorial Function and Its Relation to Determinate Sentencing Structures." In *The Prosecutor,* edited by William McDonald. Beverly Hills, CA: Sage.

McEwen, Tom. 1995. *National Assessment Program: 1994 Survey Results.* Washington, DC: National Institute of Justice.

McGee, Jim, and Brian Duffy. 1997. *Main Justice: The Men and Women Who Enforce the Nation's Criminal*

Laws and Guard Its Liberties. New York: Simon & Schuster.

McGillis, Daniel. 1997. *Community Mediation Programs: Developments and Challenges.* Washington, DC: U.S. Department of Justice, National Institute of Justice.

McGillis, Daniel. 1998. *Resolving Community Conflict: The Dispute Settlement Center of Durham, North Carolina.* Washington, DC: National Institute of Justice.

McIntyre, Donald. 1968. "A Study of Judicial Dominance of the Charging Decision." *Journal of Criminal Law, Criminology and Police Science* 59: 463–490.

McIntyre, Donald, and David Lippman. 1970. "Prosecutors and Disposition of Felony Cases." *American Bar Association Journal* 56: 1154–1159.

McIntyre, Lisa. 1987. *The Public Defender: The Practice of Law in the Shadows of Repute.* Chicago: University of Chicago Press.

McQuiston, J. T. 1995. "In the Bizarre L.I.R.R. Trial, Equally Bizarre Confrontations." *New York Times,* 5 February.

Meador, Daniel. 1974. *Appellate Courts: Staff and Process in the Crisis of Volume.* St. Paul, MN: West.

Meier, Kenneth. 1994. *The Politics of Sin: Drugs, Alcohol, and Public Policy.* Armonk, NY: M. E. Sharpe.

Meinhold, Stephen, and Steven Shull. 1993. *Policy Congruence Between the President and the Solicitor General.* Paper presented at the Midwest Political Science Association, Chicago.

Mellon, Leonard, Joan Jacoby, and Marion Brewer. 1981. "The Prosecutor Constrained by His Environment: A New Look at Discretionary Justice in the United States." *Journal of Criminal Law and Criminology* 72: 52–81.

Meltsner, Michael. 1973. *Cruel and Unusual Punishment: The Supreme Court and Capital Punishment.* New York: Random House.

Merry, Sally Engle, and Neal Milner, eds. 1993. *The Possibility of Popular Justice: A Case Study of Community Mediation in the United States.* Ann Arbor: University of Michigan Press.

Meyer, Jon'a, and Paul Jesilow. 1997. *Doing Justice in the People's Court: Sentencing by Municipal Court Judges.* Albany: State University of New York Press.

Miethe, Terance, and Charles Moore. 1989. "Sentencing Guidelines: Their Effect in Minnesota." Washington, DC: U.S. Department of Justice, Bureau of Justice Statistics.

Mileski, Maureen. 1971. "Courtroom Encounters: An Observation Study of a Lower Criminal Court." *Law and Society Review* 5: 473–538.

Miller, Benjamin. 1991. "Assessing the Functions of Judicial Conduct Organizations." *Judicature* 75: 16–19.

Miller, Frank. 1969. *Prosecution: The Decision to Charge a Suspect with a Crime.* Boston: Little, Brown.

Miller, Herbert, William McDonald, and James Cramer. 1978. *Plea Bargaining in the United States.* Washington, DC: National Institute of Law Enforcement and Criminal Justice.

Mills, Carol, and Wayne Bohannon. 1980. "Jury Characteristics: To What Extent Are They Related to Jury Verdicts?" *Judicature* 64: 22–31.

Misner, Robert. 1983. *Speedy Trial: Federal and State Practice.* Charlottesville, VA: The Michie Co.

Misner, Robert. 1996. "Recasting Prosecutorial Discretion." *Journal of Criminal Law and Criminology* 86: 717–758.

Moley, Raymond. 1928. "The Vanishing Jury." *Southern California Law Review* 2: 97.

Moody, Carlisle, and Thomas Marvell. 1996. "The Uncertain Timing of Innovations in Time Series: Minnesota Sentencing Guidelines and Jail Sentences—A Comment." *Criminology* 34: 257–267.

Moore, Charles, and Terance Miethe. 1986. "Regulated and Unregulated Sentencing Decisions: An Analysis of First-Year Practices under Minnesota's Felony Sentencing Guidelines." *Law and Society Review* 20: 253–278.

Moore, Kathleen Dean. 1989. *Pardons: Justice, Mercy and the Public Interest.* New York: Oxford University Press.

Moore, Mark, Susan Estrich, Daniel McGillis, and William Spelman. 1984. *Dangerous Offenders: The Elusive Target of Justice.* Cambridge, MA: Harvard University Press.

Moran, Gary, and Brian Cutler. 1991. "The Prejudicial Impact of Pretrial Publicity." *Journal of Applied Social Psychology* 21: 345–367.

Mortimer, John. 1984. *Rumpole for the Defense.* New York: Penguin Books.

Moulds, Elizabeth. 1978. "Chivalry and Paternalism: Disparities of Treatment in the Criminal Justice System." *Western Political Science Quarterly* 31: 416–440.

Munstermann, G. Thomas, and Janice Munstermann. 1986. "The Search for Jury Representativeness." *Justice System Journal* 11: 59–78.

Myers, Laura, and Sue Titus Reid. 1995. "The Importance of County Context in the Measurement of Sentencing Disparity: The Search for Routinization." *Journal of Criminal Justice* 23: 233–241.

Myers, Martha, and John Hagan. 1979. "Private and Public Trouble: Prosecutors and the Allocation of Court Resources." *Social Problems* 26: 439–451.

Myers, Martha, and Susette Talarico. 1986a. "The Social Contexts of Racial Discrimination in Sentencing." *Social Problems* 33: 237–251.

Myers, Martha, and Susette Talarico. 1986b. "Urban Justice, Rural Injustice? Urbanization and Its Effect on Sentencing." *Criminology* 24: 367–391.

Myers, Martha, and Susette Talarico. 1987. *The Social Contexts of Criminal Sentencing.* New York: Springer-Verlag.

Nader, Laura. 1992. "Trading Justice for Harmony." *National Institute for Dispute Resolution Forum* (Winter): 12–14.

Nagel, Ilene. 1983. "The Legal/Extra-Legal Controversy: Judicial Decisions in Pretrial Release." *Law and Society Review* 17: 481–515.

Nagel, Robert. 1990. "The Myth of the General Right to Bail." *Public Interest* 98: 84–97.

Nagel, Stuart. 1973. *Comparing Elected and Appointed Judicial Systems.* Beverly Hills, CA: Sage.

Nagin, Daniel. 1998. "Criminal Deterrence Research at the Outset of the Twenty-First Century." In *Crime and Justice: A Review of Research* (Vol. 23), edited by Michael Tonry. Chicago: University of Chicago Press.

Nardulli, Peter. 1978. *The Courtroom Elite: An Organizational Perspective on Criminal Justice.* Cambridge, MA: Ballinger.

Nardulli, Peter. 1979. "The Caseload Controversy and the Study of Criminal Courts." *Journal of Criminal Law and Criminology* 70: 89–101.

Nardulli, Peter. 1983. "The Societal Cost of the Exclusionary Rule: An Empirical Assessment." *American Bar Foundation Research Journal:* 585–609.

Nardulli, Peter. 1986. "'Insider' Justice: Defense Attorneys and the Handling of Felony Cases." *Journal of Criminal Law and Criminology* 77: 379–417.

Nardulli, Peter, Roy Flemming, and James Eisenstein. 1984. "Unraveling the Complexities of Decision Making in Face-to-Face Groups: A Contextual Analysis of Plea-Bargained Sentences." *American Political Science Review* 78: 912–928.

National Advisory Commission on Criminal Justice Standards and Goals. 1973. *Report on Courts.* Washington, DC: U.S. Government Printing Office.

National Association of Criminal Defense Lawyers. 2000. "Citizens Grand Jury Bill of Rights." Available online: http://www.criminaljustice.org

National Center for State Courts. 2002. *Survey of Judicial Salaries* (Vol. 27). Williamsburg, VA: Author.

National Center for State Courts. 2003. "A Profile of Hung Juries" *Caseload Highlights* 9: 1.

National Center for Victims of Crime. 2002. *Civil Legal Remedies for Victims of Crime.* Washington, DC: U.S. Department of Justice, Office for Victims of Crime.

National Coalition to Abolish the Death Penalty. 2001. "Here's How You Can Get Involved." Available online: http://www.ncadp.org/motivate.html (accessed 25 February 2001).

National Institute of Justice. 1982. *Exemplary Projects: Focus for 1982—Projects to Combat Violent Crime.* Washington, DC: U.S. Department of Justice.

Neisser, Eric. 1981. "The New Federal Judicial Discipline Act: Some Questions Congress Didn't Answer." *Judicature* 65: 143–160.

Neubauer, David. 1974a. "After the Arrest: The Charging Decision in Prairie City." *Law and Society Review* 8: 495–517.

Neubauer, David. 1974b. *Criminal Justice in Middle America.* Morristown, NJ: General Learning Press.

Neubauer, David. 1983. "Improving the Analysis and Presentation of Data on Case Processing Time." *Journal of Criminal Law and Criminology* 74: 1589–1607.

Neubauer, David. 1985. "Published Opinions Versus Summary Affirmations: Criminal Appeals in Louisiana." *Justice System Journal* 10: 173–189.

Neubauer, David. 1991. "Winners and Losers Before the Louisiana Supreme Court: The Case of Criminal Appeals." *Justice Quarterly* 8: 85–106.

Neubauer, David. 1992. "A Polychotomous Measure of Appellate Court Outcomes: The Case of Criminal Appeals." *Justice System Journal* 16: 75–87.

Neubauer, David. 1996. A Tale of Two Cities: A Comparison of Orleans and Jefferson Parish, Louisiana. Paper presented at the annual meeting of the Academy of Criminal Justice Sciences, Louisville, KY.

Neubauer, David. 2001. *Debating Crime: Rhetoric and Reality.* Belmont, CA: Wadsworth.

Neubauer, David, Marcia Lipetz, Mary Luskin, and John Paul Ryan. 1981. *Managing the Pace of Justice: An Evaluation of LEAA's Court Delay Reduction Programs.* Washington, DC: U.S. Government Printing Office.

Neubauer, David, and Stephen Meinhold. 2004. *Judicial Process: Law, Courts, and Politics in the United States.* 3rd ed. Belmont: Wadsworth.

Neumeister, Larry. 1996. "Criticized Judge Reinstates Evidence." *New York Times*, 2 April.

New York Times, "Federalism Despoiled." 1991, 27 June.

New York Times, "In '90s, Prison Building by States and U.S. Government Surged." 1997, 8 August, A15.

New York Times, "Supreme Court Bars Sawed-Off Shotgun." 1939, 16 May, p. 3.

Newburn, Tim, and Elizabeth Stanko, eds. 1994. *Just Boys Doing Business: Men, Masculinities and Crime.* London: Routledge.

Newman, Andy. 2003. "Investigation of Judge Touched Off Wider Inquiry." *New York Times*, 25 April.

Newman, Ted. 1996. "Fair Cross-section and Good Intentions: Representation in Federal Juries." *Justice System Journal* 18: 211–232.

Nielsen, Marianne, and Robert Silverman, eds. 1996. *Native Americans, Crime, and Justice.* Boulder, CO: Westview Press.

Nimmer, Raymond. 1978. *The Nature of System Change: Reform Impact in the Criminal Courts.* Chicago: American Bar Foundation.

Nimmer, Raymond, and Patricia Krauthaus. 1977. "Plea Bargaining Reform in Two Cities." *Justice System Journal* 3: 6–21.

Nobiling, Tracy, Cassia Spohn, and Miriam DeLone. 1998. "A Tale of Two Counties: Unemployment and Sentence Severity." *Justice Quarterly* 15: 459–485.

Nolan, James, ed. 2002. *Drug Courts in Theory and Practice.* Hawthorne, NY: Walter de Gruyter.

Norton, Lee. 1983. "Witness Involvement in the Criminal Justice System and Intention to Cooperate in Future Prosecutions." *Journal of Criminal Justice* 11: 143–152.

Nugent, Hugh, and Thomas McEwen. 1988. *Prosecutor's National Assessment of Needs.* Washington, DC: U.S. Department of Justice, National Institute of Justice.

O'Brien, David. 1988. "The Supreme Court: From Warren to Burger to Rehnquist." *PS* 20: 13.

Oaks, Dallin. 1970. "Studying the Exclusionary Rule in Search and Seizure." *University of Chicago Law Review* 37: 665–753.

Office for Victims of Crime. 1998. *From Pain to Power: Crime Victims Take Action.* Washington, DC: U.S. Department of Justice.

Office of Juvenile Justice and Delinquency Prevention. 1996. *Female Offenders in the Juvenile Justice System.* Washington, DC: U.S. Department of Justice.

Official Teen Court Homepage. 1998. Available online: http://library.advanced.org/264

Oran, Daniel. 1985. *Law Dictionary for Nonlawyers.* 2d ed. St. Paul, MN: West.

Oregon Peer. 1998. *(Teen) Court Pages.* Available online: http://www.ncn.com/~snews/peerct/open.htm

Ostrom, Brian, and Roger Hanson. 2000. *Efficiency and Timeliness, and Quality: A New Perspective from Nine State Criminal Trial Courts.* Washington, DC: National Institute of Justice.

Ostrom, Brian, and Neal Kauder. 1996. *Examining the Work of State Courts, 1995.* Williamsburg, VA: National Center for State Courts.

Ostrom, Brian, Neal Kauder, and Robert LaFountain, eds. 2003. *Examining the Work of State Courts, 2002.* Williamsburg, VA: National Center for State Courts.

Pabst, William. 1973. "What Do Six-Member Juries Really Save?" *Judicature* 57: 6–11.

Packer, Herbert. 1968. *The Limits of the Criminal Sanction.* Palo Alto, CA: Stanford University Press.

Padawer-Singer, Alice, and Alice Barton. 1975. "The Impact of Pretrial Publicity on Jurors' Verdicts." In *The Jury System in America: A Critical Overview,* edited by Rita James Simon. Beverly Hills, CA: Sage.

Padgett, John. 1985. "The Emergent Organization of Plea Bargaining." *American Journal of Sociology* 90: 753–800.

Padgett, John. 1990. "Plea Bargaining and Prohibition in the Federal Courts, 1908–1934." *Law and Society Review* 24: 413–450.

Palmer, Barbara. 2001. "Women in the American Judiciary: Their Influence and Impact." *Women and Politics* 23: 89.

Parent, Dale, Barbara Auerbach, and Kenneth Carlson. 1992. *Compensating Crime Victims: A Summary of Policies and Practices.* Washington, DC: U.S. Department of Justice, National Institute of Justice.

Parent, Dale, Terence Dunworth, Douglas McDonald, and William Rhodes. 1996. *The Impact of Sentencing Guidelines.* Washington, DC: National Institute of Justice.

Parent, Dale, Terrence Dunworth, Douglas McDonald, and William Rhodes. 1997. *Intermediate Sanctions.* Washington, DC: National Institute of Justice.

Partridge, Anthony, and William Eldridge. 1974. *The Second Circuit Sentencing Study: A Report to the Judges of the Second Circuit.* Washington, DC: Federal Judicial Center.

Paternoster, Raymond. 1984. "Prosecutorial Discretion in Requesting the Death Penalty: A Case of Victim-Based Racial Discrimination." *Law and Society Review* 18: 437–478.

Perkins, Craig, James Stephan, and Allen Beck. 1995. *Jail and Jail Inmates 1993–1994.* Washington DC: Bureau of Justice Statistics.

Perkins, David, and Jay Jamieson. 1995. "Judicial Probable Cause Determinations After *County of Riverside v. McLaughlin.*" *Criminal Law Bulletin* 31: 534–546.

Perlstein, Michael. 1990. "DA's Office Suffers as Prosecutors Flee to Better Pay, Hours." *Times-Picayune,* 22 July, B1.

Philbin, Walt. 2001. "Murder Rate Up Sharply in 2000." *Times-Picayune,* 1 January.

Piccarreta, Michael, and Jefferson Keenan. 1995. "Dual Sovereigns, Successive Prosecutions, and Politically Correct Verdicts." *Criminal Law Bulletin* 31: 291–304.

Pinello, Daniel. 1995. *The Impact of Judicial-Selection Method of State-Supreme-Court Policy: Innovation, Reaction and Atrophy.* Westport, CT: Greenwood Press.

Platt, Anthony. 1969. *The Child Savers: The Invention of Delinquency.* Chicago: University of Chicago Press.

Platt, Anthony, and Randi Pollock. 1974. "Channeling Lawyers: The Careers of Public Defenders." In *The Potential for Reform of Criminal Justice,* edited by Herbert Jacob. Newbury Park, CA: Sage.

President's Commission on Law Enforcement and Administration of Justice. 1967. *Task Force Report: The Courts.* Washington, DC: U.S. Government Printing Office.

Pretrial Services Resource Center. 1999. *Integrating Drug Testing into a Pretrial Service System: 1999 Update.* Washington, DC: U.S. Department of Justice, Bureau of Justice Assistance.

Priehs, Richard. 1999. "Appointed Counsel for Indigent Criminal Appellants: Does Compensation Influence Effort?" *Justice System Journal* 21: 57–79.

Pro-Death Penalty.com. 2001. "'Innocence' Critique." Available online: http://www.prodeathpenalty.com/DPIC.htm (accessed 11 January 2001).

Propp, Wren. 2003. "Court Suspends Mora Magistrate." *Albuquerque Journal,* 10 April.

Provine, Doris Marie. 1981. "Persistent Anomaly: The Lay Judge in the American Legal System." *Justice System Journal* 6: 28–43.

Provine, Doris Marie. 1986. *Judging Credentials: Nonlawyer Judges and the Politics of Professionalism.* Chicago: University of Chicago Press.

Puritz, Patricia, S. Burrell, R. Schwartz, M. Soler, and L. Warboys. 1995. *A Call for Justice: An Assessment of Access to Counsel and Quality of Representation in Delinquency Proceedings.* Washington, DC: American Bar Association.

Puro, Stephen. 1976. "United States Magistrates: A New Federal Judicial Officer." *Justice System Journal* 2: 141–156.

Puzzanchera, Charles, Anne Stahl, Terrence Finnegan, Howard Snyder, Rowen Poole, and Nancy Tierney.

2000. *Juvenile Courts Statistics 1997.* Washington, DC: U.S. Department of Justice, Office of Juvenile Justice and Delinquency Prevention.

Radelet, Michael, and Glenn Pierce. 1985. "Race and Prosecutorial Discretion in Homicide Cases." *Law and Society Review* 19: 587–621.

Ragona, Anthony, and John Paul Ryan. 1983. "Misdemeanor Courts and the Choice of Sanctions: A Comparative View." *Justice System Journal* 8: 199–221.

Ralph, Paige, Jonathan Sorensen, and James Marquart. 1992. "A Comparison of Death-Sentenced and Incarcerated Murderers in Pre-*Furman* Texas." *Justice Quarterly* 9: 185–209.

Rapaport, Elizabeth. 1991. "The Death Penalty and Gender Discrimination." *Law and Society Review* 25: 367–384.

Raymond, Paul. 1992. "The Impact of a Televised Trial on Individuals' Information and Attitudes." *Judicature* 75: 204–209.

Reagan, Ronald. 1981. Speech in New Orleans, quoted in *New York Times,* 29 September.

Reaves, Brian. 2001. *Felony Defendants in Large Urban Counties, 1998.* Washington, DC: Bureau of Justice Statistics.

Reaves, Brian, and Jacob Perez. 1994. *Pretrial Release of Felony Defendants, 1992.* Washington, DC: U.S. Department of Justice, Bureau of Justice Statistics.

Rehnquist, William. 1993. "Symposium Spotlights Nation's Drug and Violence Problems." *Third Branch* 25 (July): 1.

Reid, Traciel. 1999. "The Politicization of Retention Elections: Lessons from the Defeat of Justices Lanphier and White." *Judicature* 83: 68–77.

Reiman, Jeffrey. 2001. *The Rich Get Richer and the Poor Get Prison: Ideology, Class, and Criminal Justice.* Boston: Allyn & Bacon.

Reinarman, C. 1988. "The Social Construction of an Alcohol Problem." *Theory and Society* 17: 91–120.

Reinkensmeyer, Marcus. 1991. "Compensation of Court Managers: Current Salaries and Related Factors." *Judicature* 75: 154–162.

Remington, Frank. 1988. "Post-Conviction Review: What State Trial Courts Can Do to Reduce Problems." *Judicature* 72: 53–57.

Rengert, George. 1989. "Spatial Justice and Criminal Victimization." *Justice Quarterly* 6: 543–564.

Report of the Federal Courts Study Committee. 1990.

Resick, Patricia. 1984. "The Trauma of Rape and the Criminal Justice System." *Justice System Journal* 9: 52–61.

Reskin, Barbara, and Christine Visher. 1986. "The Impacts of Evidence and Extralegal Factors in Jurors' Decisions." *Law and Society Review* 20: 423–439.

Resnik, Judith. 1995. "Multiple Sovereignties: Indian Tribes, States, and the Federal Government." *Judicature* 79: 118–125.

Rhodes, William. 1978. *Plea Bargaining: Who Gains? Who Loses?* Washington, DC: Institute for Law and Social Research.

Rhodes, William, Raymond Hyatt, and Paul Scheiman. 1996. "Research in Brief: Predicting Pretrial Misconduct with Drug Tests of Arrestees." Washington, DC: National Institute of Justice.

Richardson, Richard, and Kenneth Vines. 1970. *The Politics of Federal Courts.* Boston: Little, Brown.

Robertson, Leon, Robert Rich, and H. Laurence Ross. 1973. "Jail Sentences for Driving While Intoxicated in Chicago: A Judicial Action That Failed." *Law and Society Review* 8: 55–68.

Robinson, Mike. 1996. "Abrasive, Erratic Judge Sidelined." *Times-Picayune,* 12 October.

Roper, Robert. 1979. "Jury Size: Impact on Verdict's Correctness." *American Politics Quarterly* 7: 438–452.

Roper, Robert. 1980. "Jury Size and Verdict Consistency: 'Line Has to Be Drawn Somewhere'?" *Law and Society Review* 14: 972–995.

Roper, Robert, and Victor Flango. 1983. "Trials Before Judges and Juries." *Justice System Journal* 8: 186–198.

Roper, Robert, and Albert Melone. 1981. "Does Procedural Due Process Make a Difference? A Study of Second Trials." *Judicature* 65: 136–141.

Rosen, Ellen. 1987. "The Nation's Judges: No Unanimous Opinion." *Court Review* 24: 5.

Rosencrance, John. 1988. "Maintaining the Myth of Individualized Justice: Probation Presentence Reports." *Justice Quarterly* 5: 235–256.

Rosenthal, John. 2002. "Therapeutic Jurisprudence and Drug Treatment Courts: Integrating Law and Science." In *Drug Courts in Theory and Practice,* edited by James Nolan. Hawthorne, NY: Walter de Gruyter.

Rosett, Arthur, and Donald Cressey. 1976. *Justice by Consent: Plea Bargaining in the American Courthouse.* Philadelphia: J. B. Lippincott.

Rosoff, Stephen, Henry Pontell, and Robert Tillman. 2002. *Profit without Honor: White-Collar Crime and the Looting of America.* Upper Saddle River, NJ: Prentice-Hall.

Ross, Darrell. 2002. *Civil Liability in Criminal Justice.* 3d ed. Cincinnati: Anderson.

Ross, H. Laurence. 1992. "The Law and Drunk Driving." *Law and Society Review* 26: 219–230.

Ross, H. Laurence, and James Foley. 1987. "Judicial Disobedience of the Mandate to Imprison Drunk Drivers." *Law and Society Review* 21: 315–323.

Roth, Jeffrey, and Paul Wice. 1980. *Pretrial Release and Misconduct in the District of Columbia.* Washington DC: Institute for Law and Social Research.

Rottman, David, and Pamela Casey. 1999. "Therapeutic Jurisprudence and the Emergence of Problem-Solving Courts." *National Institute of Justice Journal* (July): 12–19.

Rottman, David, Carol Flango, Melissa Cantrell, Randall Hansen, and Neil LaFountain. 2000. *State Court Organization 1998.* Washington, DC: Bureau of Justice Statistics.

Rowe, David, and David Farrington. 1997. "The Familial Transmission of Criminal Convictions." *Criminology* 35: 177–201.

Rubenstein, Michael, and Teresa White. 1979. "Plea Bargaining: Can Alaska Live Without It?" *Judicature* 62: 266–279.

Rubin, Alvin. 1976. "How We Can Improve Judicial Treatment of Individual Cases Without Sacrificing Individual Rights: The Problems of the Criminal Law." *Federal Rules of Decisions* 70: 176.

Rubin, H. Ted. 1984. *The Courts: Fulcrum of the Justice System.* New York: Random House.

Rubin, H. Ted. 1989. "The Juvenile Court Landscape." In *Juvenile Justice: Policies, Programs and Services,* edited by Albert Roberts. Chicago: Richard Irwin.

Rubin, Paula. 1995. "Civil Rights and Criminal Justice: Employment Discrimination Overview." Washington, DC: U.S. Department of Justice, National Institute of Justice.

Ruckman, P. S. 1997. "Executive Clemency in the United States: Origins, Development, and Analysis (1900–1993)." *Presidential Studies Quarterly* 27: 251–271.

Ryan, Joan. 2002. "Do We Count Strikes or Justice?" *San Francisco Chronicle,* 5 November.

Ryan, John Paul. 1980–1981. "Adjudication and Sentencing in a Misdemeanor Court: The Outcome Is the Punishment." *Law and Society Review* 15: 79–108.

Ryan, John Paul, Allan Ashman, Bruce Sales, and Sandra Shane-Dubow. 1980. *American Trial Judges.* New York: Free Press.

Ryan, John Paul, and James Alfini. 1979. "Trial Judges' Participation in Plea Bargaining: An Empirical Perspective." *Law and Society Review* 13: 479–507.

Ryan, John Paul, and James Guterman. 1977. "Lawyers versus Non-Lawyer Town Justices." *Judicature* 60: 272–280.

Ryan, John Paul, Marcia Lipetz, Mary Luskin, and David Neubauer. 1981. "Analyzing Court Delay-Reduction Programs: Why Do Some Succeed?" *Judicature* 65: 58–75.

Saari, David. 1982. *American Court Management: Theories and Practice.* Westport, CT: Quorum Books.

Sager, Jackie. 2000. "Teen Court Offers Disciplinary Alternatives for Youth." *Holland Sentinel,* 11 August.

Saks, Michael. 1996. "The Smaller the Jury, the Greater the Unpredictability." *Judicature* 79: 263—265.

Saltzburg, Stephen. 1983. "Discovery." In *Encyclopedia of Crime and Justice,* edited by Sanford Kadish. New York: Free Press.

Sanborn, Joseph. 1986. "A Historical Sketch of Plea Bargaining." *Justice Quarterly* 3: 111–138.

Sanborn, Joseph. 1993. "The Right to a Public Jury Trial: A Need for Today's Juvenile Court." *Judicature* 76: 230–238.

Sanborn, Joseph. 1994. "The Juvenile, the Court, or the Community: Whose Best Interests Are Currently Being Promoted in Juvenile Court?" *Justice System Journal* 17: 249–266.

Scalia, John. 2002. "Prisoner Petitions Filed in U.S. District Courts, 2000, with Trends 1980–2000." Washington, DC: Bureau of Justice Statistics.

Scardino, Albert. 1989. "Steinberg Live: Courtroom TV Is a Fixture, Even as New York Is Deciding." *New York Times,* 22 January, E7.

Scheck, Barry, Peter Neufeld, and Jim Dwyer. 2000. *Actual Innocence: Five Days to Execution and Other Dispatches from the Wrongfully Convicted.* New York: Doubleday.

Scheingold, Stuart. 1991. *The Politics of Street Crime: Criminal Process and Cultural Obsession.* Philadelphia: Temple University Press.

Scheingold, Stuart, Toska Olson, and Jana Pershing. 1994. "Sexual Violence, Victim Advocacy, and Republican Criminology: Washington State's Community Protection Act." *Law and Society Review* 28: 729–763.

Schelling, Thomas. 1960. *The Strategy of Conflict.* Cambridge, MA: Harvard University Press.

Schlesinger, Joseph. 1966. *Ambition and Politics: Political Careers in the United States.* Chicago: Rand McNally.

Schmidt, Janell, and Lawrence Sherman. 1993. "Does Arrest Deter Domestic Violence?" *American Behavioral Scientist* 36: 601–615.

Schotland, Roy. 1998. "Comment." *Law and Contemporary Problems* 61: 149–150.

Schulhofer, Stephen. 1984. "Is Plea Bargaining Inevitable?" *Harvard Law Review* 97: 1037–1107.

Schultz, David. 2000. "No Joy in Mudville Tonight: The Impact of 'Three Strike' Laws. . ." *Cornell Journal of Law and Public Policy* 9: 557.

Schwarzer, William, and Russell Wheeler. 1994. *On the Federalization of the Administration of Civil and Criminal Justice.* Washington, DC: Federal Judicial Center.

Scruggs, Anna, Jean-Claude Mazzola, and Mary Zaug. 1995. "Recent Voting Rights Act Challenges to Judicial Elections." *Judicature* 79: 34–41.

Segal, Jeffrey. 1984. "Predicting Supreme Court Cases Probabilistically: The Search and Seizure Cases, 1962–1981." *American Political Science Review* 78: 891–900.

Segal, Jeffrey, and Harold Spaeth. 1989. "Decisional Trends on the Warren and Burger Courts: Results from the Supreme Court Data Base Project." *Judicature* 73: 103–107.

Segal, Jennifer. 2000. "Judicial Decision Making and the Impact of Election Year Rhetoric." *Judicature* 84: 26–33.

Seron, Carol. 1988. "The Professional Project of Parajudges: The Case of U.S. Magistrates." *Law and Society Review* 22: 557–574.

Severance, Lawrence, and Elizabeth Loftus. 1982. "Improving the Ability of Jurors to Comprehend and Apply Criminal Jury Instructions." *Law and Society Review* 17: 153–198.

Sherman, Edward. 1987. "Military Law." In *Encyclopedia of the American Judicial System,* edited by Robert Janosik. New York: Charles Scribner's Sons.

Shiff, Allison, and David Wexler. 1996. "Teen Court: A Therapeutic Jurisprudence Perspective." *Criminal Law Bulletin* 32: 342–365.

Shine, J., and D. Price. 1992. "Prosecutors and Juvenile Justice: New Roles and Perspectives." In *Juvenile Justice and Public Policy: Toward a National Agenda*, edited by Ira Schwartz. New York: Lexington Books.

Shinnar, Shlomo, and Reuel Shinnar. 1975. "The Effects of the Criminal Justice System on the Control of Crime: A Quantitative Approach." *Law and Society Review* 9: 581–611.

Silbey, Susan. 1981. "Making Sense of the Lower Courts." *Justice System Journal* 6: 13–27.

Silverstein, Lee. 1965. *Defense of the Poor.* Chicago: American Bar Foundation.

Simon, Jonathan. 1994. *Poor Discipline: Parole and the Social Control of the Underclass, 1890–1990.* Chicago: University of Chicago Press.

Simon, Rita James. 1967. *The Jury and the Defense of Insanity.* Boston: Little, Brown.

Singer, Simon. 1993. "The Automatic Waiver of Juveniles and Substantive Justice." *Crime and Delinquency* 39: 253–261.

Sipes, Dale. 1988. *On Trial: The Length of Civil and Criminal Trials.* Williamsburg, VA: National Center for State Courts.

Sitomer, Curtis. 1985. "Rural Justice Affects Many, But May Serve Few." *Christian Science Monitor* (28 May): 23.

Skogan, Wesley, and Mary Ann Wycoff. 1987. "Some Unexpected Effects of a Police Service for Victims." *Crime and Delinquency* 33: 490–501.

Skolnick, Jerome. 1967. "Social Control in the Adversary System." *Journal of Conflict Resolution* 11: 52–70.

Skolnick, Jerome. 1993. *Justice Without Trial.* 3d ed. New York: Macmillan.

Slotnick, Elliot. 1983. "The ABA Standing Committee on Federal Judiciary: A Contemporary Assessment." *Judicature* 66: 385–393.

Sloviter, Dolores. 1992. "Diversity Jurisdiction Through the Lens of Federalism." *Judicature* 76: 90–93.

Smith, Brent, and C. Ronald Huff. 1992. "From Victim to Political Activist: An Empirical Examination of a Statewide Victims' Rights Movement." *Journal of Criminal Justice* 20: 201–215.

Smith, Christopher. 1992. "From U.S. Magistrates to U.S. Magistrate Judges: Developments Affecting the Federal District Courts' Lower Tier of Judicial Officers." *Judicature* 75: 210–215.

Smith, Christopher. 1995. "Federal Habeas Corpus Reform: The State's Perspective." *Justice System Journal* 18: 1–11.

Smith, Christopher, and Thomas Hensley. 1993. "Assessing the Conservatism of the Rehnquist Court." *Judicature* 77: 83–89.

Smith, Douglas. 1986. "The Plea Bargaining Controversy." *Journal of Criminal Law and Criminology* 77: 949–957.

Smith, Michael, and Geoffrey Alpert. 1993. "Law Enforcement: The Police and the Americans with Disabilities Act—Who Is Being Discriminated Against?" *Criminal Law Bulletin* 29: 516–534.

Smith, Nancy, and Julie Garmel. 1992. "Judicial Election and Selection Procedures Challenged under the Voting Rights Act." *Judicature* 76: 154–155.

Smith, Steven, and Carol DeFrances. 1996. *Indigent Defense.* Washington, DC: Bureau of Justice Statistics.

Smothers, Ronald. 1996. "Arkansas Plan to Promote Election of Black Judges Brings a Familiar Challenge." *New York Times,* 8 April.

Snell, Tracy, and Laura Maruschak. 2002. *Capital Punishment 2001.* Washington, DC: U.S. Department of Justice, Bureau of Justice Statistics.

Sniffen, Michael. 1997. "FBI Lab Problems Are Widespread." *Times-Picayune,* 14 February.

Snyder, Elizabeth. 1989. *Toward an Integrative Theory on Courtroom Decision Making: Observations on Bail Setting and Sentencing.* Paper presented at the annual meeting of the Midwest Political Science Association, Chicago.

Snyder, Howard. 2000. *Juvenile Arrests, 1999.* Washington, DC: Office of Juvenile Justice and Delinquency Prevention.

Snyder, Howard, and Melissa Sickmund. 2000. *Juvenile Offenders and Victims: 1999 National Report.* Washington, DC: Office of Juvenile Justice and Delinquency Prevention.

Songer, Donald. 1990. "Criteria for Publication of Opinions in the U.S. Courts of Appeals: Formal Rules versus Empirical Reality." *Judicature* 73: 307–313.

Sorensen, Jon, and Donald Wallace. 1999. "Prosecutorial Discretion in Seeking Death: An Analysis of Racial Disparity in the Pretrial Stages of Case Processing in a Midwestern County." *Justice Quarterly* 16: 559–578.

Sosin, M. 1978. "*Parens Patriae* and Dispositions in Juvenile Courts." Madison, WI: Institute for Research on Poverty.

Spangenberg Group. 2000. *Contracting for Indigent Defense Services: A Special Report.* Washington, DC: Bureau of Justice Statistics.

Spangenberg, Robert, Richard Wilson, Patricia Smith, and Beverly Lee. 1986. *Containing the Cost of Indigent Defense Programs: Eligibility Screening and Cost Recovery Procedures.* Washington, DC: U.S. Department of Justice, National Institute of Justice.

Spill, Rorie, and Kathleen Bratton. 2001. "Clinton and Diversification of the Federal Judiciary." *Judicature* 84: 256–261.

Spohn, Cassia, and Jerry Cederblom. 1991. "Race and Disparities in Sentencing: A Test of the Liberation Hypothesis." *Justice Quarterly* 8: 305–328.

Spohn, Cassia, and David Holleran. 2000. "The Imprisonment Penalty Paid by Young, Unemployed Black and Hispanic Male Offenders." *Criminology* 38: 281–307.

Spohn, Cassia, and Jeffrey Spears. 1996. "The Effect of Offender and Victim Characteristics on Sexual Assault Case Processing Decisions." *Justice Quarterly* 13: 649–679.

Spohn, Cassia, and Jeffrey Spears. 1997. *Gender and Sentencing of Drug Offenders.* Paper presented at the annual meeting of the American Society of Criminology, San Diego.

Springer, Charles. 1986. *Justice for Juveniles.* Washington, DC: Office of Juvenile Justice and Delinquency Prevention.

Springer, J. Fred. 1983. "Burglary and Robbery Plea Bargaining in California: An Organizational Perspective." *Justice System Journal* 8: 157–185.

St. Petersburg Times, "This Week in Review." 2000. 3 September.

Stanko, Elizabeth. 1981. "The Arrest Versus the Case." *Urban Life* 9: 295–414.

Stanko, Elizabeth. 1981–1982. "The Impact of Victim Assessment on Prosecutors' Screening Decisions: The Case of the New York County District Attorney's Office." *Law and Society Review* 16: 225–239.

Steadman, Greg. 2002. *Survey of DNA Crime Laboratories, 2001.* Washington, DC: Bureau of Justice Statistics.

Steadman, Henry, John Monahan, Sharon Davis, and Pamela Robbins. 1982. "Mentally Disordered Offenders: National Survey of Patients and Facilities." *Law and Human Behavior* 6: 31–38.

Steele, Walter, and Elizabeth Thornburg. 1991. "Jury Instructions: A Persistent Failure to Communicate." *Judicature* 74: 249–254.

Steffensmeier, Darrell, and Chris Hebert. 1999. "Women and Men Policymakers: Does the Judge's Gender Affect the Sentencing of Criminal Defendants?" *Social Forces* 77: 1163.

Steffensmeier, Darrell, Jeffrey Ulmer, and John Kramer. 1998. "The Interaction of Race, Gender, and Age in Criminal Sentencing: The Punishment Cost of Being Young, Black, and Male." *Criminology* 36: 763–798.

Steinberger, Barbara. 1985. "*Alford* Doctrine Popular in State's Courts." *New Haven Register,* 9 June.

Steketee, Gail, and Anne Austin. 1989. "Rape Victims and the Justice System: Utilization and Impact." *Social Service Review* 63: 285–303.

Stern, Andrew. 2000. "Illinois Governor Halts Executions Pending Review." *Reuters,* 23 January.

Steury, Ellen Hochstedler, and Nancy Frank. 1990. "Gender Bias and Pretrial Release: More Pieces of the Puzzle." *Journal of Criminal Justice* 18: 417–432.

Stidham, Ronald, and Robert Carp. 1997. *Judges' Gender and Federal District Court Decisions.* Paper presented at the Southwestern Political Science Association, New Orleans.

Stith, Kate, and Jose Cabranes. 1998. *Fear of Judging: Sentencing Guidelines in the Federal Courts.* Chicago: University of Chicago Press.

Stott, E. Keith. 1982. "The Judicial Executive: Toward Greater Congruence in an Emerging Profession." *Justice System Journal* 7: 152–179.

Strawn, David, and Raymond Buchanan. 1976. "Jury Confusion: A Threat to Justice." *Judicature* 59: 478–483.

Strodtbeck, F., R. James, and C. Hawkins. 1957. "Social Status in Jury Deliberations." *American Sociological Review* 22: 713–719.

Strom, Kevin, Steven Smith, and Howard Snyder. 1998. *Juvenile Felony Defendants in Criminal Courts.* Washington, DC: U.S. Department of Justice, Bureau of Justice Statistics.

Sudnow, David. 1965. "Normal Crimes: Sociological Features of the Penal Codes in a Public Defender Office." *Social Problems* 12: 254–264.

Sullivan, Joseph. 1991. "New Jersey's Highest Court Defends Its Course." *New York Times,* 4 August, p. E16.

Surette, Ray. 1996. "News from Nowhere, Policy to Follow: Media and the Social Construction of 'Three Strikes and You're Out.'" In *Three Strikes and You're Out: Vengeance as Public Policy,* edited by David Shichor and Dale Sechrest. Thousand Oaks, CA: Sage.

Sviridoff, Michele. 1976. *Bail Reform in America.* Berkeley: University of California Press.

Sviridoff, Michele. 1986. "Bail Bonds and Cash Alternatives: The Influence of 'Discounts' on Bail-Making in New York City." *Justice System Journal* 11: 131–147.

Taggart, William. 1989. "Redefining the Power of the Federal Judiciary: The Impact of Court-Ordered Prison Reform on State Expenditures for Corrections." *Law and Society Review* 23: 241–272.

Tarr, G. Alan. 1982. "State Supreme Courts and the U.S. Supreme Court: The Problem of Compliance." In *State Supreme Courts: Policymakers in the Federal System,* edited by Mary Cornelia Porter and G. Alan Tarr. Westport, CT: Greenwood.

Tarr, G. Alan, and Mary Cornelia Porter. 1988. *State Supreme Courts in State and Nation.* New Haven, CT: Yale University Press.

Thaler, Paul. 1994. *The Watchful Eye: American Justice in the Age of the Television Trial.* Westport, CT: Praeger.

Third Branch, "Courts Try New and Tribal Ways in Indian Territory." 2001. *Third Branch* 33 (October): 4–6.

Thomson, Douglas, and Anthony Ragona. 1987. "Popular Moderation Versus Governmental Authoritarianism: An Interactionist View of Public Sentiments Toward Criminal Sanctions." *Crime and Delinquency* 33: 337–357.

Thompson, Kevin. 1996. "The Nature and Scope of Rural Crime." Pp. 3–18 in *Rural Criminal Justice: Conditions, Constraints, and Challenges,* edited by Thomas McDonald, Robert Wood, and Melissa Pflug. Salem, WI: Sheffield.

Tiffany, Lawrence, Yakov Avichai, and Geoffrey Peters. 1975. "A Statistical Analysis of Sentencing in Federal Courts: Defendants Convicted After Trial, 1967–1968." *Journal of Legal Studies* 10: 369–390.

Time, "The Sausage Factories." 1974, 25 November. p. 91.

Times-Picayune, "A Week of Violence: 21 Dead, 9 Wounded in New Orleans' Bloodiest Week in Memory." 1995, 5 March.

Times-Picayune, "Court: Sentences for Crack Are Fair." 1997, 15 April.

Tobolowsky, Peggy. 1993. "Restitution in the Federal Criminal Justice System." *Judicature* 77: 90–95.

Toborg, Mary. 1983. "Bail Bondsmen and Criminal Courts." *Justice System Journal* 8: 141–156.

Toborg, Mary, and John Bellassai. 1986. *Public Danger as a Factor in Pre-Trial Release*. Washington, DC: Toborg Associations, Inc., in cooperation with the National Association of Pre-Trial Service Agencies.

Tonry, Michael. 1987. *Sentencing Reform Impacts*. Washington, DC: U.S. Government Printing Office.

Tonry, Michael. 1991. "The Politics and Processes of Sentencing Commissions." *Crime and Delinquency* 37: 307–329.

Tonry, Michael. 1993. "The Failure of the U.S. Sentencing Commission's Guidelines." *Crime and Delinquency* 39: 131–149.

Tonry, Michael. 1999. *Reconsidering Indeterminate and Structured Sentencing*. Washington, DC: U.S. Department of Justice, Office of Justice Programs.

Torbet, Patricia, Patrick Griffin, Hunter Hurst, and Lynn MacKenzie. 2000. *Juveniles Facing Criminal Sanctions: Three States That Changed the Rules*. Washington, DC: U.S. Department of Justice, Office of Juvenile Justice and Delinquency Prevention.

Torres, Sam, and Elizabeth Piper Deschenes. 1997. "Changing the System and Making It Work: The Process of Implementing Drug Courts in Los Angeles County." *Justice System Journal* 19: 267–290.

Traynor, Roger. 1970. *The Riddle of Harmless Error*. Columbus: Ohio State University Press.

Turner, Susan, and Judith Greene. 1999. "The FARE Probation Experiment: Implementation and Outcomes of Day Fines for Felony Offenders in Maricopa County." *Justice System Journal* 21: 1–21.

U.S. Department of Justice/Office of Inspector General. 1997. *The FBI Laboratory: An Investigation into Laboratory Practices and Alleged Misconduct in Explosives-Related and Other Cases*. Available online: http://www.usdoj.gov/oig/fbilab1/fbi1toc.htm

U.S. Senate Judiciary Committee. 1993. *The Response to Rape: Detours on the Road to Equal Justice*. Washington, DC: Author.

U.S. Sentencing Commission. 2003. *Federal Sentencing Statistics by State, District & Circuit*. Available at http://www.ussc.gov/JUDPACK/JP2001.htm.

Uchida, Craig, and Timothy Bynum. 1991. "Search Warrants, Motions to Suppress and 'Lost Cases': The Effects of the Exclusionary Rule in Seven Jurisdictions." *Journal of Criminal Law and Criminology* 81: 1034–1066.

Uchida, Craig, Timothy Bynum, Dennis Rogan, and Donna Murasky. 1988. "Acting in Good Faith: The Effects of *United States v. Leon* on the Police and Courts." *Arizona Law Review* 30: 467–495.

Uhlman, Thomas, and Darlene Walker. 1980. "'He Takes Some of My Time: I Take Some of His': An Analysis of Judicial Sentencing Patterns in Jury Cases." *Law and Society Review* 14: 323–342.

Utz, Pamela. 1979. "Two Models of Prosecutorial Professionalism." In *The Prosecutor*, edited by William McDonald. Newbury Park, CA: Sage.

Van Dine, Stephen, John Conrad, and Simon Dinitz. 1979. *Restraining the Wicked*. Lexington, MA: Lexington Books.

Van Duizend, Richard, L. Paul Sutton, and Charlotte Carter. 1984. *The Search Warrant Process*. Williamsburg, VA: National Center for State Courts.

van Dyke, Jon. 1977. *Jury Selection Procedures: Our Uncertain Commitment to Representative Panels*. Cambridge, MA: Ballinger.

Van Ness, Daniel, and Karen Heetderks Strong. 1997. *Restoring Justice*. Cincinnati: Anderson.

Varney, James. 1996a. "Date Sure Teen Was Quarter Killer." *Times-Picayune*, 25 January.

Varney, James. 1996b. "Killer's Family Accuses Justice System of Racism." *Times-Picayune*, 30 January, B1.

Varney, James. 1996c. "Teen-Ager Gets Death for Killing Slidell Man; Family Silent in Court." *Times-Picayune*, 27 January.

Varney, James. 1996d. "Teen Guilty of Murder Outside Quarter Lounge." *Times-Picayune*, 31 January.

Vaughn, Michael. 1996. "Prison Civil Liability for Inmate-Against-Inmate Assault and Breakdown/Disorganization Theory." *Journal of Criminal Justice* 24: 139–152.

Vera Institute of Justice. 1977. *Felony Arrests: Their Prosecution and Disposition in New York City's Courts*. New York: Author.

Vera Institute of Justice. 1981. *Felony Arrests: Their Prosecution and Disposition in New York City's Courts*. Rev. ed. New York: Longman.

Vermont Center for Justice Research. 1995. "DUI Adjudication and BAC Level: An Assessment." *DataLine: The Justice Research Bulletin* 4 (May).

Viano, Emilio. 1987. "Victim's Rights and the Constitution: Reflections on a Bicentennial." *Crime and Delinquency* 33: 438–451.

Vidmar, Neil, Sara Beale, Mary Rose, and Laura Donnelly. 1997. "Should We Rush to Reform the Criminal Jury?" *Judicature* 80: 286–290.

Vincent, Barbara, and Paul Hofer. 1994. *The Consequences of Mandatory Minimum Prison Terms: A Summary of Recent Findings*. Washington, DC: Federal Judicial Center.

Visher, Christy. 1987. "Incapacitation and Crime Control: Does a 'Lock 'Em Up' Strategy Reduce Crime?" *Justice Quarterly* 4: 513–544.

Visher, Christy. 1992. *Pretrial Drug Testing*. Washington, DC: U.S. Department of Justice, National Institute of Justice.

von Hirsch, Andrew. 1976. *Doing Justice*. New York: Hill and Wang.

Walker, James, and Susan Ostrander. 1982. "An Observational Study of a Juvenile Court." *Juvenile and Family Court Journal* 33: 53–69.

Walker, Samuel. 1989. *Sense and Nonsense about Crime: A Policy Guide*. 2d ed. Pacific Grove, CA: Brooks/Cole.

Walker, Samuel. 1992. "Origins of the Contemporary Criminal Justice Paradigm: The American Bar Foundation Survey, 1953–1969." *Justice Quarterly* 9: 47–76.

Walker, Samuel. 2001. *Sense and Nonsense about Crime and Drugs: A Policy Guide*. 5th ed. Belmont, CA: Wadsworth.

Walker, Samuel, Cassia Spohn, and Miriam DeLone. 2004. *The Color of Justice: Race, Ethnicity, and Crime in America*. 3d ed. Belmont, CA: Wadsworth.

Walsh, Anthony. 1985. "The Role of the Probation Officer in the Sentencing Process." *Criminal Justice and Behavior* 12: 289–303.

Walsh, Anthony. 1987. "The Sexual Stratification Hypothesis and Sexual Assault in Light of the Changing Conceptions of Race." *Criminology* 25: 153–173.

Wardlaw, Jack. 1997. "Foster Backs Police Changes." *Times-Picayune*, 2 May.

Wardlaw, Jack. 1998. "Accord Returns Angola to Louisiana Control." *Times-Picayune*, 25 September.

Wasby, Stephen. 1982. "The Functions and Importance of Appellate Oral Argument: Some Views of Lawyers and Federal Judges." *Judicature* 65: 340–353.

Wasby, Stephen. 1993. *The Supreme Court in the Federal Judicial System*. 4th ed. Chicago: Nelson-Hall.

Watson, Richard, and Ronald Downing. 1969. *The Politics of the Bench and Bar: Judicial Selection under the Missouri Nonpartisan Court Plan*. New York: John Wiley.

Webster, Barbara. 1988. *Victim Assistance Programs Report Increased Workloads*. Washington, DC: National Institute of Justice.

Weed, Frank. 1995. *Certainty of Justice: Reform in the Crime Victim Movement*. New York: Aldine de Gruyter.

Weisheit, Ralph, and Sue Mahan. 1988. *Women, Crime and Criminal Justice*. Cincinnati: Anderson.

Weisheit, Ralph, Edward Wells, and David Falcone. 1995. *Crime and Policing in Rural and Small-Town America: An Overview of the Issues*. Washington, DC: National Institute of Justice.

Weiss, Robert, Richard Berk, and Cathrine Lee. 1996. "Assessing the Capriciousness of Death Penalty Charging." *Law and Society Review* 30: 607–638.

Welch, Susan, and Cassia Spohn. 1986. "Evaluating the Impact of Prior Record on Judges' Sentencing Decisions: A Seven-City Comparison." *Justice Quarterly* 3: 389–408.

Welch, Susan, Cassia Spohn, and John Gruhl. 1985. "Convicting and Sentencing Differences Among Black, Hispanic and White Males in Six Localities." *Justice Quarterly* 2: 67–80.

Wexler, David B., and Bruce J. Winick, eds. 1996. *Law in a Therapeutic Key: Developments in Therapeutic Jurisprudence*. Durham, NC: Carolina Academic Press.

Whitehead, John. 1991. "The Effectiveness of Felony Probation: Results from an Eastern State." *Justice Quarterly* 8: 525–543.

Wice, Paul. 1974. *Freedom for Sale*. Lexington, MA: D. C. Heath.

Wice, Paul. 1978. *Criminal Lawyers: An Endangered Species*. Newbury Park, CA: Sage.

Wice, Paul. 1985. *Chaos in the Courthouse: The Inner Workings of the Urban Criminal Courts*. New York: Praeger.

Wice, Paul. 1991. *Judges and Lawyers: The Human Side of Justice*. New York: HarperCollins.

Wicker, Tom. 1991. "Dee Brown and You." *New York Times*, 15 May, p. A15.

Wilkey, Malcolm. 1978. "The Exclusionary Rule: Why Suppress Valid Evidence?" *Judicature* 62: 214–232.

Williams, Jimmy. 1992. "Sentencing Guidelines and the Changing Composition of Criminal Appeals: A Preliminary Analysis." *Judicature* 76: 94–97.

Williams, Jimmy. 1995. "Type of Counsel and the Outcome of Criminal Appeals: A Research Note." *American Journal of Criminal Justice* 19: 275–285.

Williams, Victor. 1993. "Solutions to Federal Judicial Gridlock." *Judicature* 76: 185–186.

Willing, Richard. 2002. "DNA Testing Fails to Live Up to Potential." *USA Today*, 7 October.

Willing, Richard. 2003. "Judges Go Softer on Sentences More Often." *USA Today*, 28 August, p. 1.

Wilson, James Q. 1973. "If Every Criminal Knew He Would Be Punished If Caught." *New York Times Magazine*, 28 January.

Wilson, James Q. 1983. *Thinking about Crime: A Policy Guide*. 2d ed. New York: Basic Books.

Wiseman, Jacqueline. 1970. *Stations of the Lost: The Treatment of Skid Row Alcoholics*. Englewood Cliffs, NJ: Prentice-Hall.

Wiseman, Jacqueline. 1976. "Drunk Court: The Adult Parallel to Juvenile Court." Pp. 233–252 in *The Criminal Justice Process: A Reader*, edited by William Sanders and Howard Daudistel. New York: Praeger.

Wold, John. 1978. "Going Through the Motions: The Monotony of Appellate Court Decisionmaking." *Judicature* 62: 58–65.

Wold, John, and Greg Caldeira. 1980. "Perceptions of 'Routine' Decision-Making in Five California Courts of Appeal." *Polity* 13: 334–347.

Wolfgang, Marvin, and Marc Riedel. 1973. "Race, Judicial Discretion, and the Death Penalty." *Annals of the American Academy of Political and Social Science* 407: 119–133.

Woods, Keith. 1993. "The Wall Builder." *Times-Picayune*, 13 September.

Worden, Alissa Pollitz. 1990. "Policymaking by Prosecutors: The Uses of Discretion in Regulating Plea Bargaining." *Judicature* 73: 335–340.

Worden, Alissa Pollitz. 1991. "Privatizing Due Process: Issues in the Comparison of Assigned Counsel, Public Defender, and Contracted Indigent Defense Systems." *Justice System Journal* 14: 390–418.

Worden, Alissa Pollitz. 1993. "Counsel for the Poor: An Evaluation of Contracting for Indigent Criminal Defense." *Justice Quarterly* 10: 613–637.

Worden, Alissa. 1995. "The Judge's Role in Plea Bargaining: An Analysis of Judges' Agreement with Prosecutors' Sentencing Recommendations." *Justice Quarterly* 12: 257–278.

Worden, Alissa Pollitz, and Robert Worden. 1989. "Local Politics and the Provision of Indigent Defense Counsel." *Law and Policy* 11: 401–424.

Wright, Charles. 1994. *Hornbook on Federal Courts.* 5th ed. St. Paul, MN: West.

Wright, Kevin. 1981. "The Desirability of Goal Conflict within the Criminal Justice System." *Journal of Criminal Justice* 9: 209–218.

Wright, Ronald, and Marc Miller. 2002. "The Screening/Bargaining Tradeoff." *Stanford Law Review* 55: 29–118.

Young, Malcolm. 2000. "Providing Effective Representation for Youth Prosecuted as Adults." Washington, DC: U.S. Department of Justice, Bureau of Justice Assistance Bulletin.

Young, Tara. 2003. "Murder Beat." *Times-Picayune,* 13 July.

Zalman, Marvin, and Larry Siegel. 1997. *Criminal Procedure: Constitution and Society.* 2d ed. Belmont, CA: Wadsworth.

Zatz, Marjorie. 1984. "Race, Ethnicity, and Determinate Sentencing: A New Dimension to an Old Controversy." *Criminology* 22: 147–171.

Zatz, Marjorie. 1987. "The Changing Forms of Racial/Ethnic Biases in Sentencing." *Journal of Research in Crime and Delinquency* 24: 69–92.

Zehner, Sharon. 1997. *Teen Court.* Available online: http://www.fbi.gov/leb/mar971.htm

Zeisel, Hans. 1979. "Bail Revisited." *American Bar Foundation Research Journal:* 769–789.

Zeisel, Hans. 1982. "The Verdict of Five Out of Six Civil Jurors: Constitutional Problems." *American Bar Foundation Research Journal*: 141–156.

Zeisel, Hans, and Shari Diamond. 1974. "Convincing Empirical Evidence on the Six Member Jury." *University of Chicago Law Review* 41: 281–295.

Zimring, Franklin, Sheila O'Malley, and Joel Eigen. 1976. "Punishing Homicide in Philadelphia: Perspectives on the Death Penalty." *University of Chicago Law Review* 43: 227–252.

Case Index

Index

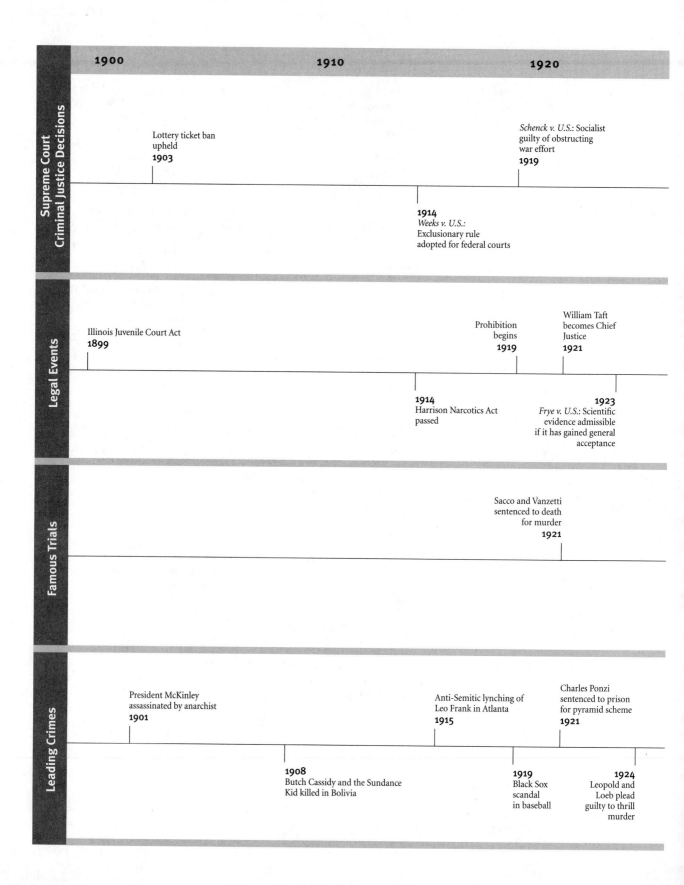

1900   **1910**   **1920**

Supreme Court Criminal Justice Decisions

Lottery ticket ban upheld
1903

Schenck v. U.S.: Socialist guilty of obstructing war effort
1919

1914
Weeks v. U.S.: Exclusionary rule adopted for federal courts

Legal Events

Illinois Juvenile Court Act
1899

Prohibition begins
1919

William Taft becomes Chief Justice
1921

1914
Harrison Narcotics Act passed

1923
Frye v. U.S.: Scientific evidence admissible if it has gained general acceptance

Famous Trials

Sacco and Vanzetti sentenced to death for murder
1921

Leading Crimes

President McKinley assassinated by anarchist
1901

Anti-Semitic lynching of Leo Frank in Atlanta
1915

Charles Ponzi sentenced to prison for pyramid scheme
1921

1908
Butch Cassidy and the Sundance Kid killed in Bolivia

1919
Black Sox scandal in baseball

1924
Leopold and Loeb plead guilty to thrill murder

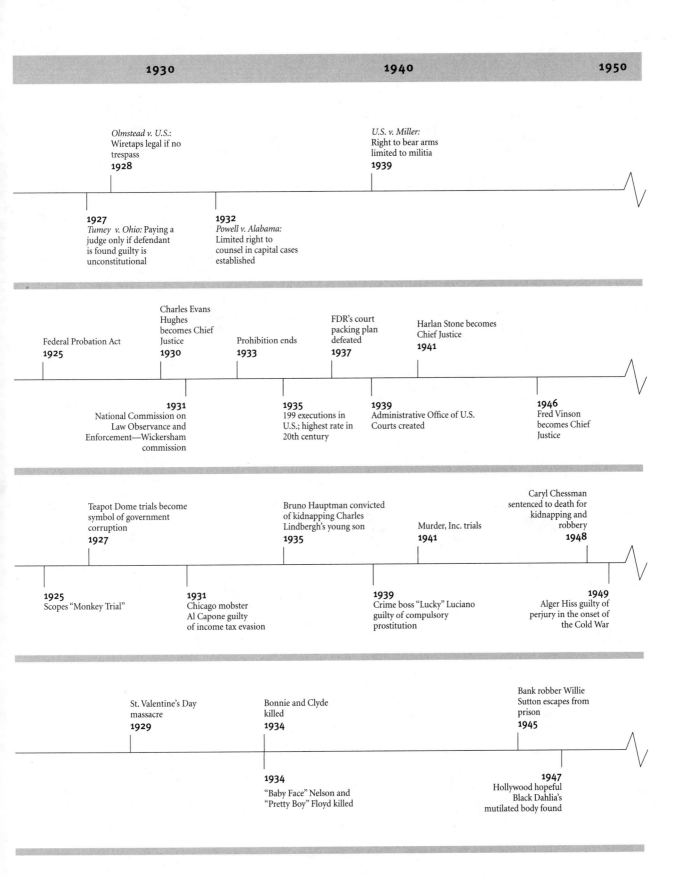

1930 **1940** **1950**

Olmstead v. U.S.:
Wiretaps legal if no
trespass
1928

U.S. v. Miller:
Right to bear arms
limited to militia
1939

1927
Tumey v. Ohio: Paying a
judge only if defendant
is found guilty is
unconstitutional

1932
Powell v. Alabama:
Limited right to
counsel in capital cases
established

Charles Evans
Hughes
becomes Chief
Justice
1930

FDR's court
packing plan
defeated
1937

Harlan Stone becomes
Chief Justice
1941

Federal Probation Act
1925

Prohibition ends
1933

1931
National Commission on
Law Observance and
Enforcement—Wickersham
commission

1935
199 executions in
U.S.; highest rate in
20th century

1939
Administrative Office of U.S.
Courts created

1946
Fred Vinson
becomes Chief
Justice

Teapot Dome trials become
symbol of government
corruption
1927

Bruno Hauptman convicted
of kidnapping Charles
Lindbergh's young son
1935

Murder, Inc. trials
1941

Caryl Chessman
sentenced to death for
kidnapping and
robbery
1948

1925
Scopes "Monkey Trial"

1931
Chicago mobster
Al Capone guilty
of income tax evasion

1939
Crime boss "Lucky" Luciano
guilty of compulsory
prostitution

1949
Alger Hiss guilty of
perjury in the onset of
the Cold War

St. Valentine's Day
massacre
1929

Bonnie and Clyde
killed
1934

Bank robber Willie
Sutton escapes from
prison
1945

1934
"Baby Face" Nelson and
"Pretty Boy" Floyd killed

1947
Hollywood hopeful
Black Dahlia's
mutilated body found

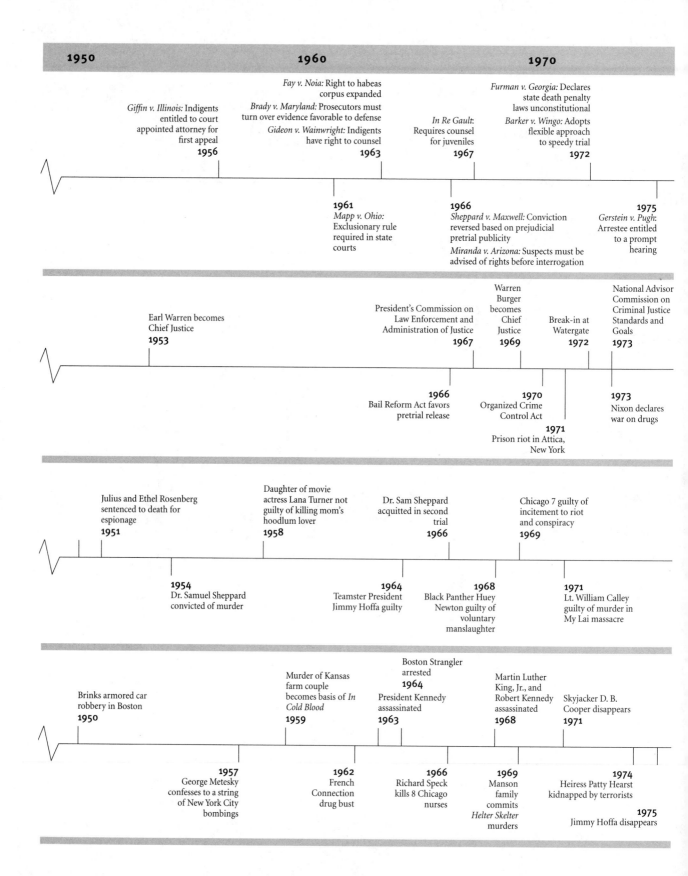

1950   **1960**   **1970**

Fay v. Noia: Right to habeas
corpus expanded
Brady v. Maryland: Prosecutors must
turn over evidence favorable to defense
Giffin v. Illinois: Indigents
entitled to court
appointed attorney for
first appeal
1956

Gideon v. Wainwright: Indigents
have right to counsel
1963

In Re Gault:
Requires counsel
for juveniles
1967

Furman v. Georgia: Declares
state death penalty
laws unconstitutional
Barker v. Wingo: Adopts
flexible approach
to speedy trial
1972

1961
Mapp v. Ohio:
Exclusionary rule
required in state
courts

1966
Sheppard v. Maxwell: Conviction
reversed based on prejudicial
pretrial publicity
Miranda v. Arizona: Suspects must be
advised of rights before interrogation

1975
Gerstein v. Pugh:
Arrestee entitled
to a prompt
hearing

Earl Warren becomes
Chief Justice
1953

President's Commission on
Law Enforcement and
Administration of Justice
1967

Warren
Burger
becomes
Chief
Justice
1969

Break-in at
Watergate
1972

National Advisor
Commission on
Criminal Justice
Standards and
Goals
1973

1966
Bail Reform Act favors
pretrial release

1970
Organized Crime
Control Act

1971
Prison riot in Attica,
New York

1973
Nixon declares
war on drugs

Julius and Ethel Rosenberg
sentenced to death for
espionage
1951

Daughter of movie
actress Lana Turner not
guilty of killing mom's
hoodlum lover
1958

Dr. Sam Sheppard
acquitted in second
trial
1966

Chicago 7 guilty of
incitement to riot
and conspiracy
1969

1954
Dr. Samuel Sheppard
convicted of murder

1964
Teamster President
Jimmy Hoffa guilty

1968
Black Panther Huey
Newton guilty of
voluntary
manslaughter

1971
Lt. William Calley
guilty of murder in
My Lai massacre

Brinks armored car
robbery in Boston
1950

Murder of Kansas
farm couple
becomes basis of *In
Cold Blood*
1959

Boston Strangler
arrested
1964
President Kennedy
assassinated
1963

Martin Luther
King, Jr., and
Robert Kennedy
assassinated
1968

Skyjacker D. B.
Cooper disappears
1971

1957
George Metesky
confesses to a string
of New York City
bombings

1962
French
Connection
drug bust

1966
Richard Speck
kills 8 Chicago
nurses

1969
Manson
family
commits
Helter Skelter
murders

1974
Heiress Patty Hearst
kidnapped by terrorists

1975
Jimmy Hoffa disappears

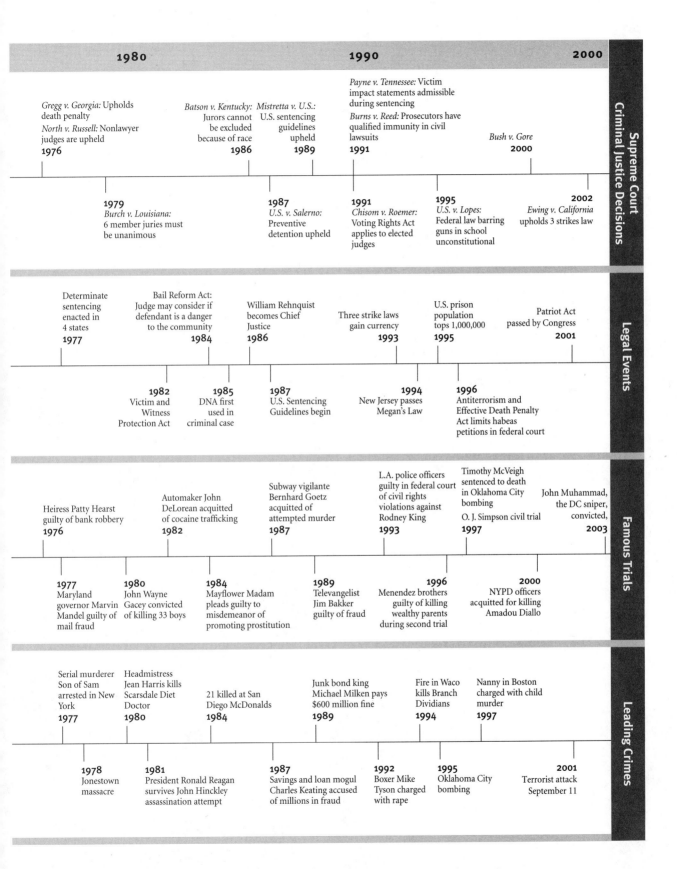

Supreme Court Criminal Justice Decisions

1980 — **1990** — **2000**

Gregg v. Georgia: Upholds death penalty
North v. Russell: Nonlawyer judges are upheld
1976

Batson v. Kentucky: Jurors cannot be excluded because of race
1986

Mistretta v. U.S.: U.S. sentencing guidelines upheld
1989

Payne v. Tennessee: Victim impact statements admissible during sentencing
Burns v. Reed: Prosecutors have qualified immunity in civil lawsuits
1991

Bush v. Gore
2000

1979
Burch v. Louisiana: 6 member juries must be unanimous

1987
U.S. v. Salerno: Preventive detention upheld

1991
Chisom v. Roemer: Voting Rights Act applies to elected judges

1995
U.S. v. Lopes: Federal law barring guns in school unconstitutional

2002
Ewing v. California upholds 3 strikes law

Legal Events

Determinate sentencing enacted in 4 states
1977

Bail Reform Act: Judge may consider if defendant is a danger to the community
1984

William Rehnquist becomes Chief Justice
1986

Three strike laws gain currency
1993

U.S. prison population tops 1,000,000
1995

Patriot Act passed by Congress
2001

1982
Victim and Witness Protection Act

1985
DNA first used in criminal case

1987
U.S. Sentencing Guidelines begin

1994
New Jersey passes Megan's Law

1996
Antiterrorism and Effective Death Penalty Act limits habeas petitions in federal court

Famous Trials

Heiress Patty Hearst guilty of bank robbery
1976

Automaker John DeLorean acquitted of cocaine trafficking
1982

Subway vigilante Bernhard Goetz acquitted of attempted murder
1987

L.A. police officers guilty in federal court of civil rights violations against Rodney King
1993

Timothy McVeigh sentenced to death in Oklahoma City bombing
O. J. Simpson civil trial
1997

John Muhammad, the DC sniper, convicted,
2003

1977
Maryland governor Marvin Mandel guilty of mail fraud

1980
John Wayne Gacey convicted of killing 33 boys

1984
Mayflower Madam pleads guilty to misdemeanor of promoting prostitution

1989
Televangelist Jim Bakker guilty of fraud

1996
Menendez brothers guilty of killing wealthy parents during second trial

2000
NYPD officers acquitted for killing Amadou Diallo

Leading Crimes

Serial murderer Son of Sam arrested in New York
1977

Headmistress Jean Harris kills Scarsdale Diet Doctor
1980

21 killed at San Diego McDonalds
1984

Junk bond king Michael Milken pays $600 million fine
1989

Fire in Waco kills Branch Dividians
1994

Nanny in Boston charged with child murder
1997

1978
Jonestown massacre

1981
President Ronald Reagan survives John Hinckley assassination attempt

1987
Savings and loan mogul Charles Keating accused of millions in fraud

1992
Boxer Mike Tyson charged with rape

1995
Oklahoma City bombing

2001
Terrorist attack September 11